Letters in a Trunk

Letters in a Trunk

A WWII Love Story

First Edition

C.L. Sniderman Barr/J.G. Barr

Edited and Introduced by Daniel R. Mazza

Letters in a Trunk: A WWII Love Story
Copyright © 2019 by Daniel R. Mazza and Vickie S. Mazza

Library of Congress Registration Number: TXu002161273

For information, please email Daniel R. Mazza at
mazzadr@icloud.com.

Book Cover (Front and Back) Design by Melissa Williams Design

Dedication

This book is dedicated to the descendants of the Barr/Sniderman family, especially, the children (Michael, Jay, Scott, and Vickie) and grandchildren (Daniel, Joshua, Jayme, Sarah, Scott, Michael, Alex, and Kenny) of George and Lottie Barr.

Special thanks to Dorothy Potash Kashuk and Evelyn Levine Plotkin, who not only are friends mentioned in the letters, but also gave me great background information on George and Lottie, and their friends, family, and co-workers during the timeframe of these letters.

In memory of Scott Elliot Barr
1954 - 1990

Preface

Following the deaths of Charlotte (Lottie) Sniderman Barr and James George Barr in 2004 and 2007, respectively, a vast collection of letters were found that were written between Lottie and George during World War II, while George was serving in the U.S. Army Signal Corps.

The following pages are transcriptions of these letters, which were written between May of 1943 and February of 1946. These letters not only give a unique snapshot of life during the war, but also the very beginning of a romance that lasted a lifetime. Reading and transcribing each one of these letters was akin to opening an individual time capsule hundreds of times, each with a hidden surprise.

As you read these letters, you will be instantly transported 75 years into the past, reliving life through the eyes of two madly in love kids from Worcester, Massachusetts. At the start of the letters, in May of 1943, Lottie, just a year out of Worcester High School of Commerce, and almost nineteen, had only recently started going steady with George. George had just enlisted in the U.S. Army, and was attending classes in Philadelphia to learn how to install and repair radios in the U.S. WWII airplanes. As you read these letters, you will be able to follow George's travels as he is shipped out to various U.S. Army airfields throughout the United States, and eventually overseas. While George does share with Lottie a good deal of his experiences while serving in the army, much of Lottie and George's conversations are about family, friends, and the love they share for one another. I don't want to spoil the surprises, both good and bad, as their daily lives and inner most thoughts are revealed, but there will be some chuckles and some tears along the way.

Other than correcting the occasional typographical error, or adding a few commas to improve the readability, the transcriptions are true to the original handwritten letters. Fortunately, in addition to these letters, Lottie and George also saved many photographs and other documents during this timeframe. If a photograph, postcard, telegram, poem, newspaper clipping, etc. was mentioned or included in one of the letters, I have included them immediately following that particular letter. Likewise, if the stationery they were using is interesting or mentioned in the letter, I have included the letterhead at the top of the transcribed letter, before the salutation. At the end of the book, where I could find them, I have included pictures of the family, friends, and army buddies that George and Lottie mention in their letters, in essence, to give a face to the name.

As you read the letters, you will notice that some words are written unconventionally, such as, to-day or to-morrow. These, and others like them, were left as originally written. You will see, especially in Lottie's letters, the spellings of some words are sometimes purposely changed or misspelled (e.g. "mother" written as "mater") to add a funny flair to her writing. As an added treat, Lottie and George frequently give the name of a song that was playing on the radio while they were writing their letters, and it is interesting to look them up and listen to them as you are reading the book, as you can't help but feel you are back in another age that has almost been forgotten.

So, grab a chair, sit back, and enjoy the trip back in time!

Daniel R. Mazza
Editor, and husband of Vickie (Barr) Mazza

Introduction

Before jumping into George and Lottie's letters, let me set the table, so to speak, with a bit of history on the two authors. Both Lottie and George's parents were Jewish emigrates from Lithuania, which, like many Jewish Lithuanians in the early 1900's, were fleeing the country due to growing antisemitic violence in Europe.

James George Barr was born on May 12, 1923 in Worcester, Massachusetts. He was always called George by his family and friends, and only upon entering the army in 1943, did he learn that his first name was actually James. As the story goes, George's mother liked the name James, but with it being known as a more "Christian" name, he was always called by his middle name of George.

George's family owned a small grocery store, aptly named, "Barr's Creamery", on 112 Water Street in Worcester. Throughout his teenage years, George helped out his father (Jacob) and mother (Rose) in the store, along with his two older brothers (Solomon & Nathan) and younger sister (Toby). The store provided the Barr family with a good to moderate income, which allowed them to purchase their own home and family automobile.

George owned a camera and very much enjoyed photography. He would bring his camera and "portable radio", which resembled a small suitcase, on picnics with Lottie and their friends and take photographs and listen to the songs of the day. Another interest of Georges' was table tennis. This interest in particular, would serve George well during downtimes while serving in the army.

Charlotte (Lottie) Loretta Sniderman was born on May 31, 1924, also in Worcester, Massachusetts. Lottie's father (Max) owned and operated a second-hand store in downtown Worcester. Lottie's family rented the second floor of a "triple-decker", a three-story house in which the home owner usually lives on one floor and rents out the other two floors. There is an interesting history regarding the construction of these triple-deckers to house the wave of immigrants arriving in the New England area in the late 1800's, and some even consider Worcester to be the epicenter and birthplace of triple-decker home construction.

Lottie's mother (Sara) had already been widowed twice before marrying Lottie's father, in 1922 at the age of 33. Sara Hoffman Sniderman had two sons (Samuel Pemstein & Irving Walker), each from her two previous marriages. While hard to imagine today, the average life expectancy in the U.S. in 1900 was only 47 years. Many commonly cured diseases today were fatal during this time period, this combined with two world wars and the Great Depression, meant that it was not at all unusual for married men and women to be widowed at a young age, which also led to many orphaned children.

Unlike George's family of many aunts, uncles, and cousins on both sides of his family, Lottie's main family relationships were with her two half-brothers and two aunts and an uncle on her mom's side. Prior to and during the time period of the letters, Lottie worked for a wholesale grocery supply company "New England Grocer Supply, Co.", and at night took nursing classes that required working at a local hospital. Lottie had a very close relationship with her mom, and hearing her mom's life experiences, along with growing up during the Great Depression, made Lottie a very independent and mature young woman, and I believe you can pick that up from her letters.

By all accounts, George and Lottie had a very enjoyable childhood growing up in Worcester, and it appears they began having feelings for one another when George brought flowers to Lottie while she was in the hospital with the flu on her 18th birthday in 1942. From that point on, their infatuation for each other only grew. So, now that I have brought you up to speed on the authors, let's jump into the letters, starting with May 20th, 1943.

§

May 20, 1943
Thursday

From:	To:
C.L. Sniderman	Mr. George Barr
65 Houghton St.	11th & Pine Sts., Gladstone Hotel
Worcester 4, Mass.	Philadelphia, Pa.

George dear,

It is astonishing how much the state of the body influences the powers of the mind. I have been thinking all morning what a delightful and interesting letter I would send this evening, and now I am so tired that my thoughts are quite giddy. I fancy myself in more of a Sara Bernhardt condition. You surely have heard of how beautifully she could portray a death scene. Well, each new and frequent illness that befalls me, puts me in a highly dramatic state and I fancy myself in the last hours of my life. But, alas, I awake the next day to find myself very much alive and quite often realize that I have taken a turn for the better.

Your new habitat sounds very nice. The idea of living in a penthouse, as you called it, must be intriguing. Although, it's not yet a week that you have gone I feel to miss you already. You most likely have been too deeply engrossed with your new surroundings to feel lonesome. But Worcester is a morgue now that you have gone. I am left completely void of all male companionship!! To this I will have to become accustomed, but it is not in my being to be happy about the situation.

My mother saw your mother this morning. It seems she feels "miz" about your sudden departure, - but then again, we could find solace in our mutual loss.

My dear, I realize to the fullest that you will be quite busy, but you will drop me a line whenever the opportunity presents itself, won't you? Take care.

Love, Lottie

P.S. If this missive sounds a bit peculiar please forgive. I am a person of many moods and this just exemplifies my present state of mind. Goodbye – L.S.

May 26, 1943
Wednesday

From:	To:
C.L. Sniderman	Mr. George Barr
65 Houghton St.	Gladstone Hotel
Worcester 4, Mass.	Philadelphia, Pa.

George dear,

I was truly worried about your accident. I wonder if you realize how lucky you are that you came through with only a few cuts and bruises. Egads, man, that was enough of that kind of excitement to last the duration. To-day's letter enlightened me to the fact that you are most alive – and kicking.

I wish to hell you could book passage on a plane for this weekend. I know it's almost the impossible, but, hells bells, this sure is going to be a dull birthday for me. Everyone loves the gift you gave me and today Edith Megans bought me some beautiful earrings that almost match, as a matter of fact, it's a very close match.

I don't know whether I mentioned in my last letter that I had my hair cut. It looks quite good. Such a drastic change from my former hair-do!! You probably wouldn't like it, but I do, so there.

I also went back to work to-day for the first time. Such a reception, my, my!! They were all very happy to see me, not because of my magnetic charm & personality, mind you, but because they were sick of doing my work. They didn't say it in so many words, but I know. Started piling me down the minute they spotted me and at 5:30 they had the gall and nerve of a tin monkey to ask why I came back before two weeks. Hell, the place probably would have gone under without my guidance (Ho-Hum)!!!

Well hon, guess that's about it. Write soon, won't you and please take care.

Love, Lottie

P.S. My new name is little Charlie, do you like it? Little Charlie.

June 9, 1943
Wednesday

From:	To:
C.L. Sniderman	Mr. George Barr
65 Houghton St.	Gladstone Hotel
Worcester 4, Mass.	Philadelphia, Pa.

George dear,

Received your letter this A.M. and between blowing my nose and wiping tears from my eyes I finally managed to get to the part where you said you were coming home. Yes, I can with much regret inform you that I have another cold. To some this is a very minor affair, but to me in the past it has meant the wrotten stench of hospitals. Can now inform you that I have taken a marked turn for the better and after a two-day vacation shall return to work tomorrow.

I'm very glad you're coming home. When will I see you? I get through work Sat. at 1 o'clock, so if you're not asleep call me at the office, the number is 5-2501, if not, call me at home after 1 o'clock.

I got a card for Pvt. Morton Herman today. He's still at Devens, and it seems he just don't like it, especially K.P., at which he has become a specialist. As a matter of fact, I gather he don't think very much of the whole army. Poor, poor, Morty, I'm afraid there isn't a thing to be done about it, unless they suddenly discover that he has two left feet or a wooden arm or something.

Not being able to go to work today I decided that I would get started on my short story or didn't I tell you that I am to become an author of the very baddest kind. I am really a sight to behold, very dramatic to say the least. Here is a description in the fullest I can give it to you. I'm sitting at the table in the dining room with a typewriter before me, papers scattered every which what way, a couple of ash trays filled with lipstick stained cigarette butts, one giving out a steady stream of smoke. I'm wearing my navy slacks with a stripped jersey and a jacket flung over my shoulders. My hair is quite mussed and between puffs on that cig that is still burning I'm trying to write you. The reason for all this get up is that a person of authority, knowing that I liked to write told me I ought to take a crack at it, so I says to myself, says I, here's a person that recognizes talent. What in heaven's name makes an amateur think she can just sit down and write a short story is beyond me, so far, I have been wise enough to throw all my attempts in the basket. Maybe some day I will become another Cornelia Otis Skinner or somethin'.

The weather here has really been something, no kiddin'. When it doesn't rain, which is very seldom, it is so damn hot that you could die. Already 18 people have been drowned in and around Worcester. One person threw herself into a well, so I suppose that doesn't really count, but all the rest were from swimming and boats. The person who threw herself in the well did so due to an unhappy love affair, she was a young woman of 80 and was afraid she would never get married so she decided to end it all (how's that for the theme of a novel, stinks doesn't)! The part about the love affair is a little doubtful, (ahem) but she was 80 and she did end it all, ho, hum.

Well guess I've written enough about nothing so I will write nothing more about nothing since I have nothing more to write anyway, so there. See you soon.

Love, Lottie

June 23, 1943
Wednesday

From:	To:
C.L. Sniderman	Mr. George Barr
65 Houghton St.	Gladstone Hotel
Worcester 4, Mass.	Philadelphia, Pa.

Dear George,

Jesus, am I hot! Oh, for the good old winter. We went on another picnic last nite and had oodles of fun. I took a picture in my bathing suit, which should be a looloo! Real sexy!! If it comes out good, - I'll hide it and never show it to anyone! We had pigs in a blanket for supper and I was so sick I nearly died.

Sunday, Edie Megans came over for dinner and then both of us were invited over to Pauline Cohan's for supper. Edie simply couldn't put on her shoes so we walked from my house to Pauline's in shorts & Edie didn't wear any shoes - just in old pair of my socks. Everyone thought we were nuts. What a picture we must have made. People looked once and then stopped to stare. They must have thought the heat had affected them - and us!!

In your last letter, you compared my flare of temper to a lightning. I was flattered - no kiddin'. I had no idea my eyes flashed like that. I'll have to look at myself in the mirror when I get antagonized next time. You're really sweet, - compliments and all.

If I ever envied anyone in my life - I did to-day. All the kids were going to their graduations & here I am an old graduate of one year that just doesn't belong anymore. It seems I've been out of school a million years or more. Wouldst that I were only five or sixteen anyway. Gotta go now, hon. Puddles of passion from your Passion Puddle.

Lottie

June 28, 1943
Monday

From:	To:
C.L. Sniderman	Mr. George Barr
65 Houghton St.	Gladstone Hotel
Worcester 4, Mass.	Philadelphia, Pa.

Dear G.,

Well, for once, something has really happened!! This morning around 5 a.m., I was very rudely awakened by nothing less than a burglar. Yes, dear, a burglar. Everyone was sound asleep, except me, when all of a once in a sudden, I heard someone at the front door. At first I thought twas my dad, then I thought twas my imagination, but the tinkering at the door continued. Evidently, he had a key but it did no good since we have some other contraption to lock the door from the inside. Well, anyway, I lay there and planned to open the door and hit him over the head with the vase you gave me. The thought scared me so much I nearly died!! My heart was beating so fast I thought it would come thru my ribs. I quietly went and woke my mother so the both of us could be scared and we were!! After fifteen minutes of planning an attack we heard him run away. I ran to one window my mother to another and we didn't even get a peek at him. We sure were scared silly and everyone laughed at us for letting him get away.

The second piece of news is that Mr. Saul Sharfman, my boss, with all the best of dishonorable intentions, propositioned me in all the immoral sense of the word. I was so stunned and shocked that I stood there with my mouth open. After a few ghastly moments, I recovered my senses and let my sense of humor get the best of me. I just sat there and roared and roared. I think he was insulted, but it really struck me funny. The kids saw him talking to me, and when they saw me go into convulsions of laughter, they got panicky 'cause they thought I was crying. When he left I told them what happened and we all had a gala time at my expense. They said I was a sucker. With all his dough, it might be worth, they said, but I couldn't be persuaded. Egads, every time I think of the look on his face and the gleam in his eye, I start laughing all over again and I am now!!

Love, L.S.

P.S. The 4th is this coming week-end. Are you coming in? I thought it was in two weeks when I spoke to you. L.S.

July 6, 1943
Tuesday

From:	To:
C.L. Sniderman	Mr. George Barr
65 Houghton St.	Gladstone Hotel
Worcester 4, Mass.	Philadelphia, Pa.

SAUL SHARFMAN
PRES. & TREAS.

NORMAN SHARFMAN
GEN. SALES MGR.

New England Grocer Supply Co.

Wholesale — NESSCO — *Grocers*
LIQUORS, WINES, BEERS
LICENSE NO. W. I. 94
41-45 ARCTIC ST.
CAMP—BAKER'S—HOTEL
RESTAURANT SUPPLIES
Worcester, Mass.

Sponsors of
NEW ENGLAND STORES "FOR THRIFTY PEOPLE"

George dear,

    I feel like an awful stinker for not writing but I had waited, hoping I could enclose some pictures we took on the picnic. They came out awful!! Not at all worth sending.

    My plans for going to Wash. have been definitely cancelled. I decided it would be unwise on my part - so in good old Worc. I shall stay - at least for the present anyhow.

    I'm trying to write this while at the switchboard and every time I get two words written the damn things start ringing. Can I have this person, my house, that person, etc., etc., etc. Some day I'm going to tell them all to go jump up a tree and branch off.

    We had loads of fun on the picnic. Laughed till I thought our sides would split. We're having just a small one to-morrow for the younger girls (me included).

    I know this letter is very drippy and I also hope you'll forgive me. This is just to let you know that I'm thinking of you. I'll write again first chance I get - when I'm not at the switchboard. I sure wish you were home now. When things went wrong - it always was wonderful having you to talk to.

Love, Lottie

July 7, 1943
Wednesday

From:	To:
C.L. Sniderman	Mr. George Barr
65 Houghton St.	Gladstone Hotel
Worcester 4, Mass.	Philadelphia, Pa.

Dear G.

Quite a coincidence when I got your letter asking me about the play. Two great minds but with one thought!! I have reserved two tickets in the middle section balcony at $.85. They are in your name. They were pretty well sold out, as a matter of fact, almost a complete sell-out. If you feel in the mood you can pick them up Saturday morning. Hell, I wish you'd hurry up and get here. I really feel lonesome. Stinkin' news about the rumors that you may take your basic down New Orleans. That means you'll never be home. It gets woiser and woiser, doesn't it?

Had a swell tennis game planned for to-nite after work, but had to postpone it due to circumstances beyond our control – that being that it rained. And here I had a swell dinner invitation that I refused because of the game. It's not the kind of nice rain I used to love to walk in, but the kind that makes you want to sit down and cry. Gee, I sure miss the walks down Massasoit Rd., and the walks in the rain and the many crazy things we used to do. Hell, I feel droopy and sentimental all over. Not good for me at all. Sometimes I think so much about various things that I feel myself going mad.

My mother is planning on going to Washington one of these weeks. Edie Megans and I will stay to-gether. Her aunt is away so we shall have a gala time cooking and learning the culinary arts.

No, dear, I haven't left my job. I think it would be quite childish to make a fuss about what Saul Sharfman said. I'm broadminded and after all you can't blame a guy for trying. You told me that yourself, didn't you?

Well, guess I'll see you before I have another chance to write. Will you call me at the office when you come in?

Love, Lottie

July 14, 1943
Wednesday

From:	To:
C.L. Sniderman	Mr. George Barr
65 Houghton St.	Gladstone Hotel
Worcester 4, Mass.	Philadelphia, Pa.

Dear G,

Hell, August 6th is not very far away is it? At least this time they're giving you ample time to think about your new plight. They just rushed your gang right off to Philly with no time to spare. How long do you get off between times now? Is it definite that you're going to New Orleans? How long are you going to be there? Egads, I have a million questions I want to ask you. It looks like I'll never get to see you in a uniform which is really very minor, altho I would love to see what kind of a soldier you'll look like. Uncle Sam will get a good man when you don an army shoot suit. Just between you and me I think this war is a stinkin' mess and I hate every damn part of it. But, nevertheless, we must grin and bear it. When are you coming in again? I guess you can start bidding farewell to all the waitresses you seem to have made the acquaintance of, eh?!!

I asked Dave, my boss, for a vacation. He was very sweet to me. He said all I had to do was ask, and all he had to do was say "No". So, I asked – and he said "No". I was so mad I cried. He explained why I couldn't have a week off, which didn't make a damn bit of difference to me. If I were smart I would have asked Saul Sharfman, but hell, I'm no glutton for punishment. Write soon.

Love, L.

July 21, 1943
Wednesday

From:	To:
C.L. Sniderman	Mr. George Barr
65 Houghton St.	Gladstone Hotel
Worcester 4, Mass.	Philadelphia, Pa.

George dear,

I honestly hope that you didn't in your generosity, give too much blood to the Red Cross. Evidently, the loss of just that one pint has made you too weak to write. Ho-hum!!

My mother leaves for Washington to-morrow morning. I think I'm gonna miss her more than I think I'm gonna miss her. I only wish to hell I were going! Yesterday at the depot I got the sudden urge to flee, and had I had one ounce of encouragement, I would have gone and bought myself a ticket too.

I started writing you last night. I was alone in a dark room and wrote between beautiful flashes of lightning. It really fascinated me. Each thunder and flash seemed so horribly mad at everyone and every thing, almost like hell and earth in a hand-to-hand battle. The letter turned out very poetic in a morbid sort of way, so I threw it away and went to bed. This morning is beautiful and my spirits much higher despite the fact that I didn't get any mail.

I have a delightful luncheon date with one Phylis Jacobson. Every time I look at her she has that fiendish look about her and immediately proceeds to tell me how hungry she is. Any minute now I expect her to start nibbling at my elbow since we still have $\frac{3}{4}$ of an hour before lunch time.

Jack Paskin, one of the boys who works here just came to the window and sends his love to you. He doesn't know you from a hole in the wall, but claims any friend of mine is a friend of his. Very friendly chap, indeed.

Well, I'm much too hungry to write anymore so with hopes of hearing from you within a few years of my life, I close with.

Much love, Lottie

P.S. Jack is also writing you something. After it passes my approval, I shall enclose it. L.

PHILCO

CERTIFICATE OF TRAINING

PHILCO
TRAINING SCHOOL
UNITED STATES ARMY SIGNAL CORPS

This certifies that JAMES GEORGE BARR was enrolled in the United States Army Signal Corps Training School conducted by Philco Radio and Television Corporation at Philadelphia, Pennsylvania, from MAY 19, 1943 to JULY 24, 1943 and has completed the prescribed course of instruction on COMMUNICATION AND NAVIGATION General Airborne equipment. Presented at Philadelphia, Pennsylvania, this 24th day of JULY 1943.

[Editor's note: While no letters from George to Lottie were found while he attended training school in Philadelphia, this Certificate of Training was found, certifying that George completed the course from the U.S. Army Signal Corps on General Airborne – Communication and Navigation, between May 19, 1943 and July 24, 1943.]

August 11, 1943
Wednesday

From:	To:
C.L. Sniderman	Mr. Pvt. J.G. Barr 11057933
65 Houghton St.	Br. T-1720 Co H. R.C.
Worcester 4, Mass.	Fort Devens, Mass.

George dear,

It was wonderful speaking to you to day. You sounded quite happy, though your letters weren't the gayest. Wish I could have gone to Devens with your mother to see you.

I went to Gloucester last weekend and had the most unusual time I ever had. I was never so impressed with scenery in my life. The place is really a fisherman's paradise. We stayed at Joe Cohen's house (Edie's cousin), and the place was a dream, formerly owned by a countess. It's in the real hoi polloi section and next door to the <u>Barr</u> mansion. Unfortunately, it is not the same Barr that is of my acquaintance, but a Barr nevertheless. It really is a mansion, complete with swimming pool and tennis courts. Will you buy that for me someday, daddy!!!

Not much has happened except that I'm thrilled to have me mater back home. She brought an album of Victor Herbert melodies, I think it's like the one you have. I'm listening to them now. She also brought me a beautiful shirt and sweater.

It's going to feel funny calling you Pvt. J. Barr - with a G.I. clip!! I can't even begin to picture how you look (oi vay)!

Write soon and I hope like hell you can come in this week.

All my love, Lottie

August 18, 1943
Wednesday

From:	To:
C.L. Sniderman	Mr. Pvt. J.G. Barr 11057933
65 Houghton St.	919th Sig. Co. Depot Aviation
Worcester 4, Mass.	New Orleans Air Base
	New Orleans, La.

George dear,

I just came back from a long walk and the wind blowing through my hair made me realize that the summer was almost gone and fall once more on its way. The days are mild and the evenings have a real autumn tinge.

I was sorry to no end that your stay at Devens was terminated so quickly. I had wanted to see you at least once more before you left. I miss you terribly. I realize even more now that my feeling for you has passed way beyond the brotherly love stage. This must seem funny coming from me..... mine has always been such a non-committal attitude. New Orleans is so damn far away, I realize its distance more than ever now.

Sunday I played a wicked game of tennis with Jackie Waxler. Our moods seemed to coincide exactly. So, after tennis we came back to my house, drank beer and talked about everything from the war situation to his breaking up with Evelyn. Then we became quite silly and after I practiced a few anti-Jap tactics on him, he left - both of us feeling in higher spirits.

Incidentally, I hope I'm not downing your spirits any by informing you that your portrait was far from flattering. I'd love to have a really good picture of you in your uniform, - so see what you can do for me along those lines.

That Thursday before you left, when I played hooky from work, it seems all my co-workers saw me and readily saw that I was not on my last stages of life. They all gave their whole-hearted approval of you. It was very funny to me, because we only saw two of them, but many more than two saw us. Such is life - ..... ain't it fun!! More of a "now you see it, - now you don't" game!! Don't tell anybody, but I hate it that way. Write soon.

Love, Lottie

August 23, 1943
Monday

From:	To:
C.L. Sniderman	Mr. Pvt. J.G. Barr 11057933
65 Houghton St.	919th Sig. Co. AVN. N.O. A.A.B.
Worcester 4, Mass.	New Orleans 12, La.

George dear,
I wish the hell it were possible for me to hop a plane - or even a train, but that's almost like asking for the moon.

Looks like my soldier isn't working himself to death!! How come you're just starting your basic? I'm glad the shots didn't have any affect on you – just a tough guy this Barr.

I was disappointed like hell that I couldn't get into Clark this year. With the soldiers all over the place there's no room for little me to increase my stagnant mind. As a consolation, I'm joining the Red Cross. I have my interview come Friday and then my physical. I wonder if they'll declare me 4-F!! I've also started taking horse back riding lessons. My first lesson is Saturday with a few more girls. Altho riding is not new to me, I'm going to start from scratch and learn the real technique. Next time you see me I shall no doubt remind you of 'dem dear old Texas gals'.

Played a wicked game of tennis yesterday and then a gang of kids including Barbara and Millie, her room-mate came over here and we had a mild cocktail party. We drank a toast to all and everyone. That's one way of forgetting your trouble.

I'm answering your boyfriend's letter and ask him to please forgive the delay, - had I remembered I would have answered it before, but don't tell him it was lack of memory.

Love, Lottie

August 25, 1943
Wednesday

From:	To:
C.L. Sniderman	Mr. Pvt. J.G. Barr 11057933
65 Houghton St.	919th Sig. Co. AVN. N.O. A.A.B.
Worcester 4, Mass.	New Orleans 12, La.

George dear,

I really haven't anything of importance to write, but maybe just getting mail will make you a little happier, so who am I to deprive you of such small pleasures. The heat here is terrific and I'm melting slowly like a sugar lump. I'm quite worried about how this army life is going to affect you mentally. I hope you won't develop an "I don't give a damn attitude." It's tough, I know, but hell, if M. Zitowitz can take it, - surely you can. Of-course, I don't mean to slur Maxie, but hells bells, I hope there's a little difference between you – mentally!!

I didn't get any mail from you to-day and you are, of course, forgiven. I realize you don't feel like spending your few spare minutes writing. George dear, there's a favor I must ask of you. If you still have the ring I gave you, I wish you would send it back for just one day. I'll send it back immediately because I want no one else to have it but you. But my father and I want to surprise my mother with a ring and that's the exact size. You don't mind, do you? I was going to call your mother and ask if she got any mail from you, but I thought maybe you wouldn't like me to. Do write first chance you get.

Love, Lottie

P.S. Tommy Dorsey is now playing "Time On My Hands" – how appropriate!

August 30, 1943
Monday

From:	To:
C.L. Sniderman	Mr. Pvt. J.G. Barr 11057933
65 Houghton St.	919th Sig. Co. AVN. N.O. A.A.B.
Worcester 4, Mass.	New Orleans Air Base
	New Orleans 12, La.

Hija fella,

Quite a shock about you being engaged, for a minute I thought you had held out on me, and after all, news such as that is nothing to keep mum about. What I'd like to know is how the hell these unfounded rumors get around so quickly. Chet Leavitt mentioned it to me before I got your letter and I didn't know exactly what he was driving at, but now I know!!

Went horse back riding Saturday and the only thing I can feel is pain. It was wonderful, or at least I thought so at the time, but after getting the after affects so strongly, I'm not so sure I was born to ride a horse.

I'm typing this letter at the office. Monday is our very slow day, or anyhow I make it slow because I really don't feel like doing a damn thing, ... So, I'm not doing a damn thing! The noise outside in the big office is terrific. Two gals are discussing the awful travelling conditions that will exist during next week-end, two others are discussing Tommy Manville and his 54 million and hoping that he would come give the Worcester dames a chance at his dough. Uh, uh, one is coming over to me with an error, -.... wait till I finish getting a bawling out!!! Oh, well, someone else made that error- thank goodness. I don't know why, but the minute something goes wrong they run to me with that accusing look in their eyes. Most of the times it wasn't my error at all, so we all laugh, - ha, ha, ha.

I had planned on going to New York for Labor Day weekend (we get an extra day off plus Monday) but we can't get reservations at any hotels. I had a lovely invitation to go to Falmouth at the Cape for the weekend, so maybe I'll take that. Personally, I'd rather stay home and get some sleep. Edie Megans and I are going to supper and the movies tonight. I guess she'll sleep over too, so that means another night I won't get any rest.

My nephew and I really get along famously. Yes, dear, there is a reason for it, you see, our mental capacity balances exactly. Sunday morning, we played baseball and he really gave me a work out, the little brat. I've learned more about ball games and pitchers and airplanes then I thought I ever could. He also plays drums so he gets himself all set in the parlor with four or five different sounding pans and then drags me over to play the piano while my mother furnishes the vocals. It's a sight to behold, no kiddin'. Nobody can ever say that the Sniderman household is such a peaceful place.

Please pardon my typing. I know it's atrocious but I honestly can't see straight. I look and feel very dissipated. You will forgive me won't you, huh, wounded would be my pride should you say NO! And if you don't like it, you know what you can do don't you dear, sweet, gentle, kind, lovable, George. (I feel very silly, woe is me.)

LOVE, LOTTIE

September 1, 1943
Wednesday

From:	To:
C.L. Sniderman	Mr. Pvt. J.G. Barr 11057933
65 Houghton St.	919th Sig. Co. AVN. N.O. A.A.B.
Worcester 4, Mass.	New Orleans 12, La.

Dear George,

First of all, let me thank you for the long, long letter I received from you to-day. I thought I would never finish reading it. Yes, dear, I'm talking about the letter you enclosed with the ring. Ya, some letter, - ..... plenty of paper...... not one word. Surely you could have signed your name, or maybe it just skipped your mind, huh, kid?!!!

I got your letter on record yesterday and it was swell. I played it all of fifty times. Funny how many things you forget to say when you get in front of a "mike." But outside of all the hemming and hawing it was great. Lottie would love more if you can do.

The heat here is slightly terrific, and plus all the work I did to-day, I was just good for nothing. Boy, to-morrow I rebel, - I'm not used to doing my work plus being at the switchboard all day. The regular operator is on vacation so I was elected unanimously to take her place. I'm so damn sick of saying "just a minute, please" that at the end of the day I was barking "Jesus Christ wait a minute"- or any how that's what I felt like saying.

After I got your record yesterday I called your mother. She told me she also got one and was quite thrilled. She wanted to hear my record but the phone is too far from the 'vic' to hear it good, and besides that, it was in a temperamental mood yesterday and wouldn't play every time. Furthermore, I didn't think she'd be really interested in the sweet things you said. Hon, I'm really a dead woman to-night, so good night. I'll write to-morrow.

Love, Lottie

September 8, 1943
Wednesday

From:	To:
C.L. Sniderman	Mr. Pvt. J.G. Barr 11057933
65 Houghton St.	919th Sig. Co. AVN. N.O. A.A.B.
Worcester 4, Mass.	New Orleans 12, La.

George dear,
I got both your letters yesterday, which of course made me doubly happy. To-day is the day in which I try and catch up on my correspondence, and altho I already have writer's cramp, I couldn't stop without writing you. I wish I had something exciting to tell you. I wish I could say I met some fascinating new people. I wish I could say I found a million dollars. However, nothing like that has happened since last I wrote you. My social life is the same, I still have no clothes and I'm still broke. And so it goes!

Life is so hellish! I should love to run away to some South Sea Isle and get away from it all. Would you like to join me? "Ariel, my love, and fly away with me! etc." I can write more words without saying anything at all. But, after all, what is there to say?

George, I'm getting that old feeling to get up and run. Wind in my sails again. I'm getting fed up with my job and everything about it. If Jackie would take his car down New Orleans, you can bet your sweet life he'd have a passenger and none other than yours truly. Would you like me to come down for a visit? Last week when we went horse back riding we took a few pictures and I'm enclosing two of them. They're awful I know but after all what can you expect – Hedy Lamarr? Incidentally, where are your pictures, and if you do take them be sure you beg, borrow or steal a dress cap to take them in.

Honey, the news that Italy surrendered just came out. My heart is thumping like mad! I can't write anymore – must run and buy an <u>extra</u>. The whole office is in an uproar. I have my own selfish, private reason for wanting this damn thing to finish.

Love, Lottie

September 12, 1943
Sunday Morning

From:	To:
C.L. Sniderman	Mr. Pvt. J.G. Barr 11057933
65 Houghton St.	919th Sig. Co. AVN. N.O. A.A.B.
Worcester 4, Mass.	New Orleans 12, La.

George dear,

This is one of those beautiful Sunday mornings in early fall when you would give your left knee to take a long walk with someone who you can talk to. Being such a thorough sentimentalist I feel the urge more than others. It's at times like this that I hate myself.

Last night Pauline Cohan came over and we had one of our brilliant discussions – brilliant on her side, - educational on mine. We discussed Cancer backwards and forwards and the war to the same degree. Russia proved to be equally puzzling to us both.

To-night my cousin Zelda and I are going to play "Unexpected Husband." I hope it's awfully, terrifically fun because I certainly could use a good laugh. I wish you had a furlough coming. I miss you something fierce. Can't you talk to the general of someone about a 2 week, 2 month or even 2 year furlough? I think twould be damn inconsiderate of the Army to deny such a small request, - don't you?!!

All week long I had the funniest sensation that something was going to happen. I can't put my finger on it exactly. Call it woman's intuition or something but that feeling persists. Its sort of a lonely, sinking, feeling. A feeling that you want something terribly, but you don't know exactly what it is. Did you ever have a sensation like that – I hope not.... It's very unpleasant. You've begun to slack up on your writing, and why pray tell should this be so? I know you haven't a thing to do all day!!! Write P.D.Q.

Love, Lottie

September 14, 1943
Tuesday

From:	To:
C.L. Sniderman	Mr. Pvt. J.G. Barr 11057933
65 Houghton St.	919th Sig. Co. AVN. N.O. A.A.B.
Worcester 4, Mass.	New Orleans 12, La.

Greetings general!

Brrrrr, my hands are positively frozen and if you think I'm kidding, run over here and see for yourself. The good old Herr Winter is on its merry way. I'm sitting here cuddling close to – myself (ha!) in a pair of heavy slacks and a jacket that George Barr gave me.

Quite funny about you having a tousle with a spaghetti, because I also had to fight my way through a delicious bowl of the damn stuff. Sunday, a whole gang of us went to the Parkway and mingled with the rest of the spaghetti lovers. Edie had her car, thank goodness, I never could have walked after eating as much as I did.

Last night I went for my Red Cross Physical. The doctor hemmed and hawed and I thought surely I would be declared 4-F, but after much deliberation he came to the conclusion that I was healthy as a horse (not the ones I ride) and put his O.K. on my application. Whew!!

I also saw Cab Calloway last nite and fell completely and madly in love with him. He sure is a righteous looking Jack. Zoot suit and all!! What a man, - sigh, sigh!! But don't worry, dear, I love you just the same even though you are white?!!

I would love to call Jackie and ask him to trek down to New Orleans, but I hate disappointment and I'm sure that's what it would turn out to be. So, you write him about my wonderful idea and if he agrees let him call and surprise me. How's that? All I can say is that if he goes – I go!!

Hells bells, honey, your pay check is not quite as much as John Jacob Astar's and so I'm mailing you a <u>package</u> of cigarettes. If there is anything else your little heart desires just yell and you'll get or anyhow I'll try and get. Take it slow – Jack and write soon.

Love, Lottie

P.S. When I say Jack, I really mean George but your James, aren't you?!!

September 19, 1943
Sunday Morning

From:	To:
C.L. Sniderman	Mr. Pvt. J.G. Barr 11057933
65 Houghton St.	919th Sig. Co. AVN. N.O. A.A.B.
Worcester 4, Mass.	New Orleans 12, La.

George darling,

It was wonderful talking to you Friday night. I love you this much for calling. After waiting until 10:30 I had given up all hopes that you'd call. But as always, you came through. I called your mother and we both laughed at how funny you must look minus your hair. For some reason, I can't picture you with a "wiffle." Friday night my brother came over and he had a grand time laughing at me watching the clock. He kept heckling me by saying that you probably were out with some other <u>dame</u>. He's a stinker, my brother, but I love him just the same. Then he kept insisting that I get married. This was of course after he had had a few drinks. He told me to quote him directly as saying - quote - I love George - unquote. All night long he kept saying he had always thought George a fine boy and that he loved George: When I tried to tell him George had been in jail three times and that he used to beat up his mother just for a laugh, he nearly killed me.

I finally got hold of some film and to-day is the day in which I shall grin my personality grin before a camera. I want to have some pictures taken, good pictures, but I want to wait till my hair grows a little longer. But if you want - (and it's up to you because the picture is for you, I certainly don't want one) I'll have one taken as I am now. Beautiful is the word for how I look this morning!! I had the reddest cherry nose you can imagine and so I started rubbing it - now my whole face is red. The news in town is very dull. Sara Sreikerg and Lou Entin are getting married to day. Sid Levine and Rita Scheyer got married a few days ago. Charlotte Cutler is marrying some guy from Boston. Everyone in this damn town are planning nuptials. Ho hum!! Write toute de suite.

Love, Lottie

P.S. Did you try to have some pictures taken, please?

September 20, 1943
Monday 8:30 P.M.

From:	To:
C.L. Sniderman	Mr. Pvt. J.G. Barr 11057933
65 Houghton St.	919th Sig. Co. AVN. N.O. A.A.B.
Worcester 4, Mass.	New Orleans 12, La.

Dearest George,

This is one night that I'm thrilled, despite the fact that I got no mail from you. I just enrolled at the Worcester Junior College for a specialized course in Journalism. I have always wanted to go to school and major in English, and at last, the opportunity presented itself and I grasped with eager hands. Of course, it's a night course and I probably won't get as much out of it as I would were it day school, but it's the best I can do, and I plan to go at it heart and soul. Wish me luck, darling.

Now for some not so good news. George, please don't be angry at me for this because I feel even worse about it than you do. I've put off writing about it hoping I wouldn't have to, - but it looks like its futile. George when you sent me back the ring I put it back in the paper you had wrapped it in and threw it into my pocketbook with the idea of giving it to my father to give to the jeweler. Well, between that time and this, I don't know what happened to the ring. Either it slipped out of my pocketbook or it may have slipped while I was putting it back in the paper. Anyhow I haven't got it. My mother knows nothing about it, of course, and my father was quite angry. Since I gave it to you, it had a double sentiment attached to it. Please don't be angry. The fact still remains that I want you to have something of mine so I'm sending you my mother of pearl and gold locket. I'm having you're initials and mine engraved on the back. This I'll never take back under any circumstances. I loved this locket and had my folk's pictures in it, but I took them out and you can put in your own pictures of your favorite pin up girl. I'm gonna miss this locket and because I like it so much I want you to have it. I hope it brings you what you want. Take care of it and I hope to hell it takes care of you. I'll mail it as soon as its been engraved.

George, your mother has asked me time and again to come up and listen to the record you sent her and to bring the record you sent me. I want to very much, but I keep wondering how she'll feel hearing you say those sweet things to me. I may be foolish, but it worries me. If it's O.K. with you, - it's alright by me. So, don't forget to let me know.

Polly Cohan went back to school to-day and I'll miss her terribly. She's simply dying to meet you. She says when she finally does meet you she's going to feel very silly because she seems to know you so well. It must become pretty dull to her to hear your name everytime she sees me. Incidentally, you're my favorite talk of conversation. I ses to her, I ses, George – he's a stinker. He didn't even buy me a corsage before he left. And he forgot to give me a birthday present. And when I went to the hospital, he didn't even come to see me. Ya, she knows all about you.

I hope you appreciate the length of this letter. I haven't written anything this long for centuries. Write toute de suite.

Love, Lottie

P.S. Please say you're not angry about the ring. More snapshots in the next letter

[Editor's note: As background for the reader, Lottie Sniderman's writing abilities had previously been recognized in July of 1937, when she was 13 years old. On the following page is an article written in the Worcester "Telegram", where Lottie won $1 for a writing contest she had entered. Also shown, is a telegram from her brother Irving "Jerry" Walker congratulating her, and a letter from the Worcester Telegram informing Lottie of her award.]

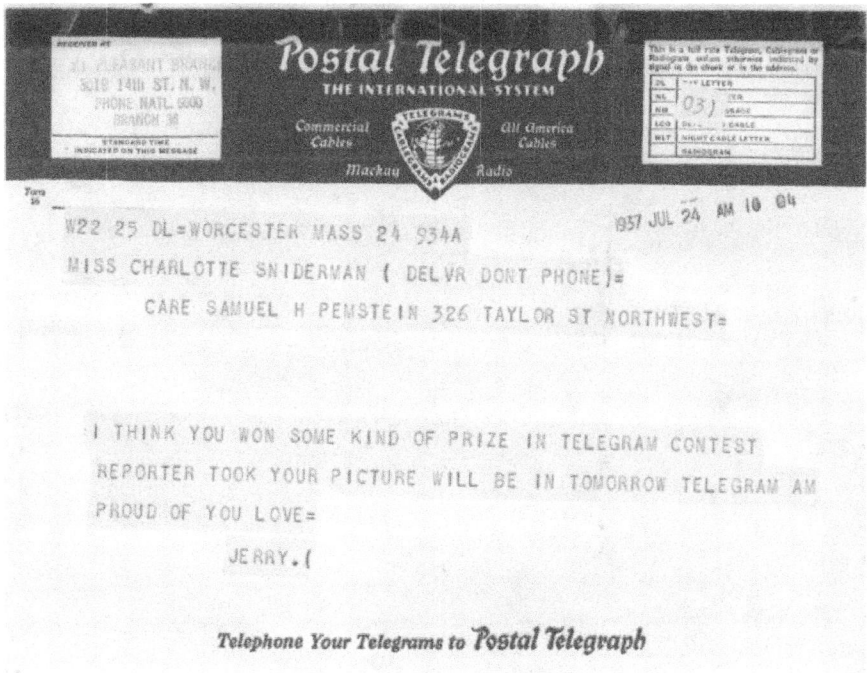

"Dick Tracy," brilliant sleuth of The Evening Gazette funnies, easily won the election to the office of "Mayor of Funnytown," but a fine letter on "Henry," whose antics appear daily in the Worcester Telegram, written by Olga DiMassa, 12, of 26 Depot square, Leominster, won first prize of $20 in the Telegram and Gazette contest for best letters on "My Favorite Funny."

Second prize of $10 is awarded to Barbara Fuller, of 45 South street, Shrewsbury, for her letter about "Winnie Winkle.' Third prize of $5 goes to Richard Mulligan, of Elmwood road, Lunenburg, for his lively letter about "Henry."

Other prizes of $1 each are awarded to Sammie Ricchute, of 10 De Marco terrace; Marie Anderson, 9 Judson road; Judith Goldman, 93 Brantwood road; Carolyn Falk, 3 Lasell avenue; Charlotte Snyderman, 65 Houghton street; Lucy Mancini, 80 Shrewsbury street, and Marilyn Beaudry, 128 Clark street, all of Worcester; and to Helen La Plante, 191 Mill street, Winchendon; Vivian Bryant, 11 Pearl street, Shrewsbury; Virginia Farquhar, 79 Mt. Vernon street, Fitchburg; Romeo Kardas, 63 Main street, Gilbertville; Vivian Vallee, 106 Cottage street, Whitinsville; Madeline Demers, Millbury road, Oxford; Janice Toppin, Box 155, Barre; Sophie Bloniasz, Franklin street, East Douglas.

Charlotte Snyderman, Worcester

GEORGE F. BOOTH
PUBLISHER

WORCESTER TELEGRAM-The Evening Gazette-SUNDAY TELEGRAM
WORCESTER, MASSACHUSETTS

Net Paid
CIRCULATION
DAILY, OVER 120,000
SUNDAY, OVER 60,000

July 26, 1937

Miss Charlotte Snyderman
65 Houghton Street
Worcester, Mass.

Dear Miss Snyderman:

We take pleasure in informing
you that your letter on "Dick Tracy" has
been awarded a prize of $1.00 in the
Funnytown Letter Contest conducted by the
Telegram and Gazette.

Your letter was very interesting
and we all enjoyed reading it. Our check
for $1.00 is enclosed.

Very truly yours,

THE TELEGRAM AND THE GAZETTE

Walter F. Hopkins

WPH:L
Enc.

Walter F. Hopkins
Contest Editor

OWNERS OF
WTAG
RADIO STATION

September 26, 1943
Sunday 8:30 P.M.

From:	To:
C.L. Sniderman	Mr. Pvt. J.G. Barr 11057933
65 Houghton St.	919th Sig. Co. AVN. N.O. A.A.B.
Worcester 4, Mass.	New Orleans 12, La.

George dear,

I'm so glad you liked the cigs, must see what can be done to make the other boys' happy, too. Would you suggest that I mail them canned samples of my salmon wiggle?!!

Don't know whether the news about you being moved to a different camp is good or bad. But being the optimist that I am, I've all the hopes that you might be stationed nearer home. Wouldn't that be somethin'! I was just sitting here thinking about you (as I often do), and I was thinking that last year at this time you were in Alabama. Next year we'll have to see that you're here, O.K.?

Ha, now for some news. Why George dear, I never knew you were a 'killer'!! I'm just beginning to learn about the women in your life! I was talking to Miriam Sigel, she works down our place, and somehow or other we began talking about you, and the conversation went thusly: "You've been going with George Barr, haven't you," she said. "Yes, why, do you know him? Yes, but not to speak to. He used to go out with my sister Ester when they were younger. He gave her his graduation picture." "Hmm", I hemmed, "what did Ester think of him". "She thought he was a <u>killer</u>". Then I fainted from laughing so much. George, of all the words to describe you, I really think "killer" is very inappropriate, or this may be a side of your personality I haven't seen yet. You're much too sweet to be a killer. Besides that, I think at that tender age your taste in women was awful. Not that I mean to be catty, but Ester and I never did click for reasons that are highly amusing to me. Remind me to tell you sometime.

I hope you had some pictures taken, and I hope it's a large size. I realize how hard it is to get a photographer, but, honest, they will be fully appreciated. Next letter may have some news about my <u>job</u>!! Write.

Love, Lottie

October 1, 1943
Friday Night

From:	To:
C.L. Sniderman	Mr. Pvt. J.G. Barr 11057933
65 Houghton St.	919th Sig. Co. AVN. N.O. A.A.B.
Worcester 4, Mass.	New Orleans 12, La.

George dear,

Well, this letter really should be something. I'll start from the beginning and try not to leave out any details. Yesterday I was sitting and thinking of nothing in particular when the telephone rang. I answered, which was very bright of me and said hello. Can you guess who it was? No? Well, I'll tell you, - it was your mother. After exchanging the usual Happy New Year greetings, she got down to what she really called about. She informed me that your brother, Nookie, and Fran were here and wanted to meet me, so she very sweetly invited me to dinner. Realizing that this was my chance to get a free meal, I accepted. Well, hon, the dinner was today and delicious to say the least. Charlotte and Bonnie were also there and the baby is adorable. After a ten-course meal, the company, your family, started pouring in. I swear in all my life I never met so many people in one day. Your mother told me not to forget to tell you that. Uncle Nathan from Laronto is in town. Fran, Charlotte, and I sat on the sofa and received and met the guests. I didn't feel so bad because they didn't know half the people either. Your mother slipped a few times and introduced us as her three daughter-in-laws. I felt very awkward!! Before dinner, your record that you sent me, was played about ten times, and Nookie kept insisting that he didn't know his kid brother had it in him. Both Fran and Nookie are very sweet and Nookie insisted that I kiss him goodbye. I'm no dope - so I did. But really, I had a super time; only I missed your not being there terribly. Sid Plotkin was in for a few days and he and Evelyn were also up for a few minutes. Jackie Waxler was operated on for a Hernia last week. I guess he was quite sick, but he's fine now and should be home in a few days. Nookie went to see him in the hospital.

George, there's no use saying I wasn't scared stiff. I was so nervous I had to take a cab up to your house. Once I got there I was O.K., but I was sure I'd spill the soup or fall down or something. But set your mind at ease, everything went wonderfully. I won't ever be able to explain in words how I felt. I experienced something I never have before, and haven't gotten over it. I think I looked pretty nice, but of-course, I wouldn't call mine an unbiased opinion!!! I wish to hell you were here. I showed everyone your picture and they thought twas very nice. Incidentally, Happy New Year, dear. I think

I've done alright by you in this letter, - I still haven't gotten over being a little nervous. Write soon.

Love, Lottie

October 6, 1943
Wednesday

From:	To:
C.L. Sniderman	Mr. Pvt. J.G. Barr 11057933
65 Houghton St.	919th Sig. Co. AVN. N.O. A.A.B.
Worcester 4, Mass.	New Orleans 12, La.

George dear,

I feel awful 'cause I didn't write for so long, but this time I have a legit excuse. Yep, you guessed, - I was sick!! Panic struck this house when I came down with a grand cold and my ears started acting up again. Me mater tucked me into bed and there I stayed till all fear was gone. I am most happy to report I am almost well, that is, I feel O.K., but they keep me a prisoner in my own house.

Your record was wonderful! I had the surprise of a lifetime when I heard Dave was in the army, and even more so that he's not far from you. The picture you sent is also good. I had a hard time recognizing Dave, - he looked so morose. My mother insists that you got fat, the only comment I have to make, is that you make a pretty cute soldier!

I did have some snap shots to send you, but I haven't been able to go downtown to get them. Next will be sure to enclose.

I've been going mad trying to amuse myself this past week. I read every book I could get ahold of, - I know all my records by heart and everyone was working so there was no one to talk to but myself and I've come to the conclusion that I'm a very dull conversationalist!! Your letters, thank goodness, have been coming every day so that took up some of my time. I called your mother last nite to tell her about the record, but she wasn't home so I'll try again to night. Am dying to see what your good picture will look like. Surely it will do justice to that handsome, masculine, press of yours, (ho-hum)! I really have nothing of any real importance or interest to tell you, and this letter is truly a bore but in my mental condition what did you want, - anyhow?!! Write soon, hon. I'm going to make some fudge to-night, if it's any good I'll send you a piece, O.K.?!

Love, Lottie

October 10, 1943
Sunday

From:	To:
C.L. Sniderman	Mr. Pvt. J.G. Barr 11057933
65 Houghton St.	919th Sig. Co. AVN. N.O. A.A.B.
Worcester 4, Mass.	New Orleans 12, La.

George dear,

Humph – so your brother wants to fix you up with a rich southern belle! Well, can't say that I'd blame you if you did want to meet her. Hell's fire, I haven't got even one car to try to entice you with and she's got a whole garage full of them. Well, can I help it if I was born beautiful (ahem) instead of rich!

Saw your mother in schule yesterday and she asked to be remembered to you. She looked very nice. I was never so bored in my life. The place was simply void of young people. There were a few gals standing around and the newly weds, Sara Sreiberg and Louie Entin. They looked so happy it made me sick to my stomach.

Too bad about the proofs not coming out. Be sure and send them P.D.Q. when you finally do get the pictures. To-day is positively beautiful. Real autumn weather. After finishing this letter I'm going to pull on a pair of slacks and a heavy sweater and take a long walk. I haven't been walking for a long time. I hate going myself, - would you care to join me?!! Egads, man, your army life really doesn't sound too tiring. I can't understand they're system at all. How long are you going to go to school and how many times are you going to take the same thing over again. Oh, well, maybe when you finally do finish your course, you'll be able to do something with my radio. Incidentally, did you get yours, your mother said she sent it to you a long time ago and you never said whether you got it or not. My bedroom radio went on the blink and poor Sol Zitowitz nearly went mad trying to fix it. Every time he'd finish, something else would go wrong. He said he never was so glad to get rid of a radio in his life. Incidentally, he sends his regards. Also, regards from an Elenore or Elaine Freedman. She said you used to deliver up her house. I don't know her from a hole in the wall and I don't know how she knows I know you, - but she said she did and I guess there's nothing I can or want to do about it. Next letter will send you snapshots.

Love, Lottie

P.S. Miss you like all hell!

October 13, 1943
Wednesday

From:	To:
C.L. Sniderman	Mr. Pvt. J.G. Barr 11057933
65 Houghton St.	919th Sig. Co. AVN. N.O. A.A.B.
Worcester 4, Mass.	New Orleans 12, La.

George dear,

    I thought surely I would get a letter from you today, but it seems like you're getting my bad habit of procrastination when it comes to missives. Last week was great – a letter every day – this week not even a post card. Fine thing!!

    Sunday nite I was sitting alone and thinking when who should call but your mother. She asked me to come over. So, I donned my duds, grabbed your record and your picture, and went avisiting. But I was darned if I'd walk alone on that dark street of yours, so I took my father along for protection. We both had a very enjoyable evening. Tobye showed me gowns and your mother told me what a good boy you were in your younger days – she was being sarcastic, of course. Your sister is really a very sweet kid. She told me she also plans to go into nursing as I once did. I had to settle for a nurses' aide class!

    I'm writing this letter in a hot and very uncomfortable office. Every once in awhile the "bull dog" (Saul Sharfman) struts by and ogles the girls. While I'm not watching him, and talking to Phylis Jacobson, I'm playing nursemaid to a darn switch-board! If by any chance, you happen to be stationed in Florida this winter, I know a little girl who's going to visit you, and I'm not kidding!

    I'm going to take out those snapshots during my lunch hour, so I'll enclose them in this letter if they're any good. I made my appointment to have some good pictures taken a week from Saturday. It's really a waste of time, money, and film but I'm doing this just to please you. Now, ain't I a good girl?

    You better write soon, my friend, or Uncle Sam will be minus a soldier.

Love, Lottie

P.S. George, the pictures were fierce! I couldn't send them, honest. Will try again when I get film.

October 19, 1943
Tuesday

From:	To:
C.L. Sniderman	Mr. Pvt. J.G. Barr 11057933
65 Houghton St.	883rd Sig. Co. Depot Avn. N.O. A.A.B.
Worcester 4, Mass.	New Orleans 12, La.

Hello!

    Please forgive my not writing, but time was one thing I didn't have. I meant well, - honest! But, why the hell should I apologize. You haven't written for years. Perchance have you been sneaking out at night with some southern gal?!! Fine thing.

    I'm down at the office now and I thought I'd write while the damn switchboard wasn't so busy. To-night I'm going to the opera, my dear! Carmen is playing and you know me when it comes to operas. Friday nite I saw "Life With Father" which was very good. I was talking to Edie Megans and before I knew it, I had made arrangements to meet her in $\frac{1}{2}$ an hour to see the play. We missed the beginning of the first act and people cursed us up and down for coming in so late, but once we got settled everything was O.K. We were both so exhausted from rushing that we didn't really appreciate it, but what I saw while I wasn't sleeping was very good. Last nite I went to a bridge, a regular old maid's affair, which was too, too boring. A few of the younger girls (me too) got together and gabbed and gabbed. I won the prize. No, not for gabbing – for cutting highest in the cards. It was a bee-utiful 5¢ ash tray!

    The girls in the office brought in some very unintelligent literature, which I'm passing on to you. You'll probably think they're very "corny" but I have a funny sense of humor, anyway. I thought them cute.

    It was very sweet of Dave to send me a card. Tell him I'll write first chance I get. Hon, I haven't anything more to write, so why the hell should I bore you. Write ----!!

Love, Lottie

October 22, 1943
Friday Night 8:45

From:	To:
C.L. Sniderman	Mr. Pvt. J.G. Barr 11057933
65 Houghton St.	883rd Sig. Co. Depot Avn. N.O., A.A.B.
Worcester 4, Mass.	New Orleans 12, La.

George dear,

Congratulations! So, you've finally started your basic and only for the seventh time! Confidentially, dear, I think you're taking the long way around to becoming a general.

I told my mother that you suggested I learn to cook. She was dismayed that you thought I didn't know how, but strictly on the Q.T. she thinks it's a pretty good idea too – so any day now I shall partake in learning the culinary arts. Just tell me what you like best and I'll send you samples so you can see how well I'm progressing.

We had quite a discussion down at the office yesterday and I was the main topic of conversation. We started talking about psychology and the girls marveled at my ability to understand people. I was flattered to say the least. They also agreed that office work was definitely not my line, to which I agreed whole heartedly. They said I had imagination and creative ability and office work did not allow me to show any initiative. If they tell me much more I'll begin to think I know something. Charlotte, the girl I work under said I could do office work very well when I put my mind to it, - the only trouble was I never or almost never want to put my mind to it. She said she and the other girls often watch me and marvel how mechanically I do my work when they know my mind is a million miles away. The trouble is they are only too, too right about me. I loathe office work and my mind is never fully on it, - therefore, some of the results are quite bad. My brother and this reporter Hal Greenberg were up the house the other nite and he discouraged any ambitions I had of going into the field of journalism. My mother on the other hand encourages me greatly. She says I'll never be happy unless I try it, and if I fail then I'll be satisfied to at least know I tried. I'm going to wait until after Christmas, and then make up my mind what I'm going to do. All I can say is that's a hell of a situation!! What do you think I ought to do, Mr. Anthony. Should I go on forcing myself to do the thing I hate or try what I want to and hear the disappointments, which are inevitable to anyone who is inexperienced. At times, I wish I were born very stupid, - then I'd be content with anything. I wish to hell you were here so I could talk to you. You're always such a comfort and I love you for it.

Incidentally, what about your pictures? My appointment is next week and I know they're going to come out lousy, but only for you would I go through taking pictures again. I thought of posing on a bear skin rug or with a bubble or somethin' – what do you think?!! And with this parting thought I leave.

Goodnight, Lottie

P.S. This had been an awful letter, please forgive – next one will be better.

October 25, 1943
Monday

From:	To:
C.L. Sniderman	Mr. Pvt. J.G. Barr 11057933
65 Houghton St.	883rd Sig. Co. Depot Avn. N.O. A.A.B.
Worcester 4, Mass.	New Orleans 12, La.

George dear,

I got your pictures today and they are grand. You look more like a general than a private. I gave you the place of honor in the living room, and there you sit watching the household. I can't understand why you haven't gotten any mail from me. I write every chance, honest injun'!

I went to Boston Saturday with my mother. We were going to stay over Sunday, but after tramping from one store to the other for hours (my mother was looking for a coat), we both collapsed in the seats of the Shubert Playhouse. We saw "Outrageous Fortune" which was very good. All about this Jewish family who were blessed with having a "fairy" for a son. My mother, bless her innocent heart, didn't get the drift of the play until I, the world wise daughter, explained. I think I'll buy a book on "How to Raise Your Mother." But don't get me wrong I love her that way and if I had a tenth of her wisdom, I'd be pretty clever. Well, to get back to what I started to say – we were so tired that we took the last train home Saturday nite. I was so tired I thought I'd never get up – but I did.

Edie Megans just called me and we talked for hours. And what a morbid conversation it was! We were practically weeping on each other's telephone. Of all the girls that both of us have met, we both think it's wonderful that ours has lasted so long and we're still terribly close. I always missed not having a sister and I guess she did too. It's swell to have someone to talk to and tell your troubles to. I miss you like awful. Twould be hotsy dandy if this damn war would take an end. My brother just called me and he has double trouble in his household. First of all, he got his card to come to Devens for a physical. This wasn't exactly pleasant news, but even worse than that his dog was just taken to the hospital with pneumonia. Poor brother, he's taking it awfully hard!! What a guy. Incidentally, he sends his regards to you. Very interested in your welfare is this relative of mine. Write soon, hon.

Love, Lottie

October 28, 1943
Thursday

From:	To:
C.L. Sniderman	Mr. Pvt. J.G. Barr 11057933
65 Houghton St.	883rd Sig. Co. Depot Avn. N.O. A.A.B.
Worcester 4, Mass.	New Orleans 12, La.

Hiya Hon,

Its been raining miserably for the past three days and the weather being what it is doesn't do very much for one's spirits. I've started writing you about five letters. Each one went into the waste basket. Not suitable was the label I put on them. Why they were not suitable, don't ask me. This one is going to be mailed good, bad, or otherwise. I decided to take my lunch with me today, a thing I rarely do, and I'm sitting in a dirty overheated conference room. I just finished eating and decided that I simply must write you. So here I am. I called my mother a few minutes ago, and she said there was a letter from you. Your letters get better with each writing.

I wish to hell I had something newsy to write you, but honest, not a damn thing has happened. Before I go any further may I take time out to wish you a Happy Halloween. The gals in the office were going to have a party, but it seems we haven't got the time. We all rush around doing nothing very busily. So again, - Happy Halloween – from one funny face to another.

Have you seen Dave Grossman lately? You haven't said anything about him for a long time, that's why I ask. There's been loads of talks, rumors I guess, that the war with Germany is nearing its last stages. It's probably very unfounded, but sounds good anyway. Worcester is going to lift the "dim out ban", so maybe I won't be afraid to go out nights anymore. Not that I go out anyway, but even a poor excuse is better than none. A big glass of beer is sitting beside me and making my mouth water. It happens to be card board, but the damn thing looks so real in another minute I'll start drinking it anyway. Fer goodness sake, when's a guy like you gonna get a furlough! Seems like you've been away forever. Miriam Sigel, Ester's sister, just came in and asked to whom I was writing. She sends her regards. Pardon me, while I light my third cigarette, - I'm sooooo nervous! Write -

Love, Lottie

October 29, 1943
Friday Night

From:	To:
C.L. Sniderman	Mr. Pvt. J.G. Barr 11057933
65 Houghton St.	883rd Sig. Co. Depot Avn. N.O. A.A.B.
Worcester 4, Mass.	New Orleans 12, La.

Hello darling,

And how's the love of my life today?! Your baby is really raring tonight and here's why. Jackie Waxler just called and we had a lengthy and gay discussion. Among one of the things we hashed over was a possible trip to New Orleans - and we ain't kiddin'!! It seems Jackie is planning to go to Florida this winter, but I wasn't going to let him off that easy so..... if we can get some gas coupons and the consent of our folks, we'll be on our way. It sounds heavenly, doesn't it? He's taking me to the movies tomorrow night and we'll discuss the pros and cons. Tomorrow also is the day that I'm taking my pictures. I'm terribly nervous, honest! I can tell you now how I'm going to look, and brother that ain't good.

I started reading "For Whom the Bell Tolls" today and it's veddy veddy good. Some parts are lousy but I guess it's professional jealousy, only I'm not professional, heck, I'm not even an amateur. Writing as of now for me is just a gleam in my eye! But it's fun, anywho, so there. Incidentally, you ought to congratulate me. I, Lottie, have given up smoking. All of a once in a sudden, every time I take a cig I get very dizzy and have a awful felling of nausea. Maybe it's the cigs, maybe it's me, but the point is, I ain't indulging anymore. Nice? Jackie also told me that Sid was planning on getting a special furlough to come home and get married, but the poor kid was shipped to another camp and quarantined for a month. They don't know if this means the fellows are sick or if they're getting ready to be shipped. Either way, it's too bad.

Gotta go now, pal. But the reason is not what you think. I suddenly feel a passion to wash my face. I know, this sounds ridiculous but I'm always getting sudden ridiculous passions. Wanna make sometin' of it?!! Will write again tomorrow, so until then, goodnight.

Love, Lottie

November 1, 1943
Monday

From:	To:
C.L. Sniderman	Mr. Pvt. J.G. Barr 11057933
65 Houghton St.	883rd Sig. Co. Depot Avn. N.O. A.A.B.
Worcester 4, Mass.	New Orleans 12, La.

Hello!

    I saw Jackie Saturday night as I wrote you, and the chances of my coming down are very slim. In the first place, Jackie can't take his car and my folks wouldn't dream of letting me go by train. I guess he's going anyway to Florida. He said he'd let me know if by any chance he was taking his car. Sunday, he and I also went to the Air Show. There wasn't much to see. A couple of Piper Cubs and a few Thunderbolts. Quite disappointing. We were standing and watching the planes when all of a sudden, we hear Harvey Coblentz's name called for a free ride. They picked names out of a hat and he was the second one chosen. We spoke to him after the ride and he evidently got a big kick out of it. He was accepted by the air corps, you know. After the air show, Jackie and I went to the hospital to see your mother, and they told us she had just left for home! So we rush pell mell down to your house. She really looks wonderful, George. You'd never know she was sick. I knew she was in the hospital when I called her to tell her I got your pictures. She also asked me to call Charlotte and tell her she was home, so meanwhile, Charlotte and Bonnie asked to be remembered to you.

    I got a very sweet letter from Dave G. today. I didn't know the guy could write such cute letters. Incidentally, I'm beginning to realize what an awful peculiar person Jackie is. He has some of the funniest ideas. I was amazed at his lack of interest in life. He really let loose Saturday night and talked a blue streak. I enjoyed every minute of it – but disagreed with all of his philosophy. He has some misconstrued conceptions of what it's all about and a marked chip on his shoulder. I guess his health has a lot to do with it. Wish I could change some of his ideas. I also saw where you got some of your viewpoints when I first met you. I think you've gotten over most of your grudges against the world. At least I hope you have. Be an optimist, like me?!!

Love, Lottie

P.S. Never be anything I am, on second thought.

November 1, 1943
Monday

From:	To:
Mr. Pvt. J.G. Barr 11057933	C.L. Sniderman
883rd Sig. Co. Depot Avn. N.O. A.A.B.	65 Houghton St.
New Orleans 12, La.	Worcester, Mass.

Dearest Lottie,

You lovely crazy kid, but how I love you for it, thinking your folks would agree to you coming all the way down here with Jackie. Not that I wouldn't give anything to see you, but it would be impossible, just think about all the angles.

The first one is getting the consent of your family, secondly, by the time you could arrange to come down here I could be shipped, thirdly, although I have faith in Jackie's car, I doubt if it could make such a long trip again without mishap. Think about it.

Darling, the thought of yours makes me love you the more. It seems that no matter how much I love you, little things you do just make me love you just that much more.

They got your boy friend good to-day. This dark and dusky morning, we were rudely awakened at 4:30. The silly reason was that the officers wanted to get an early start out to the firing range. We waited a half hour for breakfast, then off we rode to the range. There was so much fog out there that the boys couldn't fire till 1:00 P.M. I didn't fire because they think I'm the very best target setter. I was scheduled to fire to-morrow, but they still think I'm one of the very best. I get up at 3:30 A.M. to-morrow morning just to get the boys started on time.

Don't get any wrong ideas about me, I love the army. —— All kidding aside, if I didn't have you back home and I wanted to be a wolf in Uncle Sam's clothing, I'd like it an awful lot.

I thought that clipping was very good, and to spread cheer among the boys I gave it to one of the fellows to send back home to his girl. The boys really got a big kick out of it. "How true!" was the remark they made.

Goodnight kid, I'd better get to bed a little earlier to-night.

Your, George

November 2, 1943
Tuesday

From:	To:
Mr. Pvt. J.G. Barr 11057933	C.L. Sniderman
883rd Sig. Co. Depot Avn. N.O. A.A.B.	65 Houghton St.
New Orleans 12, La.	Worcester, Mass.

SIGNAL CORPS
U. S. ARMY

Dearest Lottie,

Hello darling. I've a whole hour to myself before we fall out again, so I thought I'd use it to the best advantage.

We were supposed to go out to the firing range again to-day, but it was cancelled. As yet we've been doing absolutely nothing, but we had to stay to-gether in front of one of the barracks. They finally let up on us and told us we were dismissed til 12:30.

I just came back from the mess hall where I got a couple of pieces of chocolate cake. One of the boys that I know is on, and he passed them out to me. Yesterday I fixed him up with so much fruit and milk he wanted, that way we remain one big happy family.

To-night we have another dress parade, a general or something is coming in and we have to put on a show. The last week was nice but during the night it got chilly and we're all wearing jackets. I wish it would either be hot or cold. These frequent changes in weather, well – I don't like them.

Yesterday while on K.P. two of the other boys wrote a song at my suggestion. It's not much of a song, having only two stanzas. It's sung to the tune of "Pistol Packing Mamma."

Here is what we have ----

K.P.'s Lament (until we get a better title)
They woke me up one morning, and told me I was on K.P.
Turned right ones, started snoring, now cookies after me
Chorus
Oh! Lay that cleaner down cook, Lay that cleaner down,

Cleaner carrying cookie, lay that cleaner down

\#

He bashed in all my front teeth, Blackened both my eyes, cut me down to
form fut

Now I'm about his size.

Chorus

\#

They put me the pots and pans – pretty mean of them wasn't it.

The last line is not to be sung, sort of like a Bob Hope ad lib, if you get what
I mean. This is as far as we got, and probably as far as we'll get until we get
on K.P. again.

We drove the cooks crazy with our singing yesterday. They told us
to keep quite about twenty times. If we didn't work so darn hard I could say
I had a wonderful time. We really raised hell.

I just sang my last bar.

Your, George

P.S. Of course the song is not to be printed without permission of the
writers. G.B.

November 4, 1943
Thursday

From:	To:
C.L. Sniderman	Mr. Pvt. J.G. Barr 11057933
65 Houghton St.	883rd Sig. Co. Depot Avn. N.O. A.A.B.
Worcester 4, Mass.	New Orleans 12, La.

Dear James?!

Vots de matter mit you? Don't you believe in writing letters
anymore? O.K., so your last letter was exceptionally good. That's no reason
to call it a day.

Monday night, Edith Megans and I went to see "Porgy and Bess" –
it was tres good. Especially the part where Porgy sings, "Bess ya is mine
woman now, etc." Edie and I almost fell asleep when she started to sing
"Summer Time." Ah me, if only I had a voice. I saw Phil Sobel to-day
downtown and he looks very bad. He needed a shave something fierce and
looked so dissipated. I also saw Harry Grace the other day. Phylis Jacobson
and I were walking down Front Street chatting merrily when all of a sudden
both of us stopped dead. We saw before us a mustache, - when we looked

again we realized it belonged to Harry Grace. Ugh – me no like him with or without a mustache.

Last night we had our first rehearsal for the minstrel show that I'm in – or didn't I tell you before. Sho nuff the Junior Hadassah are putting on a minstrel and yours truly is going to be an 'end man' and also in one of the specialty acts, - that is, if I don't get thrown out when they find out that I'm not as good as I told them I was.

I've got so damn many things I must do tonight that I don't know where to begin. As a matter of fact, I don't think I'll begin – much too tired to do anything where mental or physical exertion is required.

Yep, Rose Barr is getting married come Sunday. Too bad you can't be here. Very inconsiderate of her not to wait until you could come. Weddings are such happy occasions – they always make me cry.

Listen, me pet, you better start writing or this pistol packin' mama is gonna make one less soldier for Uncle Sam, see, I'm tough, see, - See?!

Love, Lottie

November 5, 1943
Friday

From:	To:
Mr. Pvt. J.G. Barr 11057933	C.L. Sniderman
883rd Sig. Co. Depot Avn. N.O. A.A.B.	65 Houghton St.
New Orleans 12, La.	Worcester, Mass.

Dearest Lottie,
Congrats' are in order, for yesterday I shot the terrific total of 145 on the rifle range with the carbine, the signal corps rifle. This qualifies me as a marksman. Now if they have enough medals to go around I'll get one. Hot stuff, that's me.

All kidding aside, 145 is fifteen points above average. A lot of the boys shot 160 and better. The story you hear about the cowboys are true, they can shoot and shoot straight.

I don't quite get what you mean, you know where I got some of my ideas of life. If I'm not mistaken I didn't get them from Jackie, because I think I have a mind of my own, although unconsciously I may have been a bit influenced by him, but I doubt it. We had many talks just like the one you had, and we both had our own opinions on things in general, some coincided some didn't.

I sure miss those talks we had, and no kidding. Just being to-gether alone and talking to each other, and you telling me I was wrong in some of my thoughts, but did I love it, coming from you. I'd rather listen to you than anyone in this cockeyed world.

Dave and I were to-gether last night for a while and he wants to know why you haven't answered. I told him that you were too busy writing me and when you got a loose minute you would answer him. Did I do right by you?

I'm glad you were up to see my mother, because I'm sure she'd like to see you, especially while I'm not around, why, I don't know, because I was an awful nuisance while at home. Thanks darling, your wonderful and I love you.

Your, George

November 7, 1943
Sunday

From:	To:
C.L. Sniderman	Mr. Pvt. J.G. Barr 11057933
65 Houghton St.	883rd Sig. Co. Depot Avn. N.O. A.A.B.
Worcester, Mass.	New Orleans 12, La.

Dearest George,

After waiting for what seemed like months, I finally got both of your letters in one day. Today I'm all a dither. I've been receiving and sending telegrams and cancelling and making plans. Next Saturday I had intended to go to Boston, but after conferring with Pauline Cohan, who is going to school in Baltimore, we decided upon New York for next weekend instead of the following weekend, and so what seems like a very mixed affair is very mixed up because we had to cancel and remake hotel reservations. We're really going to meet and mingle with the hoi polloi, since we're going to stay at the Biltmore. I'm really very excited. It's been so long since I've done any travelling, and altho I'm only staying 4 days we've crammed a whole weeks' schedule into these few days.

I read your letter to my mother. The one in which you tell me how foolish a trip to New Orleans would be. She was very happy that at least one of us was sensible. Incidentally, my mother and I went to visit your mother last night and she received so many boxes of candy, that she asked me to send you one of them. She also gave me the remains of a small cake and the gloves you asked for. I'm sending them out the first minute I get. I also heard one of the records you sent her. The one Dave Grossman spoke on and you said you sent me some negatives of pictures you had taken. I was amazed because it was the first I had heard of them. Your uncle from Washington was also there and it seems he used to live with some very good friends of ours. Your uncle and aunt from New York were there, too. I don't remember their names. They made many remarks regarding you and I, which made me blush to no end. Oh, well....! I'll try and write every chance I have this week but don't be angry if they are short because I have oodles of things to attend to. Take care, darling.

Love, Lottie

November 10, 1943
Wednesday

From:	To:
C.L. Sniderman	Mr. Pvt. J.G. Barr 11057933
65 Houghton St.	883rd Sig. Co. Depot Avn. N.O. A.A.B.
Worcester, Mass.	New Orleans 12, La.

George dear,

Trying to find a spare minute this week was almost like trying to find gold, but tonight I said to myself, ses I, "Lottie you old stinker, you had better write to George." I got your pictures today, and altho mine is not an unbiased opinion, I thought them very good. You look like such a damn tough soldier. Heck, I wouldn't like you for my tap sergeant -...... or would I!! I felt very bad because you said I didn't write to Dave. I'm sure I answered his letter. But of course, it takes much longer to get there than yours because I didn't send his Air Mail. Ask him if he got it. I was all excited when you said you were going to apply for a furlough, and you let me down with a bang, by saying you were sure you wouldn't get it. Here's hoping it comes through, - but quick!

Very sweet of your brother and Fran to have said they liked me. But I don't know how much of a compliment it is, - since they probably figured they had to say that. But don't think for a minute that I didn't like it.

The mater and I went to see the Russian Ballet at the Auditorium the other day and twas very good. I came home and tried it but it didn't look the same. Even my mother who loves me very much, said as far as ballet was concerned, I had better stick to an office! Oh, well.....?!

Yea, man, the lights are on again in ye old home town, but I still have to feel my way around. Only the signs and store lights are on – the streets are the same. I've become very charitable of late and have been selling stationary, the proceeds going to aid children in Palestine. I don't know whether I ask the right people or what, but in one hour I made 12 orders. How's that! The average is 4 orders. Very good about you planning to take up photography, - maybe you'll be able to take a good picture of me. Incidentally, you should be getting my pictures any year now. Well, hon, I gotta go to a rehearsal. I'd much rather go to sleep, but my career comes first. Do you still love me?!

Love, Lottie

November 13, 1943
Saturday

From:	To:
C.L. Sniderman	Mr. Pvt. J.G. Barr 11057933
Murray Hill Hotel	883rd Sig. Co. Depot Avn. N.O. A.A.B.
New York, NY.	New Orleans 12, La.

MURRAY HILL HOTEL
NEW YORK

Hi honey,

Well, here's your little girl in the big city and having one hell of a time! By some misfortune, they made our reservations at the Biltmore for next weekend and after calling every hotel in the city we finally got a room. We were almost ready to sleep on a bench in Central Park but luck was with us. Why does everything happen to me!! But this place isn't half bad – it's got beds anyway.

Pauline and I were just about to go out to lunch, and I am famished, but I thought I'd dash off a few words to at least tell you we got here. I'll write again when I get home. Wish you were here, honest.

Love, Lottie

P.S. Pauline says "Hi George". LCS

November 15, 1943
Monday Night

From:	To:
C.L. Sniderman	Mr. Pvt. J.G. Barr 11057933
65 Houghton St.	883rd Sig. Co. Depot Avn. N.O. A.A.B.
Worcester, Mass.	New Orleans 12, La.

Hello darling,

Well, I'm back. All I can say is that I had a wonderful time, only I wished you were there. There were so many things I saw and did that I know you would have enjoyed. Pauline and I restricted ourselves mostly to Park Avenue and 5th Avenue. Those people have money and enjoy it – so many have money and don't get any fun out of it at all. We ate one lunch at the St. Maritz Hotel, and all you could see were Minks and Silver Fox. Altho I wasn't jealous, I hate jealous people, I wouldn't mind having a few of the things they have. Someday......!

George, it's very sweet of you to want to call me, but as much as I'd love talking to you, I'd much rather you spent the money on yourself. Hell, the call only lasts 3 minutes, - a meal should last at least an hour! So, let's save all the talking until you get a furlough. Here's hoping it won't be long.

The French café you wrote me about sounds quite intriguing. You must remember to take me there on our first trip across the country. Is that a date? I took my proofs back to the photographer's today, and altho I pleaded on bended knee, she said they wouldn't be ready for three weeks. I'll mail it to you as soon as I can.

It snowed in Worcester for the first time today. It wasn't a pretty snow at all, more, I should say, of a maybe snow snow or maybe rain snow. When you figure out that last sentence please explain it to me.

Me mater is hounding me to hit the hay and I really am awfully tired. Dave Grossman wrote that the next time he saw you he was going to kiss you for me. Not that I asked him, - it was strictly his idea. George, when he finally gets around to delivering the said object will you honestly tell me whether or not ya enjoyed it!

Love, Lottie

November 16, 1943
Tuesday

From:	To:
Mr. Pvt. J.G. Barr 11057933	C.L. Sniderman
883rd Sig. Co. Depot Avn. N.O. A.A.B.	65 Houghton St.
New Orleans 12, La.	Worcester, Mass.

Dearest Lottie,

This is a heck of a way to start a letter but – I'm tired – no I'm dead. Tomorrow I'll write you all about it.

How Dave and I had dinner at Arnaud's, one of New Orleans' best and fanciest restaurants, how I drove a G.I. truck, and finally a little about my day of K.P. (are you on pins and needles? Yes?)

Darling, what made you ask if I still love you? You should know by now that I do, and I'll love you for the rest of eternity.

Lottie, my darling, I love you. I'm just sorry I have to write it and not be able to tell you personally. Until to-morrow –

Your, George

P.S. Something I shouldn't have forgotten. Thanks loads for the package, it was swell while it lasted. G.B.

November 19, 1943
Friday Night

From:	To:
C.L. Sniderman	Mr. Pvt. J.G. Barr 11057933
65 Houghton St.	883rd Sig. Co. Depot Avn. N.O. A.A.B.
Worcester, Mass.	New Orleans 12, La.

Hi honey,

After waiting all week, I finally got both your letters today. I nearly fell over at the length of one of them. Twas simply wonderful – only I'm jealous! I wanna go to hoi polloi restaurants too and have wine and all the trimmings. I'm glad at least one of us is having fun. I can just picture you in the setting you described, - both of us like things done up in a big way. Pardon me for a few minutes, please; my mother insists that I indulge in a bit of repast.

Oh, that was good, - now I feel much better!

Last night I went to nurses' aid and I had to lift an enormous patient. I could feel something inside me pull and I nearly dropped her. Well, today I couldn't stand up straight. Yes, you guessed it, - I strained a muscle in my stomach and it hurted like hell. I didn't dare tell my mother, she wouldn't have let me go anymore. Leave it to me, uh!

Your sister Tobye called the other night and she said your folks were sending you a package, among one of the things being shoes. I nearly died laughing. For some odd reason, I was under the impression that the army supplied shoes!

One of the gals came to the office with the most gorgeous orchid I ever saw. I never liked the darn things before, but now I've developed a passion for them. George, some day, when you've made your first million will you buy me an orchid, huh, pleeeze, will ya? When are you going to get a furlough? I know someone who would love to see you. Who? Why, me, of course, you silly!

When I finally was all ready to make my debut as a great dramatic actress, guess what happened. The minstrel show was postponed indefinitely. Not enough came to rehearsals because most of them are busy either working or buying for Christmas. Of course, Phylis Jacobson and I were highly insulted. We were the specialty acts, - and don't say that's why it was put off, — everyone else has. Oh, well!

The poem you sent me about New Orleans was very good. Me thinks the boys who wrote it are wasting their time in the Army. What has Edgar Allen Poe got that they wouldn't like to have.

Why did you ask why I asked if you still loved me? (Christ, I got a little mixed up). 'Twas really a very normal question. I asked - you answered - now we're all happy, - O.K.?

The other night when I went to nurses' aid, I was very, very tired. The trolley car was warm and before I knew it I had fallen asleep. All of a sudden, I woke up and saw all the people getting off, so without looking I got up and walked out too. After rubbing my eyes about ten times I realized I got off at the wrong stop. I was so mad the air was blue with curses. You know how dark it is going up to Belmont Hospital, well, I swear, my knees were shaking, I was all alone going up that dark and lonely walk. I stopped short, listened and sure enough I could hear someone coming towards me. I said the few prayers I knew and realized the other person had stopped also. Then I noticed a kerchief and at the same time she evidently noticed mine. We walked towards each other, stopped, stared, and burst out laughing. We were both sure some man was there to attack us.

Before I fall asleep while I'm writing I'd better say goodnight and pleasant dreams.

Love, Lottie

November 22, 1943
Monday

From:	To:
C.L. Sniderman	Mr. Pvt. J.G. Barr 11057933
65 Houghton St.	883rd Sig. Co. Depot Avn. N.O. A.A.B.
Worcester, Mass.	New Orleans 12, La.

George dear,

And how are you today? I feel punk and the weather doesn't do much to help the situation. Rain, rain, and then for dessert, a little more rain. This noontime Miriam Sigel and I were sitting in the upstairs office alone and eating lunch. We felt very depressed when who should come in but one of our salesmen who is a great pal of mine. I asked him if he was going downtown so we could go along and get some hot coffee. We were very sorry when he said he wouldn't be ready for another hour, so very kiddingly I asked if I could take his car and when he said "sure", Miriam and I nearly fell over. Well, that was one ride she'll never forget! We were riding all around the town in the pouring rain. I was cock sure of myself, but Mim was a little scared, a little, I should say her knees were shaking. We had a super time and the kids at the office nearly collapsed when they saw me drive up. They always said I was unpredictable, - now they have proof.

I was talking to Rhoda Cutler Saturday night and she really is thata way about Dave. I never dreamed they were really that serious. She has plans of maybe going down to New Orleans if Dave is shipped. 'Tis wonderful this love business.

Thursday, Thanksgiving, we are all going over to my aunt's house. The whole family will be there. Incidentally, 'twould be very nice if you could accept the invitation she extended to you via me.

I haven't mentioned Mike Gordon to my folks until the other day. I didn't think they knew him, but they know him very well. I guess everybody in Worcester knows everybody else. At one time or another everyone meets. Remember so very, very well. A dance, a date, a dirty trick and George. I'm referring to the dance you picked me up back at my house when the other fellow brought me home. Whatta night!! Now that I'm in a reminiscent stage, that reminds me of what your mother said last time I saw her. We started talking and she said she remembered when you came home and said that you had visited the Sniderman girl at the hospital. She didn't know who I was and I imagine she cared even less. She said she never imagined I would turn out to be my mothers' daughter, and after all this time that I would still be in the picture. Oh, well, - I'm still me and you're still you. Happy? You bet!

Love, Lottie

November 26, 1943
Friday

From:	To:
C.L. Sniderman	Mr. Pvt. J.G. Barr 11057933
65 Houghton St.	883rd Sig. Co. Depot Avn. N.O. A.A.B.
Worcester, Mass.	New Orleans 12, La.

George dear,

    I have oodles to tell you but I'll tell you the most important. First you had better sit down and take it easy. Wednesday nite I called your folks to wish them a happy Thanksgiving and then your mother told me news that nearly floored me. It seems your father had a little accident. He was coming out of the store and just going to dinner when an automobile hit him. He was taken to the hospital and, of course, he's still there but much better. Now for the good part. Your mother and I put our heads together and decided that if we called the Red Cross you could get an emergency furlough. For how long, of course, we don't know but we are trying. I'm writing all this in the hope that it reaches you before the Red Cross, because I know how tactless they can be. Your cousin has a friend that works in the Red Cross and she's going to get in touch with her tomorrow. I called today to find out if it was possible and they said it definitely was possible. So, here's hoping!

    I told you about our going to my aunts for Thanksgiving. Well, around 7 o'clock on that morning my aunt called and she was hysterical. My mother and I immediately thought it was something about your father, but she told us that they're house had burnt down. Luckily, the turkey was rescued, so we all had dinner over my other aunt's house and then they all came here to sleep, as a matter of fact, they'll be staying here for a few days. It was very lucky that my aunt started coughing, evidently from the smoke, and when she saw the whole kitchen in flames there was a panic. The place is like a fire trap anyhow, and altho they lost a lot of their belongings, they were lucky they didn't lose their lives. So, all in all, between your family and mine, we had a very nerve wracking Thanksgiving.

    Saturday night a few of your cousins and I are going to stay down at your dad's store. I told your mother I'd shoot her if she came down, altho she's feeling much, much better, she's in no condition to work. I'm hoping to heaven you can come home, that is of-course, if you want to come home and I'm sure there are no maybes about you wanting to come.

    Well, darling, I guess I've told about all of any importance. No room for trivial things tonight, too much of importance has happened. I'll keep in close touch with you if anything happens at the Red Cross and you do same. Please, don't worry about your father. Your folks are going to cause a commotion so you can have a chance to come home. Write as soon as you can.

All my love, Lottie

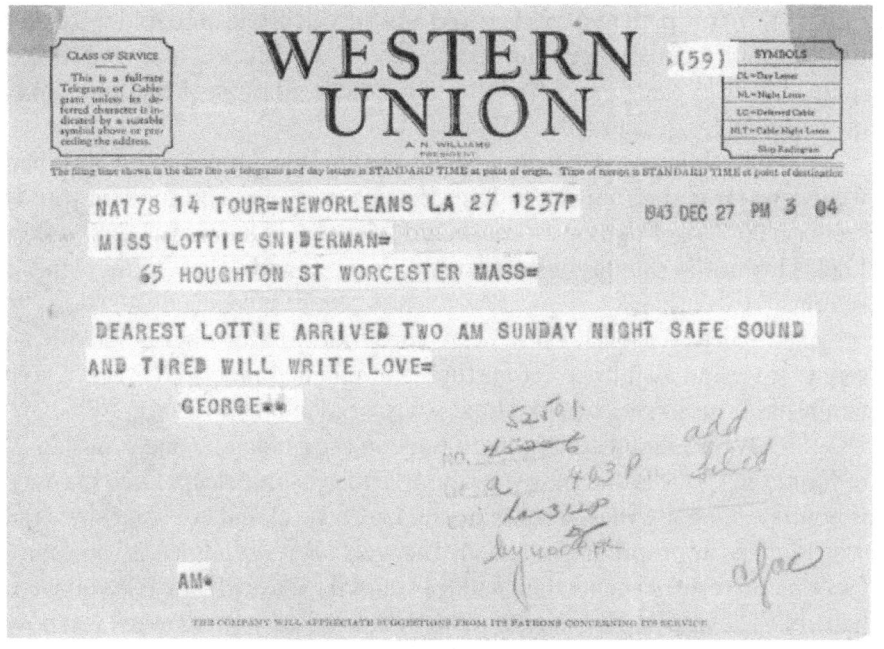

December 31, 1943
Friday

From:	To:
C.L. Sniderman	Mr. Pvt. J.G. Barr 11057933
65 Houghton St.	883rd Sig. Co. Depot Avn. N.O. A.A.B.
Worcester, Mass.	New Orleans 12, La.

Charlotte L. Sniderman
65 Houghton Street
Worcester 4, Mass.

My dearest George,

No need to tell you how I felt when the train pulled out of the station. I felt as if part of me had gone away, too. I must have stood there alone for a full ten minutes before Jackie came and got me. It was one of the most wonderful weeks I have ever had. It couldn't have been more ideal. I started writing you about three times before I got your letter, but I tore each one up because they were too morbid. I didn't think you'd be interested in knowing how much I miss you!

As I'm writing to you now, I'm still in my uniform. I love working in the hospital, altho the work is much harder than I thought. My patient, rather one of my patients, was very old and very delirious. He told me to get the hell out if I couldn't get him any hot chestnuts. He was all caged in and quite violent. A few times I had to run for the head nurse, I thought surely he was going to get out of bed. Some fun.

Dick Haymes is just going on the radio. It was much more fun when we listened together. I listen to Joan Brooks every nite and think of you. It seems everything I do now is connected with you in some way or another. Dick Haymes is singing "The Touch of Your Hand." Pardon me while I swoon.

I received a lovely New Year's card from your brother Sol and Fran today. It was an awfully sweet gesture, and much appreciated. Your whole family has been so sweet to me. I must write Sol and Fran a letter.

My dad said you slept like a rock on the train. The one consolation of your going back is that now you'll be able to get some sleep. Dick Haymes is now speaking low and singing "Speak Low." I call that our song since the words are so appropriate. Especially the words "everything ends too soon." George, there are so many things that I wanted to say to you while you were here, but I always find it easier to write than to talk. I wanted to tell you how sweet I thought you were and how much I love you. If even I tried, I don't think I could help loving you. Now all I have to worry about is that you don't forget all about me with all those beautiful southern gals to distract you.

I better go now before I get too much in "that mood." I'll write again tomorrow so for tonight, goodnight darling.

Love, Lottie

January 1, 1944
Friday Night and Saturday Morning

From:	To:
C.L. Sniderman	Mr. Pvt. J.G. Barr 11057933
65 Houghton St.	883rd Sig. Co. Depot Avn. N.O. A.A.B.
Worcester, Mass.	New Orleans 12, La.

1943
Happy New Year, darling!

Yep, here it is New Year's Eve. Have I got a date? You bet I have – with a picture, a ring and a Red Cross doll. Later Polly Cohan is coming over and we shall toast each other with a bottle of Pepsi Cola. I can just picture what you're doing tonight. Probably have a dame hanging on your arm and are having a hellava time. I hate youoooooo!

1944

Polly came over so I had to put you aside for a few minutes. It really was a very long few minutes since this is the next day. Polly slept over here and intends writing you a letter stating that I am the worst cuddle gal she ever slept with. I told her if I didn't cuddle, I couldn't sleep, and I wanted to sleep, so I cuddled. Incidentally, she was talking to Marcia Glazer and happened to mention very casually (oh yeah!) that we were going together. Marcia was very pleased and she said you were a very, very nice boy. So now that we have Marcia's approval, I don't know what we're waiting for.

I was just thinking of a night on my front porch when you told me you had promised yourself not to see me anymore. I wonder what would have happened had you kept that promise. That's a gruesome thought! By the way, George, I must admit that for the first time I lied to you. I promised I would stop smoking, and altho I hate to break promises, I had to this one. Please forgive me!

Today is a beautiful, but very snowless. It looks more like Easter than New Year's, and I have my Easter cold to prove it. Me nose is red and my throat is hoarse and I look very glamorous, so there.

How about dropping me a line sometime - you know, when you get a spare hour or two. Do you still love me?!!! (Mur-der!)

Love, Lottie

P.S. I love you.

January 2, 1944
Sunday

From:	To:
C.L. Sniderman	Mr. Pvt. J.G. Barr 11057933
65 Houghton St.	883rd Sig. Co. Depot Avn. N.O. A.A.B.
Worcester, Mass.	New Orleans 12, La.

Dearest George,

Well, another one is practically gone! Bella Sandman had a lovely shower today and Thursday Bernie Verstein will have himself a wife. Isn't that nice? They're having it at the Bancroft, - quite a nice affair. I wonder if Bella will be a blushing bride - oh, well!

Yesterday Polly and I went to see "Thousands Cheer." It was very, very good, - we enjoyed it as much the fourth time as we did the first. Yes, dear, 4 times. Twice in New York and we stayed twice to see it in Worcester. Nuts? We certainly are!!

My folks and I are having a minor battle tonight. They insist that my cold, due to previous experiences should be taken care of, and therefore, they don't want me to go to work tomorrow. I, on the other hand, insist that I am quite well, and besides that I need all the money I can get now. Tomorrow I shall let you in on who won the battle.

I called up your folks today and they are quite well. Your father is back in the store and it's my opinion that he's very happy about it.

My head just refuses to think tonight. I'm not tired and yet I can't move to do anything. I'se in a bad way and I know just what I need to cure me. Pill? No! Medicine? No! You? Uh-huh!!

Stan was in town this weekend so Edie was quite happy. Today she insisted that she didn't love him. But knowing Edie as well as I do, I know that by tomorrow the tune she'll sing will be quite different. I love her 'cause she's so undependable, - of-course that's O.K. for a gal, but don't think I'd admire that trait much in a male. But Edie isn't a male so everything is just fine! I'm getting awfully woozy now and the arms of Morpheus are calling or rather dragging me. (They're playing the "Hour of Parting" on the radio – very nice.) Goodnight.

Love, Lottie

January 3, 1944
Monday

From:	To:
C.L. Sniderman	Mr. Pvt. J.G. Barr 11057933
65 Houghton St.	37th Base Hdqt. Sqdn. N.O. A.A.B.
Worcester 4, Mass.	New Orleans 12, La.

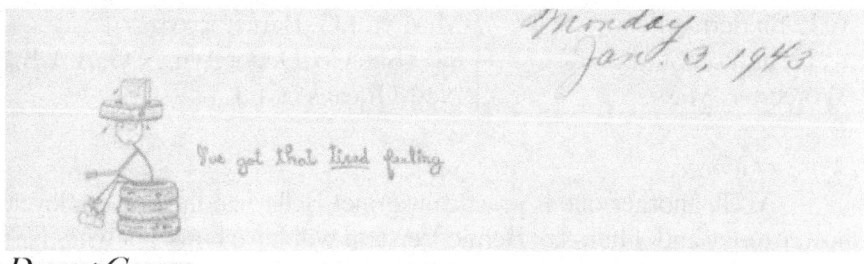

Dearest George,

I nearly laughed myself sick when I got your typewritten letter today. The spelling was so comical that it brought tears to my eyes. I could just picture you struggling away and making the air blue with curses everytime you made an error. If I ever do typewrite a letter like that please don't fire me. Who will support my 24 children and St. Bernard dog? Please, have mercy!!

Mazeltoff (Congratulations, to you) on your cousin William Barr's engagement. Her picture was in the paper the other night. She's a very lovely girl. Speaking of engagements, Sylvia Goodman is now in that class and not to Uddy Goff. Also, Pearl Ritz has become thusly and not to Joe Marcus. Surprised? I was amazed!

Polly just called to say goodbye, she's going back to school, and also to get your address. I thought she was kidding when she said she was going to write to you, but she ain't the kidding kind of a gal.

How do you like this awful stationary? I was feeling kinda low and I thought this would cheer me up – which it did. Silly, isn't it?!

For some odd reason, dear, I just can't picture you in an office. How do you like being a nursemaid to a typewriter? I'm wondering where and how soon you'll be sent to a new camp. Could be that you'll be sent nearer home.

Have you seen Dave as yet? When you do see him, ask him to forgive me for not writing, but I haven't got his new address, etc, etc, etc. I suppose you could send it to me, couldn't you. I really feel as if I should write him.

I went to work this morning (re: the argument I mentioned last nite) and I felt simply, - simply!! Tonight, we're arguing about tomorrow. Fun, isn't it?!

I dast I better go to bed now. I'll finish this, listen to Joan Brooks and then – I'll try to sleep. Goodnight.

Love, Lottie

P.S. Isn't it a shame about the Paper Doll? She just found out her mother was an old bag!

P.S.S. If Polly does write you, will you send me the letter, pleeze!

January 6, 1944
Thursday

From:	To:
C.L. Sniderman	Mr. Pvt. J.G. Barr 11057933
65 Houghton St.	37th Base Hdqt. Sqdn. N.O. A.A.B.
Worcester 4, Mass.	New Orleans 12, La.

Hello you!

I simply must thank you for that long, long letter you wrote the other day. How did you ever find the time to dash off those three sentences, and the one I didn't receive today was even longer. Oh, well, I still love, in spite of it all.

Your mater called last night and asked if I had heard from you. It was yesterday that I got your brief note and I was tempted to say "no." But I got around it by saying yes and no! I further went on to make explanations of why you hadn't written. He's busy, you know, I told her. And when she asked me what you were doing that you were so busy, I was stumped. She also invited me to Tobye's graduation, which is at the end of this month. Of-course I can't go because it's in the afternoon of a weekday. This is just a friendly reminder, but I do think she is entitled to a gift. If you're not in the chips, I shall buy her something from the both of us. If it's O.K. by you, it O.K. by me, because I'm going to get her something regardless. So there!

I just spilled a whole bottle of soda down my sweater and all over my arm. I don't know how I did it but I dood. I just tasted myself and with a nice piece of cake I'd be delicious. Would you like to taste me?

My mother and I are going visiting, so I rahlly must leave ya. Do drop me a line, that is if you can break away from your army chores – the army comes first, you know, - damn it!

Love, Lottie

January 7, 1944
Friday Night

From:	To:
Mr. Pvt. J.G. Barr 11057933	C.L. Sniderman
37th Base Hg. & A.A.B. Sq. NO. A.A.B.	65 Houghton St.
New Orleans 12, La.	Worcester, 4, Mass.

Dearest Lottie,

You're getting this letter from my new job. Truck driver at night down at the Base transportation office. I didn't take any stationary, but was able to pinch this stuff.

This morning I was asked, very politely of course, to report to the transportation office. When he found that I didn't have a G.I. license, he said that could easily be fixed up. I went to the hospital where I was checked for eyes, ears, and blood pressure. Passed O.K. Took a written drivers test. Passed O.K. Took the actual driving course, well, I wouldn't say the actual drivers course, but at least it was where the new drivers are tested. I put the truck in first, went up a slight grade, didn't have to change gears it was so small, then I backed it up. That was all. Who said that life in the army was tough. P.S. I'm now an official G.I. driver.

It doesn't make any difference that I never drove the kind of trucks the army has in traffic, but they put me on the night shift.

Last night we went into town for supper. There was a new French place that we were told to try. We had to wait a little while, meanwhile, I played the "One Armed Bandit", that is, a slot machine. I did manage to win about $.55. By this time our table was ready. We sat down and were waiting for the menu, when the waiter brought us our first course. Still waiting for the menu, he brought us our second course. By this time, we gathered that you don't see menus at this restaurant, and we found out we were right.

The dinner wasn't bad at all and the price was a minimum, a dollar and a quarter. After having supper, we walked along Canal Street to find a jeweler who would install a watch crystal for Lenny. After going into about seven places, one was kind enough to do the work. During our travels, we met the diamond buyer of one of New Orleans fancy jewelry stores. He happened 2 be a New Yorker, who's name was Cohen. Glad to see some Yankees, he told us he had just flown down from there with a batch of jewelry.

Such stuff, one remarkable piece was a $9\text{-}\frac{3}{4}$ carat diamond, which was selling at $22,000.00. I ordered two. One is going to be a pendant for you and the other a tie pin for me. O.K.? The other stuff was five and dime stuff, only $1,000 and $5,000. The crazy jerk let us handle every piece that he showed us.

Now you can say you know a guy that had a $9\text{-}\frac{3}{4}$ carat diamond in his hand. This stuff is all authentic because there were price tags on everything, except the diamond, and I think the guy was telling the truth.

About that letter from Polly, well maybe she'll write something that you shouldn't read, so I'll ponder the question awhile.

Darling, I was tempted to call you to-night, I just wanted to hear your lovely voice. Due to the time I'd have to wait, I decided to ask you if I try and call you about 12 or 1 o'clock at night. That's if it wouldn't interrupt your sleep.

I asked my sergeant if I was on any shipping list, and he told me to Denver Colo. That maybe true, but some fellows are leaving to-morrow who were supposed to go there, but are going to Nashville, Tenn. Nothing is sure in the army.

The guy that I got this stationary from doesn't know about it and I don't know the fellow, so I think when he comes back to-morrow morning to find he is all out of paper, he'll blow his top. See how much I love you, what I wouldn't do for you?

That's all for to-night, darling, and be careful of your cold.

Your, George

January 6, 1944
Thursday

From:	To:
C.L. Sniderman	Mr. Pvt. J.G. Barr 11057933
65 Houghton St.	37th Base Hdqt. Sqdn. NO. A.A.B.
Worcester 4, Mass.	New Orleans 12, La.

Dearest George,
　　Your three letters came today, so that made me three times happier than on other days. I must admit that your typing has improved tremendously. Please, dear, don't ever apply for a job down our place because you'd probably get it and then where will I be.
　　If you still like snow, you should have been in town today, and then you would have hated it. It was that nice kind of wet snow with slush every place you put your foot. And when you're crossing a street minding your own business a tiny little Mack truck comes along and covers you from head to foot, but you smile because after all it's winter and you love snow. Or anyhow you try to love it even tho it is a little dirty and instead of being a glistening white it's a mixture of gas and mud. But don't get me wrong – I love snow, honest. I brought my lunch to the office today so I wouldn't have to go out, but Mimi Sigel and I (mostly I) decided we must take a little walk and get an ice cream soda. So, the gals in the office dressed me for the storm and this was what I wore. Red boots (not mine), a plaid jacket (not mine), a trench coat (mine), a yellow kerchief (mine), and a black and red umbrella (not mine). Now do you wonder why Alvin Ecker looked twice when he saw us? Mimi was wearing a bright red coat. Alvin is in on furlough and is still the same old Alvin. He's in the best outfit, has the best breaks, etc., etc. Of-course that's only what he tells people. When he wasn't talking about himself he took time to tell me that Bob Silner has been discharged from the army. He was shot down over Burma and quite badly bruised. I guess it's mostly a mental condition – he's very nervous. He really is such a nice boy, I feel very badly for him.
　　I wish I could go to Alabama with you if you get a three day pass. It wouldn't take much coaxing at all. But since I can't go, I am hoping that you can. Goodnight, darling.

All my love, Lottie

January 7, 1944
Friday Night 9:25 P.M.

From:	To:
C.L. Sniderman	Mr. Pvt. J.G. Barr 11057933
65 Houghton St.	37th Base Hdqt. Sqdn. N.O. A.A.B.
Worcester 4, Mass.	New Orleans 12, La.

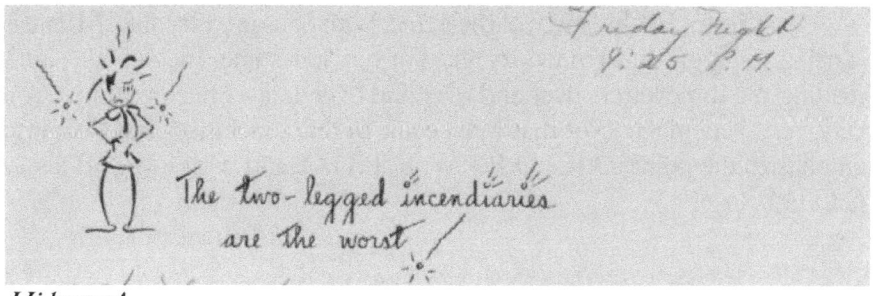

Friday Night 9:25 P.M.

The two-legged incendiaries are the worst!

Hi honey!

Pardon the blinding color of this paper but we felt in a bright mood and we happen to be two very consistent people. I know you're wondering who we is, well, it's Miriam Sigel and I. We're over my house and decided <u>we</u> must write a letter to her one and only and my one and only. So – now I present Miriam Sigel, better known as Queenie or Mimie.

[Miriam] Hello again George. Remember you said hello to me at the office? I really don't know what to say since we don't know each other very well. The radio is playing such soft and sweet music and I wish you were here to dance with Lottie – she's doing a good job of soloing around the floor. It's surprising how well she follows herself. Right now, Lottie is drooling over your picture and if she hasn't already told you so, she sure misses you too. I don't blame her – if I were your girl I'd miss you too.

[Lottie] I wrote a letter applying for a job at W.T.A.G. There was an ad in the paper so I answered just for the hell of it. Well, lo and behold, today I got an answer asking me to come for an interview. The job is doing publicity work, and you know me when it comes to anything in that line of work. The woman I'm supposed to see is going to New York so I can't see her until next week, but I know I won't get the job because it requires experience, of which I have none. But I can still hope, can't I?

Barbara came home today for a few weeks and then she's off to New York. Lucky gal she is, - but then she hasn't got you, has she?

[Miriam] The purpose of my visit was not to spend the evening here kibitzing, but to go sledding. Instead of the snow that Lottie wrote you about, the sidewalks and streets are covered with us, or ice!!! This is our second letter for the nite, so I'm just about "done-out" for words. We had a delicious supper, looked at pictures, talked, and now conclude a swell evening writing to my honey and you. It's funny how people's minds work. Numerable times Lottie will just sit at her desk, sometimes working hard – her work just won't come out right - *%&!!#%? etc. follows. She'll have a forlorn look on her pulchritudinous physiognomy (puss). All the girls think she's thinking about you. Is she? The answer will be in tomorrow's issue. $64 question!!!

[Lottie] By this stage of the game, both of us are very silly. Mimie is starting to giggle and I'm woozy and I'm very lonesome. Incidentally, after reading the three letters over and over and over again I decided I love you very, very, very much. Not that I just came to this conclusion, but I want to emphasize the point. O.K.? O.K.? Write P.D.Q. and with love and kisses C.O.F. I close.

Always yours, Lottie

P.S. Mim didn't see the last part of this letter, damn it!

January 10, 1944
Monday

From:	To:
Mr. Pvt. J.G. Barr 11057933	C.L. Sniderman
37th Base Hg. & A.A.B. Sq. N.O. A.A.B.	65 Houghton St.
New Orleans 12, La.	Worcester, 4, Mass.

Dearest Lottie,

How is my loved one to-day? I miss you like all hell. I'm just craving for you. Love is a funny, wonderful thing, it makes you feel good when you feel low and makes you feel low when you feel good. You know what I'm talking about?

I tried again to get a three day pass, but no luck. I'm on some kind of a shipment but I cannot find where.

Wired Dave to-day, I think he is back at his camp, to come up and see me. I'd like to see the son-of-a-gun before I'm shipped.

Maxie Zitowitz certainly has changed. He writes me about his love life and it's pretty damn hot. I think I'll get the girls address in case I'm shipped around Detroit.

Last night, Lenny, another fellow, and I had a farewell supper. We ate at this Italian place and had spaghetti, then a nice large T-bone steak. We also got a quart of wine, and darling, after the second glass, I got feeling good. I knew I had a little too much, but didn't give a damn. I could walk straight and everything else, but just talked. The boys got a big kick out of it. After the wine, we had some whiskey, but that stuff doesn't seem to affect me. I guess I'm becoming a bum.

Last night I made one trip out to the airport to pick up a couple of officers, so that they could sleep at our camp, that was my entire night's work.

The boys are falling out for retreat now, but I don't have to, because of my night work. I'm excused from most all formations.

I saw "Old Acquaintance" last night, before we ate, but couldn't stand it. I thought the woman in back of me was going to hit me on the head to stop me from squirming so much, but luckily, she didn't.

Your, George

January 10, 1944
Monday

From:	To:
C.L. Sniderman	Mr. Pvt. J.G. Barr 11057933
65 Houghton St.	37th Base Hq. & Air Base Sq. N.O. A.A.B.
Worcester 4, Mass.	New Orleans 12, La.

My dearest George,

I started writing you last night, but was so exhausted from working at the hospital all day that I just fell asleep on the table. I stayed at the hospital for eight hours and worked like a dog, since I was the only aid up there on a Sunday. But regardless of the work, I still love it. Both the nurses and the patients appreciate it so much.

Saturday night I went to a Servicemen's dance. It was the first and I think maybe the last one I'll ever attend. I don't know why, but it was simply awful. The boys are either awfully stupid or awfully conceited, - neither of which I could tolerate. I loved you more when I came home from that dance, if that is possible.

I'm so glad you liked "Thousands Cheer." It seems everyone thought of us when he gave her the ring. Especially when she had the string wound around it. I brought the ring into Kumins to be fixed, but after much deliberation he said he couldn't do anything. The ring is so much too large, that if he tried to bend it into my size, it would break the top. Furthermore, he said you had something done to the top to make it keep better and it would be a shame to waste all that work. Anyway, I don't really care. I love you, and I love the ring, so I don't really mind wearing the tape around it.

I was very surprised to hear Dave was in town. He didn't even call. But can't say I blame him, he's probably spending every minute with Rhoda.

The whole town is talking that we're engaged. Saturday night Rose Gerald offered her best wishes, much to my amazement, and today Phylis Jacobson came over and said she wanted an answer straight from the shoulder. She said everyone's been telling her that I'm engaged and she felt very hurt that since I work with her I didn't tell her. I quickly set her at ease. She thought maybe I wanted to keep it a secret for some odd reason. Boy, when I get engaged there won't be any secrecy about it. I'll have my picture plastered all over the paper and have a headline over it. I do wish the people would stop rushing me, - not that I mind particularly, but it does feel awfully queer to have to refuse best wishes!!

Edie Megans just called me and that gal is really in the dumps. She's had another major battle with her aunt and is seriously considering joining the WAVES. She said she simply had to talk to me and get some advice, so I'm meeting her tomorrow for supper. The poor kid is working her nerves to nothing. I wish she wouldn't join up, although at one time, I wanted to myself very much.

Friday I'm going to doctor Goodspeed about my ears. I don't dare tell my mother 'cause she'll have a fit, but they don't feel too good so I'll just have him check them. I'm playing smart this time. I like the hospital very much, but not as a patient.

I'm terribly nervous about applying for the job Monday because I want to get it so terribly and I know I won't. This is the first job I ever really wanted. Well, if I don't, - I don't, that's all!

Honey, if you tell me what kind of a tube you want for your radio, maybe I can get one for you out here. I can try anyway.

My goodness, this has been just like talking to you. I haven't realized I'd written so much. I don't know where it all came from. So, until tomorrow, goodnight and pleasant dreams.

Love, Lottie

January 11, 1944
Tuesday

From:	To:
C.L. Sniderman	Mr. Pvt. J.G. Barr 11057933
65 Houghton St.	37th Base Hq. & Air Base Sq. N.O. A.A.B.
Worcester 4, Mass.	New Orleans 12, La.

Hello darling,

The hour is exactly 12 midnight, and if my mother knew I was still up writing a letter she'd probably kill me. I'm writing you while lying on my bed, so if the writing is kinda bad, you'll understand why. I came home from the hospital about an hour ago, and since I wasn't home for supper, I found two letters from you. I'll try and do my best to find something nice for your sister. I have no idea what to get for either of us for her. Very nice of you, dear, to get that $22,000 diamond. I'm sure it'll make a beautiful pendant and the stick pin for you will be lovely. But all kidding aside, it's never the money value of a thing, it's the sentiment attached to it – or at least that's how I feel about it.

Darling, I'm sitting here thinking that I'm a very happy girl. I haven't been really happy for a long time, and the feeling is wonderful. Loving you has been doing wonders for me and I think everyone has noticed it. I've been looking around at other people and realizing how very fortunate I am. The only thing missing is that you're not here with me, but even that will be true in due time.

George, you're very sweet to want to call me, and I'd stay up all night when I'd expect your call, but it really would be foolish. I know you haven't got that extra money and the time we'd talk is really so short. So, suppose you take that money and have a good time for yourself, and while so doing, think of me. I'll really enjoy it, no kidding. It'll be like mental telepathy. But if you still want to disregard all I have written on the matter, then let's wait until you're sent to another camp, which evidently will be quite soon. I love you very much for even wanting to call.

When I buy Tobye's gift, I'll also buy a card, which I'll send to you so you can sign it and then send it back to me. It would be more personal and I'm sure she'd like it. O.K.?

I think I could write for another hour, but I really should get some sleep. Will you wire me when they send you to wherever the damn army is sending you? Goodnight, darling.

Love, Lottie

January 13, 1944
Thursday

From:	To:
C.L. Sniderman	Mr. Pvt. J.G. Barr 11057933
65 Houghton St.	37th Base Hq. & Air Base Sq. N.O. A.A.B.
Worcester 4, Mass.	New Orleans 12, La.

Dearest George,

I've been searching all over for something nice to get Tobye, but all in vain. I have absolutely no idea what to get. The stuff is so damn expensive and I don't mind that as much if it were worth the price. I'm open to suggestions if you have any. I still have time so I'll keep looking.

Fine thing! I'm here pining away for you, and you have the nerve to want to look up Maxie Zitowitz's girl friend. Somehow, I just can't picture Maxie in connection with a love life. But, of course, he may have hidden talents and the girl might have a brother for me. So there!

Your farewell supper with the boys sounded very nice. Darling, when you have a couple of drinks in you, you really are a rare treat. I never saw you drunk, thank goodness, but you seem to glow from within and talk a blue streak. You're really very cute!! I was amazed that you didn't like "Old Acquaintance." I loved it, but it was strictly a woman's picture, and you not being a woman, I could see where it would prove quite boring.

I got a letter from Barney Shapiro yesterday. He's in New Caledonia and having a hellava time. I always thought Barney just not the type for the army, but I guess I'm not a very good judge of character. I also saw Chet Leavitt today and he asked for you as he always does. He always looks at my hand and says, "engaged yet?" Then we both laugh for some reason. I never could figure it out. Silly, eh wot?!!

Mrs. Rosenbloom, the woman that lives at your house, had a little automobile accident. She was quite badly bruised, but she's not in the hospital, and I guess she's much better now. Me mater went to visit her today. Dick Haymes just finished singing "How Much Do I Love You" and I swooned dead away. That song gets me, but as you said, I always go for songs like that. Take care, darling, and get Maxie's girl off the brain or you'll have trouble on your hands.

Love, Lottie

January 14, 1944
Friday Night

From:	To:
C.L. Sniderman	Mr. Pvt. J.G. Barr 11057933
65 Houghton St.	37th Base Hq. & Air Base Sq. N.O. A.A.B.
Worcester 4, Mass.	New Orleans 12, La.

Dearest George,

Well, I went to the doctor today, and what do you think he said? Yep, he said I was good for at least a couple more years. This was very encouraging, because at times I did have my doubts, but he said my hearing was very good and that I was healthy as a horse. Not very complimentary to be likened to a horse, but he meant well anyhow, I hope!

That's what we'll do! If Dave doesn't write me a letter of apology, we won't invite him to our wedding, and it'll be a beautiful wedding, too, won't it? He'll be soreeeee!! He won't have a chance to kiss the bride.

I don't know what makes you think your letters are short. Of-course, the longer the better, of that I would never complain, but they have been very, very nice, - contents and all. You really write a very nice letter.

To-night I was supposed to go over and visit Barb, but I was so tired, I just fell asleep right after supper. When I got up it was too late to go, and besides that I had too many things to do – namely writing to you.

The other day I was called into the office. Anne Bramson, private sec. of Mr. Saul Sharfman hemmed and hawed and finally told me that I was due to get a raise. She said, as yet, it hadn't come through yet, but they are giving me a small increase in the meantime. Small is right! It will be approximately a dollar and some odd change – that will be until my raise comes through. If I only can get the job at WTAG, I'll tell them all to go to the old Harry!!

Tomorrow night me mater is being treated by me to see "Abie's Irish Rose." Isn't that nice of me? Ho-hum.

Last night I really had a nightmare. I don't know how it happened, but in dreams the oddest things do happen. It seems I went avisiting to none other than Mr. & Mrs. Barr, and I was really dressed to kill in a pair of torn pajamas and no shoes. When I got to your house there was a lot of company and I was trying to hide the tear in my outfit. It was all very embarrassing. Must remember never to go visiting in pajamas again. Goodnight, dear.

Love, Lottie

January 17, 1944
Monday

From:	To:
C.L. Sniderman	Mr. Pvt. J.G. Barr 11057933
65 Houghton St.	37th Base Hq. & Air Base Sq. N.O. A.A.B.
Worcester 4, Mass.	New Orleans 12, La.

Dearest George,

What a sweet idea of yours to put my letters in chronological order. First chance I get, I must do the same thing with yours. But I have so many of yours, I wouldn't know where to begin.

Yesterday, while on duty at the hospital, I saw something that I'll not forget for as long as I live. A woman had been waiting 48 hours for her baby to come and finally the doctors decided a Cesarean operation would be the best thing. I asked the doctor if he'd mind if I watched and he said he'd be delighted. So I donned my sterile gown, cap and mask and marched into Surgery with him. The poor husband was pacing up and down the outside corridor nearly going mad. I saw the operation from beginning to end and was so fascinated that I didn't even think about being sick. I can't describe the thrill I got when that baby let out his first yell. It was really a miracle. I don't think you would have enjoyed it at all. Dr. Goodspeed was scheduled to operate an hour later, but I figured one operation was enough for the first time.

I went for my interview today and the answer is what I expected. The fact that I don't do shorthand is not to my favor, but she said she'd let me know in a week or two. That means – no.

Darling, I don't know what makes you think I have all work and no play. Maybe that's true in a little way, but being in the hospital takes most of my spare time, and I assure you I get more pleasure out of that than I do going to a silly dance with a bunch of man hungry girls and a flank of conceited males. I'm very happy doing just what I am, - honest ingun! Sometimes the girls (my friends) and I go to the movies or to dinner or some such thing, and then writing letters takes up the rest of my time. There's not a bit of discontentment in me, - or almost, - meaning the war. Edie Megans has finally decided to go to Mississippi. I'm very glad for her, but will miss her terribly. I wish I were going, too. I wouldn't mind a trip in the least.

Very nice that Jackie Waxler has finally made up his mind. You didn't mention where he was going and for how long. I think it'll be the best thing for him.

Jackie Lubarsky and Evelyn Avers were married last night. I can't picture Jackie as a husband, - but I guess he is.

It really is a shame about the roll of film, but we can use them up when you come home. Maybe someone will take a picture of you and I together. You know the kind, you sitting down with me aside of you, my hand on your shoulder and you stroking your beard - (oh, no!)

They just finished singing "Candlelight and Wine." I took time out for a cig and a bit of reminiscing. I told a little fib when I said I wasn't discontent. I'm very much so when I think of how much I miss you. I can feel myself getting moody and that lonesome feeling is creeping up, so I'd better say goodnight darling.

Love, Lottie

January 18, 1944
Tuesday

From:	To:
C.L. Sniderman	Mr. Pvt. J.G. Barr 11057933
65 Houghton St.	37th Base Hq. & A.A.B Sq., N.O. A.A.B.
Worcester 4, Mass.	New Orleans 12, La.

Dearest George,

I can't explain the sensation I had talking to you last night. It was truly wonderful, but I missed you more than ever all day today. This morning I asked my mother if you had really called. I thought maybe I had dreamt it. You're a darling. I simply don't know what to do about you. You're too sweet for words. Now who else would think of getting me a scarf, - a little thing I really need very badly. I had planned to buy one myself, but it just slipped my mind. Did I ever tell you I love you very, very much, well, just in case I forgot to mention it, - I do – very much. But darling, even though I appreciate the thought that you even wanted to give me a gift, I must reprimand you. If I thought you had oodles of money to spend I wouldn't mind so much, but I know damn well you haven't. Honest dear, you don't have to give me gifts to show that you love me or to make me love you because I love you anyhow – gifts or no!

Edie just called to say goodbye and informed me that she is stopping in New Orleans for a short while. She will call you when she gets there and will try to see you. I'm jealous, - I want to go too!! Much to my amazement, her cousins know Mike Gordon very well and she plans to see him too. It's just a small world after all, isn't it?

I just got home from the hospital, and going down there we had a little accident. An automobile collided with the bus. A few women fell down, but no one was hurt. On the way back I was waiting for the bus when a girl came up to me and asked if I was a nurse at her hospital. I asked her where she was and she said Worc. State Hosp. I nearly fell over because she looked liked she might have been an escaped inmate. Maybe she thought the same about me, but she sure was dressed to fit the part. She wore a long Raccoon coat, a big red hat, high black boots and was carrying an enormous package. Some fun! Goodnight dear.

Love, Lottie

January 20, 1944
Friday

From:	To:
C.L. Sniderman	Mr. Pvt. J.G. Barr 11057933
65 Houghton St.	37th Base Hq. & A.A.B Sq. N.O. A.A.B.
Worcester 4, Mass.	New Orleans 12, La.

Dearest George,

I finally got a very sweet letter of apology from Dave, and while the letter was to me from him, it was all about you. He really thinks you're O.K.! I just wrote him back to tell him his apologies were accepted and that now all is well. I hope he gets it before he's shipped.

Tobye called me up last night and we had a long conversation. She invited me to her graduation and altho I'd love to go it's quite impossible, but next Friday night, I'm invited to supper and since my mother is so glad to get rid of me for a night, I readily accepted. During our conversation, she also set me wise to a few woman-to-woman details. She told me I ought to be very careful because so many gals are on the loose and you're just an innocent fella so far from home you might be taken in by one of those babes. She suggested numerous things for me to do so as you wouldn't lose your love for me. Quite a kid your sister!! She also is going to a school dance and at my suggestion was ready to fix me up with Irving Cooper, but then she was afraid of you. You bad, bad big brother!!

Very funny about you getting your money back after calling me. I even enjoyed the call even more when I heard that. I don't know why I take such good care of your money, or at least try to. It's quite obvious that you pay no heed to my advice!

I met Evelyn Levine Plotkin today and she didn't look very good. She told me all about their honeymoon and such. I felt very bad for her, but she doesn't seem to mind, so why should I? She just got a letter from Sid, which is supposed to be his last. (I still don't think she was a blushing bride!)

George, is Dave still going with Rhoda? He made a few remarks in his letter, which made me think that maybe things weren't just right with them. Do you know?

I didn't get any mail from you for the past two days. I could say that you're too tired to write, but I'll feel better if I blame it on the mailman. Goodnight dear.

Love, Lottie

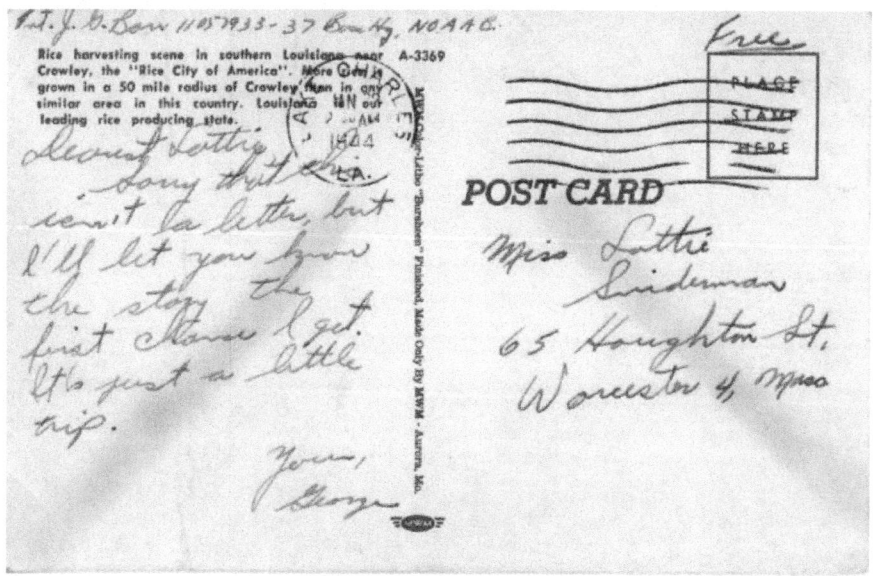

Pvt. J. D. Barr 11057933 - 37 Base Hq. NOAAC.

Rice harvesting scene in southern Louisiana near A-3369 Crowley, the "Rice City of America". More rice is grown in a 50 mile radius of Crowley than in any similar area in this country. Louisiana is an out leading rice producing state.

Dearest Lottie,

Sorry that this isn't a letter, but I'll let you know the story the first chance I get. It's just a little trip.

Yours, George

POST CARD

Miss Lottie
Sniderman
65 Houghton St.
Worcester 4, Mass.

January 23, 1944
Sunday

From:	To:
C.L. Sniderman	Mr. Pvt. J.G. Barr 11057933
65 Houghton St.	37th Base Hq. & A.A.B Sq. N.O. A.A.B.
Worcester 4, Mass.	New Orleans 12, La.

Hi honey,

Your gal is in one of those moods tonight. I feel as if I could just get up and run away. When I say run away, I mean from this horrible feeling of loneliness, which I dread. Sometimes this mood is more prevalent than at other times, and unfortunately this happens to be one of those evenings. The house is filled with my relatives, and yet I feel all alone. Their talk is just a hum drum in my ears. I can't hear a word they're saying. I walked to the hospital today. I couldn't resist it. A slow soft snow was covering anything. It was beautiful. On my way home, the snow had stopped and a million stars were twinkling in the sky. Oodles of soldiers and sailors were walking to and fro downtown and I envied them. They looked so happy and why shouldn't they be happy.

One of the visitors at the hospital came over and introduced himself as Joe something or other. He knew my name was Charlotte and wanted to know my last name. For some odd reason, I told him it was Walker, and when he asked where I lived, I said Chandler St. He then very gallantly asked if he could drive me home. I thanked him in the nicest way I could, but declined his invitation. So, you see, I'm not quite as ugly as you may think! I've become quite friendly with another nurse's aide at the hospital and she's so intelligent it's just grand talking to her. We get along famously and are planning on going to City Hospital together.

Not knowing what the devil to get Tobye for a gift, I finally found it necessary to call your mother. She told me the only thing Tobye really wanted that she didn't have was a ring. So pell mell, yesterday I ran downtown and purchased a lovely birthstone ring, I only hope she likes it.

When I started writing this letter I felt tres low, but now I can feel my spirits rising by slow degrees.

I'm beginning to wonder why I haven't heard from you. If I don't get any mail tomorrow I shall start shooting people. I'm so used to getting mail everyday that if one day passes that I don't, I'm fit to be tied.

Yesterday downtown I met Rhoda Cutler. She looked very nice and sends her regards. She always makes me feel very peculiar and I have no idea why.

Isabelle, the girl at the hospital who I was telling you about, said she'd never believe I was nineteen. She said I act so much older, that she thought I was nearer her age and she's twenty-four. That made me laugh because sometimes I feel no more than ten years old and at other times I feel as old as the hills. When there's not much to do, we go into the doctor's study and read med books. Today an intern walked in and found us sprawled out on the bed reading an Anatomy book, and a volume of Obstetrics was also on the bed. He was very nice about it when we finally convinced him that he was not in the wrong room and that our intentions were strictly honorable. We left the room feeling weighed down with knowledge and worldly worries. Ho hum.

Well, dear, I guess I'se done good by you in this 'ere letter. I'll have a little midnight repast now, and then into the arms of Morpheus. Write taute de suite.

Love, Lottie

P.S. Now that I've written such a long letter I just remembered I have no stamps to mail it with. Tomorrow I'll start bumming from the kids – that's a usual occurrence.

January 24, 1944
Monday

From:	To:
C.L. Sniderman	Mr. Pvt. J.G. Barr 11057933
65 Houghton St.	37th Base Hq. & A.A.B Sq. N.O. A.A.B.
Worcester 4, Mass.	New Orleans 12, La.

My dearest George,

Well, lo and behold! Not one letter, not two letters, but three letters all at once. Twas worth waiting for and wait I did. Your letters were really quite funny. The first one I read definitely said Denver, - the second discarded Denver plans for Texas plans, and the third put me right where I was the first time – you didn't know. How nice of the army to play quiz games!! Very nice of Emil to send you a cigarette case. That's one thing you didn't have.

Dear, I always knew the beautiful way you drive would bring you recognition and I guess it finally has. The only trouble is, I don't think you'll win any laurels of medals, do you?!!

I got a very sweet letter from Fran Barr today. She said she and Sol couldn't get over how big Bonnie had grown. They received the picture Charlotte sent them. She's taking a First Aid course down Alabama, but no hospital work, it's just for home purposes, which is very good to know. I took that course twice. It's just in case you accidently fall down and break your neck or arm or leg, so you'll know how to make it worse, before the doctor comes. The funny part is I work like a dog in the hospital and yesterday when my father had a strained back, he wouldn't let me touch him. Humph – see if I care!!

Tomorrow we're going to the Coronado for supper. That is, all the girls from the office are going, in honor of a girl who is leaving our happy little group for more money. The mercenary lucky dog. I have already told the kids and promised myself not to dance. I still remember how ridiculous those girls looked when Fran & Ira took us to the Coronado. I refuse to make a spectacle of myself, - so there!

Me mater is going high brow on me. She's having a beautiful Persian lamb coat made. From now on she refuses to walk with poor 'lil me! I'll throw mud pies at her – that's what I'll do.

Eddie, the boy who lives upstairs, or anyhow he used to, but lives in New York now, came home to see his folks who live upstairs and brought me a lovely box of hankies. Wasn't that nice, - well, I did, anywho. Gottta go now, me pet, pater is calling me for tea and crumpets. Willst thou jine us? Pray do!!

Love, Lottie

P.S. – This is no PS either but I love you!!

January 26, 1944
Wednesday

From:	To:
C.L. Sniderman	Mr. Pvt. J.G. Barr 11057933
65 Houghton St.	37th Base Hq. & A.A.B Sq. N.O. A.A.B.
Worcester 4, Mass.	New Orleans 12, La.

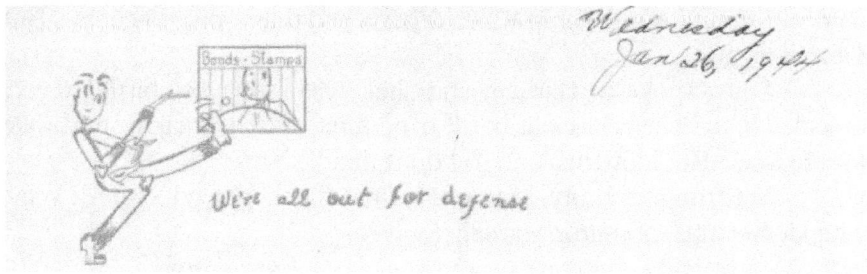

Dearest George,

I'm wondering if you'll still be in New Orleans when this letter gets there. It must be awful to know you're going someplace, but not know where or when.

Good to know your marksmanship has improved so much. When you come home you simply must take me to White City and shoot down a couple of ducks so's I can have a doll!

Last night we went to the party at the Coronado that I wrote you about. We had oodles of fun and just in case you're wondering – I didn't dance. Everyone has been telling Evelyn Cohen and myself that we missed our profession. I don't even remember doing anything particularly funny, but the kids were in stitches of laughter all night. Comedians Sniderman & Cohen we're known as now. I had 1/8 of a glass of beer, and I think that did the trick. After we ate we went to see "Madame Curie", which was excellent. Then to top off a beautiful evening, I got so mad I could feel my blood pressure rising by degrees. After the show my cousin Zelda decided she didn't feel well, and altho I know she puts on a swell act, I thought maybe she wasn't kidding this time. She was reeling back and forth as if she were going to faint. I didn't have a cent in my pocket. I borrowed a couple of bucks and ran all the way from the Palace down to the Bancroft in a pouring rain to get a cab and I left Sylvia Coblentz with her in case she did faint. Well, finally I did get a cab, and when I got back to the movies, Sylvia told me that she had suddenly recuperated and had taken a bus home. I was so wet from the rain and tired from running that I just sat in the cab and cried all the way home. I sure am a prize jack-ass – just in case you didn't know. There are times when I get so disgusted with girls that I could scream. I was still mad today, so during my lunch hour, I ran down and bought myself a new hat. It isn't exactly a thing which would keep one warm in the sub-zero temperatures, but I think it's real cute. You'd probably think it's atrocious. But it did make me feel better, so I don't care what you think of it.

Darling, I don't know whether Mike's wife bought me anything or not because as yet I haven't received anything, but if she did forget, George, dear, please don't bother to buy me anything because you told me you would. The only thing I want from you I can't have, and that's you, - of-course. But I'll wait my turn.

I just spoke to Barbara and she's celebrating her birthday very quietly. I bought her a luscious bottle of perfume, which is making me broke for the week. But I love her, and so I don't mind.

Well, my pet, I gotta leave you for my other boyfriend, - who?!! Why, Frankie Sinatra, - of course, you silly!!

Love, Lottie

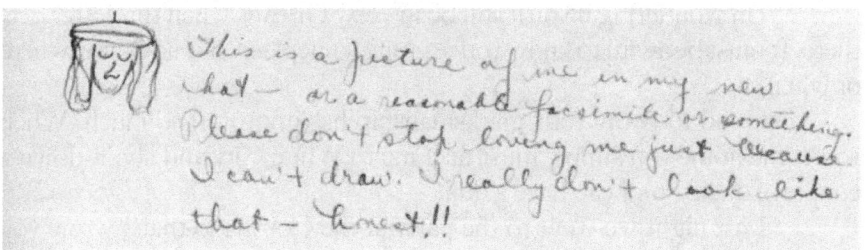

This is a picture of me in my new hat – or a reasonable facsimile or something. Please don't stop loving me just because I can't draw. I really don't look like that – honest!!

January 27, 1944
Thursday

From:	To:
C.L. Sniderman	Mr. Pvt. J.G. Barr 11057933
65 Houghton St.	37ᵗʰ Base Hq. & A.A.B Sq. N.O. A.A.B.
Worcester 4, Mass.	New Orleans 12, La.

Darling George,

I feel terrible because you feel bad about the gift. It really doesn't matter, honest. Please don't think about it anymore.

I don't remember if I told you that I got a card from Jackie, too. He wrote the card from Memphis, Tenn. That guy is sure seeing the country, - and on his own time and money. Evidently, he had been saving while he was working, and now when he wants it he's got it. Very nice!

You simply can't imagine the weather we've been having. The little kids are already jumping rope and playing marbles. I swear I have spring fever. It truly is wonderful. Snow is a thing we've had only twice this winter, and at that, it was very mild snow. I think I've changed my mind about going to Florida this winter!! Instead I'll wait till summer and come and visit you, - how's that?

My mother, she's such a dear, has been teasing me all day that she had bought me something, but she wouldn't give it to me and wouldn't tell me what it was. Finally, she relented and gave me the <u>little</u> gift as she called it. It's the most beautiful peach colored nightgown I've ever seen. It's real dainty with tiny sleeves and rosebuds and lace and every-thing. I can just imagine how unenthused you are, but I am truly excited, so please bear with me!

I have no idea where Edie is now or when she'll be in New Orleans, but I do hope you'll get to see each other. Edith Richards, the operator at the office, (remember?) always asks for you. She's an awfully sweet person.

What a dirty trick to have made you shave all for nothing. When you come home (for keeps), I'll let you raise a beard if you promise to look like Walter Pidgeon. Every time I write you now, I keep wondering if you're still there, - or where! Take care, darling.

Love, Lottie

January 30, 1944
Sunday Night

From:	To:
C.L. Sniderman	Mr. Pvt. J.G. Barr 11057933
65 Houghton St.	37th Base Hq. & A.A.B Sq. N.O. A.A.B.
Worcester 4, Mass.	New Orleans 12, La.

Dearest George,

Friday night I had one of the nicest times I ever had. I went over to your folk's house for supper, and then your mother and dad took Charlotte and I to the movies. They're really very sweet people, and both of them look simply grand. Tobye loved the ring and it fit just right, for which I was very happy. She looked very sweet. So all in all, I had a swell evening, only had you been there, it would have been super swell.

Friday afternoon you almost had yourself a gal minus four fingers. I was in a department store waiting for someone and for some odd reason I was looking at some very sharp knives. Just as I picked up a billed diller, a fellow pushing a hand wagon bumped into the table where I was standing, and evidently the jolt scared me so much that I dropped the knife, but everyone around thought I had sliced off my fingers and started coming over. They were very disappointed, - luckily for me. Also, Friday at work, I was told to go up to the fourth floor by the elevator to get a bill. The elevator is a freight elevator and I was scared stiff to work it myself. I asked one of the jerks to take me up and he said O.K., but when I told him I was afraid to run it myself, he started the damn thing with me on it and he didn't get on. It was a full couple of seconds before I realized what his idea of a joke was and I jumped off. He got scared stiff because had I been a few inches higher I could have fallen between the shaft. He was on bended knee apologizing, but we are not exactly on friendly terms as of Friday. What a day!!

Quite a time you had for yourself with all your generals and colonels. Evidently, your upper bracket friends are running you ragged. But regardless, I still think you have it purty easy, so there.

They're playing "Speak Low" on the radio and it's bringing back the lonesome feeling I've had all day. Yesterday I was sitting at my desk and thinking. I got into one of those moods and I was thinking of that Saturday morning you came down to the office and then you, my mother and I went to the movies. I kept watching the door foolishly thinking that maybe you'd come in. Then again, this afternoon was the first Sunday for a long time that I didn't go to the hospital and I nearly went mad. So, I went for a long walk and the crisp air made me feel alive, - but still lonesome. There's nothing so bad as a feeling of loneliness.

I'm glad everything is O.K. with Rhoda & Dave. She didn't tell me Dave had given her his ring, altho she said she heard that you had given me yours. She is terribly young (grandma speaking)! But have they got a definite understanding of going steady? I can't picture her sitting home nights waiting for Dave, - she's so lovely. Well, I guess it's their lives and no business of mine. I have my own life to think about, and yours to think about, and so I guess that's enough for anyone.

Well, dear, this is about it until tomorrow night. Take it easy - from the song of the same name.

Love, Lottie

January 31, 1944
Monday

From:	To:
C.L. Sniderman	Mr. Pvt. J.G. Barr 11057933
65 Houghton St.	37th Base Hq. & A.A.B Sq. N.O. A.A.B.
Worcester 4, Mass.	New Orleans 12, La.

Monday
January 31, 1944

Dearest George,

So, glad my letter tickled your fancy. I practically knock myself out trying to write you every night, but if one comes through in a month that you like, then I'm happy. At least all my efforts have not been in vain.

Well, your baby went ariding again today. One of our salesmen let me borrow his car and Mimi and I had a gala time all lunch hour. On the way back, the damn car keep stalling all the way down Summer St. and stopped completely in front of the insane asylum. All the mentally deficient came out to greet me. They thought I was an inmate out on a spree. But I wiggled a couple of the things and the car was good as new again when I finally brought it back. Heavens knows why, but regardless of what happens, I never get nervous or lose control.

I went over to the hospital to get my cap today and it looks adorable. Thursday, we graduate and me proud mater will witness the occasion.

I got a card from Edie today and she's already in Mississippi, so I guess the girl whose car she went in decided New Orleans was one place they could miss. She may have tried to call you or something. She only dropped me a card and no details were given.

It seems that all you and your gang do is have farewell parties, but you don't go anyplace. What a racket! So now you've heard rumors about Florida, have ya? Fine Thing! I'll be freezing up here while you're basking in the sun. Lottie wants to go too!!

Tonight I says to myself, ses I,..... I'se gonna do some reading. But am I? No! I received oodles of mail today and it must be answered, so here I am at my usual nightly occupation. I used to hate writing letters, but I'm getting so I kinda like it now. Everyone still laughs at the big plaster I wear around your ring or my ring. They can't understand how I can help but be annoyed, but honest to Peter, I don't even know it's there.

I took my mother to the movies Saturday night and we saw "Desert Song." So, help me I couldn't get her out. She fell madly in love with Dennis Morgan and that's all there is to that. Twice we saw it. If my poor father only knew the truth. I think she snuck away (what English) today and saw it again. I wish I had a funny joke to tell you, but I don't know any funny jokes. This is a very ridiculous letter and hardly worth the six cents that I'll have to borrow to mail it with. I guess I'd better hang up now, I'll make it up in a newsier letter next time. Actually, I haven't done so bad in this letter have I? Just let me know if I short-shipped you, don't hesitate to let me know. O.K.? O.K.!

Yours with love, Lottie

February 1, 1944
Tuesday

From:	To:
C.L. Sniderman	Mr. Pvt. J.G. Barr 11057933
65 Houghton St.	37th Base Hq. & A.A.B Sq. N.O. A.A.B.
Worcester 4, Mass.	New Orleans 12, La.

Dearest George,

Thought I decided I must do something I've not done for a long time. I wanted to read and read I did. It was a beautiful story, the kind that relaxes you completely. Then I turned on the radio and listened to a program of all Beethoven music. There was a strange morbid fascination in the music. It made me think of so many things. Beautiful things. There was no war and there were no miles between us. You were here with me and I let my imagination take a holiday. I'm having an inner battle with myself. Imagination is a fine thing, but it dwindles too soon, and you are left with reality. If I were an artist, I could paint beautiful thoughts. If I were a poet, I could put into words what I feel. Unfortunately, I am skilled in neither of these arts and have no way of self expression, but to write to you when this strange mood hits me. Please try to bear with me.

George, did you ever regret anything you had done? If you had your life to live over again, would you do it differently? Not that I mean to imply that I'm self satisfied, I'm far from that, but if I could live my life over again, I think I would have done just what I did before. Many people have told me that I'm wild, spoiled, unsettled and numerous other unflattering things. If that was the impression I created, then I'm sorry, but I can feel that since I realized that I love you I have changed. I think you are the nicest thing that ever happened to me. I'm sorry that I didn't realize that you were the one before I did. I liked you from the start because you were different. When I said "parking" was out, you didn't become angry and dash off to find some female who was more responsive to your desires. While most of the kids were off in some secluded spot, we were out walking in the snow or in the rain or just staying home talking, discussing, getting to really know each other. When I really did fall in love with you, I knew it wasn't just a passing crush until the next one came along. We built a solid foundation and I'm so thankful you had the patience. Where all the patience came from I'll never understand, but I'm so glad. I could ramble on like this for hours. I miss talking to you so much. Please don't ever stop loving me.

Love, as always, Lottie

February 3, 1944
Thursday

From:	To:
C.L. Sniderman	Mr. Pvt. J.G. Barr 11057933
65 Houghton St.	37th Base Hq. & A.A.B Sq. N.O. A.A.B.
Worcester 4, Mass.	New Orleans 12, La.

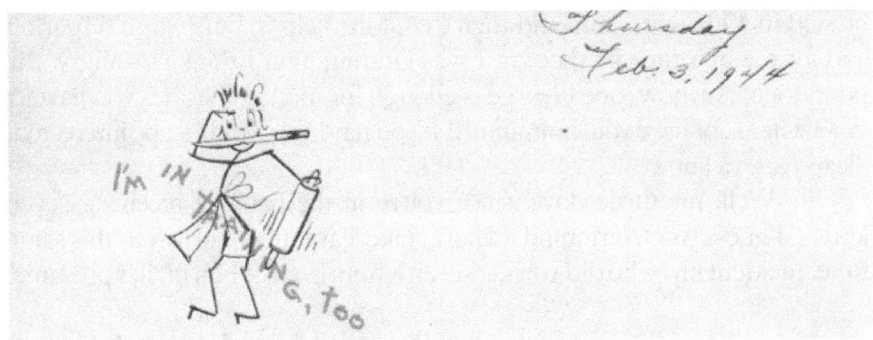

Hi honey,

Well, I dood it! Tonight, I became a full fledged nurse's Aid. The speeches they made in our honor were really inspiring, no kidding. Ah, do I feel good. I'm enclosing the insignia we are supposed to wear on our hats. I don't know what you're gonna do with it, but keep it anywho, just on accounts I love you.

What a question - .... Am I the jealous type?!! Don't rightly know how to answer that question. When it comes to material things such as money, clothes and such, I am definitely not the jealous type. So far I haven't been jealous of anything or anybody except those who are free from worry and care. Those, (incidentally, I've never met any such person,) I'm truly jealous of. And as for my being afraid that some southern gal will take you away from me, well, regardless if I do or don't want it, that's up to you. You have a mind of your own, and let me add a good mind, too, and it is your privilege to change it anytime before its too late. Then it really will be a bad state of affairs. I think you know pretty much what you want, and if that happens to be me, well then, everything is just fine and dandy, so let's drop this whole ridiculous conversation. O.K? O.K.

Evidently, you asked Mike Gordon if he knew anyone by the name of Megans. Well, you silly goose, Edie is the only one named Megans, her cousin's names are Shapiro, that is, their maiden names are Shapiro. So there!

I felt terrible about Jackie's asthma attack. He's had wrotten luck, hasn't he? When he asked me to go to Miami with him, he was more serious about his going than I thought. I'm glad he's finally done something he's wanted to.

George Dowd, a boy that works down our place, keeps asking me out. He's a very nice fellow but has a wife, a baby, and besides I have no intentions of ever going with him, but it's loads of fun stringing him along. Tonight, when he asked me to go out, I said first he'd have to tell me where we would go. He suggested some dine, but I insisted on going parking first, he said its O.K. with him, and then I couldn't help it, but I started roaring and for the first time he thought I was kidding him. I think he's angry, the poor dope! Anyhow, one George is enough for me, and besides you haven't got a wife..... or have you, hmmmm!!! If you haven't - would ya be interested, - leap year, ya know.

Well, my turtle dove, since you're in the habit of receiving seven letters, I guess you won't mind if I sorta take leave till tomorrow at this same time. Incidentally, who did you get seven letters from?!! Fan mail, I presume.

Love, Lottie

P.S. Does ya still love me?!

February 6, 1944
Sunday

From:	To:
C.L. Sniderman	Mr. Pvt. J.G. Barr 11057933
65 Houghton St.	37th Base Hq. & A.A.B Sq. N.O. A.A.B.
Worcester 4, Mass.	New Orleans 12, La.

Dearest George,

By the time you get this letter you'll have probably heard all about it, but it was such a surprise to me that I'll tell you over again. I had just gotten home from work Friday when your mother called. She told me Mike Gordon was in town and when she asked if I'd like to come along to see him I jumped at the chance. He really is a very nice fellow and talked very well of you. Incidentally, he also told me that you visited his place with a beautiful blonde! This, of-course, was not supposed to be told to me, but you know, it just slipped out. I guess my reaction was the expected one, because much to my disgrace I blushed. Everyone laughed and I was very embarrassed. I hate myself when I blush!! But seriously, he's very nice.

I nearly laughed myself sick when you wrote that you had tried to teach one of the boys to dance. Not that I don't think you're capable, but for some odd reason I just can't picture you. Another thing in your letter that brought a smile to my face was when you told me about the fellow who has three lots. So, you'll have to look further into it, huh? Well, darling, either you're kidding, or you've some money piled away that I don't know about! In either event, it's still a good idea.

Today was a beautiful day. Phylis Jacobson and I were supposed to go skating but the ice wasn't hard enough so we went for a long walk down Massaoit Rd. We were just starting back when a car started tooting the horn. We thought it was a couple of kids and put our noses right up. But the horn persisted. Finally, we turned to look and it was Phylis' mother & dad. They took us for a long ride, which I thoroughly enjoyed. Then she came over here for supper and we talked and talked and talked. I talked mostly about you.... about the fun we used to have, the silly things we did, and how we used to get so much fun out of the little things. She said she envied me because all the boys she ever went with were only interested in "parking." Pardon the drastic change of color, but I just ran short! [editor's note: Stationary paper color changed]. So anyway, we had loads of fun talking and we decided we got along quite well together. She said she liked my informality, humph, just wait till I put on the dog!

I started reading "A Tree Grows In Brooklyn" and it's very good. The type of book you can't put down once you've started.

George, your sister is really so funny. When we went to see Mike Gordon, she also came. She insisted on sitting on the same chair with me and asked a few very embarrassing questions. She noticed and scrutinized everything about me, - how I did my nails, the way I hold my cigarette, my shoes, my lipstick, - and everything else, - the little devil even whistled at me. I always missed having a sister and I always imagined that had I had one, she probably would have been like Tobye. She's an awfully nice kid. I don't know whether she likes me or not after that thorough over going she gave me. Your mother is very glad that I like the same things you like, such as, "gefilte" fish and poppy seed cake, (I don't know how to spell it in Jewish), and promised to teach me how to make all that stuff. I'll probably never learn, but it'll be fun trying anyhow.

By the by, who did you take to the company party? Now don't tell me you went alone! Was she nice?!! And with this parting thought I shall bid thee farewell; me mater is hounding me 'cause it's so late, but for you I even give up my beauty sleep. Take it easy ---

Love, Lottie

P.S. Again let me remind you to please forget about getting me something. Put the $12.00 extra you got in your piggy bank!!

February 7, 1944
Monday

From:	To:
Mr. Pvt. J.G. Barr 11057933	C.L. Sniderman
37th Base Hq. & A.A.B Sq. N.O. A.A.B.	65 Houghton St.
New Orleans 12, La.	Worcester, 4, Mass.

Dearest Lottie,

I saw our traveling orders, they read we are to leave on or about the 7th. I don't think we'll leave to-day, perhaps to-morrow. Anyway, my new address will be:

Pvt. J.G. Barr
A.S.C. Replacement Depot #2
Kelly Field, San Antonio
Texas

I'll write you when I get there.

Saturday afternoon another fellow and I went to the park. It was so nice we thought we'd like to go canoeing. Unfortunately, when we went to hire one, they had all been let out. Being in a very vivacious mood we rented bikes. We rode through the parks watching them play tennis and the kids on the swings. It was good to see people enjoying themselves without apparent worries or cares. The best part of the whole afternoon tho, was when we rode through the gardens. In one section, I stopped and the lovely aroma of roses seemed to be all around me, caressing me and soothing my troubled mind. It seemed as if you were there looking after me. When we have our own garden, we're going to have rose bushes around the whole house.

The other night I took the fellow I've been chuming around with to supper, he's a good kid, reminds me of Maxie, so when he won in a poker game Saturday afternoon (I won 8¢) he took me out for dinner.

Yesterday afternoon while at the "Y", I met Ken Davidson from Worc. He and my brother Narky used to go together, that is, they chummed around together. It was funny the way I met him, I was chewing on a hot dog and just walking around to see who I knew there. There in front of me in a Coast Guard uniform was a very familiar face. Before I could remember his name, I asked him, rather told him, "You're from Worcester", and he yelled, "Barr", Narky's brother. He's down here to get his ship and expects to be here a couple of months more.

As what we're doing in camp, nothing. Most of all the detail work is given to the men who aren't alerted for shipment, so we play ping-pong, cards, and read. I haven't really worked for so long that I'm going to be a wreck the first time I'll have to.

Your, George

February 9, 1944
Wednesday

From:	To:
Pfc. D. Grossman 31389999	C.L. Sniderman
6th Traffic Reg. Gp. T.C. A.P.O. #9497	65 Houghton St.
c/o Postmaster N.Y., N.Y.	Worcester, 4, Mass.

Dear Lottie,

First of all, let me make an excuse for this pen. I just borrowed it and it doesn't write too smoothly. I'm sorry that my letter upset you so, for I really had no intention of doing that. I just wrote what I thought, and although it sounded very morbid, I was in a good frame of mind at the time. It just proves how unpredictable I am.

I saw your honey the last Saturday in January, and he's O.K. As you probably already know, he expects to ship soon.

Well, Lottie, I've finally got my A.P.O. address. I'm somewhere on the East coast and a little closer to home than I was two weeks ago [censored] although I don't know for sure [censored] as far as I'm concerned [censored]. I really would just as soon be over as to be where I am. "So near, yet so far." I never thought that phrase would apply to me.

I'm really fine though, and I'm getting along O.K. I've been promoted to P.F.C., so you had better tell your boyfriend to have respect for his superior non-com.

There really isn't too much that I can say, but one of these days I'm going to sit down and write a nice long letter to you. Let me know if you want it to be serious, humorous, or what I'm thinking about. If my letters offed you the way the last one did, then I had better get out my little joke book and start to quote.

Well, miss, that's about it. We've got to fall out for another formation soon, and I owe a letter to Pvt. James Barr. I sure feel sorry for that guy. He's probably sweating down there while I'm freezing up here. Please write soon and get yourself some "V" mail stationery. Charge it to my account.

As your, Dave

[Editor's note: This letter was censored by an Army Examiner and was cut up in several places throughout the letter.]

February 9, 1944
Wednesday

From:	To:
C.L. Sniderman	Mr. Pvt. J.G. Barr 11057933
65 Houghton St.	A.S.C. Replacement Depot #2, Sq. #5
Worcester 4, Mass.	Kelly Field, Texas

Dearest George,

For the past few days, I've been on pins and needles wondering where you finally would end up, and today's letter set my mind at ease. So, you're agoing to be in San Antonio, - good old Texas.

Darling, I nearly cried when you wrote me that you got drunk. I always said I wanted to see you drunk, but I meant on a happy occasion and when I could get drunk with you. I don't ever want you to get that low in mood again. Promise? O.K.

I wish I could have gone on that bike jaunt with you. And we must definitely remember to have roses in our garden. Oodles and oodles of them. Why do your thoughts coincide so beautifully with mine?

We're going to have quite a nice surprise in our family next week. My brother, Sam, from Washington is coming to visit us for a few days. I haven't seen him for three years. I've almost forgotten what he looks like.

Everything here is very much the same. I just called the Union Station and they told me a trip to Texas would cost approximately $85.00. Would you like me to come and visit you? Am seriously considering, no kidding!

I went to a shower the other night, and decided then and there, that if I ever had a shower, it would not be like that one, - I hope. It was at the Lido. A bunch of cackling women came, - ate and then went home. Very "kikey." I'm going to have one that'll be done up right. Only friends and relatives, - and not the whole city of Worcester. Incidentally, you have been increased with a new cousin. Jack Snider, I think his name is Jack, and Winnie Bernstein have decided to unite.

Frank Sinatra's singing is making writing a little difficult, but I think I'm winning out. He's singing "Falling In Love With Love", and in case you didn't know, I'm mad about that song.

Guess your next letter will be from your new home, - or temporary home anywho. Write soon, darling.

Love, Lottie

P.S. After just learning your old address, - I have to start all over again. Oh well.

SOUTHERN PACIFIC LINES GRAND CENTRAL STATION, HOUSTON, TEXAS

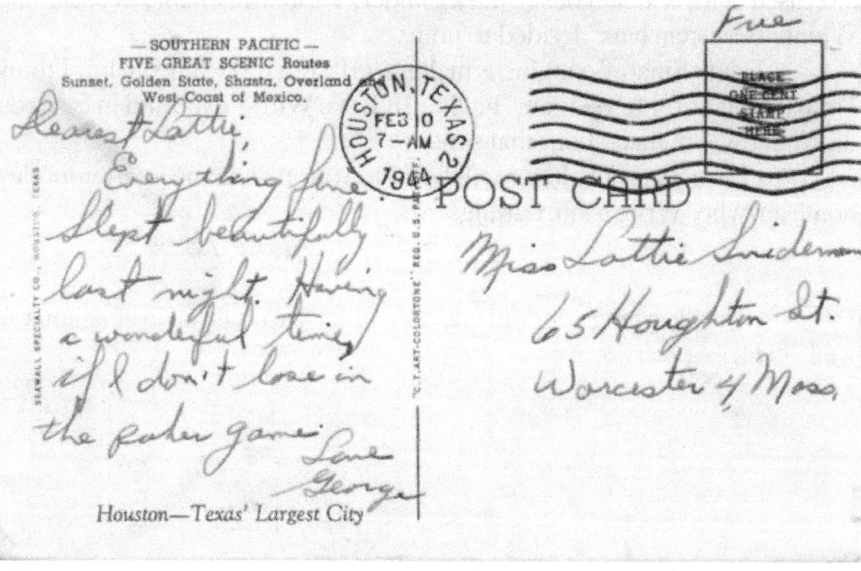

— SOUTHERN PACIFIC —
FIVE GREAT SCENIC Routes
Sunset, Golden State, Shasta, Overland
West Coast of Mexico.

Dearest Lottie;
Everything fine.
Slept beautifully
last night. Having
a wonderful time
if I don't lose in
the poker game. Love
George

Houston—Texas' Largest City

POST CARD

Free

Miss Lottie Sniderman
65 Houghton St.
Worcester 4 Mass.

February 10, 1944
Thursday

From:	To:
Mr. Pvt. J.G. Barr 11057933	C.L. Sniderman
A.S.C. Replacement Depot #2, Sq. #5	65 Houghton St.
Kelly Field, Texas	Worcester, 4, Mass.

Dearest Lottie,

I hope honey that you won't get angry at me (I know you won't), but this will have to be short. They've been making us run around, wait around, and move around, that I haven't had time to do a damn thing.

It seems that you stay in this hell hole no longer than a month, two at the most, then you are shipped to some other camp. Usually to a permanent company, or squadron, as the air corps calls them, or to a P.O.E. as a casual. In other words, no one knows, it is just a messed up affair all around. The food so far has been a hundred percent better than what we had back at the air base in N.O., but the camp routine is supposed to be terrific. K.P. and guard duty all the time.

This afternoon I had half of my clothes taken away from me because they showed the slightest wear, shoes, because when it rained water soaked thru (I haven't found a pair of shoes yet that didn't absorb water when they got wet.) As far as I can see it is just a waste of government money.

We live in huts with double decker beds, eight men to each hut.

Honey, I think I forgot to congratulate you in your graduation to a full-fledged nurses aide, but if I did, it was of the conditions back at N.O. I have the insignia in my writing kit, at the top of your picture, and I can say I am proud to have it. Thanks.

They may have sent me 600 miles further from you, darling, but they'll never be able to take my heart from you.

Your, George

February 10, 1944
Thursday

From:	To:
C.L. Sniderman	Mr. Pvt. J.G. Barr 11057933
65 Houghton St.	A.S.C. Replacement Depot #2, Sq. #5
Worcester 4, Mass.	Kelly Field, Texas

Dearest George,

Last night at 11 o'clock I finally received your telegram. I'm so glad you sent it, it made me feel more at ease to know you were there already. I called your folks this morning and your father told me they got a telegram this morning. He tried to get me before I called him, but the lines were busy. I was glad that he was glad, and he was glad that I was glad, so that made us both simply delirious with happiness and joy.

What a day at the office! I was never a person who liked being stepped on when I knew I was right so I let one of the girls have it good today. She felt very bad because after I let loose, I had a grand pout on my face. I wasn't sorry, not in the least, but I do hate arguments. Just before we were leaving to go home she noticed I was still pouting, so she ran over and hugged me and planted a kiss on my cheek. I was so astonished I just sat there and laughed, then we both laughed and everything was O.K. She said that no matter what I did or said, she could never get really angry at me. She said if she went home to supper knowing I was mad she wouldn't enjoy it (she's nuts.) The kids are so used to having me laughing all day, that when I show them I'm really human by becoming angry, they feel terrible. Yesterday during lunch hour, I was showing the kids how to do ballet. I stood on my desk and everyone (the bosses) were out, - I thought! I was just finishing my dance when I noticed that everyone was edging away from me. I turned, gasped, and saw a smiling Mr. Norman Sharfman. I was never so embarrassed. He didn't say anything, but I'm shocked when I think what he must have been thinking. So much for the office!!

Well, me friend, what's what in Texas? What are you doing and what are you going to do? Is there any chance of you going to school? Pray, write and tell me all.

Why the heck do I miss you! It would be so nice if I didn't miss you and if I didn't like you. Then I wouldn't care how far or where you were. But on second thought I'd be very miserable. I'm glad I have you to worry about, it gives me food for thought. I think about you in connection with the past, present, and mostly the future. Did I ever tell you I love you, - well I do, honest. Does you all have a place in yo heart fo me, huh?

Love, Lottie

P.S. Pardon me, but I feel silly this eve!

February 11, 1944
Friday

From:	To:
Mr. Pvt. J.G. Barr 11057933	C.L. Sniderman
A.S.C. Replacement Depot #2, Sq. #5	65 Houghton St.
Kelly Field, Texas	Worcester, 4, Mass.

[Editor's note: the poem and the information booklet for Kelly Field, San Antonio, Texas were the only two things included in the envelope. No letter was included.]

THIRTY SEVENTH BASE HEADQUARTERS AND AIR BASE SQUADRON
NEW ORLEANS ARMY AIR BASE

New Orleans, Louisiana,

I wrote a book the other day, A book to show the G.I. way,
Of how to make this Army life pay. Now figure from your 50 bucks,
The thirty two, sixty four deducts, Allotments take your twenty two,
For a wife to send it to. This leaves you with a bond to buy,
Insurance, too, in case you die. Now seventeen forty isn't bad,
For that much left won't make you mad. But wait! Stop! Halt! Desist!
Here's more to go, I insist. Laundry bills, the weekly shows,
For carfares, cokes, your money goes. These extra socks that natty hat,
The squadron's fund will take care dig in that.

You're punch-drunk now and going fast, You hope the hell it won't last.
Donate here nad donate there, You drop a quarter everywhere,
Camels Luckies, all your dough dough, you're almost broke,
You've borne up well, you're almost through, there's nothin else,
You think, that's due, Oh hell, Here comes Joe, what lousy luck,
He's come to get his borrowed buck. It shakes your faith in Army life,
Oh, to be back living off your wife!

YES SIR, SOLDIER...

THIS PAMPHLET TELLS YOU EVERYTHING YOU WANT TO KNOW...

...and no doubt the first thing you want to know is why am I here ? Well, here's why...

The ASC Replacement Depot No. 2 was established to supply men - well qualified men - to units where their particular specialities are needed. If you are a prop specialist then you won't be sent from here as an automobile mechanic.

That doesn't mean you will arrive here one day and out the next, but it means you will be here until a place is found for you. A place where you can really do a job in which you are qualified.

That is the prime responsibility of this Station, and the Depot welcomes you here.

Maybe you are one of the fellows who have been moved from here to there and you have reached the point of wondering "Why am I in the Army" ?

Well soldier, this is your last station. Everything will be done by this depot to make you feel like the army does want you.

Your food will be good.
You will be paid.
You will be fully equipped.
When you leave here you will
have a definite assignment.

In addition to providing you with the best that the Air Corps has to offer, there are many things you should know - but not through hearsay or by asking questions of those who have been here for a period of time. For instance, certain regulations of this Depot, places of entertainment or bus service available.

This pamphlet will give all this information, and more too. So read on...

ATHLETICS...

The South Kelly Gymnasium is one of the best equipped gym's in the entire Army. You can bowl, play basketball, volleyball, badminton, table tennis, handball, or box or wrestle. If you like, you can have a sandwich and a cup of coffee after your workout and shower. For outdoor athletics, you can draw some equipment from your squadron.

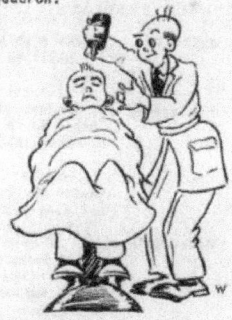

BARBER SHOP...

This clip joint is located in Building 423 and is open from 0800 to 1800 every day but Sunday. Haircuts, shampoos and shoe shines. Sorry, no pretty manicurists.

BUS SERVICE...(To San Antonio)

The South Kelly bus leaves from the south gate (opposite Theatre No. 2) every twenty minutes. The return trip starts on the same schedule from the Military Plaza in San Antonio. The North Kelly bus starts at the main gate on the same schedule and can be boarded for the return trip at any corner along Commerce Street, San Antonio. Fare is 20 cents each way - but ask the bus driver about weekly tickets. They're cheaper if you expect to make more than one trip.

BUS SERVICE... (Local)

The Kelly Field free bus runs completely around the base (in both directions) at about twenty minute intervals. The schedule is posted at each bus stop. The most convenient stop to the Depot is at the corner by the theatre.

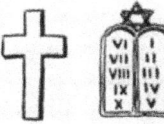

CHAPLAIN...

The Chaplain always has his door open. He wants to talk over anything that's bothering you. He is located in Building 430.

CHURCH SERVICES...

Catholic . . Sunday 9:00 and 11:00 A.M. in Chapel No. 1, Building 476.

Protestant . . Sunday 10:00 A. M. in Chapel No. 2, North Kelly, Building 1633.

Jewish . . . Friday at 7:45 P. M. in Chapel No. 2, North Kelly, Building 1633.

Greek Orthodox . . There is no service on the Base, but there is a Greek Orthodox Church on N. St. Marys Street in San Antonio.

CHECKS...

Personal checks may be cashed in the PX week days from 0930 to 2200, if endorsed by an Officer.

CLEANING & PRESSING...
POST TAILOR SHOP...

Located in Building 417.

CURFEW...

You have to be off the streets of San Antonio by 1100 on week nights or 0200 Saturday nights. If you're not, you will encounter an M. P. which may mean punishment and restriction.

DOG TAGS...

Will be worn at all times. That means around the neck.

FURLOUGHS...

Sorry, but you can't get one here unless—

(1) It's an emergency.
(2) You're just back from overseas, or
(3) You haven't had one in one year or longer.

GAS MASKS...

Will be worn every Thursday. If you don't have it on, you're liable to get caught with your pants down in a gas attack.

HOSPITAL...

If you feel ill, report to sick call, at
1000. Record must be made in the Sick
Book and this book presented to the Doctor at the dispensary. Otherwise you
will not be treated.

LAUNDRY...

Can be had on five day service at the
Post Tailor Shop, Building 417.

LIBRARY...

The library is very complete in every
respect. Drop in to read your home town
newspaper, write a letter, use the typewriter, listen to the radio or just curl
up with a good book. Building 477 from
0800 to 2100.

MAIL...

Can be picked up in Building 442 between
1030 and 1200 and 1330 and 1600 each day
except Sunday.

MAILING ADDRESS...

Your address here will be:

Pvt. John Doe, 3246531,
ASC Repl. Depot #2,
Squadron#_____,
Kelly Field, Texas

Be sure you write this in the upper left
hand corner of each envelope. If you
don't you'd better put a stamp on it,
'cause soldier it will come back.

MESS KITS...

Will be used for all meals in the Depot.
Better keep yours clean or you'll be doing a lot of double time.

MONEY ORDERS...

May be purchased in the Post Office,
Building 483.

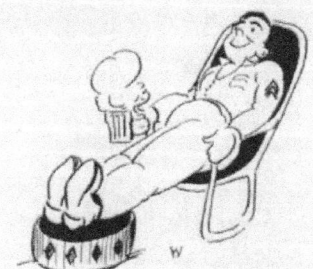

N. C. O. CLUB...

Is located at North Kelly (next to the
Service Club, Building 1025). You'll
find the entertainment excellent and
dues reasonable.

OFF LIMITS...

There are a great number of off limits establishments in San Antonio. Check with your Squadron Bulletin Board before you go to town. If you aren't sure or can't remember, ask any M. P.

ORDERS...

You'll have a trick or two of guard, soldier, so you'd better brush up on your General Orders.

PASSES...

Passes to San Antonio may be issued by the Squadron Commander effective after retreat unless you are restricted. You must be back, though, by midnight and your pass must be turned in by 0700 next morning. And of course you have to sign in and out.

POST EXCHANGE...

Building 484. Open 7 days a week from
0830 to 2200.

PROPHYLACTIC STATIONS...

Can be found in San Antonio at the
following locations: 633 E. Commerce
St. and 213 Santa Rosa St.
Also prophylactic treatment can be had
at Dispensary # 2 (open all night).
Prophylactic kits can be purchased from
the Post Exchange at a cost of 10¢.

READING ROOM...

This building is opposite Squadron 1's
Orderly Room. It will always be QUIET
for you G.I.'s who want to write that
particular "Sugar Report" or read the
latest Book-of-the-Month.
        This building will also play host
        to a series of Orientation Talks
        to be given during ' off-duty '
        hours. These talks will be given
        by G. I.'s who have been in the
        thick of it...

Hours..All day until 'Call to Quarters.

RECREATION BUILDING...

In our Area Buildings, 441 - 443, are for your recreation. There are pool tables (keep your cue out of the felt, Joe), ping-pong tables, card tables, shuffle boards and other deck games. There you will also find a radio and that piano for the 'G.I. Joe' you must force to play - but then WOW! What a mean Boogie-Woogie.

RED CROSS...

It is important that your folks understand the work the Red Cross does in checking requests for emergency furloughs. Tell them that if it is urgent for you to be called home immediately, to get in touch with the Local RedCross Chapter and explain the emergency. The Red Cross will then refer the request to your Commanding Officer for action.

RESTAURANT...

IS LOCATED IN THE PX AND IS OPEN 24 hours a day with doughnuts, coffee, hot sandwiches and a complete soda fountain

SERVICE CLUB...

Is at North Kelly, Building 1025, and quite a distance from the Depot. But a free Kelly Field Bus goes there. A long ride but you won't regret it.

SOCIAL EVENTS...

Consult the "Flying Times" (Free Kelly Field Newspaper) for outstanding social events you might want to take in. You can get your copy at the Library or PX.

SQUADRON COMMANDER...

If you're in trouble, talk it over with your Squadron Commander. He can answer a lot of $64 questions and give you plenty of good, sound advice.

TAILOR SHOP...

In Building 417 to take care of any alterations you may want to have done – or mend that tear in your trousers.

TELEPHONES...

If you want to make a phone call, you will find three booths in the rear of Building 441. Make your conversation as brief as possible.

THEATRES...

There are two on the post. If you don't like the show at the South Kelly Theatre, Building 481, try North Kelly, Building 1628.

GLOSSARY
of
GOOD OLD ARMY SLANG

Albatross	Chicken
Armored cow	Canned milk
*Army Banjo	Shovel
*Army brat	Son or daughter of Army officer
Army strawberries	Prunes
AWOL	Absence without official leave
Baby	Mustard
Barker	Heavy artillery gun
*Bath tub	Motorcycle sidecar
*Battery acid	Coffee
*Bazooka	New anti-tank gun
Bean gun	Rolling kitchen
Beans	Commissary officer
*Behavior report	Letter to a girl
Belly robber	Mess sergeant
Bible	Army regulations
Big John	Recruit
Black strap	Coffee
*Blind flying	A date with a girl you have never met
*Blisterfoot	Infantryman
*Blitz it	Polish it
*Blitz wagon, or buggy	Staff car
Blood	Ketchup
Bop-pocket	Tightwad
Bootleg	Coffee
*Bootlick	To flatter
Boudoir	Squad tent
*Bowlegs	Cavalryman
*Brass hats	G.H.Q. officer; staff officer
*Bubble dancing	Dishwashing
Buddy	Close friend
Buddy seat	Motorcycle sidecar
Bugs	Any solids found in soup
Bull pen	Military prison yard
*Bunk fatigue	To sleep or rest
Burn and turn	Game of blackjack
Butt	Cigarette
Button chopper	Laundry
Buzzard meat	Chicken or turkey
*Buzzing a town	To do the town
Canned cow	Canned milk
Canned horse	Canned roast
Canned Willie	Canned beef
Carp	To complain
*Carrier pigeon	Officer's messenger
*Carrying a heavy load	Fatigued or melancholy
*Chinese amateur	Automatic rifle
China clipper	Dishwasher
Chow	Food
*Chow hounds	Men always at head of mess line
Cits	Civilian clothing
Class "A" pass	Reward for efficiency and good conduct; permits absence at all times when not on duty
Class "B" pass	Permits absence between retreat and reveille
CO (KO)	Commanding officer
Coffee cooler	One who seeks easy jobs
Company stooge	Company clerk
Copenhagen	Chewing snuff
Cow juice	Fresh milk
Crab	Chronic complainer
*Cream on shingle	Creamed beef on toast
*Cross Bar Hotel	Guard House
Crow	Chicken
Crow tracks	Chevrons
Crumb hunt	Kitchen inspection
Dawn patrolling	To arise before reveille
Devil's piano	Machine gun
*Ding How	Everything O. K.
*Dis De Artist	Radio Operator
Dog robber	Orderly
Dog tags	Identification disks
Dogface	Enlisted man
Dog show	Foot inspection
*Dough puncher	Army baker
Draped	Intoxicated
DS	Detached service; away from organization
Dud	Unexploded shell
Duff	Any sweet edible
Egg in your beer	Too much of a good thing
Embalmed meat	Canned meat
File	Waste basket
Flying boxcar	A bomber
Foot slogger	An infantryman
*Foxhole	A crescian trench
*Frog sticker	A bayonet
Galvanized gelding	Tank
Gas house	Saloon or beer garden
Gasoline Cow Boy	Member of Armored Force
*General's Car	A wheelbarrow
*G. I. cans	Garbage
*G. I. haircut	One-inch trim
*G. I. Sky Pilot	Chaplain
G. I. War	Maneuver
*Glamour boy	Draftee; Selective Service trainee
Goaty	Awkward; ignorant
*Gold brick	One who gets by without doing his share of work
Gold-fish	Salmon
Grass	Vegetable or salad
Gravel agitator	Infantryman
Grease	Butter
Grinders	Teeth
*Guard house lawyer	One who knows little but talks much
*Halt and freeze	Assume position of attention
*Hashburner	Cook
*Hay burner	A horse or mule
*Hell Buggy	Tank
*Hen fruit	Eggs
*Hitting a pole	To climb a telephone pole
*Hit the silk	Use a parachute
*Homing Device	A pass or furlough
Hooks	Chevrons
Ink	Coffee
Iron horses	Tanks
Iron ponies	Motorcycles
Jackson	Form of address for any soldier
Java	Coffee
*Jeep	A bantam car
Juice Jerker	Electrician
Keeps dainty	Well behaved
KO	Commanding officer
Latrine rumors	Unfounded reports
*Loaded breeches	Inert, lazy
*Limp line	Men reporting at Sick Call
Little poison	37 mm. Gun
*Makings	Cigarette tobacco and paper
*Meat wagon	Ambulance
Medics	The Medical Corps
Mill	Guard House
Motor Pool	Garage
*Motorized freckles	Insects
*Monkey clothes	Full dress uniform
Mother McCrea	A sob story
MP	Military police
Mule skinner	A teamster
NCO	A Non-Commissioned Officer
North Dakota rice	Hot cereal
Old file	An old soldier
Old man	Company or Regimental Commander
*On the carpet	Called before the Commanding Officer for disciplinary action
Orderly room	Company headquarters
Paring knife	Bayonet
*Pearl diver	Kitchen Police
Pencil pusher	Clerk
*Pick up your brass	Get out of the way
Pineapple	Hand grenade
*Polishing the Apple	Flattering your superiors
*Popsicle	Motorcycle
*Pup tent	Shelter tent
*PX	Post Exchange
PX Coupons	Post Exchange checks
*Rain room	Bath house
Rats	Balls of lint on floor during an inspection of quarters
Red Leg	Artilleryman
*Refugees	Recruits or newly arrived selectees
*Regimental monkey	The drum major
*Rise and shine	Call used to awaken soldiers
Rookie	A recruit
Runner	A messenger
*Run the guard	Leave or enter camp furtively
St. Vitus Davenport	A tank
Sand and dirt	Salt and pepper
*Saw-bone	The doctor
Scandal-sheet	The monthly payroll
Seagull	Chicken
See the chaplain	Stop groaning
*Shave tail	A second lieutenant
Show tent	Motion picture theatre
*Shutter bugs	Camera fans
Side arms	Cream and sugar
*Skirt patrol	Search for feminine companionship
Slum	Food
Slum burner	A cook
Slum gullion	Hash
Snore sack	Sleeping bag
*Soft money	Paper currency
Soup	Dynamite
Steam shovel	Potato peeler
Street monkeys	Members of band
*Strictly cut plug	Well pleased
*Super report	A letter from girl
*Superman Drawers	Woolen underwear
*Swanks	A soldier's best clothes
Swill	Beer
Tailor Mades	Factory-made cigarettes
Three striper	Sergeant
Tiger meat	Beef
Tin Hat	Steel helmet
Tommy gun	A Thompson sub-machine gun
*Top kick	First Sergeant
Turned in	Reported for misconduct
Two striper	Corporal
Typewriter	30 Caliber Machine Gun
Uncle Sam's Party	Payday
*Walkie-Talkie	Portable radio receiving and sending apparatus
Wing-heavy	Inebriated
*Yard bird	A raw recruit

* SLANG EXPRESSIONS ILLUSTRATED

February 11, 1944
Friday

From:	To:
Mr. Pvt. J.G. Barr 11057933	C.L. Sniderman
A.S.C. Replacement Depot #2, Sq. #5	65 Houghton St.
Kelly Field, Texas	Worcester, 4, Mass.

Dearest Lottie,

I don't know how to start this letter because this is the first chance that I've had to do anything on my own. This morning we fell out raring to get our clothes changed, but the supply room wasn't ready for us, so we waited and waited, ready to go, but they didn't get ready until after dinner. Then we waited in line to turn our clothes in, and by that time we couldn't get our new clothes. This was lucky, because we couldn't stand retreat because our lack of uniform. After we do get our clothes, we'll have to stencil our clothes. Tho I have a rubber stamp, I can't use it, because it is not G.I.

What I've told you could have taken a few hours, but because this is the army, it took us all day. After this, we had a G.I. party. Our hut was so dirty that when we poured water on the floor, we could have made those mud pies that you wanted to throw at your mother because she wouldn't let you walk with her when she got her new coat. Now the floor is nice and clean, in fact, I'm sitting on the floor writing to you.

There is one nice thing about this camp though that I like, they have the band out for two or three hours a day, and military music fills the air, it sort of puts a snap to your walk.

Darling, it feels awful not being able to get mail as yet. I hope by tomorrow I'll be receiving at least a letter from you, but the way mail is after a transfer, I doubt it.

If I have a chance, I'm going to go into San Antonio tomorrow to see what the place looks like. It's about a half hour ride from here.

Your, George

February 12, 1944
Saturday

From:	To:
C.L. Sniderman	Mr. Pvt. J.G. Barr 11057933
65 Houghton St.	A.S.C. Replacement Depot #2, Sq. #5
Worcester 4, Mass.	Kelly Field, Texas

Dearest George,

Today is a day you would appreciate – A slow soft snow is falling serenely covering everything into fantastic shapes. Every once in awhile, the stillness is broken by the squeals of children having the best time ever. I came home from work today and just sat, looked, and envied. I envied those kids. No cares, no worries. The radio is playing soft music, and that lonesome feeling just grows. If you were here I'd enjoy it much more, this is the kind of weather we used to love.

Maybe my morbid mood got its start when I received some very bad news today. A cousin of mine in New York passed away. He had been in an incurable hospital for 28 years and his day finally came. The funeral is tomorrow in Worcester and all my relatives are here. I'll forget about it till tomorrow.

I received a very sweet letter from Fran & Sol today. Seems they really enjoyed having Jackie. I also got a letter from Dave and it was all cut up. Evidently, the censor didn't approve. I think I know where he is, although they tried to discourage all his hints. Very nice that Pauline wrote you such a nice letter. But you didn't tell me what she wrote, or is that a secret! O.K., - you'll be sorry!

My adopted grandmother, she's such a dear, gave <u>us</u> a gift today. I nearly died when I saw it. I won't tell you what it is, but someday you'll see, I hope. It gave me the most peculiar feeling. Everytime I think of it I laugh – even now I have a big grin on my face.

I was listening to the radio last night and every station seemed to be playing "I had a good man, but introduced him to a good friend and now I ain't got no man and I ain't got no friend." That was right after you told me Pauline wrote to you. Ironical, eh not! Tell me, dear, do I stand a chance. She really is very clever – (I'll kill her!) I hate women!! Or some of them anywho.

Love, Lottie

February 13, 1944
Sunday

From:	To:
Mr. Pvt. J.G. Barr 11057933	C.L. Sniderman
A.S.C. Replacement Depot #2, Sq. #5	65 Houghton St.
Kelly Field, Texas	Worcester, 4, Mass.

Dearest Lottie,

Here I am working my head off on K.P. One of the fellows was nice enough to give me this paper and another lent me his pencil, now all I have to do is write.

Yesterday I went and got my clothing. I exchanged my blouse for one that fit me better and turned in my mackinaw for an overcoat. The rest of my clothes were even exchanged. You see, to clean your clothes here takes about five days, and when you turn them in for exchange or salvage, you get new clothes issued. Most of my clothes were dirty and I just turned them in to get clean stuff. This saved me days of waiting, even though I have to pay for cleaning of the clothes I turned in.

After getting my clothes yesterday I had to stencil them. My hands are so black from the ink that it will take months to wear off, almost anyway.

To further avoid any similar trouble in stenciling I went in town and ordered a rubber stamp (something I was going to do before, but never did get around to it). Last night I went into town to get it, but when I arrived at the store, it was closed. There was a girl working there at a typewriter, so I knocked on the door. When she looked up, she saw a soldier, so immediately went back to her work. I was insistent in my knocking so she came over and asked me what I wanted. I told her, but she said she didn't have anything to do with the stamps, but would look for me. She couldn't find it, so I joined a fellow, of recent acquaintance, at one of the hotels here. He was visiting a brother of a pal of his. We talked and the boy put in a call to his wife, who remained in N.O., but couldn't get thru, then he called his folks in Cleveland, still no soup. Meanwhile we drank the guy's wine and talked some more. He was on guard today and I was on K.P., so we left and came back to camp. Then the stinkers woke me at 4:15 A.M.

Yesterday afternoon we had an interview, but it didn't do me any good. It seems the government spent money on guys like me so they won't allow us to transfer into anything else, except to air cadet and that's not for me, besides everything is closed. O.C.S. – A.S.T.P. and photography. They have too many men in the army already, but I guess if they stopped taking men in, people would think the war was already won.

The days recently have been cold, but today it is drizzling. The atmosphere is better than N.O. because it is drier, whereas N.O. is very damp.

Everyone that hasn't had a furlough within a year is getting one. It seems as if there are an awful lot, and it just makes me wish that I could go home to you. It's been almost a week now that I haven't received any mail from you and that makes matters worse.

Darling, I love you more than anything else in this world. It seems as if I neglected to tell you for almost a week and I want you to know (as if you don't). But all kidding aside, when you said that loving me was the best thing that happened to you, well it is even more so in my case. A lot better things could have happened to you, like falling in love with someone rich instead of a jerk like me. But I'm happy about the whole deal, because I'm getting the best of the bargain.

Sweetheart, I miss you so much that it really hurts. I ache all over when I think of you. I close my eyes and see you and I want to grab and hug you. The next time I'm home and I get a hold on you, you'll realize what I mean.

The boys are in now for breakfast and I probably be called to do something any minute now, and there isn't anything more to write, So-----

Your, George

February 14, 1944
Monday

From:	To:
C.L. Sniderman	Mr. Pvt. J.G. Barr 11057933
65 Houghton St.	A.S.C. Replacement Depot #2, Sq. #5
Worcester 4, Mass.	Kelly Field, Texas

Dearest George,

I was beginning to think that you had forgotten all about me. I realize now that you couldn't have possibly written to me right away. Today's letter set my mind at ease.

Kelly field is supposed to be quite a nice place. I wonder if you'll have it as easy here as you did in New Orleans. You being a lucky guy (well, you got me didn't ya!) will probably have good breaks, I hope.

My big brother Sam came home today and the family gave him quite a reception at the station. Evidently, I changed a lot since the last time he saw me because when I ran up and kissed him he was stunned for a minute, - he didn't recognize me. He wants to buy a Photostatic place after the war and wants to know if you'd be interested in going into partnership. The man that owns it wants to retire in a few years and is going to sell out for about $18,000. I don't think it's a bad idea at all, - so I told him you'd think about it. So, - think about it. Shall I make out a check for the $9,000?!! He's such a peach, me brudder. You'll like him.

We're having a little blizzard outside now and my brother and I went for a little walk just before it started. It was almost like walking with you. We talked about old times and when the three of us were kids. He told me how I once socked him in the eye and I cried so much they couldn't stop me. In all my life, I've loved four men. My dad, my two brothers, and you, of-course. Right now, - guess who tops the list? But my love for you is entirely different from any other. Do you mind my loving three other men?!! I got a long letter from Edie Megans and she plans on stopping to see you in New Orleans on her way back. – Little does she know! Goodnight dear. Try and write every chance. I'm miserable when I don't hear from you.

Love, Lottie

February 14, 1944
Monday

From:	To:
Mr. Pvt. J.G. Barr 11057933	C.L. Sniderman
A.S.C. Replacement Depot #2, Sq. #5	65 Houghton St.
Kelly Field, Texas	Worcester, 4, Mass.

Dearest Lottie,

In answer to your last question of to-day's letter, yes, I do have a place in my heart for you. When I was born, the good Lord made a special place in my heart just for you. It's been there all my life and now that the vacancy sign is down, you'll live there the rest of my life.

This afternoon we moved to some different huts and it just moved us farther away from everything. Now to make a formation we'll probably have to run for it.

While trying to catch an afternoon nap, a corporal came running in the hut and told us that there was going to be an alert. After asking him what an alert was, he told us that when we heard two long blasts of a siren, we were to fall out on the double, with gas mask, helmet, leggings, and pistol belt. After arranging ourselves at the orderly room, we would immediately take off to supply and have rifles issued to us, then we would all run out to the landing strip, and that's as far as he got and when it did happen – and – was as far as we got. We stayed out on the field for about twenty minutes, then marched back to the company area, only to be told to go back to our huts and get ready for retreat.

No, I didn't go to the company party by myself. She was a nice girl. But when Mike said that she was a beautiful blonde, he was mistaken. She was a brunette. Are you jealous? If you are, don't be, because there is no need to be as I explained in the opening of this letter. If the girls at the office want to be taught ballet, then make them pay for it. After all, the talent that you have shouldn't be given free to such an audience without some kind of compensation. If you need a manager, I'll be glad to take you as my client. Rate - 10%. Let me know as soon as you can, as I am very busy with the rest of my stars. Who do you think brought Zorina to fame and fortune? (Wait till I throw away this weed and I'll start talking sense.)

To-morrow we start on a basic program, reviewing all that we've had in military procedure and some that we didn't have. It is just to keep us busy until someone some place wants us.

I'm glad that your glad, and my father is glad that both of you got my wires, and I'm glad to have sent them.

"North Star" is playing down here and if I get a chance I'm going to see it. I hear it is pretty good.

Your, George

February 15, 1944
Tuesday

From:	To:
C.L. Sniderman	Mr. Pvt. J.G. Barr 11057933
65 Houghton St.	A.S.C. Replacement Depot #2, Sq. #5
Worcester 4, Mass.	Kelly Field, Texas

Dearest George,

Your valentine was very, very sweet. Thanks loads, dear. I surely thought you had forgotten with so many other things on your mind, - I should have known better. Please pardon the pencil, but I'm spending the evening over at the Walker household and a pen is one thing I couldn't find. They wanted to take my brother Sam out so I volunteered to stay with the children. I'm sitting here listening to the radio, the dog is at my feet, and I can picture this as being my own home a few years hence. It's an awfully contented feeling only writing to you sort of spoils it, - you should be here, not a million miles away. Someday - ......! The baby is really beautiful. Much prettier than when you saw him, - or am I prejudiced!

I met Mrs. Pilson and she asked how you were. She told me George had a little accident and is in the hospital. His injuries were minor, but enough to upset her. Harvey Coblentz is also in the hospital. I don't know what's the matter with him.

I have oodles of letters to write and absolutely no time to write them. My life is one mad dash from one place to another and doing nothing to speak of. All I know is that I'm always rushing.

It's so quiet here it's driving me mad. Every once in awhile the dog snores, - honest, - turns over, groans a few times, and goes back to sleep. Oh, for the life of a dog – never mind, - I just changed my mind. Imagine me running around on all fours and going steady with a fire hydrant. No sir, - not for me. The car just pulled in the driveway so I'll be released from my chores. Either the mail situation is bad, or you haven't written, because I've only had one letter from you. Goodnight dear.

Love, Lottie

There is no way to measure love
And there can never be
For words can't even start —
                    to tell
How dear you are to me —

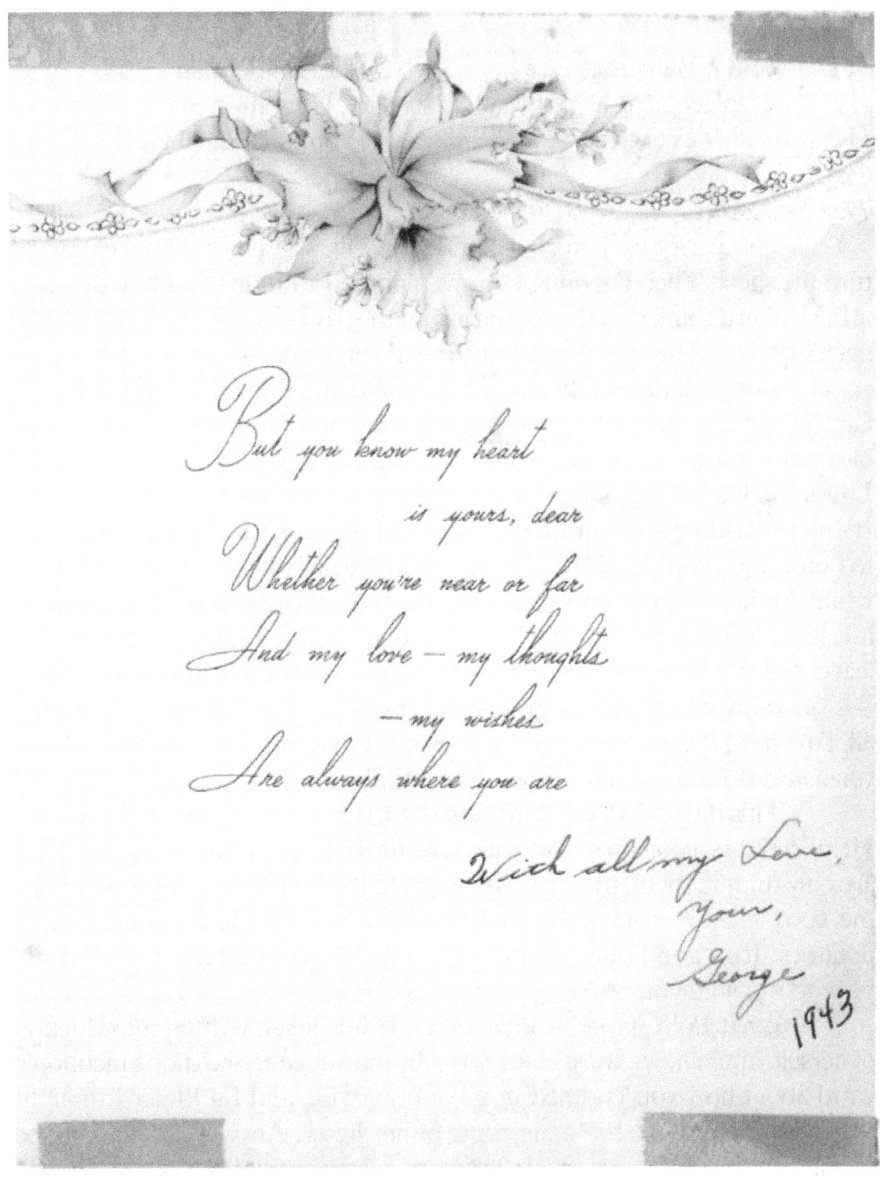

But you know my heart
    is yours, dear
Whether you're near or far
And my love — my thoughts
    — my wishes
Are always where you are

    With all my Love,
    Your,
    George
    1943

[Editor's note: This Valentine's Day card from George to Lottie was incorrectly written with a 1943, instead of 1944, years later.]

February 16, 1944
Wednesday

From:	To:
Mr. Pvt. J.G. Barr 11057933	C.L. Sniderman
A.S.C. Replacement Depot #2, Sq. #5	65 Houghton St.
Kelly Field, Texas	Worcester, 4, Mass.

Dearest Lottie,

I have a lot to write, but I probably will forget half of it by the time I turn the sheet. Then I'm on K.P. now, night K.P. I didn't find that out until 4 P.M. You'd think they'd have the list up the day before so that a fella could get a little sleep, but no, that is not the way this camp is run.

Lottie darling, I'd love to have you come down here to see me. In fact, if I knew I could get a three-day pass (they don't issue them here because of conditions) and could get out every night, I'd say yes, because sweetheart, I miss you like all hell. Then there would be the hardship of your traveling. It's no joke riding straight for two days and three nights. When I get closer to home, then you can come visit me, and I know I'm going to stay put for a while. At this damn camp, I can be shipped out at a moments notice because it is just one great pool, and when some one asks for me or anyone else, we leave, and in a hurry. I'd better stop this now before I talk myself out of it.

Now what did your grandmother give us? You have to tell me, after all, I'm one of the receivers of the gift. So, if you don't tell me, daddy will give you a lickin! I think you're a tease, a beautiful wonderful tease!

This night K.P. wouldn't be so bad, but we have a stinker for a cook. He won't let us cook up some steaks that the butchers want to give us. They are only ruining them, they're going to grind them up for hamburger. I hope the cook falls on something and breaks a leg. We de-eyed 900 lbs. of potatoes! It's a good thing that we have machines to peel them or we'd still be working on them.

What Polly wrote is not a secret. It was just a written introduction of herself, after all, we were never formally introduced. She didn't mention a word about how you 'cuddled' good or otherwise, and I told her I thought that was going to be the main topic of her letter. Anyway, I shouldn't be telling you this, because you are trying to keep a secret from me, so I won't tell you anymore about Polly's letter, besides that was about all.

Yesterday and to-day I was on detail work, moving lumber around. Big pieces, from a foot to six feet long. I never worked so hard in my life, to make it harder on our-selves we limited ourselves to one piece of wood at any one time. The corporal in charge was very mean, he wouldn't let us smoke all the time (just when we wanted to). If I get work like that everyday, it will be O.K. with me.

After loading the truck this afternoon we drove around the field, we had plenty of time to spare. We saw all the planes they have down here, including a B-29 (Superfortress). It's longer than a B-17. That is the kind (B-29) of airplane I would have worked on had I gone to Denver.

Last night I saw "North Star", but I wouldn't say it was wonderful. Propaganda all the way. While in town I notice that through the center of the city, a small river, or stream, runs through. The City built walks along the edges, planted trees, and have benches along the way. It winds itself among the streets (below street level) and reminds me of some of the pictures I've seen of Venice. Very picturesque.

Where do you think Dave is? The last letter I got from him, he was still in N.O.

You'll have to get used to this blue ink, because I have no more brown, and I got disgusted every time I ran short and couldn't borrow someone else's.

Your valentine was very cute, and I got the biggest kick out of it. All I could say when I finished reading it was, "She's Wonderful!"

"Who's wonderful," the boys asked. "Lottie's wonderful, that's who!" I answered. Lottie's wonderful!

Your, George

February 17, 1944
Thursday

From:	To:
C.L. Sniderman	Mr. Pvt. J.G. Barr 11057933
65 Houghton St.	A.S.C. Replacement Depot #2, Sq. #5
Worcester 4, Mass.	Kelly Field, Texas

Dearest George,

Writing to you tonight, is a very tired, but quite contented girl. My brother left at 4:30 this morning, and of-course we were all up to see him off. Barb and Mrs. Coppersmith just left and I've been running around all day, - so today was quite full. Barb wants me to come to New York with her to live. It sounds very good, but I'm sure my folks wouldn't be too overjoyed if I mentioned it. So, I'll have to be content with only a visit to the big city. Yesterday I got three letters from you, which was really a treat. One was especially good, but one part in it irked me to no end. What makes you think that falling in love with a rich guy would have been better for me? Everyone likes to have money that's very true. But if both of us want the same things and work together hand in hand for those things, there isn't anything we can't have – yes even money. Both of us happen to be young and willing, and even if not immediately, someday we'll have what we want.

Why didn't you tell me you took someone to the company dance? Was she pretty? Yes, I am jealous, - so there! I'll bet you didn't think of me even once while you were dancing with her. You'll be soreeeeee!!

It's pouring rain outside now and I'm tickled silly I'm not out in it. Tonight, I don't feel like getting drippy all over.... And no remarks about my being drippy anyway.

The booklet and poem you sent were very good. Your camp is a little town in itself. More amusements than in the whole town of Worcester.

George I've just hit a brilliant idea. In one of your letters you said that you kept all my letters. Well, dear, I don't know where the heck your putting them with all your other stuff, so here's where my brilliant idea comes in. Why don't you put them together and mail them back to me? If you like, I'll keep them for you, - honest. Isn't that a good idea? I'd hate to think that those missives were laying around at the disposal of someone else to read. My literary masterpieces are quite bad I know, and so are they quite personal. What do you think, - good idea? – Tou no! Anyway, I think they'd be fun for me to read over again.

I'm beginning to feel my lack of sleep. If I don't hurry up I'll fall asleep at the table. My brother slept in my bed and I can still smell the Vitalis, - tis wonderful, I'm sure to have pleasant dreams. Goodnight nacht.

Lottie

February 18, 1944
Friday

From:	To:
Mr. Pvt. J.G. Barr 11057933	C.L. Sniderman
A.S.C. Replacement Depot #2, Sq. #5	65 Houghton St.
Kelly Field, Texas	Worcester, 4, Mass.

Dearest Lottie,

The photostatic business is very nice. I wouldn't mind going into it at all and I will think about it. Of course, there are a few things that will have to be looked into before attempting to buy that, or any other kind of business. Whether the other man has standing contracts that we could take over, and whether $18,000 was a right price to pay for his establishment, and a few other details. Save your check until I can further investigate.

I'll see what I can do about writing more often. Even if I haven't anything to write, I'll try and write something. In other words, dear, I don't want you to be miserable, and anything that I can do to help you avoid being that way, I'll do.

We had a pretty busy day to-day. This morning we had some nice exercises to do in a cold wind. After that, we played ball, from there we went out on the drill field, and of course, drilled. The next thing on the program was extended order drill. Extended order drill is what you do when you are in a battle zone. Your squad leader is your boss and he leads the way. When he gives a signal, everyone obeys it. It's a silent signal so you have to keep your eyes on him most of the time.

There's nothing hard about it except when he gives the order to hit the dirt. We have some good soft ground here, so we didn't mind too much. After that, we had a lecture on gas and the precautions to take against it. Then in the afternoon we marched to the gas chamber where we went in to test our masks. The only thing about it is, when we go overseas they give us new masks. While out in that area we had smoke bombs and incendiary bombs demonstrated.

Last night one of the Jewish boys and I went to the Jewish U.S.O. It's not a bad place, but it's not very large. They showed the "Fleets In." While there, I found out that Sunday mornings the B'nai Brith has a bagel breakfast. If I'm able to I'm going to be there, and in the afternoon, they have a horseback riding school with a professional instructor who gives his time for free. So, if I have a little money for the horse, I'll go (If I don't have any duty).

I'm in our day room writing and when I came in some guy was playing the piano, or I should say, was trying to play, and he sounded as you must have sounded after the first week you took lessons. Now that is all changed, there is someone sitting in his place that knows what to do with the black and white keys. Until tomorrow sweet –

Your, George

February 20, 1944
Sunday

From:	To:
C.L. Sniderman	Mr. Pvt. J.G. Barr 11057933
65 Houghton St.	A.S.C. Replacement Depot #2, Sq. #5
Worcester 4, Mass.	Kelly Field, Texas

Hello darling,

Today is beautiful. The sun is shining and spring is in the air. Could that starry-eyed look in my eyes be spring fever? George, you're positively a dear and your mother too. She called me Friday night and said that you told her to make me a scarf. By hook or by crook you do get what you want, don't you! I went over yesterday to see it, and it is positively lovely. It's made of heavy white crepe and big enough to have two scarves. She wouldn't let me take it because the initials weren't put on as yet. But it really is beautiful. Thank you so much, dear.

Friday night Toby called and sadly relayed that she wanted to go to the movies but didn't have anyone to go with. Whether this was a hint or not, I don't know, but I caught the general idea. So, we went to the movies and saw "A Guy Named Joe." She cried from the minute we sat down to the minute we went out. It's true that the picture was sad, but it wasn't that sad. Either she's super soft hearted or I'm super hard hearted. After the movies, we went into the Mayflower, and every time I looked at Toby I could see you. It was a most peculiar feeling. When she ordered, I was sure she would say grilled American and coffee – but she didn't!

Yesterday Charlotte came over with Bonnie. She really is a very sweet little girl. She's starting to talk and sounds adorable. I never noticed that she had a dimple.

Barb just called me, and Wednesday she's leaving for New Jersey. She's going to play there a week, then four weeks in Baltimore, then to New York. She's not even excited. What a gal! I don't envy her in the least. She's practically completely bored with the ordinary things in life and doesn't get a kick out of anything that doesn't have glamor. Maybe I'm just "small time", but I'm happy without being glamorous or sophisticated. Nevertheless, I like Barb very much, she's really a swell kid.

I've been meaning to write to Edie M. but for some odd reason I never get around to it. I think she should be coming home pretty soon. Golly, but I've missed her. You never really miss a person until you haven't got them around. Which reminds me of how much I miss you. Sometimes I think this damn war will never be over. Let's think ahead awhile and how it will be when I meet you at the station and know you'll be back for good and not for just a few days. All the boys will be back, - it'll be heaven. My cousin Zelda and I always talk of what we'll do, and what our houses will look like, and how funny looking our children will be. Someday those thoughts will be reality instead of dreams. Write toute de suite.

Love, Lottie

February 20, 1944
Sunday

From:	To:
Mr. Pvt. J.G. Barr 11057933	C.L. Sniderman
A.S.C. Replacement Depot #2, Sq. #5	65 Houghton St.
Kelly Field, Texas	Worcester, 4, Mass.

Dearest Lottie,

I just came back from seeing "Jane Eyres." It is a very slow moving film, but nevertheless good. After comparing the play and the picture, it seems that the picture was more exciting and dramatic. Of course, the background music and the scenery was the thing that could improve it. There was a slight change from the play, but it was of no value.

Of course, as I predicted, it is raining and within the next few hours I'll be walking my guard tour. There is one consolation though, and that is, that the sergeant of the guard let us sleep later than is usual. You see, usually there is a certain length of time taken to practice guard mount, but because of the weather and it being Sunday, we don't have to go thru that formality. (This writing on one's knee is most difficult, especially when near the bottom.)

Last night after bowling a string at one of the local U.S.O.'s, I went upstairs where I bumped into Herby Nestor. He's stationed a little over 100 miles from here. It was funny, but I didn't feel any too joyous over the meeting, except that I know him from Worcester. I compared it with my meeting with Dave in N.O., but there was no comparison. This was due perhaps that I never had anything to do with him when I was home. Don't get me wrong, of course, I was glad to see him, but it is not like meeting someone who you really know and who you have had occasion to go out with.

I had something else to tell you but I'll be damned if I can remember it. It was not a lie!!

Your, George

February 22, 1944
Tuesday

From:	To:
C.L. Sniderman	Mr. Pvt. J.G. Barr 11057933
65 Houghton St.	A.S.C. Replacement Depot #2, Sq. #5
Worcester 4, Mass.	Kelly Field, Texas

Dearest George,

The two letters I got from you yesterday were really killers. I kept reading them over and over. You're certainly learning how to write good letters.

Today I had one grand day of running around. It being Washington's Birthday, we had the day off from work. I called Barb and since she's leaving tomorrow morning, I had to go over to say goodbye. Also, my cousin Zelda had a tea over her house today. I ran over Barb's, paid my respects, and dashed in a cab and ran over Zelda's. All the girls were there, of course, and they insisted that I wanted to make an entrance. So, I made an entrance! I nearly fell flat on my face, - could I help it if a carpet was in the way. There were about ten girls and we discussed everything backwards and forwards. I had a rum coke and then went into my ballet routine. I spent the rest of the night picking up the pennies. Some of the conversation was quite revolting. Sex took up most of the time. How silly, eh wot?!! Then we called a cab to come home in and the damn thing couldn't make the hill. I didn't mean to be mercenary, but there we were stuck in the ice and the meter was ticking calmly away. Much to my amazement he turned it off when I told him I had an earache. The girls roared, - but I didn't when he told me how much it cost. Practically my whole week's pay – <u>practically</u>.

So, you want to know what my adopted grandmother gave us, huh. Well, darling, I hope you appreciate how ridiculous I feel telling you, but I do hate keeping things from you. Now don't laugh, - .... it was towels! Yes, towels. They're really lovely, but I wonder what the heck I'm supposed to do with them <u>now</u>. We may be poor, but at least we'll be clean!!

We're having a little blizzard outside and the roads are really terrible. My mother went to a Jewish show and she isn't home yet. I'm worried sick. Now I know how she feels when I go out and come home a little later. Remember on one of the first dates I had with you, we stayed out all night and you were afraid to come up after that because you said my mother didn't like you. My mother likes you more than you think, you silly goose!

Well, darling, I gotta go sit in the window and wait for my mother. Take care.

Love, Lottie

February 22, 1944
Tuesday

From:	To:
Mr. Pvt. J.G. Barr 11057933	C.L. Sniderman
A.S.C. Replacement Depot #2, Sq. #5	65 Houghton St.
Kelly Field, Texas	Worcester, 4, Mass.

WE'VE BEEN BUSY KEEPING UP CIVILIAN MORALE IN THIS LOCALITY, OR I'D HAVE WRITTEN.

Dearest Lottie,

Yesterday I received a note from Edie Megans that she would be in N.O. on the 11th, and that she would like to see me. She is probably in Worcester by now, that is, if she went straight home, so tell her I'd still like to see her.

Your man received another toothache to-day and off he ran to the dentist. After x-raying it, they still were not satisfied, so they undrilled the filling to see what was in the tooth that made it hurt. They found an exposed nerve. That's what I told them I thought it was originally. Then the dentist sent me to the expert tooth puller. My heart was in my mouth at all times, I would have given a lot not to have been there and rid of the pain.

He looked at it, and "Mmmm'd." I could see by his expression that he was going to like this job, it must have looked nice and juicy. Then he stuck me with a needle to freeze the right side of my face. Everything was O.K., but one place, which didn't take. That's what hurt.

Well anyway, to-get down to the gruesome facts, when he pulled on the tooth, it wouldn't leave my mouth, and I can't blame it in the least. You know it has been living with me for a long time now. The next yank, broke the top part of the tooth. After that he got down to business. First, he drilled, then he chiseled, (I mean what I say, he took a chisel and hit it with a hammer) and then with a pick. He even had to cut my gum in a place so it would make things easier, then he put a stitch in it.

This is the first time I ever had a stitch and I think I'm going to be proud of it, for a few days anyway, because he's going to take it out after that.

That's that – I'm on the road to recovery and will be back on my feet right after I finish this letter. Didn't I tell you where the tooth was? Well it is in the back and even when I smile, it isn't noticeable.

Yesterday's mail also brought a card from Dave. I suppose he wrote you more than he did me, because all I got was one little paragraph. Then on the bottom he prints, "Write." So, what could I do, but write.

Also, a letter from Charlotte, telling a little incident that happened to Bonnie. It seems that Bonnie got hold of some lipstick and was trying it on. Since she didn't use a mirror, she couldn't find her lips and the stuff was all over her, and what didn't get on her body, she put on the walls and floor. I just imagined what had happened, and started to laugh. The boys in the hut wanted to know what the big joke was, so I told them. They didn't think it was funny. They're crazy.

I went to mail call in the rain, but didn't receive any mail. From now on darling, spare your mail so that I'll get a letter when it is raining, and if I have to go without some day, let it be a nice day.

Your, George

February 24, 1944
Thursday

From:	To:
C.L. Sniderman	Mr. Pvt. J.G. Barr 11057933
65 Houghton St.	A.S.C. Replacement Depot #2, Sq. #5
Worcester 4, Mass.	Kelly Field, Texas

Hi Toothless!

I don't envy at all what you went through having that 'lil nasty ole tooth out. You better take care of what you have left.

Just spoke to your mother and tomorrow she leaves for the big city. I think she wishes she was already back. And here I am very willing to trade places with her. I think I need a vacation desperately. On second thought, I think it would be very nice if you had a vacation too. Think I'll write to your C.O!! Do you think he'd oblige?

Very funny about Edie wanting to visit you. She isn't home as yet, and evidently, she left Mississippi before she got my letter telling her you were in Texas.

A few of the <u>younger</u> gals in the office and I went to Danny's for spaghetti today. It was simply delish. I ate, and ate, and ate. Walking back to the office the spaghetti was dragging along the sidewalk, - I ate so much it stuck out all over me and the calories, - oh, my!!

I haven't answered Dave's letter as yet, but tonight it's a do or die affair, and since I do not relish the thought of dying, I shall write. What I'll write I have no idea, - me and my dull mind. Also, I must write to Jackie. You and your friends are surely taking care of me via correspondence. I love it!

Bing Crosby, old boy, is now vocalizing on "I'll Be Seeing You", and what I want to know Mr. Antony is dis, - ven vill I be seeing you, - ven!! I feel very silly tonight. I don't know why, but I do.

Can't understand why you didn't get any mail from me that day it rained. I wrote to the P.O. and gave them specific instructions to deliver a letter every day it was juicy outside. Gotta go now and keep up the moral of the rest of the army, - no not the whole army!! Silly.

Love, Lottie

February 27, 1944
Sunday Night

From:	To:
C.L. Sniderman	Mr. Pvt. J.G. Barr 11057933
65 Houghton St.	A.S.C. Replacement Depot #2, Sq. #5
Worcester 4, Mass.	Kelly Field, Texas

Hi darling,

Heck, the letter I got from you yesterday was hardly worth the postage. Notice that I said hardly because even the fewest of words I get from you is fully appreciated.

Yesterday I really had some fun. One of my mother's friends came in from New York, so I took them to lunch. Across the table from us was sitting an adorable soldier. He smiled and I couldn't resist smiling back. I noticed that he kept looking at me, but I tried not to pay any attention. A few minutes later, the waitress came over and handed me a note. It seemed that Phil, the soldier, wished me to come over to his table. I told my mother, and we both laughed, so I nodded to him that I couldn't possibly. He told me not to be unfriendly, and if I could possibly get rid of the two older women, he'd like it very much if I met him in front of his car on Commercial St. He was close enough to my table so that we could talk. I told him I'd think about it, and while I was thinking, a friend of his came over to his table. He told his friend – quote – Damn it, if I had her in the back seat of my car, I'd know what to do – unquote. My mother and I heard this and both of us went into stitches of laughter. This went on for about half an hour, and just when he thought he was getting someplace, we left. Oh, well, next time I'll know better than to go to lunch with my mother. Just think - .... what an opportunity! I told you this so that you'd realize that I'm not quite as ugly as you may think, so there, humph!

George dear, I really would like to have my letters. Not for any other reason than that I don't want anyone else to read them. You don't mind do you, because if you do, I'll forget the whole thing. O.K.? O.K.

I just came back from Irene Sherr's house and it seems that she has a one and only, and I have a one and only, so you can gather who the conversation was bout. It's nice talking to someone who understands.

George, I'm going to go into Franklin Leather and see if I can get a stationery refill for your writing kit. The stationery you bought is very nice, but I'll see if I can get the same kind you had before. My mother and I put our heads together and decided that you should have a Purim bundle, so I'll enclose the stationery in there if I can get it. Is there anything in particular you would like for the Purim box? Your wish is my command sir!

I'm afraid your sister exaggerated a trifle when she said we had a five-foot snow storm. Maybe it was five inches, and I doubt if it was that. It snows one night and the next morning there's no sign of it.

My goodness I think I've just about written myself dry. Goodnight dear, and my heart's in this letter tonight, as it is in everyone I write.

Love, Lottie

P.S. I'm enclosing a little poem that I read somewhere's and it caught my fancy. I think it's very clever. L.

February 29, 1944
Tuesday

From:	To:
C.L. Sniderman	Mr. Pvt. J.G. Barr 11057933
65 Houghton St.	A.S.C. Replacement Depot #2, Sq. #5
Worcester 4, Mass.	Kelly Field, Texas

Dearest George,

Seems to me you are becoming a real ping-pong fan. I can still beat you, - so there. Your dream was very interesting, but I think it was downright ungentlemanly of you to leave me out in the middle of it. Next time I dream about you, I'll leave you stranded I the middle of nowhere too. The "bagel party" is a swellegant idea, but dear, if you eat as much as that all the time, - well, all I can say is that it's good that your father is in the business that he's in.

I got a card from your mother today and she wants you to write to her at the following address:

> 351 Clifton Pl.
> Brooklyn, New York
> c/o Capp

It was a very cute card saying that all the aunts & uncle send regards, - both the ones I've met and the ones I've yet to meet. If I'm gonna meet all your relatives, I had better start developing a memory for names, because I think 9/10 of the population is comprised of your relatives. I also got a letter from Edie and she was in New Orleans. She was crazy about the place. She wants me to meet her in New York, but financial difficulties forced me to decline.

George, just as long as you keep saying you love me, I'll be happy. Poet or no poet, pretty words or not, it makes little difference. The way you say it is the only way I want to hear it. Take care, darling.

Love, Lottie

March 1, 1944
Wednesday

From:	To:
C.L. Sniderman	Mr. Pvt. J.G. Barr 11057933
65 Houghton St.	A.S.C. Replacement Depot #2, Sq. #5
Worcester 4, Mass.	Kelly Field, Texas

Dearest George,

Before I forget I must tell you Toby sends you her love and kisses. I spoke to her last night and she made me promise that I wouldn't forget, and a Sniderman never goes back on a promise. Seems to me your little sister is carrying on a romance with Herbie. He was one of the kids we took to Mickey's that night. I'm jealous. I wish I was only fifteen and having my first heart throb. Everytime I think back, I can't help but smile. I used to have quite a time for myself! Do you remember the first girl you loved, - wasn't it wonderful? Ah me!

Went to the movies Monday night with a few of the girls from the office. We saw "Cry Havoc", and I didn't enjoy it at all. It was an excellent picture, but I guess I wasn't in the mood for a weepy film that night. The second picture was a mystery and still is to me. I never did find out who killed who and why. My boy, Frank Sinatra is going on the air now, so pardon me while I change the station and swoon. Incidentally, next week "Song of Russia" is playing and the ads say to be sure and see it with someone you love. So, darling, could you possibly manage to come home next week and take me to the movies? Silly, - ain't it?!! No letter from you today, so tomorrow should make up for it. Goodnight dear.

Love, Lottie

P.S. I just killed a moth and I'm sick, - Ugh.

March 2, 1944
Thursday

From:	To:
Mr. Pvt. J.G. Barr 11057933	C.L. Sniderman
A.S.C. Replacement Depot #2, Sq. #5	65 Houghton St.
Kelly Field, Texas	Worcester, 4, Mass.

Dearest Lottie,

The poem you sent me was very cute and stuff like that is appreciated.

This morning I volunteered for detail work. I got tired of doing basic training and seeing, or sleeping, the films that they keep on showing us. The detail was to go to a tree nursery and uproot the trees and bushes and bring them back to camp.

The place is about twenty miles from here so, of course, we had to ride out. Our truck driver was about fourth in line, but he soon was out in front leading the pack. We saw small herds of cattle and a few sheep. Most of the houses are ordinary places, but there are real beautiful homes, usually built Spanish style.

When we arrived at the nursery we dug up bushes and pulled down trees. That is, we tie ropes to the trees and then tied ropes to one of the trucks, which proceeded to pull down the trees. Then we trimmed off the excess dirt and chopped off some of the roots. Then a large trailer came and we had to load the trees on the trailer. It was hard work lifting the trees, but I really enjoyed it. Maybe I'll get a little harder if I do that kind of work for a while.

After working for about two hours, I quit and waited for the chow wagon. This was a nice long wait of an hour, then we had a lunch of an hour and a half. After all the trees were piled on the trailer, two other boys and I rode back on the trees. On the way, this driver took a different route. From one point, we could see the city of San Antonio laid out before us. I didn't realize how large it was until I saw it laid out in front of me.

There was another good part about it, we came back too late, and had to miss retreat. We felt very badly about it, and will try not to do it again.

My brother Narky writes me that he has four hours in the air and will put six more in while he is in Pennsylvania.

Got a letter from Jackie, and he has moved to a small town where he has a drafting job. He says that he thinks he is going to like it. It seems he couldn't find anything in Miami.

To-morrow we are scheduled for a parade, naturally nobody has told us anything about it. Who it's for and why it's for? The squadron needs to send a certain amount of men, and I hope they leave me behind. I don't mind watching a parade, but being in one is different.

Your, George

March 2, 1944
Thursday

From:	To:
C.L. Sniderman	Mr. Pvt. J.G. Barr 11057933
65 Houghton St.	A.S.C. Replacement Depot #2, Sq. #5
Worcester 4, Mass.	Kelly Field, Texas

Dearest George,

After today's letter, I'm practically at a loss for what to write. I know you miss me, and George I miss you every bit as much. But you can't go around complaining to the world because the world doesn't understand. Each person is surrounded by too much of his own troubles to care about everyone else's. I love you and I know you love me, that's all that matters. Had it been our good fortune to have circumstances different, we'd really be having a gay time for ourselves. But this thing can't last forever, and when it is over we'll make up for lost time, - but good. So no more sulking. I'm a fine one to talk. There are times when I think I'll burst with loneliness and no one can speak to me. I'm just one bulk of misery at times, - then I get a letter from you and I try to talk myself out of the blues by thinking that it really could be much worse. But darling, whenever you do feel low, just write away to your hearts content. I know it makes you feel better and your troubles are really mine too, so just get everything off your chest in a letter to one who understands.

Toby just called and she and your father are coming for dinner tomorrow night. Mrs. Rosenberg's mother died and she's staying with her relatives. So, the remaining Barr's will dine and sup with the Sniderman's tomorrow eve. Willst thou jine us? I wish to hell you could.

Last nite I had a dream that tops all dreams. I, - Lottie, - dreamt I got married to you, - George! It was so realistic I couldn't believe it was a dream, and yet it was silly too. There I was running down Main St. in a wedding gown. I called you up at the store and told you not to forget about the flowers and liquor. Evidently, it was a rush affair because I was inviting everyone by phone. I woke up with a big grin on my face, - but was disillusioned when my mother told me it was time to get up. Such is life. Bubble, bubble, toil and trouble! George, damn it, if your next station is going to be anywhere in the east, I'm gonna come and park myself on your front door-step. Even if only for a little while.

Sylvia Coblentz and I had lunch today and she was telling me about all the fun you kids had at Providence Jr. High. She also said she'd like to relive it. Heck, how good could it have been since I wasn't there!! Goodnight dear.

Love, Lottie

March 3, 1944
Friday

From:	To:
C.L. Sniderman	Mr. Pvt. J.G. Barr 11057933
65 Houghton St.	A.S.C. Replacement Depot #2, Sq. #5
Worcester 4, Mass.	Kelly Field, Texas

Dearest George,

Two letters from you today. Altho I was very glad today, I won't be tomorrow, because the letter I got today should come tomorrow. Complicated? It certainly is!

Your father and Toby just left and we had a very nice evening. I told Toby you said it was O.K. for me to have the letters but she doesn't believe me. And I promise not to tie them in pink ribbons, honest. Someday we'll read them over together and really enjoy them. I have everyone of yours, too.

George, do you really think I'm beautiful. I think you're a damn liar, but I love it and what femme doesn't. I think you're beautiful, too!

Tomorrow a few of the girls in the office and I are going to Boston. We'll do some shopping (window shopping), see a play, and eat in Chinatown. Something to break up the monotony. I enjoyed Boston more than I ever did the night we went. That was the last time I saw you. It seems like ages. Neither of us really appreciated it when you were in Philadelphia.

I'm really very tired, darling. It's after 12 o'clock and I can't even think what I'm writing. Goodnight dear.

Love, Lottie

March 4, 1944
Saturday

From:	To:
Mr. Pvt. J.G. Barr 11057933	C.L. Sniderman
A.S.C. Replacement Depot #2, Sq. #5	65 Houghton St.
Kelly Field, Texas	Worcester, 4, Mass.

Dearest Lottie,

Why didn't I take a few minutes off and write you yesterday? That, my dear, will all come out during the writing of this letter.

Yesterday morning I went out on a pick and shovel detail. The work we did was to dig up a square section of ground, which I called our Victory garden. I'm pretty good with a pick, you should see me, it doesn't throw me anymore. Then after swinging the pick a few times, I know just how to prop it on the ground and lean on it. A W.P.G. worker has nothing on me.

We finished our "garden" and then went back to the hut to dress for the parade, that I wrote you about. I dressed and then went down to eat dinner, but the line was so large that I decided to wait awhile (I shouldn't have left). The next time I looked the line was smaller, but if I went to eat, then I would have had a chance of not getting paid, so I went to the pay formation. I got paid a tremendous sum of $27.42, they took some money out for clothes that I got, but which I had lost, in one way or another. By this time, the regular meal had ended and all that was left was cheese and baloney, so for my dinner I ate some cookies that one of the boys received from home.

Not long after I had 'eaten', we had to fall out for the parade, this was at one o'clock. We lined up, squared off, dressed right, dressed left and etc., then piled into trucks. It was now two-thirty. When we got into town we milled around some more before we started to march. Finally, at 4 o'clock, we started, and ended about forty minutes later.

The parade, the part that I was in anyway, was rotten. The bands weren't together, so that mixed up the step. Our C.O. gave commands that we couldn't hear. All in all, it was a waste of time as far as I was concerned.

But darling, here is the payoff. Just before we left, I looked on the bulletin board to see if I had any detail for the next day, and was glad to see that I wasn't on a thing, but, when I came back from the parade, I found that someone had gotten off of a detail and my name was substituted.

After eating supper, I changed my clothes and reported for work. We had to clean about five barracks' (Headquarters and a school), day room, and the shipping and receiving building. The day room we saved for last, and at 2 o'clock in the morning we were playing ping-pong and pool, while the radio gave out with some jive.

Before going to bed, I showered so that took a few more minutes. About three o'clock I was in bed. This morning during inspection I slept. It was surprising to me that they didn't wake me and give me holy hell for not having my shoes polished and my clothes hung neatly. My clothes tho were hung neatly, neatly on the floor.

When I did wake up I felt good. I think I was supposed to be at the one o'clock formation, but we arranged it among ourselves (the fellows that worked with me) that we considered to-day our day off, because we worked last night I think that they won't bother us, because if I thought differently, I would have made sure to be at the one o'clock formation.

That is one thing I've learned in this army, the dumber you act, the better it seems to be for you. I'm G.I. Joe who don't know from nothing.

But before I close there is one thing that I definitely do know, and that is I love you.

Your, George

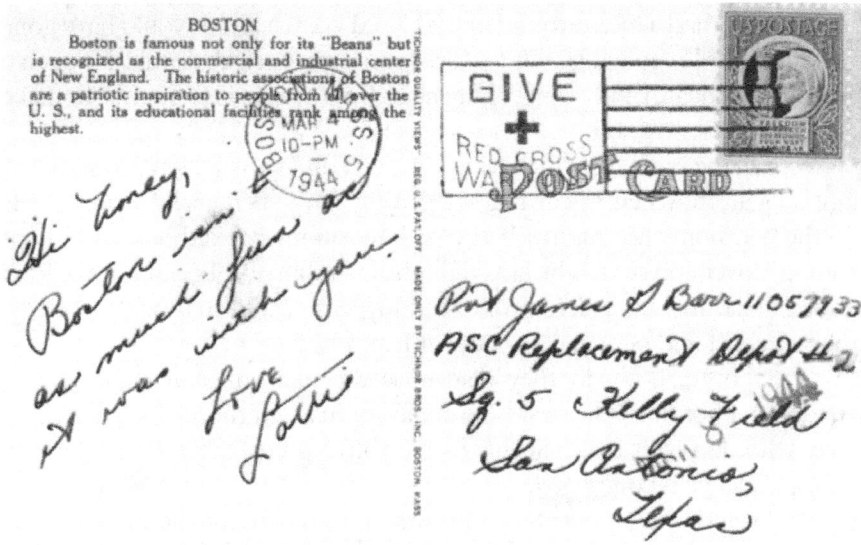

March 5, 1944
Sunday

From:	To:
C.L. Sniderman	Mr. Pvt. J.G. Barr 11057933
65 Houghton St.	A.S.C. Replacement Depot #2, Sq. #5
Worcester 4, Mass.	Kelly Field, Texas

Dearest George,

I've found out that it's a positive untruth when people say that you eventually get accustomed to being without a person. I simply can't get accustomed to being without you. I think Sunday is my worst day because I have more time to think.

Yesterday the gals from the office and I went to Boston. We got a ride into Boston and took the train back. We were so cold we couldn't stay outside, so we saw a matinee performance of "Rosalinda", which was excellent. Then I led the way to Chinatown and we ate at Ruby Foo's Den. The stuff was luscious, but I still prefer either Russian or American food. At night, we saw "Highland Fling", a comedy, which was very good, too. After the play, we grabbed a cab, rushed down to South station, -just in time to see the train pulling out. We had to wait a whole hour and I was stinkin' mad. When we finally got on our train, a sailor met a girl on the train and she really was plastered. He told her next time she came to Boston to please be sober. Her actions were quite revolting but I enjoyed it immensely! At South station, a sailor was sitting on a bench sick as a dog. Evidently, he had gotten drunk and he had a mess around him. If I had known him I would have gone over to him. He looked so white. George, don't ever get drunk. It's such a silly waste of health and money. Having a drink or two is O.K., but to make it a habit is just no good.

On the radio, they're playing "I Love You." I always have to stop and light a cigarette when I hear that song. Why am I such a silly sentimental? On the way home last night I had your letter in my pocketbook and I kept reading it over and over. The kids thought I was horrible because I wouldn't let them read it. I never let anyone read my letters, and that one especially, was too sweet and personal to share with anyone.

George, how do they distribute the mail at camp? I've always wondered. I bet that's the best time of day for many of the fellows. Are there many who don't get mail? Seems to me you're pretty taken care of where correspondence is concerned.

Well darling, gotta take me bath and prepare for the morrow. So, until tomorrow, goodnight and take care.

Love, Lottie

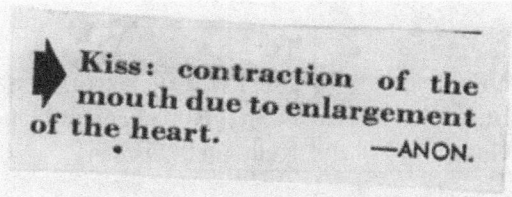

> **Kiss:** contraction of the mouth due to enlargement of the heart.
> —ANON.

March 7, 1944
Tuesday

From:	To:
C.L. Sniderman	Mr. Pvt. J.G. Barr 11057933
65 Houghton St.	A.S.C. Replacement Depot #2, Sq. #5
Worcester 4, Mass.	Kelly Field, Texas

Dearest George,

Well, today I really hit the jackpot. Eight letters. I sure make the poor mailman work from morn till dusk. One of the letters was from Dave and he's somewhere in England. He wrote a V mail, so he really didn't write much. Also, I got a letter from Jackie. It seems things didn't come out as he had planned, so he's coming home at the end of the month.

Your mother just called; she came in from New York a short while ago. She received a letter from the Red Cross again praising their son James. Little do they know! How the heck do you get away with the stunts you pull?

The Red Cross also said that if your folks wanted anything done for you, to just let them know. I suggested telling them to let you come home again. Your mother heartily agreed, but we decided that they wouldn't oblige. Too bad your parade didn't turn out so well. The best parade will be the one you come marching home in. All I want to know is when that will be. I tried to get a refill for your stationery at Franklin Leather, but they didn't have any. Anyway, I like the paper you're using now. Glad to hear you're becoming so handy with a pick and shovel. I always did love a garden, so after the war you will have steady employment planting roses for me. Maybe a piece of grass here and there would really do the trick.

Today it rained all day. Very miserable, but it was warm. Yesterday was truly beautiful. Spring must really be here because I have already had a chocolate ice cream soda. It was delish.

Edie sent me an air mail special delivery letter today. My hands shook while opening it. I thought either she was going to get married or was sick. Fortunately, neither of these was the matter. She just said that she loved me and money was no object. What a gal! Well, hon, I gotta go now, and like the washerwoman who brings her clothe to the line, - I bring my line to a close. (Ha, ha – joke).

Love, Lottie

P.S. I can't help it if I'm corny.

March 9, 1944
Thursday

From:	To:
C.L. Sniderman	Mr. Pvt. J.G. Barr 11057933
65 Houghton St.	A.S.C. Replacement Depot #2, Sq. #5
Worcester 4, Mass.	Kelly Field, Texas

Dearest George,

The Purim card you sent was a very sweet gesture, thanks dear. I got your record today, and altho I've tried and coaxed, my phonograph won't do it justice. But by working it with my finger, I managed to hear it and it's not bad at all. The only trouble is you sound so scared. Are you afraid of talking to me or doesn't the "mike" resemble me enough to make you forget that it's a "mike."

Your going horseback riding has given me the urge to go too. I will, just as soon as it gets a little warmer, and as soon as I have money. I paid my income taxes today, which makes me flat broke. What a horrible thing money is. But even though I hate the stuff, I wouldn't turn away if someone offered me a million, or a thousand, - hell, I'd settle for a buck!

The last letter you wrote took exactly two days to get here. That of-course was exceptionally good. Most of them take around four days. But you've been so good about writing that I get a letter practically every day. Did I ever tell you that you're very nice? Speaking of letters, I wrote a beautiful love letter to a boy I don't know and who doesn't know me. One of the girls in the office had to write a letter to some guy but didn't have time so she gave me his letter and let me answer it. Boy, what a job I did on that one. I mailed it before Rita could read it, - she'll probably have a proposal on her hands when he reads it.

I just dunked my hair in the ink bottle and from now on just call me blue haired Lottie. I hate myself when I do things like that. Oh, well!

I finally found some film for my camera and if it's nice Sunday I'll take some. If they're not good I'm not sending them, - as if you didn't know.

I haven't anything much of interest to write tonight, except that if you think that I chased my hat for two blocks is interesting. It really was most embarrassing. I always swore that I'd never chase a hat, but heck this was my new hat and I couldn't bear to let it go. It went rolling merrily, merrily up Grafton St. The air was blue with curses when I finally caught it.

I'm dead tired, honey, so I think I'll retire. I wish to hell I didn't have to get up tomorrow, but wishing in my case won't make it so.

Goodnight dear, Lottie

March 12, 1944
Sunday

From:	To:
C.L. Sniderman	Mr. Pvt. J.G. Barr 11057933
65 Houghton St.	A.S.C. Replacement Depot #2, Sq. #5
Worcester 4, Mass.	Kelly Field, Texas

My dearest George,

Tonight, I miss you more than ever: I feel so lonesome I could burst into tears. I'm all alone in the house, and it's so quiet, I feel all alone in the world. I went for a long walk through the fields today. It was so warm and the sun soaked right through me. I felt so reminiscent. Remember when we used to go walking or riding? I remembered when I used to go alone or with one of the girls and you'd drive up and take us back. Many times, I turned and looked today expecting to see you. But I suppose at times you feel just a lonely as I, and my writing like this doesn't help matters any.

Your last letter made me go into tantrums of laughter. You must have been in a rare mood. All the time I was reading it, I thought you must be drunk, and sure enough, as if you were reading my thoughts, you said I bet you think I'm drunk. After reading that letter over and over, I've decided that there must be many sides of your personality that I haven't seen yet! I just took a few minutes off to reread that letter and I simply can't believe, my morale was just boosted, no kidding! And to answer your question, - no I don't know what you would do with one of those....!!! I'll bet you don't even remember what you wrote, - if you don't it's a shame because I thought it was a riot.

Sid's letters were also good and I'm glad you sent them. His greeting of love really got me. I didn't know he thought you were an old bastard – that proves he loves you!

Tonight, I had a date, - Yes, I really did. With whom, you ask. Why with Max, of-course, you dope. He took me to the movies and then to eat afterwards. I really had a very enjoyable time and to top it off he even kissed me when we got home. Oh, I fear I forgot to tell you Maxies last name. It was Max Sniderman, of-course, the other man in my life. But I fear he's not entirely true to me, because after bringing me home he went out with his wife. Such troubles I have!!

Friday night my mother and I went over your house. Your dad was in New York so we went to keep his better half company. As for the letters, - she didn't mention them so I didn't either. Supposin' we just forget about them until you come home. It really doesn't matter. She did say though, that none of the stuff you sent home was unpacked. Please don't write her anymore about them, huh.

I think a law should be passed whereas I could get mail on Sunday. That's the only part about Sundays I don't like.

I saw "Miracle of Morgan's Creek" a few days ago, and really enjoyed it. If you haven't seen it and it comes your way, do see it. You'll like it. Pardon the lipstick on the edge of the letter, - those things do happen.

Goodnight dear, Love, Lottie

March 13, 1944
Monday

From:	To:
C.L. Sniderman	Mr. Pvt. J.G. Barr 11057933
65 Houghton St.	A.S.C. Replacement Depot #2, Sq. #5
Worcester 4, Mass.	Kelly Field, Texas

Dearest George,

Tonight, the funniest thing happened to me. Evelyn Cohen had a few girls over for supper and Sylvia Coblentz brought over her Ouija board. If you've never heard of it, it's part of a fortune telling board, you ask it questions and it spells out the answer. It was the first time I had ever seen or worked one and I was very skeptical. Well, I sat down and asked who I was going to marry, and it spelled out George Barr in full. I asked it when, and it said August 1944, also the war is going to be over in that month. It spelled out all the kid's names that the other girls were going to marry, and they were all possibilities. It was positively amazing. I hate to sound stupid, but I really was intrigued. Time has come to a pretty pass when I have to rely on an Ouija board for my future. But it was fun anywho.

Clif Whitcomb, our salesman, let me take his car again today, and for the first time I drove home. It was raining cats and dogs and when my mother saw me drive up she nearly had a fit. I had to promise to call her the minute I got back to the office. Incidentally, I got back safe and sound.

I was sick as a dog today from laughing. All day long I laughed. It started when Dave, our manager called me into his office. He had a slight cut on his foot and wanted me to fix it. I dragged out all the first aid supplies, and started to work. By this time, all the other girls in the office came over to watch. When I got through with his minor cut, it looked like a major operation, that's how much bandage I put on him. We were rolling on the floor with laughter. Dave was going to call up the paper and have the headlines read "Nurse's Aid Saves Managers Life"!

Edie came back from Mississippi today and she had a hellava time. This town is going to seem terrifically dull to her now. I got a letter from Polly, and she said she got a very sweet letter from you. What goes between you two, eh!!

Well, dear, the hour is awfully late and I'm awfully tired and I love you awfully much. And with this parting thought, I take leave until tomorrow.

Goodnight, Love, Lottie

March 15, 1944
Wednesday

From:	To:
C.L. Sniderman	Mr. Pvt. J.G. Barr 11057933
65 Houghton St.	A.S.C. Replacement Depot #2, Sq. #5
Worcester 4, Mass.	Kelly Field, Texas

Dearest George,

I guess you really are G.I. Joe in person. But after the war you can write a book on how you became a general the hard way. They must like the way you do K.P. Which, of-course, is very nice to know because what's good enough for the army is good enough for me, which all leads me to say that when you come home you can do all the housework. Isn't that nice of me?!!

I took Edie Megans to lunch today. She looks super and had a swellegant time. And who wouldn't if one had a cousin who was a captain and could introduce you to all the guys in the camp. Some fun!

Your mother called last night and invited me to supper Friday night. Pretty soon I'll start paying board at your house. When we finished talking, your mother and Toby were still arguing as to whether I should go to the movies with your folks or bowling with Toby. I still haven't found out who won the argument. They really are some swell people, which accounts for what makes you so nice.

I had myself a swell case of spring fever and all of a sudden, all my aspects were dampened by snow today. 'Tis was very disappointing.

I got a letter from Barb today. She's still out in Baltimore and having the time of her life.

Frank Sinatra just finished singing "All The Things You Are". I was swooning all over the place.

One of the girls in the office got sick today, and I being a nurse royale, was called on duty. I did everything I knew how and finally she was cured. If there's one thing I hate to see is anyone crying. And there she was bawling on my shoulder. After I got through with her she said she didn't know if it was my medicine or sense of humor that cured her. She really is a swell gal and much too nice to be sick. The fact that I felt like a dog myself mattered very little. I had a miserable case of the blues this morning, but while I was bringing her out of the dumps, I suddenly realized that I had brought myself out too.

This afternoon, Joe, one of the boys down our place, ran over to my desk and asked if I wanted a kiss. I was astonished, but managed a "No, Thank-you." Whereas, he said it was too bad, and proceeded to open a bag of candy kisses. Ah, me, life is full of disappointments.

Write soon darling, and do try to stay out of the guard house. I don't think you'll look very good in stripes, - but I'll love you jest the same. Tally ho.

Love, Lottie

March 17, 1944
Friday

From:	To:
Mr. Pvt. J.G. Barr 11057933	C.L. Sniderman
A.S.C. Replacement Depot #2, Sq. #5	65 Houghton St.
Kelly Field, Texas	Worcester, 4, Mass.

Dearest Lottie,

I just came back from services at our Chapel. As you know, I'm not what is known as a religious person, the reason I went there was really the lack of anything else and there was going to be women and food. But, my darling, during the services, while the Chaplin was praying, I could feel your presence. Was it silly of me? I guess it was not. Whether is anything to religion or not, I haven't as yet decided.

During the services, there came the time when a prayer was said over the wine, at this time, wine was passed out to all that were present. I had to laugh, because the glasses couldn't have been any larger than a thimble. After the services, a few went back and tried to finish up what had been left, after downing my fifth drink (and still going strong), we were stopped by the Chaplain, who explained that the wine was not to be touched. And for a while I thought I was going on a cheap drunk.

I'm glad that I went, and if I'm still here next week, I'm going to attend again.

You know that to-day is G.I. day, don't you? Of course, we've known it for a long time now, but usually down here, we would throw a few buckets of water on the floor and call it done. For some odd reason, I cannot explain it, but we gave the hut a real good going over. We scrubbed the floors, moving our bunks away from the corners, something we rarely do, polished up our stove, something we've never done, and fixed up a nice walk in front of our hut. Then we got some gravel and put it around our walk. When one of the fellows came in, he started to walk out because he couldn't believe that he was in the right place. The real funny part about it is that most of us won't to be here long enough to really appreciate our nice clean hut. Now darling, do you still think I'm crazy?

Tell Edie hello for me. That girl friend of yours, Polly, owes me a letter, and you can tell her for me that she is going to have to wait for some time for an answer for the next one she sends me.

Goodnight, sweet, I must get some sleep. I almost forgot – this 'prayer for home' I'm enclosing, is something else I liked. There is so much meaning to it.

Your, George

PRAYER FOR HOME ⸌ 320

PRAYER FOR HOME

Far from home and those I love, I find my thoughts turning to them with affectionate longing. O Thou who art with my distant loved ones even while Thou art here with me, who hearkenest to their prayers even as Thou hearkenest to mine, bless us and keep us united in spirit until we meet again. Let my memory hold them in such loving embrace that I be cheered by their imagined presence. Keep me under the influence of the ties that bind me to them, so that even in strange surroundings I may conduct myself in ways that do them honor. Keep me gratefully mindful of the blessing of their love and let me not give way to loneliness or despondency. Help me to bring cheer to my comrades, who like me are separated from their dear ones. For Thou, God, art the Father of all; Thou art the source of all love. None who puts his faith in Thee need ever feel friendless or forsaken. Amen.

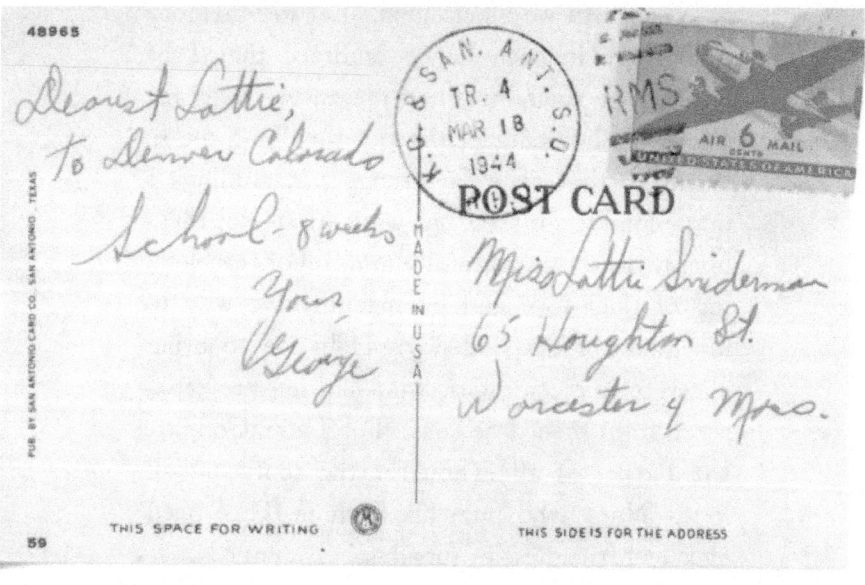

March 19, 1944
Sunday

From:	To:
C.L. Sniderman	Mr. Pvt. J.G. Barr 11057933
65 Houghton St.	A.S.C. Replacement Depot #2, Sq. #5
Worcester 4, Mass.	Kelly Field, Texas

Dearest George,

I'm glad you liked the Purim box. Here's hoping next Purim you'll be home.

Friday night, Toby, your folks, and I went to the movies after a very delicious supper. I also heard the record you sent. Toby bought some new needles and it sounds swell.

I just came home from a tea that the Hadassah had. I was one of the hostesses, - a very thankless job, but it was fun anyhow. How anyone can get so excited about a glass of punch and a piece of cake is beyond me.

I went down Water St. with my dad today and got the surprise of my life. I met Freddie Topper and he shook me little hand and congratulated me on getting married. Since this is almost an old story, I was merely surprised and not astonished, as I used to be. I asked him to whom I was supposed to be married, but he didn't know. He's stationed down at the Cape with some other Worcester fellows and they told him the glad tidings. Also, when I went to the movies with your folks, I met Chet Leavitt, and he was amazed when he saw me with them. He didn't say anything, - just looked!

Today at the tea, Sylvia Berman noticed my bracelet and said that must be the one George gave you. I don't know how in heaven's name she even knew you gave me a bracelet. No secrets in Worcester!!

Dave Isreal, our manager, called me in Saturday, and with the usual huff and puff, asked me to sit down. He asked if I would please do him a favor. Isn't that cute? But anyway, he said that he thought I deserved a raise and had spoken to the Sharfman's about it a long time ago, and I proceeded to tell him that if the raise didn't come thru pretty soon, the New England could go to hell. So to make a long story short, he wants me to speak to Saul Sharfman about raises for all the girls. All of a sudden, he gets so good to me! Tomorrow is the fatal day. I don't know why the hell he gave me the dirty wash since he's the manager. But I said I'd do it anyhow. So tomorrow I'll know whether I get an increase or if I'll be out of a job. Some fun! Sounds kinda peculiar to me.

Listen you. – I want those pictures of you, whether good or bad. You're my favorite pin-up boy anyhow. Especially, I want the one of you in your towel sarong. And no back talk, - see?!!

Incidentally, why do you want Sid Plotkin's camera? What's the matter with your own? It would be swell if you had a camera. I'm still waiting for a nice day to take some pictures.

My goodness, I guess I've written enough. So, till tomorrow, goodnight dear.

Love, Lottie

March 20, 1944
Monday

From:	To:
C.L. Sniderman	Mr. Pvt. J.G. Barr 11057933
65 Houghton St.	33rd T.S.S.
Worcester 4, Mass.	Lowry Field #1, Colorado

My dearest George,

I was amazed when I just got your telegram. Only this morning I received your letter saying that you were going to be transferred. I never expected it so soon. I called your folks and they were as amazed as I was. It seems every time you're moved, they take you farther and farther away from me. Damn this war anyway! But I suppose I should be very thankful that you are going to school and I really am thankful. Incidentally, what kind of a school are you going to and for how long? Write me all the details. Just exactly where is Lowery field?

We are having quite a blizzard now. People have been killed, traffic halted, and school stopped in the small towns. I just spoke to Toby and she's praying they'll be no school tomorrow in Worcester. I remembered when that used to be a major concern to me too. Funny how important those things used to be, - now things are so much bigger, and so much more important to worry about. I guess it all comes with growing up. Is there any chance that you'll get a furlough in the near future? I miss you so dreadfully.

Last time I went to the hospital I worked in the maternity ward and then in the nursery. A woman had just had her baby and was pretty sick. Her husband had been with her all day and he looked worse than she did. The minute I came on duty he called me aside and asked if he could please have some aspirins. He was very young and looked so scared. The babies in the nursery were screaming for food. Some of them were the homeliest little things I ever saw, but they were cute anyway. One was seven hours old and hadn't yet learned to swallow. He was pitiful. They looked so tiny and helpless. While I was feeding one of them, I wondered how he would grow up.... Successful, poor, rich or what? Sometimes I have the silliest thoughts! George, always remember that no matter how far you are or whatever happens, I love you. Write as soon as you can.

Love, Lottie

P.S. The address seems too short to be correct, but that's what you sent in the telegram.

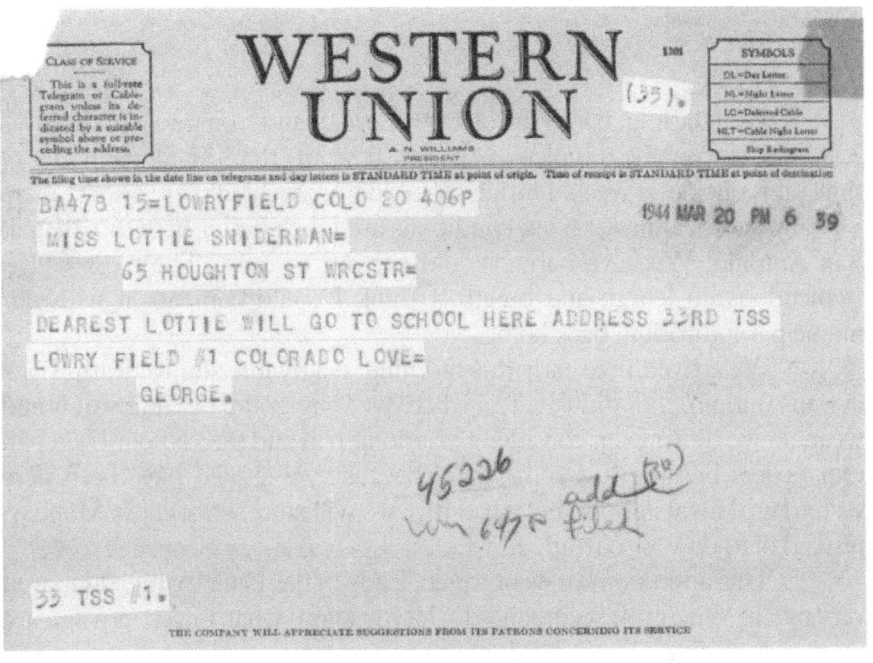

March 20, 1944
Monday

From:	To:
Mr. Pvt. J.G. Barr 11057933	C.L. Sniderman
33rd T.S.S.	65 Houghton St.
Lowry Field #1, Colorado	Worcester, 4, Mass.

LOWRY FIELD
DENVER, COLORADO

Dearest Lottie,

Well darling, here I am at Lowry Field, and from most of the boy's accounts, it won't be too pleasant a stay. It seems that the total amount of time off is one day a week. During school days, of which there are six, there isn't any passes issued. Living conditions are much better here tho, than at San Antonio. We have barracks and eat out of trays. The mess hall is tremendous, in length and breath, I think I could compare it with our municipal auditorium back home.

We arrived here early this morning, nearly freezing to death. Back in San Antonio, they didn't tell us where we were going or what we should wear, so we didn't even consider a very long trip and packed our overcoat. Our orders became lost somewhere because we should have been here yesterday. This will probably mean that we will start school next Monday, instead of to-day, as scheduled.

This afternoon we went to see "Lady in the Dark", which I enjoyed very much. When you see it, and do, let me know what I need, a wife, or a mother, sometimes I wonder about it.

Saturday morning, when I received word that I was to ship out, I was on detail. I had just asked my sergeant in charge if we could go to the other side of the field and get breakfast, because we hadn't eaten that morning. He said wait around a few more minutes to see if we had any more work to do, and if there wasn't any, O.K. Not more than two minutes later, a runner from the orderly room came and told me to pack my bags, I was shipping in a half hour. I rushed back to my hut, threw all my belongings in my barracks bag and left. I was in such a rush that I threw everything in. On the train, I had to borrow a soap towel, shaving equipment, and even cigarettes. Our bags had been sent on the baggage car, so I didn't have an opportunity to get a thing. We're still waiting for them. They better get here to-morrow or I won't be fit to line with.

When we came out of the show it was snowing, nice large flakes. If I were home, not in the army, I could appreciate it, but now it is just a nuisance. I hope that I'll be able to go skiing or skating while I'm down here tho.

We were fortunate in obtaining a Pullman for the first night, and even more lucky for me, I was able to have a lower berth all to myself. The next night was awful, we had to sleep on the coach. I could think of many better places to sleep than in an old train coach, but what can one do in such a case. There was one thing that I couldn't forget to take with me, and that was my writing kit with your picture in it. It was in my field bag and I used that as a pillow. I thought of you always, what you were doing, what you were thinking. Lottie darling, I love you with all my heart. I miss you sweet, I just hope that some day not far off, we can be to-gether for always.

Good night my love,
Your, George

[Editor's note: This was printed on the back of the stationary of George's 3/20/1944 letter to Lottie.]

March 21, 1944
Tuesday

From:	To:
C.L. Sniderman	Mr. Pvt. J.G. Barr 11057933
65 Houghton St.	33rd T.S.S. Lowry Field
Worcester 4, Mass.	Denver, Colorado

Dearest George,

Thanks loads for my little Indian. He's adorable, but as yet, I haven't named him. Have you any suggestions? He'll make fine company for Georgianna, altho she's somewhat bigger. You're really very sweet.

Jackie just called me, and he didn't sound too enthused about his journey. He already had a drafting job, - and back where he was before. Me thinks the lad is in a rut and I think he knows it. I think maybe a girl would be the answer, but he doesn't seem much interested in the opposite sex.

I just finished washing my hair, and what a job that is. It has grown very long and somewhat difficult to care for. It's still very wet, and every once in a while, a trickle of water runs down my forehead, along my nose and flops onto this paper. Little does that little drop know how many miles it will travel.

My father is making tea and has requested that I join him. I feel like something, - but not tea, but since there is nothing better, tea I shall have.

The little blizzard I wrote you about piled up 11 inches of snow. And since today was very warm, the place is flooded. The weather is very distasteful, - tonight everything seems distasteful to me. I feel in a very peculiar mood. Aw hell, I'd better sleep it off. Goodnight till tomorrow, dear.

Love, Lottie

March 21, 1944
Tuesday

From:	To:
Mr. Pvt. J.G. Barr 11057933	C.L. Sniderman
33rd T.S.S.	65 Houghton St.
Lowry Field #1, Colorado	Worcester, 4, Mass.

Dearest Lottie,

Nothing of importance has occurred since I last wrote you, regarding my stay here. We're scheduled to stay here 8 weeks and then go to Tinker Field, Oklahoma. The week we miss by not going to school here will make it 9 weeks, and then by the time we are shipped, it may be a bit longer.

And then again, it may be shorter, because they are washing a bunch out all the time. The course is supposed to be rough.

It is the repair and maintenance of equipment of the 'central fire control system.' This system enables one man to fire automatically more than one machine gun at a time. The electrical motors involved in this system are similar to ones we had back in Philly. I don't remember anything about them, in fact, we didn't have much on it.

The snow is still coming down, but now I have all my clothes, so it isn't as bad as it was yesterday. We're going to G.I. our barracks to-night, then the medical boys are coming down to oil the floor. So much colds, pneumonia, and rheumatic fever is going around that they are trying to get rid of it. What oiling the floor is going to do to stop it, is something for the medics, not me.

Last night at the service club they had a nice musical show. The band was a bit unusual. Piano, seven accordions, drums, and that's all. Friday nights they have dances here. There is a bunch of WAC's here, so I guess the dames will be strictly G.I.

I'm on K.P. to-morrow from 12:00 to 8:00 in the evening, so think of me while I work.

Your, George

March 22, 1944
Wednesday

From:	To:
C.L. Sniderman	Mr. Pvt. J.G. Barr 11057933
65 Houghton St.	33rd T.S.S. Lowry Field
Worcester 4, Mass.	Denver, Colorado

Dearest George,

I just spoke to Polly and she told me she has just written you a letter with profuse apologies for not writing sooner. She also told me about the letter you wrote her, which indeed sounded very nice. Quite by accident, Polly met Barb in Baltimore where Barb is playing now, and the report she gave me was not of the best. But regardless of what anyone says, I still like Barb. When it comes to people, I always make up my own mind as to whether I like them or not. Hearsay is not always the best. I remember when a friend of yours invented a very unflattering story about me. Remember? That I shall never forget!! I think my dislike for him was kindled in that story.

The little prayer you sent was very nice and just struck the right note. It's wonderful how beautifully some people can put feelings into words. I always wished that I could.

I got a letter from Fran Barr today, and evidently you promised them a record, which you never sent. Also, they went to a formal St. Patrick's Days shindig. Funny that Jewish people down south celebrate such an Irish holiday.

I hated going to work this morning. It was so beautiful, I just wanted to walk and walk. I was walking along and thinking, when all of a sudden, your father drove by in the beach wagon. I had to restrain myself from calling out George. That was my first impulse. I still haven't gotten used to your not being around. Goodnight dear.

Love, Lottie

March 24, 1944
Friday

From:	To:
Mr. Pvt. J.G. Barr 11057933	C.L. Sniderman
33rd T.S.S.	65 Houghton St.
Lowry Field #1, Colorado	Worcester, 4, Mass.

Dearest Lottie,

I guess the army does know how good I am at K.P., because for the last three days, that's all I have been doing. Last night when I came home I was dead tired, and intended to go to sleep immediately, because I was on K.P. again the next morning at the darky and awful hour of 4:00 A.M. Could I go to sleep right away? Like hell!!!! When the fellows G.I. the barracks, they left the section around my bed, and about five more untouched. When I did hit the hay, for some odd reason I couldn't get to sleep. Why? You ask – because I hadn't written a letter to you, even knowing you would forgive me, it took a long time for me to drop off to sleep.

I'm glad that the G.I. situation doesn't happen, like it did this time, all the time, because I would lose my faith in mankind. I was burnt up.

I worked at officer's mess this morning. I had the lovely job of cleaning pots and pans. Darling, at the time of our wedding, I won't be a bit surprised if the rabbi says to you, "Will you take this man to be your lawful wedded K.P.?" So, you think that I'll do all the housework? Didn't I ever tell you why I love you? It's because I want you to do those things for me. Now, aren't you sorry?

Darling, I'm sorry, but I think that there are a lot of questions that I didn't answer in my letters, but I was in such a whirlwind that I think I forgot some of them. So, my love, if there are, let me know and I will promptly reply.

I'm glad that you are thankful that I'm going to school. Personally, I don't think I'm going to like the school, but it is a delaying action. Although sometimes I wonder if I want a delaying action such as this, because I'll probably get just as much out of it as the other G.I. schools I went to. The trouble with this army, the air force anyway, is that it has a surplus of men, and they are trying to keep them busy. Everything is overcrowded, so you cannot transfer into anything different.

To-day, my darling, was the first time in six days that I received mail, and all three letters were from you. I felt down and out, just coming off K.P., but up I came like a rocket when I saw your letters. You are the best girl in the world, and I love you for always.

I even got a money order from my father. This month we're not getting paid, because we weren't here to sign the payroll, so I wired my dad for a bit of mazuma, and he came thru with flying colors.

I'm glad you like the "Indian," I didn't know what it was myself.

Now I know where to go when I'm sick. Yes sir, Lottie Sniderman is the best nurse around. I bet you pretty soon you'll be putting out your shingle. No kidding darling, I think it is swell of you.

I hope you don't let the snow get you 'down,' if you know what I mean. I haven't fallen, as yet, but had a number of pretty close calls. The snow is all gone from the center of the streets, but there is enough around everywhere else to keep me on my toes.

I love you, my darling, so take care –

Yours, George

P.S. 33rd Technical School Sq. Is my current address.

March 25, 1944
Saturday

From:	To:
Mr. Pvt. J.G. Barr 11057933	C.L. Sniderman
33rd T.S.S.	65 Houghton St.
Lowry Field #1, Colorado	Worcester, 4, Mass.

Dearest Lottie,

Darling, I'm now the K.P. kid! To-night again I have the honor, for K.P. is an honor, of feeding my buddy. Anyhow, it should be the last time for a while now, because we hope to start school Monday.

To-day I received a package from my folks, and is the stuff delicious. Want some? I'm stuffing myself with dates, and at the same time writing to you. You see, a way to a man's heart, is thru his stomach.

This morning there wasn't anything for us to do, so the detail sergeant got up brooms so we could sweep up the gutters on the street. Silly wasn't it, for the only thing in the gutters was a thin layer of snow, but they couldn't let us remain idle. Then in the afternoon, the sun came out and melted all the snow.

Polly wrote me a very nice letter, even tho it took me a little time to read it, I enjoyed it. She certainly is a wit. If things continue the way they are, I'll also be a wit, but I'm afraid it'll be half witted.

This afternoon I tried to get a pass, this was before I knew I had K.P., first I saw the first sergeant, who sent me to see the major, but the stinkers didn't give it to me. It seems that it is against the bosses' policy to give more than one pass a week, unless of course, of an emergency. Next time I ask for a pass, I'll have to get some emergency, like my wife having a baby, or something. If you think up a good one let me know.

Darling, I'm going to have another date, and then try and get a little shut eye, before I go on.

Your, George

March 26, 1944
Sunday

From:	To:
C.L. Sniderman	Mr. Pvt. J.G. Barr 11057933
65 Houghton St.	33rd T.S.S.
Worcester 4, Mass.	Lowry Field 1, Colorado

Dearest George,

Today is the kind of spring day you wait for all winter long. To look outside and see the sun shining makes you feel good all over. It's just the kind of day I love to go walking.... and so, I stayed home and hung curtains. Yes, dear, out of the goodness of my heart, I've taken part in the spring housecleaning chores. If by any chance, you're thinking that my hair is all tied up and that I'm wearing an apron, - well, wrong you are! As a matter of fact, I have on a pair of slacks and a sweater, plus a cigarette in one hand, and if I didn't have a smudge on my nose and a dust mop in the other hand, you'd never know I was cleaning. That's what makes me so wonderful, you never know what I'm doing.... or thinking!

I'm so sorry you're always getting stuck with K.P. Seems the army is pleased with the way you peel potatoes. But what about you going to school, and what are you going to take up. I hear tell they have a large photographic center there. Do you think by any chance you can get into that?

The Rocky Mts. sound beautiful. How'd you like to ski down them? I can just picture myself skiing. No, - not on my feet, silly!!

I'm hoping your next letter will be longer than the one I just got. Surely you can manage more than a paragraph. Take it easy, dear.

Love, Lottie

March 26, 1944
Sunday

From:	To:
Mr. Pvt. J.G. Barr 11057933	C.L. Sniderman
33rd T.S.S.	65 Houghton St.
Lowry Field #1, Colorado	Worcester, 4, Mass.

Dearest Lottie,

Now I guess you'll know I still love you, for ain't I still sending you my letters air mail, even tho they did jack up the price two more cents? Yes, dear, I love you, and always will no matter what.

I just came back from "Cover Girl", which I liked plenty. Music, dancing, and, of course, women. I'm at the Service Club and I get a big kick out of seeing all the boys writing to their sweethearts, girls, families, and friends. I'm glad that the paper shortage hasn't affected stationary.

Did I tell you my father, when he sent me some money, sort of increased the amount I asked for? Well darling, he did, by five dollars (I know, I'm mercenary) but he really is swell. Some times I used to think otherwise, but age and time, plus experience certainly bring subjects out clearly, whereas before you could only see the outline.

To-morrow morning we are to start school, but I will not be able to believe it until I am seated in a class room, and teacher rings the little bell, or a sergeant hollers "at ease", starting off our class. I hope that I'll like school, because if I do, then time will pass much more quickly, and then I'll finish school and when I arrive at my squadron at Tinker Field, I'll be able to ask for a furlough, and if all is well, such as not too many other men on furlough and other things, then who knows? Worcester is a beautiful place to be at the end of May, especially when a certain fellow's girl friend has her birthday. Every time I think of it, it makes me shiver, because so many things can happen to keep this boy away from the one he loves. Darling, I hope that all my fears are just imaginary ones.

We moved into different barracks' this afternoon. I like these better, more room and just a little bit cleaner.

In back of me is a couple with their child. I think it is a boy, but I wouldn't say for sure, but he, if it is a he, anyway, I'm going to call him a he, is about eight or ten months old. They just finished feeding him his bottle and put him on a writing table for a rest. His parents are just watching him, with love written over their faces. I can just imagine when she leaves with the child, how he will feel. I know, I had to leave the one I love, and at a much further distance.

To-night I'm going to try and write to Dave and Sid, but they're going to show a movie soon, and I'm such a sucker for free entertainment, and besides they'll have to put out the lights. Sometimes I am a stinker because it takes me some time to answer the people who write me, but at this base so far, I haven't had much time for writing.

I was very mad this morning when I found out that they don't have mail call Sundays. The hell with them, I'll get two letters from you to-morrow, instead of one. Therefore, I will be doubly joyous.

Gab is running short darling, so I'll end here.

Yours, George

March 27, 1944
Monday

From:	To:
C.L. Sniderman	Mr. Pvt. J.G. Barr 11057933
65 Houghton St.	33rd T.S.S.
Worcester 4, Mass.	Lowry Field 1, Colorado

Dearest George,

I was frantic because I hadn't heard from you, but today three letters came to set my mind at ease. I really got a kick out of the part where you thought at our wedding the rabbi would ask if I take you as my lawfully wedded K.P. Darling, if you love me because you think I will excel in the culinary and household arts, - well, I think we'd better call the whole thing off. I'm sure you'll find someone much more capable than I, - but if you care to take a chance, I promise I'll try. That's all I can do for you!!

I understand very little about what you're taking up in school. Just what is your job going to be? Are you going to fire machine guns, and why is this part in the air corps? I can't see what machine guns have to do with planes, unless you are going to be in one. I hope to hell you won't be. Is your job to fire the dang fangled contraptions or just to repair them? I feel awfully stupid.

The weather outside is very, very juicy. I was very fortunate in getting a ride home from work today with one of the salesmen. No cabs or such animals were to be had.

From the back of your stationary I could see almost all of Denver. It looks very nice. Let's remember to go back there someday.

I have been told very confidentially a secret, but I'm bursting trying to hold it in and I'm sure telling you won't matter one bit, - so I'm gonna tell you. I think my cousin Zelda is going to get married. Her boyfriend is up in Alaska and he thinks in the near future he may get a furlough. If he does, she'll have everything ready and they will trade "I do's." I was so excited I nearly burst. So far, I'm the only one that knows because should he not get a furlough, she doesn't want everyone to get excited about a wedding that won't be. I'm going to be maid of honor whether it be now or next year, - that is, if it doesn't start any family rows. I love weddings! I hope I'm not boring you, but I had to tell someone!

Well, dear, I guess baby better go to sleep now. And besides that, I'm all written out. Take care and, - be good?!!

Love, Lottie

March 27, 1944
Monday

From:	To:
Mr. Pvt. J.G. Barr 11057933	C.L. Sniderman
33rd T.S.S.	65 Houghton St.
Lowry Field #1, Colorado	Worcester, 4, Mass.

Dearest Lottie,

To-day we started school, finally. We start at 12 o'clock in the afternoon and finish at 6 o'clock in the afternoon. We haven't hit into the course yet, but had a controversial discussion on electricity. The instructor thinks one way, and we were taught another way. I don't think he is too bright, but as long as he gives us the answers to the tests, we ought to get by.

I'm sorry you brought up that incident. I had forgotten about it and no "friend" of mine ever brought it up. I'm just sorry that anything like that is ever thought up about anyone. Darling, you know Barb, and your opinion is worth more than anyone else's. O.K. let's forget it.

This morning I almost froze to death. I don't think I was outside more than fifteen minutes when my toes went numb and my face was stiff. If it is like that to-morrow, I'm going to wear a dozen pairs of stockings and my overcoat. It's snowing now, so I think it will be a bit warmer to-morrow.

If everything goes well, I'll be able to get a pass to go out, I hope. We have barrack inspection to-morrow so there is a chance that our Major may not like them, and then he will just say we'd better stay in and clean up the barracks. Oh well, such is army life, very interesting, you don't know from one minute to the next what is going to happen. Good night, darling.

Your, George

March 29, 1944
Wednesday

From:	To:
C.L. Sniderman	Mr. Pvt. J.G. Barr 11057933
65 Houghton St.	33rd T.S.S.
Worcester 4, Mass.	Lowry Field 1, Colorado

Dearest George,

Your letter that I got today just topped off the super mood I was in all day. Darling, it would be too too grand if you get a furlough for my birthday. This was the first time I ever thought of my birthday, - I surely thought you had forgotten. Let's just keep hoping.

I'm glad you got the money that your father sent you, but he also sent you some money about the time you left Texas. Have you gotten that yet?

I also saw "Cover Girl" last weekend, I thought it was swell. I'm sick, so sick, of war films. This was a most pleasant change.

I met Phil Sobel in town today. He didn't look so hot. Why the hell does he always have that dissipated look? I spoke to your folk's last nite and they told me Narkey was at the Santa Ana Air Base out in California. Outside of being very far, it's a swell place to be stationed.

I was supposed to go to a WAC recruiting campaign featuring Glenn Miller and his band tonight. We were all hyped about it and worked like the devil to get tickets. Finally, after getting the tickets we decided we were too tired to go. This proves that it's a woman's prerogative to change her mind.

I became entangled with a religious fanatic today and was disgusted after the conversation. It proved to be one of the reasons why he was issued a medical discharge. Seems to be in his family, as his brother is a conscientious objector, and is now working in a defense plant making big money.

I just spoke to Edie M. and her morale is lower than a snake's belly. Even worse than mine. If I didn't work at a place where the gals were so swell, I'd really be bad. But all we do all day is laugh. My boss asked me today if I ever got an A in conduct while I was at school. Hmm, I wonder what he meant!!!

Jesus, George, I wish you were home. Now that you mentioned a furlough, I'm counting on it, which of course is very stupid of me. But most of the fun comes in planning and waiting for the actual, - so I'm really having a riotous time by the law of averages! To heck with the waiting, give me the actual any day, anytime, anywhere.

That's about all the stuff I have to spill, that is, if you consider any of this letter newsy. And so, my love, keep my morale up and keep writing when you can.

Love, Lottie

March 31, 1944
Friday

From:	To:
C.L. Sniderman	Mr. Pvt. J.G. Barr 11057933
65 Houghton St.	33rd T.S.S.
Worcester 4, Mass.	Lowry Field 1, Colorado

Dearest George,

Your folks were tickled that you got the package. They had almost given it up for lost. And it looks like you're not the only one in your family blessed with K.P. – Narkey also has been given the honor. Some fun!

I can sympathize with your difficulties in Pauline's letter. I too have such troubles. A letter from her is left unread until I have plenty of time to decipher it. But the gal sure knows how to write. George, what do you picture her as looking like? I wonder how nearly correct or incorrect you are?

Too, too bad you couldn't get a pass. Now see, - if you had a wife (as you said) who was having a baby, you'd get all kinds of considerations. See what you're missing!!!

I just finished reading a delightful book called "You're Only Young Once." Twas very good, - and how true.

Seems the marriage bug has really bitten hard in Worcester. Sylvia Coblentz is simply dying to become Mrs. Erwin Goldman, - only trouble is he doesn't feel like being burdened with a wife. Whatta jerk. She really feels terrible. He told her point blank, - no wedding. She told him point blank, - we're gonna get married. Hmm, I wonder who'll win!

Last nite at the hospital I was on the men's Ward. It's very bad when you're a woman and you're sick, but in my opinion, it's ten times worse being a sick man. They look so pathetic. One of my patients was Abe Freedman's father, - a Mr. Winer. He insisted on calling me Miss Bloom and kept talking Jewish, - also he sang all kinds of Jewish songs. The patients were in stitches, - of laughter and otherwise!

In case you've been athinking that good ole Worcey is a dull joint, - well let me tell you about another girl who was attacked on corner Houghton & Acton Sts. It gets so that a gal is afraid to go out alone nights, - so how about coming home and protecting me?

I just got another letter from Barb and she's making it a habit of getting stinko on champagne. Maybe she's better off, - at least when you're drunk you don't think about things in the same light as you do when you're sober. Me thinks me will get stinko too.

My folks gave their Passover Order last nite and how they missed you. Last year you were kind enough to deliver it. - This year, - well, maybe next year, huh, honey. Goodnight, m' love.

Love, Lottie

Return at Teatime

By Ruth-Ellen Storey

If you should come when spring has
    spread
    Her lacy cloth of green across the
    scene,
I shall prepare thin slices of my own
    baked bread,
    With crisp, fresh water cress
    pressed in between.

Or should it be when summer's
    blazing prints unfold,
    I shall drop ice, like laughter,
    temptingly into our tea.
Or if brave autumn flaunts her
    doilies, red and gold,
    There will be doughnuts and
    mulled cider from my apple tree.

And should you come when winter's
    · fingers weave
    A frost of damask, white and
    startling bright,
Before a fire of high-heaped logs,
    you will receive
    Hot ginger cake with snow-
    whipped cream by candlelight.

And if my well-laid plan should run
    amuck—
Dear love, I'll open up a can, and
    you will take potluck.

March 31, 1944
Friday

From:	To:
Mr. Pvt. J.G. Barr 11057933	C.L. Sniderman
33rd T.S.S.	65 Houghton St.
Lowry Field #1, Colorado	Worcester, 4, Mass.

Dearest Lottie,

I just came back from services. I never saw such a large crowd of fellows there before, maybe it is because Passover is so near, or maybe it is because of the girls that come up, or even the sandwiches that are given out afterward. Anyway, it was a full house.

They even had an attendance prize – a telephone call home. My number was, of course, the one not to be called. A lucky fellow from Chicago had the lucky number. Also, coming to the services are about eight Frenchmen, most of them speak only French, but a few of them can talk just a bit of English. Now I'm sorry that I cannot remember any of my French. One of them can speak very good Jewish, so thru him, they arranged to have all of them up some family's house for the Seder.

In school, we have lessons on rotating machines, and it keeps my head spinning. It is all on motors. We are going to have a test on what we had to-day, tomorrow. I hope I can remember what the instructor was talking about.

Darling, I miss you very much, and even the services sort of bring us a bit closer spiritually, I am still lonesome for you.

Lights are going out pretty soon, so I'd better get to the end. I'll write again to-morrow.

Good night, darling —
Your, George

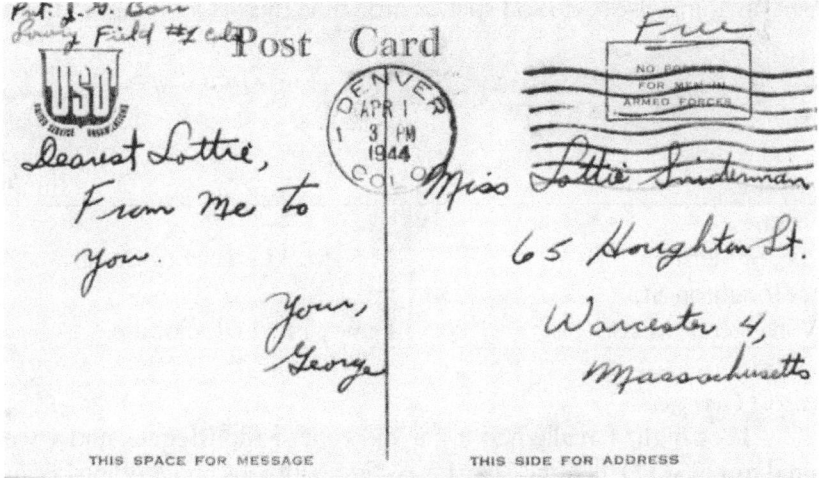

April 1, 1944
Saturday

From:	To:
Mr. Pvt. J.G. Barr 11057933	C.L. Sniderman
33rd T.S.S.	65 Houghton St.
Lowry Field #1, Colorado	Worcester, 4, Mass.

Dearest Lottie,

This morning they really gave us a work out. When we had physical training, otherwise known as P.T., this morning, I really sweat. I can see I'm not in good physical condition. Maybe after eight weeks, I'll be hard as nails, but I'm pretty damn mushy now.

When I went to mail call, no letter from you, and no letter for the last two days. I miss your letters very much.

At school to-day we reviewed yesterday's lesson and started on our test. It was one of the funniest tests that I ever ran across. There were fifty questions, these questions were on fifty individual cards. We all sat in a circle and had one card apiece. When the instructor gave the word, we passed the card on to the next person. This went on until all the fifty cards were passed out. This time my score was just six and a half points above passing, 76 $\frac{1}{2}$. It doesn't count too much, the score is just 30% of the weekly mark, and attitude is the remaining 70%.

We had a little time left over in class, so to occupy our time, I made a wheel out of one of the film reels they have in class. By putting numbers on each spoke and letting the boys bet on the numbers, I made eight cents. If they had bet large amounts of money, I could have made a fortune.

I went to the show to-night and saw two lousy pictures, but there wasn't anything else to do so I spent a little time there. Good night, darling.

Your, George

April 2, 1944
Sunday

From:	To:
C.L. Sniderman	Mr. Pvt. J.G. Barr 11057933
65 Houghton St.	33rd T.S.S.
Worcester 4, Mass.	Lowry Field 1, Colorado

Dearest George,

Last night I really had a gay old time. Edie Megans and I were invited to a USO Dance at Clark. I was a little dubious about going because

I hate going to stag dances for fear of being a wall flower, but she wanted to go and I hate being a wet blanket so we went. It turned out simply grand. I danced and danced, congas, rumbas, jitterbugging and had cut ins' galore. Twas too, too!! This was the first time I went to a dance of this kind. I also slept over Edie's last night. That is if you can call it sleeping. We talked most of the night.

I haven't had mail from you for four days now. Could it be bad mail conditions or are you slipping? Let's leave it at bad mail conditions.

Today is really a spring day. Birds are singing, trees are budding and I feel simply super. I feel as if I could take wing and fly - fly where? - To Colorado, of-course! They say this is the time of year when a young man's fancy turns to thoughts of love. Are your thoughts turning towards love? Do you love me? Today I feel full of love, - love for you, love for fellow man, and I even love my boss, - that really is going some, eh wot! I wish to high heaven you were home. It's a shame to waste all that love on Edie. She's over here for supper, incidentally, and she sends her love. Both of us feel very lovey dovey. Seems to me I had some dirt to write you, but I'll be damned if I can think of it, - me mind is a complete blank. I'll make up for this horrible missive tomorrow. I love you George, do you love poor 'lil me? Write.

Love, Lottie

P.S. Edie is annoying me, that's why I can't write or think or do or don't or anything. Me.

April 3, 1944
Tuesday

From:	To:
Mr. Pvt. J.G. Barr 11057933	C.L. Sniderman
33rd T.S.S.	65 Houghton St.
Lowry Field #1, Colorado	Worcester, 4, Mass.

Dearest Lottie,

Darling, I'm sorry that I haven't written sooner, but honestly, I've really been busy as all hell. This morning, the first thing I was ready to write you, but it seems that I had to report to the dental clinic. I don't know what it is, but every camp I go to, they inspect my teeth and supposedly fix them up so that they are in good shape. Now I have to have a few more fillings. When I got to the clinic, I had to wait almost an hour before they remembered I was there, then they told me I would have to come back in two weeks to have my teeth taken care of. Then when I came back, I had to pack one of the boys' bags and take them to the supply room. He had a slight cold, and hurt his knee during calisthenics, and it swelled up. So, when he went to the hospital to have it taken care of, they just kept him there. They were afraid of rheumatic fever, and any slight sign of it, and into bed you go for observation. He will stay there at least two weeks. I have a slight cough, but I'll be damned if I'll go on sick call, no telling what they are liable to do to me.

I want to get out of this camp, just as soon as I can, because the sooner I get out, the sooner I can ask for a furlough. Tho there is only a slight chance of me getting one so soon, I don't want to do anything to hurt my chances.

This afternoon we had a test, and I think everyone of us flunked. Will know more about it to-morrow. There weren't many questions, but it took two hours to finish it. The trouble with the school is that they throw the subject matter at us too fast to absorb it. Like this afternoon, two hours before the test we had something new, and on the test, we had questions on it. We didn't even have a chance to digest and analyze the subject matter. To-morrow we have a test on the whole course and then get a new piece of equipment.

Last night we went to see "Up in Arms" with Danny Kaye and Dinah Shore. It was hysterical. That Kaye boy is really a wit. They didn't need anyone else in the picture, because he was the whole show, although Dinah Shore did sing her best and that is good.

Lottie darling, you have me worried, two more days have gone by, and still no word from you. Please don't frighten me like this.

Got a letter from Sid to-day with a picture. He's in a tropical helmet and a bush jacket with boots. He is unshaven, and looks like the typical jungle hunter or trader, especially with four native boys around him. If Jackie hasn't any pictures of him, I'll send it to you.

Also, received a letter from my brother Narky who is in Santa Anna, Calif. He says that they are flunking a bunch of cadets, because there are just too many of them, and he's afraid he may be one of them. I hope not. – Who is going to teach me how to fly if he doesn't get his wings?

The weather here has been perfect for the last few days. I hope it keeps up. Our classroom is almost open air. There are two large doors that open on to the stairs, so we keep them open, letting all that Colorado sunshine come streaming in. I wish the hell I could get a camera that I could use. It makes me sick to see this stuff and not be able to record it.

I cannot get into photography or anything because I am on 'detached service' from another field, and am attending a G.I. school. I wish the hell they'd ask me what I want to do, instead of sending me where the hell they want me.

When we march to school, we have to sing. This is supposed to keep up our morale, I think that is what it is for. Anyway, the sergeant suggested we elect a class song leader, so I popped up with the idea of having one of the boys as song leader. Boy! Did that back fire! For now, I am class II-44's song leader. I didn't even know any complete song, but do they care? I guess not.

Sweetheart, I know my former letters where much below par, but the life I'm now living is so damn irregular that I just cannot seem to get into a writing mood. We get up at seven o'clock, eat breakfast, come back, make our beds, clean up, then go to P.T. After that, we're dead and don't want to do anything. By the time we're rested, we go to school, that is to dinner first, then to school. By the time we finish supper it's seven o'clock. Back at the barracks there is always a bunch of noise and kids coming up to you and asking you your idea of one thing or another. I guess I shouldn't complain. The other shift has to get up at 4:15 A.M. and goes to school until 12:00, then they come back and do there P.T. at 3 o'clock. The rest of the day is for themselves. That is, if they don't want any sleep.

I am all out of words now darling, as I look back at this letter I'm still wondering where the hell I got all this energy to write so much. Maybe I have a conscience and it bothered my mind, if not my mind, I assure you my heart.

Goodnight my love —
Your, George

April 3, 1944
Monday

From:	To:
C.L. Sniderman	Mr. Pvt. J.G. Barr 11057933
65 Houghton St.	33rd T.S.S.
Worcester 4, Mass.	Lowry Field 1, Colorado

Dearest George,

The only comment I have to make on your picture is "Wow!" If you were a girl you'd have it all over the Varga creations. Some figure, I'll say, oh my!!

About my getting a raise, - well, I'll tell you, it's like this. Dave, the manager, told me to ask Saul Sharfman, as I told you previously. Well, - I asked him, and told him a few added things in the heat of my indignation. So, he told me to please be patient because I was much desevervant of a raise and as soon as the O.K. comes thru from the government, I'll get it. He said he was trying to make it retroactive. I don't know if he was giving me the baloney or not, but since I have nothing better to do, I might just as well wait.

I finally got it through my thick brain what your job is about. Lottie is mighty glad that you're going to be behind the front lines.

I just had a time for myself. Zelda was over here and she brought her veil. It looked beautiful on me, honest! If Phil doesn't get a furlough now, the poor kid will be heart broken. I also had to take out my gowns that were put away for the duration. It was loads of fun trying them on. I tried on the blue gown I wore when I went to the formal with you. What memories that brought back. I don't know what I'll wear yet. Outside of being maid of honor, I'm making her a shower and taking care of arrangements for the orchestra. All this will have to be done at a moment's notice. When my mother saw me come out in the veil she couldn't stop crying. Heck, ya might think twas I. Why in heaven's name do people cry at weddings. I always do, - except at Evelyn's and Sid's wedding. Speaking of Sid, have you heard from him lately? And also, have you heard from Dave G.?

Fer heaven's sake, I owe so many people letters, and here I sit writing a novel to you. Hmmm, - I wonder why! Goodnight dear, and I'm glad you're good, - or at least making an effort. Funny, but I never did notice a halo around yer head. But I loves ya just the same, - or maybe even more so!

Love, Lottie

April 4, 1944
Tuesday

From:	To:
Mr. Pvt. J.G. Barr 11057933	C.L. Sniderman
33rd T.S.S.	65 Houghton St.
Lowry Field #1, Colorado	Worcester, 4, Mass.

HOTEL CORY
BROADWAY AT SIXTEENTH
DENVER, COLORADO

Dearest Lottie,

I guess you don't know where this is being written from, now do you? There are three of us, and two beds. We matched for the bed, but I lost, so I'll have to sleep with one of the boys.

The test we were supposed to have today was postponed until Thursday. They wouldn't tell us why, but I think it was because we did so badly on yesterday's test.

I got two packages to-day, one from my folks and one from the Torens. Two letters from you, and two cards from home. All in all, I think that I did very good. The reason I didn't receive mail from you is because of the terrible mail situation here.

We went to a dance again to-night, but it seems that the girls down here don't know what to do when they play a rhumba. They are just a bunch of jitterbugs. I'm such a <u>good</u> jitterbug that I had a swell time.

I feel sorry for Sylvia not being able to get married. If I were her, I'd tell Irwin now or never. If he was any kind of a man (I have my doubts), it would be now. I know that under the same circumstances I would get married. Do you think some nice girl would have me? All right, so I'm not funny!!!

Goodnight honey – I'm going to hit the "sack", an old army expression.

Your, George

[Editor's note: This card was in an envelope post marked 4/05/1944 from Lottie Sniderman to George Barr]

April 6, 1944
Thursday

From:	To:
C.L. Sniderman	Mr. Pvt. J.G. Barr 11057933
65 Houghton St.	33rd T.S.S.
Worcester 4, Mass.	Lowry Field 1, Colorado

Dearest George,

I just got back from the hospital and altho I'm terribly tired and depressed, I must write to you. I did a very foolish thing at the hospital tonight, - I started crying the way I haven't for a long time. When I got to the hospital, I was greeted by a mouse running up and down the ward, then a cockroach met me in the kitchen, so I was a nervous wreck to begin with. Then my patients were all terribly sick. One woman grabbed my arm (I have two big scratches) and insisted she was dying. She begged me not to leave her alone, so I felt duty bound to stay. She looked at me and started to cry. She asked me how old I was, and when I told her nineteen, she cried even harder and told me she knew I was only a baby girl. Then she started stroking my hair. You have such beautiful hair, she kept saying, promise me you'll take care of it. She was completely bald and wore a wig.

Then another woman kept telling me her legs were aching, - the day before they had cut both of her legs off. Another young girl had just had a brain operation and was completely dead mentally. She kept looking at me. Then to top it off I broke my nail and I started to bawl. I was carrying a large vase of flowers when one of the doctors saw me crying and he started to laugh. He made me sit down and talk and talk, - after that I felt much better, and I started to laugh. I really shouldn't write you about all this because I know it doesn't make very pleasant reading, but hells bells, I gotta tell someone and you always were a good listener. But don't get me wrong. - I love the hospital.

George, please take care of yourself. If you still have that cough, don't let it go. Taking care of sick people you don't know is bad enough, but when someone you love gets sick, that's a different story. So, promise you'll be a good boy. Promise? O.K!

I can't understand why you haven't had any mail from me for so long. I'm sure by this time you must have gotten my letters. I write every chance I get, dear. But, don't worry about not getting any mail, it'll probably come all together, - I still love you, mail or no! They're singing "I Love You" on the radio now – how appropriate. I'm really dog tired, darling. Goodnight.

Love, Lottie

April 6, 1944
Thursday

From:	To:
Mr. Pvt. J.G. Barr 11057933	C.L. Sniderman
33rd T.S.S.	65 Houghton St.
Lowry Field #1, Colorado	Worcester, 4, Mass.

Dearest Lottie,

I am glad that you had a good time when you went to the dance at the U.S.O. at Clark. All work and no play makes Lottie a dull girl. So, play a little. Not that you'd ever be dull to me, because you couldn't be to me. You are the one I love, and if you love someone, they never become dull to you.

Yesterday afternoon while looking thru the Coronet magazine, I saw an article, "Are You Fit for Marriage?" I took the tests that they gave, they have three of them. I think you'd like to know that I passed two of them with flying colors, and one of them I'm on the border line. My faults are small, and I know that I'm slowly improving. I flunked on, "Do You Have a Tendency to be Disorderly?" I know I'm getting rid of that habit – Army you know, and "Do You Take Out Your Discomforts and Irritations on Other People." I'm getting ones on that too. In a little while I should be eligible.

Yesterday afternoon we went shopping for a knife. It took us all afternoon to find one. Of course, we did more window shopping than anything else. At one five and ten, we selected records and had the girl play them. That itself took at least an hour.

The day was so damn nice, and plenty of picture opportunities that I got angry, and I'm going to send home for my camera. I may regret it later, but it has been so long that I've taken any pictures, I don't care, and besides it is not doing anyone any good laying in a closet back home.

The mail situation is terrible here, I don't know whose fault it is, but I wish someone would do something about it.

Lottie darling, I had more to write, but I got a lousy headache. We had another test to-day and it was a lulu.

Until to-morrow, sweet,
Your, George

April 9, 1944
Sunday

From: C.L. Sniderman 65 Houghton St. Worcester 4, Mass.	To: Mr. Pvt. J.G. Barr 11057933 33rd T.S.S. Lowry Field 1, Colorado

Hi M'Love,

How are you today? I feel simply simply, - half good – half bad. Golda Edinburg had to go back to school today, so Edie drove her back to Mass. State and I tagged along. The ride was beautiful, the day ideal and we had quite a jolly time. When we started, we felt very good, but after seeing all the gals sporting their boyfriends, we didn't feel so good, - so upon arriving in Amherst we entered a respectable place and indulged in a glass of beer. After that we felt good again. Golda showed us all around the campus and it really is a beautiful place. The soldiers have sort of taken over the college, but they move out in a few weeks, much to the regret of all the femmes.

But my dear, I'm telling you if you're not dressed from head to foot in purple you're just a social outcast. I hate the hideous color and thank the lord that I haven't anything that hue. It felt wonderful shaking winter clothes. Yes, my minks and foxes have been put away for the season.

But what's what with you. I haven't heard from you for days and since you wrote about that cough I'm worried. Please, - don't do that to me!

Do you know Paulina Shawmut? Well, she was supposed to graduate from Clark this June but was kicked out of school because she was caught doing not nice things during a final chem. Exam. Isn't that a piece of dirt? That dame is not very popular with others of her sex so everyone is taking advantage of the gossip.

Bev Kaplan or Mrs. Lan called me the other day and she sounded swellegant. Her husband (sounds funny) has been transferred to Missouri so she's staying here until he gets settled and then she'll follow. She sounded delirious with joy.

George, I miss you something fierce. Do you really think there's a chance of you getting a furlough? You just gotta! Today while we were riding I missed you more than ever. It was so beautiful and I remembered all the rides and walks we took, - it really hurt. The whole thing is so unfair. But someday------.

Goodnight darling, Lottie

April 9, 1944
Sunday

From:	To:
Mr. Pvt. J.G. Barr 11057933	C.L. Sniderman
33rd T.S.S.	65 Houghton St.
Lowry Field #1, Colorado	Worcester, 4, Mass.

Dearest Lottie,

You know where a fellow who is sick could find a good nurse's aide? Yes, my darling, I'm in the hospital. When I came in yesterday, I was sick as a dog, but to-day I'm feeling much better thank you. My fever yesterday was 101, to-day, almost gone. The only thing that bothers me now is my throat. I have to wash it out every two hours, what a bother.

Your picture is on my table beside my bed. When I couldn't sleep yesterday, I looked at you all the time. If it wasn't for you, I wouldn't have improved so fast. I told myself that you wanted me better, so I tried to get better faster.

What burned my up was that I could have gotten a pass last night, and I had to end up in the hospital. The night before, we had a Seder and the people were just fine. The supper was delicious and the wine good.

We were invited for the next night's Seder, but I couldn't attend.

Darling, I love you. That's all I think of is you, and that is all I care to think of.

Yours, George

April 10, 1944
Monday

From:	To:
Mr. Pvt. J.G. Barr 11057933	C.L. Sniderman
33rd T.S.S.	65 Houghton St.
Lowry Field #1, Colorado	Worcester, 4, Mass.

Dearest Lottie,

Good morning darling! I'm getting along just fine, too damn fine. If things keep up this way, I'll probably be out of the hospital in no time at all. I'll have to try and remain a little sick until I think I have had enough rest.

There is something I've forgotten to tell you. I hope that it will not make you angry. The day before I came here, five of us were put back in school a week. We had two instructors this week, one taught the first three days, and the other the last three, but the one who taught the last three days had the final word on our passing, or failing. I asked him why I had been put back and he told me that it was my grade in my last test. Well, if I'm dumb, it's no one's fault but my own. After he had told the five of us we flunked, we left class, because we were going to start the course over again in the morning. When the rest of the boys came back from class, they told us after talking to the instructor, he told them we flunked on proficiency. To me that was a laugh, because I don't think anyone of us should have failed on attitude, because, if anything, that was what we were best in.

Now with staying back in school, and being in the hospital, I don't know what they will have planned for me. I don't want to go back to school now, because if I continue, I will never be able to get home on a furlough for your birthday. If I don't go to school, then I'll stay here a while and be shipped to another camp.

Saturday morning, when I came in and got into my bed, I noticed something familiar about the table next to mine, but at the time I couldn't place it in my mind. About two hours later the patient got up looked over my way and, quote "What the hell are you doing here!" unquote. He was the same boy that had been sick. I didn't quite understand it because this ward was 11, and he was in 16, there was a very simple explanation for it, they had moved him.

The nurse just finished giving a delicious back rub. We get one every day, and sometimes twice a day.

Yesterday afternoon when the Coca Cola hour and the Prudential Family hour was on, it brought back some of my most enjoyable memories. – Sunday afternoon drives with you beside me, in all kinds of weather, during all the seasons of the year. And if I couldn't get the car, we'd sit in your parlor and talk and listen, ah, what happy days.

Good bye for now, sweetness – you know I love you, don't you? Well I do, so there!

Your, George

P.S. If some of my so-called buddies would come over, maybe I could get some stamps, so while I'm here you'll have to wait a bit longer for my letters. G.B.

April 10, 1944
Monday

From:	To:
C.L. Sniderman	Mr. Pvt. J.G. Barr 11057933
65 Houghton St.	33rd T.S.S.
Worcester 4, Mass.	Lowry Field 1, Colorado

Dearest George,

Finally got some mail from you today. Whatta relief! Glad to hear you came out so well on the "Are You Ready For Marriage" tests. Always good to know such things, eh? Would like to take a similar test, - but I know I'd come out with flying colors.......ahem! I just came back from having dinner with Bev. She's miserably lonesome without Alton, - but who isn't lonesome nowadays. It was just like old times getting together and having a big chat. We sure had loads to nosh over. Incidentally, just in case you didn't know it, she thinks you're one swell guy. Of-course, I think so too, - but could be that I'm prejudiced.

George, I think it would be silly of you to have your camera sent to you. It really is such a nice camera and it would be a shame if anything happened to it. Besides that, - well, - just don't have it sent if you haven't written for it already.

After yesterday's ideal weather, of-course, it rained today. It was drippy all over and I felt just the same way. Just a drip, that's me.

We got a new girl down our office, - girl? – That really is a laugh. She looks like a typical old maid school teacher who never cracks a smile. I can see she'll get along dandy with our bunch of lunatics. She'll probably love it when we get up and dance in the middle of the office and don't think we don't. Well darling, my eyes are drooping up and down like window shades. Take care.

Love, Lottie

April 11, 1944
Tuesday

From:	To:
Mr. Pvt. J.G. Barr 11057933	C.L. Sniderman
33rd T.S.S.	65 Houghton St.
Lowry Field #1, Colorado	Worcester, 4, Mass.

Dearest Lottie,

I received your very cute card and letter to-day. I know just what you mean "missing you', because, my darling, I miss you awfully much. That doesn't sound like good English, but I sure as hell do miss you. You cannot realize how much your picture helps me tho, it sure is a comfort. Every once in a while, when I take a glass of water, I look straight into your beautiful dark brown eyes and have a toast to you. The guy in the next bed, thinks that I'm absolutely nuts, whenever he sees me toasting you, but I don't care.

You certainly are going thru some experiences at the hospital. You'll be able to write a book on it after awhile. Whatever you write me always is of interest to me, and I'm glad that you do, so don't let it bother you one iota.

Jackie writes me that he intends to take some pictures of you, so he can send them to me. But, he thinks that he is going to have a little trouble with your 'camera shyness' – you show him different and don't forget, you still owe me one in your uniform.

Now about me – I'm just coasting along on what was wrong with me. I only get one medicine now, when before I got three different things, so I guess you can count me as being two-thirds well.

This morning I was very pleasantly surprised when one of my officers came into the ward and paid me. This, of course, made me feel much better mentally, then I deposited twenty bucks in the hospital's safe so I'll have a little money when I get out of this joint. I really oughtn't to call this hospital a joint, because they do treat me very nicely.

In case you are interested, my pen leaks and I get my fingers all blue whenever I write a letter. Now when I can get my hands on an auxiliary, I'll have to send the thing back to the factory & get it fixed. Ignore this last paragraph, if you ain't interested.

Your, George

April 11, 1944
Tuesday
The hour? - Late

From:	To:
C.L. Sniderman	Mr. Pvt. J.G. Barr 11057933
65 Houghton St.	33rd T.S.S.
Worcester 4, Mass.	Lowry Field 1, Colorado

Hi honey,

Boy, I sure had a busy evening. Bev was over here for supper and we laughed & laughed all about nothing. She thinks married life is sa-imply grand and thinks I'm a dope for not doing same. While she was here, Toby called and invited me to supper Thursday nite. Seems your aunt is here from New York and wants to see what I look like. Then I spoke to Jackie and he told me he sent you your camera and other things you asked for. I felt terrible when he said he had mailed the camera because it really would be a shame if anything happened to it. Also, I have a tennis date with him Sunday. Your mother thought the picture of you in the shower was adorable. She laughed at me when I told her I was embarrassed. So, help me I blushed! Then after speaking to Jackie, my brother came over and we talked until the wee hours of the night. Now my family and I have decided to have an early breakfast. Whatta family, - we do everything but sleep. I don't know whether I'm tired or just numb, - no, not dumb, numb!!

I hear tell Evelyn Issacman was really very sick. Sort of a nervous breakdown or something. Maybe I can get Jackie to visit her with me. She's really a very sweet girl.

Well, me love, I guess this will have to be short, - if not sweet. They're playing a Samba on the radio and my feet just won't be still. Shall we dance? Hell, but I miss you, - I just never seem to stop missing you.

Love, Lottie

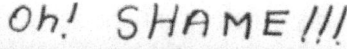

April 12, 1944
Tuesday

From:	To:
Mr. Pvt. J.G. Barr 11057933	C.L. Sniderman
33rd T.S.S.	65 Houghton St.
Lowry Field #1, Colorado	Worcester, 4, Mass.

Dearest Lottie,

Here is how sick I am – I was on ward K.P. to-day. I should never have gotten better, the way they treat a person is awful.

They really treat us fine, for yesterday afternoon and this morning they showed us moving pictures. This afternoon the Red Cross' 'Greyladies' came around. These wonderful women come two or three times a week and get cigarettes, candy, books, paper, and anything else at the P.X. that the boys want.

Received a letter from my brother Narky and he is not going to be an air cadet anymore. He said it was a long story and he would tell me sometime, the reason. I think the army just has too many men and they want the very, very best of the men.

This afternoon a lemon-orange squeezing detail also fell into my line of duties. The stuff was so good that the boy's all had seconds, and even the nurse said that it was good. She just came in this afternoon to relieve our regular nurse, so I thought it a friendly gesture to offer her a drink, she also was very pretty. After her compliment, I tried to get her to give me a back rub (I missed mine while on K.P.), but she was too smart and graciously backed out of it. I still didn't get my back rub.

The Doc said to-day, that if all goes well, I'll be out of here by Saturday.

I'm always thinking of you, darling——
Your, George

April 13, 1944
Thursday

From:	To:
C.L. Sniderman	Mr. Pvt. J.G. Barr 11057933
65 Houghton St.	33rd T.S.S.
Worcester 4, Mass.	Lowry Field 1, Colorado

Hello darling,

I nearly fell over today when I got your letter saying you were in the hospital. I hope you were telling the truth when you said you were feeling better. I don't want you ever to be sick again, - that's a command!! Speaking of hospitals, I just came back. Why is it all my patients are over ninety? Makes me realize that getting old is no picnic. George, let's never grow old, - if we can't physically, let's stay young mentally anyhow. O.K? O.K.

I got a letter from Dave yesterday. Seems he's doing pretty alright with the London belles. He also said Fanny Farmers were very hard to get in England. Subtle, - like a sledge hammer. I can take a hint, so I'm sending him some first chance. – First chance I get some money!!

George, I don't mean to reprimand you for being set back in school, because in itself it really isn't very important. But, darling, you're only going to get out of the course what you put into it. I think you've made up your mind that you won't learn anything and therefore you don't. So whatta you say, - will you rise to the head of the class? You're no dope, we both know that, and with a little effort you still may be a general. Hail the general. Think how proud your children would be. Whatta my saying?!!!

I got a letter from Fran Barr today and seems Sol is going to represent the Barr family in the navy. Your folks don't know about it yet, - so don't say anything yet. They don't know when he'll be going, - but they think it won't be long.

I just heard the latest news and it sounds pretty good. But I'll be darned if they can get me excited with a little victory, - what I want is the final victory, - and hurry up quick.

Pardon me darling, I must light me a cigarette. Joan Brooks is on the radio – remember how we used to listen to her every nite? George, about you coming home for my birthday, - well, darling, whenever you come home we'll celebrate my birthday. Didn't we celebrate New Year's Eve on Christmas Eve, so we can celebrate Memorial Day anytime. Anyway, whenever you come home will be a holiday. She's singing "I Wish I Could Hide Inside This Letter," – how appropriate. Goodnight dear.

Love, Lottie

April 13, 1944
Thursday

From:	To:
Mr. Pvt. J.G. Barr 11057933	C.L. Sniderman
33rd T.S.S.	65 Houghton St.
Lowry Field #1, Colorado	Worcester, 4, Mass.

Dearest Lottie,

Hello sweetheart, and how are you? Fine – well that's swell, because I am too. How do I know? Silly, the Doc told me so, and he outranks me so he's right and besides I feel swell. I've really had plenty of sleep and rest, and this I find is the best thing for a tired body. I'm still a little hoarse, but I do feel fine.

Last night I had a scare. The ward boy came up to me and said that I had three visitors and all old women. Now what did I ever do to have three women come to see me for. I couldn't imagine who or why they came up. I went down to see what was cooking, thinking maybe it was the woman whose house I was at for the Seder and a few of her friends. It even entered my mind that my mother took wing and had come here, but I dismissed that, because it couldn't have been more than a day or so since she received my letter that I was in the hospital. The story was that they wanted a Burr and not Barr, I politely escorted them to Burr's bed and got the hell away from them. Who wanted three old ladies visiting me anyway!

To-day I ate in the hospital mess hall, no more trays for me, plates until I get out of here. Think I'll try and stay here awhile longer.

It just started to rain here, the first since I've been down in Denver. So far, I cannot complain about the weather that they've been having here.

I'm mad as hell at my mail room, for the last two days they haven't brought me any mail – the no good sons-a-guns.

This morning I was 'king of the mop' and had to mop the floor. When you get well in the army, they make you work for your keep.

Did you know that I'm crazy about you, darling? Well I am, very much so, and I do care to let you know about it. If it weren't for you, I'd probably still be on my back, not giving a damn whether I should get better or not. See – you are my Florence Nightingale and not these nurses that we have here.

Until to-morrow my love,
Your, George

P.S. I got the day and date straight to-day, if you noticed. J.G.B.

April 14, 1944
Friday

From:	To:
C.L. Sniderman	Mr. Pvt. J.G. Barr 11057933
65 Houghton St.	33rd T.S.S.
Worcester 4, Mass.	Lowry Field 1, Colorado

Dearest George,

    I wonder if you have any idea how much your letters pep me up. Today's letter was really a lulu. You sounded in fine spirits despite the fact that you're sick. You haven't, as yet, told me what's wrong with you. I'm glad you liked the card, I thought twas cute too. Maybe I'm a mind reader or is it mental telepathy, but it's funny that you should get the card while being in the hospital. Also, funny that you toast my picture with a glass of water, and I'm insulted because your buddy thinks you're nuts for doing it because many a times I've done exactly the same thing. The hell with everyone who thinks we're nuts, - we're happy, or at least try to be, and that's all that counts. My mother and I were reminiscing today and she remembered all the crazy things we used to do. Like the time we went walking on one of the coldest nights of the year and my legs were fiery red from the cold and she was so mad. And remember the time we spent a whole evening playing hop-scotch? What may sound like a peculiar idea of fun to other people was just grand fun to me.

    I guess maybe the picture-taking bug has bitten me because I do want to have my picture taken. As soon as I have time, I must get Jackie to do the tedious job. I wrote a letter to Dave today. I wrote it down the office and with all the interruptions I'm afraid I didn't do a very good job. Well, me darlin', take care and get out of the hospital, - unless, of-course, you like it and the attention of the nurses!!

Love, Lottie

April 14, 1944
Friday

From:	To:
Mr. Pvt. J.G. Barr 11057933	C.L. Sniderman
33rd T.S.S.	65 Houghton St.
Lowry Field #1, Colorado	Worcester, 4, Mass.

Dearest Lottie,

    Another day, just another day. It's beautiful outside, but I remain inside, that is the only thing that I really miss, the nice clean fresh air with the sun streaming down. Spring fever is in me and I don't feel like doing a damn thing (pardon the ink, just refilled my pen) (I don't know how many brands it has had in it since I've been in the hospital). This ink even makes it write like a different pen.

I've had plenty of rest since I've been here, I know because I couldn't sleep very well last night and it must have been one o'clock before I finally dozed off.

Haven't received any mail for two days. If I don't get some soon I'm going over to the mail room and give those WAC's over there hell.

This morning I swept the floor nice and clean, and the rest of the day I read a bunch of short stories. I even tried to get into "Since Yesterday", its all about life in this country during the 1930's, but just didn't seem to be able to get deep enough in it to go thru the entire length of the story.

There is really one very good thing about the hospital, most all the meals are swell. To-day we had a delicious steak dinner and for dessert we had some wonderful chocolate ice cream. I haven't tasted such good ice cream since I left 'Broadway.'

So help me my minds a blank, so darling, until I get into focus again, that should be by to-morrow the latest.

Your, George

April 15, 1944
Saturday

From:	To:
Mr. Pvt. J.G. Barr 11057933	C.L. Sniderman
33rd T.S.S.	65 Houghton St.
Lowry Field #1, Colorado	Worcester, 4, Mass.

Dearest Lottie,

Last night just after we turned in, the fellow next to me looked over and said that if he had a nightmare that night to ignore him or hit him on the head with something. After asking him why, he told me that he just received a letter from his girl and she just jilted him. I wouldn't have cared, but he is one of the boys I came to Denver with and I got to know him pretty well. Just that afternoon we had been battling over who had the prettiest girl friend, he of I. Of course, neither of us could convince each other of who did.

He was telling me that they were engaged for over a year now and he even had the wedding and a silver service.

I couldn't sleep after that, it got me thinking. If I only had a little dough in the bank, I was going to tell you dear, that we'd get married on my next furlough. That's of course, if you wanted to, but I didn't think you'd have said no. Then I started to think some more. If we did get married, you'd of course, be with me as much as would be possible. You'd probably have to work, because a fifty-dollar allotment check doesn't go very far at all. Then different things would come up to keep us apart, such as restrictions, night details, or I'd be shipped and then you'd have to stay in the town until you would hear from me. You'd be alone a lot of times, maybe with no one to turn to. It just would be a hard life for any woman. Then I asked myself, did I have the right to ask you to subject yourself to such hardships. The answer was I was very selfish. But my darling, if I did have something for a start, I certainly would ask you to marry me the next time I got home.

Then if we did get married like that. We couldn't have that nice big wedding we wanted, with all our friends standing around and crying, when we'd say 'I do."

Now darling, this letter doesn't mean I'm afraid that you'll say 'no' to me one of these fine days, because, dear, we are too much in love with one another. It is just that, that little incident started me thinking.

I'm sorry to hear that Evelyn Issacman is sick, so if you see her say hello to her for me, huh? And get Jackie down to see her if you can, and I know you are the one to do it. Also, when you play tennis with him Sunday, get him to take some glamour shots of my one and only pin up girl.

Did I tell you I'm raising a mustache while being interned here? No, well I am, and as soon as I get a picture of it I'm going to shave it off. I'll probably have to use eye brow pencil on it so it will show up, but I guarantee that there is now a weeks' growth of hair.

With, as one poet put it, oceans of love, and a kiss on each wave.

Your, George

April 16, 1944
Sunday

From:	To:
Mr. Pvt. J.G. Barr 11057933	C.L. Sniderman
33rd T.S.S.	65 Houghton St.
Lowry Field #1, Colorado	Worcester, 4, Mass.

Dearest Lottie,

At long last it has come, I leave the hospital to-morrow morning to report back to my squadron for duty.

Last night one of the fellows and I went to the Red Cross building where they had a Bingo game going. There was nothing else doing, so we sat in on it. I won twice, but the only thing they had was tooth paste, shaving cream, and a few packs of razor blades. I took a package of cigarette tobacco and a box of blades. The blades I gave to the boy, because he was short of them, having borrowed one of mine early that afternoon. The tobacco I took and tried to roll my own. If there is anyone who doesn't know how to roll cigarettes, it's me. My room is just covered with the stuff.

This afternoon we went down again to hear a band. The total number of players were five, five poor players. To-night they are going to have a variety show and I think that we'll trot over there, besides, they give out ice cream and cookies.

Sunday is a day of rest, and this is all there is – no rest!! Awful isn't it, maybe I'm not well yet.

Your, George

April 17, 1944
Monday

From:	To:
C.L. Sniderman	Mr. Pvt. J.G. Barr 11057933
65 Houghton St.	33rd T.S.S.
Worcester 4, Mass.	Lowry Field 1, Colorado

Dearest George,

Boy, I really hit the jackpot today! Three letters from you, - I don't know if it's good or bad because that means no mail for you tomorrow. But anyway, I was happy today. I had to forgo the pleasure of Jackie's company at a tennis game yesterday for the simple reason of rain. All de time it rains out here. So instead I accepted a previous invitation to go to a Jewish Serviceman's Canteen. I really had a super time and realized more than ever what a wonderful thing these organizations are doing. We got there (in Ayer) about three o'clock, made sandwiches and other foods. About 5:30 the boys started coming so we served them a complete meal which they thoroughly enjoyed. During their meal one girl played the piano while Edie Megans and I tried to entertain them with a song. Knowing how beautiful I sing you can appreciate how funny it was. We never did finish the song because the boys were getting indigestion from laughter & Edie and I went into hysterics. Then Charlotte Abramson, an older man, who sort of sponsor's the canteen, and I did a chorus dance with motions and all. It really was a riot and the boys appreciated our efforts. I got home about twelve dripping wet from the rain, ore feet from dancing, a headache from smoking, and a hoarse throat from singing. Today I am completely recuperated or at least I was until supper time.

One of the girls down our office has a sister sho is away at present and this genius decided it would be fun if we went over there and cooked our own meal. There were four of us, all hungry as hell puttering around. We had steaks, which turned out delicious, as a matter of fact everything was delicious, - or maybe we were just hungry!!

Today I really got quite a shock. I received a letter from Beverly Kaplan Lan, which in itself wasn't very important, but it was addressed to Mrs. George Barr. My mother nearly fainted when the mailman asked when I got married. Must remember to tell Bev she's a bit premature!! George, I wonder if you can appreciate how much I miss you. I keep thinking of you constantly. I surely thought by this time you were out of the hospital. Hurry up, - will ya?!! Tobye called me last nite but I wasn't home and I came home too late to call her tonight. I'm terribly sorry about Narky being out of the Air Corps. How did he take it? Someone is singing a beautiful arrangement of "The Man I Love." Why does music affect me so much, - I hear a song, sweet song, and I'm a goner. Goodnight darling, - pleasant dreams.

Love, Lottie

April 17, 1944
Monday

From:	To:
Mr. Pvt. J.G. Barr 11057933	C.L. Sniderman
33rd T.S.S.	65 Houghton St.
Lowry Field #1, Colorado	Worcester, 4, Mass.

U. S. ARMY AIR FORCES *April 17, 1944*

Dearest Lottie,

Yes, darling, I'm finally out of the hospital, but not a free man by a long shot, for to-morrow before sun rise, I shall be awakened for K.P. – What a life, who's to blame? I guess I can blame myself.

After reading your little builder upper about school, I felt as low as the ground, beneath a snake's belly. Darling, I hope that you can understand me though. The folks back home may think that going to school is just a bed of roses. Well dear, it just isn't here. Not that it is hard, because I've done harder things, but that there is so many things about going to a school that you dislike, and when so many things are just so darn absurd in the running of the school. I am no longer going to school. This morning I went to see the officer in charge and he asked me why I didn't like it. I told him that I didn't think the instructors were instructors, that they couldn't put the subject matter across as well as they should, and that the tests we were being given, were the tests that the boys that go thru in sixteen weeks, were taking. There were quite a few other details, they all add up, and he even admitted to me that the instructors weren't what they should be. Now, I thought that I was going back to school, but there are no more A.S.C. men going thru, therefore, there is no class that I could go to. I cannot say that I'm sorry, because I'm not, this whole deal makes me entirely disgusted with some parts of the army. To me the whole camp system stinks!

When I reported back to my orderly room, I asked to go to see the classification officer. To see him I had to see my C.O., who'd give me a note saying that it was O.K. with him. I saw the C.O., after, I had to ask the first sergeant to get his O.K. on it, but when he found out that I was an A.S.C. man, he told me that this was not an A.S.C. field and that the classification officer would not be able to do anything for me. Now I have to wait until I get to a field where they recognize that I belong to the army. Of course, I wanted to see if I could get into photography, and they have a school here for it, but no, if and when I ever get into it (that's me always dreaming), the government will have to ship me to some photography school. What do they care how much money they spend, it all comes out of someone else's pocket.

Darling, if this letter seems a bit cynical, don't mind it. I just had four teeth filled and now since I had that last one pulled, due to a dentist who wasn't minding his business (probably, because he wanted to be home with his loved ones), I get awfully nervous. It seems when I left San Antonio, I had all the work necessary done on my teeth and nothing further was needed. But after two days on the train, it seems that I need seven fillings. The line between who is right and who is wrong in the army will never be able to be drawn.

Sweetness, you keep your camera and keep it busy. What's the good of having a camera, if you don't make use of it? I received mine to-day, and I think I fondled it just like a baby. It was like greeting an old friend. Now I hope I can get a chance to use it.

Lottie darling, I love you, day by day, more and more.

Your, George

P.S. A.S.C. = Army Service Command.

April 19, 1944
Wednesday

From:	To:
C.L. Sniderman	Mr. Pvt. J.G. Barr 11057933
65 Houghton St.	33rd T.S.S.
Worcester 4, Mass.	Lowry Field 1, Colorado

Dearest George,

The gals in our office received a very pleasant surprise today. We got the afternoon off in honor of "Patriot's Day." It was simply beautiful outside, I felt the urge to go walking or even fishing, - but instead I went thru the drudge of shopping and the pay-off is that I didn't buy anything. My uncle Dave was tendered a surprise birthday party last night. He was as happy as a four year old, - he says it's the first time anyone ever made an issue of his being born. He really is a swell guy. Jackie called me last night and we took part in very fanciful and childhood dreams. We were both married to our respective mates and extremely wealthy. I extended a standing invitation to Jackie for tea at our palatial home every day at four. Also, he said he and his wife would be delighted to sleep over sometime, but he absolutely insists that they have separate sleeping quarters, and he wants a lock on his door so that his wife couldn't sneak up on him in the wee hours of the night. Some fun! I asked him if he had seen Evelyn Issacman of late, and he completely avoided answering. I guess he means it when he says it's all over between them. Also, he had a date Saturdee nite, but refuses to tell me with whom....the stinker. I saw Sara Srieberg or Mrs. Louie Entin in town today, and she's having a babee!! That's what I call fast work! Well darling, I guess that about does it for today. I'm gonna write a letter to Fran Barr now. S'long.

Love, Lottie

April 19, 1944
Wednesday
Snowing like hell!

From:	To:
Mr. Pvt. J.G. Barr 11057933	C.L. Sniderman
33rd T.S.S.	65 Houghton St.
Lowry Field #1, Colorado	Worcester, 4, Mass.

THE CANTEEN FOR THE ARMED FORCES
OPERATED BY
The Army and Navy Commission of the Episcopal Church
DENVER, COLORADO

April 19, 44

Dearest Lottie,

How is my loved one to-day? Yes, darling, on my day off it had to snow. I don't think they know what spring is in Colorado. We've had about one decent week since I've been here.

Last night we went to a dance down the Y.W.C.A. It was a pretty nice affair, the orchestra was surprisingly good. After that we went and slept at some sort of U.S.O. where all they have is sleeping facilities. We are all kind of broke and have to watch our money. Last night one of the fellows needed some money, so he sold his hat, one with a visor. I needed one, that is, I wanted it, and so I bought it off of him for three dollars.

If it would stop snowing, I'd have a few pictures taken of me. We're now at this canteen where all the servicemen come. The food is good, and very inexpensive. I played some ping-pong and was beat by some master sergeant. He was very good and I enjoyed playing him. The fellows that I hang around with are all right, but I can beat them most of the time.

Your, George

April 20, 1944
Thursday

From:	To:
Mr. Pvt. J.G. Barr 11057933	C.L. Sniderman
33rd T.S.S.	65 Houghton St.
Lowry Field #1, Colorado	Worcester, 4, Mass.

Dearest Lottie,

I'm glad that you are making some G.I.'s happy, but I know another G.I., namely me, who would appreciate you more than those other boys.

After I wrote you yesterday it kept on snowing, in fact, it snowed like hell. Of course, I had my camera with me and my fingers were just itching to take some pictures. Even tho I had the color film in it, I took a chance and took some. One of the boys took three shots of me, so in about five weeks, when the pictures come back, if they come out, you'll be receiving a few snaps of me. The five weeks, of course, are beyond my control because the film has to be sent to the Kodak people for processing.

I think I'll be shipping next week. It may be to Oklahoma City, because two of the boys that washed out with me are going there Saturday, and if I hadn't been in the hospital, I would have been with them.

I got a kick out of Bev's address when she wrote you. I'll have to give her something for that, now what could I give her? Huh, a great big kiss maybe? No, I'd rather save them for you.

To-morrow I go to the firing range, this time to shot a 45-caliber pistol, it ought to be fun.

It was too bad that it rained Sunday, because I would like some pictures of you. We'll have to get the weatherman and give him a good talking to. If he wants it to rain, he has six other days to choose from.

Goodnight, darling. I'll be dreaming of you.
Your, George

April 21, 1944
Friday

From:	To:
C.L. Sniderman	Mr. Pvt. J.G. Barr 11057933
65 Houghton St.	33rd T.S.S.
Worcester 4, Mass.	Lowry Field 1, Colorado

Dearest George,

I've read your letter over all of fifty times, I think I know every word by heart, and I've come to the conclusion that it's one of the nicest letters I've ever gotten. The girls at the office say I say that about every letter I get from you, but honestly, this one was an exception. Darling, if you had said to me in person what you wrote about getting married, - I think you would have gotten yourself a wife! I really got a kick out of the way you weighed the pros and cons of getting married. I'm terribly sorry about your buddy's unhappy love affair. But doing that to a boy after being engaged for over a year, leaves me only to say that she couldn't have been very much of a girl. But enough about someone else's love life, we have our own to worry about, or if not to worry, to at least think about. What's this you write about raising a mustache! Surely you must be joking. Pleeze make nil of it, - after you take a picture. I stared & stared at your picture but just couldn't imagine you with a mustache.

George, I still haven't got it straight about what happened to your schooling. Evidently, you are not going to school, but what happens now? Another school, another camp, or what? Whatever does happen will be sure to be for the best anyhow, so let's not worry about it. But be sure to let me know any new details.

I just spoke to your mother and she told me how she mixed your bundle with the one going to Alabama. We had a good laugh, but she really felt terrible about it. She didn't say anything about Sol going into the navy so, of-course, I didn't mention it either. Every time I talk to your mother we keep saying if George is sent any nearer home we'll race down to see him, - we're still waiting and we will come down to see you, too.

My cousin Zelda took a picture of me in my uniform but alas and alack, it was a double exposure, - so I guess I'll just have to wait for Jackie. But now that you have your camera, how about some pictures post haste. Darling, how come you bought another hat with a visor, - you had one, didn't you? Or is my memory failing me! I went to the hospital last nite, but nothing unusual happed. I'm on the worst ward in the hospital. Everything from amputations to abortions. And some of those patients are really tough. Ever since I've been going to the hospital, at least one patient always looks at me and refuses to let me lift them. They always tell me to get someone else to help me, - maybe I look weak, or meek or something, I dunno! Also, I cut my finger on a glass and I happened to casually mention it to the nurse. She nearly broke a leg rushing to put antiseptic on it because she said one of the regular nurses did the same thing with a pair of scissors and she nearly got lock-jaw. Then an interne came in and she made him look at it and he happily said I'd pull through.

Here's some really good dirt. My cousin Lottie has been going out with some very jerky fellow, and now Edie Megans tells me everyone thinks it's me. She asked me if I had been ever out with Ozzie, and when I told her I didn't even know him to speak to, she proceeded to tell me that the whole town is talking. I was really very hurt at first, now I think it's funny. People will talk, damn them. Also, Edie Arnold Loiner is having a baby. She's out in California and sick as a dog, - the poor kid. But she's not the only one. The whole country is doing it. My goodness, I think this is the longest letter I ever wrote. I feel just like talking to you, and since I can't, I'm just rambling on and on about whatever comes into my head. Well, darling, I guess I've written just about enough anywho, so goodnight and pleasant dreams. Also C.Y.K.

Love, Lottie

P.S. Jest fer yer infirmation C.Y.K. means consider yourself kissed. Cute, eh?!

April 21, 1944
Friday

From:	To:
Mr. Pvt. J.G. Barr 11057933	C.L. Sniderman
33rd T.S.S.	65 Houghton St.
Lowry Field #1, Colorado	Worcester, 4, Mass.

Dearest Lottie,

I'm now eligible to ship off this field, for this morning I fired the sub-machine gun and automatic pistol. We fired the sub-machine gun just to get the feel of it. It was one of the new guns that General Motors just put out, it's about four or five pounds lighter than the other machine guns. After we fired them, we went to the pistol range. While firing the pistol, I thought for awhile that I was firing blanks, because I missed the target so many times. I took careful aim, fired, but no bullet holes appeared on the target. It gave me a funny sensation because I was only fifteen yards away. Someday I hope to learn how to fire that gun, because I'd like to know how to fire all the small arms that the army has.

Last night I went to the show and saw "Uncertain Glory." It was alright, but didn't have any action, something I expected with Errol Flynn. I guess I cannot complain, after all, it costs me a mean fifteen cents.

Would you like a set of my dog tags? I've been carrying them with me for about two months now, always going to send them to you, but for some odd reason I forgot. This time I'm going to place them in a separate envelope and send them to you.

To-night at 8:30 P.M. I'm going on K.P. You must be tired of me telling you I'm going on K.P. I'd like to have a buck for each time.

I'm writing this letter in our day room where they have a telephone. Just a few minutes ago, the phone rang for almost a minute before I got up to answer it. There are two rooms, the one I'm in is without the phone. There were four fellows in the telephone room and two fellows much closer to the phone than myself, but did they get up to answer it, no. When I did answer it, a mother was trying to get in touch with her son. The only thing I could do to help her was to put a notice on the bulletin board and give her the phone number of the orderly room. Just think what would have happened if no one had answered. She wouldn't quite know what to do since there was no answer. O.K., so I'm a boy scout.

Darling, everytime I start thinking of you I get that pang of loneliness. I wish the hell they'd hurry up with the damned invasion and get this war over with.

When you mentioned about your mother thinking back about those crazy things we used to do, I wonder how she ever stood me. Tell her for me she's wonderful.

Where do you get those clever poems? They're real cute - keep them coming - Now I must be going -

Your, George

April 22, 1944
Saturday

From:	To:
Mr. Pvt. J.G. Barr 11057933	C.L. Sniderman
33rd T.S.S.	65 Houghton St.
Lowry Field #1, Colorado	Worcester, 4, Mass.

Dearest Lottie,

I guess someone can give me a great big kick, a real swift one too, but how the hell was I supposed to know my brother Narky was coming up to Lowry Field to go to school. I may ship this coming week too, I hope that they lose my records for awhile.

Last night I became a butcher and had to cut meat for to-day's stew. When I first started, I cut the pieces so that they were small enough not to choke, but large enough to eat. When the sergeant saw me cutting the meat that way, he came over and showed me the G.I. way. The way I was cutting it he claimed, would take me all of last night and to-day to finish the job. After using his method, we finished three hours later.

I'm almost becoming a nurse's aide myself, I've been visiting the hospital most every day to see this fellow that I told you about. He's getting along fine now, and his comment about his broken engagement is that he is glad that it happened now, and not when he was over there.

Last night before we went on K.P. we went to the restaurant to get a few beers. In the booth opposite me there was a cute little girl, with whom I immediately tried to get acquainted with, but every time I smiled at her, she'd turn her head and hide her face in her best friend's shoulder. I found out later that she was just playing a game with me, and that she really liked me. She probably didn't know better, because she just passed her fourteenth birthday – the birthday was in months!!! With this parting thought that I'm still true to you.

Your, George

April 22, 1944
Sunday

From:	To:
C.L. Sniderman	Mr. Pvt. J.G. Barr 11057933
65 Houghton St.	33rd T.S.S.
Worcester 4, Mass.	Lowry Field 1, Colorado

Dearest George,
    I had a letter all written to you this afternoon but after rereading it, I decided it was the most morbid bit of writing that ever came out of my pen, and now that I feel in a better state of mind, I will give it another try. The reason for the morbidness this afternoon was that I had just finished reading a very sad story about a girl who locked herself away from love, and the fact that I was all alone didn't help either. When I'm alone I get very lonesome and when I'm lonesome I start thinking, and when I start thinking, that really is bad! But now the house is filled with company and the noise helps me concentrate. It's silly, but it's true.
    We were sitting around talking about the old times, when my family was flat broke but too proud to admit it, and my brother was just starting out in business and he didn't have a dime to his name. Altho I wouldn't say we're working on our second million now, - it's still better than it was. We even went back to the time when I was born and the nurse told my mother I was a boy and she was so disappointed and then she didn't believe it when the doctor said I was a girl. Then when I was about five or six, I went away picking apples and my mother ran over all the streets looking for me. Then when I got to the adolescent stage, my mother was terribly worried because I was so bashful. You wouldn't believe it to look at me now, but I had an inferiority complex and turned red from head to foot when someone looked at me. Thank goodness, I'm over that stage! It's fun turning back the years. My uncle just came in and kissed me goodnight. 'Twas very nice, - but I can think of someone else I'd prefer kissing me goodnite.
    Today was really a beautiful day but I was in no mood to appreciate its beauty. Now that it's gone I could kick myself. That's how it always is, - you never appreciate a thing while you have it. That even holds true with you. I never really did appreciate you while you were here. It took this damn war to make me realize how much you meant to me. Often times I could kick myself for all the time I wasted. But it really wasn't time wasted because I

was always aware of what a dear you were. You never let me forget it, - you were always doing such sweet things. Incidentally, did I ever tell you I love you, - yes? Well, I'll tell you again. Do you mind?!!

I was also looking through a magazine today and this issue was devoted to boy and girls considering marriage. It said that a boy should never consider marrying a girl until he's tasted her coffee, and if the coffee is no good, the marriage is off. Which reminds me, did you ever taste my coffee, - it really is delish!! It also said that a girl should always be nice to her future husband's friends, but not too nice, because it always breeds trouble!! It was really a very cute article, - also very foolish, but fun.

I'm enclosing a few examples of brides, and if you say I look like Frankenstein's Bride, - well, I'll, I'll, I'll be mad atch you!! You nasty man. And with this parting thought I take leave. Goodnite, dear and take care.

Love, Lottie

April 23, 1944
Sunday

From:	To:
Mr. Pvt. J.G. Barr 11057933	C.L. Sniderman
33rd T.S.S.	65 Houghton St.
Lowry Field #1, Colorado	Worcester, 4, Mass.

Dearest Lottie,

I really don't know what to write, I haven't done a darn thing to-day, but I just am not in the mood to write. All that was in my head to-day was you. I'm in that lonesome mood again. Lottie, darling, I miss you terribly.

The next day:----

I had to leave you last night dear, because a fellow to whom I owed money to, came to see me. I paid him and then we talked for awhile, meanwhile the lights went out.

After receiving letters from you and Polly, I felt much better. Darling, I love you, and I wish I were home so that I could ask you to be my ever loving wife. If you miss me like I miss you (and I think you do – right?), then you know how I feel not being able to see you, to hold you in my arms, and not to be able to do the little things a guy likes to do for his one and only. You see, sweet, I miss you. It is just like when you feel like having something and it seems that you'll never be the same until you get it, sometimes it will be a coke, a banana split, or a malted, what I need is you!

Polly wrote me a few addresses, so this afternoon I called a Mrs. Triefus. She is one of those people you talk to and it seems as if you've known her for years and years. She was very nice, and asked me to come and see her when I could. I told her I would if I could, but if I couldn't, I'd give Narky her address and he could do the honors for me. Polly also gave me a few addresses of some Denver girls. Think I'll look them up and say hello. Jealous?

To-day I worked in the supply room, but no matter how hard I looked, I couldn't find anything that I could "borrow", darn it. If I could get jobs like this every day, it wouldn't be bad at all – it wouldn't.

Last night I saw "Tampico," pretty good, something a bit off the war, but enough in it to let you know that we were still at war. In comparison to the last few shows here, it was damn good.

K.P. again to-morrow morning – enough said. I wrote you the complete story on school, but if there are still some doubts, let me know what they are and I'll be glad to enlighten you.

The other night after I finished writing some letters at the Service Club, I was about to leave (they were having a date dance), I spied a girl near the door. Every once in awhile, she'd look over her shoulder looking for her date, or husband. When I was walking out the orchestra started to play "Time Was" and I felt like dancing when I heard it, so I asked her if she would care to dance this one until her partner came. She cringed up against the wall and said no she didn't think so. I bide her good night and left. All she had to do to get rid of me was just to say no, and not back up against the wall until I thought she was molded into it. Life, and its disappointments – ah huh!

Thanks for the C.Y.K and the same and many of them to you.

Your, George

P.S. This pen is absolutely no good, my good one is on the way to the factory to be fixed. Good one, that's a laugh. J.G.B.

April 25, 1944
Tuesday

From:	To:
C.L. Sniderman	Mr. Pvt. J.G. Barr 11057933
65 Houghton St.	33rd T.S.S.
Worcester 4, Mass.	Lowry Field 1, Colorado

Dearest George,

I nearly fell dead when I opened your envelope today and found the dog tags. Since the letters didn't come until later in the day I couldn't imagine why you sent them. I had heard of girls getting everything under the sun, -

but never dog tags, so for some odd reason I was worried. My mother said I turned white as a ghost when I saw them. But now that I know everything is O.K., I can take time out to thank you for them. If you're wondering what I'm doing with them, well, I'm doing the same thing you did, - I've got them around my neck!

So, you were smiling at a girl, eh. Nice and considerate of you to set my mind at ease by telling me her age. I should have known better. Speaking of babies, I went to visit my nephew, Rickie, tonight. He is really beautiful. George, it's the best feeling in the world when you have a baby in your arms and he cuddles his head against your shoulder. Someday........!! My brother just called to see if I got home O.K. That guy is really a panic. Everytime I see him he keeps giving me a drink and swears to hell because I'm his sister! Whatta guy! He keeps saying, - quote – Do ya really think George would mind, - unquote.

I'm glad you like my bits of poetry. I send you everything that I think you'd like. So tonight, I'm enclosing another.

I'm sitting here writing you practically Lottie ala nude. I don't know why the hell I'm so hot. The dog tags keep tickling me. Now all the girls down the office want their boyfriend's dog tags. Me thinks you started something. Goodnite, dear.

Love, Lottie

Darling

I know you miss me when you're at a bar,
And someone's humming "Journey to a Star,"
And someone's girl is using Shalimar . . .
I know you miss me.

I know you miss me when you're One of Three,
And Two go dancing to a rhapsody,
And leave you staring at a Daiquiri . . .
I know you miss me.

I know you miss me when Sinatra sings,
And when they're playing any song of Bing's,
Or if they're zinging "Holiday for Strings" . . .
I know you miss me.

But when the endless, friendless night is due . . .
I miss you too!

—Madonna.

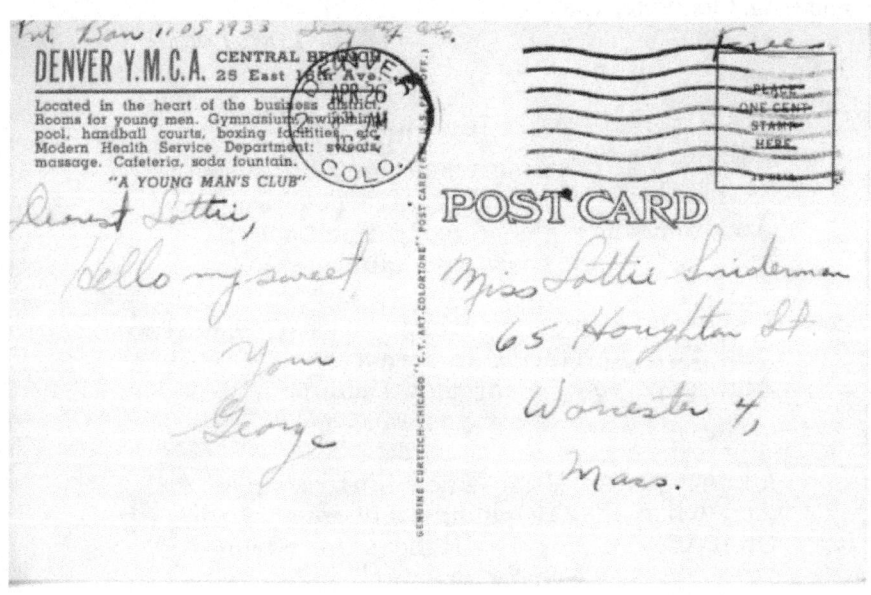

April 25, 1944
Tuesday

From:	To:
Mr. Pvt. J.G. Barr 11057933	C.L. Sniderman
33rd T.S.S.	65 Houghton St.
Lowry Field #1, Colorado	Worcester, 4, Mass.

April 25, 1944
Tuesday

Dearest Lottie,

I'm in town at the Y.M.C.A, I just came back from visiting the Mr. & Mrs. I told you about. I can now definitely state that they are very nice people. They have an apartment in one of Denver's nicest hotels, which at the end of the month, runs into something a bit more than chicken feed.

While talking to them Mrs. Triefus gave me a bourbon and soda, this must have loosened my tongue because I kept up a steady patter. I visited them just a short while because they were about to leave on a dinner date.

When Narky comes here, they want the both of us to come up so that they can take us out for dinner. Very nice people. Also, was shown a picture of their daughter, Polly's friend, nice too, and it seems like lots of dough. If I didn't have you, maybe I could become interested, but she passed out of my head just as quick as it entered. The only thoughts of love that I have are for you – don't forget it.

Darling, I love you, and love you, and love you. See what I mean? I'm just crazy about you.

This afternoon I received a tremendous bundle from my folks, but it seems half is for me, and half is for Narky, when he comes. He better hurry up or there won't be any of his half left.

On K.P. to-day I had a barrel of fun. The job I had was simple – dishing out milk to the officers, and at noon time I gave out what the cook called a Perfection Salad. To me it was a fancy dish of jello! The way he made it tho, it looked very pretty. The jello was made in a large cake pan, turned over on lettuce leaves and slices of lemon, sprinkled with paprika, and on the top, he decorated it with salad dressing. Most of the comments of the officers were – "Getting pretty fancy!" They were very surprised. I couldn't blame them. Although the cook had named the salad already, we gave it the "Penthouse Pattes Holiday's Delight" and "Lowry Field Delight."

When the first WAC officer came up, I asked her, wouldn't she like to know how to make it, she said she certainly would. I had been given strict orders to give one slice to each person and that if more than on piece was given, I'd be in the mess hall until six o'clock to-night, so when another WAC asked, "May I have two pieces?" I answered, "No, you may not." She looked very hurt, but walked away without saying anything.

Then a Lt. Colonel walked up, with a chest full of ribbons, signifying that he was an old army man. When he saw the jello, he stared at it, looked at me, but with the expression, "Sissy food!" and walked away without a word. I laughed like hell at that, I hope he didn't look around, some of those boys can get rough if they want to. I hope they send me my pen back in a hurry, because as you can see, this one is no good for anything.

It's raining cats and dogs here, I'm all alone, so I think I'll take in a movie. Very exciting evening ahead! I could go dancing, but the girls there, being girls, remind me of you, and after dancing, I just get the most lonesome feeling for you. This is a hellava world!

Take care darling, because I love you,
Your, George

April 26, 1944
Wednesday

From:	To:
Mr. Pvt. J.G. Barr 11057933	C.L. Sniderman
33rd T.S.S.	65 Houghton St.
Lowry Field #1, Colorado	Worcester, 4, Mass.

Dearest Lottie,

Yes, darling, you can tell the milkman and the paperboy to deliver their merchandise to the 487 Service Sq., 11th Service Group, Tinker Field, Oklahoma City, Oklahoma.

We are shipping Friday, so you can start addressing my letters there. I haven't heard anything from Narky, as yet, I hope he gets here before I leave.

About my hat, the one that I had, I sold when I was still down in New Orleans because we couldn't wear them down there, so when this fellow needed dough, me like a good boy, bought it off of him at a steal.

Of course, since it rained yesterday and I didn't take my camera with me, the sun came out and it was beautiful - you cannot win.

This was the first time that I was in town by myself and it made me feel lonely as hell. When I get to Tinker Field, I'll have a few fellows that I know, so it won't be so bad, I hope.

Went to the hospital again to-night. This time I talked the nurse into giving the boys a can of cold tomato juice, since I was leaving and I wouldn't be able to bother her anymore. The ward boy came over after I had filled our glasses, and asked if we were having a private stag party.

Good night, my darling, I'm a bit tired to-night, why I don't know, I haven't done a darn thing all day. Loads of love from me to you.

Your, George

April 28, 1944
Friday

From:	To:
Mr. Pvt. J.G. Barr 11057933	C.L. Sniderman
33rd T.S.S.	65 Houghton St.
Lowry Field #1, Colorado	Worcester, 4, Mass.

Dearest Lottie,

I received two letters from you yesterday and they were swell. The two little inserts were very nice, keep em coming.

Last night I went to the movies with this fellow and his wife. They are both very nice people. I've known him since Philly and also his wife. They both came from Boston. We've been on very good terms ever since Philly. In fact, whenever my mother sends me a bundle with some home cooking in it, I save a little and give it to them. Because of that, I guess they think I'm a pretty nice guy. When I said good bye to them, Marcia insisted on kissing me. I told her that you'd be angry, but she said you wouldn't because you are a swell girl. You see they know all about you, why shouldn't they, you are the only one I ever talk about.

After the movie, I went over to the troop movement section to see if Narky's train was coming in last night or to-day. They had a few shipments coming in, but not from Santa Ana, so I guess I've missed him. Why the hell couldn't they have kept me here a few more days? And just two days from pay day too - the stinkers!

I felt pretty badly last night after calling up everyone, saying good bye, and with missing Narky. I was invited to two dinners that I had to postpone! One from Polly's girlfriend's parents, and one from Polly's girlfriend's girlfriend. I went up to her house on my afternoon off. We talked and played ping-pong. She beat me too, go ahead and laugh, beat by a girl!

It just started to pour outside, and here I am at the service club without a raincoat. It better stop pretty damn quick or else I'll get soaking wet.

Did I tell you I was put in charge of the men who are shipping with me? Yup, I'm going to be a big shot. The reason they chose me is clear to see, of course. I have the ability and the leadership (I would be more sure of myself had my name been in the center of the list, and not right on top.)

Until Tinker Field my darling,
Your, George

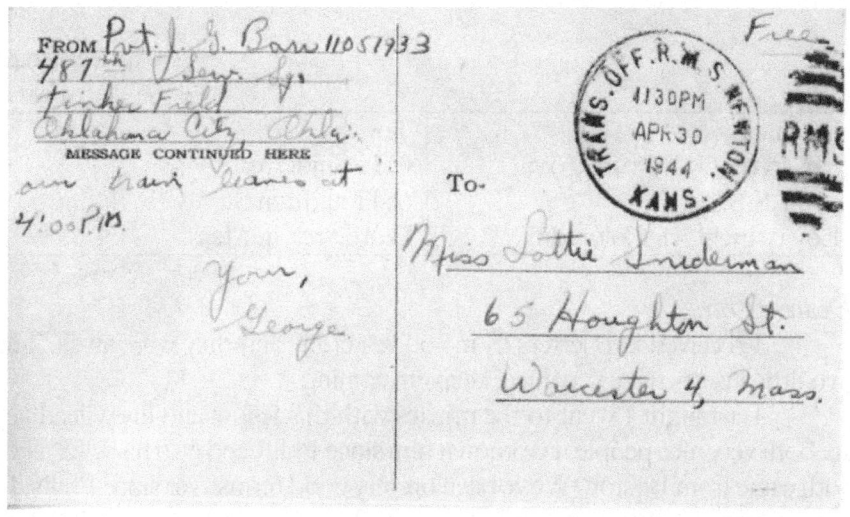

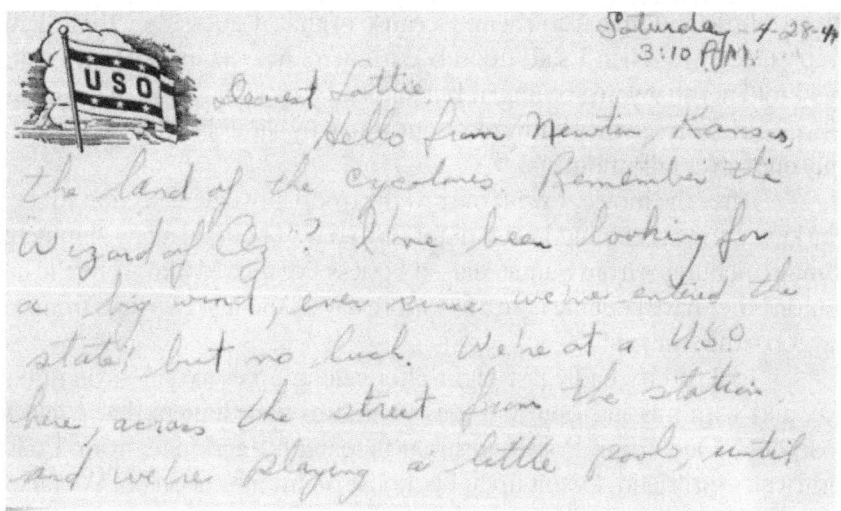

April 30, 1944
Saturday

From:	To:
C.L. Sniderman	Mr. Pvt. J.G. Barr 11057933
65 Houghton St.	33rd T.S.S.
Worcester 4, Mass.	Lowry Field 1, Colorado

Hi honey,

So now Oklahoma has you, - that's fine except I wish you were nearer home. But who can tell, if you can't come here, I may get an urge to come there. I have already inquired about the train fare. Altho it's not too much, it's an awful lot when you haven't got it. But who can tell what the future brings! I had a most exciting day today (ha – big joke). I met Barb for lunch, then had my hair done, it looks very nice incidentally, then took me mater to supper, and then Edie Megans and I went visiting her aunt who is also my adopted aunt. Edith and I definitely decided that being dateless is not very good for our morale. But there are times when I don't even mind it. Poor Edie, she is really in a bad way. Wish I could help her out, but my sex prevents me from making her happy. Or at least happy the way she wants to be. I just finished reading the most darling story. Twas all about the Stewarts, a young married couple, who got along just fine and dandy because he never objected to her having breakfast in bed Sunday mornings. I like that idea, too!

Today was simply grand. Real summer like. I felt just like doing nothing, - so I did. Very strenuous! I wish I had a whole pile of dirt to tell you, but I haven't. Only thing new is that Evelyn Labarsky, Jackie's wife of a few months, is gonna have an heir. They're very happy about it, so I am too. Who am I to complain? They're playing "I Love You" on the radio, which reminds me that I do love you, so there.

This is really a very ridiculous letter. I don't know what's the matter with me. I feel like writing, but I haven't anything to say. I'm an awful problem to myself. Will do better tomorrow, honest.

Love, Lottie

May 1, 1944
Monday

From:	To:
C.L. Sniderman	Mr. Pvt. J.G. Barr 11057933
65 Houghton St.	487 Serv. Sq., 11th Serv. Grp.
Worcester 4, Mass.	Tinker Field, Oklahoma City,
	Oklahoma

Hello hon,

Your friends entertained me royally all day yesterday. Jackie W., Sol Zitowitz, Charlie Freedman, and a cousin of Jackie's came over yesterday to take me riding. The day was simply luscious and it was just right for riding in an open car, Charlie's car. We went riding and Jackie had no trouble at all taking a picture of me. I hope they come out good. I'll send them to you post haste. Then we went bowling, my score at bowling I shall not tell you, because I'm thoroughly ashamed. As far as bowling is concerned, I'd better stick to -...... Well, I'll find something to stick to. Then we gorged ourselves on spaghetti at the Parkway. Then we went over Jackie's to look at his colored pictures, which are beautiful. Then Charlie, Sol, and I went down to Loipoon's for ice-cream. I felt in a super mood all day yesterday and all we did was laugh. I really had a very nice time. And that my dear, - was my day! Oh, yes, I also made some candy yesterday. I didn't make very much because it was the first time, but it really came out very good, so one of these days I'll make some more for you. How would you like to sample my culinary exhibits? Fancy, eh?!!

Those married people you wrote me about sound swellegant. And since any friends of yours are friends of mine, I consider them bosom pals. Remind me to invite them to our palacial little house of twenty rooms for a week-end. And why shouldn't they think you're a pretty nice guy, - I think so, so that makes you tops. Any arguments, - there better not be!

I received a charming invitation from a man about two years younger than God today to go fishing. Sure, I can just picture myself. He'll probably drown me yet, too. For myself, I don't care, but I don't think my mother or you would like it if I got drownededed!! Speaking of mishaps, I almost forgot to tello thee that I was hit by an automobile today. I was walking back to the office from lunch hour today, my mind miles away, when all of a sudden I heard wheels' shriek and then I felt a bump. He didn't knock me over just scraped my legs. I was too dazed to even get scared. Jest brushed meself off and trotted on while he sat there swearing to high heaven. De jerk!

Your mother just called and told me they got a telegram from Narky. We've been wondering if you two met by any chance. Well, darling, I wish I could write pages more, but I'm stuck for writing material so with fond regards, best wishes and etc., etc., etc. I close with all my love,

Lottie

The Trouble With Men

There may perhaps be other loves
As all my friends believe
And I have promised not to wear
My heart out on my sleeve.

I will agree that other men
May have their good points, too,
The trouble with those others is
Not one of them is you!

May 1, 1944
Monday

From:	To:
Mr. Pvt. J.G. Barr 11057933 487 Serv. Sq., 11th Serv. Grp. Tinker Field, Oklahoma City, Oklahoma	C.L. Sniderman 65 Houghton St. Worcester, 4, Mass.

OKLAHOMA CITY AIR DEPOT
TINKER FIELD
OKLAHOMA CITY, OKLAHOMA

Dearest Lottie,

When we came here, we found that our outfits were not here. My squadron is at Great Bend, Kansas. As soon as there are enough men, about thirty, we are going to go there, meanwhile, we'll just hang around, maybe do a little detail work, but I doubt it.

Our train was five hours late coming in, so we had very little sleep yesterday. About ten o'clock we went into town, walked around for awhile and then had dinner. Later we went to see "A Guy Called Joe." I liked it. While walking, I stopped at every drug and camera store trying to buy some film, but always I received the same answer.

We took a few shots and when they are developed I'll send them. The other pictures I owe you are spread around a bit. One is still in San Antonio and the other is in Denver. The fellow that took it in Denver is home on an emergency furlough, so until I can contact him, I won't be able to get it. If you can find some 120 film, please send it to me.

This morning I went to see if we could get a little money because, as yet, we haven't been paid, and at this time we are all broke. I was going to wire my father for money, but it would start to become a habit, because I did that twice in about a month and a half. I'm going to go back to-morrow to see what they can do, because to-day the whole base is getting paid and they were too busy to do anything to-day.

Hold on to your hat! While walking along the street yesterday, who should I bump into but Pip Sobel! He looked swell, except he needed a shave. The other sailor he was with had left his hat at the U.S.O., so we went back to get it. While at the U.S.O. I met about eight of the boys that I knew down in New Orleans. It was old home week for me yesterday, and I had made a remark earlier that with so many people walking the streets, I should meet someone that I knew. Pip and I are going to try and get to-gether Thursday, if possible. He isn't going to be here long either.

One of the other boys, the one that loaned me money when I came home, invited me to go to church with him last night. I went just to see what they did. It was held in the basement of the church, where they served coffee and coke. From there we went to the song room and we sang praises of Jesus! Then we went to a bible class. Here they discussed phrases from the bible and collected some dough for a present for some one of their gang that had been inducted. Before class started they passed out slips of paper that had printed on them percentages of what you attained that week. The first one was 10% for attending class, 10% for being there on time, 10% for studying, a few more and <u>then</u> 15% for giving to the church. I got 20% for being there, and on time. I guess I'm just a heathen.

But when they were going up to hear the sermon, I quit and went home. For awhile it proved interesting, but religion never did interest me too much anyway.

I'm going to see if I can get my pass now and get out of camp. Good afternoon my sweet.

Your, George

May 4, 1944
Thursday

From:	To:
Mr. Pvt. J.G. Barr 11057933	C.L. Sniderman
4503rd Eng. Sq. A.B.B.	65 Houghton St.
Great Bend, Kansas	Worcester, 4, Mass.

Dearest Lottie,

I don't know where to start, the good part or the bad part.

I'll start at the worst. This field is the worst field yet. We're going to live in huts on a flat open plain, where the wind just roars across the horizon. This is Kansas, the land of wheat – why in the hell didn't they plant wheat here instead of an airfield? The P.X. service club and movies are a fifteen minute walk and even when you get there, there isn't a hell of a lot. Town is about seven miles or less from here – population: about 10,000.

We haven't any idea what we're going to do here or why. I hope that they'll at least show me a radio. We don't have one in our hut.

While walking to and from P.X., I thought of a few cracks that I could have made at the field, it really could be worse, but now that I'm writing, it has slipped my very forgetful mind.

I think I lost it to-day, my mind, because after we got off the bus I left my small bag on it. In it was a pair of my glasses and two pair of G.I. glasses, my shaving kit, and all my clean underwear. I don't mind that so much, but I had two O'Henry bars in there also, and you know how hard they are to get!!!

When we left Oklahoma City, we left on a bus (army) at about 6:30 A.M. and came here at about 5:30 P.M. We stopped a few times. I bought two rolls of film, had some one take a picture of me, so that's another one I owe you. All the time while on the bus we played poker and I managed to win about six or seven dollars. "In every life, a little sunshine will fall!"

When I was down at the P.X., I called the next field where the bus was going and asked them to see if they could get in touch with the driver or one of the fellows on the bus and have the driver bring it back, if he has to come thru here again, or have one of the boys send it to me. That isn't what makes me mad tho – I didn't send you a telegram at Okla. City, I was broke, but now that I got paid; well darling, I hope you can forgive me. I honestly don't know what is wrong with me to-day.

Darling, you'll have to excuse this letter to-day, I know it is very bad. To-morrow a better one, O.K?

Your, George

P.S. Write me at:

    4503 Base Unit Service Group
    Engineering Squadron (Sp) Sect. J.
    Great Bend A.A.B
    Great Bend, Kansas

It took three of us to remember all of that! J.G.B.

May 5, 1944
Friday

From:	To:
Mr. Pvt. J.G. Barr 11057933	C.L. Sniderman
Eng. Sq., 4503rd A.A.F. Base Unit	65 Houghton St.
Great Bend A.B.B., Kansas	Worcester, 4, Mass.

UNITED STATES ARMY AIR FORCES   *May 5, 1944*

Dearest Lottie,

    After taking a walk to the service club, I thought I'd better write you from here, rather than the hut, with paper on my knee and smoke in my eyes.

    To-day we found out that we are overages in this squadron, they don't want us. So, off we'll be just as soon as they get ready. While talking to the officer, I asked him what he thought my chances were of going to a photography school and he said he'd find out. He took my name and wrote photography down beside it, so I know that at least he will try and find out. He seemed like a pretty good scout, and asked us how Lowry field was. We found out that he had gone thru C.F.C. school, and washed back at one time, now he is in charge of all the C.F.C. men.

    Last night it was cold as hell here, to keep warm, at least I tried, I rolled up like a cubby bear in the blankets. In the morning, one of the boys woke me for breakfast, but he thought he was shaking my shoulder, when it was my knee.

    We've been hanging around since, but we'll probably be on some detail very soon.

    There's a dance in town to-night, to which we expect to go. This will be our first chance to see it, but most of the places are restricted to soldiers, because of lack of staff. They won't sell beer to a soldier at all, because if they did they wouldn't have any for their regular trade and the boys can get all they want at the P.X.

Darling, I miss you, I've been trying to think of ways to tell you how much, but it doesn't come out in words. I just miss you, and I guess that's all. Love is a strange and wonderful thing and I'm glad that I have it. I think that to reach extreme happiness, you have to love someone and someone loves you.

Your, George

May 7, 1944
Sunday

From:	To:
Mr. Pvt. J.G. Barr 11057933	C.L. Sniderman
Eng. Sq., 4503rd A.A.F. Base Unit	65 Houghton St.
Great Bend A.B.B., Kansas	Worcester, 4, Mass.

Dearest Lottie,

Darling, I'm sending you a small package – now, before I run out of money, and it will be safer at home than it would be with me. I'm going to ask you not to open it before your birthday tho, O.K?

We just walked around the town, to their park, and just wondering. I thought maybe I'd be able to take some pictures, but there wasn't anything of interest that any other small town didn't have, so I had one picture of myself taken and I took one of one of the boys.

The dance that I went to proved to be a failure. The girls here seem to be a bunch of snobs in a funny sort of a way. I don't think that they've really been around and when the camp was built here and the soldiers came into the town, it just spoiled them. I guess they're not used to so many men at one time. I know that I felt very much out of place there. I know that if I don't meet any nice people pretty soon, I'm going to stay in camp all the time.

I received six letters at mail call and now I owe a few people letters, but for some reason or other, I don't seem to be able to get them written. One is from my cousin Anne Joselowitz, she had sent it to San Antonio and I got it a day ago. It's been almost two months ago that it was mailed. She writes me that she'd like to meet you. Sometime when you are down town, why don't you drop in and say hello. She works at the Shoe Box on Front Street, across the street from Shacks. She's a swell girl and I'm sure you'd like her and her you. How could anyone but help liking you anyway.

At camp, we haven't been doing anything, but are just waiting for them to catch up with us. I wish they'd hurry up and ship us out of here, since they don't want us, let them send us out of here.

At the park, they had two monkeys, me being a good fellow gave each one a cigarette. They ripped the paper off and ate the tobacco. I wanted to light one and see if they'd smoke it, but the boys stopped me, gee a guy never can have any fun.

How's spring coming along back home, are the trees green yet? Good bye for to-day, honey.

Your, George

May 8, 1944
Monday

From:	To:
Mr. Pvt. J.G. Barr 11057933	C.L. Sniderman
Eng. Sq., 4503rd A.A.F. Base Unit	65 Houghton St.
Great Bend A.B.B., Kansas	Worcester, 4, Mass.

Dearest Lottie,

Hello sweet, I'm writing this from our day room. In it we have some writing tables and a ping-pong table. Some of the boys are playing now, can't you hear them? Ping-pong-ping-pong, awful monotonous, isn't it? Maybe I'll play a few games before I go back to the hut.

A little while back we went on a small scale march, four miles over a nice flat highway. All the boys except my bunch wore field packs. The reason for our luck was that back at Lowry Field, they took our field equipment away from us. We were glad to get rid of it then and happier now. I didn't mind the hike in the least, in fact, a few times a week in nice weather is O.K. with me.

At mail call to-day I received a letter from the boys up at Vitoria, Kans. – the other half of our group, and he said that they found my bag and turned it into the supply room, who in turn will forward it to me, eventually.

This morning I felt pretty good because I answered a few of my overdue letters. They keep piling up on me tho because this afternoon I received some more that I have to answer as soon as I can. I have an insured package down at the main post office that I have to pick up to-morrow. I wonder what I got? Also, I received a letter from an R. Lisabitsky, I didn't know who the hell it could be. I didn't want to open it up, because then it would have been very simple, so I thought and I thought, until I finally got it. It was my cousin Rose, formerly, Barr. I can't remember my own family, what a guy!

I thought I'd go to the show to-night, but I've already seen the picture, so I think I'll stay in and read. I got a book on photography from the library and I guess I'd better read up on it if I want to take some good pictures.

I'm written out darling, so you'll have to wait until to-morrow, good night.

Your, George

May 9, 1944
Tuesday

From:	To:
C.L. Sniderman	Mr. Pvt. J.G. Barr 11057933
65 Houghton St.	Eng. Sq., 4503rd A.A.F. Base Unit
Worcester 4, Mass.	Great Bend A.B.B., Kansas

Dearest George,

It's been so long since I've written you, that it seems I have a million and one things to tell you. First let me tell you what a shock it was to learn you weren't staying in Oklahoma, but were going to Kansas. Well, now that you are there, here's hoping you'll get to like it. Your last letter sounded very unenthused, but it's always like that when you get to a new place. Incidentally, did you get your bag back after leaving it on the bus? That was a shame, you poor kid. Have you heard anything more about photography school?

Well, now I'll start on me and my great doings. Last Friday nite Jackie Waxler came over with Sol Zitowitz to bring over the pictures they took of me. But as you can see, I'm not enclosing them. They were simply awful, - so I took another chance at it. They ought to be ready shortly and I'll send them to you. Saturday afternoon Jackie and I played tennis and then Jackie took me to supper and the movies. After the movies, Jackie and I had two beers, and altho I tried my darnest to conceal it, I was drunk. I felt very peculiar all over, - awful feeling! But I really had a very nice time.

Sunday I had planned to stay in but Toby called and we went walking. It was a beautiful day or at least started to be. Midway into our walk it started to rain, and since we were near your house we went up. I finally got all my letters back, while I was up there I happened to think of it, so I took them and some great kick I got out of reading them. Then we started for the A.Z.A. rooms for a game of ping-pong, but when passing thru Water St., we decided we were hungry so Tobye insisted on buying me my supper at Ritz's [Editor's note: Ritz's refers to the Slonimsky & Ritz Delicatessen, located on 156 Water St. in downtown Worcester]. I was really angry because altho it was very sweet of her, I hated for her to spend the money on me. Then we stopped in your store and your folks wanted us to go to the farm with them, but Tobye didn't want to so we went up the rooms and played ping-pong and danced.

By this time, it was pouring so we took a cab home. I really enjoyed every minute of Sunday. Tobye is really an awfully sweet kid. And that was my weekend. Last nite my cousin Zelda had a shower at her house. It was very nice and she got a lot of nice gifts. Last nite I decided definitely that I would never make a good actress. Someone had to be toast mistress and I was unanimously elected. I got up to make my unprepared speech and my knees were shaking so that I could hardly stand. Later my mother said I became so pale she thought I would faint. But I finally got thru it and ended by toasting to myself and hoping that I'd be next, - this brought the house down and after that everyone asked me when I was getting married. My mother was beaming all over the place because everyone came over to tell her what a nice girl I was and a few more very flattering remarks. I got more compliments last nite than I have for a long time. Also at the shower was your cousin Evelyn Snider. I thought she knew I was going with you, but when she asked who my boyfriend was, I knew she didn't. When I told her she nearly fell over and exclaimed, "Then you must be Lottie!" This struck me very funny. She's an awfully nice person, - and so now we're pals.

Also, Saturday nite I met an old boyfriend of mine from Spencer. He said he had wanted to call me several times but he had heard I was married to a guy by the name of George Barr. Some fun, - I wonder who starts things like that. I got a letter from my sister in law in Washington and she's heard so much about you she would like to drop you a letter, so I'm going to send her your address, O.K? O.K.

I think I had wrote you that Dave asked me to send him some Fannie Farmers. He said he felt awful asking for them, but since you were like a brother to him and I was so close to you that makes me almost Dave's sister. Soooo, I'm sending him some Fannie Farmers, - what can ya do with a guy like that.

I'm trying to get you some film, dear, I've got my name on the waiting list and should get some next week. My goodness, I sure think this should make up for all the time I didn't write. And while I'm about it, I might as well wish you a very, very, very happy birthday, darling. I hope next year I can have a personal part in making your birthday a happy one.

Goodnite, dear,
Lottie

May 9, 1944
Tuesday

From:	To:
Mr. Pvt. J.G. Barr 11057933	C.L. Sniderman
Eng. Sq., 4503rd A.A.F. Base Unit	65 Houghton St.
Great Bend A.B.B., Kansas	Worcester, 4, Mass.

Dearest Lottie,

Thank you my darling, for your most wonderful present. I don't know where you got it, I thought it was an impossibility nowadays, but the case is the best present I've ever received on my birthday. When I started to open the package, I had two of the boy's sing Happy Birthday. The sun was out and when it struck the case it just shone, it really is beautiful. Now I know why you are broke. Thanks a million. They don't come any better than you, Lottie darling. I had the funniest sensation in the pit of my stomach when I saw what you had bought for me. I just wanted to rush to you and hold you in my arms eternally.

Yes, my dear, they have finally caught up with me, for to-morrow morning when most everyone else is sleeping, I'll be on K.P. The work should not be too hard because there will not be any dishes or trays to wash, because the boys eat out of mess kits.

I wanted to go to town to-night to see if my film was ready, but I'll have to let it go for to-night. But just as soon as I do get them, I'll send them right out to you.

After writing to you yesterday afternoon I did play ping-pong, but got very badly beat. The boys here certainly can bat that little ball around. I'll have to play them more often, maybe I'll be able to improve after a length of time.

There isn't anything else to write about, nothing new has developed about us, the weather has remained unchanged, and I haven't done anything so this is it.

Now every time I light a cigarette, I'll see your face in the flame, thanks again.

Your ever loving, George

May 11, 1944
Thursday

From:	To:
C.L. Sniderman	Mr. Pvt. J.G. Barr 11057933
65 Houghton St.	Eng. Sq., 4503rd A.A.F. Base Unit
Worcester 4, Mass.	Great Bend A.B.B., Kansas

Hi honey,

I can't begin to tell you how happy I am that you received and liked your birthday gift. I felt terrible because I had mailed it to Oklahoma and I was sure you wouldn't get it in time, but all's well that ends well, and I hope you use it in the very best of health. And now I have a complaint to make. You've aroused my curiosity something terrible by telling me you sent me something and not saying what it was, but whatever it is I know I'll love it, - only I'm angry at you for sending me anything. Darling, I know you haven't got the extra money to spend and I'd love you just as much if you had sent me a card. You're really a dear.

I just got back from the hospital and I'm dead tired. I worked in the nursery today and loved it. One father came to take his wife and baby home, - you never saw anyone so proud in your life. The baby was really beautiful, - wish it was mine. Then a funny little soldier came to the window and wanted to see his offspring. The baby was really homely – really homely, but to that guy it has the face of an angel, - and who can blame him. There are really some characters up there.

I went to an office party last nite at Cosgrove's and had a super duper time. The Sharfman's were really a riot, - all they kept calling me was the Vamp. Norman Sharfman got me in a corner and the remarks he made were quite embarrassing, - but he insisted I should be proud!! Also, he danced with me, - I was the only girl he danced with, - ho hum! Saul Sharfman insisted on taking me home, and I refused because I wanted to get home. Everyone said I was a dope for not going with him because since he had had a few drinks he was very generous and, - a mink coat wouldn't look at all bad on me. I was razzed to hell at the office today. I was really honored and flattered by their attention, no kidding. Well, darling, I guess I'd better retire for the evening. They're playing "Smoke Gets in Your Eyes", - and you know me when I hear a soft dreamy tune.

With Love, Lottie

May 11, 1944
Thursday

From:	To:
Mr. Pvt. J.G. Barr 11057933	C.L. Sniderman
Eng. Sq., 4503rd A.A.F. Base Unit	65 Houghton St.
Great Bend A.B.B., Kansas	Worcester, 4, Mass.

Dearest Lottie,

Last night after I came off of K.P., I laid on my bunk and rested. After I rested I was going to write you, but I fell asleep, guess I'm a lazy good for nothing.

When I did get up, I took a shower. This was the first time I've taken a shower with a dog tho. A few of the boys have dogs here and they treat them just as if they were their children. When the fellow took the dog out of the shower, he wrapped him up in his towel.

Monday, we are scheduled to go out on bivouac for about a week or so. We're going to have to rough it. There are going to be two planes coming out to us, that's after we clear a landing strip. One will bring mail, the other one is going to gas us.

Our C.O. told us he didn't want us to ride the farmer's horses, milk their cows, but to be especially sure and leave the sheep alone.

When I came out of the latrine last night it started raining, I had my pants in my hand, I was too lazy to put them on, so when I started to run my change fell out of my pockets. I ran back to my hut, put my rain coat on, got my flashlight, and went back for the treasure hunt. I didn't do badly at all. I came back with a loot of eighty cents.

I even learned how to use our squadron washing machine. There's nothing to it, you put water in it, soap suds, and turn a knob and the machine does the rest. When we are settled, I'll buy you a washing machine so you won't have to scrub the clothes in the wash basin.

In yesterday's mail I received a letter from Sid Plotkin, I'm sending it to you so you can read it too. He seems to have a pretty nice set up considering that he is overseas. If I ever get sent across, I'll probably have to live in a tree or a fox hole. Will you still love me then, when I'll need a shave, and be dirty and grimy? I'll still love you, I'll always love you.

I haven't heard from you in a long time now, I hope those dumb jerks in the post office get on the ball and deliver all that mail (I hope) that they owe me. This moving from place to place really screws up the works.

I almost forgot, while shaving yesterday I looked in the mirror once too often. I never did like a moustache anyway. Off it came zip, zip, zip, maybe it took another zip, but it is off, good rid of bad rubbish, and that is what it looked like.

I don't know what's the matter is, but I cannot fill both sides of this paper anymore, it seems. I'm going to have to write larger, that's all there is to it.

Your, George

May 14, 1944
Sunday

From:	To:
Mr. Pvt. J.G. Barr 11057933	C.L. Sniderman
Eng. Sq. 4503rd Base Unit	65 Houghton St.
Great Bend A.B.B., Kansas	Worcester, 4, Mass.

Dearest Lottie,

Tho it's been two days since I've written you, it seems like ages. I could kick myself for getting so far behind. The main reason was our preparing for the bivouac. The preparation has kept us quite busy. Now I see why wars take so long in winning, and we definitely are going to win. This afternoon it was quite a picnic in our hut. We all started making our packs in readiness for to-morrow morning. Each seemed to have different ideas in the correct rolling, it proved out later that most of us were wrong. Then when they were all rolled we each tried them on to see how they felt. – Heavy as hell. It's rumored we'll have to walk between fifteen to thirty miles with them on. If I can go five, I'll be doing good.

We'll be up at 4:30 A.M. to start our day, after eating breakfast we'll go on trucks for about four or five hours, then march until we hit the bivouac area. Very nice day planned for us, don't you think so? A ride, a walk, very pleasant.

This morning while pleasantly and serenely sleeping, I awoke to the sensation of something licking my hand. Without opening my eyes, I just rolled over and tried to go back to sleep, withdrawing my hand under the blankets. I really got up when I felt a tongue on my neck, I was just realizing that every thing wasn't just right in Denmark, or someplace, all it was, of course, was a little puppy dog that one of the boys brought in. I played with him a minute or two, not more, put him on the floor and slept until lunch time.

It has been hot as hell the last two days, I bet I've sweated out as much water as I've drunk. – Talking about stew beans, my love, you'll have to get drunk on at least three beers, it takes me that many, and if we're ever going to get drunk together, I don't want to see you get drunk before me!

Your last letter was a pip. I got a big kick out of, "So, you must be Lottie," who the hell did she think you were?

I just came from seeing, "Andy Hardy's Love Trouble," I had a good laugh through out the entire picture. It's something to see, don't miss it. One of the best Hardy series that I've seen, besides, the blonde twins are cute.

No doubt you've already looked at the pictures, not very good are they? I hope to improve with time. Please look after the pictures and negatives, huh. The roll that I still have in my camera contains more than one shot of me, but I still have two more pictures to take, but no time to do it in.

The other morning I was detailed to go to the motor pool clean up detail, but a call came in for a jeep and a driver. They had the jeep, but no driver. I stepped forth and offered my services, they of course, gladly accepted my offer, under the conditions. I drove that morning instead of cleaning, not that I mind cleaning up, as long as I'm not doing it!!!

When you see Toby give her the negative of my picture, they'll probably want to see my puss, goodness knows why. You won't be getting this letter air mail because I've no stamps and no one else has, sometimes I think maybe I need someone to look after me, someone just like you. Want the job, it will be hard and tiring work at times, but I really try to be good, honest injun!!

Good night darling, I'm going to see if I can get a little sleep before the whistle blows to-morrow morning.

Your, George

May 15, 1944
Monday

From:	To:
C.L. Sniderman	Mr. Pvt. J.G. Barr 11057933
65 Houghton St.	Eng. Sq., 4503rd A.A.F. Base Unit
Worcester 4, Mass.	Great Bend A.B.B., Kansas

Dearest George,

The earrings are perfectly lovely. Everyone loves them, and they look swell with the bracelet you bought me from New Orleans. I really am bedecked with jewelry from you. Thanks loads, dear.

I bought a lovely, lacey, slip for your mother for Mother's Day, - from the both of us. She was more surprised than I ever dreamed she'd be. I also bought a lovely sentimental card, - with a very appropriate piece of poetry inside. All in all, I'm very glad I bought it, - I think she was pleased too.

Friday nite Jackie, Sol Zitowitz, and Charlie Freedman came over to bring me the pictures, which I am enclosing. The pictures are very bad, but I'm sending them anywho. The boys wanted to go riding, and while they were at my house, Toby called and wanted me to go to the movies, but since I couldn't very well go with her, I invited her to go with us. We didn't do anything much, - just went riding and for ice cream at the White House Dairy. I had a very nice time, - I hope Toby did.

Last nite I saw the Sorcerer at Atwwod Hall. I didn't care too much for it, - maybe it's that I never liked Gilbert and Sullivan music particularly. Yesterday Sol Zitowitz and Jack came over in the afternoon and the three of us and Minnie Kaplan played 18 holes of golf, - I was exhausted, but it was so beautiful out and just ideal for golfing. We must remember to go sometime when you come home.

George, maybe this seems like a very silly question, but Sol and Jack said they felt a little funny about taking me out since you are away. At first I thought this very silly, but after thinking it over, I decided maybe you didn't like it. Certainly, there's no harm in it, - I like their company and evidently, they like mine, and we have a lot of fun in a very platonic way. And certainly, I'm not doing anything on the sly, - hell I've told you every time I went with them and Tobye even came with us once, and Jack came with me when I went to give your mother the gift. I hate anything underhanded and that's one thing I'll never do. Everytime I'm with those kids your name is mentioned more times than you can imagine. Last nite when Charlie tried to put his arm around me I pushed away; he looked down between us and said "Damn it, George, you're in my way." They're always saying things like, - if I should get moody for a second, - they start right in teasing me again, "Thinking about George, - thinking about Kansas?" They really take my mind off things, - and yet they never forget that there's George, - and neither do I. You always seem to be there, - and I'm glad they know how I feel.

Well, darling, I guess I'd better go back to work now, - I'm writing this at the office. It's so quiet and peaceful up here I could write for hours. Thanks again for the earrings, and just remember that I love you because you're everything I like in a guy. That's all for now. ---

Love, Lottie

May 16, 1944
Tuesday
"Somewhere in Oklahoma"

From:	To:
Mr. Pvt. J.G. Barr 11057933	C.L. Sniderman
4503rd Base Unit Eng. Sq.	65 Houghton St.
Great Bend A.B.B., Kansas	Worcester, 4, Mass.

Dearest Lottie,

This bivouac business is no good for me, especially the way they do it here. After riding on the back of trucks for about five hours, we hiked the rest of the way. We had one obstacle to pass and that was a smoke screen.

The maneuver area is in Oklahoma, where the dirt is red and soft. When the wind blows, it's like a red cloud moving across the ground. Everything that I have is red now. I know why they call the Indian a 'red skin', they must originally come from Oklahoma. Our officers got lost two times coming down here, so that added about an hour's time that we could have had for sleep. When we finally settled down, I got grabbed for a detail of digging a five foot hole, where the garbage could be disposed of. At 8:30 P.M., after working about four hours, we got down to three feet and quit, because it was too dark.

We're located in a small valley, and in the valley is a ravine, and in the ravine is an airplane. This airplane is supposed to be "mystery" ship, that landed in enemy territory, we are supposed to get it out, fix it and fly it away before the enemy locates us, and if they do, to try and keep our position.

We've been working on the plane for the complete morning and it is half raised, there are still a few obstacles to overcome. It's a lot of fun, no one knows what to do, because they've never had any salvaging experience before.

It's to-morrow now ——

I stopped writing yesterday because it was to hot, and I hardly could hold my pen in my hand.

So far, we have part of the wing of the plane up, and the body should be up pretty soon. After that, we get the other part of the wing, stay here for a few more days, and then leave I hope.

Last night at 6 o'clock I went on guard. At 10 P.M. I was supposed to have been relieved, but at 9 an alert was sounded, because earlier during the day, the 'enemy' had driven a jeep into camp, obtained gasoline for it and driven out again. The driver had used the correct pass word and no one knows how he got it. Meanwhile, the pass word was changed and the guards doubled, and patrols sent out. When darkness came, you couldn't see more than 10 yards in front of you. At one time, I was sent out to tell one of our forward guards that he wouldn't be relieved as early as he thought and to be on the look out for the enemy. I carefully went toward him keeping low and tried to avoid making any noise, I got up within five yards before he heard me. When he did he sprung up, flashed his light on me and ordered me to halt. He scared the daylights out of me and I scared him because he didn't see me, but heard the crackling of the brush. What a night!! We didn't get relieved until 12:45.

You may be interested how we wash, so I'll tell you. The only water that we have is brought to us in a tank. Once it goes dry they have to go out and fill it at the nearest town, which is thirty-two miles from here. We filled our helmets with water and use the helmet as a wash basin, very primitive, but it at least keeps our faces comparatively clean.

I received mail yesterday and was very happy to receive it. Among the letters was one from Fran and she wrote me that my brother took his physical and was classified as 4F, and now he'll try and get a job closer to home. Meanwhile he is down and out because of his classification. The service is bad enough on a fellow without any attachments, but much worse on a married man.

Down in the valley where we are living it is too hot to write, so I came up on the hill where we have a few trucks parked. I'm in one of them writing, using the wheel as my table. It's not the best in the world, but better than my knee.

You can tell the girls at the office that I'll get you a mink coat, just a soon as I can get a promotion and that they are just jealous of the boss's attention to you. By the way, how much does a mink coat cost anyway?

I have to go now, darling, before I'm captured!
Your, George

May 17, 1944
Wednesday

From:	To:
C.L. Sniderman	Mr. Pvt. J.G. Barr 11057933
65 Houghton St.	Eng. Sq., 4503rd A.A.F. Base Unit
Worcester 4, Mass.	Great Bend A.B.B., Kansas

Hi honey,

Well, I finally received the long awaited pictures, but only one of you, darn it! Why do you do things like that to me? I nearly strained my eyes trying to see your mustache, - and I've come to the conclusion that me no like.

I never was partial to them anyway, - you look dapper enough as you are, - that's the way I know you and that's the way I love you, so make nil of the 'mustachio', pleeze!

I went to see "Junior Miss" with Toby last nite. It was very good, - funny as hell! It reminded me of my youth, - ho-hum!! I'm getting older by the year and the thought is very distasteful,......such a business.

I really enjoyed Sid Plotkin's letter. His way of describing a situation is quite unique!! I liked his question asking you if you had made any further plans concerning me. – Well, have you?!!! The same day I got a letter from Bev Kaplan asking the same question, - very funny indeed.

I was supposed to go to a picnic that the office was giving tonight, but I'm dog tired, so decided to sit this one out. I'm becoming a real social butterfly. Ronnie, something or other, a boy I used to go with just called me from Spencer. He heard I was engaged and wanted a verification. He said he knows you. His name is Sidney but I've called him Ronnie for years, - he's very nice, remind me to introduce you to him someday. Everyone in my house is yelling so much that I can hardly concentrate. But don't get me wrong, - I love company!

Beatrice Goldman pulled a fast one last week by getting married. I didn't even know she was going with anyone. Bella Silver is getting married next week, I think. Jesus, I feel like an old maid. Gives you a very peculiar feeling when the people you've always thought of as kids get married. You must have felt like that at Sid Plotkin's wedding. Which reminds me that I'm gonna drop Sid a line the first chance I get.

Edie Megans, Charlotte Plotkin, Harriet Goldstein (she's the girl you once asked if she'd like to sleep with you!) and I are going to Gloucester this coming weekend. The water will probably be like ice, - all I hope is that it doesn't rain. I love Gloucester, soooo picturesque! Whatta ya say we go away for the weekend, - jest you and I on a desert isle!!! Some fun, eh kid? My father just gave me an Egyptian cigarette to smoke and I'm dizzy as hell. It looks and smells like mariwanna.

Darling, I'd like very much to meet your cousin Anne Joselowitz, but I'd feel like an idiot going into the store and saying "I'm Lottie, - how do you do." I'm sure I'd like her – if you do. If she really wants to meet me she could call me up and maybe I could meet her for lunch someday, but I just can't picture myself going into the store. Please don't think I'm snobbish or anything like that, but you can realize how ridiculous I'd feel if she'd say, - "so you're Lottie, - so what," in other words if she didn't remember my name. Hells fire, but I miss you something fierce. Please try and write more often, - the mail situation of late has been awful.

With oceans of love I remain yours,
Lottie

*W ho else — take a good
look, that's a moustache!*

[Editor's note: Above is the photo of George's mustache (you have to look
very closely) that Lottie references in her letter of May 17, 1944.]

May 18, 1944
Thursday

From:	To:
C.L. Sniderman	Mr. Pvt. J.G. Barr 11057933
65 Houghton St.	Eng. Sq., 4503rd A.A.F. Base Unit
Worcester 4, Mass.	Great Bend A.B.B., Kansas

Greeting m'love,

And how goes it by you today? Tonight, is my usual hospital night, but since my dad is in New York, I hated to leave my mother alone, so my services will have to wait for a spell, and besides that, I'm dog tired and being home is a treat. Well, New England weather is proving its inconsistency. For the past week, it has been so hot every day that everyone almost melted, - today, - bingo – we are enjoying a slight frost. Of-course, it would happen just when we were planning to go to the beach, - my luck. Everything happens to I!!

We just had some company over the house. Some of my long lost relatives from Framingham. My cousin told his wife I was about fourteen, after she told me that, I understood why she kept looking at me in that funny tone of voice. Ah, me, - I'll never see fourteen again, - ain't it awful. Hell, I wouldn't want to go through that shy, bashful, adolescent stage again.

Since my dad is in New York my mother is the breadwinner of the family; so, after work I went down to help her, - help her do nothing. Never before have I seen her so dirty. She took it into her head to clean the place out and you just couldn't miss the woman's touch, because lo and behold, she had some flowers in the window. I nearly died laughing because certainly that place doesn't need to look feminine, - but a customer had donated and my mother is as crazy about flowers as I am. We closed at a very early hour and raced home to a manless house. Not the least bit enticing, - both of us mooning about our lost lovers, - or at least far away lovers.

All the bosses were away from the office for the day, - so you can just imagine what a time we had. Evelyn Bloom decided I should be spanked, so started chasing me around the office, when she finally cornered me we decided it would be more fun if we danced, so to the amazement & delight of the other girls, we rhumbaed all over the place. Then around four o'clock another girl went out for ice-cream. Boy – home was never like this!!

I didn't get any mail from you again today. Come on, honey, you're slipping! Write P.D.Q.

Love, Lottie

I just finished reading "In Bed We Cry" by Ilka Chase and this clever bit of poetry was in it. For some odd reason, it struck my fancy so am passing it on to you.

> In Bed we laugh; In Bed we cry
> In Bed we're born; and in bed we die
> The mere approach a bed may show
> The human bliss and of human woe.

Cute, eh?

Please pardon the upward writing, - it was written while I was sitting on the floor. Silly, - ain't I!

May 18, 1944
Thursday

From:	To:
Mr. Pvt. J.G. Barr 11057933	C.L. Sniderman
4503rd Base Unit Eng. Sq.	65 Houghton St.
Great Bend A.B.B., Kansas	Worcester, 4, Mass.

Dearest Lottie,

Here it is our fourth day out and still going strong, or should I say weak, because if I don't get a decent night sleep to-night, I'll be walking on my knees. Last night we went out on a patrol for two and a half hours. The terrain here is the roughest I've ever run across. It is all hills and valleys and ravines, and each has its share of holes, rocks, bushes, and some sort of bush with thorns on it.

After patrolling our area, our officer in charge decided to attack the camp, just to see how the guards were guarding our camp. When we came close to the camp, we started sneaking up on it, one minute apart from each other. A ravine runs along the camp, so we followed that up until we were just below the camp level. When we all were gathered there, we started to climb the bank, half way up we were challenged by one of the guards, at that instant the officer sent up a flare and we let out with some lusty war hoops. The guard was so surprised he just stood there, mouth open and looked. We charged the command tent and I took the C.O. prisoner.

We got in bed about 1:30 A.M., fell asleep, but at 2:30 was awakened by a cry of "Gas!" I jumped up, put my mask on, but didn't smell any gas and started back to bed, when I saw two explosions. It was gas alright, but the wind wasn't blowing in our direction so we went back to sleep. In the morning, we found out that four of the enemy had been captured. We still have one of their officer's prisoners, but released their C.O. & first sergeant, and sent one back to the hospital. He had gotten some of the gas liquid on him and got a bad burn. The reason the C.O. and 1st sergeant were released was that the enemy wouldn't have any one to lead them on any more attacks, and these maneuvers would have to end and they didn't want to do that.

During the gas attack, one of the boys in my tent grabbed his leggings and tried to put them on because he thought that it was his gas mask. When he told us that, I thought we'd never get to sleep from laughing so much. Every once in awhile we get a good laugh here from someone's foolish mistakes. If we only could take a shower or something, go swimming someplace, or someway to really wash up I wouldn't mind so much.

Yesterday afternoon another fellow and I took off and found a small muddy pond, but we took off our shoes, stocking, and leggings, and waded in the water like school kids. Gee, but that cool mud oozing between my toes felt good. The water felt so good to the fellow I was with, that he took off the rest of his clothes and went swimming, I would have but I thought the water was too damn muddy, now I'm sorry because we're dirty as hell now and a little mud wouldn't have made any difference.

I received your letter yesterday that you wrote over two weeks ago, asking me if you should get anything for my mother from the both of us. Well it was too late for me to answer you, but to-day, Toby wrote me that you had gotten her a slip. Thanks a lot darling, you are so considerate and I didn't even send your mother, mine to be, a card. I hope she doesn't think me a stinker even tho I am one for not remembering her. Tell her I'm sorry, and I am.

I've been rushing this letter because it is getting dark and I hardly can see now, so I'd better end it here, besides there wasn't much more to write. Goodnight, precious, I miss you still.

Your, George

May 22, 1944
Monday

From:	To:
C.L. Sniderman	Mr. Pvt. J.G. Barr 11057933
65 Houghton St.	Eng. Sq., 4503rd A.A.F. Base Unit
Worcester 4, Mass.	Great Bend A.B.B., Kansas

Dearest George,

I got a great kick out of your letter explaining your maneuvers in detail. Sounds like fun, - as long as it's not the real thing.

Friday night I was over to your folk's house for supper. Nooky came in and looks great. Fran is still in Boston, but she's coming in tomorrow. He hasn't decided just what he's going to do about a job. Sunday night your whole family came over. Heck, we celebrated my birthday about a week in advance. Your folks bought me a very lovely nightgown in honor of the occasion and Toby a pair of stockings. The card that came with the gift was adorable. It was a dream, - then Toby added her own P.S. - quote, - I hope you get married real soon, - unquote. 'Twas very cute, - and heck you can't blame me for blushing. They're all very sweet, - now I know why you're like you are. Did I ever tell you I love you, - well I do - so there - any objections?!!

Speaking of birthday presents, I'm using one of them right now. My folks surprised me with a beautiful solid mahogany secretary desk. I'm really thrilled with it. After it was delivered, I had a good cry for myself. - I always cry when I'm happy.

Saturday I was sick as a dog. My aunt Mary Hoffman had a very serious operation, and I was there when they brought her in after the operation. We couldn't get any private nurses so, of course, I stayed with her. The ether fumes made me so dizzy, I nearly passed out and, of-course, seeing the waxed expression on her deadly white face didn't help any either. She recognized me the minute she opened her eyes and kept repeating my name over and over again, - even in her sleep. It gave me the most sinking feeling. I went again tonight, of-course, and she's feeling much better. My poor uncle is a wreck with aggravation. After the hospital Saturday afternoon, I was sitting alone feeling real stinko. In the most appropriate time, Jackie & Sol and the Katz twins and a few more kids came over. We went to Lillie's, and after one beer I forgot all my troubles. Then we went to White City and I had more fun than a kid. I still say that the hobby horses are the best thing in the place. Also, while we were at White City, two boys picked up and beat up two girls. One was completely knocked out and the other was sobbing. Gee, I love fights, - so long as I'm not in them.

Well, darling, I guess I'd better go to sleep. I really am tired. Speaking of dreams, I must remember to tell you I dreamt about you the other night. You were really an awful stinker. You were here for ten days, took me out about twice, and never even kissed me. I was so angry in my dream that I tore a pillow case. That's one dream I hope never comes true.

Goodnite darling,
Lottie

May 23, 1944
Tuesday

From:	To:
Mr. Pvt. J.G. Barr 11057933	C.L. Sniderman
4503rd Base Unit Eng. Sq.	65 Houghton St.
Great Bend A.B.B., Kansas	Worcester, 4, Mass.

Dearest Lottie,

What I need now is a good secretary, why – because I think that I could use some such person to help me answer all the people that I owe letters to. The mail certainly came pouring in this week, and me without a chance of answering them.

It's been a long time since I've written to you and I have a lot to write you, that's if I don't forget most of it.

The little poem that is enclosed comes from a miniature newspaper that one of the fellows received from home. The poem comes from W. Winchell's column, so you may have read it, if not, you can now.

I was very pleasantly surprised when I saw the pictures you sent me. Such cheesecake! My goodness you're wonderful, and your beautiful hair certainly has grown. If you were a blond, I could almost call you "Lady Godiva." Keep the pictures coming, I love them.

This morning my bag came in and it hadn't been touched at all. In fact, I had a small mirror in it which I thought surely would have been broken, but it was in one piece. The candy bars tasted as good as ever, and the two packages of cigarettes also came in handy.

Also in the mail I received my pen back and it works out much better than the other one I was using, much better. Your two letters were well received also, and I'm now trying to make up for the ones that I owe you.

About you going out with Jackie, darling, I have absolutely nothing to say against it. I don't care who you go out with, because I love you and you love me, and I know that you have very good judgment with whom you associate with. I want you to go with whomever you see fit and have a good time, I know that I can trust you at all times, so you needn't be afraid or restless, no matter with whom you go out with. As long as we continue to love one another nothing else really matters.

Now I'm going to try and remember what I've done and what I haven't written you. Friday of last week we were told that the townspeople of Coldwater Kansas, a town thirty-two (Just had to fill up with some ink) miles from where we were bivouacking, invited us to a buffalo barbecue and rodeo. We didn't want to go into town so damn filthy, so that night we went down to an artesian well about a mile and a half from camp. Here we stripped naked and had one of us pour water from our helmets on us. After much pumping and pouring we took most of that red dust off of us. If we only had clean clothes we would have felt much better. I think that well water was the coldest water in the world. You should have heard the shrieks and howls, or even seen us. We must have been the dirtiest soldiers outside of those in the South Pacific, or Africa.

Saturday morning, we piled into every available truck and rode into town. My "taxi" was a flat bed trailer, on which seats had been made (I should have said benches), if I had walked the thirty miles I would have enjoyed myself a hundred percent better.

When we did get into town we went to the barbecue, only to find that it was postponed till seven that evening, because it wasn't ready as yet. Meanwhile, we bummed rides on the horses that the men and the boys of the county side rode in on. You could have mistaken us for Russian Cossacks, with our rifles, helmets, leggins, fatigues, gas mask, and belt. The horses were excellent.

The ladies of the town had made us sandwiches and coffee so that we wouldn't go hungry until the barbecue was ready. After eating, we put on a small scale parade. It was too bad that we did put on the parade, although the people probably didn't notice the faults (there were so many of them), because we were awful.

The town was kind enough to have their high school band play for us, I wish they hadn't been that kind. I never knew you could change the beat of a tune so many times in such a short period of time. They were awful.

Then we went to the rodeo, where I rode some more. There was one small little horse that didn't have a saddle, and I wanted to ride it. The owner said O.K. I got on but quickly got off, and not of my own accord either, one buck and I was off, luckily, I landed on my feet. Then I got on a real fast horse. It just wanted to run, and run it did, the wind whistled past me like sixty. At the rodeo itself, all they did was ride broncos and rope calves, but it was very interesting. After the rodeo, we ate the barbecued buffalo, and went to a carnival that was in town. I just walked around it, but didn't go on any rides because of lack of funds. I had a swell time tho watching the other boys enjoying themselves. Then back to camp, but this time I got on a regular G.I. truck and slept part of the way back.

The next morning, I fired on the range, but just before I finished, an officer who was firing with me, saw a gopher about twenty five yards from us and he thought it would be nice to see if we could hit it. I got my ammunition, aimed, and bingo! The gopher was dead. This, of course, surprised me very much, because I got him the first time and he was popping his head out of the hole every once in awhile. I hope the louie wasn't angry at me for not even giving him a chance to fire at it.

All day Sunday, visitors from the surrounding neighborhood came to see the soldiers at work. All we were doing was playing soft ball. I was put on as a guide. I felt like one of these sightseeing bus drivers, explaining all that there was to explain. The women got a big kick out of our mess truck and its equipment. At night, the Chaplain put on a field service, in which all denominations can go, the people also came, and I think they had just as good a time there as we did in their town the night before.

I thought that I had written you that I had shaved off my upper lip. No? Well I did, just before I went out on bivouac.

How come my sweet, that you opened your birthday present before your birthday? Didn't I ask you not to open it till your birthday? I am glad that you like your present, I tried hard to get something that would please you, and I'm happy that they did. Wear them, sweetheart, with all my love and best wishes.

I would have written last night, but we came into camp late, and I washed myself and my clothes and went to bed. Am I forgiven?

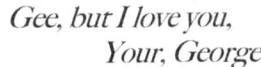

Gee, but I love you,
Your, George

[Editor's note: "Cheesecake" photos of Lottie mentioned in George's letter of May 23, 1944.]

May 24, 1944
Wednesday

From:	To:
Mr. Pvt. J.G. Barr 11057933	C.L. Sniderman
4503rd Base Unit Eng. Sq.	65 Houghton St.
Great Bend A.B.B., Kansas	Worcester, 4, Mass.

Dearest Lottie,

Hello my sweet, I wish that I could say it personally. I'd like to close my eyes and when I opened them to find you by my side. I hoped and tried to get home to you on your birthday, but I guess the gods are against us for awhile. If only some outfit wanted me, then maybe I could get my furloughs when due me. This being just a nobody is getting on my nerves, if they'd only give me some reliable job to do, I wouldn't feel so bad, but being kitchen fodder is not my idea of helping win this war.

I didn't do a thing to-day, except clean my rifle and write a few letters. About four o'clock we went into town, another fellow and I. Our reason to-day was to get a few shirts and a pair of pants pressed. We had washed them ourselves, but didn't have any way of ironing them. They are our summer uniform and the cleaners wouldn't press them, because they said they needed a different kind of press then the one that they had. Desperately, we went into a self-service laundry where we rented out irons and ironed our clean but wrinkled clothes. I don't think that I'll ever make a good ironer. I found that it is a tedious job, which requires practice and plenty of it. I hope that next time, I'll be able to get my uniforms in the cleaners so that I'll not run into such trouble anymore.

I found that I could get to see Narky in about 14 hours, now all I have to try and get is the three-day pass and wait until pay day comes around.

I received a letter from my brother Nooky (or do you call him Sol), and he wrote that he saw you, and that you're looking swell, keep up the good work. Also, my dad wrote they are going up to visit you on your birthday. Did they know that they were a bit premature?

Good night my darling,
Your, George

May 25, 1944
Thursday

From:	To:
Mr. Pvt. J.G. Barr 11057933	C.L. Sniderman
4503rd Base Unit Eng. Sq.	65 Houghton St.
Great Bend A.B.B., Kansas	Worcester, 4, Mass.

Dearest Lottie,

To-day was another quite uneventful, dull, and do nothing day. I've been trying to get in touch with an officer who'll O.K. a three-day pass for me, but whenever I go to the orderly room in search for one, no one is around to help me. I'll try to-morrow, and if necessary, the day after until I can at least talk to one and get a definite answer, yes or yes, as I'd prefer it.

This afternoon I dropped into see the dentist because I hadn't seen the one on this field as yet, but he looked my teeth over and over and said "Good job, where didja have it done," I told him and got the hell out of there before he'd like to make another good job on me.

Last night I turned the other roll of film into the drug store, so I should be getting them back sometime late next week.

I just finished talking to the photographer who took pictures at our bivouac trying to get some points from him, but they are all restricted and I can't even see them. I suggested to him to see if he could get the Colonels permission and make a montage of about a dozen of the representative pictures and sell them to the boys at cost. He thought it a good idea, and said that he'll work on it. I hope so, because I think it would prove very interesting in later and present years, you know what I mean, how I played soldier even tho it was for only a week. I asked him if there was some way of me getting in with him, but he told me that he didn't have any control on the men that came into his outfit, and he's only a sergeant. He said that he'd like me in it, but there was nothing that he could do about it.

The other day I took out a book by Alice Teasdale Hobart, "The Cup and the Sword." I liked it a lot and finished it within two days. When I went back to the library to get another book, there wasn't any that I immediately took a fancy to by reading the titles. "The Cup and the Sword", sounded very good, and proved so. I haven't read a book for so long, that when I started I thought I'd never be able to finish it, but I did. Now I know I should read much more, something else that I'll have to take care of.

You'll probably have received the chain that I sent you. It's a regular G.I. chain and made out of sterling silver, so it's good. If you are going to wear my dog tags (how can you stand them), you may as well have the best the army can offer. I'm sorry that I forgot to mention it to you sooner, but so it goes.

I better go wash up now and get some sleep. This morning I didn't get up for breakfast and since I've been in the army, breakfast is something I need to carry me thru to dinner. Awful habit breakfast, it makes you get up so early.

Goodnight dear,
Your, George

[Editor's note: The following photos may be the bivouac photos that George references in his letter.]

May 26, 1944
Friday night

From:	To:
C.L. Sniderman	Mr. Pvt. J.G. Barr 11057933
65 Houghton St.	Eng. Sq., 4503rd A.A.F. Base Unit
Worcester 4, Mass.	Great Bend A.B.B., Kansas

Hi honey,

I just got back from having supper at your folk's house. This is getting to be a habit, eh wot?! Fran had come in from Boston and we all had a very enjoyable evening. Your folks and Toby are going to New York tomorrow and they begged me to go along. I have no need to tell you how tempted I was, but then again, I wanted to be home with my folks for my birthday. Speaking of birthdays, darling, you didn't really think that I could wait that long to open my gift from you? I hope you're not angry, but my curiosity got the best of me. Also, a cute quip and comment from Fran & Sol was that they surely thought we'd get married last time you were home. Cute, don't you think! I'm sure glad your maneuvers are over, maybe now I'll get some mail, - the past week has been awful, as far as mail is concerned. Since your mother is going to New York, she gave me a whole pile of pastry to send to you which I shall do post haste, that is, if I don't eat it, - but she also gave me some for myself.

Surprises of surprises came Wednesday. I finally got my long awaited raise! It was a three dollar increase which isn't too bad considering I've only been there a year. Boy, I sure can use the extra dough.

I'm glad you liked the pictures I sent you. Me no like them, but as Jackie says, I'm prejudiced. As you have probably seen, I've enclosed another. I'm hoping to heaven you don't show them to anyone, please don't!

I got quite a kick out of your rodeo experience. I could just picture you on that unsaddled horse. I read the letter to my mother (only the part about the rodeo!), and we both had a good laugh. We also decided that you must have been extremely uncomfortable not being your usually very neat and clean self. Even my mother noticed that you used to be spotless when you came over here. That's another thing I love about you, - truthfully speaking, there are a million and one things I love about you.

Oh, yes, I have more news. Your folks bought a house. Yes, dear, a house on Hudson St. I think it's off of June St., anyway. It's a five room house, a two tenement one. Your mother has already decided that when you come home on furlough, you can sleep here because it really is so foolish to go home just for breakfast! Ouch!! So, next time home, - you live here, - everyone has unanimously agreed to the plan.

Sam Katz (one of the twins), and his girlfriend from Boston, came over with Sol Zitowitz Wednesday night. I really had a grand time listening to them argue. She wants terribly to get married, but even tho she doesn't know it, he doesn't love her enough to get married. And the arguments they were giving each other on why they should or why they shouldn't get married were really quite ridiculous. I felt like the ham in a sandwich, both of them kept asking me what I thought, and didn't I think he or she were right. I kept neutral and avoided making enemies. I hope we never have any arguments like that about getting married. To me, it's either a "You do, - or you don't want to" affair. But then again, they're really very young, - or at least act it. I feel like a grandmaw!

I just took time out for a spot of tea with my folks. And now I shall retire for the evening. Goodnight dear and pleasant dreams.

> *With Love,*
> *Lottie*

P.S. Does ya still love me?!

May 26, 1944
Friday

From:	To:
Mr. Pvt. J.G. Barr 11057933	C.L. Sniderman
4503rd Base Unit Eng. Sq.	65 Houghton St.
Great Bend A.B.B., Kansas	Worcester, 4, Mass.

Dearest Lottie,

To-day I put in my application for a three day pass, but it looks doubtful because the usual distance for a three day pass is 150 miles, and I want to go 450. If my C.O. passes it, I'll get it, if not no. Not only that may stop me, but now they are going to make us work on the line, where the airplanes are kept, doing an airplane mechanics job. It doesn't mean anything that we don't know anything about it. We'll probably end up washing the planes. The reason they gave it is that they are short of men over at the hangers.

I just came from services just now. They don't have a Jewish chaplain here, so they weren't very good, as services go. I guess most of the other boys on the field don't go because of this, there were only ten men there, just a 'minion.'

I kept busy to-day, first we put up butt cans over our area, then we got some ply wood and built ourselves a table, so that we'd have something decent to write on. For amateurs, I think we did a pretty damn good job. We even sanded the rough edges so that no one would get a sliver from handling it.

In the afternoon, I polished empty gun shells. If I can get the bullet itself from a large shell, I'll try and make you a pin and if I can do a good job, I'll send one to all my <u>favorite</u> girl friends, there are at least six of them anyway. <u>You,</u> your mother, mine, and you can guess the rest. For my dad, I'll try and make a cigarette lighter. I have the ambition, I hope the ability, now, all I need is the material.

When I dropped off last night, I went to a dance that was held next door, in our gym, from the Service Club from where I was writing you. Better I should have stayed and finished the letter. The dance stunk and that was'nt even a harsh enough word for it.

This morning I went over to the hangers and worked, that's if you call tightening three nuts work. What they wanted was mechanics, and we just hung around watching what few mechanics they did have. I did get a good look at the 'Flying Fortress' or B-17 tho. I crawled throughout the entire ship. You can't really walk thru it, you have to crawl. One of the other boys who went on the expedition has a few scrapes and bruises to prove that you have to be careful while going thru a B-17. Now I know why it cost so much money to build one of these airplanes. The amount of different equipment that it carries is tremendous. It even carries more radio equipment than I thought it would ever use, but it is there, and no doubt, for a good purpose.

If I work over at the hangers long enough, I'll be able to go up on some of the routine flights that the ship makes. Maybe to Denver.

All day long it rained, then cleared up, and rained some more. Half the sky remained clear, while the other half remained stormy. It's raining now, and I'll probably get soaked by the time I get back to my hut (I'm at our day room now.) In the afternoon, I had enough time to write ten letters, but I didn't have enough ambition to lift a pen. To-day was one of those lazy do-nothing days.

This letter, I hope, will reach you on your birthday. Happy Birthday, my darling!! May we be together very soon and live our lives in peace and happiness.

Birthdays should be happy occasions, and I hope that yours was, very much so. Your last birthday, I wasn't with you either, so this gives us even greater odds that I'll be with you on your next. Darling, I love you, heart and soul forever and ever.

Happy Birthday, again and again!
Your, George

May 29, 1944
Monday

From:	To:
C.L. Sniderman	Mr. Pvt. J.G. Barr 11057933
65 Houghton St.	Eng. Sq., 4503rd A.A.F. Base Unit
Worcester 4, Mass.	Great Bend A.B.B., Kansas

Dearest George,

    I received the chain you sent me today, and the only thing I have to say, is that you're a dear, but you shouldn't have done it. Thank-you, for being so sweet.

    Well, tomorrow marks the starting of another new year for me. What it will bring frightens me a little. So many things have happened this past year that it seems like a century. The best thing my new year could bring to me is the ending of the war. This is half a selfish and half an unselfish wish. The girls at the office were more than generous in supplying me with birthday cards and gifts. It was really terribly sweet of them. Also, I got quite a few dollars in cash from my relatives. So, all in all, I am having quite a celebration, - but by myself, which sort of dampens it. Tomorrow I'm having Bev Kaplan & Edie Megans over for dinner so maybe they'll pick my mood up. Oh, yes, I must tell you about the birthday present I bought myself, - or have I already told you? Anywho, I bought a book to help fill up the book case on top of my desk. The name of it is "The Hell of Loneliness," – you simply must read it some one of these years.

    The heat today was sweltering, - and good for nothing but loafing. But did I take it easy,......you bet I did!!

    I'm sending you a copy of my character (or at least it says so there), for some odd reason. I just happened to read it, so I thought you'd be interested to know just what you're letting yourself in for.

    I spent a wonderful part of last nite chasing a damn mosquito. Boy, was I mad. Three times I put off the light after not being able to find the little beast, and three times I could feel him laughing at me. The fourth time I was determined, so I stood in the middle of the bed and waited. – Where the hell do you think I found him? He was sitting on my arm and I swear he was smiling, - so being the big brave girl I am, I bopped him gently and he fell to the floor. After that I lived happily ever after.

    Well, m'love, that's about it for now. Take it easy and all that rot.

Love, Lottie

What TOMORROW Means to You

If May 30 is your birthday, the best hours for you on this date are from 10 a. m. until noon, from 2 to 4 p. m., and from 8 to 10 p. m. The danger periods are from 8 to 10 a. m., from 6 to 8 p. m., and from 10 p. m. until midnight.

This Memorial Day should serve to remind us of the heroic supreme sacrifices made in the past and being made now for the preservation of our constitutional rights that have and will enable us, and our children's children's children to enjoy to the fullest the blessings of the FOUR FREEDOMS. Ask yourself TODAY are you doing all you can to contribute in every way possible your bit so you will not feel a secret shame to share in the manifold blessings an Allied victory will bestow on you and civilization. Remember that it is actual and not lip service that counts. Today it should make no difference whether you are married, engaged, or in love, YOU should remember that "God grants liberty only to those who love it, and are always ready to guard and defend it," and prove by their actions that they are worthy of it.

If a woman and May 30 is your birthday unselfishness, in all likelihood, characterizes your thoughts, words and deeds. You probably do not believe in reserving one week day only for religious thoughts or charitable actions, so each and every day is apt to reflect in some way your spiritual nature and desire to be of real service to your fellow man. A natural born diplomat, you should have no trouble when it comes to handling people or selling them a "bill of goods," especially if you are convinced that it is for their own good. As a welfare worker, missionary, teacher, lecturer, actress, writer, singer, musician, trained nurse, dietitian, doctor, lawyer, business manager, sales agent, specialty shop operator, secretary, or through some patriotic service in an industrial line of activity, your accomplishments should be outstanding and your financial returns most gratifying. Favorable conditions appear to surround your future matrimonial affairs.

May 29, 1944
Monday

From:	To:
Mr. Pvt. J.G. Barr 11057933	C.L. Sniderman
4503rd Base Unit Eng. Sq.	65 Houghton St.
Great Bend A.B.B., Kansas	Worcester, 4, Mass.

Dearest Lottie,

After I tell you what I've been doing, I guess you'll think me a child. Well, I've seen children do better work than what I seem to be doing. I'm trying to build a small self model airplane. While in town Saturday, the fellow I go around with, and I, bought a model airplane. I worked feverishly for an hour and a half on it, and the shape is just forming. This, I'll have you know, is the hardest work I've done all day.

I swept underneath the tail section of 'my' plane and sat in the pilot's seat, operating one of the controls under the direction of the crew chief. Another nine lessons and I'll be able to fly the plane. One of these days I should be able to go up in one of them.

Yesterday we went to a town thirty miles from here to see a rodeo, but it was going to cost us money, and we were on our last two dollars, so we got off the G.I. truck, walked around the town's square once, and then walked back to the highway and bummed back to G.B. When we got back to G.B., we walked our feet off looking over the residential district.

At night, we took in a movie and then went to the hut and went to sleep. This morning they woke us at 6:00 A.M. It seems that the officers want us on the ball, but they don't come out for reveille themselves, so it probably won't last very long.

These postcards depict just two phases of our bivouac doings, those were all they had at the P.X. I'm also going to send you a paper from the town that we went to for the rodeo. They gave us a big write up. Pretty good too.

Darling, I'm no longer an overage in this outfit! Which means I'm eligible for a furlough!!! I asked the furlough clerk and he said about the 15th of June I can get mine! Of course, I won't be sure of it 'till I have it in my hands, but it's about time that I got some kind of a break. Let's hope that all will go well for the next two weeks.

How would you like to be my 'legal fiancée'? I'm going to see what I can do about it just as soon as I get home. Would you prefer a gold or white gold ring? I feel like a million dollars now with the expectancy of coming to see you – Happy day!

Good night, my darling, I love you.
Your, George

BIVOUAC "BOODWAH"

CHOW!

May 31, 1944
Wednesday

From:	To:
C.L. Sniderman	Mr. Pvt. J.G. Barr 11057933
65 Houghton St.	Eng. Sq., 4503rd A.A.F. Base Unit
Worcester 4, Mass.	Great Bend A.B.B., Kansas

Dearest George,

Yes, your birthday wishes came just in time. And a happy birthday it was, - at least as happy as could be expected under the circumstances. My mother, the dear that she is, surprised me with a lovely birthday cake, - candles and all. We had quite a few friends and relatives up the house in honor of the occasion and I received many unexpected gifts. Everyone was far too generous, - everyone very sweet.

The weather today was unbearably hot. I was sick from the heat at the office. I remember when summer meant nothing but fun, - now it's just a drudge. I guess I'm pretty selfish complaining, - and I'm not really complaining, just a little sad with the thought of growing up. I loved my teens. Some girls hate them, to me it was everything perfect. That's my one major fault, - I hate to lose what I love, this holds true for everything, whether it be material things or people. I always want the people I love around me, is that being selfish?

Toby wants me to go to a school minstrel show with her Friday night, but I doubt if I can make it. Reason number one being that I think my aunt is coming home from the hospital Friday, and since she's staying here, I'll feel it my duty to stay home. Another reason being that it will bring back memories of the minstrel show we went to and how we took the kids out afterwards. Of-course, I haven't told this reason to Toby, I'm afraid she wouldn't understand, but it would really be torture for me. I am a silly sentimental.

For some odd reason, I feel in not too frivolous a mood this evening. I'm hot and tired and lonesome, - I guess the reason isn't too odd after all. I hate myself when I feel like this and there is absolutely no sense in burdening you with my woes, so if you'll pardon this drippy dribble, I take leave with lotions of love.

I remain yours,
Lottie

May 31, 1944
Wednesday

From:	To:
Mr. Pvt. J.G. Barr 11057933	C.L. Sniderman
4503rd Base Unit Eng. Sq.	65 Houghton St.
Great Bend A.B.B., Kansas	Worcester, 4, Mass.

UNITED STATES

ARMY AIR FORCES

May 31st

Dearest Lottie,

To-day was pay day, so I was able to go to the P.X. and buy a few things that I needed. After splurging, I went and got sheared. That is about what it amounts to, the barber runs the cutters up my neck, around your ears, yells next and takes your forty cents, all at one time. It's an art the way they do it.

If you could see me now, you'd die laughing, at least you'd have a good time. I'm spread out on my blanket beside my hut, taking a sun bath. This reminds me of the times I bathed in the sun on our roof in Philly. It is almost six o'clock, so I won't get much of a burn. I'd rather simmer than burn all at once, don't you think so?

When you told me that my parents bought a house, I just stopped reading your letter. You can imagine my surprise, because I have yet to stop in the middle of one of your letters. Have you seen the place as yet? When do they expect to move in? Thanks for the invite, I may use it very soon, I hope.

We now have our own hanger, I guess this means we'll be here for a little while anyway. It hadn't been used for a long while and we had to clean it up. I don't know why we have a complete hanger because it really is a large place and we don't have more than one plane in our squadron and just two pilots for that plane. Maybe they intend getting some more planes and equipment. I hope that this is true and then maybe I'll get a chance working on something, and maybe in a year or so, I'll be promoted to a P.F.C. or something.

I can get a three day pass, but the catch is that they won't make it out for Denver. They'll make it out for 150 miles and then I'd have to chance it. If my furlough wasn't coming up, I would take the chance because there is very little chance of being caught, but it is that small chance that I won't take at a time like this. Maybe I'll be able to get a pass after my furlough. I'd better stop talking about my furlough, just in case it doesn't come up, which would make us feel pretty damn low.

Last night I went to see "Between Two Worlds," I was in the 5% of the entire house that liked it, someone is wrong, and I hope that it wasn't me.

You ask do I love you? Yes, I love you, darling, with all my heart, soul, and body.

Your, George

June 2, 1944
Friday

From:	To:
C.L. Sniderman	Mr. Pvt. J.G. Barr 11057933
65 Houghton St.	Eng. Sq., 4503rd A.A.F. Base Unit
Worcester 4, Mass.	Great Bend A.B.B., Kansas

Dearest George,

I'm thrilled with the news that you may get a furlough. No need to tell you how excited I am. Tis truly wonderful.....– now all we have to do is pray, and pray I will.

The weather here is still terribly hot and I'm still Lottie ala nude, - or practically. I have no more clothes on than I have to, to keep my modesty.

I went to the hospital last night and worked on the accident ward and much to my disgrace I got sick to my stomach. A man was brought in from a hit and run accident and he was soaked with blood. Everything was fine until I had to help the nurse clean the wounds. I started swaying a little and then the interne sent me out. I tried to blame it on the heat, but he gave me a knowing look and just said, "Sure pal, it's the heat." I took a big gulp of water and then went back and I was O.K. Another funny thing happened and very embarrassing, to say the least. A man came in and said he thought he had appendicitis. The head nurse came down and told me to undress him and put him to bed. I was damned if I'd undress him, so I told him to take off his jacket and shoes. When the nurse saw him fully clothed in bed she nearly had a fit, and if it wasn't for one of the student nurses, I would have gotten hell. Imagine me undressing a man, - humph!!! So very indignantly she said to get him a Johnny and put him to bed properly, - by this time it was 10 o'clock so I threw a Johnny at him and beat it out of the hospital but fast. When I signed up for duty I didn't realize all that I was letting myself in for, - but don't get me wrong, - I love it, - but not the "undressing a man" part.

I had to leave you for a few minutes cause I had to wash my hair, and washing my hair is some job since it's so long.

Now I'm going to finish this letter and go to sleep for a change. Last nite my mother and I sat up till one o'clock and talked. We had much to discuss after the letter I received from you yesterday. The only final conclusion we came to is that you're every bit a dear and I love you. Goodnight.

Love, Lottie

June 2, 1944
Friday

From:	To:
Mr. Pvt. J.G. Barr 11057933	C.L. Sniderman
4503rd Base Unit Eng. Sq.	65 Houghton St.
Great Bend A.B.B., Kansas	Worcester, 4, Mass.

Dearest Lottie,

Under separate cover, I'm sending you a few shots of myself and a few other interesting pictures. I have the negatives of a few shots taken at our bivouac, and am going to have them printed, then I'll send them to you. They were taken by Bob Orgain, the fellow I hang around with.

Thanks loads for the cake and stuff, it sure came in handy and was good.

We're still cleaning our hangar. Yesterday they had us cleaning the windows and to-day oil pans. These pans they put beneath the engines of the planes, so that the drippings will not oil the floor.

I had a plane tragedy, when I put the wings on my model I put them on wrong, one wing was longer than the other. While trying to fix it, I broke the hell out of it. Now I'm building myself a new wing, so it will be a bit longer until the day that it will be finished.

The wind is blowing pretty damn hard out here, everything that you have is full of sand, even sand gets into your mouth and between your teeth. I've bit many times only to find sand grains in my mouth.

Darling, please have a few extra copies of me made up so that I can send them to my brother, Sid, and Dave, O.K?

Starting the 5th of the month I have to go to class one hour a day for a plane spotter course. Even if I wanted to take the chance in seeing my brother, I wouldn't be able to now, because while going thru this course, no one will be able to get 3-day passes or furloughs. We finish the 15th so that shouldn't interfere with my furlough, but it comes too close to even make me smile.

If I continue getting the sun like I have been doing for the last few days, I should be brown as a nut by the time that I get home. I'm working without a shirt most of the time and every once in awhile I go outside to do something or other. So, if you see a medium, dark, gruesome, soldier walking up to you in the next three weeks, don't run away, because it may be me.

Your, George

DIRTY FACE!!

CHEESECAKE !!

June 4, 1944
Sunday

From:	To:
C.L. Sniderman	Mr. Pvt. J.G. Barr 11057933
65 Houghton St.	Eng. Sq., 4503rd A.A.F. Base Unit
Worcester 4, Mass.	Great Bend A.B.B., Kansas

Dearest George,

I started out this morning feeling in a jubilant mood, but thanks to yer friend Jack and his pal Sol Zitowitz, I feel lower than a snake's belly. Sol called me early this afternoon and asked me to go riding with he, Jack, and another girl. Everything started out fine when all of a sudden, a quarrel came about. It seemed a minor thing, but as such things do, it grew and grew into a major battle. The worst about it is that I don't even know why they're mad and I haven't the slightest idea why I'm mad, except that they said a few uncalled for remarks. I think Jack thinks you're angry at him because I've been seeing him, - as a matter of fact, he's told me so. I've meant to tell you a hundred times to draft him a line, but I always forget. Now he thinks I'm his life long enemy when I'm nothing of the sort, but when he said so, my pride and anger held me from telling him so. George, I hate arguments and I felt miserable about it all day, but I've thought the situation over and now I feel a little better. If only I could find some reasonable excuse for the outburst. Jack said many things, but I don't exactly understand what he meant, but I'm almost sure he was referring to your being angry at him which is very stupid on his part. But the hell with it. But I do have sort of a sickish feeling inside because of it.

The minute I closed my eyes last night I started dreaming of rings. Big rings, small rings, all kinds, - even a purple ring. I guess there was a very good excuse for what I dreamt and I enjoyed every minute of it. Darling, if we do become "legally engaged" - as you put it, I have some very disappointing news to tell you, - that being that no one will even be slightly surprised. I'm mad, cause I'm always surprised when people get married or engaged, and I want them to be if I'm going to join their union. But seriously now, I'm hoping you will get the furlough after both of us being all excited about it. I was very happy when I heard the news and called your mother immediately, but she brought up a point that sort of hit me hard. George, this furlough doesn't mean going overseas, does it?!! Something inside me says, "of-course not, - you dope," - but then again, -.... Oh, well, I'll just keep happy by thinking what I want to think. I wish you were home now. I could use your brand of sentiment and understanding. Incidentally, Maxie Zitowitz was in town for the day and I hear tell he is quite the lady's man, -

in other words, a wolf on the loose. Now honestly, can you picture Maxie as a wolf? He always was a riot, - now he must be doubly so.

Well, my darling, I feel in much higher spirits now than when I started this missive. Goodnight & pleasant dreams.

Love, Lottie

June 4, 1944
Sunday

From:	To:
Mr. Pvt. J.G. Barr 11057933	C.L. Sniderman
4503rd Base Unit Eng. Sq.	65 Houghton St.
Great Bend A.B.B., Kansas	Worcester, 4, Mass.

Dearest Lottie,

I'm mad, I just broke the rudder of my airplane completely off. As a plane builder, I stink. As a worker, I do wonders.

They have me on the swing shift changing the engine of a B-17. It's a rush job and there are three shifts working day and night to get it going again. Meanwhile, we won't have a day off. When it flies again, then we'll be able to resume our normal way of life. For a guy that doesn't know much about motors, I did a lot of work, at least I got enough oil and dirt on me to prove that I did something.

Yesterday morning we were supposed to have inspection, but when the time came for it, no officers came around. We waited and waited, meanwhile all of us laying on our bunks, or sacks, as they are known as in the army, of course, we all fell asleep and didn't wake up till noon. If the inspecting officer had come around it would have been our necks.

I wanted to go swimming to-day too, but the only thing I could do was put on my bathing suit and simmer a little while in the sun. I'm going to go to work in about an hour and a half. I hope that the other shifts have the engine in the plane already, but I doubt it. I wish they'd hurry up with the thing because I'd like to go up for a ride to see what the earth looks like from about five, ten thousand feet.

My furlough is now coming up the 21st of the month, if they keep postponing it any longer I'll have gray hair.

Darling, I can't write anymore because something is bothering me, but I'm going to try and call you to-night and see if I can straighten matters out.

Your, George

June 6, 1944
Tuesday

From:	To:
C.L. Sniderman	Mr. Pvt. J.G. Barr 11057933
65 Houghton St.	4503rd Base Unit Eng. Sq.
Worcester 4, Mass.	Great Bend A.B.B., Kansas

My dearest George,

I feel that this letter I'm writing to you now is the most vital I've ever written and the most important to us both. There is no need to tell you how much your telephone call aroused everyone. It was the shortest but the most wonderful three minutes I've ever had. Your call came at two o'clock in the morning and, of-course, no sleep came to me after that. Your proposal of marriage came as such a surprise and was so important that I couldn't put off thinking about it for a minute. By eight o'clock I finally fell asleep from sheer mental exhaustion. Of-course, I didn't go to work Monday morning, - too much had to be discussed and talked over. George, after I finished talking to you Sunday night my first impulse was to go ahead with plans for a wedding. I thought it was a wonderful idea, but after hours of solid thinking, I became a little frightened and I knew that I'd have to consult many people before writing you anything drastic. I spoke to my folks first, and then yours, and though both families were equally surprised and, of-course, not entirely for the situation, they were perfectly grand. Both said it was our life and too important a decision for anyone to make but us. Well, darling, I knew how you felt, - so it was all up to me. Believe me, George, I've gone over every possible point and weighed each factor pro and con a million times. My head aches with trying to think out the best possible thing for both of us. George, if only you were here so I could talk to you, - it would make things so much easier, but you're not and this is what I've decided:

George, if I could go along with you I wouldn't hesitate a minute at marrying you. But we both know this is almost impossible. I'd have to live alone and work, for surely we couldn't get along on your allotment, and I'd be in a completely new country with not a person I know or could turn to. Maybe you'd be able to see me week-ends and there might be times when you'd be restricted. This would only worry both of us into a state of frenzy. You'd be worrying about me and I'd miss you more than ever. Then again, although I haven't thought of it until now because I think it's vital to my decision, but it's inevitable that you'll be sent overseas. We'd be no better off than we are now. Only aggravation would tense our nerves because we'd have to be separated so shortly after being united. So, my darling, this is my opinion. I hate having such an important matter thrust upon me, but I'm trying to do what is best and what will insure our future happiness. I hope you understand, - I'm sure you do. When you come home on your furlough, we'll go ahead with plans for becoming engaged. That, in itself, is enough to make me so excited that I hardly know what I'm doing. Our families will get together and have a little celebration in honor of the occasion. And another good thing is that my boss has given me permission to take my summer vacation at a moment's notice and if need be, I can have a few extra days to be with you. We'll make this a glorious occasion and eliminate heartbreak, which would follow if we got married. Then again comes before my mind, Sid Plotkin's wedding. Remember, that night we swore we'd never have one like that. I always wanted a wedding, - complete, - the works. Then a honeymoon and then plans for a future with a home and everything else that comes with making a lifetime full and happy. I want you beside me to help plan not my wedding, but our wedding. If we wait, we have a lifetime of happiness to think and dream about, - after this war is over, dreams also will be over, - only reality and the nicest kind of life will be ours. But I love you more than ever for asking me to marry you, and giving me the thrill of thinking about it, even though it was for a short time. This will show that we are big enough and wise enough to overcome any obstacle, big or small, and not run headlong into disaster. So, let's lay away, for a short time, wonderful plans for a wedding until we can plan together, and let's instead plan for our engagement. I have no more to say, George, I'm hoping with all my heart that you understand. I love you very much.

Lottie

June 7, 1944
Wednesday

From:	To:
C.L. Sniderman	Mr. Pvt. J.G. Barr 11057933
65 Houghton St.	Eng. Sq., 4503rd A.A.F. Base Unit
Worcester 4, Mass.	Great Bend A.B.B., Kansas

My darling George,

I read your letter over and over again. Your plans for the wedding sound so simple, - and so wonderful. I wish with all my heart that it were that simple. I don't think you're selfish in wanting to get married, - I think it's natural, - and I want to get married as much as you do. But this is one time we must not let our hearts rule our heads. You say that our wedding would take care of us for a while. Darling, that's not being mercenary; it's being truthful and this is one time we need frankness and truthfulness. It is true, - we would have enough money to see us through for a while, but darling, after the war we will need the money so much more and for so many better purposes. No doubt we will want a home and I know you have no money to speak of, - so our wedding gifts would start us off on the right foot. Then again maybe you'd want a business, - so a home would be set aside for awhile and we'd have the money for that. If we get married now and spend all we have, after the war we must start from scratch. Last nite I wrote to you about the hardships both of us would have to endure. Please don't think I'm selfish, - I've thought about it more and more, and I'd go through a million hardships if I thought it would be best for us both. But it would do neither of us any good. I have no more to say, - if you still think it would be wise for us to get married, then we'll consider it all over again. I'm willing to listen to anything you have to say against what I have written. I think if you were here, my darling, you would have gotten yourself a wife. But let's not be foolish. The cartoon you sent me was adorable, - and just a little thing like that almost made me change my mind. You're so terribly sweet.

Darling, how long is your furlough going to be for? Your way of figuring adds up to 21 days. If this is so, - I think it's too, too wonderful. We'll have a hell of a time. With me not having to go to work, it will make it even more wonderful. Instead of having a wedding party, - what say we have an engagement party. If we can't have the best thing, then let's settle for the next best, and right now being engaged to you is the best thing I can think of.

Please say you're not angry at me for wanting to hold off the wedding.

Goodnight, darling,
Love, Lottie

P.S. Bella Verstein and Bernie are going to be three. I guess it's not very important now, but I just thought I'd tell you.

June 7, 1944
Wednesday

From:	To:
Mr. Pvt. J.G. Barr 11057933	C.L. Sniderman
4503rd Base Unit Eng. Sq.	65 Houghton St.
Great Bend A.B.B., Kansas	Worcester, 4, Mass.

Dearest Lottie,

I got a kick out of your little episode at the hospital. What are you going to do with me when I go out and have a night with the boys and get plastered? Put me under a cold shower with my clothes on and leave me stay there? Of course, I hope that it never happens to me, but I was a bit curious.

To-night for supper, the mess sergeant fried us up some steaks, because we were "good" boys and did our work. Around our mess hall, they are planting flowers, so off I went to help them, meanwhile leaving the sink where I was helping wash the pots and pans. They forgave me because I was such a help in the garden. None of us know a damn thing about flowers or gardens, but since I told them I worked with an experienced gardener at Kelly Field, they thought maybe I did, so I was chief gardener for the day. P.S. I dug the holes for the flowers, watered them and took all the stones out of the dirt.

Why Jackie should be peeved at you, or me, I can't imagine. My records show that I answered the last letter that I owed him, and that it is his turn to answer mine. I keep all the letters that I have to answer and when I answer them, I tear them up so I know that letter is taken care of. Of course, I may have made a mistake, or he may be angry because I haven't sent him any pictures, and he did go to the trouble of sending my camera to me and a roll of film. I'm going to write him a subtle letter and try and straighten things out. I just hope that I'm the one that erred and not he, because I don't want anyone to be nasty to you because of some stupid, childish grievance.

No longer am I on swing shift. The plane that I was working on is in the air and there isn't any other rush job, thank goodness.

At our plane spotting school, it's a picnic. The instructor keeps calling the engines on a plane, motors, and the mechanics keep yelling back engines. In the army, the motors are engines. Just motors that are worked by an outside source such as electricity, are known as motors. This is getting me mixed up, so I'll stop.

Until to-morrow au revoer, my love.

Your, George

June 11, 1944
Sunday

From:	To:
C.L. Sniderman	Mr. Pvt. J.G. Barr 11057933
65 Houghton St.	Eng. Sq., 4503rd A.A.F. Base Unit
Worcester 4, Mass.	Great Bend A.B.B., Kansas

My dearest George,

I received your telegram yesterday and you can't begin to imagine how I felt. It was the most beautiful thing I've ever read and the dearest thing you could have done. I was so afraid you wouldn't understand. I feel a million times better now.

Your folks and Toby were up here this evening. As a matter of fact, - they just left. Your mother and I had a man-to-man talk, and I guess she is much relieved that we are postponing getting married. She said she felt that way only for our own good, and I know she means it. Toby was disappointed at having to wait to have me for a sister-in-law. I never dreamed that I'd come so close to getting married so soon. The girls at the office have been riding me something fierce. I've told them nothing about even thinking of getting married, but two girls at the office started a rumor that I was getting married on your next furlough, - never realizing how true their rumor almost was, - so now whatever I say denying the rumor, they don't believe. The poor kids are gonna be oofly disappointed, - do you think they'd settle for an engagement?

So, you got a kick out of me putting a man to bed with his clothes on, eh! Well, darling, should you ever come home saturated with intoxicating beverages, I'm afraid you won't be able to count on my disrobing you. Under the shower you'll go, - clothes and all! Can't you just feel that icy water down your back, brrr!! But, - what would you do should I ever come home in a slightly stinko condition!!!!!

I saw Phil Sobel downtown Saturday and he looks great. He has a beautiful tan and I think he's gained a little weight.

George, you said that the letter your father sent you was a pip, but you didn't give any details. I'm really curious about what he had to say. Why do you say that you never realized you'd have to eat your own words? It must have been pretty stiff, - by the way you sound. Do write and tell me all.

Well, darling, every day brings you a day nearer to coming home. If you don't hurry up, I'll be a nervous wreck. Do you know the exact date yet?

I'm really quite tired. We've had three shifts of company at the house today and my head feels like a drum.

Goodnite, dear,
Love, Lottie

P.S. I saw the picture "Up In Mabel's Room" and I thought it was a riot. If you have the chance, see it. L.

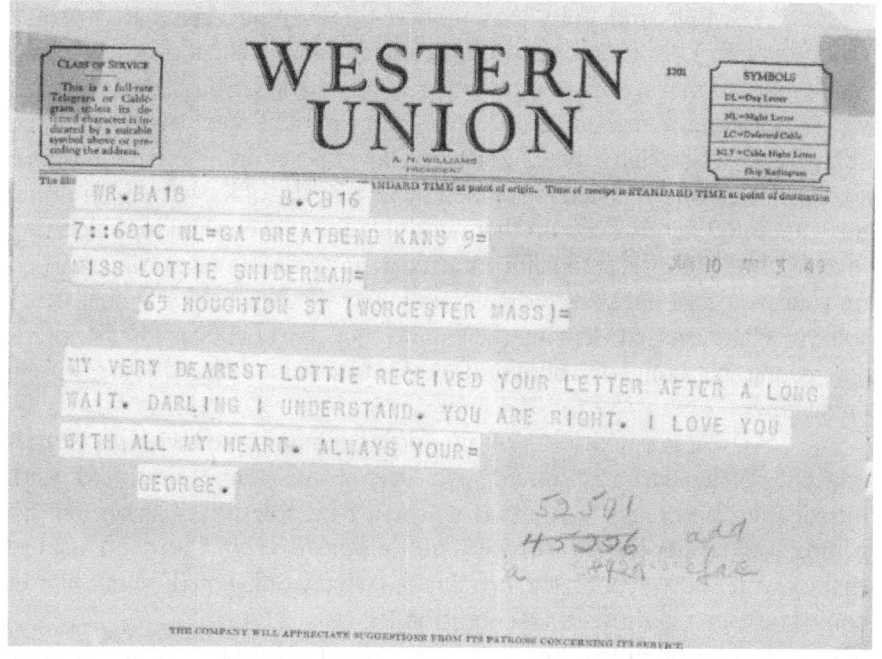

WESTERN UNION

WR-BA16   U-CB16
7::601C NL=GA GREATBEND KANS 9=
MISS LOTTIE SNIDERMAN=
65 HOUGHTON ST [WORCESTER MASS]=

MY VERY DEAREST LOTTIE RECEIVED YOUR LETTER AFTER A LONG
WAIT. DARLING I UNDERSTAND. YOU ARE RIGHT. I LOVE YOU
WITH ALL MY HEART. ALWAYS YOUR=

GEORGE.

June 11, 1944
Sunday

From:	To:
Mr. Pvt. J.G. Barr 11057933	C.L. Sniderman
4503rd Base Unit Eng. Sq.	65 Houghton St.
Great Bend A.B.B., Kansas	Worcester, 4, Mass.

Dearest Lottie,

After receiving your letter, my mind was immediately relieved. I was expecting it Thursday, but it didn't come until Friday night. I'm not angry at you, darling, how could I get angry at you. I was going to write you sooner, but it seemed that what I was going to say seemed to have two meanings, so I decided not to write until I could give you one meaning. I am not angry at you, I love you even more, because you could make such a decision with such a clear head. For one so young and lovely, you have wisdom that far outweighs your years. I'm lucky even to be able to love you and you love me. We'll wait, even tho it will be hard.

I'm peeved at something my dad wrote me tho, it seems that a Mrs. Greengus was the one who was the first to tell my dad. I don't care who knows I love you, but I would have liked my family to know that I asked you to marry me, before anyone else. Sweetheart, I read your letter over and over again, and it was marvelous. I'm sorry that I had to cause you so much concern and worry. Darling, you can't imagine how much I love you, it can't be put into words.

For the last few days I've been helping wire up a B-17. It's not much, but I'm in our radio shop. You can't call it a shop, but it's a beginning. We only have an empty room, but we hope to get equipment in soon, then we'll be able to repair our own radios, instead of sending them out, as we do now. I hope I'll be able to get a tube for my radio at home, and some batteries, until we get our own supply room for radio parts, I can't get a thing.

Everything is O.K., darling,
Your, George

June 14, 1944
Wednesday

From:	To:
C.L. Sniderman	Mr. Pvt. J.G. Barr 11057933
65 Houghton St.	Eng. Sq., 4503rd A.A.F. Base Unit
Worcester 4, Mass.	Great Bend A.B.B., Kansas

Dearest George,

I'm so glad you feel that my decision was the right one. If you only knew how much time and willpower it took to write it. I think I wasted more stationery that night than I ever did. But it looks like I'll be going to a wedding anyhow, - my cousin Zelda is finally getting married. Her beau is coming in from Alaska in about four days, and they'll be wed shortly after. I've been hoping all along that you'd be here for the wedding, - it's still possible. Darling, in the letter I received today, you mentioned not a word about your coming home. As the time draws nearer, I'm on pins and needles. I'd appreciate a wire as soon as you know definitely when you'll be here, - and also the time your train comes in. I don't want to waste anytime before I see you.

I had a very pleasant surprise this evening. Your cousin Ann Joselowitz called me. We talked for awhile and since we're both anxious to meet each other, I'm meeting her for lunch Friday. She sounds very sweet. Also, the other night, Pauline Cohan called me. She's home for her summer vacation. Her friends in Colorado thought both you and Narky were very nice. Maybe when you're home you'll have a chance to meet Pauline.

I went to a shower for Sylvia Coblentz Goldman last nite. We had a very nice time. A few of the girls chipped in and we bought her a lovely blanket. She has a very nice cedar chest, but had nothing in it, - or at least she didn't have until last night. She's quite disturbed over the fact that she hears from her husband about once a week. He's really a jerk!

I was walking down the street today when a soldier grabs my arm and asked what I'd do if a strange soldier walked up to me and started talking to me. The strange soldier happened to be Sid Stein. I was awfully glad to see him. He looks very well and sends his regards to you. I was so surprised to see him I nearly fainted. That old gang of mine......!!!

George, I don't know how my aunt could have told your father about us wanting to get married. That Mrs. Greengus you mentioned, - happens to be my aunt. I called your folks Monday morning and they were the first ones to know outside of my folks. Neither my mother nor I mentioned a word to anyone else. It could be that she was kidding, - but it came pretty close to being the truth. I really feel very badly about it, but there's nothing that can be done now. I don't blame you for being peeved.

I saw "Going My Way" this evening. It was very good and Sylvia and I both had a good cry, altho there was nothing particularly sad about it. Then we both had laughing fits when we saw each other crying. Such is life, - ain't it wonderful.

Goodnight dear,
Love, Lottie

[Editor's note: Contained in the envelope of the 6/14/44 letter from Lottie to George, was the following poem:]

```
Sitting on my G. I. bed
  My G. I. hat upon my head,
G. I. pants - G. I. shoes
Everything free - nothing to lose,
G. I. razor, G. I. comb
G. I. wish that I were home.

They issue everything we need
Paper to write on, books to read
They issue food to make you grow
G. I. want a long furlough.
Your belt, your shoes, your G. I. tie
Everything free - nothing to buy.

You eat your food from G. I. plates,
Buy your needs for G. I. rates,
It's G. I. this, and G. I. that,
G. I. haircut, G. I. hat,
Everything here is government issue,
G. I. wish that I could kiss you!
```

June 19, 1944
Monday

From:	To:
C.L. Sniderman	Mr. Pvt. J.G. Barr 11057933
65 Houghton St.	Eng. Sq., 4503rd A.A.F. Base Unit
Worcester 4, Mass.	Great Bend A.B.B., Kansas

Dearest George,

Your letter of today brought more disappointment than you can realize. I felt lower than a snake's belly on hearing that your furlough was postponed, - but I suppose there's nothing that can be done, and we'll just have to wait another week. I did so much want you to be at Zelda's wedding. Phil isn't coming for a few more days and the wedding is scheduled for Saturday night, so I was ticked silly because I was sure you'd be here. I hate the whole damn army, - they can't do this to me, I keep telling myself. But I guess they can and they did. Oh, well, - let's hope that this is the worst disappointment we'll ever have. Only trouble is that I had the office vacation schedule planned so that I could take my vacation now. I'm hoping to hell I can rearrange things. Because it would be ridiculous to stay out while you weren't here and work when you are. I'll have to do some fancy talking and maneuvering tomorrow. Already me little brain is working overtime thinking of how and what I'm going to say.

My dad got your card today, and my mother – the pin, and through me they send their heartiest thanks. They were very pleased, no kidding.

Toby and I had a foul game of tennis yesterday afternoon. The weather was beastly hot, and as a result we didn't feel very much like playing. While down the lake we met Maxie Zitowitz, who was home for the day. He looks remarkably well and boy – whatta wolf. He was sitting near the tennis courts surrounded by a bevy of women. Whatta guy. He drove Toby and I to my house and after we ate supper, Toby and I started for the movies, but after we walked two steps we felt a drop of rain, so rushed back home. We stayed here all evening and had a very nice time. We were very tired, so we lied on my bed and listened to the radio. Toby was hugging me just right, and I nearly fell asleep. Then about ten o'clock my folks and I walked her home.

I had lunch with your cousin Ann Joselowitz Friday and she's really very sweet. I had forgotten that she was from Africa. She talks with a very slight, but very pleasing accent. And so, we finally met and I did feel like the idiot that I knew I'd feel like when I had to say, - I'm Lottie! But she broke the ice very nicely.

I just finished speaking to your mother and we both discussed our troubles over your not coming. But there's one consolation. Think how nice it will be thinking of how nice it will be when you come home! Confusing, eh wot!

Pauline sends her bestest regards and apologies for not writing, - but she really didn't have the time, - unquote. –

In one of your recent letters you asked if I thought there were more than two classifications of people, - good or bad. Well, - I most definitely think there is a middle class, but that class stands no distinction. One of my teachers once said that he never forgets his very bad pupils or his very good pupils. The ones that were average usually slipped out of his memory. I think that holds true with good and bad people. Most of the people are just averages, - neither good nor bad, - they just live ordinary lives. I think those people are happiest. The bad ones are afraid of being found out, and the very good ones (I doubt if there are any saints,) are always afraid of doing something bad, - therefore, these two classes are generally very nervous people, or at least that is my point of view. But I disagree entirely with your friends who say there are only good or bad people. So, my darling, that's my point of view and another thing we both agree on.

Don't feel too bad about them postponing your furlough, - it could have been worse.

Goodnight dear,
Love, Lottie

[Editor's note: Contained in the envelope of this June 19, 1944 letter was the following poem:]

```
I think about you often, and I'd write
    you every day

But there's so very little that it seems
    worthwhile to say;

It either rains or it doesn't rain --
    it's either hot or cold,

The news is all uninteresting, or else
    it's all been told,

The only thing that matters is the fact
    that you are there

And I know I'm here without you, and it's
    lonesome everywhere.

I think about the way you smile, and I
    recall your touch

And the distance lends enchantment
    and I miss you very much.
```

June 21, 1944
Wednesday

From:	To:
Mr. Pvt. J.G. Barr 11057933	C.L. Sniderman
4503rd Base Unit Eng. Sq.	65 Houghton St.
Great Bend A.B.B., Kansas	Worcester, 4, Mass.

Dearest Lottie,

It has been rumored from official sources, that one Miss Lottie Sniderman is going to have a visitor within the next week. He leaves to see her on the night of the 25th, 1:30 A.M. Sources also state that he has signed his furlough papers, which makes everything practically in the bag, except for tornedo, fire, or earthquake. He will be home soon, underline soon.

Yes, darling, I signed my furlough, now all I have to do is wait, and it's killing me. I don't know what else to write you, I'm so happy. Going to the movies, or what I did to-day seems of no importance whatsoever. A dream in the making is coming true and that's all my one track mind wants to know.

Darling, when you get this letter, I'll probably be on the train, so there is no use of you writing me until I get home. It has been a long hard road, but I can see the end.

Darling, you can't imagine how I've missed you, I love you so much.

Your, George

P.S. I'll write you just as soon as I have the furlough in my hands & I'm out of camp. J.G.B.

The engagement of **Miss Charlotte Sniderman**, daughter of Mr. and Mrs. Max Sniderman of 65 Houghton street, to Pvt. James George Barr, Army Air Forces, son of Mr. and Mrs. Jacob Barr of 57 Arlington street, is announced by her parents. Both were graduated from High School of Commerce. Miss Sniderman is employed at the New England Grocery Supply Co. Pvt. Barr is

July 17, 1944
Monday

From:	To:
C.L. Sniderman	Mr. Pvt. J.G. Barr 11057933
65 Houghton St.	Eng. Sq., 4503rd A.A.F. Base Unit
Worcester 4, Mass.	Great Bend A.B.B., Kansas

Dearest George,

I really admired myself for behaving so well at the station, - you too were remarkably calm and collected, but when I got home I really let loose. When my mother saw me crying, she started crying, and when Sandy saw my mother crying, she started crying, so all in all, we had quite a session, but after I let loose that pent up feeling, I really felt much better, or at least as well as could be expected under the circumstances. Your two telegrams were a great relief. And so now we settle down to wait, - either for peace or another furlough. The house was filled with company all day Sunday, which kept me from thinking too much. Your folks and Toby were among the guests. Your mother brought me six beautiful hand towels and one enormous bath towel. They're really lovely. Of-course, I had to take everything out of the chest and show it to your mother, which altho it was quite a job was even more of a pleasure. Around ten o'clock when everyone but Irving and your folks had left, Irving went down Water St. and brought back beer and delicatessen. We had a delicious time. Also, Toby and my nephew hit it off quite well, and she has a date with him tonight. I felt ancient when I saw them go.

I finally finished all the thank-you notes and they're on their merry way, thank goodness. Me thinks you were let off awfully easy.

Edie Megans was also in quite a low spirit Sunday. Dave has also gone back, and we're left alone to console each other. Damn it, - this is an awful situation.

Your mother is going to the beach for two weeks and I may go out and spend a week-end with her. I really would love it.

Charlotte is coming back from her vacation tomorrow, which will relieve me quite a bit. I worked like a dog, but I'm not one bit behind in my work, which will be a pleasant surprise to her. Come to think of it now, - I don't see how I ever kept those ungodly hours and then was able to work all day. Maybe it was because I knew each minute with you was precious.

Well, my darling, I must write Barb and Bev all the news. They don't even know I'm engaged yet. Write the first chance you get.

With Love, Lottie

July 18, 1944
Tuesday

From:	To:
C.L. Sniderman	Mr. Pvt. J.G. Barr 11057933
65 Houghton St.	Eng. Sq., 4503rd A.A.F. Base Unit
Worcester 4, Mass.	Great Bend A.B.B., Kansas

My dearest George,

Your letter was terribly sweet and I know you understand how I feel. And we will be very happy together always. What does it matter if we break a few dozen dishes now and then!!

I'm quite a tired gal this evening. Worked all day, - then entertained the first shift of company. Sam and Jeanne went out for dinner, so I took Sandy for a walk. I went into a store to buy her a sweater and nearly fell dead when the salesgirl said to Sandy - quote, - see the nice sweater your <u>mommy</u> is buying for you! - unquote. How do you like that mommy stuff, - cute eh, wot!! I felt as if I had already started on the first of our twenty four. Twas a very nice feeling too, - believe it or not. Then we came home and I really felt maternal when I had to bathe and put her to bed. Such fun. I wish they would leave her here with me. Now I have to wash and wait for the second shift of company to come.

About the "small change," - there are really no thanks due to me. I wouldn't have done it if I didn't want to, and I got just as much pleasure out of giving it to you as I hope you'll have spending it. I always said what was money for if you couldn't spend it - but I guess we both found out that was not the best policy. Oh, well, it was a good idea anywho. Well darling, I really must dash, - the front door bell is ringing.

Au revoer and oodles of love,
Lottie

P.S. I love this fiancée business!!!

July 19, 1944
Wednesday

From:	To:
Mr. Pvt. J.G. Barr 11057933	C.L. Sniderman
4503rd Base Unit Eng. Sq.	65 Houghton St.
Great Bend A.B.B., Kansas	Worcester, 4, Mass.

Dearest Lottie,

It's hot here, very hot, and to think that last week I could go down the lake and cool off if I wished. The space of time is so short, but it seems so far away and long ago. I've been going to mail call waiting for your letters, but of course, it is still to early, but I think maybe the mail has been able to get thru faster than usual. Maybe to-night.

I slept most of yesterday away, didn't do a damn thing. After supper Bob and I went into town. He had to get a money order his father sent him and I wanted to see if I could get Buzzy the medal that I promised him. There are a few crummy ones, but I wouldn't think of getting those, I'll wait a little while longer, what else can I do?

To-day at dinner we had some nice large pieces of watermelon, what memories that brought back, our engagement party, the night we finished what was left. Darling, we had a wonderful time to-gether. In our victory garden, or should I call it our peace garden, remind me to grow watermelons.

Helped paint a fence to-day, once they know you can do something they let you keep on doing it.

Did I tell you I got a letter from Sid and Dave? Anyhow, Sid wants me to send him a carton of Camels. So, I went out to get him a carton, but you can't buy a carton, you can only get three at a time. It was a good thing that Bob was with me, because between two trips apiece we got the entire amount. Then after wrapping it, I went to mail it to Sid, meanwhile, I took one of my uniforms down to get them cleaned. First, I couldn't mail the cigarettes until I show them the written request, so I had to take the package back because I didn't have the letter, being ignorant of the correct procedure, secondly, the cleaners were too crowded for work, and won't take anything until Friday.

Darling, I miss you,
Your, George

July 20, 1944
Thursday

From:	To:
Mr. Pvt. J.G. Barr 11057933	C.L. Sniderman
4503rd Base Unit Eng. Sq.	65 Houghton St.
Great Bend A.B.B., Kansas	Worcester, 4, Mass.

Dearest Lottie,

How are you to-day, darling? I have yet to fall off to sleep peacefully and easily. My mind is always with you and no matter how tired I am or how badly I want to sleep, I stay awake thinking of you. Lottie dearest, I'm so in love with you.

Late yesterday afternoon Bob and I went swimming. The water was surprisingly warm and we had a good time. The beach is very sandy and clean and I was sorry that the sun wasn't out so that I could stretch out and get some vitamins.

This coming Saturday, our outfit is going to have a "Beer Bust." I don't know what the arrangements are, but I'm going anyway, maybe if I drink enough beer, I can get stinko, I'm in the mood.

Also, last night I went in to see if I could get myself some stationary printed up for myself. When its all done, it will be in pad form so that I'll be able to use it in the folder that I got when I was in December, remember the one that I keep your picture in? After I get it, I don't think I'll need to bother about buying any more for quite a long time. I just hope that the war ends before I ever use it up. I'm going to send most of it home to you, and then whenever I need any writing material, you can send me a pad and some envelopes. O.K?

Some more of the boys are going to school in Dayton Ohio, as yet, we don't know who, but I hope that I'm one of them. Being an overage may put me out of the running tho. Well, what comes comes, and the way things are, I have no control of the outcome. All that I can hope for is that whatever happens, it will happen for the best.

Have my folks been up to see the cedar chest as yet?

Your, George

July 21, 1944
Friday

From:	To:
C.L. Sniderman	Mr. Pvt. J.G. Barr 11057933
65 Houghton St.	Eng. Sq., 4503rd A.A.F. Base Unit
Worcester 4, Mass.	Great Bend A.B.B., Kansas

Hello darling,

Edie M. was over for supper tonight and now we're taking time out to write to our respective beaux. I just finished showing Edie everything in the cedar chest, and of-course, we glowed over every article. A while ago we were lying on the bed, - just talking to our hearts content and reminiscing, - of how she met Dave, - of how I met you, - and of how completely content and happy we were – or could be if there was no such thing as having to go back after a furlough. But in spite of it all, if you have something and someone to plan for it makes things so much easier. Sylvia Coblentz Goldman asked me today if we ever quarreled and was amazed when I said never. I don't think she fully understood when I said no one could ever quarrel with you. She and Irwin had a battle on their honeymoon, - big deal!

Edie and I went to see "Claudia" last night at the Little Theater and it was darling. Everytime I looked at Edie, - I kept wishing it was you and she felt the same – only she wanted Dave. Such troubles! I was over to Dorothy Potash's for supper Wednesday night and had a surprisingly enjoyable evening. She really is such a sweet kid. All she wants out of life is a man, - and morning, noon, and night, that's all she talks about.

I got a card from your mother today. She's at Revere Beach for a few weeks and asked me to come down for a weekend. Me thinks me will take her up on it.

I'm sorry you had such a lousy trip back, honey. But who the hell was the dame that was going to give you a ride back to camp? I don't mind (much) if you lose your money in a crap game, - but to spend it all on a dilly, - well......I can also go back to my red head. Ugh, - what a gruesome thought!!! With so many interruptions from Miss Megans, I'm finding it quite difficult to concentrate on what I'm writing to you, - if I should happen to mention the name Dave where the name George should be, - please understand.

I bought myself a pretty nice picture album, - now all I need is for you to send me some pictures, - and I don't mean of a squirrel either!

I got another letter from Dave today and he said he finally got a letter from you. He still doesn't know we're engaged, - so evidently, he didn't get our card from Boston. Ah, Boston, - what pleasant memories, - with the exit sign over my room!!! We did have fun, didn't we?

Well, dear, Edie and I are going down the corner to mail our letters now and then we'll sit up all night talking. If your ears burn, you'll know the reason why. Incidentally, Edie sends her love.

> *Goodnight, m'love,*
> *Lovingly, Lottie*

July 21, 1944
Friday

From:	To:
Mr. Pvt. J.G. Barr 11057933	C.L. Sniderman
4503rd Base Unit Eng. Sq.	65 Houghton St.
Great Bend A.B.B., Kansas	Worcester, 4, Mass.

U.S. ARMY AIR FORCES   *July 21st*
Friday

My darling fiancée,

What do you know, our hut has just been transformed into a barber shop. Bob has the hair clippers I brought back, and he's practicing on one of the boys. We were at the P.X. and the fellow mentioned he needed a haircut. We convinced him that Bob could do as well a job as the barber, or even better. Now he's in the chair, oops I should have said, on the edge of a bunk, finding out whether our statements are true or false. P.S. There of course is no charge, as yet.

How's "mommy" getting along with the children? Darling, you're going to be the best mother a child ever had, after all, look at the background you had.

Last night I saw "Home in Indiana," which made me ache all over for you. When those kids were making love, no older than ourselves, well, I wished you were beside me.

Did I tell you of the rumor that I may go to school, it will be for a short time on blind instrument flying in Dayton Ohio. I haven't any definite proof of it yet, so we can't count on it.

How do you like "Sad Sack"? Take care, darling, I'll be back tomorrow.

> *Your, George or Fiancée*

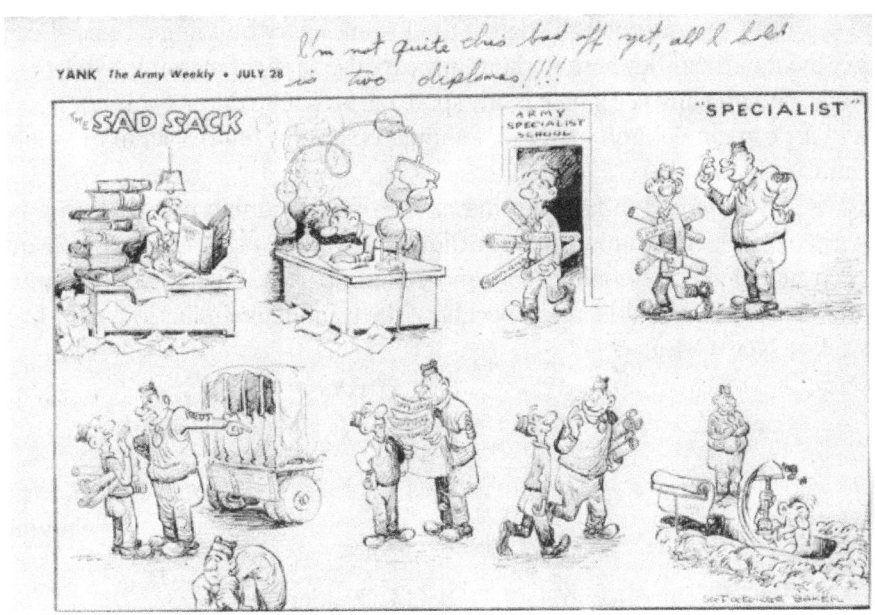

July 22, 1944
Saturday

From:	To:
Mr. Pvt. J.G. Barr 11057933	C.L. Sniderman
4503rd Base Unit Eng. Sq.	65 Houghton St.
Great Bend A.B.B., Kansas	Worcester, 4, Mass.

Dearest Lottie,

This afternoon is the time that I'm going to see if I can get drunk. I don't know whether I'll be able to drink enough beer or not, but what the hell, a fella can try.

Last night at the base gym there was a "Sadie Hawkins" dance. We went in fatigues and the girls wore anything they could think of, mostly shorts – wahoo!!! I had a more enjoyable evening than I would have had if I stayed in the hut, so it was alright. I danced alright, about three fourths of a number. I didn't feel like dancing too much, and I didn't feel like cutting in on some girl that I didn't even know. I don't know what's gotten into me, but other women don't interest me at all. I remember in New Orleans at the dances, I used to dance most of the numbers, but since then, well, – do you think I'm in a rut? Like hell I'm not, it's just that I'm always thinking of you, and this ersatz isn't at all to my liking! Darling, when I dance I want you in my arms. I'll dance no doubt but just to keep in practice.

If I can get enough spare parts I think I'll try building a radio. I can get most of the tubes here without any expense to me. I'm going to write to Solly Zitowitz and see if he has any spare parts that he doesn't want or need, and if I can get enough material, I should be able to build a set in my spare time.

Starting Monday morning, some of us, meaning me, have to take parts of our basic training that we didn't have at the other camps that we'd been at before. It shouldn't last more than a week. We won't do much anyway, so why should I cry, especially if the training is similar to what I had back at New Orleans.

Bye for now.
Your, George

July 23, 1944
Sunday

From:	To:
Mr. Pvt. J.G. Barr 11057933	C.L. Sniderman
4503rd Base Unit Eng. Sq.	65 Houghton St.
Great Bend A.B.B., Kansas	Worcester, 4, Mass.

Dearest Lottie,

You may or not believe this, but you should get this letter at least two hours earlier than you would have if I had gone to the show and written you after the movies. Since I didn't go, thru no fault of my own (no late show to-night), you should get it earlier than I thought you would. If this doesn't make sense, then cross it off, or better yet put a match to it.

This afternoon was lovely and I enjoyed myself very much at the little pond here, but I wished like hell, that you were here with me. (The comma between "hell" and "that" shouldn't be there, I was going to cross it out but then if I did there would be no need of this sentence - please omit the comma, thank you.) I was in the water most of the time, which surprised me, because I didn't think I could swim so long. Oh well, - "The army's made a man out of me, man out of me, man - (oh hell!) ect."

At our "beer bust" I had a good time. No, darling, I didn't get drunk, why? It's this way. When I started out I had all the intentions in the world to, but when I got there, I came late, so many were drunk already that I said no, I didn't want to be in their condition. I had a good time tho, I drank my capacity of beer, about 8 or 9 small glasses, had a fried chicken meal, and watched all the goings on.

I went into Great Bend before I went to the party, because the proofs of my stationery were to be ready and I wanted to O.K. them. When

I got there, to the party, Bob already was feeling high, as a matter of fact, too high, so I took him for a walk. You should have seen us. We each had a few, and I had one arm holding Bob. As soon as we left the beer tables, Bob threw up, so I threw his beer away and after the walk and an hour afterwards he was O.K.

We, of course, had a song fest, everyone, most everyone (I think the Chaplain, the C.O. and myself were the only sober ones) was drunk. After awhile they were just lying were they fell, until we carried them onto the grass under a nice large tree. There were fights every five minutes, but fortunately, no one was hurt seriously.

About six o'clock, I saw that Bob had enough, so I took him over to a nice soft place in a grassy area and put him to sleep. He woke up a few times, and he was sick. When he felt better, about eight o'clock, I took him over to were we had the cokes, and sat him down and made him put his hands into the ice water, and splash it on his face. After all this, and another walk he was able to take care of himself. Nurse's aide, that's me. Then I went for a swim.

I'm glad that you weren't with me, it was rough, everyone drunk, every tree a latrine, guys fighting and swearing, no place for a lady. Many of the boys had to be carried into a truck, transported back to camp and put to bed.

One of the boys woke up in front of the mess hall, another woke up in the hangar, and of course, they didn't remember how they got there. There was even three barrels of beer left that the boys finished this afternoon. Oh well, boys will be boys!!!

I'm sorry dear, but I'm almost sure that I forgot to thank you for that sweet card, the first thing you sent me, I meant to, but darling it slipped my mind somehow. Thanks darling, the feeling is mutual, and I think you're a sweet kid and I love you.

Wow! Where did I get this energy to write so much, - must have been that invigorating swim.

Good night, my sweet, with barrels of love.

Your, George

July 23, 1944
Sunday

From:	To:
C.L. Sniderman	Mr. Pvt. J.G. Barr 11057933
65 Houghton St.	Eng. Sq., 4503rd A.A.F. Base Unit
Worcester 4, Mass.	Great Bend A.B.B., Kansas

Greeting m'love,

 Sundays are always bad days, - there's nothing to do but feel lonesome, and I'm very much so. I got two letters from you yesterday and I've read them over so many times that the paper is worn thin! Your letters get nicer with each writing. I also received a lovely letter from Barb yesterday. She was not only surprised, but thrilled to learn about our engagement, and sends her best, best wishes. I only wish she could have been here for the party.... And the watermelon!

 My folks and I went to visit the Walker's today. It was Rickie's 1st birthday, and I'm happy to say he was very much impressed by the ceremony. I wish we could have children as nice as he, - only ours will have dimples. He really is such a doll.

 I just can't keep away from the radio today. The news about the revolt in Germany is so wonderful that I feel good all over. Everyone says the end is very near, - and oh, how I love to hear that. Can't you just picture what it will be like to be home for keeps? I love thinking about it anyway.

 I just took time out to kill an enormous bird, - well it was a big fly anyway. Ugh, - how I hate those things. You and your tent, - phooie!!

 Darling, I think it's wonderful that there's a possibility of your going to school in Ohio. Heck, I could come to visit you there. It's not so terribly far. Wouldn't that be super swell? Incidentally, your beer party sounds like fun. I hope your planning on getting stinko for me too. I feel in the mood. Shall we drink a toast?!!

 I wish you were here. I don't feel like sleeping, but I have no one to stay awake with. My family is wonderful, but they are of little consolation when I want you. The hell with everything, I'll go to sleep and dream about you anyhow. And so goodnight dear,

Lovingly, Lottie

When God gave out brains
I thought he said trains
And I missed mine!
When he gave out looks
I thought he said books

And I didn't want any!
And when he gave out noses
I thought he said roses
And I ordered a big one!

When he gave out legs
I thought he said kegs
And I wanted two fat ones!
When he gave out ears
I thought he said beers
And I ordered two long ones!
When he gave out chins
I thought he said gins
So I said give me a double, -

God, Am I a mess!!

July 24, 1944
Monday

From:	To:
Mr. Pvt. J.G. Barr 11057933	C.L. Sniderman
4503rd Base Unit Eng. Sq.	65 Houghton St.
Great Bend A.B.B., Kansas	Worcester, 4, Mass.

JAMES G. BARR   Army Air Forces

My darling fiancée,

With the strains of the "Bolers" in my ears, I'm starting this missive.

My first day of basic proceeded to be just as monotonous as I had expected. I imagine I shouldn't feel badly, because one of the tech. sergeants that also has to take it, has returned from a 23-month stay in New Guinea.

Do you like my stationery? I haven't as yet obtained all of it, because the rest of the printed sheets aren't dry yet, but I'll be able to get them as soon as I'm in town again.

About school, the school quota is already full and they aren't able to take care of us, but our officer said he is going to try and get us in someplace in Georgia. I asked him and he said that if he can get us into school, I'm going – my name is on the school list. I asked if there were any chance of sending me to school anywhere in New England, or close by, any school, I didn't care what kind, but that would have made me too happy, and a soldier can't be that, and besides there aren't any up there.

Thank Edie for the hello and tell her I'm still waiting for that letter she promised me. If she doesn't hurry up, tell her that I won't let her get drunk at our wedding, or even kiss the groom.

I think I'm supposed to answer a question that you wrote me this morning, but I'm in the service club and don't have your letter, so you'll have to wait until to-morrow.

Your, George

P.S. With this stuff to write on, I feel exclusive as hell, think I'll become an officer – what say! J.G.B.

July 24, 1944
Monday

From:	To:
C.L. Sniderman	Mr. Pvt. J.G. Barr 11057933
65 Houghton St.	Eng. Sq., 4503rd A.A.F. Base Unit
Worcester 4, Mass.	Great Bend A.B.B., Kansas

Hello darling,
    I really haven't much of anything to write today, but I thought I'd write even if only to say I love you. It was miserably hot today, - I thought surely I'd melt, and to top it off, I nearly slapped Saul Sharfman right across his ugly face. Maybe he thinks he's cute, but I think he's downright vulgar and I told him so. So, what did he do? – He patted my shoulder and said to take it all as a joke. He's really a b____!!! Maybe I got so mad because I was so hungry and while he went home to eat a hearty meal, I had to work till six. Ah, - well, every dog has his day and I have absolutely no right to complain. But I do miss you so terribly.

    I just spoke to Edie and when I told her I got two letters from you today, she told me not to feel so swell 'cause she got two from Dave. I'm so glad she's in love too. Now she knows how I feel, - and what a wonderful feeling it is. I also got a letter from Bev today and she is also thrilled that we're engaged. So now I guess everyone's happy! Incidentally, I'm still getting engagement congratulation cards. Never knew I had so many friends.

    Darling, if you go to school in Dayton, just what are you going to study there, and for about how long? I wish you'd go to school again, and besides that, Ohio is much nearer home.

    I have oodles of letters to write, but I have no ambition to write to anyone but you. Ain't I the stinker!!

Polly is coming over in a few minutes and we'll probably go for a little walk. It won't be the same as the walk I had with you. Did I ever by chance happen to mention that I love you, - well, I does, - so there.

S'long for now dear. Will be back tomorrow.

Love, Lottie

P.S. One of the guys down our place has been pestering to take me out. His wife and baby are on vacation and he figures now's his chance. His name is George also, and Jesus he's homely. If you ever try that kind of stuff on me when I go on vacation, - I'll, I'll, - well, I'll be mad atch you!! C.L.S.

July 25, 1944
Tuesday

From:	To:
C.L. Sniderman	Mr. Pvt. J.G. Barr 11057933
65 Houghton St.	Eng. Sq., 4503rd A.A.F. Base Unit
Worcester 4, Mass.	Great Bend A.B.B., Kansas

Dearest George,

I can gleefully let you know that we are the recipients of another engagement gift. I received a ten dollar ($10.00) check surrounded by good wishes to us from Uncle Ike. He said he had looked around for something to buy us but couldn't find anything he liked and he was sure we could make good use of the money, - and that we can. So, at the first opportunity, I shall deposit that sum in our account. Ain't dat nice! Also, he said he would do much better by us at our wedding time. Very nice to have relatives, eh wot?! Also, my mother gave me two lovely sets of towels, and also my grandmother gave me another set of towels. They're really beautiful. Can't see what the devil I'm gonna do with so many towels, but housewives of long standing tell me you never have too much of those things, - so who am I to quibble. Besides that, I love to look at them.

Your mother just called me and it sure was a surprise to me. I thought she was having a grand time at the beach. It seems that Toby pulled a fast one and got quite sick from something she ate. So, your mother came back on the double. Both Toby and your mother are going back again Sunday for another week. She had a date tonight, - so I guess she's quite better. Also, Evelyn Issacman called me a little while ago. Jesus, but she sounds like an unhappy kid. She no sooner gets back to town, and she wants to run off again. She's staying with Evelyn (Red) Snider for the short time she will be here. What's the story!!! I received a lovely invitation to spend a weekend in Maine with one of our salesmen. If you remember, I wrote that he asked me up to his lodge once before. He's a very nice guy and I'd love to go, - but, - can't you just think of the scandal! My father would love to choke him for even asking me. Hmmm, - I wonder why!!!

It's still fiercely hot out here. What a swell week for the beach. Do I regret having taken my vacation when you were here? - not on your life!!

Well, darling, I gotta write me uncle a thank-you letter, and then to bed. When I finally do get to bed I only have to get up again to play games with a damn mosquito. Such troubles.

Goodnight dear.

Love, Lottie

P.S. Last nite I finally wrote a letter to Sid Plotkin, and also Dave. (I'm such a good girl!) L.S.

July 26, 1944
Wednesday

From:	To:
Mr. Pvt. J.G. Barr 11057933	C.L. Sniderman
4503rd Base Unit Eng. Sq.	65 Houghton St.
Great Bend A.B.B., Kansas	Worcester, 4, Mass.

Dearest Lottie,

Lucky us! We have the afternoon off. They got our schedule mixed up somehow, so we're free for the afternoon. I'm at the service club now, otherwise I wouldn't be writing, this is the coolest spot on the base. If all goes well, I'll see my brother Narky next Tuesday. I hope that they'll let me go to Denver. I want to see whether he looks like his picture, or the studio did the job. If they did, then maybe I'll have them do a job for me.

This morning we had an interesting lecture on "booby traps", and demolition of equipment. After the lecture, we went out to a field and blew a bunch of holes in the ground, all I got was a head ache.

During the lecture the officer said something about T.N.T. not going off if it was treated roughly, I'm glad that I knew it, because the next second he threw it on the floor. You should have seen some of the surprised expressions on the boy's faces. I think they were more surprised that it didn't go off than if it had. We're just a bunch of boys having a good time.

If I didn't want to finish up on my letter writing, I would have gone swimming, but since I've duty, duty before pleasures.

Darling, if I do go to Ohio, which isn't too far, (700 to 800 miles) I was going to ask you to come up. How would you like to take a trip if they send me to a school, a school were I'd be in a city, and not a camp? If I happen to be sent to a school, we can talk over more definite plans.

I know what you mean about Sundays. Everytime I got out of the water, I sort of looked around the beach for you. I was very disappointed not to find you there. Nothing seems right anymore unless you are with me.

Did you take my mother's invitation?

Where is Barb now? I'm glad that she's happy about the whole affair. Is she still traveling with the U.S.O. group? Give her my best, second best. First, darling, is always for you.

That was a cute poem, but of course, it doesn't apply to you, because darling, you were born with all those lovely, sweet things that made you attractive to me. Brains, beauty, poise, personality, and those million and one things that I love about you.

Why is it that Dave writes to you more than he does me, is it that he loves you more than me, or do you answer him faster than I do?

Here I'm on a new page, only to sign off. My darling, your letters are just like I read in the reader's digest – a fine miniature furlough!

Your, George

July 27, 1944
Thursday

From:	To:
C.L. Sniderman	Mr. Pvt. J.G. Barr 11057933
65 Houghton St.	Eng. Sq., 4503rd A.A.F. Base Unit
Worcester 4, Mass.	Great Bend A.B.B., Kansas

Dearest George,

Your stationery is simply devine, - and quite swank to say the least. I was a little sorry that you couldn't go to school in Ohio, but the fact that you will go to school is good news anyway. Even if there are no schools in New England, there are some in New York and around that area, - try and work on it, darling. And if you do go to Georgia, - I can always decide to spend the winter in the sunny climates, eh wot?

Last nite the younger girls in the office had a weenie roast at one of the cottages down the lake. We ate like pigs and had a swellegant time. After that we decided to go to White City, - and so we did. Since I was lacking in funds, I couldn't go on everything, but we did go on the bug, the whip, the baby horses, and spent more money in the penny arcade. I felt just like a little kid and it was wonderful. As a matter of fact, when the gang of us piled on the bus, we started raising hell, and some people who were sitting <u>near</u>

where I was <u>standing</u> noticed my ring. They were mumbling back and forth and naturally when I saw them looking at my hand I listened. They came to a definite conclusion that it couldn't possibly be an engagement ring. We all roared, - it was really very funny. The kids said I didn't even look old enough to have dates. I was wearing my saddle shoes, an old shirt (maybe a little short), my trench coat, and a ribbon in my hair. Come to think of it, I looked like little orphan Annie!!!

I came home from work tonight and was so exhausted I thought I'd lie down for a few minutes. I knew I had slept a long time when I suddenly jumped up and ran to the clock. It said 7:30 and I thought I was nuts, because I thought I was on my lunch hour. It was a very peculiar feeling. I forgot to notice that I had my shorts on and that it was slightly dark. It's a good thing I looked at the clock or I would have gone back to work. Sometimes I think I'm a little peculiar, - everyone says its love that does things like that to a person. Wonderful thing, this love business!!

Your letter today was so short that it was hardly worth the postage. Surely you can do better than that. Hell, you didn't even tell me you loved me, - maybe you don't, - who knows? Are you gonna take the cedar chest and go home to mother?!!!! Funny, ain't I? Goodnight, m'love.

Lottie

July 27, 1944
Thursday

From:	To:
Mr. Pvt. J.G. Barr 11057933	C.L. Sniderman
4503rd Base Unit Eng. Sq.	65 Houghton St.
Great Bend A.B.B., Kansas	Worcester, 4, Mass.

Dearest Lottie,

This has to be a quickie, because we had a storm here, which knocked the hell out of our lights until now. I've been waiting since eight o'clock, and it's now ten thirty and the boys want the lights out, but I have to write you, what can they do about it, nothing because they know how much I love you.

This afternoon I found that my pass was O.K.'ed, so I went and bought my ticket and found out the train schedule. I'll be able to be in Denver for two days. I wired Narky that I'll be there about 10 o'clock Tuesday morning.

This is the reason for the quickie. To-morrow morning I'm going on a three day bivouac.

Last night after I got my train ticket, I humped back to camp, meanwhile we had a terrific thunderstorm. It didn't last long and it left two large rainbows in the sky. They completed a semi circle on the horizon, very beautiful. I don't think I ever saw a more wonderful rainbow. The colors in one of them were brilliant. We may have them back home, but we can't see them for the hills and houses, here where it is level as far as the eye can see, is where you can see the entire rainbow. What a haul I could have made if I could have gotten the pots of gold under each rainbow.

The mosquitos are going to be terrific to-night. I'll probably wake up and my bites will be playing 'loops a daisy' with each other.

I bought a "Yank" magazine and I'm sending you "Snafu". I always get a big kick out of it. In a few months, all the "Snafu" (It's the "Sad Sack" & not "Snafu", but it all adds up to the same guy) cartoons are being published in book form. I'll get it and send it to you and you can enjoy the lighter side of the army.

That's all for now darling. I'll be dreaming of you.

Your, George

P.S. I may drown in the night, it looks as if another storm is brewing. J.G.B.

[Editor's note: The following comics and news articles were found in an envelope from George to Lottie, post marked July 28th, 1944. No letter was included in the envelope, although they were referenced in George's 7/27/44 letter]

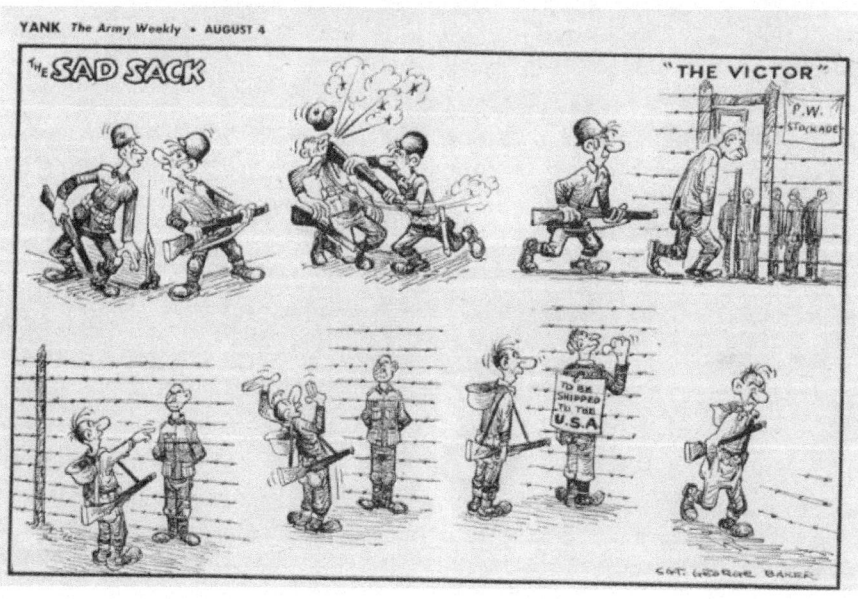

PUNNERY RANGE

The demure young bride, a trifle pale, her lips set in tremulous smile, slowly slipped down the long church aisle clinging to the arm of her father.

As she reached the low platform before the altar, her slippered foot brushed a potted flower, upsetting it. She looked at the slipped dirt gravely, and then raised her child-like eyes to the sedate face of the old minister.

"That's a hellava place to put a lily," she said . . .

* * *

The little boy was sniffing . . .

"Sonny," said a matron to him, "don't you have a hankie?"

"Yes," he snapped, "but I never loan it to strangers."

* * *

Courtship is a period during which a girl decides whether or not she can do better.

* * *

Clothes make the man, but with a woman they just serve to show how she's made.

* * *

'Tis sweet to love,
But, oh! how bitter
To love a girl
And then not gitter.

* * *

Here's to the happy, bounding flea,
You cannot tell the he from she
For they both look alike, you see.
But he can tell . . . and so can she.

* * *

Guard: "Halt! Who's there?"

Voice in the night: "You shut yer _____ mouth, or I'll come and knock yer _____ head off."

Guard: "Pass, friend."

* * *

Corporal: You still have insomnia? Have you tried counting sheep?

Private: That's no good. I counted 10,000 sheep, sheared them, combed the wool, had it spun into yarn, made the yarn into suits, took them to Boston and lost $200 on the deal.

"What ya trying to do," asked the waitress as the dogface left a nickel for a tip, "seduce me?"

* * *

Nothing on wings can travel as fast as a rumor in the barracks.

* * *

DEFFYNITION: LOVE — The most most fun you can have without laughing.

* * *

Add Last Words: If you'll zip your lip for a minute, sir, I can explain why I didn't finish cleaning the latrine.

* * *

Doctor: "How's the patient this morning?"

Nurse: "I think the sergeant is regaining consciousness. He tried to blow the foam off his medicine."

* * *

Synonyms—Hollywood marriage and three-day pass.

* * *

Siberian dogs are the fastest in the world.

Trees in Siberia are very far apart.

* * *

Of all the things I had to be
I had to be a lousy tree,
A tree that stands out in the street
With little doggies round my feet.
I'm nothing else but this, alas,
A comfort station in the grass!

* * *

I hate he, I hate he,
I wish he were die.
He tells me he love me
But oh how he lie.
Don't it awful?

* * *

The reasons that girls wear sweaters are perfectly obvious.

The Retort Logical

A city girl was persuaded to take a job in a country feed store. She had been warned the farmers there-abouts were great joshers and she was determined not to be "taken in" by them. The first morning a farmer came in and asked for some shorts (ground corn) for his pigs. The girl replied, "I'm sorry but we are out of shorts. How about some brassieres for your cows?" — Lions Roar.

* * *

You can tell a roadhog even in the theater. He always takes the arms of both seats.

* * *

"Oh Mary had a little lamb
Whose heart she so preferred:
But she couldn't wait and quickly wed
A wolf who'd been . . .

July 28, 1944
Friday

From:	To:
C.L. Sniderman	Mr. Pvt. J.G. Barr 11057933
65 Houghton St.	Engineering Sq., 4503rd A.A.F. Base Unit
Worcester 4, Mass.	Great Bend A.B.B., Kansas

Hello dear,

I have a feeling this letter is gonna be sort of a repetition of last week. Edie is again sleeping over here and again we have discussed the parties by the name of George and Dave. We felt like doing something, - so what did we do but go for a bus ride. Very exciting! It's so damn hot here we're practically stripped. Don't you wish you were here?! I still insist that you would blush!!!

I've been meaning to tell you that my brother Jerry finally got the franchise on frigerators, radios etc., that he was going to Chicago for. We're all so glad for him because so many other much bigger men were after that contract. Already he was offered a $25,000 profit for the contract, but it's worth a hundred times that.

Next weekend Edie and I are going to New London, Conn. And on the way, we'll stop to have dinner in Providence. What are we going to New London for, you ask? To buy clothes? – No, – To pick up some sailors? - well, - ... No! To visit some friends of ours – uh huh, that's it!!! Some of Edie's relatives have been asking us to come out for years, so we've finally decided to go. Speaking of Edie, she says she will drop you a line in the very near future and she sends her love, - for she really does love you, you know. Fine business and right under my very nose too.

I didn't get any mail from you today stinky. You had better write me, because the day I don't get any mail from you I'm unbearable. I've been working like a dog all week, darling, but I always manage to find 24 hours a day to think of you. Evelyn Bloom is getting married in October and bidding farewell to New England Grocer. How I wish it was I. I really envy her. You see, she and her guy are more fortunate than we, since he is not in the army. Think of all the weddings they'll be when this war is over. Your friends and my friends, - everything will be just joke and honky dory. No more worries about being separated.

Your mother called me and said she had found the picture I asked her for, and also another one of you when you were about a year old. I must go up and get them the first chance I have. Also, she said she met someone who asked her how she was going to get along with only five rooms when the boys come home. She quickly set his mind at ease by telling him that the two older boys were married, and the younger one was well on the way. So now it looks like I'm really stuck with you, - and how I love it.

Well, dear, me little head is splitting and I'm dog tired, so goodnight and pleasant dreams.

Lovingly, Lottie

July 29, 1944
Saturday

From:	To:
Mr. Pvt. J.G. Barr 11057933	C.L. Sniderman
4503rd Base Unit Eng. Sq.	65 Houghton St.
Great Bend A.B.B., Kansas	Worcester, 4, Mass.

Dearest Lottie,

I'm back in camp now, but we're only going to sleep here. Last night was so miserable for everyone that our officers thought it wise to go back to camp and in the morning, go back to our bivouac area.

We didn't get to sleep until one o'clock last night. It was awful, those mosquitos never had as much fun in their entire damn lives. The only reason we were able to sleep, was that over the opening of our pup tent, we threw a blanket and stuffed up the remaining holes. After making sure that a mosquito couldn't come in or out, we turned on a flashlight and killed every little bastard, then exhausted, we fell asleep. Now the mosquito bites are enjoying as hell.

The only thing we did was fire all day. Most everyone fired but about five fellows, I'm one of them, and we'll fire to-morrow morning.

The only constructive thing that happened to me was that I got a little darker.

Oh yeah! We also had very hungry grasshoppers, they ate holes in my shirt and about five small holes in one of my blankets. They weren't satisfied with all those weeds out there, they had to have a good G.I. meal.

The ice cream was very good, it was almost Peach Royal, I almost got a peach in mine. I made one mistake about who made the ice cream, the farmer's wife made the recipe, we had to crank the stuff. From now on I'm going to buy my ice cream at the corner drug store.

So long for now, when I come back to-morrow night I'll be a seasoned soldier.

Your, George

July 30, 1944
Sunday Nite

From:	To:
C.L. Sniderman	Mr. Pvt. J.G. Barr 11057933
65 Houghton St.	Eng. Sq., 4503rd A.A.F. Base Unit
Worcester 4, Mass.	Great Bend A.B.B., Kansas

Dearest George,

Last night Evelyn Issacman called me, but I wasn't home so she called your mother and asked if she knew where I was. It just so happened that my mother and I had just left the store and were going into S. & Ritz for supper so Evelyn came down and met me there. Then we went up to see Toby, - she had another attack of indigestion, and tho I feel bad for her, she rightly deserved it. After being as sick as she was, she sat down to a repast of pickles and watermelon. Whatta combination! She's much better now and she and your mother left for the beach today.

After visiting Toby, Evelyn came home with me and we really had an enjoyable evening. Since her folks and her were going to the farm today, she asked me to come along, and I grabbed the chance. As a matter of fact, I just got back. We had a lovely time, of-course, - but it wasn't the same as when you were there. The twins kept me pretty well occupied, - as a matter of fact, they didn't leave me alone for a minute. They really are good kids. Then I played poker and lost a whole dime, - lucky in love, - unlucky in cards, - that's me. Am I sorry? – Not on your life! Evelyn did something that was very sweet. While she was in Conn. She went into a gift shop and saw two potholders that she thought I would like, so she bought them for me. One is a little pair of pants and is positively adorable. There's a note attached which says, "If the plate is too hot, don't take a chance, - just turn around and grab you pants." Isn't that cute? I thought it was terribly sweet of her and I wonder if she realizes how much I appreciate the gesture.

Darling, if you are stationed in Ohio or any place near enough so that I can come, you can bet your boots I'll be on my way. It sounds too good to even plan on. So, lets keep on praying.

Last time I heard from Barb she was in Seattle Wash. I think now she's in Utah and she's still with the U.S.O. The tour winds up in New York around the middle of Sept. Gee, I'd like to see that gal.

Edie Lainer called me this morning and was going to come visit me, but I went away, so I guess she'll be up sometime this week. She and the unborn baby are doing just fine.

Incidentally, Beatrice (one of the twins) thinks you are handsome and wants you to marry me, hurry up quick, so that she can call me her cousin. Ain't dat sompin!

My dad hasn't been feeling too well of late, and frankly I'm worried. We're trying to get him to go to a doctor, but he's stubborn as all the other men.

Well, dear, I'm kinda tired. Will sign off till tomorrow at this same time.

Lovingly, Lottie

August 1, 1944
Tuesday

From:	To:
C.L. Sniderman	Mr. Pvt. J.G. Barr 11057933
65 Houghton St.	Eng. Sq., 4503rd A.A.F. Base Unit
Worcester 4, Mass.	Great Bend A.B.B., Kansas

Dearest George,

You are by far the sweetest person I have ever had the pleasure to know. Who else but you would have thought to send the Anniversary card? You are really a darling and the card was muchly appreciated. The clippings you sent were also very good. Darling, you have no need to worry over my dear boss, Mr. Saul S. He really is quite harmful, - even though he doesn't mean to be! Yours truly can surely take care of that "has been" who thinks he still is.

Very nice that you finally can go to Denver. I guess it's too late to tell you to say hello to Narky for me. Oh, well, maybe someday I will be able to deliver my greetings in person. Last nite Edie Arnold Lainer was over here. She is getting bigger and better by the hour. Yale is tickled silly that she's having a baby. She looks very well considering. We sat & talked and talked about absolutely nothing. That gal has always bored me stiff, - but she still was my company and I tried my best to entertain her. That really didn't require much work since she talked continually from the time she came till the time she left. But don't get me wrong. - I love her just the same!

George, I have a little bad news for you. I hope you won't take it too much to heart since nothing can be done about it. I felt terribly, but I've gotten over the first shock. Maybe if you'd have been home it wouldn't have happened. I came home from work, - picked up the newspaper and there in large print I saw that the Hovey Estate, all 15 acres, had been sold to a biological research company. They really didn't pay too much and I'm sure we could have met their price of $30,500. Life is full of disappointments, eh wot!!

The heat gets woiser and woiser. If you're wondering if I worked very hard today, let me enlighten you. I came back to work after lunch, - went up to the conference room and there, Dot Potash and I sat until about 2 minutes before 5:30. We smoked about a package of cigs and about 3:30 sent out for sundaes. We sang every song we could think of, and giggled ourselves sick. And that's what I get paid for! Dot and I decided that we're gonna ask for another raise.

We got another card of congratulations from Capt. Bill Lewis and his wife. She's the former Zelda Bass and they're really very nice people. They're all the way down Oklahoma and heard by special broadcast that we're engaged. Ain't dat somepin?!

Goodnight, m'love. See you in my dreams.

Love, Lottie

August 2, 1944
Wednesday 12:45 A.M.
Y.M.C.A.
Denver, Colo. U.S.A.

From:	To:
Mr. Pvt. J.G. Barr 11057933	C.L. Sniderman
4503rd Base Unit Eng. Sq.	65 Houghton St.
Great Bend A.B.B., Kansas	Worcester, 4, Mass.

Dearest Lottie,

At precisely 10:32 I found my brother Narky, it was a fifty-fifty deal, we both found each other on 17th St. He was walking one way, and I, of course the other. It is swell being to-gether, its almost been a year to the day since I last saw him.

The train ride was the most miserable ride I ever had to endure. The train was so crowded, that I walked on the chairs from one car to another. Boys were just strewn on the aisle and everywhere else. I managed to find a corner in between two cars where I lowered myself to the floor. Half of me was in one corner and the other half in the other corner. You could have drawn the outline of a Z on my contorted body. But do I complain? No, it was worth it, and I'd do it many, many times over.

We had dinner, then boarded a tram, they're trams in Denver, not trolley or strut cars (when in Rome, ect.), and travelled out into the surrounding mountains. We got off at the nearest stable and got us two, 1812 vintage, cow ponies. The ride lasted for three and a half hours. My body wasn't a bit sore, well it wasn't when I stood up in the saddle all the way back.

Our objective was to go to Lookout Mt., where the remains of Buffalo Bill are buried. After trying to get our horses up too steep an incline, we decided that our necks were much more important than a good see from the top of that famous man's grave.

No kidding, darling, but the scenery here is really beautiful, I have so many places to take you after this war. We'll have to extend our honeymoon indefinitely, and see the country, so we'll be able to tell our children the wonderful country that they live in, during peace time.

Darling, I wish the hell you were here with me. This room reminds me so much of the ones we had in Boston - even tho no red light.

Tho I'll have to leave here Thursday afternoon, I'll have your letters to read and make me happy. This saying hello and goodbye are too damn synonymous. When I do go back, I hope the hell that there are orders to go to school, because if they don't come pretty quick, I'm afraid that the school deal will have fallen thru.

We took pictures to-day, and I hope that they will come out good. We had a fellow serviceman take our pictures to-gether on horseback, well, I hope that the horses at least come out good. I was fortunate in being able to get ahold of another roll of film, so dearest, you should be getting some pictures of me - what a horrible thought!!!

I have to get a little rest now, dear, so good night, and may I dream of you.

Your, George

P.S. Lottie, my brother, Narky, Narky, my fiancée, Lottie. Now that you two know each other you should be very dear friends, soon relatives. –

[Editor's note: The next part of this letter was written by George's brother, Nathan "Narky".]

My Dear Future Sister-in-Law, now that we have been formerly introduced, I can speak to you as a brother. I know from Charlotte's reports that you are very charming and I know that George will prove himself worthy of your love. If he don't - just let me know and I'll paddle his fanny.

The very, very best of luck to you both and I hope it will be real soon that I'll be dancing at your wedding, as a <u>civilian</u>.

Love, Narky

[Editor's note: Pictures referenced in George's letter dated 8/2/44 of him and his brother Narky, horseback riding in Denver, CO]

August 2, 1944
Wednesday

From:	To:
Mr. Pvt. J.G. Barr 11057933	C.L. Sniderman
4503rd Base Unit Eng. Sq.	65 Houghton St.
Great Bend A.B.B., Kansas	Worcester, 4, Mass.

Denver, Colorado

THE CANTEEN FOR THE ARMED FORCES
OPERATED BY
The Army and Navy Commission of the Episcopal Church

My darling fiancée,

  This my darling, is being written to you just before we go out to dinner with the Triefuses. I wrote you about them when I was stationed here, they are the parents of one of Polly's school mates. I called up to say hello, and she invited us to dinner, how very nice of them. It was very funny, but I called her and said that I didn't think she'd remember me, when she said, "you're one of the Barr boys," I know some people have remarkable memories, but hers tops all I've ever known. It's been almost four months since I've talked with her over a telephone. It was a nice feeling to have someone recognize you in a strange place.

This afternoon Narky and I went swimming, a much easier exercise than what we did yesterday. He has to be in camp at ten o'clock to-night, so I'm going back with him to see if I can get a bunk in his barracks. I hope that he can get another pass for to-morrow also. I'll be leaving Denver at 4:45 P.M.

What did he write in the letter I sent you last night, rather this morning, or isn't any of my business? Here I thought I'd be able to censor it, shucks!

I wish that I had a pocket full of money so that I could buy you everything that I see. At least I have good wishes, soon I hope that I won't just have to wish.

I have to run, - alright I'm going to walk, now.

All my love, my dearest,
Your, George

[Editor's note: Pictures of George and his brother Narky in Denver CO on 8/2/44.]

August 2, 1944
Wednesday

From:	To:
C.L. Sniderman	Mr. Pvt. J.G. Barr 11057933
65 Houghton St.	Eng. Sq., 4503rd A.A.F. Base Unit
Worcester 4, Mass.	Great Bend A.B.B., Kansas

Dearest George,

Well, - I guess we finally got this "love" business straightened out. So sorry I made you angry, - will try not to do same again. Stinky, - what the devil are you sending me now. Remember you're the guy that said he was gonna save his money, but I love you for it anyway. If you're gonna write and tell me you've sent me something, why the hell don't you be a sport and tell me what it is? Now I'm dying of suspense. If it doesn't come tomorrow, I'll pass out from a nervous collapse.

Can just picture you and Bob in your fox holes. You'll really are getting to be hard seasoned soldiers. Me thinks you have no need to learn how to shoot a gun, - not unless you're aiming to shoot me when you get back. That would be novel. Can't you just see the headlines – "Soldier Rushes Home to Shoot Fiancée." Ugh, - gruesome, eh wot!

Now for some more serious business. George, for sometime now something has been worrying me and I don't know whether or not to write you about it. One of my old boyfriends, upon learning that I was engaged, has made quite a fuss. He doesn't believe that it's the real thing. I'm trying to take care of the situation in my own way, so that if possible, I can avoid enemies. You see, he always thought he was the man in my life, and naturally was shocked to hear I was engaged. George, I haven't written to you about this because I thought it might worry you, and that's one thing I don't want. I'm writing you about it now because I have a guilty conscience about it all, - I mean about all this going on (and it has been for some time) and you not knowing anything about it. I was afraid maybe someone else would mention it to you, and you'd be at a loss for what to say. If you want me to, I'll write out everything in detail, but if not, believe me everything is as right as it always was and you're still the only one I love. Unless, you ask me, I'm not going to mention any names because I don't know how you'll take it. I don't want you to be angry at him because I'm sure he'll get over it, and I want all three of us to be friends because, while he isn't the one I'd choose for a husband, he still is a nice boy. I feel much better now that I've told you. You can be sure that I'll never be able to keep any secrets from you because it would worry me to death. George, always remember that I love you, - come what may. If you want to know the whole story, I shall tell it to you. I can guarantee it would sound more like a novel than the truth. But if you want to forget about it, we'll never mention it again, - till death us do part, etc., etc., etc. My whole family has been worried about the situation, but I'm not, because I love you, and no one and nothing in the world can change that. So much for that, -

Goodnight darling,
Lovingly, Lottie

To
MISS LOTTIE SNIDERMAN
65 HOUGHTON ST.
WORCESTER
MASS.

From 31389999
D. Grossman
6th TRR. REG Cp.
A.P.O. 519
%P.M. N.Y.C.
Aug 2 1944

Dear Lottie,

Congratulations, Hon, all the luck, and happiness in the world. I'm tickled pink that you two guys did become engaged. I think you're going to make a swell couple. That guy sure is a lucky apple.

Received a letter from your hubby and he seems to be walking in the clouds. Love sure must be "wunnerful."

Just to make this letter dull, — I'm well and feeling fit as a fiddle. I've been taking life easy this past week but I don't think it will be too long before we're busy again.

I guess the army is trying to domesticate George. He wrote and told me he had K.P. as soon as he returned from his furlough. "Dear Mom, army life is wonderful."

Loads of luck, again, I'm sure looking forward to that wedding.

all my best,
Dave.

V—MAIL

August 4, 1944
July 4th
Friday

[Editor's note: Apparently, George is making a reference to July 4th, as that is the day he and Lottie were engaged.]

From:	To:
Mr. Pvt. J.G. Barr 11057933	C.L. Sniderman
4503rd Base Unit Eng. Sq.	65 Houghton St.
Great Bend A.B.B., Kansas	Worcester, 4, Mass.

Dearest fiancée,

Darling, this past month seems like we've been separated by an eternity of time. I have the most marvelous memories of our last two weeks to-gether. If I had to do it over again I would, even more so, because I'd know the pleasure and enjoyment that I get from our love. Let's hope that it won't be two many months before we are to-gether 'for better or worse.' (I'm getting the better and you are getting what's left).

Wednesday night, Narky and I had an elegant dinner and time with the Triefuses. We met their daughter Ruthie, Polly's school mate, but it was for about five minutes, because she had a date. I had sent their address to Narky, but when he looked them up, Mr. Triefus took him to his daughter's home for dinner. Narky wrote and told me that he thought Mr. Triefus was just doing his duty, and didn't really want me to call them up again. I told him he was mistaken and since he hadn't met Mrs. T., that we should call them up. Sure enough, they were delighted to have us, goodness knows why. Narky has changed his mind about them entirely, and intends on calling them again if he has a chance. He finished school and is awaiting orders to go to gunnery school.

That night, we slept in camp and remained there until I left in the afternoon. I looked up one of the boys who was still left because he was in the hospital, the one that was jilted. He was glad to see me and I him. He doesn't know what will become of him, but he hopes that he may be able to get a discharge.

Finally, I got a medal. I had to go to four different places before I found what I wanted. Knew it has to satisfy Buzzy.

As yet, I haven't written to Fran and Jerry, but hope to get around to it to-day.

Bob has been shipped out on detached service, someplace in Oklahoma. He's setting up or tearing down huts, possibly if I had been here instead of Denver, I would have gone also. I guess this means school isn't too near at all, because Bob was supposed to go to school even before me.

Lottie, I finally have my extra stationery wrapped, now I have to get it down to the Post Office. Hold on to it until I ask for a few pads and envelopes. Hoah Kay? You're sweet and I love you.

I received a letter from Bernie Goodstein, who's about 60 miles from here, he wants for us to meet. Maybe I'll be able to do it next weekend, I'm going to try and plan on it anyway.

I gotta go now my darling, but a happy Anniversary and may we be to-gether for all the rest.

Your, George

August 5, 1944
Saturday

From:	To:
C.L. Sniderman	Mr. Pvt. J.G. Barr 11057933
65 Houghton St.	Eng. Sq., 4503rd A.A.F. Base Unit
Worcester 4, Mass.	Great Bend A.B.B., Kansas

Dearest George,

In case you're interested, I'm writing you while I'm in the girl's room at the office. It's too damn hot to do anything else. I think the temperature is close to 100° and everyone is all washed out. Edie slept over again last nite. Golda Edinburg and Jeannette Baskin came over and we went riding. There was a big moon and Golda felt like kissing a soldier, so we rode all over town looking for a tall soldier for Golda to kiss. It really was a riot, - incidentally, the only one we could find that was tall enough was colored and Golda absolutely refused. Thursday Polly, Edie, & I went out for supper and the movies. We saw "Mr. Skeffington." Twas very, very good, and we all had a good cry for ourselves.

Narky's note was very cute and muchly appreciated. Does he look as good as his pictures? How the hell could you kids go horse back riding for hours. I was tired just thinking about it. Incidentally, Jeannette Baskin said she just couldn't picture you engaged. She said she could still picture you in knee pants in grammar school. This place is filling up, - Evelyn Cohen, Phylis Jacobson and Sylvia are in here. I find concentrating quite difficult. - I'm back in the big office now and sweltering. Dave just came in and said we could leave at 12, - yippee!!!! I'll finish later, darling.

Well, I am now in Union Station waiting for Edie. I told you we were going to New London for the weekend, didn't I? Well, we are. It's so hot I don't know how the devil we're gonna travel. My mother called and said I had a letter from you. I'd love to go home and get it, - but then again, there's something to look forward to when I get back.

I don't know if you're gonna be able to read this or not, - the window seat isn't the best place in the world to write a letter. I wish to hell you were going with me. Did I ever by chance happen to mention that I love you? - Yes? O.K., so I'm repeating myself, - any objections. There's a god damn fly annoying me, - I think I'll go kill him.

So long for now, dear.
Lovingly, Lottie

Boardwalk and Beach at Ocean Beach, New London, Conn.

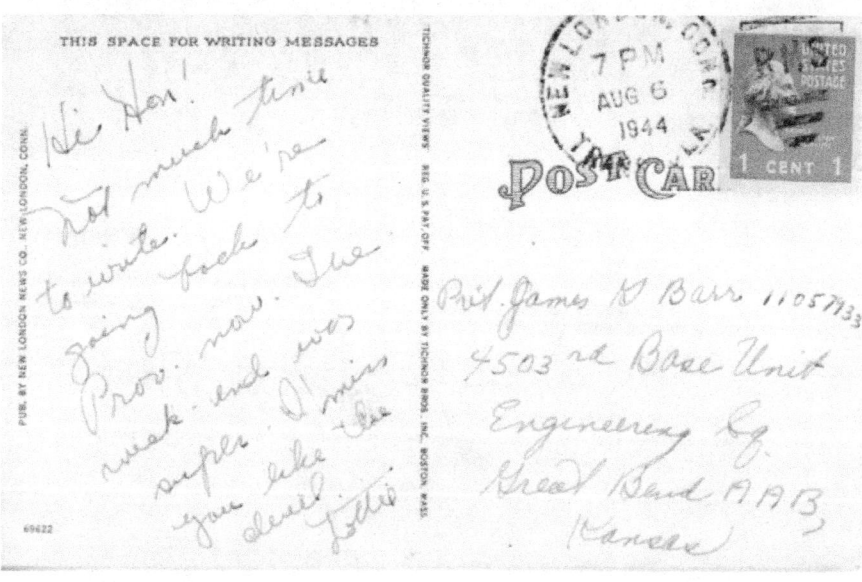

THIS SPACE FOR WRITING MESSAGES

Hi Hon!
Not much time
to write. We're
going back to
Prov. now. The
week-end was
super. I miss
you like the
devil.
Lillie

Pvt. James K Barr 11057M33
4503 rd Base Unit
Engineering Sq.
Great Bend AAB,
Kansas

CUSTOM HOUSE TOWER, BOSTON, MASS.

We ate at ? ornin, ~ what memorys, remember!!

U.S. CUSTOM HOUSE, BOSTON
is the highest building in New England. The
new tower reaches 505 feet in the air and is
a total of 30 stories in all.

Hi Hon!
We're just
coming back
from Boston
altho this
won't be
mailed till
Tues. Got
loads to tell
you. Love
Ladie

We'll all are busy

Pvt. J. M. Barr
11057933
450 3rd Base Unit
Eng. Sq
Great Bend AAB.
Kansas

HOTEL PIERONI, 7-8 PARK SQ., BOSTON—FAMOUS FOR ITS SEA GRILL

Pieroni's

OTHER GRILLS AT 13 STUART ST. AND 601 WASHINGTON ST., BOSTON

When in Boston, stop at HOTEL PIERONI and dine
in one of PIERONI'S famous SEA GRILLS. Established 1895. — The rooms really
looked that old,
didn't they!

Remember?!!!!

POST CARD

A "COLOURPICTURE" PUBLICATION, CAMBRIDGE, MASS., U. S. A.

PLACE
ONE CENT
STAMP
HERE

August 7, 1944
Monday

From:	To:
C.L. Sniderman	Mr. Pvt. J.G. Barr 11057933
65 Houghton St.	Eng. Sq., 4503rd A.A.F. Base Unit
Worcester 4, Mass.	Great Bend A.B.B., Kansas

Dearest George,

The hanky is darling, - I'll surely not waste it on anything as minor as my nose. Thank-you, dear. Your trip to Denver sounded very nice, but I'll bet you didn't have half the fun that Edie & I had. Could be because your boys and we're girls! Well, I told you in the numerous post cards that we sent, that I'd tell you all about it, - so here I go.

We took the bus to Providence Saturday and had a very miserable & very hot ride. It was so hot in Worc. that all the stores closed at 4:30, - even we got out at 12, as I told you, I think. When we got to Providence, we washed and started looking for someplace to eat. We went into some very nice place called the "Old France" and sat down minding our own business. At the next table to us sat this sailor. He asked us where we were from and proceeded to start a conversation. Well, he had just come off the train from Calif. and was dead tired. He asked us to join him for dinner, and after arguing back and forth a little, we finally did. He turned out to be a very wealthy and very charming person. He showed us around Providence a little, then put us on the train and said goodbye. So much for Gregory.

The train to New London was mobbed, - all servicemen. So, Edie & I put our suitcase in the vestibule & sat on it. Also, standing in the vestibule were these 3 darling sailors. One had a bottle of scotch and was serving everyone who'd come by. We didn't stop laughing from the minute we got on the train till we got off. So much for Johnny, Jimmie & David.

Saturday night we stayed with Edith's cousins, of course. They are three sisters & a brother who are three old maids & a bachelor. They made life a little miserable for us with their constant nagging about smoking & not eating enough, but they were very nice all the same. Sunday, we went to the beach & it was beautiful. Edith and I decided it would be an ideal place for the four of us to rent a home for the summer after we're married.

Around 6:30 Sunday we started back for Prov., but on the train, we decided since the train was going to Boston, we might as well go too, so we changed our tickets & went to Boston. On the train sitting in back of us was a soldier with the same insignia as Dave, so Edie asked him if he was from the camp, and sure enough, he lived in the barracks next door. So, of-course, we started a conversation with him. He was very nice to us, - bought us candy and everything. He got off at Prov. So much for George. – When George got off the train, three sailors got on, and since they had to stand, Edie asked them if they would like our seats. They of-course refused, but one of them sat in the seat with us. So, Edie & I, & the sailor had another conversation. He was from Alabama & was studying to be a dentist before he enlisted. He got off at Back Bay, – our trip to south station was a rest period.

We got off in Boston, checked our bags, washed and went to Pieroni's to eat. The same Pieroni's where we stayed. I wanted to ride up the rickety elevator, but Edie wouldn't let me. We sat down and the place was mobbed. We had a double table and since it was so crowded, two sailors asked if we'd mind if they sat at our table. Of-course we said no (by this time we were used to it), and we started talking. They had just come back from 13 months in Africa and couldn't get over how wonderful it was to see American people again. They also insisted on paying for our dinner, took us back to South Station, bid us farewell, and again we were on our way. We had to stand most of the way to Worc., but we were so numb we didn't mind. Then to top it off, the cab driver was so drunk that he nearly hit every tree on Houghton St. And that was our trip to New London!! Whatta time.

In Prov. I bought you a copy of Bob Hope's book "I Never Left Home." You simply can't buy it in Worc., – they sell out so fast (damn this pen, anyhow!) I'll mail it out to you tomorrow.

Edie got a letter from Dave today and he's shipping across very shortly. The poor kid's a wreck, – can't blame her in the least. I don't care if you don't go to school, so long as you stay in the country.

Darling, I've really got writer's cramp now. This is the longest letter I ever wrote in my life.

Goodnight darling, pleasant dreams and despite all the sailors, I still & always will love you very much.

Lovingly, Lottie

P.S. Tonight is very cool, – fall is in the air, there's soft music on the radio and golly how lonesome I feel. There's nothing so bad as a feeling of empty loneliness. L.S.

August 8, 1944
Tuesday

From:	To:
C.L. Sniderman	Mr. Pvt. J.G. Barr 11057933
65 Houghton St.	Eng. Sq., 4503rd A.A.F. Base Unit
Worcester 4, Mass.	Great Bend A.B.B., Kansas

Darling,

My first impulse was to send you a telegram today when I received your letter. But I thought you'd get scared, and anyhow I knew I'd have to write you the whole story. I had no idea my letter would make you feel uneasy and make you worry. I wouldn't have you worry for the world. When I wrote that I had a guilty conscience, I only meant that I thought it was unfair for you not to know about him, - and I'm not ashamed of anything that has been between Maxie & myself. I always knew you knew about Maxie, altho you never said a word about him. If you had, I would have told you a long time ago what I'm going to tell you now. Maxie & I were more than just friends up until about a year ago. Even before that time, altho we were very good friends, we battled constantly. All the time that Maxie spent being nasty, you were working overtime being sweet to me and I couldn't have helped loving you. While I liked Maxie, I want you to understand that I never loved him, - never. I knew what loving a person was when I fell in love with you, - until that time it was vague to me. It seemed that after you gave me your ring last December, Maxie started writing again and begged me to write him, which I did. I told him nothing about us because I was afraid he'd think I was using you as a means for making him jealous and I didn't want him to even mention your name in that light. My letters to him were very platonic, while his were a little more than that to me. When we became engaged, I had planned to write him, but Phil Sobel told him before I had a chance. Naturally, he was very surprised and quite excited. I've written him explaining everything, - why I didn't tell him about you before, and all other details, he understands and his best wishes are ours, honestly. George, please believe me, there's absolutely nothing to worry about because there's absolutely nothing between Maxie and myself. If it hadn't been you (and thank heaven it is), it would never have been Maxie. I feel very bad now that I've mentioned all this at all, because altho I'm trying to make you understand, words seem very futile. Please, don't dislike Maxie, because he doesn't dislike you for being the better man. I still want the three of us to be friends. He has recognized fully the fact that I'm engaged and in love with you and respects the situation. If only I could see you to make you understand that everything is as right as it always was and always will be. I'm really terribly worried about all this.

Instead of being worried, you should really be flattered that someone else wanted me, and I chose you (you lucky kid!) But I'm really glad you know. Someday Maxie, his wife, and you and I will laugh about all this, and my children will think their mother was a hussy. Not only do I love you, but my folks think you're super, my brother is in love with you and my pal (your sister-in-law), thinks you're divine.

As I re-read your letter, I find one thing that puzzles me. You said, "you didn't want to say anything that would hurt me and no matter what, that nothing could come between us." I can't seem to understand what you mean. Everything between Maxie and I was so innocent & harmless that I can't possibly understand what you could say that would hurt me. Please explain, - that paragraph really has me worried.

And now enough about Maxie. He is really something in the past. There's too much about the future to think about to even let the past interfere for a minute. Now I hope you have nothing more to worry about, - I love you, - you love me, and Maxie loves the other 90 million girls that are left. But I'm still going to be on pins and needles till I hear from you in answer to this letter. Funny how we dig things out of the ground to worry about.

Goodnight, darling, and remember I'm always yours,

Lottie

P.S. Sidney Brunelle got married tonight. He was the guy that said he'd never get married until after the war. Ha! Would you like to be the next one to marry on a furlough? – I would!!

From B-17 (6144)   August 12, 1944
Altitude 8,400 ft.   Saturday
Flying South

From:	To:
Mr. Pvt. J.G. Barr 11057933	C.L. Sniderman
4503rd Base Unit Eng. Sq.	65 Houghton St.
Great Bend A.B.B., Kansas	Worcester, 4, Mass.

My dearest fiancée,

Things cannot be any sweeter than when I'm able to see you and hold you in my arms. Tho this time it was comparatively short, I'd do it many times over if I have the opportunity. While riding thru the clouds, many times I'd see your loveliness, I'm always thinking of you. Darling, I love you so much.

After you left me, we waited till 12:30 for the captain, then it wasn't until one o'clock that we took off. Tho we have seven original men, we picked up five more who are going south.

This fight is turning out to be a sight seeing tour. The main reason we took the flight was to bring a large box, I don't know what it contained, to Newark. It had the captain's name on it, so it may have been a personal reason. At Newark, they asked him the purpose of the flight because we wore a tire to the fabric and had to replace it. The captain told them if they call Sperry Gyroscope Co. in N.Y. and gave them the proper identification code, they would probably tell them, knowing of course, that they didn't possess such a code and didn't have the authority for it even if we did fly a secret mission. I guess the captain wanted a little vacation. Why the hell didn't he stay in Newark longer!!!?

We flew to Mitchell field N.Y., where they changed the tire and wheel for us, then we went to Langley Field Va., about 25 miles of Norfolk, north of it. We slept at Langley and took off at 8:00 A.M. for Orlando, Fl., which is about half way down the coast of Florida and a little inland. From there we're going to Atlanta Ga. or New Orleans, or Atlanta to New Orleans, I don't know exactly, as yet.

The weather has been ideal for flying, clear all the way and pretty cloud formations above and beside us. We passed Savannah Ga. a few minutes back, and we're flying along the coast now.

I hope your relatives in Long Island appreciate a nice girl like you and show you a good time.

For a minute, I thought we were going to have to turn back at Langley because we saw gasoline escaping from the top of the tank, it stopped in a few seconds, just overflow.

Gee, but I love you stinky! How I'd love you in my arms again!

Your, George

P.S. Radio fine.

This is being mailed from camp. We didn't go anyplace except Shreveport La., then back to G.B. I'll write the rest later.

August 14, 1944
Monday

From:	To:
Mr. Pvt. J.G. Barr 11057933	C.L. Sniderman
4503rd Base Unit Eng. Sq.	65 Houghton St.
Great Bend A.B.B., Kansas	Worcester, 4, Mass.

Dearest Lottie,

You now see a very angry person in front of you! Not a half hour ago, I came off of guard duty. Guard duty is something that has to be done in the army, altho I don't relish it, I know I must do my share and don't mind it as such. But – but when I'm given two and a half hours notice that I'm going on guard duty was also annoying, but when I wasn't relieved for over two extra hours, that's when I really burnt up. My relief is on detached service in New Jersey and they didn't find out until an hour after I was overdue on my shift. I was going to stay on for eight hours straight, but fortunately, the officer in charge, came back from a little plane ride and took me off because there was no longer any need for guards. I was guarding an airplane that had had radar, but it was no longer on. Gee, but I want to go home!!! This war can't last forever!!

Life is funny in its ways, in your last letter you wrote that if you could only see me, regarding your affair, which wasn't your affair, and then before I even got the letter, we had already ironed everything out. Lottie, darling, love is grand, and it is grand loving you.

Your card from Pieroni's really brought back pleasant memories. One thing is certain tho, we are slowly improving our tastes.

We didn't go to any of the places that I mentioned we were going to go to. After we left Langley Field, Va., we went to Orlando Florida, then to Shreveport La., and then to G.B. I don't think I was so tired in all my life, even Sunday morning I was groggy. To relieve the situation, I went swimming and enjoyed the full benefits derived from the sun and water, after about four relaxing hours of that renewing combination, I felt like going on another trip. If I could see you again, I would have gone on a similar trip, just after we landed Saturday night, see how much I love you.

While I'm writing this, there's a super duper poker game going on beside me, not nickels and dimes, like I play occasionally, but quarters and up, well - maybe they can afford it, I cannot.

I hope to get to-morrow off, and if I do, I intend going swimming again.

When I was in town yesterday, I saw an inexpensive book on arrangement of flowers, total cost of thirteen cents. I thought you may like it, because of the flower pot on the chest, and the other flower pots you have, and those we hope to have. I'll send it to you first chance. Oh yeah, I remember that we forgot to give me "I Never Left Home."

I'm going to write my folks now and then hit the hay. Goodnight darling, and pleasant dreams.

Your, George

August 14, 1944
Monday

From:	To:
C.L. Sniderman	Mr. Pvt. J.G. Barr 11057933
65 Houghton St.	Eng. Sq., 4503rd A.A.F. Base Unit
Worcester 4, Mass.	Great Bend A.B.B., Kansas

Dearest George,

Well, here I am back again, - and I still can't believe it all did happen and that I did see you. The cab driver waited for me while I packed and checked out, and then drove me to the station. I didn't have any trouble at all getting to Long Beach, but I was terribly hot and terribly tired. I had a grand time at the beach, - not doing anything but lying around in the sun and the water was tres excellent. In that short time I was there, I got a beautiful tan. Wish you could see me now. – I really look good for a change.

Sunday my cousin Lou drove me to the train station at Long Beach, and we got there just in time to see the train pull out. I was miserable because that meant I would miss my train in Grand Central, - so Lou grabbed my bag and I ran after him and he drove me to the next stop, but since we were held up by a draw bridge, we missed the train there too, so again we started running, and he drove me all the way to Jamaica Plains where I made the train in about $\frac{1}{2}$ second. I met my father in Grand Central and from there on I left everything to him. Your brother Sol called me Saturday nite but I wasn't home so he called again Sunday morning. My mother, your father and Toby were the welcoming party when I got home. I never answered so many questions so fast in my life. Your mother is coming home from the beach tomorrow. So, I'll have to go through the whole routine again.

Your father called this morning and said he received your telegram. Last nite when I got home I found two letters from you and it seemed so strange reading what you had just told me yourself. The cab driver was very nice to me. He said it was the first time since he drove a cab that anyone was ever on time. He also said that my <u>husband</u> was a nice fellow. I smiled and didn't argue with him. I'm dying to know what the secret mission was. Whatever it was, I'm very glad about the whole thing. I'm glad I didn't know you were leaving Friday, because if I had, I wouldn't have come and I wouldn't have seen you. But even those few hours were something we can always remember. If you ever come up around this way again, you can be sure I'll be Johnny on the spot, - but it'll mean my job. Dave was ready to fire me this morning, but Charlotte told him Saturday that if I went she would go to, so this morning Dave was exceptionally nice to me. He called me in his office and I was ready for the business, but he only asked how you were and about my trip etc.

I can't understand why Charlotte would leave if I got fired, - she said she nearly cried when she even thought how close she came to losing me. Guess the jerk kinda likes me, - but I like her awfully well, too.

Darling, I laugh everytime I think about how angry you were at that sailor. You're silly, - but I love you for it. You'll never know how empty I felt when I went back to the hotel, - it just wasn't fair. But twas better than not seeing you at all.

Well, darling, I guess that about finishes this missive for tonight.

> *Goodnight, dear,*
> *Love, Lottie*

P.S. I received your stationery, - I never saw so much paper in my life. L.S.

P.S.S. My cousin Lil gave me a simply exquisite bracelet, - or rather two of them. One (the genuine) was advertised in the New York Times Sunday and I'm enclosing it. Even the remake cost plenty of dough, but I was crazy about it so she gave it to me. Please notice the price of the genuine. You can buy me one like it for our 75th anniversary. Me

August 15, 1944
Tuesday

From:	To:
Mr. Pvt. J.G. Barr 11057933	C.L. Sniderman
4503rd Base Unit Eng. Sq.	65 Houghton St.
Great Bend A.B.B., Kansas	Worcester, 4, Mass.

Dearest Lottie,

No letter to-day, or yesterday, but how could you when you were with me, huh? Darling, I love you, all day long you are with me spiritually. I do nothing without thinking of you. So, you see sweet, I love you.

This morning I woke late and went thru my day as planned. First, I washed my 'personals' (my undies), rested, ate dinner, and took off for the old swimming hole. At the pond, I swam and swam and played around like a porpoise. When I got tired I rested in the sand and smoked a cigarette, also trying to kill all the flies on the beach. When some G.I. trucks went back to camp, I hopped on and rode back with them.

After eating supper, I went to the movies to see "Summer Storm." The picture proved much better than I had hoped for. The only unfortunate thing tho, was that the lights would go out every once in awhile for a moment or so, very annoying, but that was what we were having, a summer storm.

Now I'm back in the hut and finishing up my day, and that is writing letters, again I owe plenty. That's the main reason I no longer receive any mail, I have everyone's letters and they don't have mine.

As you can see by this letter, nothing very exciting ever happens to me. The only thing exciting anymore is when I'm with you.

So, my precious, until another day.
Your, George

August 16, 1944
Wednesday

From:	To:
Mr. Pvt. J.G. Barr 11057933	C.L. Sniderman
4503rd Base Unit Eng. Sq.	65 Houghton St.
Great Bend A.B.B., Kansas	Worcester, 4, Mass.

Dearest Lottie,

For a little while I thought this letter would not have got written to-night. We are having another one of our Kansas storms, and the lights were out for some time. It seems that as long as there are a few flashes of lightning, the lights go out. For a few minutes, we even burnt a candle for light. Sticking on top of an old ash tray, it reminded me of that honky tonk place I was in, in New Orleans. Very romantic, but what good is that when you are all alone with just men? No, good!!

To-day one of our boys took the final step. He got married in the chapel with just a few of the boys with him. Her parents weren't here and neither were his, that I don't like. He got a three-day pass, what a honeymoon they'll be able to have. It was unique, in that the wedding supper was held in our mess hall. Just the people that attended were there and that's all. This is not for us!!!

I don't know how we ever get into religion, but we manage every once in a while. To-night we argued about everything imaginable. It's funny, but Bob had very definite ideas on religion until he got in this hut. He had gone to Sunday school most of his life and was brought up to believe everything that was taught him. I asked him so many questions that make him think for himself, that he's quite confused. It's all for the best tho, a man should think about what people tell him. These discussions are good for the mind anyway.

I learned a little more about the operational functions of one of the radio sets that our ships carry, so that in about six more months I ought to know a little something about what I'm in the army for. I hope the war ends much sooner than that tho.

I've still many letters to answer, but unfortunately, I won't be able to to-night, it's too late.

You may think us crazy after I tell you what we did, but I feel justified. We were waiting to take a shower all night, but the rain kept us in. Finally, Bob and I stripped and got into our raincoats and went to the shower room. By the time we got up there we were soaked, if the rain wasn't so cold we probably would have showered in the rain. Anyway, (the lights were still out) we got into the shower, Bob was across from me and the only part I could see of him, and vice versa, was where he wasn't tanned. It looked like a pair of white shorts suspended in mid air. We don't make much money, but we have a good time.

Good night darling,
Your, George

August 17, 1944
Thursday

From:	To:
Mr. Pvt. J.G. Barr 11057933	C.L. Sniderman
4503rd Base Unit Eng. Sq.	65 Houghton St.
Great Bend A.B.B., Kansas	Worcester, 4, Mass.

Dearest Lottie,

I just came from seeing "Mr. Skeffington", which only reminded me of you when you wrote that now you have a suntan you look good. This brought back, 'A woman is beautiful only when she is loved.' You've always been loved, but since I love you the most, you are more beautiful to me than anything else in my life.

I'm happy to know that you rested and had a good time at Long Beach. If you say that the bracelet is exquisite, then it must be, and I must buy you a similar one in a few years.

I got a big kick out of Charlotte's threat to Dave. Tell her I love her for it, will you, and I can't blame her for loving you, I know many good reasons why. Don't worry about jobs, because when I get home, all you'll have to worry about is our twenty-four children and having supper ready for me when I come home from the office. The children should be an easy job in comparison to taking care of me. If you don't believe me, ask my mother.

I hadn't received a letter from you for so long that I was in heaven when I got this one. In fact, I read it as many days as I didn't get any mail from you.

What did my mother have to say about me going on a plane ride? I know she's always been against it, but when so much good was done by it, I guess she would have no objections. I'm glad that she had a chance to get away this year for so long, or does it seem long?

Darling, guess what – I found Buzzy's medal and will send it to him after I answer all my other letters. It takes me an awful long time to catch up, because I don't write more than two or three letters a day. If it wasn't so hot during the day I'd write more, but when it's hot, I'm in no mood to do anything.

Everytime I take your picture off the shelf to write you, I kiss you, and before I put it back on the shelf, I kiss you again. You, my darling, are my favorite pin up girl. I love you so much.

All my love ----
Your, George

August 18, 1944
Friday

From:	To:
C.L. Sniderman	Mr. Pvt. J.G. Barr 11057933
65 Houghton St.	Eng. Sq., 4503rd A.A.F. Base Unit
Worcester 4, Mass.	Great Bend A.B.B., Kansas

Hi honey,

I sort of ran out of my own stationery so I'm using a little of yours, - you have so damn much I was sure you wouldn't mind, do you? You do, - well, that's too bad because it's too late now and anywho, I'm sure you don't mind since you're getting it back in the end anyway.

The weather is so hot, - it's positively unbearable. Even we got out of work early today. The other stores and offices have been closing at 1:00. We just had a delightful thunder storm, - it shook me right out of my size 5 shoes.

Last nite my mother and I went to visit your folks. Your mother looks wonderful, - brown as a berry. I also noticed last nite that your father looks especially good. You know, he's quite a good looking man. Your mother bought me a lovely apron, - now you'll have to do the dishes because I know you wouldn't want me to spoil my pretty apron, - or would you!

Sylvia Coblentz Goldman & I went to see "Tender Comrade" the other night and had a crying good time. It was the saddest picture I've seen in a long time, - some of the scenes brought back memories of my own.

My other boyfriend just called and gave me a nice kiss via telephone. My other man being Seymour of-course. The twins are staying here for the week and I promised to take them out. So, tomorrow night, Toby, the twins, and I are going out to the movies if it isn't too hot, - if it is too hot, I don't know where the hell I'll take them, but I think it's gonna be more fun for me than it's gonna be for them.

Your mother gave me the picture of the three of you in the Indian suits last night and I keep looking at it. If my baby is as cute as you were, I'll be perfectly satisfied. I was thinking of all the things that happened to you from that time till now. The most unfortunate, of-course, being your relationship with me. I bet now your mother wishes you were a girl instead. Wonder what kind of a girl you would have been had you been a girl. Probably awful, - O.K. - so I didn't mean it!!!

Well, dear, I guess I'd better go drop a few thank you notes. It seems I'm always thanking people for something or other, - maybe it's because people are nice to me, - which makes me very happy, - so what am I complaining about.

Goodnight, m'love,
Love, Lottie

George Barr, Nathan "Narky" Barr, and Sol Barr in the "Indian Suit Picture" referenced in Lottie's letter dated 8/18/44.

August 19, 1944
Saturday

From:	To:
Mr. Pvt. J.G. Barr 11057933	C.L. Sniderman
4503rd Base Unit Eng. Sq.	65 Houghton St.
Great Bend A.B.B., Kansas	Worcester, 4, Mass.

Dearest Lottie,

I hope you like the pictures, there are three others that I'm sending the negatives home, so that Jackie can enlarge them. Now you owe me some of you. I also sent my dad two packages of K-rations that I "found" in a B-17. One is a breakfast, and the other is a dinner. I was going to send them to you, but I didn't think that you'd want them, maybe you'd like to see it, but not to keep them, and my father will get a big kick out of it, so he gets them. If you want some I'll see if I can pick some more up.

After spending a hard day, bruising myself, wandering thru the B-29, I felt pretty low in the mouth when I received no mail to-day. The rest doesn't matter much, but I had hoped there would be one from you. You tell the postmaster next time you see him that I don't like him anymore. And if he wishes that he get back in my good graces, to hurry up your mail.

I almost had to work to-morrow, but fortunately, I have a good boss, and he chose someone else to work. Now I'll be able to go swimming. There is nothing so good as to lie down in the sun and rest.

I haven't anything else to write darling, but maybe the little poem that is also enclosed will help explain.

Your, George

P.S. Did this get by with only one stamp? J.G.B.

August 19, 1944
Saturday Night

From:	To:
C.L. Sniderman	Mr. Pvt. J.G. Barr 11057933
65 Houghton St.	Eng. Sq., 4503rd A.A.F. Base Unit
Worcester 4, Mass.	Great Bend A.B.B., Kansas

Dearest George,

In dear old New England, there is no happy medium, - last week hot, - this week comparatively freezing. Pardon me while my teeth chatter. Last nite I took Evelyn Issacman and the twins to the movies. Toby, Arshy, & Etty were also with us, but they went to see Danny Kaye in "Up In Arms", while the twins had already seen it. So, we saw some awful war torn propaganda picture at the Warner. The twins loved it, - so what does my opinion matter. Today I took my mother to see "Up In Arms" and it was wonderful. Danny Kaye is really some guy. Must be nice to have him at a party!

The wedding that your friend had was every bit romantic, - and not at all a bad idea – but I'm afraid we'll never have one like that. My family would never forgive me if I cheated them out of the chance to dance at my wedding, and besides that, I want everyone there, - I know you do too.

Yesterday I met Edie for lunch and we decided to do a little window shopping. The first window we looked into looked promising, so we went inside the store. Ten minutes later we both came out with new dresses. They were so darling, we couldn't resist, - but the price wasn't so darling. We thought it would help boost our morale. It's really funny how we try to find excuses for the things we do that we know we shouldn't have done, but hell, a girl does need more than one dress! Wonderful thing these charge accounts. Now I'm worried sick about how I'm going to pay for it. Such troubles I have!

The minute the weather gets cool, I proceed to get extremely lonesome. It never fails. I can always depend upon my mood to change as the season does. I think I'd rather stand pain than loneliness. But nothing can be done, so I'll just have to grin & bear it like the rest of the population. But there's absolutely no consolation in the fact that millions of others feel the same as I. I really shouldn't be writing you about how lonely I feel, - that doesn't help you in the least, but people always miss people they love, and I'm no exception.

Tomorrow morning my dad is going to the doctor and I'm going with him. He's not feeling at all good, I'm really worried. I guess tomorrow we'll find out just what's wrong with him.

Well, darling, it's pretty near 1:00 A.M. now and I'm really beat. Too bad there's no mail on Sundays. Guess I'll go kill a few mosquitos and then call it a day.

> *Goodnight dear,*
> *Lovingly, Lottie*

P.S. Thought you might be interested to know that our bank account now has a balance of $94.00. I've been trying my darndest to put back what we took out and I think I've done pretty good. L.S.

August 21, 1944
Monday

From:	To:
C.L. Sniderman	Mr. Pvt. J.G. Barr 11057933
65 Houghton St.	Eng. Sq., 4503rd A.A.F. Base Unit
Worcester 4, Mass.	Great Bend A.B.B., Kansas

Dearest George,

Your letter of today was very sweet. I can assure you I read it over more than once, - even more than twice. Yes, you're right, - a woman is beautiful only when she is loved.

My lonely feeling grew worse and worse yesterday. Everyone was away for the weekend and I thought I'd go mad sitting here alone just thinking. So, since my dad had to get some medicine down Water St., I said I'd walk down for it. I stopped in the store to see your folks but they were busy so I didn't stay long. Incidentally, your father went to New York yesterday for a few days' vacation. He looked very sharp. I started walking home again and since I passed Evelyn Issacman's house I thought I'd drop in. But as luck would have it, she wasn't home. Her folks insisted that I stay for a while so I did, and before I knew it an hour had passed and Evelyn was back with her boyfriend. He's some soldier she met on a train and he's at Cushing General Hospital in Framingham. He was wounded in Italy, and after eight months of being in the hospital there, he was sent back here. He's originally from New York. So, by this time, it was time for supper and they insisted I stay, - so I did. In the meantime, your mother and Toby came up also. They were as much surprised to see me there as I was them. So, I made a salad (I made, - how do you like that, - and it was good too) and we all had supper. Then the Issacman's wanted me to go to the farm with them, but that meant your mother and Toby would have to go home alone since your father had already left for New York, so I didn't think I ought to go. So, your mother and Toby came back home with me and we had a very enjoyable evening. Mr. & Mrs. Issacman liked me because I wasn't bashful, - little do they know how I used to blush when anyone so much as looked at me. Your mother told me that they are very anxious for me to cultivate a friendship with Evelyn. Evelyn was kissing me all over the place. It's such a nice feeling to be liked.

During the course of my visit, Evelyn dragged out the old picture album, and lo and behold, there was my own dear sweet little George cuddled up close to some dame from Boston. Also, this same gal was at the beach with you and you both looked very, very chummy. Your mother thought it was a riot when I started burning up all over the place. Funny how you never mentioned your other love life to me, - you killer diller, - you. It just shows to go ya, - ya can never trust a man!!!

I just finished putting some more pictures in my album. I love to look at pictures. Hey, whatever happened to the ones you took. Tomorrow I'm going to bring a roll in to be developed, - here's hoping they're good. I'm glad you found Buzzy's medal. He'll be glad. I hope you also wrote a letter with it.

Well, darling, I gotta go take a bath and then to bed. I've just been listening to the church bells and they're clanging away for all they're worth. Sounds as if maybe peace has been declared, - but I guess not, - that's much too much to hope for.

I love you very much.
Lovingly, Lottie

P.S. There was just a special bulletin on the radio asking the people to please stop calling the police stations & the WTAG to inquire about the whistles. It seems everyone thought it was a celebration of some sort, - but I was wrong too, - it was not a church bell. The truth is that the Hartford train coming into Worcester had its whistle stuck and they can't shut it off. Such excitement, - such noise, - and all for nothing. L.S.

August 22, 1944
Tuesday

From:	To:
Mr. Pvt. J.G. Barr 11057933	C.L. Sniderman
4503rd Base Unit Eng. Sq.	65 Houghton St.
Great Bend A.B.B., Kansas	Worcester, 4, Mass.

Dearest Lottie,

I received your letter on my stationery and it even looks good getting it back that way, especially when it's from you. Is that why I haven't received as many letters from you as I hope for? You know what is mine is yours, you know that, don't you? So, use it.

I'm about half way thru "I Never Left Home." Bob, (I know him personally) is just as good a writer, as he is a comedian. Thanks loads, and I'm sure the boys will appreciate it almost as much as I did, after all you did send it to me.

What else have you gotten that you're sending 'Thank You' notes? Why tell me how nice people are when you don't tell me why they are so thoughtful?

To settle the argument about who's going to do the dishes, I'll either have to do one or two things. Either buy you a dish washing machine or get you a maid, which is your preference? Me, I prefer a pretty blonde!!!! – O.K. you can have the washing machine, gee – you always have your way!!!

But, darling, all kidding aside (except for our twenty-four), we'll eat from paper plates.

Yesterday I received a pair of shoes from home, and while I was putting a polish on them, who should walk in, but Bernie Goodstein. I didn't think he ever received my letter because I wasn't sure of his address. Here I am all set to spend a quite evening in the hut and write (I had only written six letters while at work and was still ready to go a few more.)

We ate in my mess hall and it was his first time eating from mess kits for over a year. The guy never had it better. If you remember how he looked in December when I was home and we were all at the 620 Club, well he looks twice that now.

Luckily, there was a dance in a town about 20 miles from here to go to. The base was supplying transportation, and the townspeople the girls, maybe I should say the females. I usually think about girls as pretty little things. They weren't even little. What the hell do I care tho, I have my dream girl, as if you didn't know. I love her too, would you like to know her name? Why, it's on the front of the envelope this letter came in.

Bernie, did all right tho, he got a name, address, and telephone number. I wasn't sure people out here knew what telephones were.

Don't mind me tho, because some day if we ever go thru Kansas, you may not think it is civilized, well at least they don't practice cannibalism.

I'm glad that you saw my folks and it sure did this heart good to know that they are looking well, and I'm sure they feel well when you go to see them, because darling, when they see you, they see part of me – the good part.

Good night darling, and I'll be dreaming of getting a letter from you to-morrow – Bob Hope will never take the place of you.

Your, George

August 22, 1944
Tuesday

From:	To:
C.L. Sniderman	Mr. Pvt. J.G. Barr 11057933
65 Houghton St.	Eng. Sq., 4503rd A.A.F. Base Unit
Worcester 4, Mass.	Great Bend A.B.B., Kansas

Hello darling,

The pictures you sent are very good. I liked the ones where you and Narky showed your he-man chests, - or reasonable facsimile!! The clipping was also good, - and very true. I love that kind of sentiment. Incidentally, the letter did come through with one stamp.

I worked like a dog today at the office. I get busier and busier, and the Sharfman's get richer and richer. Charlotte said she absolutely refuses to let me leave, - even when I get married. She suggests I bring the twenty-four children down the office, - can't you just picture what a happy little scene that would make. Dave would pull the two remaining hairs right out of his head. Every two minutes Sylvia and I run into the girl's room for a cig. I talk about you continually, and she talks about Erwin continually. We can plan our whole life in the space of time it takes to smoke a cig. She was stinkin' mad at Erwin because he asked for money and when she didn't have it to send him immediately, he blew up. Nice guy! So, she borrowed money and sent me to mail the money order. He even starts an argument via letters. I hope we never quarrel over money when we get married. But on second thought, we won't have any money to quarrel over!!

Tonight, I simply must write a letter to Dave G. I received a letter from him ages ago and it still isn't answered. So, tonight's the night.

Edie Arnold Lainar called a few minutes ago, and wanted me to go for a walk. Just because she's having a baby, she thinks I should walk, - big deal.

Well, m'love, not much more to write tonight. I don't know why you haven't been getting many letters from me lately. Must be the mail situation, - what else.

Goodnight dear,
Love, Lottie

August 23, 1944
Wednesday

From:	To:
Mr. Pvt. J.G. Barr 11057933	C.L. Sniderman
4503rd Base Unit Eng. Sq.	65 Houghton St.
Great Bend A.B.B., Kansas	Worcester, 4, Mass.

Dearest Lottie,

Darling, you are wonderful. You are good for me, I'm the most fortunate guy alive to have a girl like you. Most women are supposed to spend money, but you my darling save it. You may say you worry about buying a dress, but you know definitely that it will be paid for, for if you didn't, you wouldn't have bought it. I'll bet it's pretty, because one of your many marvelous characteristics is the choice of clothes, and on you they look good.

Just as soon as I pay my brother back the money I borrowed from him, I'm going to try and send a few bucks home for our little nest egg. The $7.50 bond will help, but I'm going to try and add a little more whenever I can.

I just started reading a serial in the 'Colliers' magazine called "Earth and High Heaven." It's a love story, but interwoven in the plot is the conditions of the marriage of a Jew and a Gentile. I think that you'd like to read it. It starts in the Aug. 26th issue. Clifton Fadiman, Eddie Cantor, Louis Brimfield and others give praise to it, so I'm not all alone in my opinion. The story strikes home.

To-night I saw "Buffalo Bill." While I was in Denver it was given such a build up that I went to the show here expecting, - expecting what I don't know, but I was a bit disappointed after seeing it. If I had seen the picture without any impression in my mind, I would have enjoyed it much more – it was still entertaining.

Darling, you're marvelous, taking out so many people, I'm going to make it up to you, and when I get home I'm going to take you out. Whenever we have a chance we'll go out and have a good time, and people will say, "There are the Barr's enjoying themselves, don't they go well to-gether." And the women will say, "Isn't it too bad, and she was so young and beautiful too, and to have to get stuck with him." – Like I always say, women don't know what they're talking about half the time. No kidding sweet, we will have fun together!

I received a letter from home to-day, or I received an envelope from home, the letter was for Narky. I'll send it to him, and he'll no doubt send me mine. That's what makes life interesting, little things like that happen.

I had a squadron detail to-day, clean the latrine, day room, chapel, and cut grass. Well, I helped with the former, but when I started to try and cut the grass and it didn't cut, I got mad. When I examined the mower, and saw that the blades were round instead of square, I dropped the mower and quit.

The damn lights went off a minute ago, and the last sentence was written by flashlight. Now everything is O.K. What a place!!!

You are lonesome and so am I, in fact, when I passed the telegram office to-day, I felt like wiring you – "Lottie, I love you," but just that might have started you wondering what had gotten into me. I love you anyway, even tho I didn't send the wire.

> *Good night my little spare rib –*
> *Your, George*

August 23, 1944
Wednesday

From:	To:
C.L. Sniderman	Mr. Pvt. J.G. Barr 11057933
65 Houghton St.	Eng. Sq., 4503rd A.A.F. Base Unit
Worcester 4, Mass.	Great Bend A.B.B., Kansas

Darling,

I have no idea why you don't get mail from me regularly, since I write you every night. Maybe I've been putting on the wrong address or something, - but that is quite impossible. Maybe you'll get them all at once. I know exactly how you felt when you were with that young couple. I've experienced the same feeling many times. Someday we'll make up for all the time lost. I also received your booklet on the arrangement of flowers, - and very nice too.

Edie Megans is over here tonight. We finished supper and then hashed over all the good old times. She sends her best love. I've been having a little trouble with Edith, as far as Dave is concerned. She's writing him a very drastic letter now, and I don't like it. Will write you more details tomorrow.

Very nice girl who gave you the film. Remind me to thank her someday and also dislike her, - or didn't you know I was the jealous kind!!!!

Darling, I don't see why you don't accept the dinner invitation that couple extended to you. You might go and pretend that it's us a few years hence. Only we'll probably have the patter of little feet all over the place.

The war news today has been so wonderful that I feel good all over. Paris gone, Romania on our side, and Marseilles is gone. Darling, I think we'll be together much sooner than anticipated. It's good thinking about it anyway.

They're playing nice soft music on the radio now and I want you near me more than you can imagine. Are there any more little plane excursions in view?

Well, my love, I guess that's about all for tonight. I feel very nervous and restless tonight, - maybe because I'm so damn lonesome.

> *Goodnight dear,*
> *Love, Lottie*

August 25, 1944
Friday

From:	To:
Mr. Pvt. J.G. Barr 11057933	C.L. Sniderman
4503rd Base Unit Eng. Sq.	65 Houghton St.
Great Bend A.B.B., Kansas	Worcester, 4, Mass.

Dearest Lottie,

When I received two letters from you this morning, I was in heaven. I felt light and gay and just good all over. I always feel good after receiving a letter from you, but two at a time – it's great.

I hope that your dad is feeling much better. After all it's senseless in getting sick, he is old enough to realize that. I really wish he's O.K. at this letter writing.

I'm rejoiceful knowing you had a good time Sunday. You must be becoming a good cook. It's not everyone who can make a good salad, you know. If I had tried, it probably would have been thrown out.

Yesterday I had K.P. again. That is one thing that they made sure I don't miss, that and shots. Bob was on K.P. to-day and I'm now eating some of the cookies that he managed to bring back with him, they're good too.

I got a kick out of that girl in Boston. It seemed so long ago, in fact I had forgotten all about it. How I got to go with her is still one of the mysteries of life, no doubt I was still young. I grew up tho. The way you wrote, you might think I was a wolf, Aooooo! 'Nough said for that!

I feel sorry for Sylvia, but she had plenty of time to make up her mind for what she wanted in a man, if you can call Erwin a man. You're not fooling when you said we won't argue about money, whether we have it or not. Darling, we are no longer two different people, with different thoughts and ideas. We're a team in where we work together, to get the most out of what we have.

This letter may become more messy than it is, because Bob is questioning me every minute for a word of some sort so he can work his crossword puzzle. The only reason I'm helping him is so that I can get the funnies after he is thru, but I'm very little use to him, so I'm not sure whether it's worth the effort or not.

For the next month or so our outfit is going to teach a newly formed group how to operate a hangar. Now we're a bunch of instructors. There are more men running around in the hangar that no work is being done at all. I feel pretty good about the whole affair because I know a little more than any of the boys we have. Most of them tho, have been in England for quite some time.

Our outfit, according to higher ups, is so good that they wouldn't send us overseas until we teach a few new groups how it is done. Then we're supposed to leave, but that is rumor, but it came from one of the officers.

When I enlisted, I wanted to get my training and go overseas, but now it is too late. The main reason is that I have you, the other, even tho I'd like to see foreign lands, might mean I'd become part of the enormous policing force that the allies are bound to have. Nope, my mother never brought me up to be a soldier. P.S. The army is doing a bad job of it too.

If you were asking me about Evelyn, well, she's a sweet kid and all that. Once in awhile would be nice, but too often, I think, might make you disgusted. Of course, I can't judge, it has been a long time since I've seen her, and with her getting away from her mother might have made the world of difference, besides, you are the wise one.

I'm so glad every time you write me that you love me. Even tho I know it without a doubt, it makes my heart skip a beat or two. I love you with all my heart too, this also makes my blood race thru my veins.

Good night my love.
Your, George

P.S. I'm glad you like the pictures. J.G.B.

August 25, 1944
Friday

From:	To:
C.L. Sniderman	Mr. Pvt. J.G. Barr 11057933
65 Houghton St.	Eng. Sq., 4503rd A.A.F. Base Unit
Worcester 4, Mass.	Great Bend A.B.B., Kansas

Dearest George,

Yours is a very cold Lottie tonight. I'm clothed in my slacks, a sweater, and your jacket. Remember that poem about New England, - if you don't like the weather just wait a minute, - well it certainly held true today. Going to work this morning it was freezing, at lunch time it was raining, after lunch it was sweltering, - and now its freezing again. Good old New England.

I was quite surprised that you saw Bernie Goodstein. I saw him last time he was home which was about the beginning of the summer and you are certainly correct, - there is an awful lot of Bernie. He looked just like a little barrel, or a big one! At that time, I told him if he ever saw you to give you my love, - I've seen you twice since then and he's just getting around to it. I'm glad you liked Bob Hope's "I Never Left Home." I thought it was very good myself. Which only goes to prove that again we like the same things. Which is a very gratifying deduction, eh wot!

So, you'd like a blond maid, eh? Well, darling, since we're going to be so fabulously wealthy, I don't see why I can't have a red headed butler. If that meets with your approval, - then the blonde maid is O.K. with me (I bet your thinking "De hal mit you, dear!).

Last nite Edie, Harriet Goldstein and I went for a spaghetti supper and then to see Danny Kaye, - again!! I think he's simply wonderful. Harriet nearly went nuts. She hadn't seen it before and we couldn't resist telling her what was coming. Oh, yes, about Edie & Dave, - well, for the present it's all off as far as she's concerned. I felt terrible when she told me because I thought they would really get together. But she's not sure about her feelings toward him and doesn't want it to go too far until she is sure. She slept over here and all night long she kept saying she just couldn't picture me married. Maybe it was because I had my butcher boy pajamas on and I was jitter bugging all over the place. My hair was hanging long and I must admit I looked very young, - and felt even younger. I had a giggle spell and couldn't stop laughing. Edie kept saying, - poor George, - I'll have to warn him. Darling, do you really think you could learn to put up with me!!

Labor Day weekend Evelyn Cohen, Dottie Potash, Sylvia Coblentz and myself are going to Boston. We have rooms at the Sterling and we should have a good time. While Evelyn & Dottie are out wolfing, Sylvia and I will stay in the hotel writing letters. I can just imagine what will go on in the hotel with the four of us sleeping together. Sylvia & I are sleeping together and she's going to wear her black nightie just for me, - hells fire, - I can't imagine what for!!!!

I just spoke to Polly and she sends her love, - whatta business. Edie kisses you all over the place when you're here, Polly sends you her love, and Charlotte (at the office) says she's going to kiss you next time you come down. I don't know whether they really like my choice or whether the man shortage is getting them down. In either event, I'm going to post a "Hands Off" sign on you next time you come home.

George, I miss you something fierce. It's awful not having you around, - after all this time I'm still not used to it.

I brought some more money in the bank on our account and the girl said - quote, - well, now you're in the 3 number bracket - unquote.

Evidently, she's watching our account grow too. We have exactly the flat rate of $100.00. I'll admit it's not much, - but it's better than nothing.

Holy cow, I didn't realize I wrote so much. I really must dash, - you whilst forgiveth me, ain't cha!

Lovingly, Lottie

August 27, 1944
Sunday afternoon, - and beautiful too.

From:	To:
C.L. Sniderman	Mr. Pvt. J.G. Barr 11057933
65 Houghton St.	Eng. Sq., 4503rd A.A.F. Base Unit
Worcester 4, Mass.	Great Bend A.B.B., Kansas

Hi honey,

Today is really gorgeous, - what a pity to spend it alone, - or with Pauline. We're going to do something exciting, - like a tour through the woods or going to the movies.

This morning I had some workout. I was rudely awakened by Buzzy pulling the covers off me and then he decided I should learn how to wrestle, - so I learned, - but the hard way. He received the medal you sent him and was prouder than if he'd earned it himself. Rickie was also here this morning. What a baby! You should see him dance, - better than his aunt to say the least.

Yesterday me mater and I went window shopping, - and oh, - all the money we could have spent. Then we had lunch and went to the movies. We saw "Double Indemnity" and it was surprisingly good. Then we had supper down Water St., stopped in to see your folks, and came home. Ain't dat thrillin'! Tomorrow night Toby and I are going out to dinner and then she wants to buy a dress. I'm really afraid to go because every time I go with someone to buy a dress, I also come home with one. Satan, get thee behind me!

I took out the pictures yesterday that Edie & I took at the beach and they're awful. I don't know whether to send them to you or not, - I'll decide when I finish this letter.

You made me sound as if I were simply wonderful saving that money. It really wasn't wonderful at all, - I wish I could have done better. But honey, if we want the things we like (and we both like nice things), we're gonna have to save because they're no other ways we can get them. I'm much to independent to take things from either my folks or yours. So, - we'll work, we'll save, - and we'll have.

I've just looked over the pictures and decided that me no send. I've got another roll of film, and if these come out better I'll send them. Can I help it if I'm not photogenic!

So, good afternoon, darling.
Love, Lottie

August 28, 1944
Monday

From:	To:
C.L. Sniderman	Mr. Pvt. J.G. Barr 11057933
65 Houghton St.	Eng. Sq., 4503rd A.A.F. Base Unit
Worcester 4, Mass.	Great Bend A.B.B., Kansas

Dearest George,

Yours truly now feels like a second Mr. Anthony! Edith just called and has a very guilty conscience about Dave. She hasn't received a letter answering her letter telling him that she wasn't in love with him, but feels that he ought to have another letter on the subject, - so she had Harriet Goldstein write him a letter, and after reading it to me I finally persuaded her to throw it in the waste basket. It was full of explanations and sympathies, which I was sure he wouldn't want from a third party. So again, I persuaded her to write to him herself, making the letter very platonic and very friendly with no love angle attached. I know every word in the letter since I dictated it and she was very pleased with the results. Maybe it was so good because I can call myself experienced at it, - after Maxie. It's hard to write a letter of that nature and still remain friends. That, my dear, is what is known as tact.

I was a little happy and a little distressed over your letter today. The part about becoming an instructor is great news, - the part about going overseas makes me a little weak in the knees. Of course, you say in about a month or two, and many things can happen in that time, but George, should you go across, a part of me will also go. I can't bear to even think of it, - and I'm going to try not to until such a thought becomes necessary. We both have a way of putting our thoughts away until the time comes. But I do want you to keep me posted on any news, rumors, or otherwise, just so that I won't be too shocked.

Toby, Evelyn Issacman, and myself went shopping tonight for a dress for Toby & Evelyn, and much to the disappointment of all of us, we couldn't find a dress for either of them. I saw quite a few dresses that I liked but it didn't go well with them, either the style was wrong or the price was wrong. As for Evelyn, she felt quite miserable tonight since her boyfriend that I wrote you about is no longer her boyfriend. All I can say is that it was an awful short romance and she's talked herself right into the idea that she's a born spinster. If she keeps up that whining and nagging trait, she'll not only not get a boyfriend, but she'll lose her friends, as well. I realize she's a spoiled kid, but I can't stand a person who whines and complains all the time. But don't get me wrong, I still like her and I still think she's a nice kid. She was nice enough to buy me my supper tonight and then before we went home Toby insisted on buying us sundaes. Ugh, - more calories!

Saturday while my mother and I went walking downtown, we found a tiny blue baby's booty. This is supposed to be good luck, so my mother insisted I keep it. I still had it in my hand when we went into your father's store – you can just imagine the look of astonishment. I wasted no time in explaining, - and they all thought it was very funny. Your dad suggested I either wear it on my lapel or send it to you to scare you. Would you have been scared, darling? After all, it happens in the best of families. Aren't you glad we're not one of those families?!

Well, dear, I've just about written myself dry. Take care.

Lovingly, Lottie

August 29, 1944
Tuesday

From:	To:
Mr. Pvt. J.G. Barr 11057933	C.L. Sniderman
4503rd Base Unit Eng. Sq.	65 Houghton St.
Great Bend A.B.B., Kansas	Worcester, 4, Mass.

Dearest Lottie,

Before I forget, I'd like to ask you to send me three pads of stationary, three and three, and about fifty or so envelops. Just wrap them up at your leisure, and post them, also at your leisure, just so long as I get them in a week or two. O.K? Thanks, you're a darling.

I feel like a monkey, the way I've been crawling around the planes today, a tail would have come in handy many times. One time I could have wrapped it around one of the wooden beams on the ceiling and worked on the tail of a B-17. But I had to be content and climb a small crane, so that I could do my work. I was mad, here I had on a nice clean pair of fatigues, and I had to get them and myself filthy. I didn't mind getting dirty myself, but my fatigues!!! I really don't care, besides I was able to put my hands on three tubes that I may be able to make into a radio after I can get the rest of the necessary material. You'd think that I'd be able to get a bunch of stuff, being a radioman (ahem!), but it is almost an impossibility, I have patience.

Putting up one of the antennas this morning, I devised a method of attaching it to the ship simpler than it was being put on before. The other way took three or four tries, whereas it now takes me one. All you have to do is file off a portion of a little thig-a-magig and there you have it. It's nothing much at all, but it makes me feel good to be able to do things in the shortest way, maybe it's because I'm lazy.

I'm almost finished with "Marriage is a Private Affair", and the more I read it, the better I like it. It is very excellently written and it keeps you on your toes trying to see ahead of the story. If you have a chance read it, it's by Judith Kelly, you'll like it.

Within thirty days we are to give our hangar up to the new group. What will happen then is still vague and uncertain. It's even rumored we'll go on a six week bivouac, I hope it's just latrine rumor. We're practically living under field conditions now, what more could they ask? The only difference between bivouac and G.B. A.A.B., is that instead of having huts, we'd be living in tents.

The only thing that really hurts is not being able to be near you Sweetheart, loving you is what brought to me from my boyhood into my early manhood. If it wasn't for you, I think I'd still be a child, and wouldn't be able to take some of the things the army has. If it wasn't for you, I wouldn't know what I'm fighting this war for, when I first enlisted I was still a child, I didn't know why I had gotten in, now I know why I should have gotten in. Enough of being philosophical, all I wanted to say was that I'm very dearly in love with you.

Goodnight my love.
Your, George

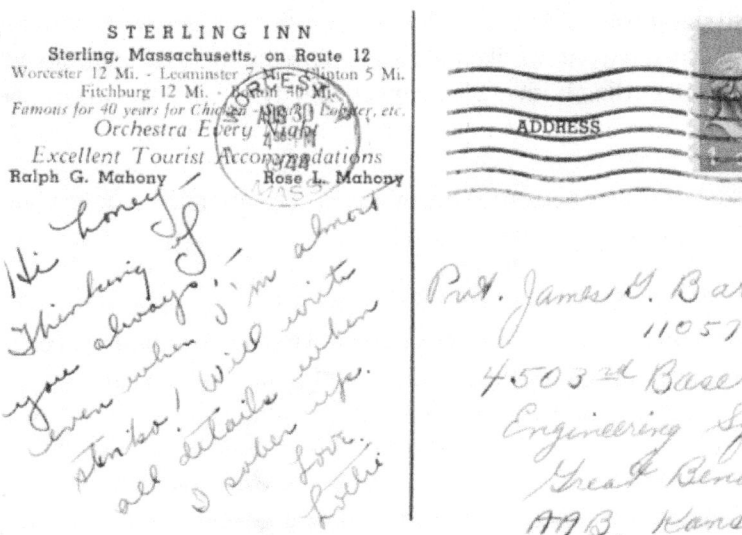

August 30, 1944
Wednesday

From:	To:
Mr. Pvt. J.G. Barr 11057933	C.L. Sniderman
4503rd Base Unit Eng. Sq.	65 Houghton St.
Great Bend A.B.B., Kansas	Worcester, 4, Mass.

Dearest Lottie,

I'm sorry that the pictures didn't come out any too good, but you not being photogenic?! Why, darling, of course you are, do you think for a moment I'd pick out a wife that I couldn't take a good picture of? I proved that you are when I took pictures of you when I was home. You have all the assets of a pin-up girl, and then some. You little devil you are gorgeous, and I love you, not only for your physical being, but more important, your spiritual self. I couldn't have found another girl, even similar to you, if I searched the four corners of this world.

The only obstacle you have to overcome is letting your picture be taken. When you sit in front of a camera, think that it is the person who is going to get the picture. Look at it, as if you were looking at the person, whether it be me, your parents, or anyone else who you think will see it – simple isn't it?

I'm really happy that Buzzy liked the medal, I thought maybe by this time he would have forgotten all about it, but I see I don't know as much about children as I ought. I'm going to try my darndest to be a good husband to you, and a good father to our children. I know with your help I'll be both.

I thought you might like Sid's last letter, but since he wrote it to me, I thought maybe he wouldn't like me to, but since he was giving me advice, or statements regarding both of us, then I changed my mind, so I'm going to send it to you. After all, we are no longer two separate, different people, we are one.

The letter hasn't changed my mind and I doubt if it'll change yours, but I think his letters are worth reading.

I didn't do a thing all day long except lounge around the hangar. Won't do anything to-morrow, but get paid and wait to get paid. What a dull life this army is becoming. Don't misunderstand me, I don't mind it, because I know how they can change this dull life, and I don't think I'd like to try it.

Last night we had a miserable storm that almost blew our hut away. The wind was strong enough to blow the tops of some of the huts off tho. Our hut managed to survive, but how it did it is one of those little wonders. The walls came in at least six inches everytime a gust of wind hit it. Stuff would be knocked off the shelf and the rain dripped in, but luckily it dripped on the floor and not anything of any value.

I was surprised this afternoon to receive a letter from Harvey Coblentz, he's up in Nebraska some place. He thought it would be nice to write because we're about 400 miles apart. This adds another one to my list of correspondence. I love to receive letters, but to answer them, that's an entirely different story. Maybe because they are so ordinary run of the mill class, but since people write me, they expect answers and probably overlook a small matter like that, but to me it's no small matter. A person has to improve tho, even tho it's from repetition.

Good night, sweet —
Your, George

August 31, 1944
Thursday

From:	To:
Mr. Pvt. J.G. Barr 11057933	C.L. Sniderman
4503rd Base Unit Eng. Sq.	65 Houghton St.
Great Bend A.B.B., Kansas	Worcester, 4, Mass.

Dearest Lottie,

I have just returned from one of the huts, where I had a very interesting conversation with a sergeant. All sargeants are not dumb, even tho people are given that impression by the movies and irritated G.I.'s. For a long time now I've wanted to take a correspondence course in something, mainly photography, but I've let it slip thru my hands. At one time, I wrote and found out about the course. The tuition fee at the time stopped me, but now, as far as I've been able to find out, the army itself is sponsoring such a course at two dollars. I'm going to fill in the application and send them the required amount.

Later on, when I finish the course, I hope to take something in the line of math, maybe a little English (at least I need some solid spelling lessons). It is not so much for myself that I want to learn, but for what the future holds for me. No longer do I have that, - I don't give a damn – attitude. I definitely do give a damn!

After I get home I'm going to be a bread winner, and at the right time, a father. When a child of ours asks me a question, I want to be able to answer it so he'll be able to understand and remember, not like me – to understand, but not to remember. I haven't forgotten about you, my main reason, because if it weren't for you, I'd probably be in town getting rid of my pay on some foolish thing. At some later time, I'll want to "throw" my money away, but now is not the time. If for some reason, I get out of this mood, wanting to enlarge my education, give me a good talking to, remember!!!

I wouldn't have been one bit scared, if you had sent me the booty, but I doubt if I would be able to stand up – I would have been shocked! Darling, we don't need any good luck charms as long as we have our love, that is all we need to get along.

I'm as sorry as you about Edie and Dave, because we both know what a person is missing when they are not in love, but as things turned out for us, and many other couples, it will be right with Edie.

Sweetness, don't worry about the rumor of us going overseas. Nothing more has been said about it, and no doubt it will be forgotten. In any case, if we do go across, it will be work behind the lines and not up in the front. If I thought, and I should have, that it would upset you so, I never would have written you unless I was absolutely sure. We will put off such thoughts just like you said, besides what would they want with a radio repairman that can't even repair a radio?

I hope to go to Wichita, Kan. for the holidays, my three-day pass application is in, and should be signed without any trouble. There is supposed to be a pretty large Jewish population there, so I should feel a little at home.

> *Good night, my love.*
> *Your, George*

August 31, 1944
Thursday

From:	To:
C.L. Sniderman	Mr. Pvt. J.G. Barr 11057933
65 Houghton St.	Eng. Sq., 4503rd A.A.F. Base Unit
Worcester 4, Mass.	Great Bend A.B.B., Kansas

Dearest George,

I just had quite a surprise. The telephone rings and who should it be but Barbara. I haven't seen her yet, but I can tell she's quite changed. Her manner of speaking and way of expression are definitely not the same. I guess a change should be expected, but somehow, I wished that she wouldn't be different from what I remembered. But I'm just an old softy sentimentalist anyhow.

The party for Evelyn Bloom at Sterling Inn turned out to be a huge success. I don't remember whether or not I told you that Evelyn Cohen, Dot Potash, Mimmie Sigel, and myself, wrote the program and also were cast as the singing "Four Angels", - only Dottie & I turned out not to be so angelic.

We got on the stage, - Dottie looked at me and I looked at her and in the middle of our song we had hysterics of laughter. The audience was rolling on the floor watching us laugh. We pinched & hit ourselves, but we continued to laugh, - finally our quartet turned into a duet, when Dot & I had to sit down. In one of our songs we forgot the words and the four of us couldn't control our laughter. It was the funniest thing you could imagine. Dave Israel says he hopes and prays that when the rabbi says "Do you take this man, etc., etc.," - that I don't go into hysterics again. Everyone said we should have called ourselves the Two Angels and the Two Devils. It would have been much more appropriate.   After the program & dinner, all the salesmen were buying everyone drinks and everyone felt a little high. There was a whole tray of silverware on the table near my pocketbook and someone decided it would be just the thing for my hope chest. So, when I got home I found 6 forks, two butter knives, 4 teaspoons and two cutting knives in my bag. I knew it felt heavy, but I thought it was the drink I had. The whole thing was really a riot.

Last night Edie & I went out to eat and then she slept over here. We gabbed and gabbed till the wee hours of the night and now I feel like a holy wreck. This nightlife is getting me down.

When you wrote, "don't smile" at your wanting to get a pipe, I went into another fit of laughter. I know you're not doing it because I asked you to, but regardless, I still think you're a darling and I still maintain that you're just the type to smoke a pipe. So, - make way for the tobacco pouch.

Hon, dare you doubt my word when I say Sylvia & I will write letters at the hotel. I didn't mean that we'd stay in all day and just write volumes of our past & present life, but you can be assured of a penny postcard anyhow. Humph!!!

Got quite a kick out of you reading books on marriage. At a very critical time you'll probably leave me flat and reread the 3rd chapter, - just so's everything will be strictly according to the bible. But all kidding aside, one does learn a lot from reading. I have very little time for reading these days, and besides that, I blush, so you'll have to inform me of all the details that a prospective bride should know, - and I'll just have to take your word for it. Now you wouldn't kid a gal, would ya!! Or would ya!

And by the by, the Jewish Holidays are on the 18th and 19th.

Also, chuckled about your description of your hut, - and the pin up girls. I imagine tis quite a Rogue's gallery. Did you ever think of charging admission fees? Nothing like making a little money on the side.

Well, darling, I guess this is where I get off. And remember, - I love you, - with or without a pipe!!

Lovingly, Lottie

September 2, 1944
Saturday

From:	To:
Mr. Pvt. J.G. Barr 11057933	C.L. Sniderman
4503rd Base Unit Eng. Sq.	65 Houghton St.
Great Bend A.B.B., Kansas	Worcester, 4, Mass.

Dearest Lottie,

I received your postcard to-day and am waiting for the story letter!

Yesterday I was detailed to clean our stones. We had a portable machine to help clean them with, but the thing vibrated so much that at the end of the day, I could hardly keep from shaking myself. We had a total of five stones to clean up, but at the end of the day we had only completed three. Yes, we didn't take off one minute, we worked hard all day long! I don't know who is going to clean the other two, but I hope I'm not one of them.

After G.I.ing the hut last night, I went to services at the chapel. I met that girl who was supposed to have that date with Nate – remember I told you about it. After the services, she and her family and three other G.I.'s drove me into town. I was going to a U.S.O. dance that was to be held in the auditorium and it so happened that she was going also, but she had to go home and change because it was going to be formal. I told her that you could get ready in ten minutes if you had to, so she went out to break your record. It took her fourteen, so she isn't as hot as she thinks she is, or she never needed to be in a hurry before.

While waiting, I saw that they had a candelabra, which was beautiful. It was a large one, about two feet high, made of silver with the branches of it similar to most Chanukah ones. It can be completely disassembled and the branches can be rotated into different positions. I asked Mrs. Feldman, her mother, where she had gotten such a pretty thing, and she told me that she brought it with her from Poland.

When we got to the dance I danced a set with her, she's a good dancer, but nothing in comparison to you. I made a big impression on her, because after the first set I went to get some cigarettes and when I came back she was dancing with some other fellow. The dance was a pretty affair, but the girls out here, phooey. If I didn't have you, I'd be going crazy like the other boys that haven't, as yet, given their heart to someone. You know darling, that if they didn't have music at dances I wouldn't go?

If I had remained in bed all day I would have accomplished just as much as I did at the hangar. Since we've turned over the hangar, we've been standing around idle.

There's a carnival in town to-night, so I'm off to take it in.

I'll see you to-morrow, after all, you are the one I love!

Your, George

September 2, 1944
Saturday night - late

From:	To:
C.L. Sniderman	Mr. Pvt. J.G. Barr 11057933
65 Houghton St.	Eng. Sq., 4503rd A.A.F. Base Unit
Worcester 4, Mass.	Great Bend A.B.B., Kansas

HOTEL   STATLER   BOSTON

Saturday night late

Hello darling,

    I told yo all that Sylvia and I would write letters, - and here's one just to prove it. Our room is lovely and we're raising hell aplenty here. There are five of us. We got in Boston around 3:30, went shopping and George, if you could have seen all the money I could have spent. As it was, I didn't buy a damn thing.

    Sylvia just gave me her pen, which is much better than the hotel pen. Well, now to continue with our doings. We went to Chinatown for supper and then to a play called "Last Stop." It was perfectly stinkin'. Then we came back to the hotel, got undressed and ordered beer and sandwiches. We're all very, very silly, and look even more so. Zelda is lying on the bed, curlers stuck all over her head. Dottie is setting Evelyn's hair, and Sylvia is yelling that someone stole her bobby pins. Amongst all this racket, I'm trying to write to you. The kids said that my mid-drift pajamas are going to waste and they offered to call the bellboy for me. Hmmm, maybe I'll take them up on it.

    Zelda sends her best love and the rest of the gang chimed in with their regards. Dot had a notion that she wanted someone to kiss her, so Zelda is now obliging. The radio was shut off at twelve o'clock so Evelyn is giving out with the vocals. Right now they're all laughing at me for a reason I dare not tell you!!!

    Well, darling, will give you a full report of tomorrow's doings at this same hour, same place, same gal.

With lotions of love I remain yours,
Lovingly, Lottie

P.S. The kids just dared me to write – quote – George, I love you madly – unquote. What a silly thing to dare me to write. L.

HOTEL STATLER, BOSTON, *Park Square at Arlington Street*

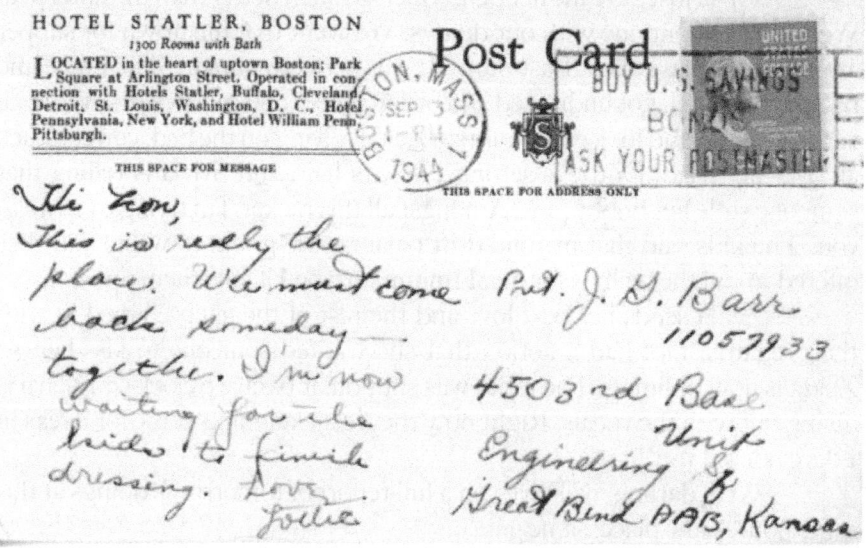

MAIN RESTAURANT AND SEA GRILL, HOTEL PIERONI, 7 PARK SQ., BOSTON

OTHER SEA GRILLS AT 13 STUART ST. AND 601 WASHINGTON ST., BOSTON

When in Boston, stop at HOTEL PIERONI and dine in one of PIERONI'S famous SEA GRILLS. Established 1895.

This place has a very sentimental value if nothing else. I never go into Boston and not stop here at least once.
Love,
Lollie

POST CARD

Pvt. James G. Barr
11057933
4503rd Base Unit
Engineering Sq
Great Bend
AAB, Kansas

September 4, 1944
Monday – Labor Day

From:	To:
C.L. Sniderman	Mr. Pvt. J.G. Barr 11057933
65 Houghton St.	Eng. Sq., 4503rd A.A.F. Base Unit
Worcester 4, Mass.	Great Bend A.B.B., Kansas

HOTEL STATLER BOSTON

STAY *Hotels* STATLER *in* BUFFALO CLEVELAND DETROIT ST. LOUIS WASHINGTON
NEW YORK Hotel Pennsylvania   PITTSBURGH Hotel William Penn

Good morning dear,

I feel as if I have a terrific hangover, - but how the hell can you have a hangover when you didn't have a drink?

Yesterday we had brunch around 10'clock, then went into the commons and took eight rolls of pictures. Heck, at least one picture should be good enough to send you. Then we came back to the hotel, dressed, and went to the movies. We saw "I Love A Soldier", and this was the first time I ever remember sobbing in a picture. I usually cry, - but here I was sobbing like a dope, - but I wasn't alone, - the tears of the five of us could have flooded the theater. It was just the kind of picture that hits the nail on the head, - especially when you do love a soldier, - and I do. Then we went to Bob Burger's for steaks, - and now we are all sick as dogs. Either from the late hours or the food at midnight. George, this town is really jumping. More servicemen than you can imagine. I keep thinking of the weekend we were here together and I feel lonesome as hell. It's at times like this, that I wish we were married. At least I could be with you sometime, - now I just have to watch other people have a good time. This hotel is the place we should have stayed, altho it is terribly expensive. Our room has white furniture and rose-colored drapes and spreads. A nice radio, - which I missed terribly in the other joints we stayed at, - but they hold memories and hours spent together with you, so I guess that makes them better than this place.

Darling, I love you, now and always, but at times I feel so lonesome I could cry. It's funny how I can feel so all alone with a room full of people.

Well, the gals are hounding me to take my shower so I'd better go. They're playing "I've Got You Under My Skin" on the radio, - how appropriate for how I feel.

S'long, dear,
Lovingly, Lottie

September 4, 1944
Saturday, Our 2nd Anniversary

From:	To:
Mr. Pvt. J.G. Barr 11057933	C.L. Sniderman
4503rd Base Unit Eng. Sq.	65 Houghton St.
Great Bend A.B.B., Kansas	Worcester, 4, Mass.

My darling Fiancée,

Two months now we've been engaged, but we've belonged to each other since the beginning of time, and that is the way our love shall always be, ageless. Dates remembered usually bring up memories of the past, but this date brings up loving, longing memories, memories that will stay with me for my life. Sweetheart I love you, and always shall.

Your letter to-day kept me in stitches. You – an angel! I can just picture you with your golden halo, or is that a hat! I don't know what you are going to do with uneven numbers of silverware, you'll have to return to the scene of the crime and make up the deficit. Darling, this often worried me, when angels walk thru doors, is it much of a hindrance? I'm just kidding, but when I put my arms around you, I'd hate like hell to have to combat a pair of wings.

Give Barbs my regards (I'm afraid to say "love", explain that to her will you,) and Edie, well I still owe her a letter. This afternoon I received a letter and a picture from a cousin of mine. The picture is of his son, not a very becoming picture, but it goes with part of the letter. Just as soon as I answer him I'll send it to you. It's a mimeographed letter that he sends to all his relatives and friends.

I'm in the service club now after coming from seeing "Two Yanks Abroad", very comical. The club is fixed up very prettily with all their card tables neatly covered with green napkins, and atop of the tables they have long green candles. They are going to have a dance here pretty soon, and me needing a shave!

I saw Dave Jall this afternoon, the lucky kid has a furlough coming up the middle of the month. I told him if he gets into Worcester to give you a call. I wish I were going home with him, even going home by my lonesome.

I don't know as much as you think I do, even tho I've read a book. One thing is certain, I won't leave you for chapter three or even the last chapter. Nature is wonderful, before they had books, people still were able to get along very nicely.

I can see that I'll never be able to finish this letter now, the music has started and every girl is dancing, the ratio is about four to one, so some of the boys are just standing around. Me, I'm a bit different than you, I like solitude when I write.

Goodnight dear, and a very happy anniversary to you.

Your, George

[Editor's note: The mimeographed letter that George references, along with the "not very becoming picture" are below and on the following two pages.]

Arthur Leonard Glick

August 21, 1944

Dear Unk: George

It's me again, just as noisey as ever, only mommy and daddy think more
so. Seems a guy can't have a little fun around the house. When I play
fire engine, it is too noisey; when I play choo choo train, that's too
noisey; even when I play soldiers, that's too noisey. Gee, a guy can't
even shoot off a cannon without being yelled at. I guess mothers and
fathers are just sissies. All they do is put their fingers in their ears,
shake their heads and yell, "Keep quiet, you!" But I suppose I'll have
to put up with them, humor them and give in once in a while. Don't
think that I am getting soft, but it's the best way to get my daily ice
cream when the Good Humor man comes around.

It won't be long now before we go back home to the city. Two weeks more,
to be exact, and I'll be sorry indeed when that day comes, because here
I have the run of a big house and am out in the sun from morning until
night. I just can't picture myself being locked in an apartment until
mommy is able to take me down to the park. Of course, it will be nice
being able to go to the zoo, and seeing all those funny animals that
daddy used to show me in my picture books, but give me the beach any
time. I love the water and daddy says it won't be long before I am
able to swim like a fish. Daddy likes the beach too. Could it be because of those new one-piece bathing suits the girls are wearing?

Incidentally, Grandpa's at it again, and here it is:

A SON OF THE BEACH

I like to feel the wet sand squish between my toes;
A sailor bold on dry land don't care where he goes.
The castles that I build there, I stamp on with both feet,
To sit on them I don't care, they're not a steady seat.

Though other kids may lay claim to beach toys that I own,
With shovel raised I take aim and sock them 'till they groan.
The dirty sandy clam shells that scratch me as I run
May have some awful fish smells but chewing them is fun.

I like to see a big wave roll up on the beach
My daddy says I'm so bravo, I jump on it and screech.
It spins me round and knocks me down just like a rubber ball,
I imitate a circus clown but I'm not scared at all.

Mother says, "It's just four" — must be getting back,
Cutely I say, "Once More", finesse is my attack.
Almost time for "hommy"* kind of sleepy too,
Guess I'll humor mommy, "My day's" nearly through.

   * Primitive English for "rations"

That describes pretty much what my whole day generally is. Incidentally,
fellas, how do you like the attached picture? Daddy is now trying to
teach me to spell Pepsi-Cola. Always looking for a way to make money!

Mommy and I have grown into real pals in the past two months. You can
see by the same picture that I am now a little man, being able to handle
my "affair" all by myself. I even run errands for my mommy and help
her dry the spoons every day after dinner. That, coupled with the chore
of putting daddy's slippers away every morning, constitutes my family
responsibilities (or am I being taken for a ride). And talking about
rides, each week-end I spend quite some time on the merry-go-round, or
could it be that daddy takes me just because he wants to play "Catch
the Brass Ring".

-2-

At any rate, we have had lots of fun together this summer and I'll be sorry when it's over.

Of course, you all heard that Uncle Allen has come home for a while. Gee, he looks swell and we had some grand times together. He is due back at some camp in North Carolina the end of this week. Let's hope he stays here.

Please write and let me know "what's new in your camp".

Lots of love from mommy and daddy, and a great big kiss from me.

Your nefoo

Arthur Leonard *Glick*

Hu you fella. this is a copy of a "monthly bulletin" we get out to our friends - this has been going on since my burial. 2½ yrs ago — Nooky suggested I send one to you — Write in & let us know how you like and what is new with you —

Willie

September 5, 1944
Tuesday

From:	To:
C.L. Sniderman	Mr. Pvt. J.G. Barr 11057933
65 Houghton St.	Eng. Sq., 4503rd A.A.F. Base Unit
Worcester 4, Mass.	Great Bend A.B.B., Kansas

Dearest George,

Well, here I am back in the home city again. We really had a riotous time. By just telling you that the five of us were in one room is enough for you to realize the racket that went on. Every night everyone was hanging out the windows, carrying on a conversation with anyone that would care to listen. Everyone was swapping soldiers, sailors and girls. The place was stinkin with looie's and higher ups and everyone was polluted. Unfortunately, we had no male companionship, - but not that we couldn't have had!! It was really a free for all, - and through all this, damn it, we kept our dignity. Monday, we saw the play "Wallflower", and twas really very, very good, - and also very, very risqué, - maybe that's why it was very, very good!! We also went to a Swedish restaurant for Smorgasbord – I think that's how you spell it, - anywho it was delish. We took the bus home at 6 o'clock and then went for spaghetti at the Blue Goose. And so, ended a very pleasant weekend.

I also got a letter from Sid Plotkin, and a very sweet letter it was. He also enclosed a $10.00 Chinese bill. Someday when we go to China, we'll have some small change. I can tell you now that his letter to you was nothing like his letter to me. I'm really glad you sent it to me. Darling, do you really think we'll be sorry for not getting married? When people write like Sid does, you really get to thinking. Would be nice if we could have a Christmas wedding, - and peace as an especially nice gift. It's funny how you have your mind all made up to do one thing, and then suddenly you think maybe it's not the right thing at all.

Darling, I think it's wonderful that you're going to take a course in photography. I hope you haven't changed your mind by now. Also, I think the idea of you taking other courses in Math & English is super. You'll never be sorry for what you learn. But as I've said before, you only get out of a thing what you put into it, - so go to it, I know you can.

So, you don't think you made much of an impression on the girl who was kind enough to drive you to the dance? Well, darling, if you mentioned me at all, I'm sure that's good enough reason. Would you like to go with me, if I were engaged to a different boy? I'm sure you'd keep away, too.

While I was in Boston, I saw some beautiful pipes and I really wanted to buy you one, but I'm sure by this time you've decided that cigarettes are quite satisfactory, - or have you?!

I'm going to mail you some of your stationery tomorrow. I hope it's enough. If it's not, I can always send you more. I'm glad you liked "Marriage Is A Private Affair." I'm going to try and read it too.

Well, me pet, I guess that about does it for tonight. I have millions more letters to write, I haven't yet decided whether I have the ambition or not. So, until tomorrow night, goodnight dear.

Love, Lottie

P.S. Sylvia said all night long I kept asking her to hug me, - and also said I was very much of a cuddler.
P.S.S. My dad went to the doctor again today and he has a heart condition. He said it wasn't serious, - I hope he's right. I can't help worrying about it. Me

Chinese $10 Bill from Sid Plotkin, referenced in Lottie's letter.

September 5, 1944
Tuesday

From:	To:
Mr. Pvt. J.G. Barr 11057933	C.L. Sniderman
4503rd Base Unit Eng. Sq.	65 Houghton St.
Great Bend A.B.B., Kansas	Worcester, 4, Mass.

Dearest Lottie,

After going to a field class on gas decontamination this morning, I had absolutely nothing to do. To occupy my mind I wrote letters, this one makes the eighth to-day. If I can write as many to-morrow, I'll be caught up on all my letter writing and even have one left over for Edie. By the way, how patient is Edie? Has Dave written her as yet, or is it still too early?

A funny thing happened to-day, while rummaging around in my barracks bag, I found an old letter of yours. It was written last February and tho it must have been cold at home, your letter really warmed my heart. It is a very sweet and lovely letter and I love you for it.

I made a slight miscalculation in the time that I'd like my stationery. It better come quickly, or else I'll have to stop writing letters. I'm down to my last six envelopes, and about twenty sheets of paper.

Darling, do you have a stupid boyfriend! Because I had a little time, I monkeyed around with my camera, and naturally it doesn't work. I hope that my insurance covers me for repairs. I think that there is a gear that is not catching, and if I can get a smaller screw driver I'm going to take a look see where I didn't look before, because I couldn't get at it. I'd feel worse about it if I had film, but since I have none, then the camera wouldn't, or couldn't, take pictures anyway.

Goodnight, my darling
Your, George

P.S. I was going to give you the wristwatch ending, by winding things up, but I thought better of it. J.G.B.

September 7, 1944
Thursday

From:	To:
C.L. Sniderman	Mr. Pvt. J.G. Barr 11057933
65 Houghton St.	Eng. Sq., 4503rd A.A.F. Base Unit
Worcester 4, Mass.	Great Bend A.B.B., Kansas

Dearest George,
I think you're a darling for smoking a pipe, - but please don't do it because I asked you to. If you don't like it, well, just don't do it. It really isn't that important. As a matter of fact, it isn't important at all, - I love you no how.

Very nice of the sergeants to take you to the movies, - me thinks me will find a couple of sergeants to do same for me. Surely, you wouldn't mind, wouldja?!!

So, Bob has himself a gal too, eh. Nothing like a little romance to stimulate the soul. Which brings to mind something I read, - quote – Love is just a friendship set on fire – unquote. Very good, don't you think?

I think it's a super idea our stopping in New Orleans on our way back from Bermuda. I always did want to see that place. So, let's plan on it, - O.K.?!

Toby called me last night and gave me all the details of the dance she went to. I nearly died laughing when she said there were a lot of older fellows there, - about seventeen or eighteen. Isn't that cute? Well, I guess I felt that way about it too when I was fifteen, which seems like centuries ago. But many times, I feel no older than her. I heard from various sources that she looked darling at the dance and was quite the belle of the ball. Ah, to be young again! Gone is my happy youth, - to make way for an even happier marriage.

Yes, dear, I have noticed the moon and with a pang of pity in my heart to have to watch it alone. But better days are coming. The evenings are getting cool now and I can just picture us sitting in front of our fire place listening to soft music. Isn't that a pleasant thought?

Enclosed you will find a miniature esquire sheet written by Evelyn Cohen who works in our office. She really has a marvelous sense of humor. Write me if you like it. Speaking of the office, I didn't do a damn thing all day long. Dave watched me a couple of times, but was in quite a good humor so didn't say anything, - at first. Finally, at 5 o'clock he said – quote, - whats a matter with you, haven't cha got nothing to do all day, - all day long you bla, bla, bla with everyone in the office. At the time, he said it I was talking to Sylvia and it was so true that we both went into hysterics of laughter where upon he got very angry, grabbed me into his office and was gonna spank me. The kids were howling, - it was really very funny.

Well, me love, I'se gotta go now. You willst forgiveth me, wontcha? So, this is your little chichadee signing off for this eve.

Love, Lottie

September 8, 1944
Friday

From:	To:
Mr. Pvt. J.G. Barr 11057933	C.L. Sniderman
4503rd Base Unit Eng. Sq.	65 Houghton St.
Great Bend A.B.B., Kansas	Worcester, 4, Mass.

Dearest Lottie,

I finally wrote a letter to Edie. Do you get to read my letters to her too? What did you think I'd say to Polly, that you wanted to read my letters to her?

Sid does write a very nice letter and I'm glad that you liked both of them. Darling, do you honestly believe you'd change your mind again, that is to marry before the ending of the war? I doubt it, for when the plans were made, you say, let's wait. If it was a year ago, we would have been married, but as things are now, we'll wait and have a wedding the way we both want one. When we get married, we'll know that we'll always be to-gether and no army order will separate us. Hasn't everything turned out for the best, or at least seems so?

Loving you has been the nicest thing in my life, and it will remain the finest thing in my life. I know if it weren't for you I wouldn't be a thing worth having. It's you that keeps me mentally alive, whereas I'd be a what during the day and a wolf at night.

This afternoon I went out on a B-24 to put up an antenna. This was the first time that I put antennas up on a 24, so when I walked out on the tail surfaces I wasn't sure whether it would hold my weight or not. The wind was rushing across the ramp and I had to lean into it, or else I might have blown over. While putting the wire up I could feel the section I was standing on vibrate up and down. I didn't feel safe up there for one moment. When I finally did get back to terra firma, I asked the crew chief just how much weight the tail could hold, 'at least a couple of tons', he told me. And here I was afraid my weight would make it collapse. Someday if you ever happen to get on the tail of a B-24, you may be skeptical yourself!!

I went to the chapel again, but I wasn't too impressed with the chaplain that gave the sermon. He beat around the proverbial bush too much.

I was very glad to hear that you had a good time on your three-day pass. We'll go on many of them when I'm back for good, and we'll stay at the Statler too.

I feel pretty good, I don't owe one letter to anyone. Edie finished me off. Now I'm finishing you off.

Good night dear, pleasant dreams,
Your, George

September 8, 1944
Friday

From:	To:
C.L. Sniderman	Mr. Pvt. J.G. Barr 11057933
65 Houghton St.	Eng. Sq., 4503rd A.A.F. Base Unit
Worcester 4, Mass.	Great Bend A.B.B., Kansas

Dearest George,

You really are a darling for remembering our second anniversary. I've been wondering if you'll be as thoughtful on our second anniversary of marriage as you are now. Ten to one you'll never even remember, - if you don't, I'll kick your pretty little teeth in!!

How nice that you broke your camera. Nothing like being a little destructive, I always say. Now let's see how good you are at fixing things.

Sylvia Coblentz wanted me to come over her house tonight and I had all intentions of doing so, - but after supper I sat on the sofa and merrily fell asleep. I was so cold and miserable when I got up that I couldn't move. So, - believe it or not, - I sat cuddled up on my mother's lap and we talked. Ever since I can remember, when anything bothered me, or I was sick, I always used to sit on my mother's lap. It's the most comforting feeling in the world. Or didn't you know that I was still just a baby at heart. George, I miss you something awful. Why doesn't this damn war end so you can come home to me?

We had quite a bit of company here tonight. My uncle kisses me every time he looks at me. Never knew the guy was so affectionate. It's too bad he hasn't any children, he'd make an awfully good father.

Edie Megans is going to New York tomorrow for a week and I'm jealous. I want to go to, - but in spite of it all, I think I did enough travelling for awhile, - unless you decide to come out this way again.

George, you remember the rabbi that was at our engagement party and wanted to make a written engagement? Well, yesterday he died. He went to a convention in N.Y. and fell down a flight of stairs and fractured his skull. When I heard this, I was sorry we didn't let him do what he wanted to, - maybe it would have made him happy before he died. Oh, well, I guess it's too late now.

For some odd reason, I find concentrating very difficult this evening, and I know this is a very drippy letter. I'll do better tomorrow, honest injun. I wrote letters to Dave & Sid last night. I wrote them Vmails because I didn't have anything to write.

Goodnight dear,
Love, Lottie

Poem
I'se so tired
I'se so weary
Pick I up
And kiss I dearie!

September 10, 1944
Sunday

From:	To:
C.L. Sniderman	Mr. Pvt. J.G. Barr 11057933
65 Houghton St.	Eng. Sq., 4503rd A.A.F. Base Unit
Worcester 4, Mass.	Great Bend A.B.B., Kansas

Dearest George,

I'm sorta glad that today is coming to an end. I don't think I could have stood it much longer. All afternoon I helped Toby move various and assundry articles to the new house, and running up and down stairs a million times plus lugging boxes, didn't do me any good considering I hadn't slept much the night before. When I came back from helping Toby, I found my dad in just one piece of misery. So, we started calling doctors, but on a Sunday, of-course, no one was home. Finally, Dr. Goodspeed's nurse called him in Boston and he called us back immediately. He couldn't come from Boston in a few minutes so he suggested we call Dr. Leel. He just left the house after giving my dad a good examination, and the verdict is a touch of pneumonia. The man is positively burning up with fever and my mother and I feel so damn useless. But he gave him some codine pills, which put him to sleep. The store will have to be closed, of course, and he'll have to stay in bed. It's funny but I never could imagine my father sick. It seems so horribly strange not to have him running here and there always trying to do something for somebody.

Incidentally, while rummaging through closets of your house, I came across your riding boots, and I nearly had a bird. There was dust a mile high on them and had things piled on top. Darling, just for your further info, boots should be filled with paper and oiled with Vaseline when not in use. So, I took them home with me and I'm gonna do a job on them. Maybe it doesn't matter to you now, but you'll appreciate it when you have to wear them again. Oh, - don't thank me, - jest gimme a kiss!

The pictures and cartoons you sent were real cute. Your mother said the pictures were so small she couldn't even see you. Also, your dad said he sent you money to have a good photo taken, - well, what happened, - he positively refuses to take those snapshots as a consolation prize!

Saturday, I had lunch with Sylvia and we went looking at antiques. The prices they ask are far beyond my means, and besides that, I can't tell whether they're authentic or not. Also, Saturday Evelyn Bloom left her job and on saying goodbye we both started crying. She's getting married next month, but wants a month to buy things and sort of get organized. I'm going to take a month off too, - I hope.

Well, dear, I'm really dog tired, so I guess I'll try to catch my 40 winks. Goodnight, - and be good.

Love, Lottie

September 11, 1944
Monday

From:	To:
C.L. Sniderman	Mr. Pvt. J.G. Barr 11057933
65 Houghton St.	Eng. Sq., 4503rd A.A.F. Base Unit
Worcester 4, Mass.	Great Bend A.B.B., Kansas

My dearest George,

I can't write much tonight, except that my father is very, very sick. I've done nothing but attend to him since I came home from work. Despite all my efforts with sponge bath, alcohol rubs, and what not, his temp remains well above normal. I'm really sick with aggravation. I just put him to sleep, but I have to wait up until its time to take his medicine. Tomorrow morning I've got to rise bright and early to nurse him as much as I can before I go to work. My mother is exhausted from running back and forth all day long, so I just made her go to sleep too. The house is deathly quiet right now and I feel as if you were right here with me, - I feel as if I'm talking to you instead of writing.

It must be a good feeling to know that all your correspondence is taken care of. I have a million letters to write, but heaven knows, I'm in no mood to write a cheery missive, - and after all, no one wants a letter full of someone else's troubles. I'm writing about it to you because I feel that you're a part of me, and besides that, I gotta have someone to talk to.

I don't know what made me think of it now, but did you send your brother Sol back the money. I certainly hope you have, - it's been a long time now.

The letter you sent me with your cousin's picture is very, very cute. A novel idea, to say the least. And whatta pose on the kid. I guess that's what you'd call an action photo!!

In tomorrow's letter, I'll send you a few of the photos that we kids took in Boston. They're really very bad of me, - but this is to test your love for me. If you love me after you look at those pictures, then yours is really a true love.

Darling, I'm very tired, so I'll go finish my last chores and then try to sleep. I miss you so terribly.

Lovingly, Lottie

September 12, 1944
Tuesday

From:	To:
Mr. Pvt. J.G. Barr 11057933	C.L. Sniderman
4503rd Base Unit Eng. Sq.	65 Houghton St.
Great Bend A.B.B., Kansas	Worcester, 4, Mass.

Dearest Lottie,

While sitting in my part of the hangar, reading some O.C.S. literature (funny books), a major walked in. When you are in the army, you are supposed to snap to attention, but our outfit has been so lax in military courtesy that I looked up at him and continued reading on. That I don't think he liked. Then he started giving me a lecture on keeping the floor clean and not throwing cigarette butts and matches on the floor. I just yes sired him all over the place until I thought he was going to really get angry at me, I didn't give a damn because he wasn't in my outfit, and they never told me anything about not siring too much. He finally left, a bit disgusted I think. That was my day at the hangar.

At the gym last night, they held a boxing fest. It will now be a weekly affair if they can get enough fellows to compete. The fights were pretty good, and if they offered furloughs for the winners, I'd gladly take a chance. Although maybe I'd do better as a wrestler, I had ten minutes' experience in the afternoon. Bob and I started to play around. We both have a few scratches on our arms and backs. What a fight, first I was down, then he, then the both of us. He won one round, me the other, but no one won the third, we couldn't have had a third if we wanted to. I'm just waiting to become a civilian again so I can get back into shape. What a mess the army has made out of me.

Thanks darling, for the package, altho you made a slight error. You sent me five pads with my name and just one pad without. It doesn't make any difference just as long as I have something to write on and can keep my correspondence up.

I hope your dad is feeling better. Tell him he has to keep well, because he has to give you away at a wedding soon, I hope, and then those twenty-four grandchildren will want to have him play with them. I hope he is feeling better.

The 15th of the month and we put on our O.D.'s. Winter must just be around the corner. The nights here are really getting quite chilly, I have to sleep under two blankets and sometimes then, I'm even cold. What I need is you, my love to keep me warm!

Did Edie quit her job or is she on vacation? How is she getting along with her love life, any answer from Dave? Let me know, after all I must know what's happening in our family!

I'm going to mail this before the morning mail goes out, and then rush to work.

Bye bye my love,

Your, George

September 13, 1944
Wednesday

From:	To:
C.L. Sniderman	Mr. Pvt. J.G. Barr 11057933
65 Houghton St.	Eng. Sq., 4503rd A.A.F. Base Unit
Worcester 4, Mass.	Great Bend A.B.B., Kansas

Dearest George,

I haven't had any mail from you for two days now and I'm really worried. I hope nothing is wrong. If I don't get any mail tomorrow, I'll go nuts.

My dad is feeling slightly better today, and so we all feel slightly better. That's how it is in my house, - if one of us is sick, we're all sick. This will be the first holidays that he won't go to Shule. He says he is going to try to go, - but I doubt it very much. So far, he can't even budge from his bed.

Today was one of those rainy and gloomy days when all the world looks sad, - and I guess my mood fits right in. Charlotte noticed this morning that I felt kinda low and she figured she'd try to cheer me up, so after lunch, she came back with a whole box full of pastry, all done up in pretty paper and ribbons. The idea was so sweet and I was so surprised that I couldn't help but feel better. She's such a darling.

Your mother calls up every day to inquire about my father. I had promised to help her fix up the new house, but it's quite impossible for me to go now. I really feel terrible, but I have to relieve my mother. She has her hands full all day.

Surely by now you've seen the pictures. Awful, - ain't they? Well, what did you expect, Lana Turner?!!

I've really done so much of nothing lately that I'm at a loss for what to write. I could write you that I'm simply swamped with dates, - but that wouldn't make you very happy, and besides that, you'd know it ain't so. So, I'll have to write the same ole kind of boring letter I always write. But I can wish you a very, very, happy New Year, with hopes that next year we'll spend it together. And I think now there are some possibilities of that wish coming true.

And so now I take leave, -
Goodnight darling.
Love, Lottie

September 14, 1944
Thursday

From:	To:
Mr. Pvt. J.G. Barr 11057933	C.L. Sniderman
4503rd Base Unit Eng. Sq.	65 Houghton St.
Great Bend A.B.B., Kansas	Worcester, 4, Mass.

Dearest Lottie,

Another dull, drab day. Even tho I did a little work this afternoon, which kept me pretty occupied, life now is just a daily routine. I'm waiting anxiously for the coming of the weekend so that I can come in contact with other faces and other means of living. I guess I'm in that, 'I don't give a damn mood' again, something I've hoped I had gotten out of entirely. After my pass, I think I'll be different, the excitement of last month in me, wants to be replenished.

I think I'll do a little sewing on my O.D. uniform to-night, nothing else to do. I finished another book on the life of Lincoln from 1864 to his death, and I finished the serial in the Colliers magazine, my writing is caught up, and I don't have any women in town to go to, so what is there left for me to do?

While I sew, I'll be thinking of you, just as I'm now doing and have been since I stopped thinking on which side of a B-29 does which wire go? Thoughts of you keep me content, otherwise, I guess I'd moan just as loud as the next fellow on how rough the army is and what raw deals we've gotten.

Before I ever was in love, I used to think that I'd tell my dreamed one that I loved her just a few times and that would be all that would be necessary, but darling, it makes me feel all the better telling you I love you time and time again, its almost as needed as air to breath. Precious, I love you more and more each day, like nature, the older it gets the more beautiful it is.

Good night darling,
Your, George

September 15, 1944
Friday

From:	To:
C.L. Sniderman	Mr. Pvt. J.G. Barr 11057933
65 Houghton St.	Eng. Sq., 4503rd A.A.F. Base Unit
Worcester 4, Mass.	Great Bend A.B.B., Kansas

Dearest George,

I've still had no word from you, - this makes five days, and there's no need to tell you how anxious I am. Your mother called a while ago and said she had mail from you today. I can't imagine what's wrong.

George, my father is very, very sick. Yesterday we took him to the hospital, and as yet, we don't know what's really wrong with him. The doctors took X-rays today, but we won't know the results until Monday. Tonight, I really broke down in the hospital, - something I try not to do in front of my mother, but he was so doped up and he looked so pathetic I couldn't stand it. This business of going to the hospital twice a day is getting me down. I go on my lunch hour and again at nite. If only I could see some slight improvement.

The expected hurricane came last nite at 1:00 o'clock and my mother and I stayed up through the whole thing. It wasn't as bad as expected, but enough to make us very nervous. A tree was downed a few houses away from us, - that was about the extent of the damage on this street. It started clearing around 3 A.M.

The house has been swamped with telephone calls with regards to my father. My head feels like a mass of steel on my shoulders. I'm terribly worried because I haven't heard from you. Goodnight, dear.

Love, Lottie

September 20, 1944
Wednesday

From:	To:
C.L. Sniderman	Mr. Pvt. J.G. Barr 11057933
65 Houghton St.	Eng. Sq., 4503rd A.A.F. Base Unit
Worcester 4, Mass.	Great Bend A.B.B., Kansas

Dearest George,

I finally received four letters from you (all at once), which certainly put my mind at ease. They were evidently held up by the hurricane, as I suspected. Even though I had a pretty good idea of why I didn't receive any mail, the waiting was enough to drive me mad.

George, my father is a very sick man. He's shown absolutely no improvement since he's been in the hospital and there's no need to tell you how worried we all are. The doctors had a consultation today and decided the only thing to do was take him to Boston. So, Saturday morning we're taking him to the Pratt Institute, which is supposed to be one of the best hospitals in the country. He's going to have a private room and nurses. The best that he can possibly have will be given him. So now all we can do is wait. This constant waiting for everything is maddening. Your folks call up everyday, and Monday night they insisted we come over to the Sara Barr's for awhile. They wanted my mother and I to come for dinner too, which was very sweet of them, but we didn't feel that we'd be very good company. So, we spent the evening there and forgot our troubles for awhile.

There's excitement aplenty going on in Worcester since the four high schools went out on a strike. They absolutely refuse to go to school until 2 o'clock, and have been striking since Monday. They meet every day in front of the City Hall and at Elm Park and are becoming quite violent. The police had to put twelve of the kids in jail. They've been on the radio, - one program featured the four principals and another, a committee of two kids to represent the pupils. They even threw tomatoes at the superintendent and threaten the kids with violence if some of them want to go back to school. Wish to hell I could join them. They've got a lot of spunk and I give them credit. The kids say they were instigated by the teachers.

I'm sorry I made a mistake in your stationery. To tell you the truth, I didn't even notice it. I'll send you some more first chance I get. I don't know where my head is lately.

Darling, I think the idea about the champagne is tres excellent, - and is positively a must do, - broken glasses and all! But hell, when it gets to be our fiftieth anniversary we'll be dead broke buying glasses. Oh well, we'll do it no how.

Glad you liked the slang dictionary. I met this man from the Jewish Welfare in Boston and they give those things out to the servicemen, then so upon hearing that I had friends in the service, he gave me about a dozen. I sent one to you and one to Dave Grossman, the rest I gave out in the office – they also have loved ones who would get a kick out of it.

I can't see why you didn't go to Arkansas with Bob. 'Twas very nice of him to invite you anyhow.

I didn't realize how very much your letters meant to me, dear, until I had to go a few days without them. I was truthfully not fit to live with.

Well, guess I've done right by you this eve. Will give you more low down tomorrow.

Goodnight dear,
Love, Lottie

[Editor's note: This card was enclosed in an envelope postmarked Sept. 21, 1944, from George to Lottie.]

[Editor's note: This card was also enclosed in the same envelope postmarked Sept. 21, 1944, from George to Lottie. Apparently, George signed for both of them, and then he mailed New Year's cards out to Lottie's friends, making a great impression.]

September 21, 1944
Thursday

From:	To:
C.L. Sniderman	Mr. Pvt. J.G. Barr 11057933
65 Houghton St.	Eng. Sq., 4503rd A.A.F. Base Unit
Worcester 4, Mass.	Great Bend A.B.B., Kansas

Dearest George,

Not much news to write you tonight. Things are still the same, - my dad is still sick and we're still worried. Your mother called a short while ago and was very sweet. If my mother stays in Boston while my dad is in the hospital there, she insists I stay at your house for the week. I really appreciated her thoughtfulness and may have to take her up on her hospitality. I told Dave that I couldn't come in Saturday and he was very good about it, - that means I'll probably be fired!!

A good percentage of the kids went back to school today, and just as good a percentage continued striking. They're main thought now is whether or not they'll get into Life magazine.

My mother & I are going mad from sheer boredom. We try to bolster each other's morale, - but our effort is to no avail. I'm so exhausted mentally that I can't even see straight. The kids down at the office are doing a good job of helping me forget while I'm working. I think I'll get my mother a job at the office.

On the way back from the hospital, I dropped my mother off, and then went for a nice long walk. The leaves are just beginning to turn and the woods look beautiful. The air smells so clean and healthy. I could almost feel you walking beside me and even though you weren't there, I was talking to you. Had anyone seen me, they would have thought me a lunatic.

I think I forgot to mention that your uncle Bennie Torren called me up Sunday to wish us a happy New Year, - also your brother Sol. Sol was in for the holidays with Fran. I was sorry I didn't get a chance to see them.

And by the by, m'love, there's been no mail from you again today. Perchance some dilly in Wichita has kept you busy. If so, - good for you and can't say I blame you any. Nevertheless, - just remember.......!!

Well, guess I'll say bye bye for now. Pardon the dullness of the letter, - but I'm sure you understand.

All my love,
Lottie

When in Boston, stop at HOTEL PIERONI and dine in one of PIERONI'S famous SEA GRILLS. Established 1895.

Hi honey,
Back in Boston & Pieroni's again. Only wish it were under more pleasant circumstances. Dad is feeling about the same, no change at all. Will write you more details later.
Lovingly, Lottie

BUY U. S. SAVINGS BONDS

POST CARD

Pvt. J. G. Barr
11057933
4503rd Base Unit
Engineering Sq
Great Bend
A.A.B, Kansas

September 25, 1944
Monday

From:	To:
C.L. Sniderman	Mr. Pvt. J.G. Barr 11057933
65 Houghton St.	Eng. Sq., 4503rd A.A.F. Base Unit
Worcester 4, Mass.	Great Bend A.B.B., Kansas

My dearest George,

First of all, I must thank you for the New Year's card and tell you how sweet you were to think of signing my name. Edith called me a short while ago, and when she got the card, she was touched beyond words, and said some more flattering things about you, which made me feel good all over, - I won't tell you what she said because your head might swell. Also, Fran called me, and she also thought it was one of the most thoughtful things you could have done. So, you see my darling, it takes only a little thing like a card to show people you think of them, - and they always appreciate it. You're terribly sweet.

Friday nite Irv, mother, and I rushed my dad to the hospital instead of Saturday as scheduled, because the hospital called and said if we weren't there by seven o'clock Friday, we'd have to wait ten days for another bed. Mother & I stayed until Sunday nite and we're both dog tired from running back and forth. So far, they've done nothing but examine him, and he feels no better at all. He's at Pratt Institute, which is a diagnostic hospital, - more like a luxurious hotel. I was going to go to Boston again tonight, but Irv said

I'd probably pass out from exhaustion, so he went. We called today, but the hospital always give the same report, - resting comfortable.

Evelyn Issacman just called and thanked us for the New Year's card.

I'm so glad you were so royally entertained during the holiday. It shows there are some swell people wherever you go, - but heck, you're a swell person to entertain.

George, I feel like a dope for not thinking to send you a Gazette myself. I'm going to mail you one tomorrow and regularly after that. Surely you wouldn't want one every day because the news would be stale. But now that I think of it, it is a nice feeling to get a hometown newspaper in your hands.

While waiting between visiting hours in the Boston hospital, my mother & I had nothing to do but go to a movie, - so we saw "Since You Went Away." George, I wept from the minute I sat down to the minute I got up. It was one of the saddest things I've ever seen, - the whole place was in tears. I felt just like crying so the picture did me good. Darling, I missed you more than ever after seeing that show. I could have kicked myself around the block for not getting married and being with you all this time. At least we would have had a little time together. You have no idea how I miss you. Everything I plan, and do, and think, seems wrong without you to talk it over with. But someday......

Goodnight dear,
Lovingly, Lottie

September 28, 1944
Thursday

From:	To:
C.L. Sniderman	Mr. Pvt. J.G. Barr 11057933
65 Houghton St.	Eng. Sq., 4503rd A.A.F. Base Unit
Worcester 4, Mass.	Great Bend A.B.B., Kansas

My dearest George,

Please forgive me for not writing as often. I do so only because I'm at a loss for what to write. I know how you feel about my dad, and to tell you what the doctors found out would only worry you. All I can say is his condition is critical. We took him home from Boston Tuesday, - there was nothing they could do for him.

My brother Irv came up Monday nite to prepare us for the worst, and I don't have to tell you what went on here. My mother was completely hysterical, and I, not much better. We sent for my brother Sam from Washington and naturally he came immediately. We have a night nurse for him and he is as comfortable as we can possible make him. My mother doesn't know what he really has, - only my brothers knew, - but the doctor thought it wise for me to know too, - and I'm glad I do. Of-course, my dad doesn't know how sick he is, - he never will. All I can say, George, is that I'll never forgive myself for not getting married. All that man lived for and talked about was my marriage, - everything was me. Never will I forgive myself.

Your folks were up here last night. They think he looks very good, - he really does, - considering. That's the heart-breaking part. Your mother was looking at me last night, - she must have been thinking how awful I look. I do look awful. She said I was making the situation worse than it is. I smiled and nodded my head, - but no one knows better than I that the situation could not be worse. But what sense is there in telling everyone about it.

Tuesday, I couldn't go to work, - after my brother broke the news, I was afraid to leave my mother alone for a minute. We were given to understand that we must be nothing but cheerful and my mother has been a major. It's not easy to laugh and joke with him when you're brimming over with tears and aggravation inside.

My darling, I shouldn't be writing like this to you. The mileage between us will worry you about how I'm going to react. I feel like a tower of steel, I have to be, - for my mother's sake and also for my dad's. I'm resigned, - there's nothing, nothing that can be done by me or anyone else, - save God. He's had the best medical attention possible, - money was no object. I know I've written too much about the subject, but I'd choke to keep it all inside me.

I'm glad you had such a nice time at the Glassiers. And I'm looking forward to that date in January. It seems years away; but I guess I have no alternative but to wait.

Edie was over here this evening and she thought your letter was so sweet that she let me read it. Surely you don't mind, do you, - or do ya! It was almost as good as receiving another letter from you myself, - please notice the almost. George, you're sweet, and good and fine, - everything I could have hoped for, and I love you very much.

Goodnight darling,
Love, Lottie

P.S. Please don't worry if you don't hear from me as often as usual. I'll try my best to keep you posted. C.L.S.

September 30, 1944
Saturday Nite

From:	To:
C.L. Sniderman	Mr. Pvt. J.G. Barr 11057933
65 Houghton St.	Eng. Sq., 4503rd A.A.F. Base Unit
Worcester 4, Mass.	Great Bend A.B.B., Kansas

My dearest George,

Well, tonight yours truly feels a little higher in spirits. We've gotten hold of another doctor, and altho he hasn't seen my dad as yet, we feel that after all, something may be done for him. Irv called up this doctor, and told him the whole story and how the other doctors said there was absolutely no hope and this new doctor thought it was almost impossible. He said that with all this new medicine out and so much being done for other people, he doesn't see why nothing can be done for him. So, we're all waiting anxiously for tomorrow's examination. I was just telling dad's nurse about this doctor and she said he was a wonderful man. Darling, I know I shouldn't raise my hopes too high, but in my mental condition, I'll grasp at anything.

By the way J.G. – is you or is you ain't my baby?!!! No letter again from you today, - and you know darn well if I don't get a letter Saturday, my weekend is ruined. So, get on the ball there and make with pen!

My brother Sam went back to Washington last nite and he sure hated to leave my dad. Mother was asleep, and of-course, my dad, - Sam and I were sitting on the sofa talking. I was all snuggled up to him and he had his arms around me. We both decided that we'd pretend I was Jeanne and he was George. It was very comical to say the least. I said I thought he looked wonderful in civvies again, and he said I should take better care of the children. We both decided that no matter how hard we pretended, it just wasn't the same. And understandable too, dontcha think?

Your mother called up today (as every day), and she insists I get out of the house tomorrow. She fully understands that I'm not used to being in the house as much as I have been lately. She's very sweet. Incidentally, you'd be surprised to see all the weight I've lost. I did want to lose some weight, - but certainly not this way.

Darling, I miss you so terribly much, - but still I'm glad you're not home now. This is positively the hardest thing I've had to face yet. My mother keeps telling me that this is the time to prove how strong my character really is, - it's not easy. But now I've regained some hope and I feel good all over.

'Nite, m'love.
Lottie

P.S. Do you want some more plain stationery, - or with your name on it? I've forgotten which you said you had too much of. L.S.

September 30, 1944
Saturday

From:	To:
Mr. Pvt. J.G. Barr 11057933	C.L. Sniderman
4503rd Base Unit Eng. Sq.	65 Houghton St.
Great Bend A.B.B., Kansas	Worcester, 4, Mass.

Dearest Lottie,

    I bought Toby a necklace and I'd like you to give it to her on her sixteenth birthday. It is on Nov. 6th. Of course, it is from the both of us, so you needn't get her anything. But what I tried to do here, I couldn't succeed, so maybe you can. I don't like the clasp, maybe you could get one that has a safety on it.

    I think when you see it you'll like it.

Your, George

P.S. If you can have it engraved also, it would look nice, but use you own judgment. J.G.B.

October 2, 1944
Monday

From:	To:
C.L. Sniderman	Mr. Pvt. J.G. Barr 11057933
65 Houghton St.	Eng. Sq., 4503rd A.A.F. Base Unit
Worcester 4, Mass.	Great Bend A.B.B., Kansas

My dearest George,

Well, - it looks like our family is no better off than two weeks ago. Yesterday afternoon my dad was taken again to St. Vincent Hospital. He had his first X-ray treatment today and altho it's too soon yet to look for results, - were hoping that this may be of some help. Now I'm more worried about my mother. She's terribly nervous and cries continually. Even tho it practically kills me, I'm trying to be as cheerful as possible. The only time she's really bad is when I go to work and she's all alone. It's ironical how much unhappiness can enter a house in such a short period of time.

The news that there's a possibility that you may go to school is wonderful. I'd be tickled silly if you did, - let's keep hoping. About my piano lessons, darling, there's nothing I'd like more, and I've been inquiring about teachers. But I'm afraid that thought will have to be laid aside until my dad recovers. I have neither the time nor the patience to practice, - but someday, dear, when everything is back to normal, I'll start. It was sweet of you to remember anyhow.

The town is buzzing with the prospect of a wedding in view. Naty Tolbot, the fellow who was missing for three years came home yesterday and he and Irene Sherr are planning their nuptials. He's got a three week furlough, so it should be taking place any day now. Irene is the gal who told me I'd be nuts to marry before the end of the war, - it's so easy to hand out advice to others.

Your pal Maxie Z. is in town and the stinker didn't even call to say hello. I saw him ride by in a car, - he didn't see me. Also, Harvey Coblentz is in town.

The weather is positively freezing here. They said this winter would be a cold one and it's starting out just as they predicted. Already I'm a frozen gal, - can you suggest a remedy?

I received a very indignant postcard from Bev today because I haven't written. Of-course, she doesn't know what's been happening around here, so I don't blame her for being angry. She says she's coming home any day now, - the reason I don't know. It seems everyone is coming home except the person I want to come home. But when you do, we'll make up for all time lost, - we always do anyway, don't we?

Well, darling, now I gotta go to sleep and look forward to tomorrow's letter, - and how I look forward to them.

Goodnight dear and pleasant dreams,
Lovingly, Lottie

October 2, 1944
Monday

From:	To:
Mr. Pvt. J.G. Barr 11057933	C.L. Sniderman
4503rd Base Unit Eng. Sq.	65 Houghton St.
Great Bend A.B.B., Kansas	Worcester, 4, Mass.

Dearest Lottie,

You know how I feel after hearing the news of your father, darling, I wish I had words to express myself, but I haven't, - all I have is understanding. We are so close that I'm sure you understand. I tried to think of something to write, but it was all superficial.

Dearest, I want to know anything that ever bothers you, because that makes us closer by knowing our troubles, large or small.

Talking to you was marvelous. As yet, the operator hasn't called to collect any money. For your information, I was in the phone booth for fifteen minutes, deducting the time I put the money in and the time that we were cut out, I think we had ten glorious minutes, altho we did say goodbye half the time.

The fellas are getting away with murder here, I guess the operators must be G.I. wives, because the calls are going thru fast, and very few are paying for talking longer than three minutes. I know that if they were Kansas people, it would never happen.

Yes, I worked hard at K.P. To-day I was in charge of the G.I. cans where we wash our mess kits. After each meal, I had to spill the water out and then refill the cans. I felt like a water boy bringing water to an elephant in a circus and just as tired. My aching back.

Darling, I marveled at your composure and your sense of humor, and it makes me feel good to know that you are such a marvelous woman. I love you, even tho I told you that over the phone a few minutes ago, I still, and will always love you.

It's getting late dear, so I'm off to bed.

Your, George

October 3, 1944
Tuesday

From:	To:
C.L. Sniderman	Mr. Pvt. J.G. Barr 11057933
65 Houghton St.	Eng. Sq., 4503rd A.A.F. Base Unit
Worcester 4, Mass.	Great Bend A.B.B., Kansas

My dearest George,

You have no idea how good I felt talking to you last night, - it was almost as good as having you home. You have a knack of showing up or calling just when I need you most. The funny part about it is that I knew you'd call, - I've had that feeling all week long. So when the telephone rang, - I was almost sure who it'd be. I just called your mother and told her I spoke to you, and of-course, she was very glad. Darling, it's things like that that make me love you more and more.

Today I was surprised again, - another engagement gift from Edith (the switchboard operator) and Charlotte (the girl I work with). They gave me a lovely glass vase, trimmed with gold, and also a lovely card, which specified that the gift was to the both of us. The vase means more to me than you can imagine because it was a gift given from the heart and not an obligation gift. They're really very sweet to me, - heavens knows why. They also made me promise that I'd send you their love. I think it would be a nice gesture if you'd drop them a little thank-you note. They're always asking about you, dear. You can send it to the office and address it to: Miss Edith Richards & Miss Charlotte Rodway. They'd really appreciate it.

I just got home from the hospital and my dad seems slightly improved. Even a slight improvement means so much to us, - so we're all hoping it'll continue, - but as for a complete recovery, - I know it's impossible. You can guess without my telling you what his ailment is.

As bad as I feel about my own troubles, I guess you always have room to hear the brunt of someone else's. Sylvia had a nice weeping spell on my shoulder today and I wept with her. It seems her married life ain't what it's cracked up to be. Erwin seems to think more of his gosh damned family than he does of his wife and it really hurts. Seems he called up his mother a few days ago, and said how much he'd missed her, - but no call to Sylvia and neither did he mention that he missed her. His folks get letters more regularly than she. It's fine to love your family, in fact, I think it's awful not to – but he seems to forget that Sylvia is his wife, and obligation is due in her direction. Thank God, my worries about you lie in an entirely different direction. Didn't we always say we were an ideal couple? Let's always keep it that way, darling.

> *Goodnight dear.*
> *Lovingly, Lottie*

October 3, 1944
Tuesday

From:	To:
Mr. Pvt. J.G. Barr 11057933	C.L. Sniderman
4503rd Base Unit Eng. Sq.	65 Houghton St.
Great Bend A.B.B., Kansas	Worcester, 4, Mass.

Dearest Lottie,

After just getting the pants beat off of me in ping- pong, I'm writing to you for consolation. Will you give it to me?

After a very strenuous day, in bed, I thought I 'd go to the show, so I put on a nice clean uniform, you never know who'll be sitting besides you at a G.I. movie theater, I trotted on down to the show. Unfortunately, there was going to be a U.S.O. show first and the line extended as far as the eye could see. Very leisurely I walk up the line until I met some of the fellows in my outfit, and greeting them like long lost brothers, I melted in with them so as the rest of the G.I.'s wouldn't know that I had committed any crime.

P.S. It wasn't worth it!!!

Darling, from your letter and the phone call last night, you want us to get married on my next furlough. Right or wrong? There is no need for you to feel badly for not getting married last time. At that time, everything pointed toward waiting and we thought it was for the best. But if we do get married the next time I'm home, I don't know if you'll be able to come back with me. This, of course, can't be decided until then. Fate can be good to me just so long.

My dearest, you know that I love you so much that I want you to be happy always, and whatever we decide will make me happy to know that you are happy.

Lottie, just thinking back of the times we were to-gether makes me feel good, and proud. Loving you is the flame in my life. During those times, we lived to-gether almost as man and wife. Remember, you even made me my breakfast, - and it was good too. You are so good and pure and unselfish; if God made land bound angels, you are one of them.

You know I didn't mind you reading Edie's letter, why should I? Did I ever keep anything from you secret? No, - at least you haven't found out any, or have you?

By the way of good entertainment, be sure to see "Arsenic and Old Lace." It's the funniest picture I've seen in a long time, you'll laugh yourself into the aisles. Maybe you'd better sit in the center of the seats and tie yourself down, I don't want to hear about you making a spectacle of yourself!!!

> *Good night my love,*
> *Your, George*

P.S. Your voice is still in my ears, and I love it. J.G.B.

October 4, 1944
Wednesday

From:	To:
C.L. Sniderman	Mr. Pvt. J.G. Barr 11057933
65 Houghton St.	Eng. Sq., 4503rd A.A.F. Base Unit
Worcester 4, Mass.	Great Bend A.B.B., Kansas

Dearest George,

I received Toby's locket today and it's positively lovely. No one can ever say you haven't a good taste. I'll have the clasp changed and the locket engraved first chance I get.

Saw dad tonight, as every night, and he's just about the same as yesterday. He gets these awful coughing spells that knock the hell out of him, - when the spell passes he feels pretty good, - but to see him suffer is unbearable.

Received a letter from Evelyn Issacman today. She's back in Waterbury, Conn. and asked to be remembered to you. She's got herself a job in some defense plant, - and is enjoying her social life very much, - at least that's more than she had in Worcester.

I smiled to myself as I read the part in your letter where you said your folks must be tickled to have Bonnie with them. Strange as it may seem, darling, I'm afraid you're a little wrong. Your folks are swell, - the best in-laws any one could ask for, but having a baby around the house all the time is an imposition and understandable too. They had their children and now they're ready for a little peace and quiet. When they come home from the store they want to relax and not hear a baby cry. I know they love Bonnie and altho your mother says she doesn't mind having them there, I know that they'd prefer for Charlotte & Narky to have their own home again. I hope to high heaven we never have to trouble anyone with our offspring. People love children, other people's children, for a visit, - but for any length of time the novelty wears off, - like everything else. It's only human nature & psychology. So, ends another lesson on life, - maybe I'm wrong, - but I think I've seen and heard enough about the subject to think I'm quite right.

I received an invitation to Irene Sherr's shower today, and altho I'd love to go, my heart wouldn't be in it. Nevertheless, a gift must be given her, - and I'm just wondering what she'd like. I think money is about the most practical since I don't get into town at all now.

My aunt Rose & Zelda were discussing people we like and dislike this evening, and they both agreed they liked you the first time they met you, - that goes double for me too, honey. How well I remember the little conversation we had on our first date, - you were so sweet I couldn't help liking you.

Goodnight dearest,
Love, Lottie

October 6, 1944
Friday

From:	To:
C.L. Sniderman	Mr. Pvt. J.G. Barr 11057933
65 Houghton St.	Eng. Sq., 4503rd A.A.F. Base Unit
Worcester 4, Mass.	Great Bend A.B.B., Kansas

My dearest George,

My dad just received the card you sent him to the Boston Hospital and the inscription you wrote certainly hit the spot. He's crazy about you anyway, - and calling him dad really clinched it. Today he was feeling very well and looked very well. I couldn't believe it myself, - my hopes have again been renewed.

George, the reason for my anxiety and worry was not something that I thought up myself. The last doctor he had told my brother that he could live no longer than two weeks. My brother thought it only fair to prepare us for the shock, - so one nite he came up and told us. I don't have to say anything further. The next day he was brought home from Boston and they expected him to go that night, - but some miracle kept him alive. Then dad suggested we bring another doctor because he knew he wasn't getting any better and altho we never mentioned any such thing, he said he knew he was going to die. To hear him talk was terrible, - he told us to take care of mother, what to do with the store and everything along that line. Now all that seems like a horrible dream because the doctor said altho he'll have to stay in the hospital about two more weeks he'll come out a well man, - or well for a time anyway. Whether his illness will start up again later is something he can't say.

Darling, you were right in guessing that I wanted us to get married on your next furlough because the only thing dad lives for is to see us married, - you know that. But the way things look now, it seems that we can wait and have the big splash we planned on. And so, it looks like our wedding plans are still as previously planned, - I do hope nothing goes wrong to spoil it. As for my marvelous composure and sense of humor, I'm afraid I wasn't really that courageous inside. But I very well know that people don't like to see anyone crying and downhearted all the time, - so I kept what I felt to myself, except what I wrote to you. Yes dear, - everyone saw me when I laughed, -

but no one saw when I cried. My mother says that's what you call a strong character, - well if that's what it is, I got it!!!

Edie Arnold Lainer just called and asked me to extend her regards to you. She's expecting her heir next month, - and looks it too. That's the only bad part about having a baby.

I guess my George is the most experienced K.P. in the army. Will let you show me what you've learned when we have our own little house, - it'll save butler expenses anywho!!! Well, my darling, - guess this finishes another day. Goodnight.

Lovingly, Lottie

October 9, 1944
Monday

From:	To:
C.L. Sniderman	Mr. Pvt. J.G. Barr 11057933
65 Houghton St.	Eng. Sq., 4503rd A.A.F. Base Unit
Worcester 4, Mass.	Great Bend A.B.B., Kansas

My dearest George,

Well today I really hit the jackpot, - three letters from you today. I got a kick out of the newspaper picture, altho you do look awfully silly. The kids in the office just wouldn't believe it was you.

I just got back from the hospital and my dad isn't feeling so good at all. He was feeling so good Saturday that we had our hopes all up, - tonight we only got more disappointments. And to add to my troubles, my mother is having trouble with her teeth, and so she feels like hell too. Whatta life.

For your information, Bev is coming home on furlough and not to expect a blessed event, - or at least not to my knowledge. Alton is being transferred to Florida so she's going to spend some time here while he gets acclimated and finds a place for her to live. She loves the life of an army wife, - altho, of-course, she's quite lonesome at times, - but she wouldn't think of not being with him while she can.

Darling, sometimes I think you're so naive, - I'm referring, of-course, to your advice to Sylvia. Even tho he is a jerk, - and even tho I'm quite sure she knows it, - that doesn't stop her from loving him. Love asks no questions, - it comes and asks no excuses!! Besides, even if she did want to break their marital ties, don't you think she ought to give it an even chance? They were only married ten days and then he left. But why the hell should we worry about other people's troubles? Let's just be thankful we haven't any difficulties of that nature, - and let them work out their own problems.

I bought an overseas box today and I'll make up Dave a Christmas package. I haven't heard from him for quite some time now, - I hope nothing is wrong. He appreciated the other package so much, but I guess he didn't have the nerve to send me another request, - so I'm doing it on my own. I'm only tickled that I don't have to send you an overseas package.

Sunday I helped my mother clean the house and boy was I exhausted. Since my dad got sick the house has been neglected something awful and if there's anything I hate, it's a dirty house. It looks pretty good now, altho it's no where near finished.

I spoke to Edie today and she's in a terrible state of mind. She's so terribly lonesome, - and how well I know what a terrible feeling it is. It's funny for me to try to cheer her up when I'm dying of loneliness myself.

Your folks were up to see my dad Saturday and brought him some fruit, which he appreciated immensely. We told your mother that we (my mother & I) might be over Sunday night, but when we saw that my dad was feeling punk again we didn't feel we'd be very good company. Besides that, I haven't had a chance to buy your mother anything for the new house. So, first chance I get, I'll try to remedy that situation.

Well, dear, guess this about finishes today's missive. I'm going to write a letter to Evelyn Issacman now and then retire.

So long, m'love,
Lovingly, Lottie

P.S. Glad you like my stationery, since most of it goes to you anyway. C.L.S.

George - at U.S.O. dance

1944

October 11, 1944
Wednesday

From:	To:
C.L. Sniderman	Mr. Pvt. J.G. Barr 11057933
65 Houghton St.	Eng. Sq., 4503rd A.A.F. Base Unit
Worcester 4, Mass.	Great Bend A.B.B., Kansas

My dearest George,

The girls at the office received your letter today and I can't begin to tell you how pleased they were. I'm awfully glad you wrote them, - they think you're super anyway, so it sort of added the finishing touches. Just shows how little it takes to please some people.

Just came back from the hospital and dad is feeling much better. We know he's feeling much better because he's starting to complain, - and that's always a sure sign!!

So, sorry you didn't enjoy your little jaunt to the football game. Twas very nice that you found time to send your mother and me a card, - altho it didn't take the place of a letter which I didn't receive yesterday.

Frank Sinatra just finished singing "The Very Thought Of You" and now they're singing "Goodnite Sweetheart." Soft lights and sweet music is the setting as I'm writing this letter, now, - only thing missing is you and believe me that's no small thing.

The leaves are falling all over now, which only reminds me of our walks. It's a very lonesome sight to see the trees becoming bare again. Only another lonely winter to look forward to, - but the prospect that there may be a furlough due is something to look forward to.

I received a very lovely letter from Barb yesterday and also a very nice picture of her sitting at a baby grand piano. Me thinks she's getting a little tired of travelling around our fair country. The letter she wrote came from Georgia.

Your mater just called me and asked to be remembered to you. You know dear, it wouldn't hurt at all if you wrote home more often, - they worry so much about you even tho you don't realize it.

Irene Sherr's shower is tonight and as you have probably guessed I didn't go. I wanted to go very much because I haven't been anywhere for what seems like years. But my mother was too tired to go and I didn't want to leave her alone, - so here I am stuck in the house as usual. It's really not that bad tho, - because I feel pretty tired myself. Your mother is worried about me, - she said if I kept on running back and forth to the hospital there wouldn't be anything left of me!! I told my dad I wanted to lose ten more pounds and he nearly bit my head off, - he thinks I'm skinny, - ain't that funny!! I'm the fattest skinny person I ever saw, - don't you think. You better come home before I waste away to a ton.

Goodnight dear & pleasant dreams.
Lovingly, Lottie

Barbara "Barb" Coppersmith. Stage name: Barbara Carroll.

October 12, 1944
Thursday

From:	To:
C.L. Sniderman	Mr. Pvt. J.G. Barr 11057933
65 Houghton St.	Eng. Sq., 4503rd A.A.F. Base Unit
Worcester 4, Mass.	Great Bend A.B.B., Kansas

Dearest George,

There is nothing I'd like more than to have a puppy, - and after putting the idea to my mother, I nearly had her sold. But when I told her the dog hadn't even been born yet, she nearly died laughing. She said we would discuss it further after the dog was born. But darling, even if you could get a puppy and even if my mother said I could keep it – how the devil would you get it out here. Unless, of-course, you brought it yourself, - or if I came out to get it, - either one is a pretty good idea, eh wot?!!

Since today was Columbus Day, we got the afternoon off, - so I hung around town for awhile and then came home to help me mater clean the house. It's pretty nearly finished and looks damn good, - even if I have to say so myself!

The part of "Since You Went Away" that was cut out was really a very cute part. They or rather she decided they should get married immediately and have a baby, but he thought they should wait. Then it showed them saying goodbye at the train with her screaming, "Darling I love you," as the train was pulling out. It was very, very touching and brought torrents of tears from the audience.

I finally received a very cute letter from Dave today. I was really beginning to worry about him. And also, a letter from Pauline. Both send their love to you.

I, of-course, went to the hospital today and dad is feeling just fair this evening. The thing that pleases us most, is that he's eating quite well now, - which is really something. He worries so much about the store being closed that it drives him nuts.

The war news looks pretty good tonight and an optimistic viewpoint is again in the air. It seems like this damn war will never end.

Everyone said Irene's shower was lovely, - I really wish I could have gone. One of these nights I gotta go up to pay my respects and give her my gift. Darling, what's this I hear about them reopening O.C.S.? Have you heard anything about it?

My mother went down Water St. tonight, which leaves me all alone and lonely. I always said I hated being alone, - even for a minute. Don't know what I'd do if tweren't for a radio. I feel terribly restless tonight, - how about dropping over for awhile to keep me company!!!

Well, here come my mother and my aunt & uncle. Guess it won't be so quiet now.

Goodnight, m'love,
Lovingly, Lottie

TO THE ONLY ONE

With you, though we've not left this land,
I've traveled far and high. I've crossed
The endless clouds of stars that fill
The cold, dark reaches of eternal space.
I've trod the sun- and wind-swept wastes
Of the Saharan plain, and have seen
True beauty in smoke-smudged towers of cities
Big and small. And I have heard music
Where all was noise and discord once before—
  Before you came.

My soul, once a philosophic configuration
Of my mind, was born full-grown
When first you crossed my way
So long ago. I did not realize or,
Still better, was not able then
To know how to walk with head
Above the clouds that mask all reason
And all thought in every earthly striving
Toward a goal. This you have done for me
  By being you.

And so with pen in hand I sit
And try with all the power I have
To find the words to speak for what I feel.
But those mere words cannot express such
Deep emotion. It must be felt
By one who too can see
Beyond the walls of this, our ordered life
And see the beauty of the commonplace
And hear the music where all was noise before,
  And such a one are you.

October 13, 1944
Friday night

From:	To:
C.L. Sniderman	Mr. Pvt. J.G. Barr 11057933
65 Houghton St.	Eng. Sq., 4503rd A.A.F. Base Unit
Worcester 4, Mass.	Great Bend A.B.B., Kansas

My dearest George,

I just got back from Irene Sherr's house. She had sorta an open house so everyone could see her gifts, and believe me, she got some beautiful stuff. Poor Irene looked rather tired and bagged from all the excitement, but she looks so happy. She & Nate are going to Boston for a few days, and then Sunday is the wedding. Her wedding gown is gorgeous, she'll look beautiful.

The poem you sent me is darling. Wouldn't it be nice if they let you come home to start a family? Heck, you deserve a head start if we're gonna have twenty four!!! Sylvia & I worked together all afternoon up in the conference room today, - what a hard days work we put in!! From 2:30 to about 4:30 we sang continuously, - every old torchy song we could think of. Of-course, in between time we smoked about a half a pack of cigs and then some refreshments. By five thirty we were so hoarse we couldn't talk.

By the by, I think I forgot to tell you that I got a new coat. It's grey and belted, on the military style idea and strictly shorty. I think its quite nice looking, - wish to hell it was paid for. Just you wait until you have to start paying for my clothes, - then you'll know what trouble really is.

We think that maybe my dad will be able to come home Sunday. I certainly hope so, - it would make it wonderful all around. They took some X-rays today and we'll know what the story is tomorrow.

I'm meeting Bev for lunch tomorrow. As yet I haven't seen her. Since my dad's been sick I've neglected my friends something awful. Sylvia has asked me over a number of times, but I hate like hell to leave my mother alone. Irene bet me that the next time you came home there would be a wedding. She said she never dreamed she would be married before me, - especially to Nate. Just shows to go ya!

Well dear, Lottie is awfully tired and weary and lonesome and everything else that makes a not too happy gal. Will do better tomorrow night, honest injun!

Love, Lottie

October 15, 1944
Sunday Nite

From:	To:
C.L. Sniderman	Mr. Pvt. J.G. Barr 11057933
65 Houghton St.	Eng. Sq., 4503rd A.A.F. Base Unit
Worcester 4, Mass.	Great Bend A.B.B., Kansas

My dearest George,

I had a wonderful day of complete rest today, - something that is really a treat to me. After I came back from the hospital at 3 o'clock, I had my lunch, washed my hair and then relaxed. Boy, did it feel good. A couple more days like this, and I'd be a new gal.

Had lunch with Bev Saturday, she sends her love to you incidentally, and we had a long gab session. Wish to hell I was going to Florida with her. If by any chance, you happen to be transferred down around that sector of the U.S.A. - you're gonna have little me on yer hands. Won't that be nice?!! Also, saw "Marriage Is a Private Affair" yesterday, the first movie I've seen in weeks, and I must say twas very enjoyable. They brought out some veddy, veddy good points. I loved the scene where they were lying in front of the fireplace, - could very well picture us doing precisely the same thing. Someday......

I blush for same to think you actually enjoyed the U.S.O. act where the girl's bra became loose. Such beasts are these men! Might think you never even looked at a Petty drawing!

The doc looked at my dad's X-rays yesterday and was extremely pleased. He said he should be coming home by the middle of the week, altho he'll have to go back to the hospital every day for a treatment. We can hardly believe that he's getting well. I spoke to yee mater this afternoon and she also was very happy upon hearing the news of Mr. S. She said it was true when you always used to say God was good to us. I told her God was good to you only because you got me, - she laughed because she knew it was soooo true, - or did she?!!

Me uncle was in from Boston today, - Uncle Ike, you know. Again, was rehashed the situation of him not being invited to Zelda's wedding, - as a matter of fact, of no one being invited, 'cept yours truly. He said he was damned if he'd give her a wedding gift, - but yet he promised us a handsome gift. Also, he gave us a very nice engagement gift. Ah me, - what have we got dat gets em!! Could it be our beautiful faces, our charming character, - or just luck? Nevertheless, the whole situation is quite satisfactory.

They're playing all these sad songs on the radio tonight, - and even tho I feel pretty good in spirit, these morbid laments make me feel lonesome all over again, - as tho I'm not always lonesome. Oh, well, this war can't last much longer, - can it? – or can it. Anything in cans cost points, you know.

And with this parting thought I take leave.
Love - me.

October 16, 1944
Monday

From:	To:
Mr. Pvt. J.G. Barr 11057933	C.L. Sniderman
4503rd Base Unit Eng. Sq.	65 Houghton St.
Great Bend A.B.B., Kansas	Worcester, 4, Mass.

Dearest Lottie,

I have all day off because my K.P. yesterday, wonderful. I didn't get up until 10:30 and I felt swell with so much sleep under my belt.

The supply boys are issuing fleece lined jackets and pants for the expected winter, so I had to get mine. They're bulky heavy things, when my camera comes back, I'll have a few shots taken, and then I'll let you see how I look in them. You may have seen them in newsreel pictures at one time or another. They are used as flying clothes too.

I'm taking it easy now in our day room, otherwise known as the "4503rd Kit Kat," swellegent aren't we?! We have a very nice bar that the boys built. It really looks like the real thing. Empty beer and whiskey bottles on the shelf to give it a live atmosphere. They do sell drinks here, but they're just cokes. There is even neon lighting and carpets!

Darling, I love you. Two wonderful letters from you to-day! You are marvelous! How can a guy help but love you when you are so good to me?

I received a poem that I sent you, what is the story, mistake? I also got that little poem too, so you want a man! Do you think you'll find one? A girl of your beauty and talents shouldn't find it hard.

O.K. we'll talk about the puppy after it is born, but if I can get a nice one, then I'll bring it home with me on my furlough. By that time, it should be old enough to travel, don't you think so?

I hope that dad is home by the time you get this letter, I know how much you want him home, where he belongs.

Maybe I shouldn't have gone to the show last night, because there is nothing for me to do now. Here I have a day off, but what good is it, I'd have it just as easy if it was a working day for me. Life is sometimes a bit ironical.

You seem to be working hard also, with your conference room sessions! I'm glad tho, if you work too hard you might get soooo thin!

Your coat sounds nice and chic. Maybe by the time I have to buy your clothes, you'll have so many that you won't be in need of a thing. Don't think about it sweet, because I'll always want to buy things for you, and I know that you'll only let me when you are sure you're in need of it. See, you can't worry or disillusion me one little bit!

The cartoon you may like, I'm also sending a copy to my parents so that they can feel sorry for me too! My dad is liable to send back that it's the funniest thing he's ever seen, or so what!

Your, George

P.S. That Grossman guy owes me two letters, what have you got on him? J.G.B.

October 17, 1944
Tuesday

From:	To:
C.L. Sniderman	Mr. Pvt. J.G. Barr 11057933
65 Houghton St.	Eng. Sq., 4503rd A.A.F. Base Unit
Worcester 4, Mass.	Great Bend A.B.B., Kansas

Greeting, m'love,

Hate to inform you that yours truly feels positively stinkin'. I spent a delightful day in bed, - it's been so long since I've been sick that I forgot how to enjoy it. This rushing around and grabbing a bite here and there has been raising havoc with me. But I fear I shall recover in due time, - the due time better be no later than tomorrow, - my job, you know! Why the devil don't you hurry up and come home so I won't always have to be worrying about a crappy old job. Oh, - I hate myself when I feel like this!

Received an invitation to a shower given by Sara Ulman in honor of her brother's girl. If my dad is better and if I have the moola to buy her a gift, I shall go, - otherwise, I'm afraid they'll have to struggle along without me. Also, received an invitation to a tea given by the Hadasah at the Coronado. Oh, my, - I'm such a social butterfly!!

Today when I'm deathly sick, my face pale, people standing over my bed crying, my mother bent over my bed, looked longingly into my droopy eyes and asked slowly, quietly if there was anything I wished? I summoned all my strength, heaved a little sigh, and then smiled. All I said I wanted was to wait for the mailman with a letter from George. About ten minutes later, the bell rang, everyone was breathless, - at last the mailman had come and now my last request could be granted. But was it granted? No, - the mailman had no letter from George. Everyone grew pale as they told me the news, - the sad truth, - no letter!! It was too much for me, I couldn't stand it any longer. You can guess the rest...... it is too sad an ending for me to write!!!! The moral of this story is, - why the hell didn't you write me a letter when you could have guessed that I was gonna be sick!!

Just took time out to kill a tremendous mosquito. I hid on him and when he came out I gave him the business. Now I'm gonna wash my face, brush my hair, brush my teeth, put on my pajamas, climb under the blanket and then toss & turn because it's too early to sleep. Ain't I silly?!!

Goodnight & pleasant dreams!
Love, Lottie

P.S. They say a letter without a P.S. is like a date with out a goodnite kiss, - so here it is!

October 17, 1944
Tuesday

From:	To:
Mr. Pvt. J.G. Barr 11057933	C.L. Sniderman
4503rd Base Unit Eng. Sq.	65 Houghton St.
Great Bend A.B.B., Kansas	Worcester, 4, Mass.

Dearest Lottie,

This is a good outfit that I'm in! Why? Because we are a bit short in the amount of privates and corporals – sergeants will start pulling K.P. starting to-morrow morning. They eat just as much as anyone else, so there is no excuse why they shouldn't pull K.P. just as we poor unfortunates have to.

I told you that I was going to report to our officer this morning, but it has been postponed until to-morrow morning because two of the boys were on detail. It looks as if I'll have a long vacation, if things keep up as they are.

Our mascot is liable to pup-ulate any minute now. If I can get a cute little pup, I shall. Whenever you get a chance, you can send me a variety of my stationery, also envelopes. O.K.?

I answered a letter from Anne this morning and she wants to know why she hasn't heard from you. I told her that you would whenever you got a chance, because you have been very busy of late.

After reading "The Man in the Iron Mask," I'm still in a quandary about half of the plot. It was the most mixed up affair I've run across in all my reading. I didn't like it anyway, because it wasn't like the picture!

This has been a terribly short letter, but to-morrow should be better.

Your, George

October 18, 1944
Wednesday

From:	To:
C.L. Sniderman	Mr. Pvt. J.G. Barr 11057933
65 Houghton St.	Eng. Sq., 4503rd A.A.F. Base Unit
Worcester 4, Mass.	Great Bend A.B.B., Kansas

Dearest George,

Stayed out of work again this morning and would have done better to stay home this afternoon. But I felt duty bound to go to work, - so I went.

I still feel quite miserable, altho I'm trying not to give into myself, as is my usual habit. By tomorrow I should be feeling chipper again, - I hope.

Your letter of today was very sweet. Darling, you don't have to say what you feel to make me understand. There's a bond between us that is much greater than words, - the ability to understand the unspoken word. Love is a funny thing, - and has many different reactions. Some people can speak right out what is in their hearts, - we have not that ability, - so we have shown our affections by actions and little things said & done. To me it is far better to love a person and not to be outspoken than to be able to speak words of love and not have them mean anything. I like us just the way we are, - don't you?!! You are so right in saying that things are different when we're apart. All planning and thoughts of the future has to be done alone, - and so the joy is only half as great, but when the time does come we'll make up for lost time, - the hours we keep should count for double time!!

Your mother told my mother that she wanted me to come to dinner Friday nite. I only wish I could, - but I wouldn't have the heart to leave my mother alone. I hope your mother understands. I really feel guilty about not going up to the new house yet, - but I can only be at one place at a time, unfortunately.

Incidentally, Edie Megans informs me that you owe her a letter and also requests that I send her love to you. Must be nice to have two femmes in love with you.

Today was very warm, - more like July than October and it felt good. I hate the thought of winter coming so soon. George, I miss you so terribly. It seems like years to wait till I'll see you again. I suppose I'm really selfish, - some girls haven't seen their boyfriends for two years and more. I suppose in one way we've been quite fortunate, but I don't consider myself as such when I get so lonesome I could cry. Everything seems so dull & drab, - nothing to look forward to except another day's work. Oh, well, I hate myself for complaining. At least you're still in the good old U.S.A. and that's a helleva lot to be thankful for. So, I brace my shoulders, keep my head up high, smile pretty and greet the world with a cheery hello. No good at all brooding over something that can't be remedied. Goodnight my love, - and don't forget, - keep smiling.

Love, Lottie

Love Letter

The weary moon will soon be fast asleep,
    The moon is cold and pitiless as doom,
And yet we have a rendezvous to keep,
    Within the shadows of a quiet room . . .
The candlelight tints beauty on your face,
    The wine will steal reality away,
And vows we make can quietly efface
    The terror of a new, unwanted day . . .

And so it goes for those who chase a star,
    The search may end in heartbreak and defeat,
But there is always magic where you are,
    A magic that is tremulous and sweet . . .

And who will have more lovely scars to show,
If you and love should ever chance to go?
                                    —Don Wahn.

October 18, 1944
Wednesday

From:	To:
Mr. Pvt. J.G. Barr 11057933	C.L. Sniderman
4503rd Base Unit Eng. Sq.	65 Houghton St.
Great Bend A.B.B., Kansas	Worcester, 4, Mass.

Dearest Lottie,

Your letter to-day brought many cheery laughs from my fat face. I could just feel the way you felt when you were writing the letter, there was nothing but good fortune in it all the way thru. Thank uncle Ike for me, as you already did. Hello to Bev and anyone else I've missed.

Also in my mail I received a nice letter from Lenny, the fellow I paled up with in Philly and New Orleans. He sends his regards as he always does.

This morning we finally went on a tour of inspection of the blind landing equipment on this field. I was astonished at what I was shown. They need qualified radio technicians such as radio studios have. It's really a joke trying to have us ever repair anything of that sort. It is a bit secretive, because we had to sign in and sign again when we left. The equipment is all mobile, so that it can be moved just as fast as a change in the wind occurs. As you know, when the wind changes the planes use different runways, and these mobile blind landing trucks park at the edge of the runway so that everything will be extremely accurate.

If they think I'll be able to do it, it's O.K. with me. About the school – letters are being sent to the school only saying, not yet! Meanwhile, the officer in charge is trying to get some literature on it and will try and teach us a little about it, so that when we do go to school, we won't be totally green, and will be able to have it easier at school.

Did you hear that Toby took two rolls of pictures, but that not one of them came out? I think I'll have to disown her!! Even when you took pictures they came out! – O.K. take that knife out of my back, you know I can't wear anything not G.I.!!!

Don't think I wouldn't mind going to Florida, this place is going to be too damn cold for me. I can just imagine me trying to buck a forty-mile gale at o°, brrr.

Say hello to dad, he must be home by now. And darling that can business, oh!

Until to-morrow, sweet
Your, George

October 19, 1944
Thursday

From:	To:
C.L. Sniderman	Mr. Pvt. J.G. Barr 11057933
65 Houghton St.	Eng. Sq., 4503rd A.A.F. Base Unit
Worcester 4, Mass.	Great Bend A.B.B., Kansas

Hi honey!

Whew, - I'm exhausted!! Just finished having a jam session with myself and I'm really knocked out. I was listening to Gene Krupa beat it out, and I got the urge to give out with a little jive, and so I did. I can't understand how I used to do it hours at a stretch. Guess I'se gettin' old!

Today for once in my life I was jealous. Sylvia came in to work and informed us that on next Saturday she was leaving for Alabama to join her spouse. She received a letter yesterday saying that he had found a room and that he wanted her to come out, - and so she is. She's being smart, - they asked nobody's advice, - just made up their minds and are going through with it. I can't understand why she didn't go down there a long time ago. Hells bells, - but how I wish I were going to see you.

Darling, that mascot of yours better come through with some puppies, because I've got my family all set on the idea. It would be swellegant if you could bring it with you. The kids in the office nearly died laughing when I called the animal hospital today to find out how long it took for a puppy to be born. I tried to tell them I was just curious, but they insisted that I was expecting, - they told everyone that Lottie was gonna have puppies any day now!! Incidentally, it takes 63 days, in case yer interested. Can I help it if I'm curious, - blame it on my youth!

My dad isn't home as yet, and probably won't be until the beginning of next week. It seems this week just flew right by. Maybe because I was home for a day & a half. At any rate, the time is passing so quickly. I'll be old and grey before you know it. Remember, - you said you'd love me when I was fat & forty.

Zelda was up at the hospital tonight and she said she expected Phil home around December or January. Would be nice if you come home around the same time. But, of course, you needn't wait until then, if you can possibly make it sooner, would be super swell for me. This year we gotta celebrate New Year's Eve together. Last year we sorta kinda got gipped.

Well, my love, - I'm cold & tired and I feel droopy again. It's so damn quiet in here it's driving me nuts.

Goodnight & sleep tight
Lovingly, Lottie

P.S. Cartoon was tres cute. You should be glad you haven't a wife to take all your pay away.

October 19, 1944
Thursday

From:	To:
Mr. Pvt. J.G. Barr 11057933	C.L. Sniderman
4503rd Base Unit Eng. Sq.	65 Houghton St.
Great Bend A.B.B., Kansas	Worcester, 4, Mass.

Dearest Lottie,

I was a latrine orderly to-day and the rest of the time I have off. One of us had to pull guard to-night and two more had to go on detail, we matched out to see who would be the lucky one to have the rest of the day off. Who else but me!

Now if there was something like this Miss Lace around here, maybe I'd be thinking up things like that. Wow!! Now don't get angry darling, for you are the only one I love.

I got a letter from Harvey Coblentz and he informed me that Uddy Goff is about 90 miles from here. Toby is going to get his address for me, and if I ever get a chance, I'll try and go up to see him to say hello.

About fifteen fellows got a boost in their ratings yesterday. Of course, I didn't get any. There are many reasons for it, one, I haven't been with this outfit as long as the rest, two, I haven't had any schooling in what I'm supposed to know, three, I guess they don't think I deserve any. But as long as the ratings are now open, after we go to school we should get a stripe. I don't care about the stripe, but I do care about the raise.

Last night Bob and I went into town, because we got tired of staying in the hut all the time. We went to the U.S.O. and hung around, played a little ping-pong, and wrote a few letters. We then got a coke and annoyed the counter girls at a local drug store. What an evening, exciting as a trip to the morgue.

This life is starting to really get on my nerves, nothing to do in the line of work, nothing to do around camp, nothing to do in town - nothing! Why the hell can't they just send us home, that would be the best way of raising our morale. When is this damn thing going to end?

Darling, if I didn't love you I don't know how I'd react to army life, but for one sure thing, I wouldn't be the way I am now. I'd be classified as just another G.I. and I'm glad that I'm not just another G.I.

Your, George

October 20, 1944
Friday

From:	To:
Mr. Pvt. J.G. Barr 11057933	C.L. Sniderman
4503rd Base Unit Eng. Sq.	65 Houghton St.
Great Bend A.B.B., Kansas	Worcester, 4, Mass.

Dearest Lottie,

I don't know what got into Bob and I last night, but it did. We cover our beds with our shelter halves to protect the blankets from soot and dust. On the shelter halves, there are some buttons, so we opened the springs on one of the beds and put the buttons through and then closed it. Of course, we waited up until the fellow came in, and you should have heard him swear when he couldn't pull the shelter half off of his bed. Wow! I guess we're just a couple of devils!

It's a good thing that I'm no longer an overage, because overages are shipping out next week and some may go to P.O.C. Bob is an overage and he is going, if this had happened a month ago, I would have been the one to ship out, because I was the overage at that time. Lucky me.

Lottie, you can give the postman hell if you don't receive letters from me more regular. The only thing I can do is write them, but I wish like hell I could be the one to deliver them. And what's the idea you getting sick, huh? What if I got another unexpected trip east, and you're in bed. So from now on you'll have to be a well girl. I wish I were there to take care of you, because you won't take care of yourself.

I put in a heavy day to-day, slept in the morning and G.I.'d in the afternoon. It seems that last week the officers didn't like the looks of the hut, so this week they are going to be strict. We really did a good job this time. All the beds and clothing were taken out so we have plenty of room to work in. The brooms flew, the dust blew, the water flew, then the mops, after that barrage the place was clean, you know, spic and span!

Oh yeah, another thing about inspection. The colonel said no nude pin ups, so our adjutant told our C.O. Our C.O. said it was his outfit and if the boys wanted pin ups, they could have pin ups. So, we are going to have pin ups and the colonel is going to have kittens! Oh well, what's a civil war in such a world war. Good night, darling.

Your, George

P.S. From now on you'll stay well, huh? J.G.B.

October 21, 1944
Saturday

From:	To:
Mr. Pvt. J.G. Barr 11057933	C.L. Sniderman
4503rd Base Unit Eng. Sq.	65 Houghton St.
Great Bend A.B.B., Kansas	Worcester, 4, Mass.

Dearest Lottie,

Our work in cleaning up our hut didn't go in vain, for we got a report of very satisfactory. Pretty good!

Another day going by and nothing accomplished. What a life. Last night I went down to the service club and ran across a fellow I met when I was down in New Orleans. We started talking when another fellow came up and asked me where I came from, because he knows that we've met before. I told him of all the places I've been, but he still couldn't place me except that at one time we were introduced. The only thread that I could give him was that I knew Phill Shack, but I had never gone out with him, so we couldn't have met that way. He comes from Webster, but he said he didn't come down to Water Street very often and it wasn't there that he saw me. What kind of a face have I that people come up to me and say that they know me. Pretty soon I won't be able to walk down the street without someone stopping me and saying, "Didn't we met someplace?" Just a popular kid, that's all.

You tell my sister in-law, she's crazy as hell, I don't owe her a letter, for she is the one who owes me. I've been keeping up my letters pretty good and don't owe but one letter, and that is to my uncle in Washington.

What did you go to work for if you were still feeling punk? I know that it is hard for them not to have you there, but I don't think the place will fail.

I haven't been in bed all morning because of inspection. It must be pretty cold by now, so I'm going back to heat it up. Bye now.

Your, George

October 22, 1944
Sunday

From:	To:
C.L. Sniderman	Mr. Pvt. J.G. Barr 11057933
65 Houghton St.	Eng. Sq., 4503rd A.A.F. Base Unit
Worcester 4, Mass.	Great Bend A.B.B., Kansas

Dearest George,

If there is anything I simply hate it's having a cold, and boy, I've got a beauty!! Between sneezes and trying to catch a running nose, I shall endeavor to write you a letter. My head feels as if someone was inside with a shoe stretcher. Nuff said about that!

Friday received a wonderfully short letter from you, - twas really not a letter at all, - a better description would be to call it a consolation note. But bad as that was, Saturday you did much better because I didn't even get a postcard. Could it be that the postman wanted to be a stinker, or was it that me little boy just neglected to drop his old gal a few lines. O.K., - forget all about me, - see if I care, - I call that situation nothing but a humph!!

Working six days a week just doesn't seem to be enough for me, so today I worked for the Walker Electrical Supply. Seems me brudder, in a fit of temper, fired his bookkeeper and now he's stuck, - but good. So, calling upon me for my worthy services I had no choice but to oblige. I didn't do much, - just made out some bills and filed a heavy stack of letters, but in my condition, all I wanted to do was sleep.

I was gonna mail you some stationery tomorrow morning, but I'll be damned if I can find a box. So, I'll see what I can dig up at the office tomorrow and mail it out as soon as possible. Was glad to hear that you took my suggestion about writing more letters home, I spoke to your mother tonight and she said they received three letters last week, which pleased her to no end. You're such a good boy?!!!

Evelyn Issacman was in town today and she called. Seems she's got a very good job in a defense plant as a clerical girl, - but her social life so far has been nil. I got the impression that she was not unhappy – but yet was not too happy either. She's a funny gal. Also, spoke to Freda Reck & Edie Megans today and they send their bestest. Both were over Freda's house trying to get stinko on ginger ale and a cherry. If you've got a good imagination it could work!!

My dad is coming along quite nicely. The doctor said he should be home around Wednesday. The man in the next bed to my dad still insists he wants to adopt me. So, all day long they argue about how much I'm worth, - dad thinks there's not enough money in the whole world to buy me. Bill said if he had ever had a daughter, he would have liked her to be just like me. Silly man, - isn't he?!!

And now my darling, I take leave again. Would love to have you to snuggle up to right now. Too bad a pillow hasn't got arms.

Love, Lottie

[Editor's note: On the following page is a newspaper article on Lottie's half-brother, Irving Walker, and his Electric Supply Co. that she references in her letter. It appears that this article may have been published sometime in 1943, but is provided to give the reader a little more context and background of Irving Walker and his business.]

Fluorescent Lighting For Daylight at Midnight

IRVING WALKER

The new Fluorescent lighting is now being featured by the Walker Electrical Supply Co., 89 Mechanic street, center of electrical equipment for industrial, commercial and home use.

'The Fluorescent tube is the latest development from the General Electric laboratories," says Irving Walker," and it is the closest artificial light yet devised to approximate actual daylight conditions."

Mr. Walker points out that a 20 watt Fluorescent tube gives approximately as much light as a 200 watt incandescent lamp; so the savings realized by using this type of lighting are readily discernible. In many cases an ordinary Fluorescent installation will return the entire original installation in less than a year.

One local factory manufacturing sprinkler systems was using ten 400 watt mercury vapor high intensity units. These were replaced by ten two-tube Fluorescent units consuming 80 watts of current, and the light in that area was actually doubled, according to Mr. Walker. And the greenish yellow illumination of the old system was replaced with the glareless daylight effect of Fluorescent lighting.

Dental laboratories, draftsmen, paper manufacturing plants and many others have found that this new light source has greatly increased efficiency and reduced eye fatigue to a minimum.

Fluorescent units are now available for the inexpensive illumination of retail establishments with a quantity and quality of light that was not thought possible two years ago, without a heavy investment in lighting fixtures and a subsequent marked increase in the light bill.

The Walker Electrical Supply Co. is thoroughly prepared to survey individual lighting problems and make recommendations for the use of the new Fluorescent lighting. Further details may be had by dialing 4-5311.

1943

October 22, 1944
Sunday

From:	To:
Mr. Pvt. J.G. Barr 11057933	C.L. Sniderman
4503rd Base Unit Eng. Sq.	65 Houghton St.
Great Bend A.B.B., Kansas	Worcester, 4, Mass.

Dearest Lottie,

Although to-day was a beautiful day, just like the old autumn days we used to enjoy and will again someday, I slept most of it away. It wasn't until dinner time did I budge from bed. Bob and I then went to see "Our Hearts Were Young and Gay." It was very different from the drab war pictures of late.

After supper, I slept a few more hours and then we took off for town. Here I am at the U.S.O. enjoying myself by drinking their free coffee and cake. There is nothing doing back at camp, and nothing doing in town, but there are more lights here.

Last night I also spent at the U.S.O. and saw an old movie, but had an awful time when the projectionist put the third reel in backwards and upside down. He monkeyed around for a half hour trying to straighten it out, when he found he had the wrong reel in. He located the correct reel and every thing ran smoothly after that.

Starting to-morrow morning for an entire week, it is up to me to see that the boys have hot water all day long. I have to be a furnace man this week. How will you like me black faced? Oh yeah!

Now, if I can get an airmail stamp you'll get this faster.

Your, George

October 23, 1944
Monday

From:	To:
Mr. Pvt. J.G. Barr 11057933	C.L. Sniderman
4503rd Base Unit Eng. Sq.	65 Houghton St.
Great Bend A.B.B., Kansas	Worcester, 4, Mass.

Dearest Lottie,

No wonder this furnace job lasts only a week, if it were any longer the man tending it would suffocate in no time. My lungs are full of that coal gas now, and I'm coughing to beat the band. I'm going up to see the general this afternoon and have them convert to oil. Why only ten miles from here there is a large oil field. How much work would it be to pipe the oil directly to the field and have oil burners, instead of coal furnaces. Look at all the man hours and man power it could save. I never should have joined the army, but should have offered my services to the War Labor Board, don't you think so? And why not!

I'm sending you another letter or report from my "little" cousin of New York. Wherever they get their ideas it's a good place.

I received a package from my folks and what do you think I found in it. You'll never be able to guess, but it was three bananas! I think I'll go into the side show business and let people look at them for a nickel. Want to be my first customer? You, I'll let in for free.

If everything goes well, we ought to be seeing some puppies any day now. I got the biggest kick out of you finding out how long it took for a dog to have puppies. You could have asked me and I would have told you. It wouldn't have been so exact, but about sixty days would have put it close enough.

When they do come, I'll try my damndest to get one of them. You see many of the boys want the puppies, and it will take a lot of fast talking to get one, but don't worry, if there is any possibility of getting one I will, otherwise, I wouldn't have asked you about it.

I also sent my dad that "Pay" cartoon, but he didn't get as big a kick out of it as you did, in fact, it cost him five bucks!

You'll have to excuse me while I go to see an old flame about some hot water.

Your, George

October 24, 1944
Tuesday

From:	To:
C.L. Sniderman	Mr. Pvt. J.G. Barr 11057933
65 Houghton St.	Eng. Sq., 4503rd A.A.F. Base Unit
Worcester 4, Mass.	Great Bend A.B.B., Kansas

Dearest George,

Well, - your little girl is sick again. Remind me never to get my feet wet, because in doing so Saturday, I really got myself a beauty of a cold. They sent me home from work Monday afternoon and I've been in bed since, - but feeling much better tonight, I persuaded me mater to let me get out fer awhile. I really hate myself, - gravel fall Gertie, a real sad tomato, that's me. My mother & your mother had a good laugh at my expense today. They said the rabbi would probably say to you - quote, - do you take this runny nose to be your wedded wife, - unquote!! I laughed a sarcastic laugh and said to myself – humph, I'll show 'em, - and I will too. But I need you so badly to look after me.

While in bed I had nothing to do but read, so I read "Leave Her to Heaven" – a new novel and very good. Read it if you ever come across it. It's all about a gal who is really a b____, a bad woman!!! (Lottie, watch yer language!). Also, just finished listening to a story on the radio, the main characters being named Lottie & George. I didn't mean to listen to it, but when I heard the names I dragged my mother over to listen too and we both laughed & laughed. It was really funny hearing our names, - and knowing it wasn't us.

Got three letters from you yesterday, which was super swellegant. Do you know I love you? O.K., - so you do! I'm tickled silly that you're not an overage. Hell, I'd go nuts if they sent you across. Also, I hope you'll be going to school soon and for a long time. Do you know if the school is in Kansas or where? Jeepers, - you don't give me any info at all.

Had a long giggly conversation with Edie tonight and we decided that I loved her madly and she loved me passionately. If anyone was listening in on the line they'll be saying not nice things about us. Darling, do you love me madly & passionately?

Got some real good news on my dad today. If all goes well, he'll be home tomorrow afternoon. He's as happy as a boy, - and so are we all. It'll be so wonderful having him home again. Now if I only had you home, my little world would be complete.

By the by, has our puppy been born yet. I feel like an anxious father. Geroge, will you be an anxious father, - all twenty-four times? Will you pace up & down the corridor and drink black coffee, - it's customary, you know. Or will you be aloof and let me suffer alone, - you stinker. How the hell do I get on subjects like this anyhow?

I feel like writing you volumes tonight, because I feel silly and I feel we could laugh long and loud if we were together and I hate everything that's keeping us apart. Mother sat on my bed today and we talked long about you and me and of our wedding and if I was sorry we didn't get married (the first time she's asked, incidentally). She said all my life she's tried to give me what I wanted, and now what I wanted and needed most, she couldn't do a thing about. She's terribly dear and sweet, but I guess all girls feel that way about their mother.

My throat aches from smoking and my eyes are blurred from reading and my pants are tight from, - well they're just tight. For some odd reason, I'm wearing my riding breeches. I always wear the silliest things at the silliest times, - but I love riding pants. I remember last winter when I put on my bathing suit & everyone thought I was delirious. Or didn't you know that at times I'm unbearably ridiculous. You're gonna have an awful time getting used to me. I usually do these things before I go to bed, - that's why you've never seen me at my worst. They're playing "Don't Take Your Love from Me" on the radio and I could cry from sheer loneliness. Do you miss me?

Goodnight my darling.
Lottie

October 25, 1944
Wednesday

From:	To:
Mr. Cpl. J.G. Barr 11057933	C.L. Sniderman
4503rd Base Unit Eng. Sq.	65 Houghton St.
Great Bend A.B.B., Kansas	Worcester, 4, Mass.

Dearest Lottie,

It sure feels funny to be a corporal, and no longer a private. While stoking the furnaces a little while ago, I heard someone yell corporal, but I just kept on throwing coal into the fire. When it was repeated, I looked around to see what was cooking, and there was a measly P.F.C. wanting to ask me something. I hope he didn't think me rude for not answering the first time, but it will take a little while to get used to my new position.

Naturally with a rise in rank, I'll get a raise in pay, naturally. Darling, would you send me the name of our bank and our account number so that I can have the army deposit ten dollars a month from my pay? This way I won't spend it on unnecessary stuff, and when I do need a little, why I'll have it.

Last night I went to another U.S.O. show and had a good time. When it finished, Bob and I went to the service club where we played about a dozen games of ping-pong, then adjourned to our hut for a peaceful night's sleep.

We've been ordered to have our stripes on by Saturday, (still spell like a private, will have to get a corporal's pen) or they'll give us hell. That would be alright, but the supply room doesn't have any stripes, and won't have until next week. I've been able to get four sets, but need about seven more, so I'll have to go down the P.X. and make a purchase. What do I care for money now, I'll be rich soon!

Since our day room has been fixed, this is where I spend most of my writing time. Also, I can always see a nice hot poker game going on all hours of the day. It's been a long time since I've participated, but I'm glad that I don't miss the game. If it became a habit, I'd probably leave you, after we are married, for a game with the boys every night, and lose my week's pay. That would be bad!!!

More news – I'm no longer in blind landing, which will mean, I'm pretty sure, that I'll not be going to that school I was supposed to have gone to. I'm back in radio, where I first came in. When the school list was sent in, my name was on it, but no doubt it will be taken off. They did that so one of the other boys could become a sergeant. If they had left things the way they were, he'd have remained a corporal, this way they could give him another stripe. Don't try to figger it out, for that is the army. I start working again this coming week.

No letter from you yesterday and still none this morning, I have this afternoon to go.

Your, George

October 25, 1944
Wednesday

From:	To:
C.L. Sniderman	Mr. Pvt. J.G. Barr 11057933
65 Houghton St.	Eng. Sq., 4503rd A.A.F. Base Unit
Worcester 4, Mass.	Great Bend A.B.B., Kansas

My dearest George,

Today found me again smitten to my household by the weariness of illness, - but a marked improvement is evident. As a matter of fact, I could have gone to work except for the fact that I wanted to be home to greet my father on his arrival, - and that I did. He is feeling only pretty good, due to the treatment he had this morning and due to fatigue. Each day will find him better, I hope.

Three letters again from you today. Darling, you're marvelous!! Your mother also received a missive from you this A.M., and upon conversing with her, she revealed to me that she can't understand it. Also, spoke to Toby. She's dismayed over the fact that a sweet sixteen birthday party has been denied her. Which brought to mind that happy occasion of my own. Where the hell were you at that time, dear? Evidently, our acquaintance hadn't been made. See what you missed!!

George, I just can't seem to picture you as the camp furnace man, - and imagining you in blackface is completely beyond me. Altho, come to think of it, - it may be flattering at that!!! O.K. - cantcha take a joke?!

I thought surely the puppies would be born by now. What the devil is taking so long! Maybe the matter ought to be investigated. Your kid sister must think me a genius of some sort or other. She's forever asking me to get her a date. I certainly would if I could, but hells bells, I couldn't even get a date for myself. Upon telling her thusly, she laughed & laughed, - said my dating worries were over. Altho that does make me feel very complacent, - it also makes me feel ancient. The funny part is that I don't even miss not going out. It even bores me to hear other people moaning about the lack of available date bate. Oh hum, - I'm content to jest sit 'ere and wait. The only thing I swear not to do in the interim is learn how to knit. Knitting always reminds me of an old maid. And please, darling, don't ever let me be one of those things. A spinster's life just ain't fer me!

My hair is flip flopping all over my head in one big untidiness. I'm too tired to worry about my appearance just now. I just happened to notice it when I looked at myself in the glass over my desk. Pardon me, - I just yawned, - and I'm terribly all in.

Goodnight dear,
Love, Lottie

October 26, 1944
Thursday

From:	To:
Mr. Cpl. J.G. Barr 11057933	C.L. Sniderman
4503rd Base Unit Eng. Sq.	65 Houghton St.
Great Bend A.B.B., Kansas	Worcester, 4, Mass.

Dearest Lottie,

You may now call me "The Keeper of the Flames," three of them to be exact. Bob christened me that and it kind of took! I have just three more days to go tho, then they'll call me something else, of course, the title may not be as romantic.

Darling, you know what? - Then I'll tell you. I received a letter from my brother Sol in which he tells me to forget about that amount I owed him. I had sent him five, but still owed him fifteen, but it was given to me by Fran and Sol like a present. The reason, this is my reasoning, Sol didn't give it to me in the first place, because I think he was a bit leery of what Fran would have to say about it. Rather than endure a woman's wrath, it was given with a pay it back as soon as you can attitude, but Fran came to the rescue and said that since they've never given me anything since I came in the army, now was their chance. Boy, and I do appreciate it, and I told them so.

How is your dad doing? He should be home by now. Be sure and give him my love, will you? Thanks.

It's a beautiful night, the moon is bright, the air is fresh and clean, but you are the one thing that is missing. This is the kind of night we'd go down the corner for an ice cream or something, and end up by walking around the Jr. High School, then down Rice Lane and back. How I loved those walks, just you and I, what I wouldn't give to do it right now. Darling, would you care to join me, because I'm walking now, holding your hand and thinking how beautiful you are, and how the moon makes your hair glisten. Now you're climbing on the wall of the school and I'm holding your hand so you won't fall.

Then we turn on Grafton Street and music is coming from one of the houses, there seems to be always music in those houses, we too shall always have music. There's the big billboard with a girl in a bathing suit, advertising something, she may be skiing now. Cross the streets with the lights against us, and I have to pull you away from the pedestrian push button, on down the street until, "We'd better turn back." I know you loved those walks to-gether just as much as I did, and we'll do it again, you'll see.

With pleasant, wonderful memories in my heavy head, I'm going to sleep, so I can dream of you.

Your, George

October 26, 1944
Thursday

From:	To:
C.L. Sniderman	Mr. Cpl. J.G. Barr 11057933
65 Houghton St.	Eng. Sq., 4503rd A.A.F. Base Unit
Worcester 4, Mass.	Great Bend A.B.B., Kansas

Dearest George,

Congratulations, darling. I suppose now you'll be demanding corporal respect from me, - but to me you'll always be just plain Stinky Barr. But all kidding aside, - I think its super and I also think you deserved it. The money will probably be muchly appreciated. Also, mazeltoff on the arrival of the puppies. How come she only had four, - the kid's a slacker, - and don't you dare ask me if I could do better!!!!

By special request of my boss today, I went to work this afternoon. I really didn't feel up to it, - but the girl I work with is out sick too, which left our department in a helleva mess. He's been so damn decent to me that I just couldn't refuse.

My dad had a very bad day today. We had the doctor again & he's given him some more medicine. He coughs continuously and we feel so damn helpless. He's gotten very thin and looks quite bad. Darling, I'm afraid I was a bit too hasty in being so optimistic. I feel as [Editor's note: the next part of this sentence was cut out of the letter, I believe it was the part on the back of the page in a P.S. note that was the subject of the edit.] never did solve a problem.

Just spoke to Edie and she also is in a helleva state of mind. Her main trouble being men is quite different from mine. But can't do a thing to help her out on that score.

I wish I could think of something gay and amusing to write you. But I have very little contact with the outside world, so naturally I hear very little news. Altho Toby did tell me that Casey Davidson is in town and is looking skinny as ever. That guy really got a good deal. He's been stationed in Washington ever since he enlisted in the Navy, which was a long time before the rest of the kids. Wish to high heaven you'd be stationed in Washington or there abouts. But I suppose to have you in the country is plenty to be thankful for.

Darling, I don't feel very cheerful tonight, so I'm gonna have a hot drink and try to go to sleep.

Goodnight dear
Lovingly, Lottie

P.S. Becoming a corporal at least deserves a kiss so, - [Editor's note: The rest of this P.S. appears to have been cut out of the letter.]

October 27, 1944
Friday Nite

From:	To:
C.L. Sniderman	Mr. Cpl. J.G. Barr 11057933
65 Houghton St.	Eng. Sq., 4503rd A.A.F. Base Unit
Worcester 4, Mass.	Great Bend A.B.B., Kansas

Hello dear,

Finally found a box in which to send you your stationery, you should have it very shortly now. I don't understand what happened, but you have a marked surplus of envelopes or so it seems. I'm sending you the remainder of the stationery, but I've kept quite a number of envelopes. If you want them, I'll send them under separate cover. You should have enough to last you awhile now.

Had a big talk with Charlotte Barr (confusing, eh wot!) this P.M., and she's quite lonely and discouraged, as the rest of the mob. She said if Narky isn't here by midnight on the eve of the 15th of November, she's gonna take a trek out there. Poor kid, I really feel sorry for her, - it's really an inconvenience not having your own home with a baby, but the setup out in Florida sounds swell.

Had a lovely invitation to go beering tonight, - with Edie & Golda Edinberg. They're a couple of stew bums if I ever saw one. But I suppose that's one way of fergetting yer troubles.

My dad feels a little better today, altho he's been terribly groggy. I also feel muchly improved, thank you!

Your cousin's letter and picture were darling. The idea is really very clever. They must have a lot of spare time to sit down and compose a masterpiece like that. We'll teach our children to do their own dirty work. And as far as the photography setup, - well dear, - if it's gonna be like he described, we better look for a house with an extra room. I'll be damned if I'm gonna serve photography soufflé' instead of chicken soup!!

Wore me new coat today and the gals think it's quite ultra, ultra, - but of-course! Now my mother says I ought to get a hat. I think she sits home and thinks up ways for me to waste my money, - how much of an increase do you get in your monthly bonus now?

Really had an unusual evening tonight. My mother decided her hair was a mess, - soooo I set it for her and while I was in the mood, my aunt squeezed in a manicure. Now everyone looks sa-imply deviche, - 'cept me!! But why do I have to look bootiful, - I ain't got no one to impress.

Well, me lovin' baby, so ends another chapter in my life.

Goodnight & pleasant dreams,
Love, Lottie

October 28, 1944
Saturday Nite

From:	To:
C.L. Sniderman	Mr. Cpl. J.G. Barr 11057933
65 Houghton St.	Eng. Sq., 4503rd A.A.F. Base Unit
Worcester 4, Mass.	Great Bend A.B.B., Kansas

Hi honey,

Had quite a hectic day today and I'm not kidding. I haven't been able to get into town for so long, that today I decided it was a must do. So, at exactly 1 o'clock I dashed downtown for what supposedly was going to be a few minutes. So, what happened, - I met a woman who used to work down our place and she asked me to join her for lunch, - so I did. Then I started dashing around the stores buying various and assundry articles for which I was badly in need. I was crossing Pleasant St. when all of a once in a sudden, I dropped a bundle and stooping to pick it up I didn't see a truck that was heading my direction, - and so we very nearly had a collision. I was thoroughly embarrassed when every body stopped to stare. Too bad I gipped them out of a bloody accident. I finally struggled into the house, - laden with bundles, my hair all over my face when who should be here but your mother and dad. They must have thought me quite a ridiculous sight.

Darling, I think your idea about saving money is swell, but I can't understand why you want it directly taken out of your pay. I have a better plan, - Just as soon as you get your pay, take out the amount you want to save and send it to me immediately, and I do mean on the double. In that way, when I get the money from you, I'll try to add some of my own to it and then make the deposit. We really should save, you know, and I think you ought to learn the responsibility or the ability of saving without it being directly taken from you. Now don't let me down, - I'm counting on you. If you don't think my idea will work out then we'll do it your way, - O.K.? - O.K.

I'm a little disappointed in your not going to school. Your explanation of why and how come was much too complicated for my dull mind. So, what happens to you now, - don't spare any details.

Received a long letter from Pauline today and she sends her bestest. She'll drop you a line first chance she gets.

I fixed up my dad good tonight. Since he's been sick, he hasn't had a haircut and looks like a musician. I decided something should be done, - so I make two braids on top of his head and tied them with a red ribbon. I thought he looked adorable, - my mother, evidently didn't, because she was in stitches of laughter!! My brilliant work just isn't appreciated, dats all. Dad feels pretty good today and is starting to look better, too.

They're playing "I'll be Loving You Always" on the radio and I swoon every time I hear it. For some odd reason, I think it's beautiful.

Can't understand why you didn't get any mail from me for two days. Heck, I spend the best part of my life writing to you, - trying to keep you happy and the damn mailing system has to gum up the works. But don't worry dear, when you come home we'll never write a letter, - or almost.

Again, I bid thee farewell until tomorrow, same time same place, same gal.

Lovingly, Lottie

October 30, 1944
Monday

From:	To:
C.L. Sniderman	Mr. Cpl. J.G. Barr 11057933
65 Houghton St.	Eng. Sq., 4503rd A.A.F. Base Unit
Worcester 4, Mass.	Great Bend A.B.B., Kansas

My dearest George,

Well, tonight is the night the goblins are out, ghosts on the prowl and witches riding their broomsticks. The moon is full and so big you feel you can touch it if you stand on your toes. All this goes to make an atmosphere just right to be sitting in front of the fire with the one you love, - laughing, joking, and just being plain happy. The air is crisp and makes you feel healthy. In your letter of today, you brought to mind the walks we used to take, every detail was remembered by me, but I love you even more for remembering too. It was wonderful the way we could be happy, not mingling in crowds at the night clubs, not spending loads of money, just being together, being young and being foolish and loving it. Darling, those days are not over, they have just taken a leave temporarily and will resume again the minute you come home.

Had a very, very pleasant evening at the folks' house last night. I was telling your mother last time I spoke to her that I hadn't been out of the house at night for nine weeks. I wasn't complaining, I just happened to mention it and so she insisted I come over for supper and stay for the evening.

After supper, some of your relatives came over and a poker game started. I went in with good intentions, and had we played for high stakes, I would have lost my shirt. Charlotte & I played partners, which helped the situation immensely. As far as being a poker player, - I better stick to playing piano!! You know the old saying, - unlucky in cards, but lucky in love. One of your cousins, I think his name was Jay, was amazed to learn that I was engaged. He thought I was sooooo young. If he tells me that when I'm forty, I'll be complimented.

Met Edie for lunch today and discussed the why's and how's of this thing called love. She received a letter from Dave and it was very, very platonic. She doesn't feel bad, - just worried about her fickle nature. We had wonderful plans for doing some shopping after lunch, - but you know women when they start talking, - and we happen to be no exceptions.

Received a letter from Dave Grossman (you know, - that measly little Pfc), and it was mostly censored. I was so mad I could have screamed. It was a Vmail, so all in all, I didn't get much of a letter, but he did say that he wrote to you.

It was wonderful of Fran and Sol to make void that debt. That warrants a damn nice gift when the baby is born. Tell them I send my thanks too. Gee, I really think that was swell.

Well dear, I've got oodles of letters to write, so I'm sure you'll forgive me if I take leave.

Goodnight and remember to
Love, Lottie

P.S. Someone is singing "When You're Away Dear" – how weary the lonely hours, etc., etc. - How true. Me.

October 31, 1944
Tuesday

From:	To:
C.L. Sniderman	Mr. Cpl. J.G. Barr 11057933
65 Houghton St.	Eng. Sq., 4503rd A.A.F. Base Unit
Worcester 4, Mass.	Great Bend A.B.B., Kansas

Dearest George,

Just entertained some very unexpected guests, - and frightening also!! It seems that on Halloween now a days, a whole gang of kids in costume get together and go from house to house. If you don't give them anything for showing you their costumes, they are supposed to keep ringing your bell and break your windows. Fortunately, I had a big bag of candy prepared, - so they left in sheer joy. They were really adorable, - the point is, you're supposed to act very frightened and I really gave them a show.

Charlotte called me this P.M. and asked me to go to the movies with her & Dotty. I really would have loved to, but my mother had made plans to go out, so I naturally had to stay in. Speaking of my dad, - he really had a day today. It was really beautiful out, so he and my mother went down to visit my brother's new place, - or didn't you know that he had already moved into that building he bought on Union St.? Irv was positively amazed to see them and was also very thrilled. He's starting to look a little better now, altho he's still quite weak.

Also, spoke to Toby this evening and it looks as if she finally got her wish. Some fellow invited her to the Mu Sigma semi formal, and naturally, she is quite pleased. She'll look like a doll. Ah me, - where is my lost youth!!!

I was sorry to hear that Bob is leaving for San Antonio. You no sooner get to know a person, and they or you ship off for someplace else. That's how it is in the army.

Glad to hear that the pups are doing so nicely. Scratch their necks for me, - or isn't that what your supposed to do to dogs! Never having been a dog (no comment, please), I wouldn't be an authority.

I just called Udie's house and got his address for you, which is as follows:

S. Sargent J.F. Goff 31070555
60th Bomb Sqd.
Smokey Hill Army Air Force
Salina, Kansas

That's all for tonight, dear. Goodnight.

Lovingly, Lottie.

Broadway Sonnet

Only a fool can hope for love to last . . .
    And so we will be fools a little space,
Nor hide our eyes when skies go overcast
    Nor yet bemoan our meager time of grace . . .
We will find inns along the shadowed street,
    Knowing full well that every inn must close,
We will find roses, scarlet-hued and sweet
    Knowing how brief the life on any rose;

But in some moment when the fire leaps high . . .
    I may set down some magic words for you,
We may find songs too beautiful to die . . .
    We may find banners waving in the blue . . .

Only a fool can hope for love to last . . .
Only a greater fool lets love go past!

           —Don Wahn.

November 1, 1944
Wednesday

From:	To:
Mr. Cpl. J.G. Barr 11057933	C.L. Sniderman
4503rd Base Unit Eng. Sq.	65 Houghton St.
Great Bend A.B.B., Kansas	Worcester, 4, Mass.

Dearest Lottie,

This afternoon I sent you some letters. Maybe you can steam the stamps off, and reuse them, there must be a fortune posted on those envelopes.

Throw me a trash can! I was on the ash can detail this morning. "Dusty Dan" Barr I was known as! What a way to make a living – phooey! Among all the ashes there are usually a few empty fifths, now I wonder where the boys get it, this being a dry state.

While at the shop in the afternoon, we got a call to move a speaker. Off we rushed to maintenance control, wherever that was. We rode around in a Jeep for nearly a half hour questioning every one we saw, but no one knew where the damn place was. This field isn't very large so we finally stumbled upon it. When we saw the work to do we were mad, because it was a telephone man's job, not ours. Since we were there we said the hell with it, and started to see if we could do the job. It proved to be very simple, so simple in fact, that anyone of the fellows working there with the least bit of initiative could have performed the job just as well as we did.

Just as we were about to leave, a sergeant came up to us and told us they'd probably want the damn thing moved in a few days, because they're not quite set up. We told him that he'd better get in touch with the right people next time, because we sure'n hell wouldn't come up there again. No doubt, we'll eat our words in a few days!

I have a day off coming to me this week, but I don't know which one to take off. I can't take Sunday off, the one that seems right, because to me it is the end of the week, because no one can have that day off. Saturday is already taken and I think Friday is too. I don't want to-morrow off, because it is too close to my last day off, what a way to figger, O.K. so I'm crazy!

Some lucky Joe is getting a discharge to-morrow. Sometimes I wish that I were eligible for one also, but who wants to get out of the army because of some disability.

I think I'll trot down to see "Mr. Lucky," nothing else to do, and as I remember it, it was good. Good night, dear.

Your, George

November 1, 1944
Wednesday

From:	To:
C.L. Sniderman	Mr. Cpl. J.G. Barr 11057933
65 Houghton St.	Eng. Sq., 4503rd A.A.F. Base Unit
Worcester 4, Mass.	Great Bend A.B.B., Kansas

My dearest George,

Your letter of today was very sweet and was reread many times. So, glad you still love me. About your giving the bananas to your friend's baby, - well, all I can say is that it's a typical thing that you would do. You're terribly sweet.

Had plans to go shopping for a gift for Sara's sister-in-law to be with Charlotte Saturday, but Golda Edinberg just called and invited me to a tea at her house, which is Saturday also. I'm gonna try and kill two birds with one stone since Charlotte will have to go home early anyway and stay with the baby. You know how it is, - it never rains but it pours. Then Sunday is the shower, Monday Toby's birthday, Tuesday election, Wednesday Edie's birthday, etc., etc. Then for the next month there won't be anything happening.   Speaking of the election; I had the pleasure of seeing Mr. & Mrs. Dewey today. I was walking back to work from lunch and got entangled in the crowd of republicans who came to pay their tribute. Dewey spoke in front of the Union Station for about half an hour and didn't receive much of an ovation in our fair city. Everyone was yelling 'Phooie on Dewey', and other not too complimentary remarks. He is a very good looking man, - much better than his pictures, but his speech stunk, and it's not that I'm prejudiced.

Had a religious argument with one of the devote Catholics in our office today. We both got to a boiling point, but didn't come to blows fortunately. It wasn't exactly an argument, - more of a friendly debate and after all was said and done we were broadminded enough to shake hands and be pals. That's the kind of argument I like. It's very stimulating to the mind.

I'm so hot right now I feel as if I could melt. It's very warm outside and we have our heat going full blast for my dad. I guess a person is never satisfied, - cold, - it's too cold, - hot, - it's too hot. Oh, well.

I'm so mentally and physically exhausted tonight that I'm practically falling off the chair. If only I could sleep for just a week; I'd feel like a walking vitamin pill. When we get married don't you dare to wake me up in the morning!!

Well, dear, nightie night again and remember, - it's you I'll always

Love, Lottie

November 3, 1944
Friday Nite

From:	To:
C.L. Sniderman	Mr. Cpl. J.G. Barr 11057933
65 Houghton St.	Eng. Sq., 4503rd A.A.F. Base Unit
Worcester 4, Mass.	Great Bend A.B.B., Kansas

Hello darling,

You really don't know how you've spoiled me. I didn't get any mail yesterday and I was miserable. Today I had to wait till the late mail came, - I was beginning to feel discouraged. I'm so used to getting mail every day.

Got a kick out of you having your fortune told. And about the red head, all I can say is, - humph. And as far as the bundle she is supposed to bring you, - well dear, even babies are sometimes referred to as bundles!!! Fine thing.

Just spoke to your mother and she tells me you wrote home that you were already looking forward to your January furlough. Can let you know that the feeling is very mutual. January seems like a long ways off, but it really isn't. We'll have to spend another weekend in Boston, - but not at Pieroni's!!!

I have five million things I could do tonight, but I don't feel like doing a damn thing. I don't know what's the matter with me, - all I want to do is sleep. But you know what they say, - no rest for the wicked. Do you think I'm wicked?!!!

My dad is coming along quite nicely. Altho he still coughs, it's nothing like it used to be. He was all set on going to the store tomorrow, - but by the act of forced persuasion we convinced him he should wait until next week.

O.K., darling, - have your way about saving. After all, it is your money and if you want to send it directly, - it's alright by me. The name of the bank is the Bay State Savings Bank, - 511 Main St. The serial number is #30953. I'm quite sure you have to have the book to make the deposits. I'll find out, and if so, I'll have to send it to you. That's all for tonight, m'love. Take care and beware of redheads!!

Lovingly, Lottie

November 5, 1944
Sunday

From:	To:
Mr. Cpl. J.G. Barr 11057933	C.L. Sniderman
4503rd Base Unit Eng. Sq.	65 Houghton St.
Great Bend A.B.B., Kansas	Worcester, 4, Mass.

Dearest Lottie,

Did I say I was going to take to-day off? How mistaken I was! Very early this A.M., I was violently awakened by my boss sergeant who politely stated, "Let's go!" So, I went. This morning while he was at breakfast, he asked one of the K.P.'s where I was, the K.P. is a hut mate and also a co-radio man, - ahem, radio man, - "Still on his sack, probably," was his reply. P.S. All day long I worked! Gee, a fella never can have any fun.

It seems that everyone had off to-day except the sarge and I. There was work to do fortunately, or else I would have been very peeved about the entire affair. We had a hundred-hour inspection of the radio equipment of a B-29. All it includes is to check the moveable equipment. The tubes are checked, the sets are cleaned and tuned up, then we give them a bench operational check, which is similar to operation on the plane, only there are a bunch of meters showing us how the sets are working. With just the two of us, it took almost a complete day. We found just two poor tubes. The sets played, but in the army, if they check poor you have to replace it before it goes entirely bad, saving a radio operator a bad time when he's up flying.

I finally received a letter from Dave. It was really a long one too, I guess he felt badly about not writing sooner, because he really outdid himself. He also mentioned you on very complimentary terms. He told me I was a very lucky guy to have a girl like you, and don't I know it. I'd send the letter to you, but, - well it was written to a guy that's in the army, if you know what I mean.

I took in the camp movie after supper just for a little relaxation. I was glad that it was a picture that I could rest, tho at moments I did show emotions. The name of the picture, if I remember correctly is "An American Romance".

So, the Republican city of Worcester is a 'Phooey on Dewey" place. What an election this has turned out to be. Now after admiring Dewey and you find him handsome, do you want me to raise a mustache? Like hell!

Give a little of my love to Edie on her birthday for me, will ya' huh? Thanks, you're a dear and I love you, yes even more than Edie!

You should be at the shower now, if it is still going at 10 P.M. If you are, I hope you are having a lovely time.

Good night, dear, and very pleasant dreams.

Your, George

P.S. I now have a pin up cartoon, and have place for the second edition of the dozen. You're doing fine, but how about me?!

November 5, 1944
Sunday Nite

From:	To:
C.L. Sniderman	Mr. Cpl. J.G. Barr 11057933
65 Houghton St.	Eng. Sq., 4503rd A.A.F. Base Unit
Worcester 4, Mass.	Great Bend A.B.B., Kansas

My dearest George,

At this writing, I can inform you that you (or your picture anyway) are in a very precarious position. I happened to be listening to the radio in my bedroom and they happened to be playing music that can't be enjoyed alone, soooo I fetched your picture and set it in the middle of the bed amidst a heap of discarded lingerie, a dress and other miscellaneous articles that one takes off when one disrobes and makes ready to retire. Can well nigh say that you looked very masculine sitting on top of a pile of feminine articles. Jesus, but I miss you.

Went to the tea at Golda's yesterday afternoon and it was really very nice. Among the people there was Edith Gordon and she was telling me that you were her first flame. She has just become engaged to Harold Freedman, - an old story, of-course, so the engagement was no surprise. Those kinds of affairs are usually very stiff and very boring, but this one was really nice.

Tonight, I was at the shower for Jack Ulman's fiancée and it was nice also. I met Charlotte & we went together and also bought the gift together. We ate, played bridge, Charlotte won the prize, and then your dad drove me home.

Last nite after the tea, I didn't feel very much like going home because it was so early, so I trotted myself down to your house and Charlotte, Dot, and I talked about everything under the sun. Charlotte is really a good kid, I like her. She has the strength of her own convictions. At the shower, tonight, I met more & more of your relatives. Seems like there's no end to them and they all asked about you.

Tomorrow is Toby's birthday, so I'm taking her out to dinner, where upon I shall present her with the gift. She looked adorable tonight. Some people had the nerve to insult the kid by saying she looked like me. I was truly complimented.

Irv & Fran were over with the kids today and Ricky is positively gorgeous. I could have taken a bite right out of him, - and believe me he's got something to bite. In two seconds, he turned the house upside down.

It's getting terribly cold these days and I dread the coming of a cold winter, - except the part where you come home. Before we know it, it will be Thanksgiving, - then Christmas, Merry Christmas, dear, - then New Year's, - Happy New Year, dear, and lo and behold, spring is on its way. Boy, I sure make the seasons fly, eh wot!!

I'm racking my brain for news to tell you, but it seems I'm all written out. So come kiss me goodnight, - and then I'll go to bed. And with this parting thought I take leave.

Lovingly, Lottie

November 6, 1944
Monday

From:	To:
Mr. Cpl. J.G. Barr 11057933	C.L. Sniderman
4503rd Base Unit Eng. Sq.	65 Houghton St.
Great Bend A.B.B., Kansas	Worcester, 4, Mass.

Dearest Lottie,

This month is surely creeping by, I wish it would hurry up and get it over, then it will be just one more month to sweat out a maybe furlough. If I'm home on New Year's, do you want to get drunk with me? If you do, who gets under the cold shower first? Well, ladies before gentlemen, you know. I can just see you, hair hanging over your face, and maybe a silly grin on your lovely lips. Oh, my god, what a mess! What am I saying, I've never seen you drunk, and if you do get stinkin', I bet you are the prettiest drunk I'd ever hope to see. I don't care drunk or sober, I love you.

If I worked yesterday, I loafed to-day, what a system the army has. My day off was to-morrow, now I have to postpone it until Wednesday, because I have latrine orderly to-morrow. What a way to help win the war!

At two o'clock I quit and went back to my hut and took a lovely afternoon nap. I didn't get up until supper time, and then I would have slept thru it if one of the boys hadn't awakened me and asked me if I was going to chow. Better I should have stayed in bed, chow this evening was terrible. We have three sets of cooks and the ones on to-night, should be digging ditches, the other two aren't bad. Are you going to cook me up a good dinner when I get home, you know your breakfast was delicious, but how about a dinner?

I think we're due for a little snow soon, the wind is blowing and the clouds are clouding, and I can just feel it coming on, or is it that snow can fall this time of the year?

Toby's sixteenth birthday is to-day. It seems like an awful long time since her birth. I can remember when my mother was having her, I was just a kid then and didn't know what was going on. Then Toby was born and I strutted around telling everyone that my mother got a baby girl because I had told her to. Are you going to oblige our children if they put in a special request? Now sixteen years have past, in no time at all she'll find a boy, then they'll want to get married, and we'll give them our blessings and feel just a bit older. She's a cute kid, even tho she is my sister, I think since she has known you, she has become better looking, maybe it is because your personality has affected her and it shows up in her face. I know she likes you better than her sister-in-laws.

Until to-morrow, my darling,
Your, George

November 7, 1944
Tuesday

From:	To:
Mr. Cpl. J.G. Barr 11057933	C.L. Sniderman
4503rd Base Unit Eng. Sq.	65 Houghton St.
Great Bend A.B.B., Kansas	Worcester, 4, Mass.

Dearest Lottie,

Here I am again, same guy, same girl, same place. Starting to-morrow morning, we start work at 6:45 A.M. (mail just came in, you'll have to wait until I read your letter; excuse me) and don't finish until 4:15 P.M. Before we report for work we have to report to an officer so he can take a count of us. They think that this will help get the planes into the air, but all it will do is just screw up the works. Until this new colonel came in, the field had been doing poorly, now it is even worse. The more stuff they throw at us, the less work they are going to get put out. The only trouble is that we'll have to wait until this colonel screws up enough, so that he'll get replaced.

O.K., I'll beware of any red heads I see, in fact, I'll give them two good once overs.

I'm glad to hear that your dad's coming along fine, but the more he stays away from the store, the better it will be.

No, I don't think you are wicked, what made you ask me that? Just because you need some rest and can't get it? Hey, maybe I'm wicked, I need some rest myself!

I don't think I'm going to need the bank book, because they'll put the balance on their own sheet every time they receive a deposit, and when they get the bank book, they'll add it up then.

I don't want to spoil any of your nice thoughts about my furlough, but it is still two months away. I don't think I have to say anything else about it, because time is the enemy of a soldier.

We will go to Boston again.

Your, George

November 8, 1944
Wednesday

From:	To:
C.L. Sniderman	Mr. Cpl. J.G. Barr 11057933
65 Houghton St.	Eng. Sq., 4503rd A.A.F. Base Unit
Worcester 4, Mass.	Great Bend A.B.B., Kansas

Dearest George,

Amid the hustle bustle of a terrifically noisy office, I shall endeavor to write you a letter or, - reasonable facsimile. I couldn't write you last nite because we had a little company and the radio was going full blast, - everyone listening for the election returns. It was quite exciting, - altho I think everyone knew who would win out.

Took Toby to dinner Monday nite and she was really crazy about the locket. It looked very sweet on her. I took her to Cosgrove's (that's where she wanted to go) and I think she was impressed by the high-class stew bums!! At any rate, we had a very, very nice time and the nicest part was that she was really surprised about the locket.

When you wrote to me a few days ago, you sounded quite depressed. And you apologized for writing as you did. Darling, you don't have to put on the gay blade act with me, - I want to know exactly how you feel and exactly what you think. These lonesome moods get down everyone sometime and I'd feel hurt if you didn't miss me, because heaven only knows how much I miss you.

The Jap propaganda leaflet you sent was very interesting, but it also made my blood boil. Plaguing a guy's mind with thoughts like that is really low down, - but I guess people in war go to any extent, especially rats like they are.

I received your letters, - or my letters that I sent you that you sent me back. Confusing, eh wot?!! They made very dull reading, - for me anyhow. Darling, do you find my letters dull? If so, I shall take a correspondence course in how to make love via letters or how to get your man in ten easy lessons!!! Aren't I silly at times, how will you ever stand me?!!

Me matre just called and said a missive is waiting for her darling little daughter from her darling little boyfriend which made my darling little mother's darling little daughter very happy. (Oui vey, - I wouldn't go through writing that again.)

Well dear, my lunch hour draws to a close, so I shall take my little pile of junk and go back to work. How I ever finished this letter is beyond me. During the course of this letter, there has been a political and religious argument, a giggle session, and a very long discussion on shoes. And for this my dear, we got paid today, - but don't get me wrong, - when we work, we really work. And so now I bid you a very, very good afternoon and remember, -

Love, Lottie

"Now don't get excited, George—it's just that they didn't have any space for me in a regular room."

November 8, 1944
Wednesday

From:	To:
Mr. Cpl. J.G. Barr 11057933	C.L. Sniderman
4503rd Base Unit Eng. Sq.	65 Houghton St.
Great Bend A.B.B., Kansas	Worcester, 4, Mass.

Dearest Lottie,

I finally have my day off! I got to bed at 11 o'clock last night and didn't get up until 11 this morning. It was one of the best rests I've gotten in a long time. When the boys got up this morning, they didn't make any noise, and if they had the light on, I was unaware of it.

Last night I went to town, and was going to take in a movie when I met our supply clerk and his wife and we started to pass the time of day. They also were going to a movie, but had seen all the shows, and were undecided what to do. I suggested they go to a town ten miles from here, since they had a car, and there was nothing doing here. They asked me if I'd like to go along, I jumped at the chance. A nice ride in a car with people I knew was just the thing I needed to get me out of the dumps. We had a very nice time, at least I did. They are two nice kids and I don't think I enjoyed myself so much since the last time we were to-gether in Newark. It was a different kind of enjoyment, but I really appreciated their company, and I hope they did mine. After we had a bite to eat and a cup of coffee, they drove me back to the base, right to my row of huts. It was swell.

After getting up I took off for town because I wanted to take a few pictures for my course. I had to wait for the damn bus nearly a half hour, and nearly froze to death doing it. The wind was blowing fiercely and I didn't take my overcoat, like I should have. When the bus went by the city hospital I got out. After looking it over I took four pictures of it from different angles and called it a day for my picture taking. I had to take pictures of some sort of building, so I thought the hospital would do fine.

Yesterday afternoon, I thought would be a good time to photograph Shavetail and her offspring. I took their box outdoors, laid Shavetail down near it, and the puppies took their natural course and started feeding.

I snapped the shutter twice before I realized that I made a double exposure, I could have kicked myself. Here film is hard to get, and I go and waste one! Would you like the honor of kicking me? Is that nice, you kicking the man you are to marry?! Shame on you. I took a good picture of them, and of course, you shall be a recipient of her photo.

To-night I'm going to another card of fights at the auditorium. They've been getting better and better every week, so to-night should be a real fast contest.

Good bye for now, my darling,
Your, George

[Editor's note: Above is the picture George took of Shavetail. "Shave tail" is army slang for a 2nd lieutenant.]

November 9, 1944
Thursday

From:	To:
C.L. Sniderman	Mr. Cpl. J.G. Barr 11057933
65 Houghton St.	Eng. Sq., 4503rd A.A.F. Base Unit
Worcester 4, Mass.	Great Bend A.B.B., Kansas

My dearest George,
     Had planned to write you a nice long letter last nite, but I should know better than to plan anything in advance. When I came home from work I found my dad in bed again, - a completely changed man. We immediately

called the doctor, but there was very little he could do for him, - he was running a temp. of 104° degrees. My brother came over immediately because, - well, to be perfectly frank, we thought last night would be the night. We gave him pills to ease the pain and sponge baths every half hour. By eleven thirty we were pretty well done for from not eating & exhaustion, - neither my mother nor I had eaten supper. Irv tried to make us go to bed, but of-course we wouldn't, so we worked it on shifts. We didn't dare leave him alone for a minute so Irv stayed up for two hours, then my mother, then I. The sleep that I did get wasn't very restful since I was all dressed and my nerves just wouldn't let go. By six o'clock we all fell asleep, - at eight I got up washed, gulped a cup of coffee, and Irv drove me to work at about 9 o'clock. When I came home for lunch today his temp. was back to normal and he felt pretty good again. The kids in the office said I looked like a walking ghost this morning and I felt it too. But now dad is sleeping, he's got no pains, - so again, we're hoping. We don't know what the reoccurrence was from. Whatta life.

I fully understand what Dave's letter to you must be like and I think I'd get a kick out of reading it, - but if you no wanna, - you no wanna!!

Darling, if you're home by New Year's, and I hope to high heaven you are, there's no doubt about our getting stinko. We'll drink the places dry. And, - eh, - ahem, - you my dear, will be the first under the shower, - clothes and all!!! Toby tells me when you come home you promised to take her night clubbing. The kid has the right idea, - she wants to go formal!

So, sorry you no like the army chow, - and I'll be delighted to make you dinner when you come home, - but you gotta promise that good or bad you'll eat it. Since we're talking about the culinary arts, - how about telling me what you like so I can learn how to make it. Since you like my breakfast we have nothing to worry about, - but even I know that I can't give you eggs three times a day, - or can I?!!!

I got a kick out of you saying that you didn't know what it was all about when Toby was born, - because I didn't know until, - well, - I should have known before because I was well along in my youth. It never even dawned on me to ask, - to tell the truth I never cared. Times have certainly changed, - eh wot?

Well darling, I guess you know without my telling you that I'm a little done in. I wish I had you here with me now, - I know it would lighten the burden so much.

Goodnite & pleasant dreams
Lovingly, Lottie

November 11, 1944
Saturday

From:	To:
Mr. Cpl. J.G. Barr 11057933	C.L. Sniderman
4503rd Base Unit Eng. Sq.	65 Houghton St.
Great Bend A.B.B., Kansas	Worcester, 4, Mass.

Dearest Lottie,

Hello dear, it has been a long time since I wrote, but I've been a bit busy. Thursday I came back from work and intended writing you, but didn't feel like doing a damn thing. It was much too early to even think of going to bed, so I suggested a poker game. Remind me not to do things like that, I lost four bucks.

Then yesterday afternoon at three o'clock we were told we were going on D.S. (detached service) up to Salina, Kans., that's if we wanted to go. Of course, no one backed out, except two married men, because Salina is a better base and town.

You may want to know how come this came about. Well, remember I told you what was happening on our field, all the "chicken" being thrown around? Our C.O. didn't have any control over us, because the base took over. He didn't like the idea, and knew we didn't relish the set up either, so we went "over the hill" sort of legitimately. He couldn't send the entire outfit up, but there are at least one third of us up here. Next week he hopes to be able to send some more of the boys up here. This way the fellows that the base had, won't have any longer than he can help it. The other boys that aren't faring out too badly will stay there. When we are on D.S. we don't have to pull details like K.P. and the like, I like.

We left camp at five-thirty and came up here about eight-thirty. When we arrived, they had a nice barrack ready for us. It is much warmer this way and cleaner. I live on an upper bunk, because I like high places, but the real reason is that once your bed is made, no one messes it up, while the man in the lower bunk goes crazy if he tries to keep his bunk straight because everyone lays on it, sits on it, and just messes it up.

I tried to locate Uddy this morning, but he was at work, so I'll try and find him some other time.

I doubt very much if we'll do much work while we are up here, I doubt if we'll be up here more than five to six weeks, then by that time the captain should have time to straighten things out, or that the colonel of the base is thrown out.

When you write me, still use my old address and put on D.S. Salina, so that the mail clerks will know to put it aside to be sent up the same day. O.K?

I'm glad that we did come up here. I need some sort of change and I got it.

Your, George

November 12, 1944
Sunday

From:	To:
C.L. Sniderman	Mr. Cpl. J.G. Barr 11057933
65 Houghton St.	Eng. Sq., 4503rd A.A.F. Base Unit
Worcester 4, Mass.	Great Bend A.B.B., Kansas

Hello darling,

It seems like ages since I've received mail from you. No letter Friday, Saturday was a holiday, Sunday no mail, - if I don't get a letter tomorrow, I'll be fit to be tied.

Saturday morning Fran, Irv and the kids came over after the parade and boy what a racket they made. That kid is such a doll. The house was a mess, - but we loved it. Just after they left, your mother & father came over and we spent a very enjoyable afternoon. Since we can't go out to see people, it's swell to have them come over here.

This morning Irv came over again and he gave me quite a bit of news. In a few weeks, he expects to go out west and is going to hit Kansas City. Now if you can possibly meet him there, - of-course I don't know how far it is, - but if you could, you'd be assured of having a helleva time and he's dying to see you. So, let me know just how far a distance it is and I'll let you know exactly when he'll be there.

Had some very unexpected guests this afternoon, - it was really quite funny. About 2 o'clock I answered the telephone only to hear a boy say hello. It is so seldom that I get calls now from male admirers (my ring fixed that, - and I love it), that I was profoundly shocked. Anywho it was this kid Ronnie from Spencer, he had just heard that I was engaged and would it be alright if he came up to pay his respects. After I told him that I thought twas very permissible, he came up with a friend of his. We sat and talked, had tea, remembered old times and then they left. After they left I had the most peculiar sensation, - that of being much older and far wiser than he. I've known Ronnie for about six years and he hasn't changed a bit. He thinks he's quite clever and worldly, - since he was my guest I let him rave on and on. He kept talking of you as my husband and admiring your picture. I wished to high heaven you were here, - it felt as though you should be with me. Darling, I miss you so terribly. Everything seems so empty without you.

My dad is feeling a little better again, - we've had so damn many scares. But thank goodness that's all we've had.

I've really not very much to write you tonight since I haven't heard from you what seems like ages. Your sister-in-law Edith went to Boston for the weekend, which leaves me without our usual nightly conversations, which I truly miss. Damn it, sometimes I feel so all alone I could cry. If Irv was going out west by car, you can bet your boots he'd have a passenger. But as it is, I'll have to struggle along until your furlough.

> *Goodnight dear & pleasant dreams*
> *Lovingly, Lottie*

P.S. My mother bought me (or us) a lovely sheet & pillowcase set with Mr. & Mrs. Embroidered on the border. They look lovely in my cedar chest, - but would look much better in use. Oh well!! Just me.

November 13, 1944
Monday

From:	To:
Mr. Cpl. J.G. Barr 11057933	C.L. Sniderman
4503rd Base Unit Eng. Sq.	65 Houghton St.
Great Bend A.B.B., Kansas	Worcester, 4, Mass.

SERVICE CLUB
Smoky Hill Army Air Field
SALINA, KANSAS

Nov. 14
Monday

Dearest Lottie,

Your little fella' spent a dull and boring day. We went to work this morning bright and early, but what did we do, radio work? No! We had to string telephone wires. After we quit for lunch we didn't go back, because the sergeant said if they want telephone wires strung, they can get telephone line men and not radio men. It will be all right, because he saw our officer and he gave his O.K.

One of the fellows that I came up with, got an infected finger and was hospitalized last night for it. This afternoon we visited him. He'll be well in a few days, but he has to stay in the hospital because of the many sulfa drugs he had to take to prevent blood poisoning.

I just came back from seeing "For Whom the Bell Tolls," it was excellent. I could have killed a couple of G.I.'s that were in front of me for their loud talking and uncalled for comments. I enjoyed the show very much.

Now I'm at the service club, which is next door to the show. The club is much better than the one at Great Bend. It is like the one we had at Denver. After writing you last night I went and sang with the boys. You should have heard us, it was a riot. We'd be singing the words and then we'd whistle or hum the rest. Me, I whistled all but the titles!

We finished up the roll of film in my camera. I'll bring it down for processing to-morrow when I go into town for my dinner invitations.

Good night darling, I'll always love you.
Your, George

November 13, 1944
Monday

From:	To:
C.L. Sniderman	Mr. Cpl. J.G. Barr 11057933
65 Houghton St.	Eng. Sq., 4503rd A.A.F. Base Unit
Worcester 4, Mass.	Great Bend A.B.B., Kansas

Hello darling,
Today was wonderful, - three letters from you, guess it was worth waiting for.

Must have been nice going out with your friend and his wife. Only wish I could have made it a foursome.

Very nice that you finally found a building to photograph for your course, but darling, why the hell did you have to pick a hospital. Surely you could have found something more cheerful than that!! But I guess when a guy is cold and erred after waiting for a bus, a building is a building, - even a morgue. Am looking forward to the pictures of Shavetail and her brood. Guess she's much easier to photograph than me, - probably much more photogenic. But just wait till I have a litter of pups, - then I'll let everyone take a picture of me too!!!

I like the nerve of you telling me never to play poker unless I win. Guess this is a good time to ask you why you don't practice what you preach. So there!!! Umph.

After your lengthy explanation of why and how come you are in Detached Service, I still don't know what the devil it's all about. What exactly are you supposed to be doing (notice I said supposed) and why is it a better base. How come you'll be up there for five or six weeks and what happens after that. Gee whiz, - ain't I the inquisitive brat.

Got a nice letter from Sylvia today and naturally she loves being with Erwin. He gets quite a bit of time off, which makes everything super. Also, got a letter from Bev today, and she also is delirious with joy. Seems everyone is exceedingly happy but me, - damn it. Bev & Alton expect to be home sometime in December or January, - also Zelda expects Phil home around that time. Now for you to come home would make the whole situation ideal. I gathered from your letter that you didn't want me to dream up any false hopes about your furlough. But I love thinking about it so much, - so please don't dampen my aspects now. I'm the kind of person who never gives up hope. Whether that's a good or bad trait remains to be seen.

They're playing such gorgeous songs on the radio tonight. All dreamy melodies, - soft & soothing. Right now, they're playing "I'll be Loving You Always," which was always one of my favorites. Before that, - "You & the Night & the Music," - "Lover Come Back to Me," etc., etc., etc. They always said music soothes the savage beast, - but I'm neither a savage & I hope to high heaven, I'm not a beast, - so what have you? I know, - a very tired gal.

It's very hot in the house tonight & I'm wondering if you'll excuse me while I take off my sweater. Ah, that's better. Now your fiancée is practically ala nude, - but I have my pearls on so it's not so bad.

Well, m'boy, eyes are drooping, spirits sagging, nerves on edge, morale at low tide and mental status is in a rut, so I guess I'd better take my leave. Tomorrow presents a new day, new troubles, and a new letter I hope.

Goodnight darling.
Lovingly, Lottie

November 14, 1944
Tuesday

From:	To:
Mr. Cpl. J.G. Barr 11057933	C.L. Sniderman
4503rd Base Unit Eng. Sq.	65 Houghton St.
Great Bend A.B.B., Kansas	Worcester, 4, Mass.

Dearest Lottie,

This coming straight from the music room at the service club, I hope you enjoy the elite company with whom I'm with. We are all long hairs, in fact, mine is so long that I'm going to have it cut.

At the completion of your letter last night I was drawn to the dance that was being held downstairs. This was a gala occasion, because Donna Reed and Jean Porter were going to dance with us G.I.'s. Of course, I danced with them, but wasn't able to distinguish them until later on. I started to dance with Donna Reed, I was going to be a gentleman and just dance, I wasn't even going to talk. She started the conversation first and asked me, "Hello, what's your name?" I answered, "Jimmy, what's yours?" I didn't have time to record the look on her face, but her facial expression did change, just then a G.I. tagged me, for which I was grateful. I danced with both of them, but found that Jean Porter was the better of the two, better looking, better dancer. They're just like the girls back home, but much different than the girls of Kansas. I thought sure I was going to get a movie contract after they met me, but since I made no impression (good one), I just wouldn't go back and dance with them again. I guess I showed them!!!

This morning when we went to work, we were told that there was no place for us there. So, of course, that made us so angry that we went back and hit the sack. This was a good time to write letters so I got dressed in my Class A's and went to the service club to write. I did pretty well, I managed to write four letters this morning, which puts me even with all my correspondence.

Because there is no work for us to do, I'm afraid that they may ship us back, that I won't like because this is a much better deal all around.

Well my brother Narky is on his way home. He should be home sometime to-morrow, this letter should come after his arrival. He is even going to kiss you for me, but I think that's just an excuse! The lucky guy! I want to kiss you. I miss you so much, you should be beside me, listening to this lovely music, we could make believe that we are back at the Pops.

Take care, my lovely darling.
Your, George

November 14, 1944
Tuesday

From:	To:
C.L. Sniderman	Mr. Cpl. J.G. Barr 11057933
65 Houghton St.	Eng. Sq., 4503rd A.A.F. Base Unit
Worcester 4, Mass.	Great Bend A.B.B., Kansas

Hello darling,

Mazeltoff! Edie Lainer had a baby girl this afternoon. She and Yale wanted a girl very badly, so they'll probably be in seventh heaven. It seems almost impossible that Edie, whom I've known for so long is actually a mother. I'm jealous!!

Had no mail from you today, - what's the big idea, - huh? Dontcha know I'm counting on you.

My dad was happy as a boy today, - for the first time in almost three months he went to the store. Irv had a boy pick him up around ten A.M. and my mother stayed with him until about four this afternoon. He was quite tired, of-course, but it was wonderful going into the store today and finding him there. I just spoke to your mother and she was also tickled about dad. The only thing is that he's lost so much weight.

Had a big talk with your sister-in-law Edith and she sends her love, - all her love. That's a fine deal, now all I need is for you to send her all your love. Or didn't you know I was of a jealous nature.

We had some long lost relatives over the house tonight, and one immediately upon seeing me, preceded to ball me out because she wasn't invited to our engagement party. To tell the truth I never even thought of asking her. She's one of these very excitable people who gets on my nerves, - but I guess she means well. Have promised to invite her to the wedding, - now all I have to do is forget. At the rate we're going we should have approximately 5000 million people at the big affair. Just imagine kissing & shaking hands with an astronomical figure like that. Maybe better we should elope!!

Your mother said Narky is expected this week. Charlotte told me the 15th. Well the 15th is tomorrow. I wonder if Bonnie will remember him.

Me mater has a cup of hot cocoa waiting on the table for me so I think I'll partake in a little repast. Wouldst thou care to jine me, wouldst lovest to havest thou. O.K., - nuff of that stuff. Goodnight m'love and remember,

Love Lottie.

November 15, 1944
Wednesday

From:	To:
C.L. Sniderman	Mr. Cpl. J.G. Barr 11057933
65 Houghton St.	Eng. Sq., 4503rd A.A.F. Base Unit
Worcester 4, Mass.	Great Bend A.B.B., Kansas

Hello darling,

Your letter sounded so cheerful today that I felt good all over. Guess it is a small world after all. I'm glad you saw Udie, - did you give him my regards? I always did like Udie. And about meeting those girls from

Commerce, - that is a coincidence and can just imagine how you felt. Wonder what you'd do if you saw me walk in the door, - and wouldn't I love to surprise you too. If it were only possible, darling.

Had a great day in the office today. Dave was out of town all day so we rushed our work in the morning, which left the afternoon for other things. Zelda & I came back from lunch about three, had a cigarette, went to our desk and proceeded to annoy the rest of the office. At about four o'clock one of the girls went out for sundaes, which we made last till about five. Well five o'clock is certainly too late to start working so we had another cigarette and then before we knew it five thirty had finally struck. Tomorrow Dave is going to be back so I guess they'll be no more fun.

Tonight, I really should wash my hair and I'm torn between doing that or listening to the opera. Something tells me the opera is going to win out. Just mailed an adorable card to Edie Lainer & Irene Grace White, - or didn't you know that she had a baby too. Yes, dear, babies are quite the rage this season. I mailed both cards from the both of us, - taking care of your end of social obligations too.

Since I had that sundae at so late an hour, I sorta killed my supper. Now I'm famished, but I don't know what to eat since it's so late. Ah me, - I do have my troubles. I think I'll go eat a sour pickle and a banana. Did you ever eat a combination like that!! I'm sick before I even start. Pardon me, - I'll be back P.D.Q. Time has marched gallantly on.

I settled for some Corn Flakes and bananas, - I think I'll leave the pickle for tonight. Now I feel like having someone wash my face, undress me, putting me to bed and kissing me goodnight. Ah, what sheer joy that would be, - having someone kiss me goodnight I mean. But since none of these varied tasks can be accomplished by wishing, I shall endeavor to do them myself, and then I'll kiss your picture goodnight. It won't be the same I know, - but hells bells what can a gal do. And with this parting thought I take leave. I hope your letter of tomorrow will be as happy as the one today, because darling, when you're happy, I'm happy.

Goodnight & remember you have
All my love, Lottie

November 15, 1944
Wednesday

From:	To:
Mr. Cpl. J.G. Barr 11057933	C.L. Sniderman
4503rd Base Unit Eng. Sq.	65 Houghton St.
Great Bend A.B.B., Kansas	Worcester, 4, Mass.

Dearest Lottie,

Last night I spent a very lovely evening at Ann and Dante's place. Dante is her husband's name. I liked him just as soon as I met him, in fact, I like the name itself, Dante. I told you another fellow was to come up also, but for some reason he didn't show up. So, what did they do, but practically made me eat his share. No kidding, I ate chicken until it came out of my ears.

I got a big kick out of their silverware. One night some of Dante's friends insisted upon him bringing them up the house for dinner. He told them he'd be glad to but they just didn't have enough silverware for so many people. They said they'd take care of that, and when they came up they brought a bunch of G.I. spoons, knives, and forks, so now the Zamarro's, that's their last name, have plenty of silverware. To-morrow night they are having spaghetti and they invited me up again. Dante is bringing up a few of his friends also. He put in for separate rations, because two meals he eats at home and the other in camp. If he does get separate rations, he'll have to eat at the restaurant, so I'm bringing him some of our temporary mess passes. This way he'll be able to eat in the mess hall and he won't have to buy his one meal on the base. I can get a bunch of extra passes, so no one is the loser.

We're back working again, they took us back, but still don't want us. We have a communication officer up here and he got us back in again. I fixed one piece of equipment and helped install another piece of equipment. The rest of the day I was out checking to see if the planes had certain pieces of equipment, but I think it was just a deal they cooked up to get some of us out of the shop.

In a few days, I expect to go on the night shift, just as soon as they get the duty roster straightened out. I don't care, just as long as I can get into a little work so I can learn some damn thing. The stuff I have been doing, anyone could have done without any knowledge of radio whatsoever.

Winter is trying with all its might to get going around here. The weather is getting to be real frigid. I'll be getting red flannels pretty soon if it keeps up.

I received your first letter yesterday since I've been up here. I guess the mailman back in G.B. isn't on the ball. About what I like, I like you very much. Food I'm not too particular, and I don't think I have a favorite dish, except once in awhile I like a nice fat juicy steak. What ever you make, you'll know I'll like – at least for a little while anyway.

Good night, darling.
Your, George

November 19, 1944
Sunday

From:	To:
Mr. Cpl. J.G. Barr 11057933	C.L. Sniderman
4503rd Base Unit Eng. Sq.	65 Houghton St.
Great Bend A.B.B., Kansas	Worcester, 4, Mass.

Dearest Lottie,

It's a miserable day and I would have loved to have spent it with you, because if I were with you I wouldn't care how the weather was. The only consolation I could get was to sleep until noon.

Last night this place was a mess. A bunch of the boys got drunk and when they came in, they put the lights on and just about raised the roof. Some of them wanted to tear down the bulletin board and this morning when I found it in the same old position, I was quite surprised! Yes sir, for a dry state, the boys must get drunk on the air. But isn't it funny the air doesn't seem to affect me that way – must be something else.

I just came back from seeing "The Princess and the Pirate." It was just as funny as I expected it to be. If you get a chance, see it the first day it comes to Worcester, because otherwise people may spoil the best part of it for you.

I'm writing from the barracks this afternoon because I have to go to work soon. I wish I were one of the fellows who isn't here. Out of about fifty men there are just two of us in the barracks. It's a lonely and desolate place now.

Uddy must be back from his three day pass that he took this week so I guess I'll look him up again the first chance that I get.

I got a letter from Maxie Z. the other day and it seems as if he started to fall for this nice girl, but when they were alone at her house one evening she told all. Maxie said he was so shocked that he just got up and left! What surprised me was that Maxie should get serious with a girl.

He told me after that night, he went into the dumps and didn't do a thing for about a month. He didn't even write home. He said his mother thought he had been shipped to China someplace. He must have had it bad or else he wouldn't have been that down and out.

Of course, I wrote him a nice cheery letter, at least I hope it was cheery. I'll let you know what happens, if anything.

Tell Yale and Edie that I'm happy about their new offspring and they had better get on the ball if they want to keep up with us once we get started.

Now about Edie, why should you be jealous of her, you know once she finds a fella' she's going to want me to return all her love that she sent to me, via you!!

I know just how you felt, to go into dad's store and see him at his work. When he's happy, I know you are, and when you are, you can bet your last dollar I am.

Off to work, darling.
Your, George

November 19, 1944
Sunday night

From:	To:
C.L. Sniderman	Mr. Cpl. J.G. Barr 11057933
65 Houghton St.	Eng. Sq., 4503rd A.A.F. Base Unit
Worcester 4, Mass.	Great Bend A.B.B., Kansas

Hello darling,

Well, it finally happened. Narky and I finally met. Your mother called and invited me to dinner Friday night, and so I finally got a squint at yer brother. I can readily say that I liked him very much, and we talked as if we'd known each other for years. Of course, I don't know what he thought of me, - but if he didn't approve of your choice, he was kind enough not to show it. I think I liked him mainly because he reminded me of you. His manners and way of speaking revealed quite easily that you were brothers. He is very easy to talk to and it's quite obvious that he is insane about his wife & baby. While I was there, Sol called and I guess he came in early this morning for a few hours. Fran couldn't come to Worcester because the doctor said he didn't want her to travel. Oh yes, Narky made me a very lovely plastic star and also an initial L to wear on a chain. It was very sweet of him.

Yesterday after I finished work at the office, I went down to work in my dad's store. Not that I did any work, - I just had to stand around, which is even more tiring than working. This business of going to the store every day is making a wreck out of my mother.

I can't understand why neither Donna Reed or Jeanne Porter didn't encourage your coming to Hollywood. Evidently, they were afraid of competition for their own men. But it was nice of you to at least try to dance with them.

It's swell of Ann & Dante to have you up to dinner. Tell them that when we have our own home they can come to dinner any time they like. If you like 'em, - I like 'em!! I wish I could have been there for the spaghetti dinner, - you know how mad I am about spaghetti.

I just wrote a letter to Dave, - finally. I feel like a stinker for not answering him sooner, but I just about manage to write to you every nite and then pop into bed.

Edith Richards, from the office, just called and said she was listening to some beautiful music, which made her think of me. So, she called and told me to listen too. Wasn't that sweet. Right now, they're playing "I'll Be Loving You Always." Darling, I love you very much and its true I will be loving you always.

Well dear, this about winds up another day. I feel particularly lonesome tonight, - I need you so badly.

Goodnight darling,
Love, Lottie

P.S. Narky did deliver that kiss from you, - the minute I walked into the house. It was very nice, but I prefer to have my kisses delivered in person. Just me.

November 20, 1944
Monday

From:	To:
Mr. Cpl. J.G. Barr 11057933	C.L. Sniderman
4503rd Base Unit Eng. Sq.	65 Houghton St.
Great Bend A.B.B., Kansas	Worcester, 4, Mass.

Dearest Lottie,

If I have to keep working on B-29's, I'll be able to become a contortionist. Last night I got into more awkward positions than I ever thought were possible. You just can't work comfortably in those 'large' B-29's, there isn't any room inside to move around. Then they have the nerve to want us to take calisthenics – they ought to work in a 29 for one night, then they'd change their minds.

It really doesn't bother me, I really like it. I'm doing something, keeping busy. We had to put an antenna up on a B-17 also. It had rained just a little, and the wings were very slippery. One fellow stayed on the ground and held onto my legs, while another braced his feet against mine and still another was sticking his head out a window holding a flashlight. We don't make much money, but we have a hell of a time.

In the shop my sergeant was showing me how to tune up one of the transmitters. When I started to do it by myself, I pressed one of the buttons too soon and screwed up the entire settings. Maybe in a few months I'll get to know how to do it.

Next week I hope we go on the day shift, or the graveyard shift. This afternoon shift isn't good for anything, we work, eat, and sleep.

I love you, sweetheart
Your, George

P.S. I know – but I'm leading a quiet life, will do better to-morrow. J.G.B.

November 20, 1944
Monday

From:	To:
C.L. Sniderman	Mr. Cpl. J.G. Barr 11057933
65 Houghton St.	Eng. Sq., 4503rd A.A.F. Base Unit
Worcester 4, Mass.	Great Bend A.B.B., Kansas

Dearest George,
Received two swell letters from you today. One in the morning, and just when I was starting to feel a little down in the mouth, one came in the afternoon. You time them perfectly, darling. Also, got a swell letter from Barb today. I haven't heard from her for so long that I had almost given her up for lost, but like a trouper, she came through with a six-page letter. She expects to be home sometime around Christmas and then head for overseas. Don't tell anybody, but she's more than a little scared, and I can't say that I blame her.

Darling, I feel like a heel about you having to write your mother for a sweater. I know it is really my place to make one for you. But honestly, George, I just haven't the patience to sit down and knit. I really envy people who can do it, - but I'm afraid it jest isn't for me, - well, not yet anyway. Maybe when I'm having a baby I'll feel duty bound to start knitting those cute little things that always reveal to the husband what's going on, - as if he didn't know anyway!!

The music room at the service club sounds super and it will be a 'must do' when we have our own home. Also, we must have a good supply of liquor in our liquor cabinet, - just in case we ever feel like indulging. As for our children, - well I do think that thought is a bit premature, - and besides that it makes me feel way too old before my time. First let's have our fun, - then we'll worry about the offspring.

I spoke to Irv tonight and you are right, it's Kansas City, Missouri, that he expects to be in, - but not till the first of the year. So, I guess there's a little time ahead.

Well, another Thanksgiving is just around the corner. I remember saying last year that this year everyone would surely be together, - but it looks like we'll have to wait for another year before I can give you the honor of carving the turkey. It seems just a short while ago that we were engaged, but already its five months, - nearer to six months. Seems like twice that length of time since I've seen you. I miss you so terribly.

The air is very cold tonight and just looking out of the window I can see that clear white soft snow flakes are beginning to fall. It really makes a beautiful picture, - when you're in a nice warm house, - on the inside looking out.

Whenever the approach of a new season comes, I seem to miss you even more. Winter always finds me thinking that we should be together in front of a big open fire, - just sitting and dreaming, with soft sweet music playing. Yes, I think of all these things during the course of a day and because I am a dreamer, I am happy temporarily. But when I awake to the cold reality, - I'm not quite so high in spirits. I'm terribly selfish about the people I love, - I want them with me always for always. I'm not the only one that's lonesome I know, but I'm sure they care very little about me and I care very little about them. I really am selfish.

Well darling, as the guy in the movie said,

All my love, all my life, -
Lottie

P.S. Happy Thanksgiving, darling. No turkey for me this year, - so eat a share for me too. Me.

November 21, 1944
Tuesday

From:	To:
Mr. Cpl. J.G. Barr 11057933	C.L. Sniderman
4503rd Base Unit Eng. Sq.	65 Houghton St.
Great Bend A.B.B., Kansas	Worcester, 4, Mass.

Dearest Lottie,

I just came back from town, I had gone in after dinner to pick the pictures up. I'm sending them to you to-morrow because I have to let another fellow see them. There are just three of them, but in a few weeks, I'll have some more because they're having some prints made of the other fellow's roll.

This morning I intended going into town, but when I woke at 9:00 o'clock, it was freezing, so I pulled the covers around me and went back to sleep. The men on the day shift had let the fire go out in the barracks.

I saw Uddy this afternoon and he sends his love, - talk about Edie, will you!

When the cats away the mice play, huh? Shame on you! – I'm glad you enjoyed yourself on your afternoon off though.

Our minds run in the same channel, because on a letter two days ago, I said that when you are happy, so am I, then in your letter yesterday, there was a similar phrase. Isn't it nice to know someone who thinks the same as you? Darling, do you think our love has anything to do with it? – Why sure!

We spent another night fighting another B-29. No kidding, I'm going to write to Washington to draft some midgets, they'd sure come in handy in the type of work we're doing. It keeps me in shape anyhow.

If that's the way you're going to feed me, bananas and pickles, we're going to eat out. If we eat out, all my money will go for food, then I won't have any money left to buy you pretty things, so my sweet, you'd better think of a better menu than that. It's not that I have anything against bananas or pickles, but for a meal, no!

If you run across any #120 film, dear, send it to me, please. I won't be able to start my second lesson until I get some more film. It's a good thing that they're giving me a long time for each lesson, otherwise, I'd have to quit now.

So, everyone is getting babies huh, they'll have to go some to beat us. We're going to have the cutest and smartest baby (or should I say babies) of them all! They'll all need that head start!!!

I'm going to have to dash back now and get my clothes ready to have cleaned, then I have to change, eat, and go to work.

Boy, I wish this month and next month would vanish overnight!

Your, George

November 21, 1944
Tuesday

From:	To:
C.L. Sniderman	Mr. Cpl. J.G. Barr 11057933
65 Houghton St.	Eng. Sq., 4503rd A.A.F. Base Unit
Worcester 4, Mass.	Great Bend A.B.B., Kansas

My dearest George,

For days now I've been planning on writing you this letter. For weeks, I've been going crazy thinking about it. Wondering if I should say what's on my mind, - wondering how to approach it, - wondering how you would feel about it and postponing it until I couldn't any longer. So tonight, I finally decided that the only thing to do was lay my problem before you and then wait for your reaction. So here goes.

Darling, last June when you asked me to marry you, I wanted to very much and had I had any idea of what the future held, there of course, would have been a wedding. But after all the circumstances were analyzed it seemed the wisest thing to wait until the war was over. And so we heeded all good advice and planned to wait. Then in August, fate reared its ugly head and my dad got sick. Not until last month did we know how really sick he was and the shock was naturally very great. George, my father is not getting better, - I don't think I ought to fool myself any longer. He feels fine while he has no pains and his pains are relieved only by feeding him one pill after another. When the potency of the pills wears off, I don't know what we'll do but suffer with him.

Darling, you know as well as I how much my father loves me and how much I love him. You know how my mother felt about me getting married during this mess and also your mother, - both having our best interests at heart. Well, dear, my mother and I have had a lengthy discussion, as a matter of fact, she approached the subject that had been on my mind since dad got sick. We don't know how much longer he has, - maybe a month, maybe two months or maybe even a year, and the only last thing that would make him happy is to see me married to you. He loves you like nothing less than a son.

Dearest, I don't know if you will have a furlough in January or not, you don't know either, I know, but if you should have a furlough I'm hoping that you will see that it's best for us to get married. Darling, to be perfectly frank, I don't know if my dad can hold out till the wars end.

If you do come home and if we do get married, we can have quite a nice affair. It won't be an elaborate affair, - I don't feel as if I want one now, but we'll be able to have our relatives and friends and make it the nicest possible wedding. We can have it at the Bancroft, and of-course, I'll wear the traditional white. If we do wait and my father won't be able to see his only daughter married, then of-course, there will be no celebration at all. I've seen weddings like that before and they were more like funerals, - I couldn't stand anything like that. From words your mother has dropped here and there, I think she feels the same. She hasn't said anything definite, but I'm sure she would agree with what I have written. We haven't got any money, I know, but people before us have gotten married without money too. We will, I hope, get some money as wedding gifts and this we can use to go on a honeymoon. There's plenty of time to worry about money for a home when you come back for good and not just a furlough.

So, darling, where last time you left the discussion of getting married entirely up to me, now I'm turning the tables and leaving it all up to you. What the future holds for us no one knows. You may be shipped overseas, its true, I've thought about that, but then again there is a chance that you may stay here for another while. That's a chance we'll have to take.

Of-course, all that I have written is pending on a furlough, maybe fate will be kind to us, - or under the circumstances maybe the Red Cross could do something. In either event, I'll be on pins and needles till I hear from you. I love you very much.

All my love, - all my life.
Lottie

November 22, 1944
Wednesday

From:	To:
Mr. Cpl. J.G. Barr 11057933	C.L. Sniderman
4503rd Base Unit Eng. Sq.	65 Houghton St.
Great Bend A.B.B., Kansas	Worcester, 4, Mass.

Dearest Lottie,

In the first place, no cracks about me standing with my eyes shut. I told the guy to tell me when he was going to take the picture, but did he? As you can see - no! I don't care tho, Shavetail and her brood came out pretty good. They, the pups, must be pretty big by now, it's been almost two weeks since I've left Great Bend.

That zoot suit I'm wearing is warm, but the hardest things to navigate in. I can just imagine myself trying to maneuver around a ship in one of those, when there is hardly enough room for me as it is.

Last night we took it pretty easy, most of the time we stayed in the shop and just hung around. I wish we were off this night shift, to-night

Frankie Masters is here and then there usually is a U.S.O. show that we miss. I'll live thru it tho. At least I'm getting my sleep.

Spent an hour or so just now in the music room listening to some good stuff. The names? I don't know, but they listened good.

I wrote my teacher a nice lengthy explanation why I couldn't process my own film and I told him that I had that kind of experience already, so if it is O.K. with him, I'll just take the pictures (when I get the film) and let a store do the photo finishing. I hope it goes over.

Your, George

November 23, 1944
Thursday Nite
Thanksgiving

From:	To:
C.L. Sniderman	Mr. Cpl. J.G. Barr 11057933
65 Houghton St.	Eng. Sq., 4503rd A.A.F. Base Unit
Worcester 4, Mass.	Great Bend A.B.B., Kansas

My dearest George,

Well, here it is another Thanksgiving, - another Turkey festival without you. We had planned on having no one at all, but thank goodness, my mother saw fit to at least have my aunt Mary & Uncle Dave for dinner. It wasn't much of a celebration, but we did eat till the food came out of our ears and we did have a good time. About four thirty, Zelda & I went to the movies and saw "Mrs. Parkington." I really enjoyed it very much. Maybe it was because you told me to see it or maybe it was because I hadn't been to the movies for so long that it was a royal treat to me.

After the movies, we went into the Mayflower and any minute I expected to hear you order a grilled American and coffee. Zelda and I had a good time, she telling me about little things Phil did, and I telling her about little things George did. We both decided that we were terribly, terribly lonesome. It doesn't seem possible that Thanksgiving has come and gone and Christmas is well on its way.

I got quite a kick out of Maxie being so terribly disappointed in love. I really should have felt sorry for him I guess, but it's just that I can't picture Maxie as the second party in a love affair. He just doesn't seem the type.

Spoke to Charlotte yesterday and she invited me over the house tonight, - she was having a few friends over. But when I got out of the movies, it was too late, and besides that my folks and I are invited to supper tomorrow night. If I came too often they might get sick of me. Narky & Charlotte are leaving Saturday morning.

It's getting to be terrifically cold way up here in New England. I need my love to keep me warm. Probably by now you've received my letter of yesterday. I can't help thinking of what your reaction will be. Can't help thinking about it, is putting it mildly, - I stayed up till three o'clock in the morning yesterday trying to figure out what you would say. But since I don't know what you will think about it, all I can do is wait. It seems I spend the best part of my life just waiting.

Darling, I was just rereading your letter and there's one part about the Maxie Z. versus girl affair that I don't comprehend. You said when they were alone in her house one night she told all and he was so shocked he left. What I want to know is what do you mean she told all?!!!

Well, darling, it's getting late, Lottie's getting tired and besides that there's no more to write.

So, goodnight dear, and may we spend next Thanksgiving and all the others that follow together.

All my love, Lottie

November 24, 1944
Friday

From:	To:
Mr. Cpl. J.G. Barr 11057933	C.L. Sniderman
4503rd Base Unit Eng. Sq.	65 Houghton St.
Great Bend A.B.B., Kansas	Worcester, 4, Mass.

Dearest Lottie,

Last night when I came for my mail I had four letters, but the best part was that two of them were from you, two grand letters.

I'm glad that you like Narky, he is a good guy. I know if it weren't for him, I'd be the most slovenly person you'd ever hope not to meet. I learned a lot from him. You'll have to let me see those presents he made for you, but I knew about them a long time ago.

It may be a long time again when I see Anne and Dante. Dante has been shipped, via air, to Texas. I didn't see him, but I heard some of the fellows talking in the mess hall. I wonder if I miss her, or her cooking! – What a heel I must be.

So, Barb is going overseas, good for old Barb, I think she's more of a soldier than I am. When she gives out with some Boogie Woogie, the boys will forget about the battles they have been in. Me, I'd like to hear her myself. I always did like the way she played "To-night We Love."

Yes, yesterday was Thanksgiving, but for me, in name only. At the mess hall, if you wanted to, you could bring a guest. All the married men brought their wives, and some even had the parents and children with them. At first it was nice, but soon I got so lonesome for you I couldn't eat. I just wanted to get out of there. The meal itself wasn't so extra good and with that kind of an atmosphere, I just wanted out. The fellows I was with couldn't understand my attitude, because usually I'm the last to finish, then I smoke a cigarette, but yesterday when you are supposed to take your time, I wanted to go.

After dinner when I usually write you, we went to see "Dough Girls." I didn't feel in any mood to write to you. I'm glad that I went to the show, because it was very funny, and I just laughed throughout the entire picture. See it when you can.

I hope that we get off of this damn night shift pretty damn soon. It seems as if I haven't time to do anything. Then when I want to write, my mind doesn't function well at all, maybe I'm half asleep most of the time. I know I have a heck of a time trying to fall asleep after I finish work.

Until to-morrow, my wonderful sweetheart.

Your, George

November 24, 1944
Friday night

From:	To:
C.L. Sniderman	Mr. Cpl. J.G. Barr 11057933
65 Houghton St.	Eng. Sq., 4503rd A.A.F. Base Unit
Worcester 4, Mass.	Great Bend A.B.B., Kansas

My dearest George,

Just came back from a very pleasant evening at the Barr estate where me mater, me pater, and me were invited to dinner. Mr. & Mrs. Hurwitz were also in attendance and later in the evening we were honored with the presence of their daughter Dorothy. Among numerous things that I did during the course of the evening, I bid adieu to Charlotte & Narky. Always having had a particular dislike for saying goodbyes, I also did not enjoy this one.

On behalf of the departure of my newly met brother-in-law (to be), I presented him with a quart of Canadian Club. I nearly broke my neck trying to sneak it out of this office so the other girls wouldn't see. A very good friend of mine who happens to be a liquor salesman smuggled a bottle of the precious stuff for me. I knew Narky wanted it because he asked me to try and get it for him, - of course, remuneration was out of the question. He of course tried to argue the point with me saying in view of the circumstances, I needed the money as badly as he, - but me being a stubborn brat, would not adhere to his pleas. Nuff said 'bout dat.

Received two delicious letters from you today and am looking forward to the pictures. Darling, I'm trying like all hell to get some film for you, - will use all my ingenuity.

Your mother showed me the sweater she made for you and it really is lovely. Even if I had made you one, it wouldn't have been as nice, - so I guess you're better off all around.

Your old sister-in-law Edie M. is sick again. I don't know what the devil is the matter with the gal, but she just doesn't feel right. She's in a very low state mentally and physically. She wants me to take a trek out to Kansas so she can come too. Hmmm, - not at all a bad idea!!

We had quite a snow storm here tonight. Your dad called for us, and the roads were so damn slippery we slid all over the place. When he drove us home, the snow had stopped, but it was still terrifically cold and slippery. Ah, good old New England, you know, with its torrid summers and frigid winters, - no happy medium at all.

Well my sweet, time to pop into bed and get some shut eye. Tonight's a good night for cuddling!!

Au revoir & pleasant dreams.
Love, Lottie

November 26, 1944
Sunday

From:	To:
Mr. Cpl. J.G. Barr 11057933	C.L. Sniderman
4503rd Base Unit Eng. Sq.	65 Houghton St.
Great Bend A.B.B., Kansas	Worcester, 4, Mass.

SERVICE CLUB
Smoky Hill Army Air Field
SALINA, KANSAS

Dearest Lottie,

Maybe I should have started, Dearest Wife, because darling, I've always wanted you to be mine. The reason I didn't object to postponing our marriage before was that I thought just as you did, that it would be better to wait. My sweet, I love you and we will get married the next time that I come home.

Darling, did you know I couldn't sleep last night, as if you cared. I tossed and turned, smoked and walked, until finally at five o'clock, I fell asleep. So many thoughts were racing thru my mind, I wanted to call you last night, but I received your letter too late to do anything about it. I'm now waiting to call you. This time you'll have to pay, for dearest, your honey is broke (as usual) and can't loan any money, Christmas next month you know, and the boys are broke, like me.

The thoughts that went thru my mind; when am I getting my furlough, who's coming to the wedding, where we'll spend our honeymoon, should I wear tails - then I remember I'm in the army - and other little details like that.

How I wish I could be with you and help plan the wedding. I feel so useless here, I want so much to talk to you, be with you, the fact is, darling, I'm crazy about you.

I even thought about whether I should bring some liquor back for the boys, you know I don't get married every day! I thought where am I going to get the money to do the things a prospective groom is supposed to do. I did want to have our wedding with our money and not to spare any expense, I wanted to show you off to the world, darling, I love you very much.

I'm going to see if I can get thru to you now.

To our forthcoming marriage
Your, George

P.S. I never did believe in long engagements. J.G.B.

November 26, 1944
Sunday

From:	To:
Mr. Cpl. J.G. Barr 11057933	C.L. Sniderman
4503rd Base Unit Eng. Sq.	65 Houghton St.
Great Bend A.B.B., Kansas	Worcester, 4, Mass.

SERVICE CLUB
Smoky Hill Army Air Field
SALINA, KANSAS

Nov. 26th 1944

Dearest Lottie,

Yes, darling, I'm still nervous, even tho I'm not supposed to admit it. I just finished a letter to my parents, I hope it was a good one.

Lottie dear, if you want me to see if I can get my furlough any special day in January, I think I can have it postponed until the day we want it, or do you want me to get it just as soon as I can. If I get it around the 2nd or 3rd of December, would that give you enough time for plans. I'm going to see what my furlough situation is to-morrow, but will you wire me the day, if you have one you like, that you want me home. Otherwise wire me that you want me to take my furlough as soon as I can get it. If I do get my furlough when it is due me, which will be the 26th of December, then the next Sunday is the 31st. New Year's Eve, so my sweet, wire me:

Cpl. J.G. Barr 11057933
247 B.U. Squadron
Barracks #256
Salina A.A.B. Kan.

This afternoon I went and saw "Meet Me in St. Louis." I thought from what I saw at the previews, it wouldn't be too good, but I was pleasantly mistaken, it proved to be pretty good.

I didn't have to go to work to-night because I was latrine orderly to-day. Because it was Sunday, I didn't do a thing. This afternoon, after throwing a few shovelfuls of coal on the latrine furnace, so the boys would have some hot water, I went to see Ted Fio Rito and his band. They put on a pretty good show, now if I had to be at work, I never would have been able to see him. So, you see my darling, I'm not working myself to death, not by a long shot!

My, but this paper is awful large! From now on, I bring my own stuff.

Good night darling.
Your, George

November 27, 1944
Monday

From:	To:
C.L. Sniderman	Mr. Cpl. J.G. Barr 11057933
65 Houghton St.	Eng. Sq., 4503rd A.A.F. Base Unit
Worcester 4, Mass.	Great Bend A.B.B., Kansas

My dearest George,

It's been a delirious two days to me since you've called. I was going to write you yesterday, but I've been so nervous I couldn't put pen to paper. They say that every prospective bride has a crying session before she finally gets married, well I've shed enough tears from Sunday until now to fill a river. So far, the only good thing that has happened from Saturday till now, is my talking to you and our decision, - from there on its been hell. I'm not going to spare any of the gruesome details because you're as much a party to the crime as I am. The only difference is that I'm here and have to take it on the chin. A happy bride, - yes, I personify a very happy bride, - all I've had so far is heartache and aggravation. People always told me that everyone goes through the same kind of trouble, but I always laughed and said at my wedding there would be no difficulties, - well, I admit I was wrong.

So far, everyone has voiced their opinions except me, - it seems I have no right to say anything. The only one who has let me open my mouth is my mother. The only definite thing I can write you is that I love you very much and at this minute I need you very badly. A big wedding, with friends and relatives, music playing, people dancing; yes, that's the kind of wedding every girl wants, and I happen to be no exception. But Irv & Fran seem to think this a very evil desire, - what right have I to want such things. Me who is a little nobody, - my dad so sick in the next room, - it seems I'm a terribly wicked and selfish person to even think of anything like that. I have no money, - I have no authority, - I have nothing but your love, which at this minute, is the only thing that really matters.

Its been suggested that I forego all dreams of marrying in white and be a little more practical. What could be nicer than a house wedding with people stepping on top of each other and just have the bare essentials such as "do you take this man to be your lawfully wedded husband, etc., etc., etc." Or we could be married in the "Shule", which is quite proper, or we could do numerous other things, which will make the affair very legal and end it at that. Well, up to this point I don't know where I'm at. The problem has been confronted to me if my dad can take the excitement of a fairly large wedding. Well, how the devil should I know, and because I could not give a reasonably intelligent answer, I shed more tears, - which to my way of thinking is very stupid on my part, but nevertheless, uncontrollable. Your folks showed no great surprise when I broke the news and also showed the proper enthusiasm. They are coming over Wednesday nite to discuss the matter further.

There's so many numerous details that I have to discuss with you, I don't even know where to begin. To begin with, whom do you want for best man? Second, where will we go on our honeymoon, at which hotel and for how long? Will you take your blood test here or in Kansas (I personally don't think it's valid in Kansas, I'll find out)? If only I knew definitely when you'll be here, they'll be a million things that will have to be done when you come home before the wedding, such as, a ring and license. Right now, I'm much too weary to think about anything more. Please forgive me if I sound a little down in the mouth, - I'm terribly happy about us getting married and I guess that's all that's really important. Tomorrow I'll brace my shoulders and stick my chin up in the air, - I don't want you to think you're gonna have a jelly fish for a wife. Incidentally, how will you feel having a wife on your hands?!!!

Goodnight darling.

Always yours, Lottie

P.S. I promise to be more cheerful tomorrow. Me.

November 28, 1944

Tuesday

From:	To:
Mr. Cpl. J.G. Barr 11057933	C.L. Sniderman
4503rd Base Unit Eng. Sq.	65 Houghton St.
Great Bend A.B.B., Kansas	Worcester, 4, Mass.

Dearest Lottie,

When I finally found our officer, he told me he was going to call Great Bend and find out when my furlough was due. He has a list of the fellows who are due furloughs and about when they'll get them. He told me he could get me a date, and if circumstances were good, then I'd be able to leave on that date.

Because I don't know the exact date you want it, I'm waiting until you send me that telegram. Here is another little item you may be interested in, my furlough is for 15 days – travel time allotted to me will be seven days, then my sweet, I have a very good chance of asking and receiving a five-day extension. Making a grand total of 27 days. Wow!!!

Darling, how are you going to invite the people, by invitation or some other method? If it is by invitation, please send me about five of them, I'd like to send them to Dave, Sid, and a few more of the fellows that I made friends with since I've been in service.

For my best man, I'm going to write Sol and ask him, since Dave cannot be there. You know darling, that I miss that guy like I do a brother. We've been to-gether for such a long time and know one another so well, that at times we used to fight like brothers.

Your two letters of yesterday tickled me. Your letters, sweetness, are masterpieces, I don't know why you ever think that they are anything but. Just compare one of yours to one of mine and you'll see what I mean.

As if anyone would get sick of you being around. You know darn well that you are part of another family by now, and you are welcome just like any other member of the family, that is the way you want me to feel about our big entire family, isn't it? And that is the way it is for both of us.

Now about Maxie – It seems as if the girl that Maxie was referring to, had had affairs with men in her time and that she even had a two-year-old child, of which she didn't know the where abouts. Poor Maxie, I can just imagine how he looked when he heard that. Now you know too, but it still remains to our knowledge and no one else's.

If I get a chance I'll write a little note to Edie and try to cheer her up, if my letters are cheery. Tell her she can't be sick, or else she'll miss the affair of the year.

I'm waiting on pins and needles until I learn what you have planned for us. I know whatever is planned, it will be good, but I can't help but feel of no help whatsoever, way out here in the wheat fields of Kansas.

I bet if Narky didn't like you (I'm sure he did), then that quart of Canadian Club put you up on top with him, that's his favorite drink. I remember he used to bother Sid Burach for same when he worked for, I think also New England.

What did my folks and your folks, our folks, say about the coming big event. Are you having any trouble with our relatives, I should say the ones on my side, it seems as if I have more than my share. Do my folks want them all or what?

I wish I could be with you on those cold frosty nights, the kind that are good for cuddling. I hope darling, that I can do the honors and soon too. I think I'll go out and find some women to practice on, it's been a long time since I've held you in my arms, I may have forgotten how. Ouch!!! O.K. I'll wait until I have you in my arms – my but your knife is sharp!

All my love, all my life,
Your, George

P.S. It's too bad that someone else thought of those lines before I did, I think they're mighty good. J.G.B.

November 29, 1944
Wednesday

From:	To:
C.L. Sniderman	Mr. Cpl. J.G. Barr 11057933
65 Houghton St.	Eng. Sq., 4503rd A.A.F. Base Unit
Worcester 4, Mass.	Great Bend A.B.B., Kansas

My dearest George,

Can readily say that I am in much higher spirits in this writing than the last letter I sent you. Mainly because much has been accomplished. Your folks were over to dinner this evening, and darling, they were wonderful about everything, if ever I loved them, it was tonight. They realized fully that a big wedding as we all want is impossible and as far as they were concerned anything we decided is O.K. with them. Again, let me repeat myself, they were wonderful.

Now let me give you some details. A wedding at the Bancroft proved quite unsatisfactory because your relatives are very religious and the Bancroft isn't. So, we've decided to have it at the Beth Israel Synagogue, which is very nice, and the reception will be catered downstairs.

As to the date, - darling, of-course I'd love to have you as soon as possible, but we can't have the wedding much before January 7th. In the first place, I have to get things straightened out at the office, secondly, we'd never get hotel reservations now for anywhere before New Year's, thirdly, we have to give the people we're inviting some time and also the Beth Israel and caterers have to be given notice. So as things stand, the wedding will be Jan. 7th at about 2 o'clock in the afternoon, which will give us ample time to go away the same day. If we had the wedding at night we'd either have to stay in Worcester after the wedding or travel all night, - both are equally unsatisfactory to me. So now my only worry is can you come home around the 3rd or 4th of the month, - of January, of-course. If you can, then we'll have enough time to discuss things a little further, have a blood test and get a ring & license. The third comes out on a Wednesday, - then we'll have Thursday, Friday & Saturday before the big day.

Oh, yes, about the people coming, - they'll be only aunts & uncles and a few cousins. All told, it will amount roughly to about 75 people. Darling, if there's anyone special you care to invite, just let me know. I can't think of anyone except Jackie & Maxie if he's home. My mother is having a tea for me on the 12th of December and Fran is having one for me on the 30th of December. Seems I will be a busy little beaner.

I'm going to work up till Christmas and then I'll have two weeks to myself before the wedding. Also, we ought to decide where we'll go on our honeymoon and make reservations at a hotel. It seems to me that the only place we can go is New York, and as for a hotel, there are millions of them. I'll leave that up to you. The two nicer ones are the Biltmore and the St. Moritz, - but expensive, the next best bet is the Lexington, the Taft or the Statler, - I haven't seen either of these three, but I guess they're pretty good. You write and tell me what you think about that score.

Either tomorrow night or Friday night our folks and myself are going up to the Beth Israel and see the hall and make definite arrangements. The only thing that worries me is you, - you seem to sound so definite that you can come anytime that I'm going ahead with plans. Darling, - I'm hoping against hope you'll be able to get your furlough for that time and also let me know how many days. I'm counting on 21, but of-course, we're not sure.

All in all, I'm very mixed up!!! For the past two days, I haven't been able to eat a thing. The nervousness and excitement plus the uncertainty of everything has completely taken away my appetite. I'm afraid on our honeymoon all I'll do is eat.

Darling, here I am raving on and on about our wedding but it doesn't feel as if I'm talking about myself at all. It all happened so quickly I just can't believe it. I'm afraid I'll wake up and find I was dreaming.

I was sorry you had such a lonely Thanksgiving. Maybe next year we'll be together in our own home. Wouldn't that be wonderful?

It seems I have a million things to ask you and tell you but I'll be darned if I can think of any more now. Please help me by telling and reminding me of all the things that have to be done if I've forgotten anything. After all, this is the first time I ever got married and you can't blame me for being more than slightly bewildered.

So, goodnight for now my darling.
Lovingly, Lottie

P.S. I just can't picture you a husband, - or me a wife. We look so damn young!!!

November 29, 1944
Wednesday

From:	To:
Mr. Cpl. J.G. Barr 11057933	C.L. Sniderman
4503rd Base Unit Eng. Sq.	65 Houghton St.
Great Bend A.B.B., Kansas	Worcester, 4, Mass.

Dearest Lottie,

Another day bringing me closer to you, a day when we'll become as one, when people will wish that all our troubles will be little ones. Only one, I love you forever.

Last night I received a bundle from the folks and the sweater was in it. Aren't mothers wonderful, the sweater fits well and looks super. I just hope darling, that you'll never have to knit any sweaters under similar circumstances. I got a big kick out of the fellows I work with. Last night when we went for a cup of coffee, I took with me the 'maun' cake that my mother sent me. When I offered them a piece, all they wanted was a small piece, to try. The first taste was enough. Between the three of us, it didn't last long at all. I get a good deal of pleasure out of seeing some of the boys tasting some good old Jewish baking, and I think in all this time, just one of them didn't like it at all, which, I think, is a pretty good record.

I took in "Frenchman's Creek" yesterday afternoon. It was a good show, and this afternoon I'm going to see "Together Again." There isn't much to do except sleep or go to the movies, and I've slept too much recently. Why, the last two weeks I've been getting between eight and ten hours of sleep nightly, quite a record!

If you'd like, you can call me Chief Long Hair, but by the time you receive this letter I'll have gotten paid and then shaven.

Now I have to run down to the post office to get a stamp and this letter will be on its merry, airy way.

Love always
Your, George

November 30, 1944
Thursday

From:	To:
Mr. Cpl. J.G. Barr 11057933	C.L. Sniderman
4503rd Base Unit Eng. Sq.	65 Houghton St.
Great Bend A.B.B., Kansas	Worcester, 4, Mass.

Dearest Lottie,

No word from you for the last two days, I know it is not your fault, but I'm on edge to know what's going on. I haven't been getting to sleep this last week for an hour or two after I hit the bed. I catch up on it, my sleep, on the waking up time, but that hour or two before I fall asleep is the hardest part of the day for me.

Last night the moon was full, the night clear, everything perfect, but the most important thing missing was you, my darling. It's getting colder and colder and I need you more and more.

This morning, all right, afternoon, when I woke, I found myself rolled up in a ball and the covers over my head. When I stretched my feet out I hit the cold spot down at the bottom of the bed, swift as a flash, I was back in my original position. I wish someone would take care of the stoves in this barrack, the day men leave them alone because they're at work and the night men are in bed, what a life!

I hope we get paid to-day. The C.O. is supposed to come up from Great Bend and pay us, but I don't know what time he's due, he even may wait a few days until it warms up a bit. I don't care, I don't need money in the army, they feed me, clothe me, board me, now what do I need money for – I'm ready for a section 8 now, sir!!!

Darling, would you still love me if they gave me a section 8? Just because there would be something wrong with me mentally, shouldn't make any difference, should it? Oh, it would, huh! O.K. Then I won't get a section 8. I may be a bit unbalanced, but not unbalanced enough, I guess I'll have to sweat this damn war out like I am.

I had three letters to answer to-day, but did I do it, no. Time, there was plenty, but ambition, none, so they'll have to wait. Got a letter from Bob and he says hello. I can see him now when I write him and tell him we are to be married.

Good afternoon, my darling
Your, George

P.S. Pay Call 3:30 P.M.!!!! J.G.B.

December 1, 1944
Friday nite

From:	To:
C.L. Sniderman	Mr. Cpl. J.G. Barr 11057933
65 Houghton St.	Eng. Sq., 4503rd A.A.F. Base Unit
Worcester 4, Mass.	Great Bend A.B.B., Kansas

My dearest George,

Got two super letters from you today, - one of which brought especially good news, - that of your furlough's possibility of an extension. As yet, I've received no word from you in answer to my night letter. I'm hoping I'll get some word tomorrow. Your mother & dad went up to see the Rabbi this evening and they said he's a grand guy. They said they nearly burst out laughing when he asked them if the both of us were Jewish and if this was our first marriage. Your mother was quite embarrassed when she had to tell him I had three previous marriages to my name!!!

Darling, I called City Hall and they said a blood test taken in Kansas is perfectly O.K. in Mass. Providing it is used within 30 days. So, I think you'd better take it some time next week or there abouts, just in case we can't get it through fast enough in Worcester. I'll take mine around that time too. Just as there won't be any added aggravation. Also, your dad informs me that a marriage license has to be at least five days old before you can get married, - if so I'll have to get the license myself altho I'd prefer it otherwise. I'll find out definitely what the story is there.

Now let me tell you about some more worries I have. My brother Irv was over the house tonight and when I told him the date of the wedding he nearly had a stroke. It seems he has to go to Chicago on the 6th of Jan. for a very important deal, - and the whole thing has me worried sick. He's going to try to arrange things so he can leave a day or so later, - but I'm not sure he'll be able to.

There are going to be no invitations, dear, - mainly because there's no time to have them printed and secondly, the affair won't be large enough to warrant invitations. I do wish you'd write Dave a nice long letter though, and also Sid. Also, if you have time it would be nice to drop Edie a few words.

I'm glad the sweater fit you, - your mother did a beautiful job on it. Damn it, - someday I'll learn to knit if it kills me. That's all the dope for tonight.

All my love, Lottie

December 1, 1944
Friday

From:	To:
Mr. Cpl. J.G. Barr 11057933	C.L. Sniderman
4503rd Base Unit Eng. Sq.	65 Houghton St.
Great Bend A.B.B., Kansas	Worcester, 4, Mass.

Dearest Lottie,

I'm going to feel wonderful having a wife, especially when the wife is going to be you.

I feel like a stinking, low down heel, not being able to be with you to help plan the wedding. I see no reason for you not getting married in white. Your father, I know, definitely would want you to get married that way. If it's a matter of money, well, darling, we'll be getting an allotment of $50 a month and the $10 allotment that is going to the bank, so if we need to, we can borrow the money necessary and pay it back month by month.

Where will we go for our honeymoon and for how long, I also thought of that, and I thought maybe a week or longer in New York. When I know definitely when we are getting married, I could write or wire a good hotel for reservations. But of course, the length of our honeymoon will have to be considered by our bankroll. If you have any ideas on the subject let me know.

I wrote you that I'd ask my brother Sol to be best man. The license, if I'm not going to be home long enough, you'll be able to get. My blood test, because it is the army's, I think will be O.K. in Massachusetts. If not, I hope to be home a few days before we get married anyway.

I've been waiting for the last two days for a telegram from you telling me when we'd get married, but as yet, I haven't received it. If I don't get one to-night, I'm going to send you one to-night.

I'd like to know, were my folks against the wedding of your liking? And about you being a jelly fish wife, what an absurd idea. You are so far from being jelly fishes that I can't even start to picture you as being such.

Darling, I know what you are going thru and I feel like hell about it, I wish I could do something about it, but this darn distance is the damndest thing. Take care my darling.

Your, George

P.S. How come you underscored your last name? Would it be that you're going to change it, or have you some other reason? J.G.B

December 3, 1944
Sunday

From:	To:
Mr. Cpl. J.G. Barr 11057933	C.L. Sniderman
4503rd Base Unit Eng. Sq.	65 Houghton St.
Great Bend A.B.B., Kansas	Worcester, 4, Mass.

Dearest Lottie,

Your telegram finally came. It seems ages before I received it. If I hadn't gone down to the telegraph office the day before, checking up on it, I may never have received it. When they sent it from Worcester, they misspelled my name as Bass, so at the orderly room, they sent it back to the telegraph office saying that there never was such a man in that outfit. After I was notified that it was on the base, I went down and got it, but it seemed that everyone I met afterwards knew I had a telegram, and asked me if I had gotten it yet.

The dopes at the orderly room, if they had read the entire address and looked up my barracks number, they could have compared serial numbers, but no, they're just wasn't anyone by that name in the outfit. After looking at the telegram, you can see it was bounced around a bit before I received it.

When I went up to check on my furlough, the officer marked me down for the 2nd of January. I asked him if he'd make sure about it, and if I wouldn't have to bother him until I got my furlough. He said that in all probability I would get it the 2nd, but I better check with him again in a week or so, to make doubly sure. Then, darling, he said, "This outfit is surely going to hell! It seems as if every one is getting married!!" The nerve of the guy!

Oh, yes, my precious, who is going to have the honored privilege of marrying us? I don't care who he is, except that I'd rather not have the rabbi who married Narky and Charlotte, I don't know his name, but he lives on Providence St., on the corner of Harrison. Personally, I think he stinks.

I hope to be home the afternoon of the 3rd, so that should give us time to get the license & if my test isn't good here, I think I can get it within two days at home.

Did you know I'm waiting impatiently until the day we are wedded? Darling I love you very much. You are dearer to me than anything, or anyone else in this or any other world. I'm a much better person since I've loved you, if it hadn't been for your love, there is no telling what kind of a guy this army life may have made me. It isn't that the army life would have made me anything, it is just that, I would have allowed myself to be made.

What time is the wedding scheduled for? Will we have to spend the first night in Worcester, or will we have enough time to get out. How many do you expect to have there?

I'm going to love having you for my wife.

Your, George

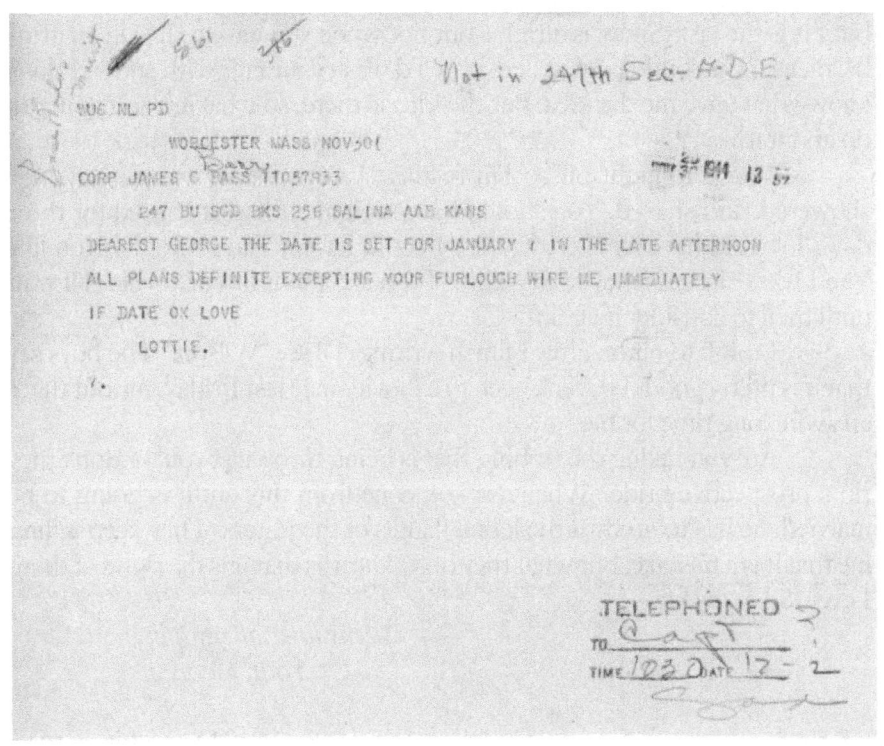

```
9US NL PD
          WORCESTER MASS NOV 50(
CORP JAMES C BASS 11057933
     247 BU SQD BKS 256 SALINA AAB KANS
DEAREST GEORGE THE DATE IS SET FOR JANUARY 7 IN THE LATE AFTERNOON
ALL PLANS DEFINITE EXCEPTING YOUR FURLOUGH WIRE ME IMMEDIATELY
IF DATE OK LOVE
     LOTTIE.
```

December 4, 1944
Monday

From:	To:
Mr. Cpl. J.G. Barr 11057933	C.L. Sniderman
4503rd Base Unit Eng. Sq.	65 Houghton St.
Great Bend A.B.B., Kansas	Worcester, 4, Mass.

Dearest Lottie,

Five months have passed since that wonderful day of our engagement. Now, a little more than a month away, we'll be celebrating a more joyous occasion, our wedding day. So, you think I'll be one of those thoughtless husbands and forget our anniversary? If I do, just hit me on the head with something.

I was just talking with some of the fellows and they brought a question up in my mind. Would our wedding have anything to do with leap years? Trying to pull a fast one on me, huh! Leap years or otherwise I don't care, I love you anyway.

The snow is snowing and the ground is mushy and I'm splattered with the stuff. This is the first real snow we've had, and I wouldn't care one bit if it is the last. Snow is alright, but not when you have to live in an army barracks. I think if I had you here now I'd wash your face with snow, I don't know what gave me the idea, but the idea is there, so what are you going to do about it?

I have to-night off so I'm resting. I slept the morning away, ate, showered, and shaved. You should have seen me, I hadn't shaved for three days. I should have let it grow, then I could have a Van Dyke. Do you like Van Dykes? I guess they're all right – if you are about fifty years old. I'll wait until then to consider it again.

I think to-night, after I finish writing, I'll see "Wilson." The boys say that it is pretty good. I haven't been to a movie since last Friday, my but that's an awful long time for me.

Are you taking the ribbing that is being thrown at you, or don't they rib a prospective bride? Whenever someone from this outfit is going to be married, he has to go thru the lethal flames of the jesters. They keep telling me that it is a mistake, but what they don't know is that it is the rightest thing I ever did in my life.

All my love, all my life
Your, George

December 4, 1944
Monday

From:	To:
C.L. Sniderman	Mr. Cpl. J.G. Barr 11057933
65 Houghton St.	Eng. Sq., 4503rd A.A.F. Base Unit
Worcester 4, Mass.	Great Bend A.B.B., Kansas

My dearest George,

My mind has been muchly relieved since Saturday nite when I got your telegram. If you leave on January 2nd it will be perfect. From now on the time is going to fly by before we know it. The "Shule," the rabbi, and the caterers have been taken care of. Now all I have to do is see about the number of people and the music. Darling, you'll never know how much I wish this was all over, - guess the excitement is too much for me. It's a good thing a person doesn't get married every day!! I'm going to take my blood test in about another week or so, and also get the license.

Darling, I told Dave Israel about our getting married today and he was very good about it, - only he won't give me all the time off that I want, so I guess I'll be looking for a new place of employment. He wants to give me two weeks, which is hardly enough. I want at least a week before you come home and then naturally all the time off while you are here. If I take two weeks as he says it'll mean I get up and go to work while you stay home and sleep, - now what do you say about that. After all, - you will be my husband, - so I told him I'd make my decision after I heard from you. From now on you wear the pants in the family!!!!

Jackie Waxler called this evening and we had a nice big chat. He related some news that nearly floored me, - nearly? - Why, I fainted dead away, they threw water all over me, but I just couldn't be revived, so let me pass on this bit of gossip to you. It seems your friend George Pilson is by this time married or well on the way. - No, - not to Jeanne Berger, but a little English girl out there, - who is incidentally, not Jewish. Maybe you're not as surprised as I was, - but I still can't get over it. Oh, well. - nuff said 'bout other people!

Your mother is tickled that you like the sweater so well, - and why shouldn't ya, huh?!!

Got two letters from you today, which means that tomorrow, - no mail. I'm glad that you're going to feel wonderful having a wife – because everyone at the office is going to try to talk you out of it, - the stinkers!! Oh, by the by, - this bride will definitely wear white. The kids say I'm going to be a typical bride, - even to the blushing part. Jesus, I never did learn how not to blush.

About our honeymoon, - I think New York is super and we'll stay about a week. When you wire or write for hotel reservations, tell them to hold them because we probably won't get in till late, - and don't forget the date, - it's for the week starting Jan 7.

About my underlining my present last name on one of my letters, - well that was done purely out of sentiment. You see, I won't have it very much longer and I want it to be as proud as possible while I still have it. Silly, eh wot!! Don't say I didn't warn ya!!

Darling, please don't worry if you don't hear from me every day now for a little while. There are so damn many things to be done and so little time to do it in. I'll try my best to write you every nite, but just in case I slip up once, don't get excited. But come hell or high water, - please don't you get slack about writing. Goodnight, m'love.

Always yours,
Lottie

P.S. Heard an awfully good definition of marriage today, - "Marriage is when you find your other self, and when you lose her, its like losing yourself, - and without her, you're but half a person." Isn't that beautiful? Me.

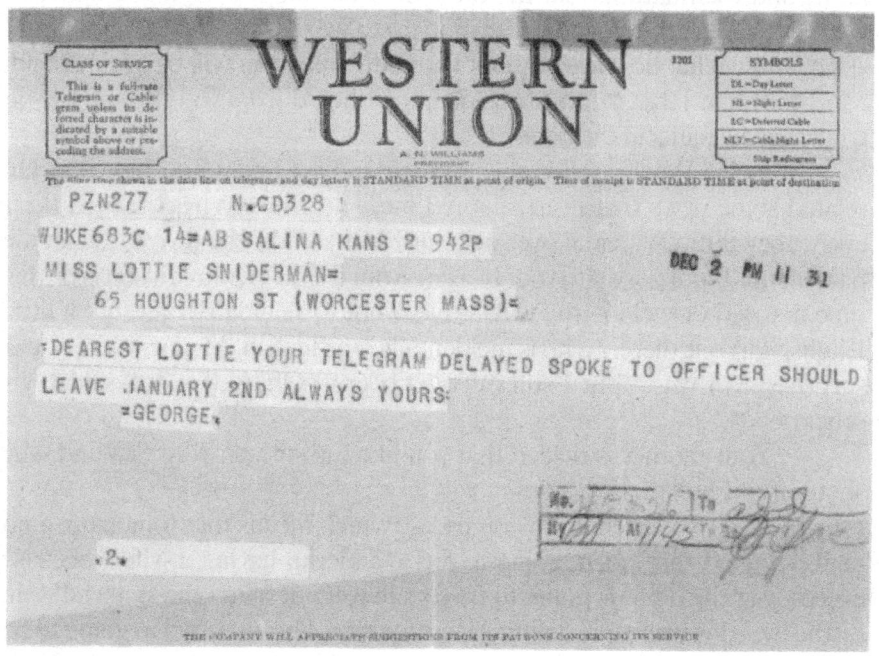

December 5, 1944
Tuesday

From:	To:
Mr. Cpl. J.G. Barr 11057933	C.L. Sniderman
4503rd Base Unit Eng. Sq.	65 Houghton St.
Great Bend A.B.B., Kansas	Worcester, 4, Mass.

Dearest Lottie,

It had been almost four days since I last received any word from you, so you must know how I felt when last night I received two swell letters from you. I think you are handling our wedding first rate, and if I were there with you I'd probably be in the way anyway.

This is a fine time to be telling me about your previous marriages! Here I thought I was going to marry a sweet innocent girl, and now I find out she is very experienced!! Now you'll have to be the one who will guide me, for, my love, this is the first of my marriages. Oh, to be so disillusioned!!

Darling, I've invited Jackie already and will write Maxie, but I'd like you to ask Anne, Rhoda Cutler, and Evelyn Plotkin. I'll write Sid and Dave and Edie, the first chance I get. I hope I'll have time to write at least one of them to-day.

New York does seem about the best place to go under the conditions. I'll see what I can do about getting reservations at a nice hotel. There are a few fellows in the outfit from New York, so I'll ask them for a couple of good bets. Don't worry about that, there are always a few empty benches in Central Park.

Darling, I'm almost positive that I'll be able to be home about the 3rd. I know if something does come up, my officers will fight to get me home in time. Just as long as things ride as they are then there is little need of any doubt.

I'll take my test next week, but I hate like hell to give up any of my blood, I'll need all the energy I have, and the way I've been eating myself, I'll need it.

Your, George

P.S. What makes you think we look too young to be married? Down south they marry a bit younger than ourselves. J.G.B.

December 6, 1944
Wednesday

From:	To:
C.L. Sniderman	Mr. Cpl. J.G. Barr 11057933
65 Houghton St.	Eng. Sq., 4503rd A.A.F. Base Unit
Worcester 4, Mass.	Great Bend A.B.B., Kansas

My dearest George,

Your future wife just came home from the Policemen's Ball and twas very enjoyable too. Your mother and dad had an extra ticket and asked me to join them, - so I did. They had quite a crowd, - all young kids, - when your mother & dad kept remarking about the youngness of the crowd they made me feel ancient. Oh, well, - maybe I am!!!! They had very few servicemen, - I should say about ten all told.

I could see by the looks of my wire that it was quite delayed. It's a wonder you got it at all.

The rabbi who is going to marry us is new in Worcester and is supposed to be very good. He's a young man and very modern. His name is

Gutherman, - if it makes any difference. I haven't seen him as yet. The wedding is for about 2 or 2:30, - what time it will actually turn out to be I can't say. We should have around 75 people, which I think is a very nice number, altho I think there will be much more than that coming to see the ceremony. If it's at all possible, I would like to leave Worcester Sunday night and not stay over, - but we'll discuss that when you come home.

The whole office has been calling me a child bride, - the nerve of them. But I suppose when you compare the ages of some of the girls to mine, I am quite a child. But I always did advocate that a girl should marry before she was fifty!!

I can't wait for Christmas to come so I can leave work and have time to do all the things I should. It's awful having to rush everything on a lunch hour.

It'll be swell if you can come home on the 3rd of January. Then we'll have a few days to get re-acquainted before we get married. Doesn't that sound silly?!! I'm trying to think if there's anything about the wedding that I've neglected to tell you, but I'm so damn tired my mind refuses to function properly.

The first shower is Monday night and my mother is a wreck from cleaning the house. This shower is going to be exclusively for the women in my mother's organization. Tuesday night is the one for your cousins and mine, - the older ones I mean. Either Wednesday or Thursday nite I think the kids in the office are having a party for me, and then the following Monday, Edie is having a tea in my honor, and then on the next Saturday, Fran is having her tea for me.

Now you can see for yourself what a bride goes through, - and I love every bit of it!! My only regret is that you won't be here to share it. But there will be so much more that we'll share for the rest of our lives.

And so now I take leave, dear. Goodnight & pleasant dreams.

Always yours, Lottie

December 6, 1944
Wednesday

From:	To:
Mr. Cpl. J.G. Barr 11057933	C.L. Sniderman
4503rd Base Unit Eng. Sq.	65 Houghton St.
Great Bend A.B.B., Kansas	Worcester, 4, Mass.

Dearest Lottie,

I didn't have a chance to write this afternoon, and we aren't doing anything here at the shop, so of course, I'm writing you.

We're having quite a time here, there are two civilian radios here and everyone has worked on them, but as yet, they haven't been repaired. I stay away from them except to see how they are making out. In fact, darling, I keep away from most everything, except the little things that I know about, and those are very few.

You might wonder about why I didn't have a chance to write you this afternoon and I'll tell you. I went to see "To Have and to Have Not." I liked the picture very much, but I like any picture Humphrey Bogart is in. I guess I'm just a born romanticist. In all his pictures, his women are full of life and fire, just like you. I think that's the first thing that attracted me to you, was that life. I must have fallen for you the first time I met you, I was too young to realize it at first, but after seeing you and being with you, just proved that my instincts were right. Things must have been planned that way a long, long time ago, because aren't you my little spare rib.

I'm so excited about our coming marriage that I toss and turn for what seems hours, every night before I can fall asleep. It's a good thing I can sleep late or else I'd be a wreck. You know that I wear my coat to the mess hall, and wear my overshoes to work. That's something I never do, but I just won't take any kind of a chance to mess me up. Darling, I love you so much, so very, very much.

This will have to be mailed to-morrow, but I feel much better knowing that it has been written. By the way, if I don't forget, I'll send you a few more pictures of myself.

Good night, my darling.
Your, George

December 7, 1944
Thursday

From:	To:
Mr. Cpl. J.G. Barr 11057933	C.L. Sniderman
4503rd Base Unit Eng. Sq.	65 Houghton St.
Great Bend A.B.B., Kansas	Worcester, 4, Mass.

Dearest Lottie,

I hope you like the pictures, they weren't taken by my camera, otherwise, they would have taken clearer pictures. The sergeant, the one with the shirt on is the fellow that I chum around with now. He and I have been in the same hut to-gether since my arrival at Great Bend, but he had his pal and I was paling around with Bob, now that we know each other better,

I think he is more of a regular fellow than Bob was. Bob just took a lot of understanding, that's all.

I've written to a few hotels in New York, and will write to a few more this afternoon. Darling, how much do you think we'll be able to have for our honeymoon, you know that our wedding presents will have to take care of that. I wish that I had enough money so that we wouldn't have to rely upon our wedding presents, if I could have only foreseen my coming marriage when I was going to school in Philadelphia, I could have saved at least three hundred dollars. Darling, I'll make it up to you someday, it will have to be after the war, but I will.

When I got up this morning, I felt dopey as hell, and still do, I didn't have a very restful sleep. Maybe to-night I'll be able to get a decent rest.

Jackie wrote me and he said that he'll try and get some film so that he can take pictures at the wedding. I hope he can get kodachrome, because they are much better than regular film. Another thing darling, if you want pictures of us, our wedding pictures, maybe you should make an appointment at J. Carrol Bramns. When our children ask us, "What did daddy do in the big war," we can show them the picture and say, "Daddy was a soldier."

Good bye for now my sweet.
Your, George

*Smile. & watch the birdie
we smiled, but no matter
how hard we looked we
couldn't see any birdie*

Salina Kan, 1944, [?]

Picture 1 of 3 from George Barr letter dated 12/7/44

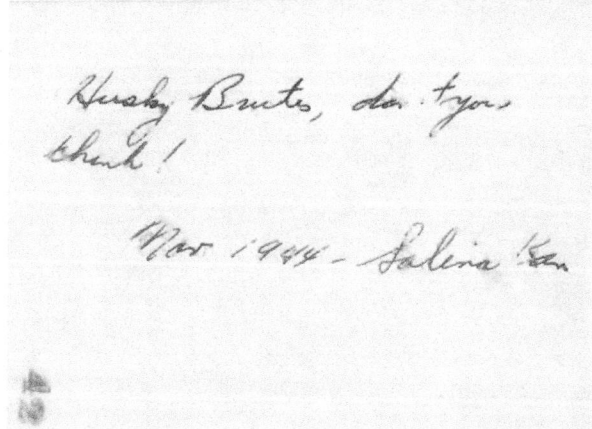

Picture 2 of 3 from George Barr letter dated 12/7/44

You should have seen the guy taking the picture.

Salina Kan. Nov. 1944

Picture 3 of 3 from George Barr letter dated 12/7/44

December 8, 1944
Friday

From:	To:
Mr. Cpl. J.G. Barr 11057933	C.L. Sniderman
4503rd Base Unit Eng. Sq.	65 Houghton St.
Great Bend A.B.B., Kansas	Worcester, 4, Mass.

Dearest Lottie,

Would you be very surprised if I told you I got up early? By early, I mean I got up before noon, one hour before noon. I like it much better this way, because I can wash up before dinner, instead of rushing to the mess hall, then coming back to wash up. I'll have to do it more regular.

Last night I received a letter from Narky that was dated the 19th of last month. All the address he had was Eng. Sq. Great Bend, Kan. How they managed to get me, shows me that our postal system is pretty damn good. Why he didn't put down 4503rd, I don't know, except that he must have been half asleep, or drunk at the time.

Did you know our niece Bonnie, could write? Neither did I until she wrote me a sentence. But they can't kid me, I know that Narky held her hand!

Another did you know – did you know that I haven't had any letter from you since Monday? I realize you are busy as hell and am even selfish in telling you about it, but darling, I'm going crazy waiting to hear from you. I know that to-night will bring me a letter or two from you, but you know how I feel. I suppose after we're married, you'll never write to me!!

Back at the shop we should be getting some work in. The last few days have been excellent for flying and I think the flying squadrons have taken full advantage of the weather. When the ships fly, we work. Our slogan is "Keep 'Em Flying."

I wrote to Edie finally, also Maxie and Sid. As yet, I haven't written to Dave, but I will in a day or so.

This is all my dull mind can think of, so my sweet, I bid you a good afternoon.

Your, George

December 8, 1944
Friday nite

From:	To:
C.L. Sniderman	Mr. Cpl. J.G. Barr 11057933
65 Houghton St.	Eng. Sq., 4503rd A.A.F. Base Unit
Worcester 4, Mass.	Great Bend A.B.B., Kansas

Hello darling,

Had intended to write you a letter early tonight and then get a good night sleep, but it started dashing rain outside and I couldn't resist just sitting and watching it. So now the hour is late, me head is tired, but come hell or high water, I'll finish this letter.

I spoke to the leader of some band tonight and engaged him for the wedding. I hear tell he's very good, - I hope so. Last nite we had a little excitement in the house, - as if we need anymore. Around 1:30 A.M. the phone rang and naturally I thought it was you, - I was almost afraid to answer it. When I finally did answer it, some man said this is the officer on the beat of Mechanic & Front Sts. and there's been an attempted theft in our store. They took a big rock and threw it through the window and he wanted someone to come down there. Naturally, I wouldn't wake my dad and tell him anything like that, so I started to get dressed and go. But of course, my mother wouldn't hear of it, - so we called Irv, - he in turn called the Fire Dept. and they went down and boarded it up, Irv also went down there but there was nothing he could do. This morning my mother and I diplomatically broke the news to my father. Never a dull moment in this household!!

Darling, I don't think you'll ever forget our anniversary. You remember so well our engagement anniversary that I'm sure I'll never have to remind you about our wedding anniversary. Fine thing, - whatta ya mean has our wedding got anything to do with leap year!! I'll have you know Corporal Barr, that leap year or no leap year, you didn't have a chance. Didn't you know that when I make up my mind that I want something I never let it go until I get it? So, you see, you were sunk from the start!!

I never knew you were so fiendish. Why should you possibly want to wash my face in the snow?!! Remind me to do same to you should we happen to have a little blizzard on our honeymoon. No, darling, I do not like a Van Dyke, - not now or when your fifty. You can have anything your 'lil heart desires, - but no mustache in any form or fashion. If you grow a mustache, I'll smoke a pipe!! Won't we be a gruesome twosome?

Are you kidding!! You should hear the ribbing I have to endure, - from all sides!! All I hear down the office is there goes our child bride. But I can took it like a man. Those guys have a nerve telling you it's a mistake to get married. We'll be the craziest and the happiest people that ever got married.

I'll try and make you a good wife, darling, honest. As soon as I learn to cook I'll be all set, - and I'll be a good cook too, - I hope, for yer sake. Let's always stay young, - or for a good many years anyway. Just because we'll be married, it doesn't mean that we can't do all the crazy things we used to do. We'll always be happy, - I know we will, and I'll always love you. This month is going to be terribly long just because I want it to hurry up and go. Goodnight dear.

And remember, - always love,
Lottie

P.S. Someone is singing "The Very Thought of You." Me.

December 9, 1944
Saturday

From:	To:
Mr. Cpl. J.G. Barr 11057933	C.L. Sniderman
4503rd Base Unit Eng. Sq.	65 Houghton St.
Great Bend A.B.B., Kansas	Worcester, 4, Mass.

Dearest Lottie,

Yesterday when I told you I'd receive some mail from you that night, I didn't expect such a wonderful surprise. The bracelet is grand and, of course, I love you for it. While I sorted the mail for my letters and saw the package, I knew instantly what it was going to be. Even so, you didn't have any stickers on it saying, "Do not open until X-mas," so I opened it and all the boys that saw it readily agreed that I'm a mighty lucky fellow to have such a swell girl, who is going to be my wife shortly. They keep telling me that you are going to get the short end of it tho, when you get me. The nerve of the guys! Even if it is true.

Last night business really picked up at the shop. We kept going all evening and even worked an extra two hours to boot. A captain called a few times during the night to come down and check a plane and we kept holding him off, because we had other work to do. He became insistent, so one of the fellows went down. A half hour later the captain is on the phone again asking were the man was. We told him that he must be down there because he left a long time ago. He was so burnt up that he asked for his name and said that if we couldn't find him soon, that he'd have the M.P.'s after him.

Then the sergeant sent me down to check up. While walking thru a hangar to get to the hangar where the ship was supposed to be, I saw the plane in that hangar. I got on the phone immediately and told the sergeant what I found. He said that I must be crazy, because the other guy phoned and had the equipment out of the ship, and wanted someone to pick it up. The captain had been notified that the equipment was out, so he was satisfied, but he didn't know that it was out of the wrong plane.

Anyway, I took the equipment out of the correct ship and after we had our midnight meal, we came back & put the equipment back in the other ship. What a night!!!

To-night we have off, so we're going to have a nice steak supper pretty soon. I hope they have some good steaks in this town, for I haven't had a decent steak for a long time.

Bye for now, sweetness.
Your, George

December 10, 1944
Sunday

From:	To:
Mr. Cpl. J.G. Barr 11057933	C.L. Sniderman
4503rd Base Unit Eng. Sq.	65 Houghton St.
Great Bend A.B.B., Kansas	Worcester, 4, Mass.

Dearest Lottie,

Another note being dashed off while I'm supposed to be at work – shame on me!

I did do a little work this evening, don't get me wrong, I don't goldbrick all the time. We almost froze our tiny little toes off, it gets mighty damn cold working out here on the line. It gets rough especially when we have to work without gloves. They should fly airplanes in the winter made out of plastic or wood, metal is too cold to handle.

After writing you last night we went and got ourselves a good steak. I was very surprised, because I didn't think that they knew what a good steak was. I'll have to go back again and see if they can feed me like that two times in a row.

You tell Dave that I think he is quite considerate for letting you have two weeks off and that you'll do anything he wants you to, then you can tell him to go to hell! If I get my extension and you want a week off before the wedding, you wouldn't be back to work for at least five weeks. Darling, I know that you like the kids you work for and with, but don't you think it silly to have just two weeks. Hell, if it wasn't so cold up here and dad was well, I'd want you to come back with me. So, wifey, you can tell Dave that you'll need much more time.

So, I'm going to wear the pants in the family, am I? You say that now, but later I'll have to beat you so you'll see things my way, so to avoid that, we'll have to work this on sort of a 50-50 basis.

Guess who walked in and surprised me this afternoon, Bob. He is with a new outfit that moved onto the field last night. If it weren't for him, this letter would have been written an hour or so later. How come? I was assigned by the boys to go down and get sandwiches at the P.X. and when I got there, there was a line a mile long (it was very long anyway), but fortunately, I saw Bob half way down so I walked up to him and had him get my order. I'm sorry that I forgot to tell you about George Pilson. Jackie had written me about him, but I didn't think that it rated a lime, so I forgot about it. I'm glad tho, because I think that Jeanne Berger is a pretty nice girl.

I'm going down and see if I can take my blood test to-morrow, then if I have a chance, I'm going to see if the Louie has gotten any definite word on my furlough. It's a sure thing, but if something does happen, then I want a little time to fight it. I'm not taking any kind of chances.

If this letter is a little messy, you'll have to excuse me, because so am I, and so is this G.I. pen that I'm using. It writes O.K., but the ink is in a lot of other places than the point.

Here is something you might be interested in. Those two radios that I mentioned a few days ago, they are still inoperative. No one is able to find out what's wrong, I suggested buying new ones, as yet I don't know if they've taken my suggestion or not. I'm afraid that one of the men is going to take a sledge hammer and really fix them up.

Don't you worry about anyone talking me out of marrying you. I know a good thing when I see it and I don't intend to be talked out of it!!!

> *Goodnight, darling, and pleasant dreams.*
> *Your, George*

December 10, 1944
Sunday nite

From:	To:
C.L. Sniderman	Mr. Cpl. J.G. Barr 11057933
65 Houghton St.	Eng. Sq., 4503rd A.A.F. Base Unit
Worcester 4, Mass.	Great Bend A.B.B., Kansas

My dearest George,

I was just about to sit down and write you a letter thinking that I had no news of interest to write. All of a once in a sudden the bell rings, - the door opens and who should walk in but Maxie Z., Jackie & Sol Zitowitz.

Maxie looks super and was very, very surprised to hear we were going to get married. He said he received a letter from you sometime last week, but you didn't mention a word about it. His furlough comes up sometime in January and he's going to try to make it for the wedding, but if he can't, he'll meet us in New York during the time we're there. Sol & Jack said they felt lost having no prospective wives, - seems they're gonna start shopping around, - jest like fer a pair of shoes!!! Altho I looked simply miz when they came up, I was glad to see them. I had just finished washing my hair, it was all rolled up in a towel and I had not a drop of lipstick on. What a mess, - but what could I do.

I can hardly wait for tomorrow to come since the first party is tomorrow nite. We've already received one gift and it's lovely. My aunt Rose gave us a set of cocktail glasses, - something we'll probably need once we get in our own home. I'm not going to put them away so you'll be able to see it when you come home. Your dad has already bought the liquor for the wedding and it's all getting very, very exciting. Do you realize darling, that in less than a month we'll be married!! Fer goodness sake's that not very long. Maxie reminded me that now that I'm gonna be a married woman I'll have to settle down. It'll be like the taming of the shrew. But won't you love it, - I will?!!

Got no letter from you yesterday and I was good and mad. You can't do this to me! Guess there's no more to write about tonight, - except that now that the time draws nearer I miss you more and more. Guess this is a question of how near and yet so far.

All my love always
Lottie

December 11, 1944
Monday

From:	To:
Mr. Cpl. J.G. Barr 11057933	C.L. Sniderman
4503rd Base Unit Eng. Sq.	65 Houghton St.
Great Bend A.B.B., Kansas	Worcester, 4, Mass.

Dearest Lottie,

This afternoon I went down to the hospital to take my blood test, but was told that in some states a form must be sent to the soldiers to be filled in by the medical officer here. I've already sent a letter to City Hall requesting such a form or whatever is necessary. I doubt very much if I need such a thing, but I'll have to appease the doctor here.

Last night Bob and I were going to see "Hollywood Canteen," but before we went to the theater we stopped at the service club for a bite to eat. As we were walking out the door we noticed that there was a small crowd gathered on one side of the club, so naturally we went to investigate. It was a Pepsi Cola man with a record machine, recording the voices of the G.I.'s. I didn't have time to think of anything to say, and when there is a crowd of people around, I'm practically speechless, so I read one of the prepared speeches of the Pepsi people. I know it was a bit hammy and I don't remember very much of what I said, but it was either that way, or no record for you.

Darling, you remember what I told you about my brother's wedding, the champagne? Listen to this – when I wrote him, I kiddingly told him that if he wanted to be best man, that he'd have to get us that bottle that I was cheated out of last time. He wrote back and accepted my terms. Fran and Sol send their love.

I asked Sol if it was a surprise to him and he said no, because everyone in New York knew about it before he did and they told him, and I guess Fran was the first to tell him. My father called New York, that's why my letter to him was beaten.

Last night just before I turned in, one of the boys came in dead drunk, and he wanted some one to put him to bed. He sleeps in an upper bunk and it would have been an impossibility for him to climb up there. Obligingly, I helped him undress, hung up his clothes and shoved him into bed.

Then he has the nerve to ask how many letters he got from his wife, because he was expecting two of them, I guess she writes every day, and here he was out getting drunk with some old whore! If for any damn reason, I ever even think about such a thing, I just hope someone shoots me.

All my love, all my life.
Your, George

December 13, 1944
Wednesday

From:	To:
Mr. Cpl. J.G. Barr 11057933	C.L. Sniderman
4503rd Base Unit Eng. Sq.	65 Houghton St.
Great Bend A.B.B., Kansas	Worcester, 4, Mass.

Dearest Lottie,

I've just returned after an hour and a half at our orderly room. The reason I went up was to keep check on my furlough. It seems as if I had to sign some form of furlough application, something that we didn't have to do while up here, but now it is supposed to be necessary. They don't have any blanks here, so my officer called Great Bend and had them make one out for me. My officer told me that I needn't worry about it and it will come out right. He doesn't realize how much I am worried about me getting my furlough on time. He must have a lot of faith, so I will too, which also means you will too.

How are all your showers coming along? Why would you want me to be there, men aren't invited to showers, they're strictly her affairs. I'd look mighty silly at one of those affairs anyway, one man and all those women. The showers are for you, so you'll have to attend them by yourself, and carry me along in spirit.

Last night I was running up and down the line, dodging men and airplanes. One 29 was ready to fly and two transmitters were out and we were called to do a quick repair job. We fixed one, nothing wrong except the dial setting, something the radio operator could have done, and the other one wasn't even properly installed. We took that one out because it would have taken too much time to put it in and the plane flew without it. That's about all we've been doing, it seems, is fixing other people's mistakes.

Lots and lots of love.
Your, George

December 14, 1944
Thursday

From:	To:
C.L. Sniderman	Mr. Cpl. J.G. Barr 11057933
65 Houghton St.	Eng. Sq., 4503rd A.A.F. Base Unit
Worcester 4, Mass.	Great Bend A.B.B., Kansas

My darling George,

I feel like a damn stinker for not writing for so long, but I have a feeling this is going to be long enough to make up for the days lost. First of all, darling, let me thank you for the pin, - it is gorgeous and will look lovely on my new suit, - the suit I bought to go away in. Also, I'm glad you liked the bracelet. I know you had felt bad because you had lost your last one, and anyway I had wanted to buy you one then, if you remember, - so I got you one now. Also, I finally received your letter today in answer to what I should do about my job. Here's the story. For a week now, Dave has been hounding me about how foolish it would be for me to leave, so finally I told him that I had written you all about it and whatever you said to do would be O.K. with me. I knew damn well what you would say, but I gave him the benefit of the doubt. Yesterday he cornered me again and I got so angry at him that I said I had already received your letter, and you said you absolutely didn't want me to work. He got very excited and immediately made plans for hiring a new girl. When he told Charlotte I was leaving she spent the rest of the afternoon bawling. I felt miserable about it because I'm crazy about her, - but the point is that I'm much more crazy about you than I am about her and I wouldn't think of working while you were here. So, the hell with Dave, and to hell with the job, - you're much more important to me, and besides that, I'm getting sick of the place. So, my darling, for as long as you're here we'll have glorious days together, we'll make up for all the time lost in the past and all the time we will lose until this damn war is over.

And now to begin with Monday night. My mother had the tea for the ladies of her branch and everything was lovely. They gave us a very, very lovely blanket. Tuesday nite was the shower for yours' and my cousins, and oh, my gracious, what a mob. Everybody came and I still don't know where we put everybody. We had everything from soup to nuts to eat and we received some very lovely gifts.

Whether you're interested or not I'll innumerate some of the gifts, - that is, the ones I can remember. We received two sets of lovely dishes, - one dinner and one breakfast set, - 2 blankets, towels, sheets and pillow cases, - tablecloths, book ends, glass cooking pots, and some underwear, etc., etc., etc. There was much more, but I can't think of them, - oh yes, your folks gave us a check of ten dollars and we got some money from two of my aunts.

Then there was the party from the office last night, and what a party it was, - the only thing missing was you, - also I missed you so terribly Monday and Tuesday nites. I remembered how at the engagement party you were with me every minute and I missed your not being with me now. To get back to Wednesday nite, - it was at the Bancroft in the Baroque Room and the whole table was set with white and pink baskets and favors. In back of my chair was hanging a great big wedding bell and in front of me on the table was a soldier and a bride, and on either side, were two long pink candles. On my plate was a beautiful corsage of roses and sweet peas and for a half hour straight they had the orchestra play music dedicated to me such as – "I Love You Truly", "Oh Promise Me", "I'll be Loving You Always", the Wedding March, etc., etc. Like a great big sissy, I started to cry.

Then after the dinner they presented me my gift, which is the most beautiful, beautiful silk puff I have ever seen. It's as light as a feather and pale peach in color. So, I guess now with two blankets and a puff, we should keep warm. The general opinion seems to be that we'll be warm even without covers!!!

Oh yes, Tuesday nite at the shower around nine o'clock the bell rang and I went down to answer it, - a man handed me two enormous vases of flowers and four corsages. I told the man he had the wrong house, but he said no!! I finally carried them up the house and each card was signed George. The corsages were for your mother and mine, Fran & me. It seems that Irv sent them and signed your name. How's that for a brother-in-law!! I tried to thank him for you but he said he didn't know what it was all about, - so don't you mention it to him, or maybe you should, - I don't know.

Also, while we're on our honeymoon, Irv is going to Chicago, he's leaving right after the wedding, and for the following weekend after the wedding he has a suite reserved in a Washington hotel. He doesn't know when he'll get there, it's reserved for Sat, Sunday, and Monday, and he said if we want to stay there for the weekend until he gets there, it's O.K. with him. If we have enough money to go to Washington, we'll go. O.K? O.K.

Darling, I must remember to tell you not to forget that you're going to wear your Garrison Cap at the wedding. I refuse to let you wear an overseas hat. Also, I understand of-course, that we'll have to use our wedding gifts for our honeymoon. And please don't feel badly about it, because it's the only thing we can do. We'll worry about money for our home when the war is over, - we'll manage somehow, I know.

Another thing about our wedding, dear. I'd love to have Rhoda Cutler and Evelyn Plotkin at the wedding, but it's quite impossible. The caterer refuses to cook for more than about 75 people and we've got more than that with just relatives. Anyway, Rhoda is away at school and I'll handle Evelyn Plotkin by inviting her to Fran's tea. I don't think you realize dear, that the reception is only for our relatives and very close friends, - certainly Rhoda isn't very close to us and neither does Evelyn mean very much to us outside of being Sid's wife. If Sid were here we'd naturally invite both of them and if Dave were here we'd invite Rhoda, but under the circumstances, I hardly think it's necessary. But I have invited Ann Yoselowitz – also Rose & Harry Lizabetsky are coming.

Darling, I didn't want to mention this to you before because I thought you'd feel bad about it, but now I guess it's O.K. It seems a few weeks ago, I noticed that all the wood in the cedar chest was cracking up as if someone had cut it with a knife. I felt terrible about it and didn't let it go unmentioned. I wrote a letter to the Raeder's telling them all about it and since I didn't receive any reply, I thought they just disregarded it. But today your mother called and said Ethel Raeder had called her and said that the factory was going to send me a new one. So now everything is O.K., and I'm happy. Or didn't you know that your future wife never likes to be cheated out of anything. I never care how much I pay for a thing if I like it, - but I also want to get my money's fair value. Dear, you'll never have to beat me to make me see things your way, - I'm always willing to have my mind changed if I think the other person is right. Of-course, when I think I'm right I'm pretty hard to sway, - but I think we'll manage very well without having to break those pretty dishes we just received.

Darling, your mother apologized to me for making the check only ten dollars. Apologies were hardly necessary, - I thought it was swell!! So please write and tell her that I thought her gift was lovely, because it most certainly was.

My goodness gracious, - I told you this letter was going to be long, but I never dreamed it would be this long. I swear I've got writer's cramp. And so now dear, I bid thee goodnite, and many, many pleasant dreams.

Always yours,
Lottie

December 15, 1944
Friday

From:	To:
Mr. Cpl. J.G. Barr 11057933	C.L. Sniderman
4503rd Base Unit Eng. Sq.	65 Houghton St.
Great Bend A.B.B., Kansas	Worcester, 4, Mass.

Dearest Lottie,

Just came back from Salina to Great Bend. An outfit moved out of here and I imagine that this field is short of radio men, so I guess we are elected to fill in the shortage. Since it's about two weeks before I get my furlough, I can keep close tabs on it.

The ride down was much better than the ride up, because this time we stopped twice in a few towns for a cup of coffee and a little rest.

I thought that I'd be able to write you last night at work, but unfortunately, I had to work. They ran us ragged until quitting time, then I went back after work to help one of the fellows locate his wallet that he lost. We were lucky, because we found it in the first ship that we looked thru.

Also, last night, to further inconvenience me, I got stuck in the mud with our truck. We tried to push it out, got mud all over ourselves, but still it wouldn't budge. Finally, we called up for a tractor and that did the job very neatly.

We were supposed to report to our officer this morning, but we didn't get up till 10:15, and by that time he sent over another fellow to tell us that we were going back to Great Bend. It seems that now, since there aren't so many men down here, we have breakfast at 8 o'clock in the morning, which means we can get an extra hour of sleep.

I imagine that K.P. will roll around mighty quick, now that we are back, Sunday I think will be the day. It won't be bad, because there aren't as many men to feed as there used to be.

Coming back to G.B. we passed the mail truck, so that I'll have to wait until to-morrow to see if I got any letters.

Darling, I miss you terribly and can hardly wait until I'm home. You've been in my mind constantly and I love you for it. It still seems hardly possible that we'll be man and wife soon. Do you think I'll turn out to be a wife beater?

Goodnight my darling,
Your, George

December 16, 1944
Saturday

From:	To:
Mr. Cpl. J.G. Barr 11057933	C.L. Sniderman
4503rd Base Unit Eng. Sq.	65 Houghton St.
Great Bend A.B.B., Kansas	Worcester, 4, Mass.

Dearest Lottie,

This morning I went and took my blood test. The report on it will take about a week. That business about forms is a lot of baloney to our medics here. I went in this morning and within fifteen minutes I was out again. They take the blood and send it down to the hospital where it is tested, then the report is sent to them and they make out a certificate for me. By the way, do you know who gets the certificates afterwards, City Hall, or does the rabbi have to see them before he can perform the ceremonies?

Darling, before I do anything about changing my allotments you'll have to say O.K. This is the way it will be – I have two allotments now, one for a war bond at $7.50 a month, and one for our bank account for $10.00 a month. I'll have to get rid of the bond allotment, it will be the best. That way it will leave me about $24.50 a month. The other way will give me $2.50 more, but the $7.50 will be in bonds, and if we needed a little money, they would have to be converted into cash. Your answer, please. How does it feel to be a wife, helping her husband plan?

Starting to-night, I work on the same shift that I worked when I was at Salina. I think I'll be the only one down there to-night, so there won't be much work done.

I'm off to see if the mail is in. Here's hoping!

Your, George

December 17, 1944
Sunday

From:	To:
Mr. Cpl. J.G. Barr 11057933	C.L. Sniderman
4503rd Base Unit Eng. Sq.	65 Houghton St.
Great Bend A.B.B., Kansas	Worcester, 4, Mass.

Dearest Lottie,

Except for Hotel St. George, the hotels that I wrote to are full for the 7th, as you'll be able to see, for I've sent you their replies. I'm still waiting for an answer from the Lexington, which should be here by to-morrow, then I'll wire. I never imagined that so many people stay at hotels.

Last night I received a letter from you that must have walked here!! You wrote it the 7th and I didn't get it 'til the 16th. It's a wonder that the Worcy police got there in time to stop the attempted robbery, usually thieves can walk away with the entire place before our police know about it. It's a good thing that you didn't go down, because the robbers would probably have come back and taken you, you are of priceless material!

Toby wrote me about one of my cousins coming into the store and leaving you a present, and Toby wrote me that she also got something for you. Where are you putting everything? Guess we'll have to get another chest or something.

So -- I didn't have a chance, huh?! You never let go until you get what you want! Was I a hard guy to get, I didn't want to give up easily. Things that are hard to get - once attained, are much more appreciated!

I'm very glad that I'm what I am, in the army, because otherwise I'd stand a good chance of being in the infantry. I think that almost one third of the air corps are being transferred into the infantry. Those that are supposed to be air corps technicians are exempted. I'm glad that I enlisted, otherwise, who knows where I'd be.

I was right about last night, I didn't lift a screw or anything, and I imagine it will be the same to-night. Oh hum, the hard working soldier! I wonder how I'm going to stand up under work when this is all over with. You'll have to throw me out of bed every morning, so that I'll at least get there on time. Do you still want me? Are you sure you know what you are doing? Oh, you poor kid, you'll have to spend the rest of your life with me, and am I going to love it, because darling, I love you.

Your, George

P.S. I don't know why we need an orchestra – we could sing for them!!! No! O.K. J.G.B.

We are sorry . . .
Your request for a reservation comes on a day when we find our hotel booked to capacity because of the many reservations we accepted before yours was received.

The demand for rooms is very heavy which places us in the most unwelcome position of not being able to accommodate all of our patrons. This is a source of keen disappointment to us, but the circumstances are beyond our control.

We regret that we cannot make a reservation for you on this particular trip but we hope that you will give us an opportunity to serve you on future visits.

Very truly yours,

J A Froise

OFFICE MANAGER

HOTEL PENNSYLVANIA, NEW YORK

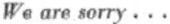

FIFTY CENTRAL PARK SOUTH **ST. MORITZ** ON-THE-PARK NEW YORK

Dear Cpl. Barr;   12/11/XX

We regret that we are unable to accept your reservation as we are already overbooked for that date.

S. GREGORY TAYLOR
President

The
BILTMORE
DAVID B. MULLIGAN, PRESIDENT

MADISON AVENUE AT 43RD STREET

New York City

TELEPHONE - MURRAY HILL 6-7920

ADJOINING GRAND CENTRAL

December 11th, 1944

Cpl. James G. Barr
4503rd B. U. Eng. Sq.
Great Bend, AAB
Kansas

Dear Cpl. Barr:

We are sorry to advise you that we will be unable
to accept your reservation for a week or two commenc-
ing January 7th as we are booked to capacity.

Thanking you for writing us, and hoping that we may
have the pleasure of serving you at another time, we
are

Cordially yours,
THE BILTMORE

C. M. FLUGHAM
Office Manager

FD

"MAKE NEW YORK YOUR VACATION CITY AND THE BILTMORE YOUR HOTEL"

HOTEL TAFT

Times Square's Largest Hotel, 2,000 rooms with bath from $2.50. New "Direct Reception" radio, servidor, circulating ice water, in each room.

ADJACENT TO

Radio City, 100 theatres, retail and wholesale districts.

Grand Central and Pennsylvania R. R. Stations 5 minutes by taxi.

B. & O Motor Coach connection at door. I. R. T., B. M. T., 6th Ave. and 8th Ave. Subway stations, Capitol Bus Terminal, just around the corner.

WE ARE VERY SORRY . . . .
but we have no rooms for the
period you specify.

   Please be assured of our
desire to serve you whenever
possible.

Alfred L. Lewis

MANAGER

POST CARD

PLACE
1c
STAMP
HERE

Cpl. James G. Barr,
11057933,
4503rd B.U. Eng. Sq.,
Great Bend, AAB, Kansas.

WICKERSHAM 2-4400   CABLE ADDRESS "LEXTEL"

HOTEL LEXINGTON.

LEXINGTON AVENUE AT FORTY-EIGHTH STREET

NEW YORK 17, N.Y.

CHARLES E. ROCHESTER
VICE PRESIDENT AND
MANAGING DIRECTOR

December 14, 1944.

Cpl. James G. Barr, 11058933
4503rd B. U. Eng. Sq.,
Great Bend, A.A.B., Kan.

Dear Cpl. Barr:

In reply to your letter of December 7th, we
note that you anticipate spending a week or
two in New York City sometime in the future,
accompanied by your wife, and we would be
pleased to provide a nice suite for you,
consisting of a parlor, bedroom and bath, at
the rate of $15.00 per day.

Thanking you for your valued inquiry and
trusting that we will have the pleasure of
reserving accommodations for you, we are

Very truly yours,
Hotel Lexington

G. W. Miller
Resident Manager

GWM:a

December 17, 1944
Sunday

From:	To:
C.L. Sniderman	Mr. Cpl. J.G. Barr 11057933
65 Houghton St.	Eng. Sq., 4503rd A.A.F. Base Unit
Worcester 4, Mass.	Great Bend A.B.B., Kansas

My dearest George,

Again, I've neglected you for two days, - but not of my own choosing, - more because of necessity. You know the old saying – "the spirit is willing, but the flesh is weak."

So now let me start with my doings as of Friday. Friday afternoon I had a very unexpected luncheon with a one Mr. Louis Burack, who happens to be one of our salesmen. I was walking downtown with him and he asked me to join him for lunch at the Bancroft, - so I did. He is really quite the gentleman, - the only trouble was that he looked like me grandfather. When I got back and told the kids at the office they nearly collapsed because he very rarely pays any attention to anyone, - but ever since I've been working there he's been exceptionally nice to me.

Friday nite Mrs. Coppersmith came over and brought us a lovely gift. It's a small wooden fruit or nut dish with two candle holders to match. 'Twas tres sweet of her.

Saturday afternoon went shopping with me mater and as we were coming home we bumped into Sir Jack Waxler. He cordially invited me to see a play with him at Clark that nite and after pondering the situation, I decided it was a very nice idea. So, I went. But a very, very funny thing happened. As we were going into Clark, I met many girls that I knew and since the announcement of our marriage was in Saturday's Civic Leader (I am enclosing it, incidentally), they all came over to wish us well. They all paid their respects and then very dumbfoundedly looked at Jack. I don't know what they thought, but they all looked very silly with their mouths open. After the play, which was very cute, we went to some Italian place for pizza and beer. The combination left me quite sick!!

Jack is a good kid and we had a long gab session about him and his women and they both seem to worry him. Poor Jack says with all his friends getting married he feels quite lost. Oh, well, - nothing I can do for him on that score. By the by, I hope you don't mind or feel angry about Jack taking me out. It's really the most harmless thing I can think of. Today being Sunday I did nothing but relax and boy did it feel good. After I finish this letter I shall bathe and retire for the P.M.

I received your record, but I'm madder than hell because our Vic has become temperamental and refuses to play. I'll have to get hold of someone with a phonograph.

Tomorrow eve is Edie's tea and the kids are all hepped up, - of-course, I'm not at all, - oh no!!! Darling, do you realize that three weeks from today at this hour, everything will be all over and we'll be Mr. & Mrs. - Aintcha excited?!!!

Darling, the idea 'bout the champagne is super swellegant. But we're not going to open it at the wedding. We'll take it with us and then guzzle when we're alone. Won't it be fun to sip champagne on our honeymoon? Sol is a darling and I love him — like a brother!! Polly is home on her Christmas vacation, but will miss the wedding by one week. I thought surely, she'd be able to make it.

Tuesday nite we're having a Christmas party from the office at the Englebrekt Club. It's going to be a real Swedish meal. Last year you came at the tail end of the party and then we went to Boston. This year your furlough is going to be much more important to us both.

Well, me darling, this concludes another weary note of dribble. Will write you tomorrow nite and tell you all about the party.

All my love always, Lottie

BARR — SNIDERMAN

The marriage of Miss Charlotte Sniderman, daughter of Mr. and Mrs. Max Sniderman, 65 Houghton Street, to Cpl. George Barr, son of Mr. and Mrs. Jacob W. Barr, 7 Hartshorn Avenue, will take place Jan. 7 at Beth Israel Synagogue.

Rabbi Sidney S. Guthman will perform the ceremony which will be followed by a dinner-reception at the synagogue.

The bride will be gowned in white slipper satin en train with a fingertip length veil of white tulle falling from a coronet of simulated pearls. She will carry a Bible with an orchid marker and sweet pea streamers.

Miss Charlotte Namath will be maid of honor, and Mrs. Philip Siegel, matron of honor. Sol Barr of Newark, N. J., will be his brother's best man.

Following a wedding trip to New York, the bride will make her home with her parents while her husband is in service. He is a member of the Army Air Force, stationed at Great Bend Army Air Base, Kans.

Both the bride-elect and Cpl. Barr are graduates of the High School of Commerce. He was formerly active in the local A. Z. A. She is a member of Junior Hadassah and is employed by the New England Grocer Supply Co.

December 18, 1944
Monday

From:	To:
Mr. Cpl. J.G. Barr 11057933	C.L. Sniderman
4503rd Base Unit Eng. Sq.	65 Houghton St.
Great Bend A.B.B., Kansas	Worcester, 4, Mass.

*Dec 18th
monday*

Dearest Lottie,

I forgot my pen back at camp, and I'm somewhat unfamiliar in handling one of these fat U.S.O. pens, so you'll have to forgive me on my writing.

Darling, Evelyn Plotkin must come. I promised Evelyn and Sid that they'd be invited to the wedding. I pulled a boner at our engagement and I don't want it to happen again. And Rhoda, well, I'd want her at the wedding because of Dave, and I also told him that she'd be invited. Please see what you can do, because I don't want to make any disappointed friends.

This morning I received your wonderful long letter. Your brother would do something nice like that, I think he's swell. If we can make Washington we will, and I don't see why we wouldn't be able to.

Even before you mentioned it, I had planned on wearing my Garrison Cap, it's now in the cleaners for blacking and cleaning.

Last night I helped repair one of the fellows (damn this pen!) radios. He belongs in our hut, but he lives off the post with his wife. Because I wouldn't take army money for fixing it, he's invited me and the other fellow to his house for supper some night. I have another set that has to be fixed also, I'll have to see what can be done with that. By the way, the way I fix radios is to let my sergeant fix them while I watch!!!

In a few more days, I think I'll be going on the day shift. Our outfit has been given authority to be a parent training unit. Its job is to train outfits that are scheduled for overseas shipment. We've been a training unit ever since our beginning, but our authority has just been given to us. Now all they have to do is have someone teach me so I can teach them. – Why don't they just send me home until this war is over with?

The party that the girls threw sounded wonderful, wish I could have been with you. I would have loved to have danced those numbers with you.

Here it is my day off and I don't have any idea what to do. I was going to go to the movies, but I think I've seen them all. I'd better check up on them tho, because I wouldn't want to miss any of Roy Rogers' pictures with his horse Trigger! Wahooo!!!!

Off I go hunting for a stamp, I forgot those also when I left camp. I hope I don't forget to show up at the wedding. What an awful thought!!

Your, George

P.S. Please don't forget about Evelyn and Rhoda. J.G.B.

P.P.S. I've already wired for our reservation at the Lexington. J.G.B.

December 19, 1944
Tuesday

From:	To:
C.L. Sniderman	Mr. Cpl. J.G. Barr 11057933
65 Houghton St.	Eng. Sq., 4503rd A.A.F. Base Unit
Worcester 4, Mass.	Great Bend A.B.B., Kansas

Hi honey!

I know I promised to write you last nite and tell you all about Edie's party, - but I didn't get home until about 2 A.M. – so I knew you wouldn't mind if you had to wait until my lunch hour. I'm up in the conference room now with Zelda, Dot Potash & Mimi Sigel and amidst all the distracting variations of noise, I shall endeavor to write. How I'm managing to hold a pen in my hand is quite a miracle. I'm sitting with my legs under me, - my hair falling over my eyes, a cig in one hand and pen in another. Oh my, - such troubles!!

Well, anywho, Edie's party was positively lovely. There were about 18 girls. We played bridge for awhile, then I opened my gifts, which incidentally, were lovely and then had a late supper. For supper, we had hot rolls stuffed with tuna, tea or coffee, all kinds of crackers with jams & cheese, and for dessert we had chocolate cake with ice cream and hot fudge. Doesn't that sound scrumptious? I promised to do the same for Edie when her time comes, providing I don't have fifteen squalling brats all over the house.

The practical jokers at the party wrapped up some very lovely gifts (ahem), which they thought would be very practical under the circumstances, - I shall not innumerate, but I'm sure with an ounce of imagination you can guess. We really had a lot of fun. After the party, Edie Gordon drove some of us home and it was so slippery that the car skidded and almost landed us into a lamp post. Darling, if this missive happens to be a bit sticky – take no offense, - I just dropped it on a piece of unfinished apple pie.

Tonight, I'm on the go again, - the Christmas party. Jesus, I'll be glad when all the parties are over and I can get some rest, - but don't get me wrong, - I love it. George, do you mind if on our honeymoon, I sleep for $\frac{3}{4}$ of the time? I finish work this Saturday, which will give me one week before you come to finish up some odds and ends.

Well, m'love, the clock strikes 2:30, and back to work I must go. This last week of working is like agony. I can't even begin to concentrate on what I'm supposed to be doing. We're having quite a snow storm outside, - more like a little blizzard. Remember last year you were so mad because it didn't snow once while you were here? Wonder if we'll have that kind of luck this year. And so now goodbye darling, - wish you were here so I could hit you with a snow ball.

All my love always,
Lottie

P.S. Will write again tonight to make up for this letter – this is just an extra dividend.

December 19, 1944
Tuesday

From:	To:
Mr. Cpl. J.G. Barr 11057933	C.L. Sniderman
4503rd Base Unit Eng. Sq.	65 Houghton St.
Great Bend A.B.B., Kansas	Worcester, 4, Mass.

Dearest Lottie,

After leaving you yesterday afternoon, I took a stroll around town and met that fellow who lives in our hut who invited me up for supper. He was shopping for a Christmas present for his wife and asked if I cared to join him. I went along gladly, for I was just killing time anyhow. We first shopped for a bedspread, altho I didn't see why he wanted to get her a bedspread, just because she said that they needed one. After going thru store after store (a total of three stores, it's a big town), he settled for a slack suit.

When I told him I thought I'd go catch a bite and then maybe take in a movie, he asked me to go home with him. His wife works at a grocery store in Great Bend, so she didn't come to the apartment until an hour later.

As apartments go its considered pretty good for this town. It has just two small rooms, bedroom and kitchen and the kitchen isn't even separated by a door. They have a small range and ice box, and all this cost them ten dollars a week. Boy, do the people take advantage of the G.I.'s here, altho I guess it's a shame all over.

Because she didn't expect me for supper, she said I'll have to return again, this time for steak. We had chili last night, I eat the stuff, but I don't particularly care for it.

I'm glad that the cedar chest incident has turned out. I received a letter from Mackie and he told me that he went down to see you. The letter that you told me about it, came after your manuscript. Darling, you're marvelous.

Also, I received the Civic Leader and I read our write up. I noticed that it was the longest write up in the column. Who do you know at the Leader?! The description given in the paper of what you'll wear sounds wonderful, you're going to look beautiful. Whether with a bridal gown or not, you look beautiful.

Starting to-night, the entire outfit is going on the graveyard shift. I don't know how long it is going to last, but the C.O. is going to try and see if we can work the shift till Christmas and then change to days afterwards.

Bye Bye now.
Your, George

December 20, 1944
Wednesday

From:	To:
Mr. Cpl. J.G. Barr 11057933	C.L. Sniderman
4503rd Base Unit Eng. Sq.	65 Houghton St.
Great Bend A.B.B., Kansas	Worcester, 4, Mass.

Dearest Lottie,
Last night when we came to work we were almost floored by what we had in store for us. All the radios on the field, of a certain model, had to be modified for a new change. We didn't have a chance to rest, and to-night will no doubt, be the same. One of the fellows hooked up a wire in the wrong place and had to do his work over again. We thought the place was on fire when we saw smoke coming out of his set.

To-night at the base theater our outfit is putting on a comedy relating to "An Overseas Hero Stationed at Great Bend." It's supposed to be a pretty good show, so naturally, I'm going to trot down and see it later this evening.

I've sent you a few pictures that were taken in our mess hall this Thanksgiving. The women are the men's wives and girl friends. The captain is pictured with his mother, he isn't married, the poor fellow!!

I asked the Lexington to wire me if our reservations had been accepted, and this afternoon, while I was peacefully slumbering, I was awakened and a telegram thrust into my hands. Everything is set now, now all there is left for me to do is be there!

I built the fire a little while ago and this place is roasting. We can't cool it off by opening the shutters, because they have been nailed down.

Just think, in two weeks I'll be home again with you in my arms. What a paradise that's going to be. I haven't taken my mind off of that wonderful moment for months, darling. I love you very dearly, or did you have a little suspicion of that fact.

At the P.X. here, it is getting to be pretty difficult to obtain the brand of cigarettes that I smoke, and not only that, they've raised the price by one cent! Isn't that a shame? Thinking that we might run into a little trouble getting smokes, I wrote my dad to get me two cartons of Philips and one carton of Chesters. If you don't think that one carton is enough for you, you'd better ask him to get you another carton. How is the cigarette situation back home?

I received a letter from Toby reminding me of my promise to take her out when I come home, so we'll have to try and make it. O.K.?

Good night, sweetheart,
Your, George

[Editor's note: Below, and on the following pages is the Lexington Hotel reservation acceptance telegram, and the Thanksgiving photos referenced in George's letter]

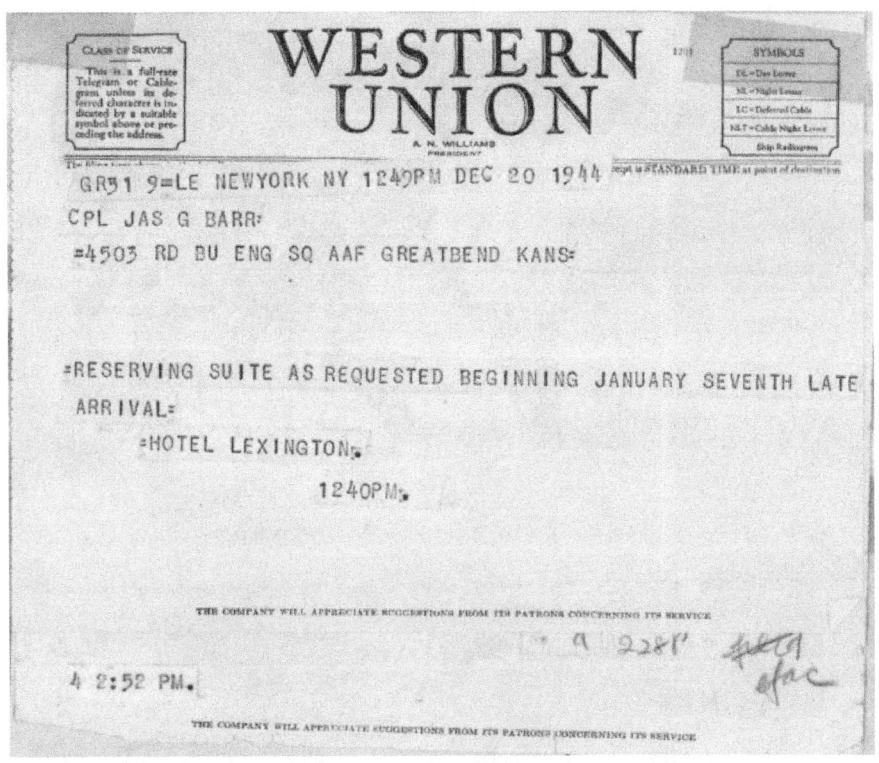

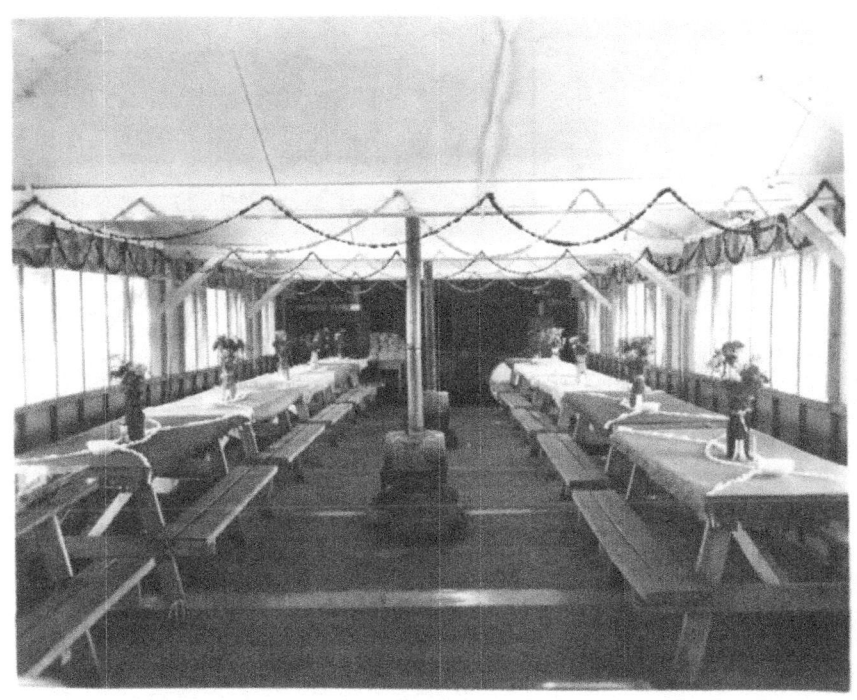

December 20, 1944
Wednesday

From:	To:
C.L. Sniderman	Mr. Cpl. J.G. Barr 11057933
65 Houghton St.	Eng. Sq., 4503rd A.A.F. Base Unit
Worcester 4, Mass.	Great Bend A.B.B., Kansas

My dearest George,

At this writing yours truly is quite a frozen young lady. It must be 50° below outside. We just can't get the house heated tonite.

Last nite was the Christmas party, - and what a party it was. Everyone was stinko, - even me. I'm what they call a sociable drinker and there were some I just couldn't refuse, especially when they drank to our coming marriage. I think I had about ten offers to go out last nite after the party, and I told each one I'd be delighted to go, - the fun came when I put my coat on and they all stood around waiting for me. I finally managed to duck out with a guy who promised to take me straight home, - and he did. Also, I think he was the only one who was not entirely drunk, - by the by, his name is George, - but bears no resemblance whatever to the George I intend marrying.

We received more of a gift this year from the Sharfman's than we did last year, - this year I received $17.34, - last year it was $8.96. The small change really gets me!! Also, we got a box of dried fruit candy from our accountant and a box of chocolate from the Sharfman's. Charlotte gave me a beautiful wallet, Edith Richards gave me two lovely towels, another girl gave me a box of stationery and still another a box of perfumed soap. All in all, I'd say I had a very successful Christmas. When I came in and saw all the gifts on my desk, I nearly fell over. Unexpected, to say the least. Already Charlotte says she dislikes the girl who is going to take my place, - the poor girl hasn't even been hired yet and already she's handicapped. Some fun.

Got no mail from you today, which sort of spoiled my day. Guess the Christmas rush is going to cramp my style as far as the mail situation is concerned. Darling, I miss you terribly, - more now than ever, - it seems that these $2 \frac{1}{2}$ weeks will never pass. Incidentally, have you written for reservations at a hotel?

Of all the awful things to happen, some how or other, I caught a delightful cold. It's really maddening and I'm going to try and get rid of it pretty damn quick. It's such a funny feeling to have to take such good care of myself, - I'm not used to it.

Every damn radio program specializes in Xmas carols, - if I weren't such a devote Catholic, I might get sick of them. Ho-hum!

Felt in a very silly mood all day today and all the kids kept saying "Poor George, - he doesn't know what he's letting himself in for." Me oh my, - nobody loves me!

Goodnight J.G.
Always yours,
Lottie

December 21, 1944
Thursday

From:	To:
Mr. Cpl. J.G. Barr 11057933	C.L. Sniderman
4503rd Base Unit Eng. Sq.	65 Houghton St.
Great Bend A.B.B., Kansas	Worcester, 4, Mass.

Dearest Lottie,

I'm a dopey little boy this evening. At 10 o'clock this morning I went to bed and got up at 5 to eat. After having my meal, which one it is, I don't know, I went back to sleep. It's now nine thirty and I feel like going back to sleep, whatta life!

Heck, why should I feel angry about Jack taking you out? Don't you know that I'm happy if you can go out and have a little fun? We had this out before, don't worry about it.

The show that the 4503rd put on last night was really good. They rewrote words to popular tunes, which were a hit in themselves. The latrine song was the favorite of them all.

Last night it started snowing so hard that we thought sure we'd have a blizzard. About an hour later our fears vanished, as the snow did likewise. If it had kept up, I would have had to get a pair of snow shoes to get around camp.

If these last twelve days don't hurry up and fly by, I'm going to be a gray headed soldier. I've spent some slow time, but never anything like this. How foolish I was when I was a child, when I said I'd never get married!! Now I can hardly wait until I'm joined with you in the holy bonds of matrimony. Do you know why I can hardly wait? - It's because, darling, I love you so very much.

Sweet dreams, darling,
Your, George

"B L A C K O U T S O F '4 5 (03RD) "

- The Adventures of an Overseas Hero in Great Bend -
(Written and directed by Sgt. Henry Piffl)

Scene I
"GOOD-BYE TO JERKVILLE"

The Mayor .... Pfc. Carl Heim   Joe Sharp .... S/Sgt. Edward Smith
Little Girl .... Miss Reina Silverman

Scene II
"RECEPTION IN GREAT BEND"

First M.P. .... T/Sgt. George Bogantz   Lt. JAFFE .... Pvt. Alan Stratton
Second M.P. .... Pfc. Germe Trombetta   Strange G.I. .... S/Sgt. Johnny Crouch
Joe Sharp .... S/Sgt. Edward Smith

Scene III
"WITH THE NUTS IN OUR HUTS"

C.Q. .... Sgt. Henry Piffl   G.I Dream .... Pfc. Carl Heim
Joe Sharp .... S/Sgt. Edward Smith

Scene IV
"WHAT A MESS"

K.P. Pusher .... Pfc. Germe Trombetta   M.P. .... S/Sgt. Edward Smith
Mess Dictator .... Pfc. Carl Heim   K.P. .... Pvt. Alan Stratton
Secretary ...... S/Sgt. Johnny Crouch   C.Q. .... T/Sgt. George Bogantz

Scene V
"JOE'S UNFULFILLED DESIRES'

Joe Sharp .... S/Sgt. Edward Smith   Latrine Trio .... S/Sgt. Edward Smith,
Latrine Orderly .. Pvt. Alan Stratton   Pfc. Carl Heim and Sgt. Henry Piffl

Scene VI
"WHAT PRICE COKE?"

P.X. Girl ...... S/Sgt. Johnny Crouch   Joe Sharp .... S/Sgt. Edward Smith

Scene VII
"NO INFORMATION PLEASE"

The Guard ..... T/Sgt. George Bogantz   The Spy .... Sgt. Henry Piffl
Joe Sharp .... S/Sgt. Edward Smith

Scene VIII
"YOUR CPD IS RATIONED TOO"

The Topkick .... Pfc. Carl Heim   Gabriel Hecter...T/Sgt. George Bogantz
The Bottomkick ... Pvt. Alan Stratton   The Editor of The Great Bender ,......
Drew Pearson ...... Sgt. Henry Piffl   .... Pfc. William Duggan

Scene IX
"EXIT FROM GREAT BEND"

First M.P. .... T/Sgt. George Bogantz   The Topkick ....Pfc. Carl Heim
Second M.P. .... Pfc. Germe Trombetta   The Corpse .... S/Sgt. Edward Smith

- - * - -

Piano Solos & Accompaniments by Cpl. A. B. del Moral. Lt. BETHEA played by
Pfc. Wm Duggan. Stage Settings by Cpl. Irving Leckovitz & constructed by 4503rd
Utilities Sect. Costume Creations by Q.M.Corps. Produced thru the cooperation
of Lt.Col. JAMES H. CLARK, CO - Lt.Col. CHARLES H. ADAMS, Executive Officer -
1st Lt. HENRY N. MORRISON, Special Service Officer.

December 21, 1944
Thursday

From:	To:
C.L. Sniderman	Mr. Cpl. J.G. Barr 11057933
65 Houghton St.	Eng. Sq., 4503rd A.A.F. Base Unit
Worcester 4, Mass.	Great Bend A.B.B., Kansas

My dearest George,

Another day is passing bringing us closer together. In this sub-zero weather I sure need you to keep me warm. Today I started to take home some of my personal belongings from the office. I still can't believe that Saturday I work there for the last time.

Despite all the petty squabbles and arguments, I loved working there, - and if the kids weren't so damn nice to me, it would make leaving much easier. Even today, Dave asked me if my mind was definitely made up. Charlotte insists that when I come back he'll give me back my job. Altho I'd love to believe it, I know he never will. With him it's more a matter of principle now. Oh well!!! Anyhow, if things go well, I'd like to come down and spend some time with you in the spring.

I'm glad you already have our reservations at the Lex. I hope you made sure that it had a private bathroom. Also, I hope they hold the reservation until we get there, which might be quite late.

Thank heavens you weren't put into the Infantry. Outside of it being a lousy branch of the service, - they also are the first to go across. So far, darling, you've been very fortunate, - now all we have to do is pray it keeps up. I can see now that it was a good thing you enlisted. Sometimes it's so hard to see what's good and what's not good.

Come hell or high water, I'm going to take my blood test next week. I've been putting it off only because I couldn't find a doctor. This town is completely devoid of doctors.

I went down to the bank today and made a small deposit, - they also added on the $10.00 that you sent. I'm afraid darling, that when you come home we'll have to draw on our account. I'd like to leave a little something in there, but we'll discuss it further when you come home.

My dad isn't feeling good at all these days. We had the doctor tonight and he gave him another kind of pills. I wish I didn't know what they are – but I'm afraid I know only too well. From now on my mother and I will be on pins and needles until the wedding is over. In all ways, it seems these two weeks will never pass.

Bought some more thank you paper today, and again I shall start the tedious task of giving our appreciation. Seems to me you're getting away oofly easy!!

Goodnight dear, Lovingly, Lottie

December 22, 1944
Friday

From:	To:
Mr. Cpl. J.G. Barr 11057933	C.L. Sniderman
4503rd Base Unit Eng. Sq.	65 Houghton St.
Great Bend A.B.B., Kansas	Worcester, 4, Mass.

Dearest Lottie,

To-night is my night off, so I told one of the fellows who works days to wake me at noon. Four-thirty this afternoon I got up and wondered what had happened to him. A few minutes later he came in, and when I questioned him about not waking me up, he said I was crazy, because he had tried to about six times, only for me to tell him, "Get the hell away!" I don't have the slightest remembrance of any such thing. If he had wakened me, I would have had just two hours of sleep, but I thought that it would have been enough. I'll get up early to-morrow morning and do the things that I have to do.

First I have to see if my test is ready, then do down after a shoe ration stamp, and then trot off into town to get my hat.

Would have wanted me at Edie's tea, just as you wanted me at the other parties? What about the gift from the practical jokers? I bet you wouldn't have had to use any rouge for a few days afterwards!! I'm glad that you had a nice time anyway.

To-night I'm going to a dance at the gym, and practice upon my dancing, and of course, to say goodbye to all my girl friends. Aren't I a cad!!

Last night I kept busy, just with G.I. work, and then with a set that someone else wanted me to look at. I guess they ask me to look at it, because the other fellows charge to fix them. Hell, I'm only too glad to get a little practice. The only trouble is that I haven't any parts to replace for the bad ones. I get a lot of help from my sergeants, otherwise, I'd really be working on them for days at a time. I'm learning tho.

There's one consolation about working the graveyard shift, and that is when I wake up, I look beneath my pillow and get my mail. Isn't that wonderful service? I read your letter and then I can count one more day off the list. Two weeks from this Sunday and we'll be taking each other for better or better. We're going to make a wonderful team, don't you think so? I definitely do!

Your, George

December 23, 1944
Saturday

From:	To:
Mr. Cpl. J.G. Barr 11057933	C.L. Sniderman
4503rd Base Unit Eng. Sq.	65 Houghton St.
Great Bend A.B.B., Kansas	Worcester, 4, Mass.

Dearest Lottie,

Here I should be taking a little cat nap before I go to work, but no, I'm writing to you instead, and only because I love you. I wouldn't do it for anyone else.

This morning I got up early, turned my laundry in, and then went to get the report on my blood test. They didn't have the report, but they filled in the necessary papers already. Now there is nothing else for me to do except wait for my furlough, which I'm finding out to be a very long wait, I never realized how long a day was.

Oh yeah, also picked up my nice clean hat from in town. I never should have gone to town just for the hat, it was too cold! By the time I came back to camp, it was time to eat. After supper, we went to see "Ministry of Fear." The author is a stinker!!! At the start of the picture, I figured out the spy, in the middle, I changed my mind about him, and then at the end – the man who I thought would be the spy, at the beginning, but changed my mind in the middle, proved to be the snake in the apartment; excuse me, grass! I can't figger that last sentence out either, I just write the stuff.

Our Uncle Barney and Aunt Jennie from Wash. wrote and said that they are very sorry that they won't be able to attend our wedding, but wish us the best luck in the world. Barney has a back injury, which doesn't enable him to travel, especially during the cold season. When we are in Wash. we can drop in to see them also.

When I went to mail call, I said to myself, I said, "There'll be a nice letter from Lottie to-day," but did I get a letter from my darling wife to be very soon, no! I think that I'll have you write me a letter every day while on our honeymoon. When I go down to get the evening paper, you'll set out my slippers and pipe beside the fireplace and then you'll write me a letter. Then when I come back you'll have mail call for me. – Won't I ever think of any good ideas!!! (To your way of thinking).

With this lovely thought as a reminder, I love you, I bid you good night.

Your, George

December 25, 1944
Monday

From:	To:
C.L. Sniderman	Mr. Cpl. J.G. Barr 11057933
65 Houghton St.	Eng. Sq., 4503rd A.A.F. Base Unit
Worcester 4, Mass.	Great Bend A.B.B., Kansas

Hi darling, -

And a merry Christmas to ya! I spent a delightful Christmas day in the house. It was very nasty all day, - snow and rain and slippery as hell. We had a little company in the afternoon, which made the time go a little faster. After they left, I immediately started to write thank you notes, - a procedure, which I've sadly neglected. I wrote twenty-five and called it a day, - I still have about thirty more to go.

Since Saturday, I feel like a man without a country, - it was really sad saying goodbye to everyone in the office. Dave kissed me goodbye, as did Saul Sharfman, and most of the girls. I promised them we'd come in when you got home.

In the afternoon, I felt in kind of low spirits, so Zelda persuaded me to go to the movies with her. My mind was so restless that I didn't enjoy the picture very much, I think the name of it was "Something For The Boys."

I'm taking my blood test Wednesday, darling, and when you get your certificate, mail it to me and I'll get our license.

I'm glad you like the description of what I'm going to wear. I'll sound nice, - even if I don't look it. Oh well, you knew what you were getting into!!!

Darling, I've been thinking about your allotments, and which one it would be best to get rid of, and this is the conclusion I've come to. To my way of thinking, I think it best that you continue buying the bonds and cancel the ten that goes to the bank. The bond money will come in very handy when it's due, and besides that, it's the patriotic thing to do. Furthermore, it'll leave you a couple of extra dollars. So darling, - buy bonds.

And now dear, for the not so good part. This is something I've put off telling you, hoping that I wouldn't have to, - but now I see that I must. George, when I spoke to your folks about our wedding they were swell about it, as I told you. I made out the list for some 75 odd people. As you know we planned to have the reception downstairs in the Beth Israel, - well the general opinion seems to be that my dad could never stand up with all that crowd and so much excitement, so I think maybe the reception plans will have to be changed. I'm not sure about it, - as a matter of fact, I'm not sure about anything anymore, - all I know is that I'm getting married. I'm glad people only get married once!!

Well, dear, guess that's about all for now. Will write you more tomorrow. Now that I'm not working, I'll make it my business to write you every day as I used to. Please forgive me if I've been neglecting you.

Always yours,
Lottie

December 25, 1944
Monday

From:	To:
Mr. Cpl. J.G. Barr 11057933	C.L. Sniderman
4503rd Base Unit Eng. Sq.	65 Houghton St.
Great Bend A.B.B., Kansas	Worcester, 4, Mass.

Dearest Lottie,

Last night I started writing to you, but because unforeseen circumstances arose, I was unable to go any further than the first paragraph. You'll have to forgive the boys, it was Christmas Eve and they were feeling very merry. By the way, they all wish us happiness on our forthcoming marriage. We broke open the bottle on a toast to that.

Our area didn't get any sleep until early this morning, everyone tried to pass off as Santa, but some how or other they didn't succeed, even tho their noses were quite red! At one o'clock this morning they came in and woke everyone and asked them if they wanted to go up in a B-29 that was just taking off. Of course, we all agreed, just so that they'd leave. They left, but not before they opened up all the shutters - trying to freeze us to death.

A bit later, they came in, but this time I caught them unawares, I grabbed my pillow and let them have it right in the face. One of them wasn't as drunk as I thought, because he picked it up and let me have it. This time they woke every one up for K.P., if it wasn't for one thing, they get you up for another.

For our Christmas dinner, we had the works, and very nice too. The difference from the Thanksgiving meal at Salina to what we had here was like day and night. The cooks really outdid themselves.

Whenever the fellows bring their wives with them at some affair, such as our Christmas dinner, I miss you very much. It makes me jealous to see those fortunate guys with their loved ones beside them. If I had you beside me, then they'd be jealous of me, because of my beautiful wife.

I can hardly wait until this week passes by. I'm nervous as a cat, can't eat, can't sleep, all I can do is think of you and that's good.

> *Merry Christmas my darling,*
> *Your, George*

> December 26, 1944
> Tuesday
> One more week!

From:	To:
Mr. Cpl. J.G. Barr 11057933	C.L. Sniderman
4503rd Base Unit Eng. Sq.	65 Houghton St.
Great Bend A.B.B., Kansas	Worcester, 4, Mass.

Dearest Lottie,

Here I am sucking on some delicious chocolates, aren't you jealous? If you are, why I'll buy you a box of Fanny Farmers if you like.

I got a check from my dad of fifty bucks, so that I can come home. I had written him that I'd need the money, and he came thru with flying colors, as he always does.

Again, I checked up on my furlough, and the furlough clerk said he didn't want to see me again until after I get back. Now all I have to do is go to the orderly room next week, pick up the furlough papers, and I'm off. I can hardly wait until next Monday, I'm certainly going to start the New Year off right.

Did I forget to mention that I put in a day of K.P. to-day – how did that happen, must be getting forgetful for some little reason or other.

Don't worry about your job, you'll be getting fifty dollars a month – mmm, just like me when I was a buck private. You must be marrying me for my money, having nothing else!

You can quit writing to me for awhile now. If you did write, I don't think I'd be here to receive them. Oh well, you'll be able to tell me all about it when I get home, which should be about 1:59 P.M. Wednesday afternoon on the Knickerbocker.

I can't think of a thing to write, my mind is on my furlough, you, and our future happiness. So, before I break it up, I'll say good night until to-morrow.

> *Your, George*

December 27, 1944
Wednesday

From:	To:
C.L. Sniderman	Mr. Cpl. J.G. Barr 11057933
65 Houghton St.	Eng. Sq., 4503rd A.A.F. Base Unit
Worcester 4, Mass.	Great Bend A.B.B., Kansas

My dearest George,

I have a vague feeling this is going to be another manuscript, - that is if my head can remember all the things that are on my mind. I think in yesterday's letter I laid the groundwork to prepare you for a change in the wedding plans. Well, what yesterday was just a plan, - today became a reality. The main point being, of course, that my dad is very sick and it would be an impossibility to take him to the Beth Israel. So my darling, disappointing as it may be, - and come hell or high water the plans will not be changed, - unless, of course, something unforeseen happens. The wedding will be at 1:00 o'clock at my house, - the reception will be also at my house and should start between 2 and 2:30. I will wear white as originally planned because, altho to me it seems impractical, my dad won't hear of me wearing anything else. A train leaves for New York at 5:10 and we'll be on it, - or at least I hope we will!! We've planned a very nice reception in the house and I'm sure it will turn out O.K. So, that my darling, is how we'll be married. Nothing like we wanted or planned, I know, - I'm sick with aggravation about the whole thing. If only you were home and it was all over with, I think I could just sit back and breathe easy for anything else. I'm only hoping that you won't be too disappointed, - because after all, the main idea is that we'll be married, - and that's all that really counts. Nuff said 'bout dat!!

I took my blood test today and was all prepared to have a minor operation. The whole thing took about a second, - I didn't even feel it. I went up to file our marriage intentions yesterday and it was really funny, - "Raise your right hand please, - Do you solemnly swear etc., etc., etc., etc............ -- - two dollars please!!! I just couldn't help it, - I started to laugh. When she said two dollars, please, I went into hysterics. Here I was thinking how damn important I was, and she brought me down again by making the procedure so automatic. Now I'm waiting for your blood test certificate so I can get the license. Please send it as soon as you can, dear.

Last nite I went up to your house to help Toby dress for the formal. She looked like a doll, - the kid she went with was also darling looking. Jackie came up to take pictures of the kids. He wanted me to go skating with him and I was dying to, but I called home and my mother was all alone with my dad and he was quite sick. So, Jackie came home with me, we had some hot chocolate and then talked. He's such a good kid. I was feeling kind of stinko last nite, about the wedding and all, and he was trying so hard to cheer me up. I must admit I felt a little better. Also, yesterday I got a belated shower gift from Ethel Raeder. She gave us a lovely hamper (you know, - what you're gonna put all yer dirty clothes in!). What I'm going to do with it in the meantime is really a problem! Oh well!

Darling, if you have a chance, I think you'd better write the Lexington and tell them to make sure and hold the room because we won't get there until about 10:30, - and if we miss the 5:10 train we have to wait for the next one which leaves at 9:20. For some odd reason, things like that worry me.

Talk about cigs being hard to get! Why my dear, what the devil are cigarettes. They are absolutely an impossibility in Worcester. There's only one place that has 'em and that's Barr's Creamery!!

The idea about taking Toby out is fine by me. I'm sure we'll be able to find the time..... if we can find the money!!! George, don't forget to wire me when you're leaving and what time you should be here. Talk about wires, - I just got the bill for your collect call, and jest in case you're curious, the bill was $8.36. I thought it would be at least ten!!

I also received the pictures you took of the dinner. But really darling, I would have enjoyed them much more had you been in at least one of them. You're some guy!!!

We're having quite a blizzard outside. I feel just like going for a walk. I think you'd enjoy a nite like this. Maybe I can order one up for you when you get home.

Well, me darling, I think I've done right by you this P.M. Don't forget, - only 9 more days and you'll be a man with responsibilities on yer hands!!

All my love,
Lottie

Picture of Toby Barr and her date for the formal referenced in Lottie's letter dated 12/27/1944.

December 27, 1944
Wednesday

From:	To:
Mr. Cpl. J.G. Barr 11057933	C.L. Sniderman
4503rd Base Unit Eng. Sq.	65 Houghton St.
Great Bend A.B.B., Kansas	Worcester, 4, Mass.

Dearest Lottie,

I was going to write a little sooner, but we have a saxophone player in our hut and he was trying to learn to play a fife. I've heard him play the sax, but don't want to hear him play the fife. Also, living with me is an inventor. He comes in and tells us the troubles he is going thru trying to check his invention. Our C.O. has given him two weeks' time to work on it and he's working day and night, almost, to finish it. It runs, but he hasn't been able to check the efficiency of the engine. That's what he invented, an engine to run 20% more efficient on the gasoline now being used. The inventor is even now out working on his pet – oh well, we still aren't crazy – yet!

Another one of those letterless days for me, which doesn't make for happiness on my part. I bet you that I'd rather receive a letter from you, than you a letter from me, yours are so much better.

Went to work again to-day, very little to do, but no sooner do I have a day of work, when the day afterwards I have some kind of a detail, tomorrow's is latrine orderly. "Polishing Sam the latrine man." 'Nough said about that.

I sent a little letter to our Uncle Barney and family telling them we are going to miss them at the wedding, but if things go well, we'll be able to visit them, if and when, we are in Washington.

Darling, I love you very much, so I'm going to sleep now and dream of you.

Your, George

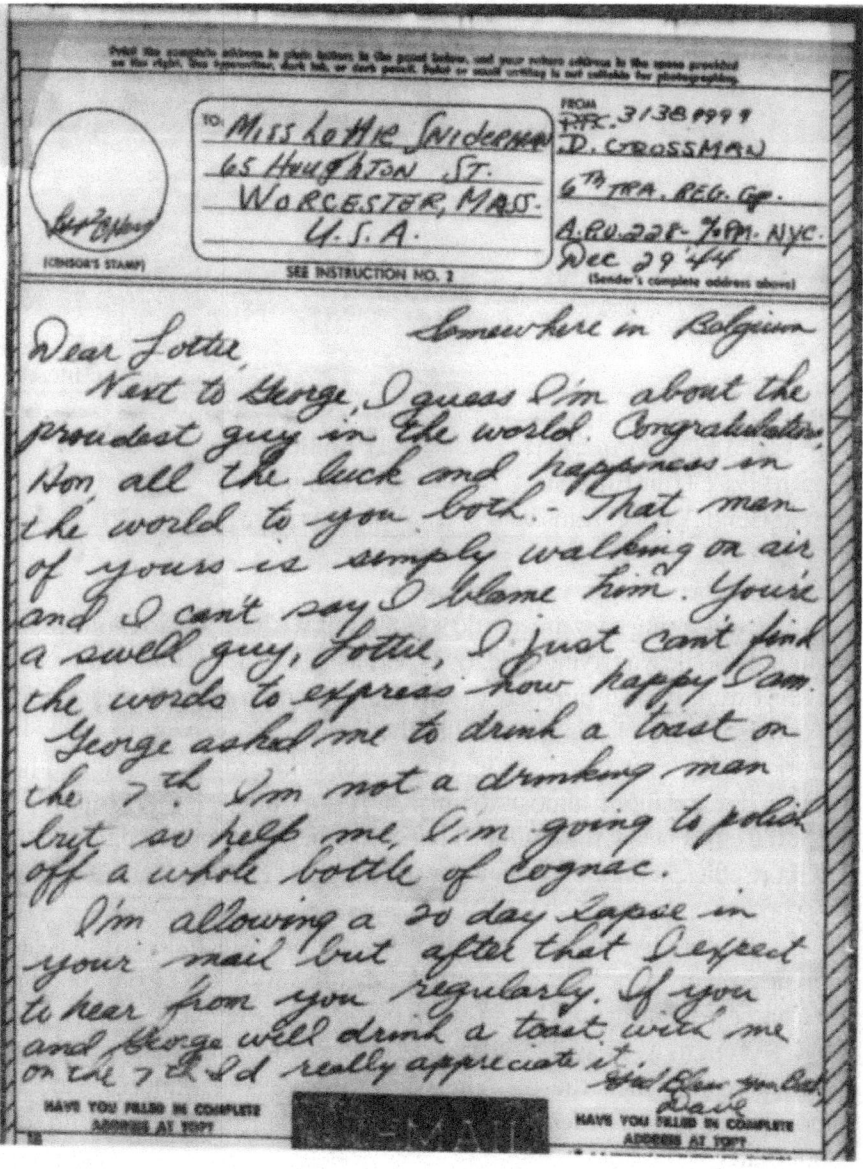

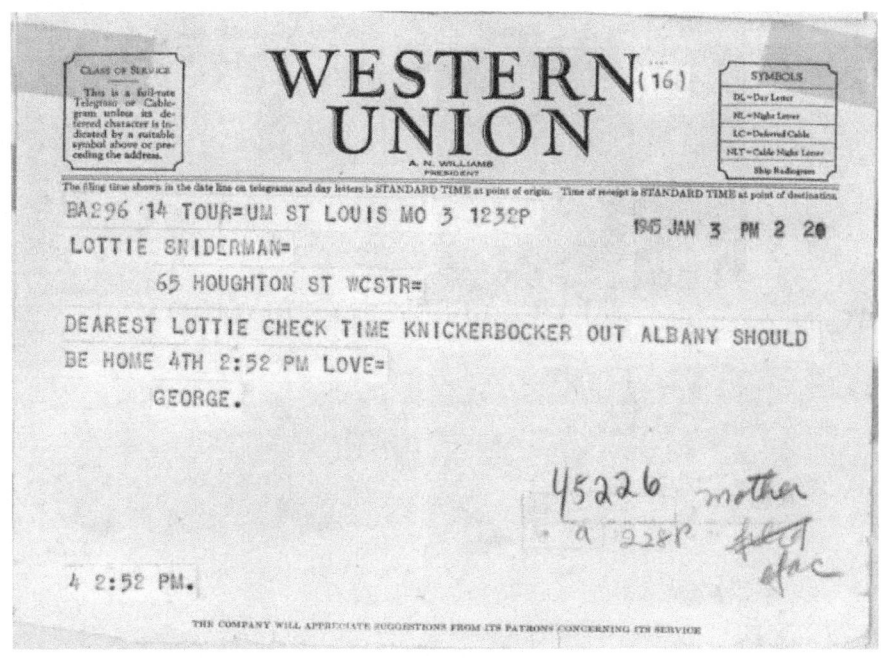

[Editor's note: This is a telegram that George sent Lottie on January 3, 1945. The Knickerbocker was a passenger train that ran between Albany, NY and Boston, MA in the 1940's.]

SERVICE CEREMONY PRINCIPALS

Principals in recent ceremonies were Corp. James George Barr and Mrs. Barr (Charlotte L. Sniderman), left, and Master Sgt. Garabed Kassabian, Army Air Forces, and Mrs. Kassabian (Rita Desrosiers).

Corp. Barr, son of Mr. and Mrs. Jacob Barr of 7 Hartshorn avenue, and Mrs. Barr, daughter of Mr. and Mrs. Max Sniderman of 65 Houghton street, were married at the bride's home on Jan. 7. After a wedding trip to New York, Mrs. Barr will live with her parents and Corp. Barr will report to Great Bend, Army Air Base, Kan., where he is a radio technician.

Sgt. Kassabian and Mrs. Kassabian were married Jan. 6 in the rectory of Church of the Holy Name of Jesus and will live in Atlantic City, N. J. Mrs. Kassabian is the daughter of Mrs. Delina Desrosiers of 109 Canterbury street, and Sgt. Kassabian is the son of Mr. and Mrs. Martin H. Kassabian of 29 Glen street.

JAN. 7, 1945

BARR-SNIDERMAN

Miss Charlotte L. Sniderman, daughter of Mr. and Mrs. Max Sniderman of 65 Houghton street, and Corp. James George Barr, Army Air Forces, son of Mr. and Mrs. Jacob Barr of 7 Hartshorn avenue, will be married at the home of the bride tomorrow at 1 p. m. Rabbi Sidney Guthman of Beth Israel Synagogue will officiate. A reception will follow.

Miss Charlotte Namath, cousin of the bride, will be maid-of-honor and Mrs. Philip Siegel, another cousin, will be matron of honor. Sol Barr of Newark, N. J., brother of the bridegroom, will be best man.

The bride will be gowned in white slipper satin, cut entrain, and a fingertip length veil of white tulle styled with a coronet of seed pearls. She will carry a Bible with an orchid and sweet peas cover corsage.

Miss Namath will wear a pink gown of satin and net and will carry an old-fashioned bouquet. Mrs. Siegel will wear an orchid gown of net and satin and will carry an old-fashioned bouquet.

The bride has chosen an aqua suit, brown squirrel coat and brown accessories for traveling. After a trip to New York, the bride will live with her parents while her husband, who is stationed at Great Bend Army Air Base in Kansas, is in service. Corp. Barr is a radio technician.

JAN. 6 - 1945

BARR — SNIDERMAN

The marriage of Miss Charlotte Sniderman, daughter of Mr. and Mrs. Max Sniderman, 65 Houghton Street, to Cpl. George Barr, son of Mr. and Mrs. Jacob W. Barr, 7 Hartshorn Avenue, will take place Jan. 7 at Beth Israel Synagogue.

Rabbi Sidney S. Guthman will perform the ceremony which will be followed by a dinner-reception at the synagogue.

The bride will be gowned in white slipper satin en train with a fingertip length veil of white tulle falling from a coronet of simulated pearls. She will carry a Bible with an orchid marker and sweet pea streamers.

Miss Charlotte Namath will be maid of honor, and Mrs. Philip Siegel, matron of honor. Sol Barr of Newark, N. J., will be his brother's best man.

Following a wedding trip to New York, the bride will make her home with her parents while her husband is in service. He is a member of the Army Air Force, stationed at Great Bend Army Air Base, Kans.

Both the bride-elect and Cpl. Barr are graduates of the High School of Commerce. He was formerly active in the local A. Z. A. She is a member of Junior Hadassah and is employed by the New England Grocer Supply Co.

JAN 1, 1945

The engagement of Miss Charlotte Sniderman, daughter of Mr. and Mrs. Max Sniderman of 65 Houghton street, to Pvt. James George Barr, Army Air Forces, son of Mr. and Mrs. Jacob Barr of 57 Arlington street, is announced by her parents. Both were graduated from High School of Commerce. Miss Sniderman is employed at the New England Grocery Supply Co. Pvt. Barr is stationed at Great Bend Army Air Base, Great Bend, Kan.

JULY - 4, 1944

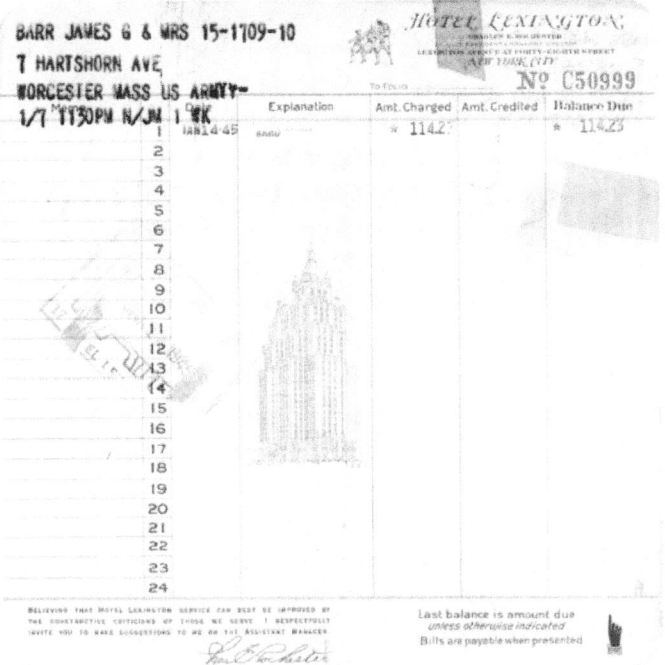

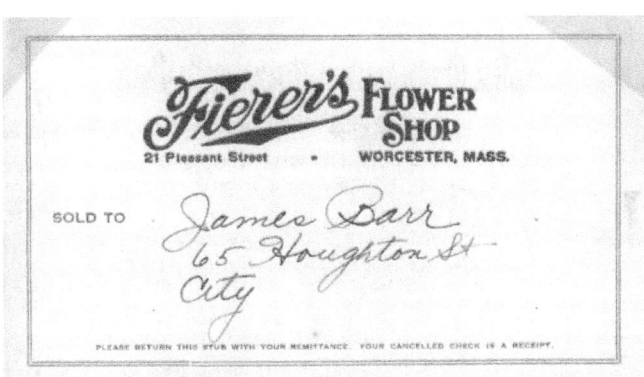

Certificate of Marriage

(Hebrew ketubah text)

This Certificate Witnesseth that

On the _First_ day of the week, the _Twenty second_ day of the month _Tebet_ in the year 5705, corresponding to the _7th_ of _January_, 19_45_, the holy Covenant of Marriage was entered into at _Worcester_, _Massachusetts_, between the Bridegroom _James G. Barr_, and his Bride _Charlotte Sniderman_.

The said Bridegroom made the following declaration to his Bride:

"Be thou my wife according to the law of Moses and Israel. I faithfully promise that I will be a true husband unto thee. I will honor and cherish thee, work for thee, protect and support thee, and provide all that is necessary for thy due sustenance, even as it becometh a Jewish husband to do. I also take upon myself all such further obligations for thy maintenance, during thy life-time, as are prescribed by our religious statute."

And the said Bride has plighted her troth unto him, in affection and in sincerity, and has thus taken upon herself the fulfillment of all the duties incumbent upon a Jewish wife.

This Covenant of Marriage was duly executed and witnessed this day, according to the usage of Israel.

Sidney S. Guthman
Rabbi

Charlotte Sniderman
Bride

James G. Barr
Bridegroom

Abraham Fishman
Witness

Sidney S. Guthman
Witness

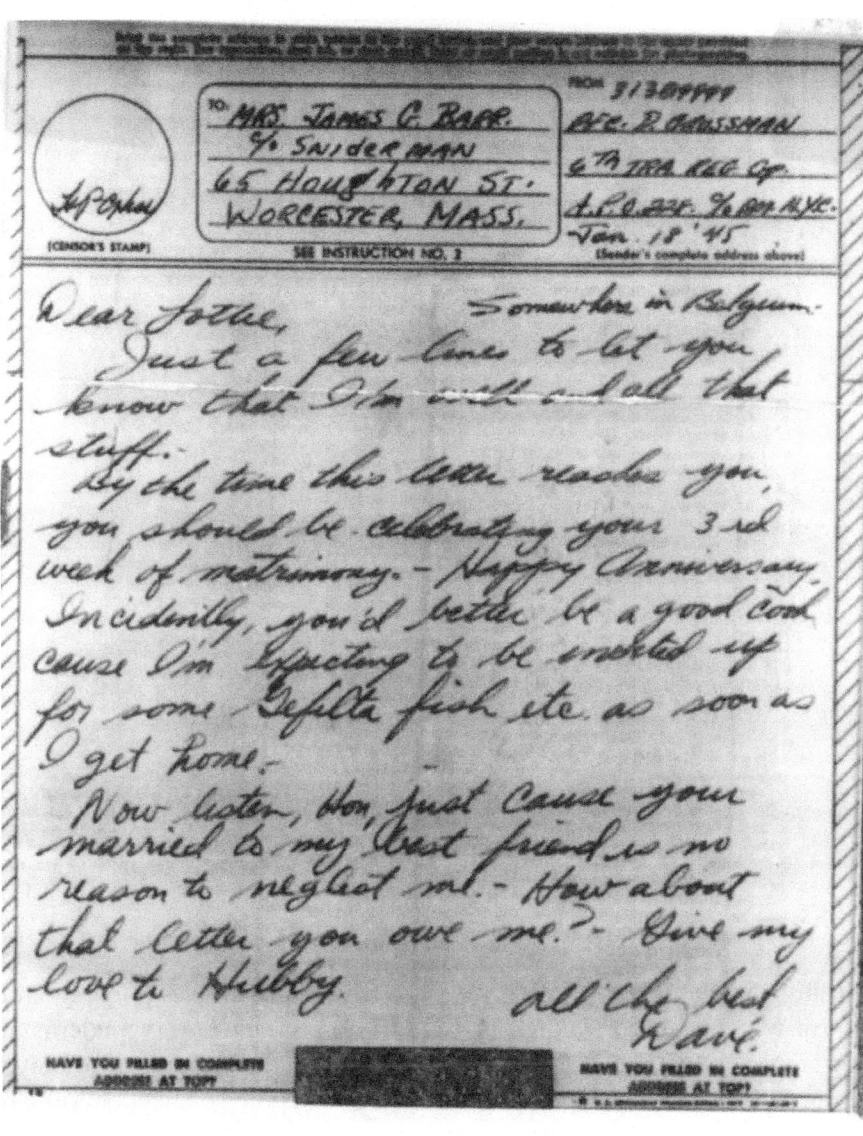

MAX SNYDERMAN

Max Snyderman, 60, of 65 Houghton street, died at St. Vincent Hospita yesterday. He had lived here 40 years. He was a Spring street merchant.

He leaves his widow, Mrs. Sarah (Hoffman) Snyderman; a daughter, Charlotte, wife of Corp. James G. Earr, and two sons, Samuel of Washington and Irving of Worcester. He was a member of the Workmen's Circle Branch of Worcester and the Sons of Abraham Synagog.

The funeral was this afternoon at his home. Rabbi Jacob Weisenberg of Shaarai Thorah Synagog officiated. Burial was in B'nai Brith Cemetery.

FEB. 5, 1945

[Editor's note: As can be seen by these newspaper articles, George and Lottie were married on January 7, 1945 and Lottie's father, Max Sniderman, died on February 5, 1945. One can only imagine all the emotions Lottie was feeling at this time; The joy of getting married and going on her honeymoon and having George home for almost two months, and the sadness of losing her father, and then having his funeral and burial just days before George was to leave for Great Bend, Kansas.]

February 11, 1945
Sunday

From:	To:
Mrs. J.G. Barr	Mr. Cpl. J.G. Barr 11057933
65 Houghton St.	Eng. Sq., 4503rd A.A.F. Base Unit
Worcester 4, Mass.	Great Bend A.B.B., Kansas

My dearest husband, -

It's only 2:30 o'clock, - you've only been gone about 2 hours and yet I feel the necessity of writing to you. The house seems unbearably empty without you, - everything I touch, everywhere I look, and everything I do, reminds me of you and brings a lump in my throat. Your shirt is still hanging on the bedroom chair, your hat is still on the piano, and as I sit here chewing gum, I can just hear you say you won't kiss me until I throw it away.

We did have a long time together, ... but hardly long enough. I always did say that a pain of loneliness was far worse than a physical pain, - and I'm so terribly, terribly lonesome.

Jack was kind enough to take me home, but he didn't stay at all. I don't think we said two words to each other coming home. He's such a good boy, - but hardly any consolation when it's you I love and want. When the train started pulling out I started running after it, but then I stopped because I thought I'd bust out bawling and I didn't want to spoil it.

Something in my head keeps yelling 'what are you going to do without him' and I keep answering myself, 'I don't know, - I don't know.' At this time, I also am thinking that Dave Israel said we'd get sick of each other for 21 days and nights constantly, - that statement proves what a god damn fool he really is. Being with you constantly for the rest of my life still won't be enough for me. Last nite you said you felt sorry for the people who haven't fallen in love yet. I feel sorry for them too, - they simply don't know what they're missing.

Well, my darling, what else can I write you? Maybe this sounds ridiculous, but I feel much lighter of heart now that I've written you a few words. It's funny that even though by now you are miles away, I can still feel you comfort me. Darling, I love you so very, very much.

Your loving wife-
Lottie

February 12, 1945
Monday

From:	To:
Mrs. J.G. Barr	Mr. Cpl. J.G. Barr 11057933
65 Houghton St.	Eng. Sq., 4503rd A.A.F. Base Unit
Worcester 4, Mass.	Great Bend A.B.B., Kansas

My dearest George, -

You can't imagine my surprise when I found your valentine last nite, darling. It was terribly sweet of you, and a surprise, which certainly hit the spot last nite. I couldn't help laughing when I found it in that particular drawer, - but that was one time I didn't mind.

Tonight, sometime you'll probably be back in Kansas. Did you have any luck on the train, - ? Oh, come now, - don't tell me you read the magazines all the way back!!!!

My mother and I had planned on going downtown today, but she was too tired, so I nearly went mad staying in again. Last nite we had a house full of people. My mother had a group of her friends and Edie Megans, Golda Edinburg, Franny Wilson, and Zelda came over to see me. I really appreciated their coming over last nite, - I was so damned lonesome. We received another pile of cards and oodles of candy.

I hated sleeping alone last nite, so I made my mother come in with me. I hugged her and she hugged me, but honest dear, - it twasn't the same!!!! So finally, after tossing and turning for what seemed like hours she went into her own bed and I proceeded to hug my pillow as of days gone by.

I spoke to your mother last night and she said the baby is very cute and Fran is doing fine. The name is Martin Barry Barr, - not half as distinguished as Michael Paul Barr, - or is it?!! Well, ours will be more intelligent anywho, won't he?

I received another letter from Dave Grossman today and he's very angry at me for not writing for so long. Will take care of him when I finish with my husband, oh, how I like the sound of that!!

Well, darling, I hope I get a wire from you tomorrow, I'm on pins and needles. Write me as soon as you can.

Your loving wife,
Lottie

P.S. – Kiss me quick!!!

P.S. — *Kiss me quick!!!*

February 14, 1945
Wednesday

From:	To:
Cpl. James G. Barr 11057933	Mrs. James G. Barr
4503rd Eng. Sq.	65 Houghton St.
Great Bend, Kansas	Worcester 4, Mass.

Dearest Valentine,

How does one start the first letter to his wife? There are so many things that I want to tell you and yet, I don't know where to start. It's been so long that I've written a letter that I'm afraid that I've forgotten how, almost anyway.

I don't think you were out of my mind for one moment since I pulled away from you at the station. Lottie, Lottie, is the only thing that runs thru my mind. The more I think of you, the more I get to love you. I thought that I loved you as much as a person could love someone, but I'm finding out that I was wrong, and that I can love you more and more as the minutes go by.

Early yesterday morning, when I finally got into my bed (almost four o'clock) and even tho I was exhausted, I couldn't fall asleep. I felt so very peculiar to be sleeping alone, no one to hug, or have hug me, no one to talk to, no one to kiss. I was very much alone.

At nine I was up and went and got my barrack bags, signed papers for your allotment, gave the liquor to the orderly room and officers, who appreciated it very much, then after dinner, I went back to sleep. Later I got up again, straightened out my clothes and such, then got all cleaned up and hit the sack. I was a very tired boy, I'll have you know.

Millions of letters were waiting for me and even a little wedding present from Bob. It's a very lovely baby cup that is made of sterling. I'll have to write to him very soon. Also, got a letter from Anne inviting me up to

Salina for dinner again. Three letters from Sid, two from Dave, one from Morty, and many more. If I don't get writer's cramp in a week, I'll either have a strong hand, or I didn't write!!!

One of Dave's letters was written on the seventh of Jan. He had a bottle of Cognac in front of him, which he was going to drink a toast to us when he finished the letter. Dave's a damn good kid.

When I got on the train at St. Louis, I met Anne Feldman (the only Jewish girl in town) with her husband to be (to-day they'll be married). He's from my outfit and it has been a little over a month romance – quick, wasn't it. I'm invited over to their house this Saturday. They think I'm a pretty lucky guy to get you, even after seeing the tintype!!!

As yet, I haven't gone back to work, but the fellows tell me that there isn't much doing, so I'll be able to rest – after to-morrow, I'm the K.P. Kid again!!!

How are things at home? I wish I could have remained there for my life time, but Uncle seems to think it unnecessary.

The first chance I get I'll mail the present to you, which should be this afternoon or to-morrow. It is a cute little cup with "Baby" inscribed on it. Leave it to Bob!!!

I think that is about all for to-day.

Your valentine husband,
George

P.S. Ain't I romantic! I love you just the same anyway!

February 14, 1945
Wednesday

From:	To:
Mrs. J.G. Barr	Cpl. James G. Barr 11057933
65 Houghton St.	4503rd A.A.F. Base Unit, Eng. Sq.
Worcester, Mass.	Great Bend A.B.B., Kansas

My dearest George,

I received your sweet telegram yesterday and altho I was mighty glad to get it, it only made me doubly lonesome. I was going to write you a nice long letter yesterday, but I started washing and I didn't realize how much dirty clothes I had accumulated in all the time that you were here. Anywho, after that I still felt ambitious so I cleaned my closet and my drawers and boy, - what a job that was. Today I spent the best part of the day ironing. I received another letter from Dave G. today and he finally received my Xmas package. The stuff must have been stale as hell, - but he said it was swell, so that's all that counts.

Last nite as tired as I was, I just couldn't sleep. I thought I would go mad. I got out of bed and got myself a nice big apple, found a last month's Reader's Digest and started to read. I started reading an article on Venereal Disease and it scared me to death. Darling, I hope you won't be persuaded by any of the other boys to partake in a little of that kind of fun. It's silly of me to think of it because I have the utmost confidence and trust in you, - but that damn article started me thinking!! After reading that I went to sleep.

Received a letter from Fran Barr today thanking us for the gift. They seemed very appreciative and it was a very cute letter. It seems that instead of Martin Barry keeping Sol awake, - Sol kept Martin Barry from sleeping. Sol sat by his crib all night, - he said his son was talking to him. Fathers are really very cute. Also, Fran likes being a mother very much and recommends it highly. Well..............?!!

The radio warned everyone to prepare for another blizzard yesterday, but nothing happened, - only a mild snow. But it's so damn slippery that my uncle Dave fell down two times coming home today. Boy, was he mad!

I sent your folks and Toby a Valentine from us yesterday and they were most surprised. They were very cute Valentine's too. Also, received one from Edie Megans, who is again ailing. She's in bed and thinks she's got the Grippe.

Also, some news on the Irene vs. Naty battle. As you know, Irene has an apartment in Boston, but she's looking for all kinds of excuses not to go. So, Mrs. Sherr had a talk with Natey and it seems he's not the quiet meek little boy he's cracked up to be. Mrs. Sherr called up my mother this morning and was crying for all she was worth. It seems Natey told Mrs. Sherr that he didn't want her giving Irene advice on how to run her life and he told Irene if she's so crazy about her job, then she should have married her job. Of course, he's perfectly right, but he really surprised them by finally speaking up. So, whether Irene will go to live with him or not is still a mystery. Jesus, I just happened to think how I would feel if you happened to be stationed in Bedford. I think I'd even walk there just to be with you. But, of course, there's no doubt about my love for you, - and there seems to be with the Talbots.

Things in the house are not so good, dear. My mother is really fed up with going to the cellar fifty times a day and still its cold in this damn house. Just after supper she went down to fix the steam and burnt five fingers on her right hand. You can just imagine what went on here. I'm trying my darndest to make her go away, but she just won't go. I'm hoping everything will straighten out soon or I'll be a nervous wreck too.

Well, my darling, and so ends another daily report from Mrs. J.G. Barr, - and I hear from very good sources that she's terribly in love with her husband.

Goodnite dearest.
Lovingly,
Lottie B.

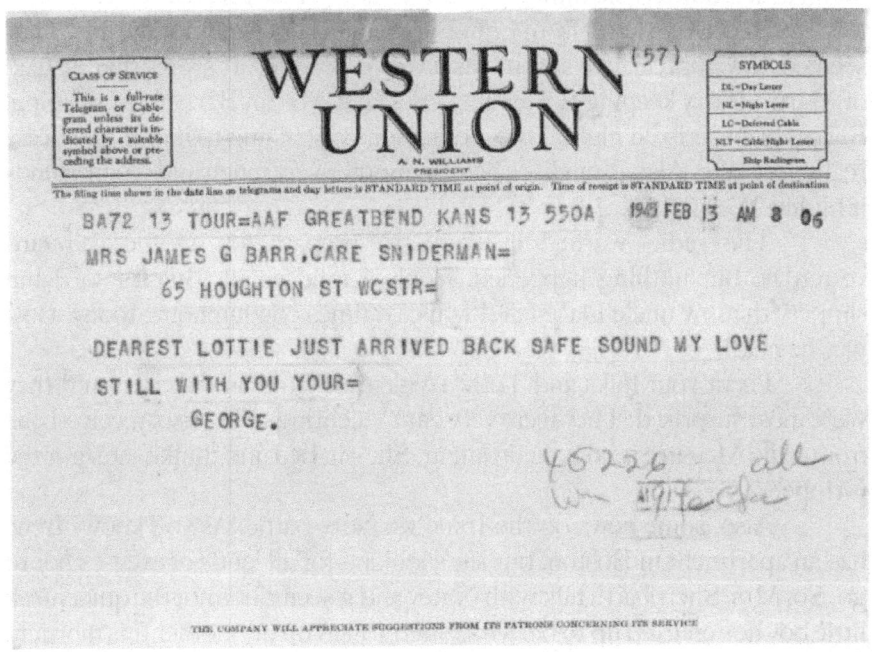

February 15, 1945
Thursday

From:	To:
Cpl. James G. Barr 11057933	Mrs. James G. Barr
4503rd Eng. Sq.	65 Houghton St.
Great Bend, A.A.B. Kansas	Worcester 4, Mass.

My darling wife,

The valentine you sent me was beautiful, but how did you manage to get it here right on Valentine's Day? I always said you were wonderful.

I still can't get used to not having you near me. It seems as if I'm not myself, there definitely is something missing – and it definitely is you! Darling, I love you.

Last night I went to the show to see "Tomorrow the World," which was what I considered excellent. The acting and the story were real good. Also, a new kid made a grand hit with his adult performance. The plot dealt with a Nazi boy brought to this country, and shows how the German children of Hitler are brought up. A Jewess, Betty Field, and a professor, Fredric March, who she loves, try to convert him to the American way. They both have a pretty rough time with him, but of course, he finally sees the light and everything turns out as what was originally hoped for.

You know I should have brought back many more pints of liquor, because I sold one pint, the last one, to-day for five dollars, and the fellow was glad to get it for that price.

I wrote Bob a nice letter yesterday and thanked him for the gift. Also, the gift is on the way for you.

We're in luck, kid, for I got under the wire and they're going to start your allotment on my next pay. The bonds will still be sent to my house, but you are now my beneficiary. The allotment will be sent to your house, so if there is going to be a change of your address, let me know and I'll change it. O.K.? – O.K.!

Good night my sweet,
Your husband, George

February 15, 1945
Thursday

From:	To:
Mrs. J.G. Barr	Cpl. James G. Barr 11057933
65 Houghton St.	4503rd A.A.F. Base Unit, Eng. Sq.
Worcester, Mass.	Great Bend ABB, Kansas

Hello my darling,

Today I was back at my old occupation of waiting for the mailman, - but no luck. By tomorrow, I should have a letter, - that is, of course, if you wrote to yer 'lil ole wife!!

Spent a very dull day today. My aunt Rose came up in the afternoon, so we sat and talked for a few hours, - outside of that, I sat around thinking, - thinking of how much I miss you. I wish to heck I could start working again, - it would take my mind off things, - at least temporarily.

Last nite I really had myself a jolly old time. I went to bed with yer old pal "The Torch of Life." This time I really read it through giving it my undivided attention and I think I understand now what the author was trying to put across. I still had to laugh at some of the descriptive words!! Had I read the book before we were married, I never would have understood it. Even last nite I had to read some of it over and over again before it penetrated. Sometimes I wonder whether I was really naïve or just plain stupid. Oh, well, the book says the only way you can really learn is through experience and if you can quote the book, - so can I, - so there!!!

Darling, I have the funniest sensation all over me. A feeling I can't exactly put into words. I feel a terrible longing sensation all over my body. I feel like crying, and yet I can't, I feel very restless and there's nothing to relieve the tension. Everything I touch reminds me of you, sometimes I can just hear you talking, - calling me, Cookie, - I can see how irritated you were when I annoyed you. I'm sorry, darling, because I annoyed you, but it was just because I wanted you to myself every minute, because I knew what a long time it would be before I could be near you again. I'm really very selfish about the people I love.

Well, darling, it may be difficult to understand why I do certain things, - but I really don't intend to be annoying. Maybe it was because my affection for you was pent up for so long. I don't know.

Fer hevven's sake, I hope I get some mail from you tomorrow, or I'll be completely good fer nothin'.

Goodnight my darling,
Always yours,
Lottie

P.S. – Have you got any pennies for Michael?!!! I'm not doing so good.

February 16, 1945
Friday

From:	To:
Cpl. James G. Barr 11057933	Mrs. James G. Barr
4503rd Eng. Sq.	65 Houghton St.
Great Bend, A.A.B. Kansas	Worcester 4, Mass.

My beautiful wife,

What wouldn't I give to be beside you instead of so many miles from you? How can I feel married when my wife isn't near me? I fully realize that I am married and am very happy that I am, but when you will be able to be near me, I'll be that much more. I also have a suspicion that you feel that way too!!!

This morning I went to work, but of course, I didn't do a thing. In fact, in the middle of the afternoon, I went back to my hut and took a nap. It's funny, but I seem to need rest, I get tired awfully easy lately. What I need is a wife, when do you think you'll be able to help me out?

I've only received that one letter that you wrote, the same afternoon that I left, so I still don't know yet if you've made any plans on what's going to happen back home, so when you have decided, let me know.

The last few days had been very nice, but the weather has turned colder and we've had snow flurries. Who knows, maybe the blizzard that I left in Worchester is coming out to see me.

We've just had another religious discussion – join the army and become religious. I think I'll become a recruiting officer, find a WAC to replace me, and then come home to you. Good idea, don't you agree?

Darling, I still can't believe that when I go to bed soon, you won't be coming into the room soon, putting out the light, getting into bed with me and putting your cold, but lovely feet against mine to warm them. I wish I had that small crack, to see you thru, you talked about!

Goodnight my love,
Your husband, George

February 16, 1945
Friday nite

From:	To:
Mrs. J.G. Barr	Cpl. James G. Barr 11057933
65 Houghton St.	4503rd A.A.F. Base Unit, Eng. Sq.
Worcester, Mass.	Great Bend A.B.B., Kansas

Dear Mr. Barr (my husband),

No letter from you again today and at this point I don't know whether to be angry or worried! Surely, - they'll be some mail tomorrow. If not, I'll go stock raving mad. Mad, mad, - do you hear?!!!!

Met Edie M. for lunch today, and finally got around to giving her a birthday present. I asked her what she wanted and she said a photo album, - so that's what she got. It cost a fortune, but it was a beauty and I figgered she well deserved it.

I received a tremendously long letter from Beverly today and she told me some real exciting news. She and Alton are expecting a blessed event in September. That means, of-course, that they just about found out for sure. I'm really all excited for them. By the by, Michael's fund is slowly but surely increasing!! Your folks were up here this evening and no sooner did Pop set his foot in the door, I promptly relieved him of his pennies. He only had six, - but heck, tis better thern nuthin'. They only stayed for a short time because they came up late. They were coming from Mrs. Solomon's house. Her son is home on furlough so they went to see him.

Barbara was due to come home this evening, but she called up her house and they are so rushed with rehearsals, that she can't come in until tomorrow nite, - and even at that she can only stay for Sunday. Ruthie, her sister, called and told me all this because she knew I was waiting for Barb to call.

I called Dave Israel last nite and left word for him to call me back because he wasn't home. So, this morning he called and was as bright and pleasant as that bastard could be. Anywho he asked me what I wanted (as if he didn't know) and I told him since you had gone back to camp I was getting ready to go back to work. So, - without letting me say another word he said he wanted to talk to me personally. I'm going down the office Monday A.M. and if he does take me back I'm not going back unless I get a raise. Hell, this is one time I can be independent. Anywho, I'm still planning on coming down in spring, honey. That is, of-course, if things go right and ..... if you want me to come out.

Well, my darling, another day has ended. Now I retire (alone, damn it!). Still miss you, guess I will until I'm with you.

Always yours,
Lottie

P.S. Am enclosing puzzle to prove I'm not so dumb after all, - ha!

CROSSWORD PUZZLE

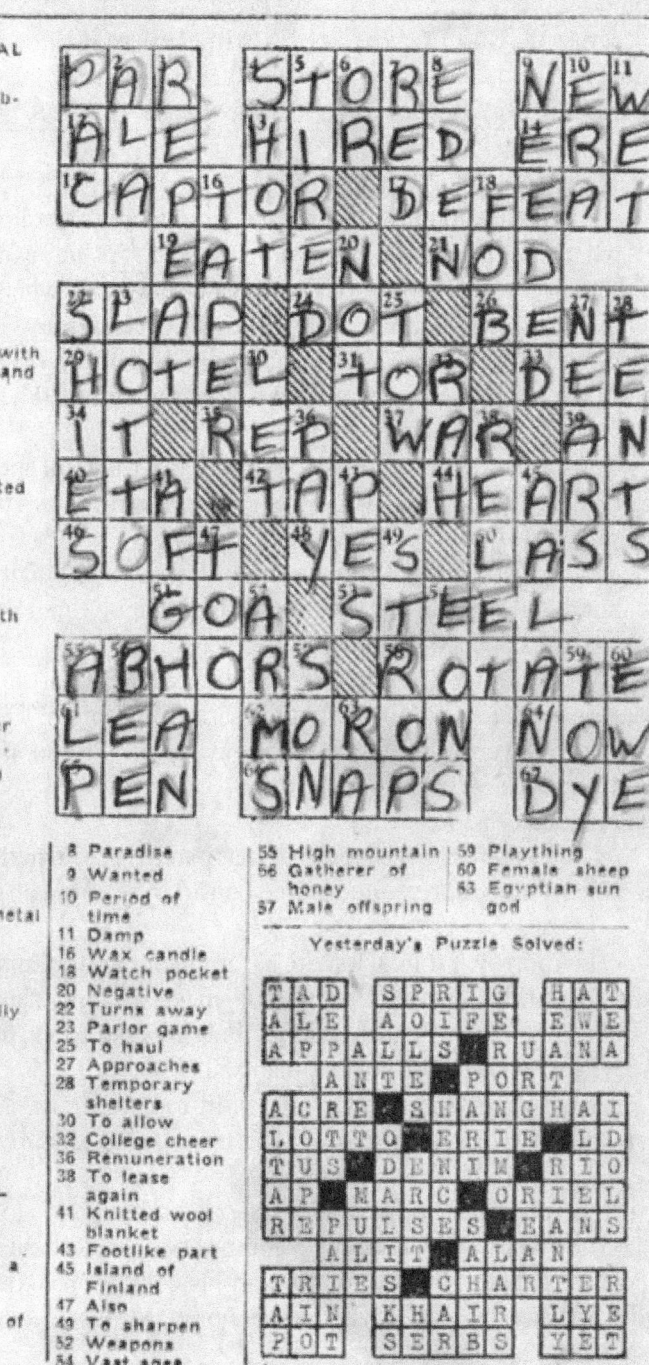

HORIZONTAL

1 Equality
4 Retail establishment
9 Recent
12 Beverage
13 Rented
14 Before
15 One who captures
17 To whip
19 Dined
21 To bow
22 To strike with the open hand
24 Speck
26 Twisted
29 Lodging house
31 High, pointed hill
33 River in Scotland
34 Neuter pronoun
35 Corded cloth
37 Armed conflict
39 Indefinite article
40 Greek letter
42 To knock
44 Vital organ
46 Gentle
48 Affirmative
50 Young girl
51 Tibetan gazelle
53 Priority metal
55 Hates
58 To revolve
61 Meadow
62 One mentally deficient
64 At present
65 Sty
66 Breaks suddenly
67 To change color of

VERTICAL

1 Moccasin
2 Wing
3 To iterate
4 Discharged a gun
5 Weary
6 Correlative of either
7 Crimson
8 Paradise
9 Wanted
10 Period of time
11 Damp
16 Wax candle
18 Watch pocket
20 Negative
22 Turns away
23 Parlor game
25 To haul
27 Approaches
28 Temporary shelters
30 To allow
32 College cheer
36 Remuneration
38 To lease again
41 Knitted wool blanket
43 Footlike part
45 Island of Finland
47 Also
49 To sharpen
52 Weapons
54 Vast ages
55 High mountain
56 Gatherer of honey
57 Male offspring
59 Plaything
60 Female sheep
63 Egyptian sun god

Yesterday's Puzzle Solved:

Grid answers:
T A D | S P R I G | H A T
A L E | A O I F E | E W E
A P P A L L S | R U A N A
| A N T E | P O R T
A C R E | S H A N G H A I
L O T T O | E R I E | L D
T U S | D E N I M | R I O
A P | M A R C | O R I E L
R E P U L S E S | E A N S
| A L I T | A L A N
T R I E S | C H A R T E R
A I N | K H A I R | L Y E
P O T | S E R B S | Y E T

February 17, 1945
Saturday

From:	To:
Cpl. James G. Barr 11057933	Mrs. James G. Barr
4503rd Eng. Sq.	65 Houghton St.
Great Bend, A.A.B. Kansas	Worcester 4, Mass.

Dear Mrs. J.G.

Right this minute I feel like kicking myself right up the ____, you know what! Not one minute ago, did I break a lens in my new glasses! I'll send them to Dr. Glixman and then he can call you up when they are ready – then you can pay for them and ship them back. I know now why I got married, so I could have a wife to pay my bills. But don't worry about the money. I'll send you some around the first of the month. There's no rush for them, so don't go out of your way.

This afternoon, I received your letter of the 12th, and also one from my folks, dated the twelfth. We didn't even get our money's worth out of air mail!

I'm glad you liked the valentine. I would have put it some other place, but then I wouldn't be sure of you finding it on time. Besides, I closed my eyes when I opened the drawer!!!

We had an inspection this morning, which wasn't up to any decent standards, so next Saturday, we get the same thing again. To show the men that he didn't have any hard feelings, he gave us the afternoon off to go to the movies. I guess he's trying to make them feel like louses. I say them, because our hut passed O.K.

I'm going to town to-night to that party I was invited to. I hope that I'll be able to have a pretty good time considering you won't be there with me.

To-morrow I think I'll write letters all day and try and catch up with my mail. So far, I've answered very few to make any kind of a dent in the pile I have. I'd better answer them or they'll never write to me again, and then where will I go when they holler "Mail Call!!"

I miss your huggin' and your kissin' too, but most of all I miss you! Gee that's poetry!!! Now you're getting to see what kind of a husband you have. P.P. huh? O.K. Pretty Punk!

Have you gone down and taken out a subscription for me as yet? I'd like to know, because Walter W's column is two weeks behind in the paper we get here!!! I read, or started to read his column in to-day's paper, and found I had already read it when I was home. Modern Kansas, up to date Kansas, Kansas, phooey!!!

Your husband, George

P.S. How about throwing that gum away? I'm just kidding. Papa.

February 17, 1945
Saturday nite

From:	To:
Mrs. J.G. Barr	Cpl. James G. Barr 11057933
65 Houghton St.	4503rd A.A.F. Base Unit, Eng. Sq.
Worcester, Mass.	Great Bend A.B.B., Kansas

My dearest George,

    I received the first letter from my husband today and what a wonderful letter it was!! I too, my darling, find that I love you more and more with each passing day. And I know that my love for you will be ever increasing as the years go by.

    Thank Bob for me also for sending the wedding gift, - altho it is a bit premature, - or at least I hope it is!! I thought I would die laughing. Was he being funny or just optimistic?!!! Cute idea, nevertheless.

    Dave Israel called me up this morning and told me to come down today instead of Monday. So down I trotted all prepared for a good speech. But when I got there I received an amazing reception. Norman Sharfman fell all over me, as did also the salesmen, etc., etc. Anywho, Dave said, - quote – ahem, ahem, - I take it you want to come back to work. And yer wife said very icily, - "yas, dats de general idea." And before I could say another word he said I was hired. But little Lottie didn't let it go at that, no sireeee. I asked him for a raise and he said he couldn't say definitely until he spoke to the Sharfman's but he said he was almost positive that it would be arranged. I also told him that there was a possibility that I might go out to Kansas and he said we would discuss it later. All he wants me to do is come to work Monday, - then we'll have a confab with the Sharfman's and if the arrangements aren't to my satisfaction, he said I was at liberty to leave any time without any fuss. Jesus, he made me feel so damned important. I honestly don't understand it!

    Mother, aunt Mary, and I went to visit Fran today. Irv is in New York. Who should be over there, but Alma Hersh. I just don't see the connection, do you?!

    Barb finally got home tonight. I spoke to her, but it was too late to see her, so I'm hoping I can see her tomorrow. She sounds swell, - same old Barb. I'd be disappointed if she changed.

It's as cold as hell in Worcy. I wish Spring would hurry up and come for two reasons. No fun at all going to sleep in a cold bed, - alone!!!!
Goodnite until tomorrow, dear.

All my love, all my life.
From your wife.
Lovingly, Lottie

P.S. Well, it rhymes, anyway!

February 18, 1945
Sunday night

From:	To:
Mrs. J.G. Barr	Cpl. James G. Barr 11057933
65 Houghton St.	4503rd A.A.F. Base Unit, Eng. Sq.
Worcester, Mass.	Great Bend A.B.B., Kansas

Hello darling,

Just one week from today we said goodbye at the station. It's only a week, - but it feels like you've been gone years. Golly, but I love you.

We went over my aunt Rose's today for dinner and had a delicious time. After dinner, I went over to see Barb. Outside of being and looking very tired, she looks and feels swell. Once I got over there they didn't let me go home. Her sisters and their husbands were there and a few cousins. They made me eat another tremendous meal and after that a scotch and soda and I swear I got high. Barb started playing the piano and I was singing these sad songs and then I started giving an exhibition of rumbas and Jewish dances. They were all in hysterics!! I was glad I had the drink, because outside of them being made happy, I also was lifted out of the dumps! Mrs. Coppersmith said next time they felt blue they would call me up to entertain. Now that I think of it, I must have been quite ridiculous.

My aunt Becky was over here this P.M. and you'll never believe all the compliments she paid you. Remember when I told you she said her daughters couldn't marry ordinary fellows like you and Phil. Well, she certainly has changed her mind about you. She thinks you're positively wonderful and darling, it made me feel very proud. I know I love you, but I want everyone else to love you too, and it makes me so happy to hear all the nice things they say about my husband.

Jesus, tomorrow I go back to work. I don't know how I'm ever going to get up. I'm so broke that I keep borrowing money from my mother and how I hate that! By the by, how are you doing for money, - have you gotten paid yet?

My head is throbbing away, bang, bang, clang, clang. That will loin me not to drink!!

And with this parting thought I take leave for this eve. (I'm just fulla rhymes lately!).

All my love,
Lottie

February 18, 1945
Sunday

From:	To:
Cpl. James G. Barr 11057933	Mrs. James G. Barr
4503rd Eng. Sq.	65 Houghton St.
Great Bend, A.A.B. Kansas	Worcester 4, Mass.

SERVICE CLUB
GREAT BEND AAF, KANSAS

Feb 18th

Dearest Lottie,

This morning I was very pleasantly surprised to receive a letter from you, why, because it's Sunday and I thought that they had discontinued Sunday mail call.

Dearest, you can put all your little fears away about me going out and having fun with women. Even tho it might be hard for you to believe that I was a virgin, being in the army and so forth, I was until I married you. One of the main reasons that I never indulged was because I read and heard lectures on venereal diseases a long time even before I had any definite sex interest in women. I never did want to take any chances on having any of my future children crippled. Another reason, which started a little while after I got to know and love you, was that if I had, and now if I did, I wouldn't be able to get as close as we are now, something would have left me. Maybe it is respect for myself, maybe it's because I hate a cheater, I don't know what to call it, but you needn't worry about me having any intimate relations with any other women. Nuff said.

Tell mother that I was very sorry to hear she burnt herself. After all, if it was really bad, then you'd have to do the cooking, then where would she be able to eat. O.K., so I'm kidding.

I've written so much to-day that my hand feels the strain. I wrote two real long letters, one to Dave, the other to Sid. Also, got a few more in so I should be thru in a few more days, I hope!

Last night I had a pretty good time, at least I spent an evening. I went with another fellow, he's the guy that had me call his mother while we were in New York, remember at Zimmerman's? We got them a little gift that we picked up at one of the stores here. It wasn't much, but they got a big kick out of it. All we got them was a pair of baby shoes we saw in a five & ten. One good feature about going up there was that they drove us back to camp.

When she got on his lap and they started kissing, I had to turn my head. Lottie, I couldn't stand looking at them, I was jealous!! But I felt much better when I took out our wedding pictures and everyone said what a beautiful bride you were and what a lucky guy I was to get you.

I felt sorry about you having to wash so many clothes. Darling, don't forget to add a washing machine to the other things we have to get when we get settled. O.K. you can put down a maid too.

Don't feel like writing to any more people, had enough sleep to-day, nothing else doing, so I think I'll go see what the movies have to offer.

Just spoke to your husband, and all he said was that he loves his wife very dearly. Knowing you the way I do, I can't say that I blame him.

Your husband,
George

P.S. Got a kick out of Lottie B. Papa.

February 19, 1945
Monday

From:	To:
Mrs. J.G. Barr	Cpl. James G. Barr 11057933
65 Houghton St.	4503rd A.A.F. Base Unit, Eng. Sq.
Worcester, Mass.	Great Bend A.B.B., Kansas

My dearest husband,

Received your sweet letter today and I'm sure glad you got the valentine on time. I mailed it right after you left, that probably accounts for why you got it so soon. I hope you got as big a kick reading it as I did buying it!

Well, went back to work today and had a little trouble. Evelyn Cohen is leaving the office and Dave thought it was an ideal set up for me to take over. I tried it all morning and quickly decided it jest wasn't for me. I knew the kind of work she did beforehand and I always considered myself lucky not being in her department.

Well, at lunch time I thought the situation over and came back and told Dave that either I get back my old job or I hit the road. Sooooooo, - he gave me back my old job with a little compromise that don't particularly appeal to me. But I figgered I might as well stick it out because I'm still planning on coming to Kansas. So, I won't be down there too long anyway and besides that, as I said before, I need the money.

Incidentally, if that boy your dad told you to look up in Coffeeville is the same fellow that Edie Potash is married too, well, that's fine. Because Edie is down there with him now and she loves it in Kansas. Besides that, if you ever get a 3 day pass, we can go out to visit them. I don't know Joe, - but Edie is swell and Joe is supposed to be too. She went out there for three weeks and now she's decided to stay there as long as he's there. Her sister Dot works down our office. Now all we need is for Phil to be stationed in Kansas. Zelda is going wherever he's going, and hell, - I don't blame her!! I certainly want to be with my husband as much as she does with hers. My mother wants me to go because she knows my heart is in Kansas anyway and she still plans on going to Washington. So, - now I can't wait for Spring to get here. It's all very exciting. I hope everything turns out well.

I'm glad you got the matter about the allotment cleared up. Boy, fifty bucks all for little ole me, - to put in the bank!! Or maybe we should invest it in liquor and make some money. Boy, five bucks a pint is pretty good money.

Well, hon, guess I better sign off for tonight. Will be back tomorrow at this same time, same place, same gal, and as much love as ever.

Goodnite dearest.
Your loving wife,
Lottie

P.S. Hug me!!

February 20, 1945
Tuesday

From:	To:
Mrs. J.G. Barr	Cpl. James G. Barr 11057933
65 Houghton St.	4503rd A.A.F. Base Unit, Eng. Sq.
Worcester, Mass.	Great Bend A.B.B., Kansas

My dearest husband,

I can't understand why you've only received one letter from me since you've been gone. I've written faithfully every day. By this time, you should be getting them regularly, - or at least I hope so.

Your letter of today made me very happy. I'm glad you want me to be with you because you know I feel the very same and also because I have all intentions of doing so. My mother and I are starting to plan accordingly. If things go right I should be with you early in April. If you have any ideas of where I could stay and etc., etc., I'd love to hear about them. Also, how do the chances look of you staying in Kansas. I know this is a silly question, - but are there any more rumors flying around about breaking up your outfit?

I've only been back to work for two days and I'm quite exasperated with the situation. I should have adhered to your advice and not gone back there. Maybe it's because my mind is on so many other things that every little trivial thing annoys, - at any rate, I'm not at all happy there.

Dave & Mary went back home tonight so we are quite alone. They were supposed to go home Sunday, but we kept postponing them. Tonight, they left and it's terribly lonesome and quiet.

We're having another little snow storm tonight and I really dread going out tomorrow. It's terrifically slippery, - I nearly broke my neck a hundred times. It was only by the grace of God that I didn't fall.

I really have very little to write you tonight. Maybe because nothing has happened. At any rate, I'm still terribly lonesome, - I'm sure you know that without my telling you. And I won't be happy until we're together again.

Goodnite dearest.
Your loving wife,
Lottie

February 21, 1945
Wednesday

From:	To:
Cpl. James G. Barr 11057933	Mrs. James G. Barr
4514th A.A.F. B.U., Tinker Field	65 Houghton St.
Oklahoma City, Oklahoma	Worcester 4, Mass.

Dear Cookie,
After a very terrible trip down here from Great Bend, we are located at Tinker Field. Coming down here I had three blankets wrapped around me and still I froze. We were fortunate enough to leave in the middle of the worst blizzard that Kansas had the displeasure of having all winter long.

When the trip was half over, we stopped to refuel, so that gave us a chance to get out of the trucks and get a cup of coffee and warm up. Warm up I did, for I took off my shoes, put on another pair of stockings and didn't put them back in (my feet) my shoes until they thoroughly thawed out.

We are now in the 4514th, which is made up of the 4503rd & the 4504th Service Groups. This makes it just twice as large as we had it back in Great Bend. Our C.O. is still back there, and we don't know if he is coming down with us or not, but three fourths of the others are with us.

We are lucky in the respect that we have nice warm barracks and are closely situated to the movies, service club, and P.X. Back in Great Bend, we had to hoof it for nearly a half mile for any of those conveniences. Another nice thing is that we no longer have to eat out of mess kits.

To-morrow we go to work in the shops here, so I think we'll stay around for a little while anyway. If we are here in the spring, and you do come down, there will be at least one Jewish couple I can introduce you to and possibly more. Remember the couple that I wanted to call when we were in Boston, well he is in my outfit now, because he was in the 4504th. Also, another fellow I knew got married and his wife is coming here. How long she'll stay I don't know, for she's having a baby. Oklahoma City is much nicer than Great Bend could ever hope to be, this is at least a City!

As yet, I haven't received your Monday mail telling me about your job, if you got it back, with the raise and all. We'll get the mail in a few days I imagine.

This afternoon, I washed and washed, until I thought my back would break. It's a good thing that I did, otherwise I'd have to go around naked or else in dirty clothes. I hope that they dry before I go to sleep, because otherwise, I'll have a lot of work putting them away at 6:15 in the morning when we have to get up. Things are going to be a little more G.I. here than at G.B., such as inspections, wearing a certain uniform, curfew, marching to work and eat, but I think I'll be able to pull thru alright!

This morning while we were lying around in the barracks, a few of the fellows got their instruments out and played awhile. I asked them to play "Take Me In Your Arms", and when they did, I closed my eyes and I could almost feel you in my arms. Sweetheart, I love you so very much, every minute that we are separated is agony.

Until to-morrow.
Your loving husband,
George

February 22, 1945
Thursday

From:	To:
Mrs. J.G. Barr	Cpl. James G. Barr 11057933
65 Houghton St.	4503rd A.A.F. Base Unit, Eng. Sq.
Worcester, Mass.	Great Bend A.B.B., Kansas

LOTTIE

Thursday
Feb 22, 1945

My dearest George,

Today being Washington's Birthday is a welcomed day of rest from the office. But the day happens to be good for nothing other than staying in the house. It has been raining torrents since last night and the city is virtually flooded. But I have so many letters to answer that this is really an opportune day.

That was a wrotten trick, - breaking your glasses. I shall look into Dr. Glixman when I think they should be ready. Also, I've inquired about having the paper mailed to you and have found out that it must be paid in advance. Shameful as this may sound, it is never the less true, - I didn't have the money. But I have given in the order and Wednesday when I get paid, I shall go over and pay them. I don't think I was ever as broke as I am now!

There really seems nothing to write you, since nothing of importance has happened. Oh, what a dull life without you.

I spoke to Edie Megans this A.M., - she's working and really sore about it. She sent George Freedman a Valentine and just received a letter in answer. It seems that his hopes again have been aroused. She told me she'd read the letter to me tonight. Said it was really cute. I feel bad for him, he was crazy about "E", but she couldn't see him at all. Seems her mind is still with Stanley, whom she hasn't heard from for months, - the stinker!!!

By the by, - how do you like my new stationery?!! I was going to have the full name put on, but it takes too long and I was muchly in a hurry.

My mother & I invited Mrs. Ciborowski for lunch today. She came down for breakfast at ten, stayed until 12:30, went upstairs to make her beds, and came down again at 1 o'clock for lunch. If her husband didn't come home for dinner, she'd probably eat with us again. It's swell having someone like that around.

Well, my dearest husband, can't think of another damn thing to write, so pleeze forgiveth me if I take leave. I really dislike today intensely because there's been no mail!

Your loving wife,

Lottie

P.S. – I'm all out of gum, - what shall I do!!!

February 22, 1945
Thursday

From:	To:
Mrs. J.G. Barr	Cpl. James G. Barr 11057933
65 Houghton St.	4503rd A.A.F. Base Unit, Eng. Sq.
Worcester, Mass.	Great Bend A.B.B., Kansas

My dearest George,
    I really haven't anything to write you tonight because I wrote you a letter this afternoon, but it's just that I feel particularly lonely tonight. I just heard someone singing "Take Me In Your Arms" and also "Every Time We Say Goodbye I Die A Little." Tonight, is one of those nights when tears would come easy to me when I'm alone in my bed with no one to see or hear me. Even you won't be there to comfort me, take me in your arms and pat my hair. Darling, I love and miss you so terribly much. Nothing seems to take my mind away from you.

Goodnite dearest.
Lovingly, Lottie

February 23, 1945
Friday

From:	To:
Mrs. J.G. Barr	Cpl. James G. Barr 11057933
65 Houghton St.	4514th A.A.F. B.U., Tinker Field
Worcester, Mass.	Oklahoma City, Oklahoma

My dearest George,
    I nearly had a heart attack this morning when I received your telegram. It came to the house and my mother had it transferred to the office. It was so unexpected that the girl had to repeat the message three times before I could compose myself. It wasn't until this afternoon that I got your letter saying that you might be transferred, - so the telegram, which was very unexpected, came as quite a shock. Well, at this point, I don't know whether to be happy or sad about the transfer and I will control my emotions until I hear from you what the set-up is. If you're going to remain in Oklahoma, I'll be tickled silly because that's one country I'd love to see. Write me all the

details as soon as you know yourself. Oklahoma is supposed to be a beautiful country. I wish I knew what the story is so I could get excited.

I also received the baby cup today, which is really a beautiful thing. I brought it down to the office and Dave nearly had a fit, altho he didn't ask any questions! Even if he asked, I still couldn't tell him!!!

Dave G.'s letter was really sad. He must have been feeling p.p. (pretty punk!) to have written a letter like that. I would have given anything to have had him at the wedding. Of all the people we had, there were really very few that we really wanted. But, we'll make up for it someday.

Mother & I had dinner at Mary's tonight, and a good dinner it was. She made some more chopped herring and I wanted to send you some, - but quickly put the idea out of my head. It would smell up the whole baggage train.

Darling, I know what you mean when you say you were jealous when that girl was kissing her boyfriend. I'm jealous just thinking about it. Please, dear God, let George stay in Oklahoma so I can come to see him. AMEN!

Received a letter from Bev today. They are coming home at the beginning of March and Bev is quite thrilled about having a baby, - I think I wrote you that she was that-a-way! The only bad part about it is that it's overseas for Alton after this furlough. I feel bad for the poor kids.

I met Barb's sister today and Barb isn't going overseas. One of the girls in the outfit flunked out in her physical, - so that means none of them go. Mrs. Coppersmith is in seventh heaven and Barb isn't too sorry either. I guess it's all for the best.

Well my dear husband, I guess I've written enough to keep you happy for one day. Don't forget to write me all the latest news.

Always yours,
Lottie B.

P.S. Now I have to learn your address all over again! Damn the army anyway!! Mama

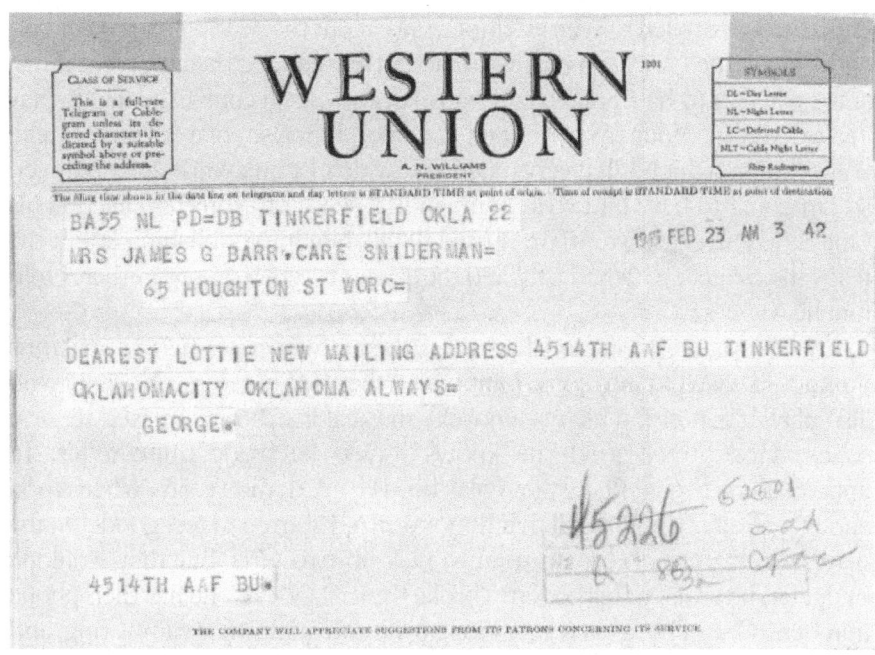

The filing time shown in the date line on telegrams and day letters is STANDARD TIME at point of origin. Time of receipt is STANDARD TIME at point of destination.

BA35 NL PD=DB TINKERFIELD OKLA 22

1945 FEB 23 AM 3 42

MRS JAMES G BARR.CARE SNIDERMAN=

65 HOUGHTON ST WORC=

DEAREST LOTTIE NEW MAILING ADDRESS 4514TH AAF BU TINKERFIELD

OKLAHOMACITY OKLAHOMA ALWAYS=

GEORGE=

4514TH AAF BU=

THE COMPANY WILL APPRECIATE SUGGESTIONS FROM ITS PATRONS CONCERNING ITS SERVICE

February 25, 1945
Sunday

From:	To:
Cpl. James G. Barr 11057933	Mrs. James G. Barr
4514th A.A.F. B.U., Tinker Field	65 Houghton St.
Oklahoma City, Oklahoma	Worcester 4, Mass.

My darling wife,

No, dear, I haven't forgotten about you even tho a few days have elapsed. Friday night when I was going to write, that was the time we had a G.I. party. This was something that I didn't have since I left Lowry Field. I almost fell out of the window while I was cleaning them. Then I had promised to go to services with a few of the boys, so into town we went, for they don't have Jewish services on the field.

Services were quite peculiar, because the English prayers were read by women of the congregation and the sermon was also given by a woman. Quite odd I thought. Then, of course, we went upstairs after services to have tea and sandwiches, that finished Friday night.

Saturday night I was going to write you as soon as I got into town, but I didn't. First, Norman and I went looking for a suitable photo album that I wanted, but after looking in a dozen places, we couldn't find the kind I wanted. Then we were going to see the "Three Caballeros," but that was entirely too crowded to even attempt to sweat out the waiting line. We finally ended up at the U.S.O., where we danced a few dances, then we went down stairs where they had a piano and Norman played. Of course, he had to play "Take Me In Your Arms" again for me. He also played an original composition, which I like very much and which I think you'll go crazy over, so I'm going to have him write it up and I'll send it to you. It's called "This One Sided Sweet Love Affair." I tried to talk him into publishing it, but the fellow he wrote it with had a tiff and they cannot seem to get to-gether. I told him he was crazy.

Next, we went and had a few beers, which seemed to make us hungry, so we went into some joint where they had hot dogs. Norman who also plays a 'tonette', which is a novelty musical instrument, played request songs. He's pretty good (he knows it), so he made quite a hit. In appreciation, a civy filled our coke bottles up. I didn't say 'when' soon enough, so after drinking all that liquor down, I started to feel good. On the way back to camp, Norman tried to pick up two girls, but they wouldn't budge, so he took out his 'tonette', broke the ice, and now he has their phone numbers. One of the girls wanted to know if you made me wear my ring, and when I said no, she was very much surprised. It's funny how I can't pick up any women with my ring on.

We wanted to sleep over in town, but we couldn't get a hotel room for love of anything. When I hit the sack back at camp, I fell asleep right away, I was groggy from that drink, but it wasn't until I woke up a few of the boys. I guess I'm a no good stinker!

We're working pretty steadily in the hangars and we can't goof off like we could at G.B. It's rough. We're changing antennas on B-29's. In fact, they are having a lot of changes put into them.

My outlook in our stay here has changed, it doesn't look as if we'll be here as long as I thought, but that's the army for you.

As yet, we haven't received any of our mail, something got screwed up someplace, maybe to-morrow. It's hard to take not getting any mail from you, I miss you so much. Lottie, I'm not me without you, there's no getting away from it.

I'll have to see what I can do about keeping you better posted. O.K.?

Your loving husband,
George

P.S. Notice a little change in address. Papa

February 25, 1945
Sunday

From:	To:
Mrs. J.G. Barr	Cpl. James G. Barr 11057933
65 Houghton St.	4514th A.A.F. B.U., Tinker Field
Worcester, Mass.	Oklahoma City, Oklahoma

My dearest George,

I certainly won't be sorry to see today end. It has been a terrifically aggravating day, - from all sides. We went over Irving's tonight, and what started out to be a very pleasant evening, turned out quite the opposite. Irv got a few estimates on the value of the store and what they offered certainly set us back on our heels. The maximum amount was $250, and rather than sell it for that, we'd rather give the damn store away. My mother wants to stay there and see what she can sell, - Irv thinks the best idea is to give everything, lock, stock, and barrel to the Russian Relief. It seems such a god damn shame to give what my dad worked for, for so many years, away for naught. What the final outcome will be I don't know.

The second blow I had tonight was about my brother Sam. I was telling Fran about my plans to go to see you while mother stayed in Washington, - well, Sam is due to go into the army March 1st. Mother doesn't know a thing about it yet, - what will happen when she finds out is another thing I don't know.

Thirdly, Edie M. is very sick. She's had all kinds of treatment for her stomach, but to no avail. Tuesday, she has an appointment for X-rays. And that was my day Sunday. My head is just splitting and even if I go to bed I know I won't sleep.

Yesterday I went into your folk's store and Toby let me read the letter you wrote home. Darling, I had no idea that you aren't going to stay in Oklahoma. Whether you like it or not, - I'm worried. And I will be until I have reason to be otherwise. I had no mail from you Saturday so I still don't know if anything has happened or not. This damn uncertainty of everything is driving me crazy. I like your optimism in saying that there's a chance of you being shipped nearer to home. Darling, no one in this world would like that to happen more than I, but somehow, I can't put my heart into believing that maybe you will be. I love you so damn much and I need you so terribly. Why can't something go right for me? The only real good thing that has happened to me is your being in love with me and our being married.

I wouldn't trade the little happiness we had for all the money in the world. I love you very, very much, George, and come what may, it will never be otherwise. Everything seems to be so empty tonight. I feel all alone in a great big world. Maybe I'll sleep it off, - I certainly hope so.

Darling, Dr. Glixman sent your glasses to your folks and when I was in the store, your mother gave them to me, but I don't know whether to send them to you now or wait. So, tell me what to do. If you want them, I'll send them immediately.

I hope you'll excuse this very miserable letter. I'm sure tomorrow the world will seem much brighter, - if I get a letter from you it will.

Goodnight darling,
Always yours,
Lottie

P.S. Michael's account is growing very nicely. Dave gave me a whole hand full of pennies today. Mama

February 26, 1945
Monday

From:	To:
Cpl. James G. Barr 11057933	Mrs. James G. Barr
4514th A.A.F. B.U., Tinker Field	65 Houghton St.
Oklahoma City, Oklahoma	Worcester 4, Mass.

Dearest One,

If I get this letter written at all to-night, I'll consider myself pretty good. There's so much racket going on in here a person can't think or even talk! We have four musicians here and they're all playing, but not good, and too loud.

Three letters from you to-day, the first mail I've received since I left G.B., and it is wonderful. I would have loved to have seen you pixilated, when you get drunk with me you pass out.

I had to laugh when I read in your letter asking me how long you think I'll remain in Kansas, and here I am, but in Oklahoma! This couple my father wanted me to look up, isn't the one you mentioned. Sorry, maybe you know someone in Okla.?

I had it very easy to-day having B.O. (barracks orderly, to you). I worked almost a half hour the entire day, the rest of the time I read, wrote a few letters, one to Sam and one to Irving. I also got the music and the words for that song I wrote you about. He has to put the chords in it, then I'll send it to you. He put the chords in that he thought were good, but when he asked the advice of a piano player (he hopes to be a concert pianist some day), they started to change them around. I'll send it to you one of these days.

After writing you last night we sat down to some U.S.O. show and Norman and I got a box of cookies apiece - for not having our birthday yesterday. The M.C. wanted some service man who had his birthday yesterday, so when no one answered, he just picked on us. They were very good too. Being still hungry, we went and had a good steak dinner.

We still hadn't seen the "Three Caballeros," so when we walked by the show and saw that there was a small waiting line, we bought our tickets. While waiting, Norman played his 'tonette' and everyone had a swell time. We raised hell and finally the usher told us to stop, but our audience booed him so much he walked away. To get rid of us, he came back and had two seats for us. Norman's 'tonette' certainly comes in handy!!

It will be a happy day when you can come out with me. We'll get a bottle and we'll get nice and happy and have a hell of a time. We'll rumba and dance and any other thing that our feet desire!! I'll hug you and kiss you, and hug you and kiss you, and ----- I could go on and on!!! Loving you is my health tonic.

I'm going to sleep now to dream about my sweet lovely wife.

Goodnight dearest,
Your loving husband,
George

P.S. Our uncle from Wash. saw Sam and he also sends his regards to you. Papa

February 26, 1945
Monday

From:	To:
Mrs. J.G. Barr	Cpl. James G. Barr 11057933
65 Houghton St.	4514th A.A.F. B.U., Tinker Field
Worcester, Mass.	Oklahoma City, Oklahoma

My dearest George,

Altho one could have easily drowned in the rain today, to me the sun shone brightly because I received two letters from you. One was still from Kansas, the other from Oklahoma.

I thought I'd die laughing when you wrote about the boys contributing to the Michael Barr Welfare Fund. Not at all a bad idea, - by the time Michael is born, we should have a small fortune in pennies!

Well, at least today's letter gave me a vague idea of what you are doing. You say you are working in a shop, - what kind of work you are doing you neglected to tell me. If someone should say to me, "what is George doing" – and I told them he works in a shop, they'd probably say what a shame that you weren't in the army! So pleeze, my darling husband, enlighten me.

Had a very pleasant surprise this P.M. A short while ago your mother called me and when I asked where she was, she said home, - but I could very plainly hear a baby yelling. Well, to make a long story short, Narky, Charlotte & Bonnie came home today. Narky is due to report in California around the 12th of March, so Charlotte will stay here and work. Meanwhile she'll stay with your folks, and then when her folks go into their own home, she'll go with them.

Narky told me absolutely to go to Oklahoma if I had the chance. He made it sound so easy that I feel like a stinker for not leaving tomorrow. But then I tried to explain it wasn't as easy as all that, - but he sure gave me the added encouragement I needed about going. Darling, every minute we are separated is agony for me too. I only hope that things turn out so that I can come down. If you only knew how much I want to come.

Just spoke to Barbara and this life of ease is driving her nuts. I think she'll go back to New York sometime next week. It's still pouring outside, a nice night to sit in an automobile and listen to the rain beating down on the roof, soft music and cuddled up to someone you love. Well, we can dream, can't we?

And so, my darling ends tonight's missive.

Goodnite & pleasant dreams.
Always yours,
Cookie

February 27, 1945
Tuesday

From:	To:
Cpl. James G. Barr 11057933	Mrs. James G. Barr
4514th A.A.F. B.U., Tinker Field	65 Houghton St.
Oklahoma City, Oklahoma	Worcester 4, Mass.

Dearest Lottie,

Here's "This One Sided Sweet Love Affair", I hope you like it. You'd better, for I spent a good half hour copying it from the work sheet!

Your letter of to-day was the letter you wrote me when you got my first letter, a 'few' days late, but just as good as if I had received it before. You said in this letter you have expectations of getting a raise. Did the Sharfman's come across, or are you getting the run around?

Last night Norman and I went to the P.X. where we got a few things and then went for a beer. There's a piano in the beer hall, so right away Norman started to play. Near the piano there was a WAC and she invited us over to their day room, so that she could hear him, the noise that the G.I.'s make in a beer hall is terrific. We went over and I never saw such a collection of bags in my life. The pay off was when one of the WAC's stopped the conversation and said that "Damn it, here I've been shacking for two weeks now, and I'm not even legally married." When I heard that I almost dropped!!! The other WAC's didn't even move a muscle! What a bunch of women! By the way "shacking" is living with a man or woman. Norman wants to go back again to-night to see if he can get himself a shack mate.

We had a terrific snow storm, so of course, there was plenty of snow to shovel. Our detail was to clean off the top of a warehouse. After pushing snow over the roof for about an hour and a half, we got tired and quit. Of course, the only reason we quit was that there was no one around to check up on us.

I get a big kick out of Norman, because when I'm sitting down and thinking of you and I have that far off look in my eye, I catch an occasional glimpse of him and he has the funniest expression on his face. I guess my love for you shows up on my face and he knows just what I'm thinking.

So, Becky threw a few nice remarks about me? What did I ever do that I should be able to have her compliment me? It was your idea to walk her home, you're the gentleman of the family, and of course, the lady.

I signed the payroll for seventy bucks to-day!! I'll be able to send you lots of dough when we get paid to-morrow or the next day! That's if you consider $40 – much money.

I also got me a nice photo album yesterday, now I'll have to fill the pages with pictures. Has Jackie called you up about the pictures as yet?

I think your rhyming is beautiful. Although, I can't write poetry, I still can say, Darling, I love you very much.

Your loving husband,
George

February 28, 1945
Wednesday

From:	To:
Mrs. J.G. Barr	Cpl. James G. Barr 11057933
65 Houghton St.	4514th A.A.F. B.U., Tinker Field
Worcester, Mass.	Oklahoma City, Oklahoma

Hello darling,

This is my second try in writing you a letter. I started earlier this evening with the intention of doing a lot of things tonight, - namely answering an accumulation of letters, - but we had a pile of company and the noise was so loud that I couldn't even hear meself think. Well, anywho, I tore up the first attempt, so here I go again!

To begin with, - yer lil ole wifey is quite the busy bee these days. We opened the store yesterday and I go down there on my lunch hour and after work. We posted Sale signs on the window and my mother and I are trying to push out whatever we can. As you know, there isn't very much, - we don't have the right sizes in anything, but nevertheless, we've taken in a few dollars. At least it's better than giving it all to the Russian Relief, - the remainder we will give to them, though.

I'm having a little trouble with your new address, the post office stamped right on top of it, so I'm putting down what I can figure out.

So velly sorry, darling, that the wedding ring cramped your style in picking up that girl. By the by, who is Norman, - is he a new or old acquaintance?!! Tell him if I ever meet him, he'll have to keep playing "Take Me In Your Arms" constantly, also "Meet Me In St. Louis, Louieeee!" Whenever I hear that song I instinctively think of our honeymoon. Also, the title of his song sounds very good, I'm hoping he will write it up for me. If it's any good, I'll have Barbara plug it when she goes to New York. Also, how were the girls that he picked up, - or didn't he use those phone numbers yet!

Darling, why has your outlook on staying in Oklahoma changed? Have there been any new rumors, - or isn't there much work, - and if you do get transferred, have you any idea where? There are millions of questions I want to ask you, but when I come to write, I can never think of them. Anyway, any of the questions I would ask would be silly, because most likely your answer would be "I dunno!"

I'm mailing your glasses and your envelope tomorrow morning. You should have them in a few days.

The weather is starting to bring on a bad case of spring fever for me. I don't feel like working, or anything, - just sitting and dreaming. Zelda is also smitten with the same ailment, so you can imagine how much work we accomplish. At 5:15 we both start rushing like hell.

Today was pay day and boy – what a relief. I was never so broke in my life. Now if I didn't have to pay my income tax everything would be supper duper. But I don't want them to put yer wife in the clink! By the by, - speaking of yer wife, I have been re-christened by Edith Richards. My name is now Chocolate, - you know, for Chocolate Barr. Everybody agrees that it's a very sweet name.

Spoke to Edie M. today and she feels a little better. She took those X-rays, but as yet, does not know the results.

Fer hevven's sake, I'm tired. My head is wiggle woggin all over the place.

Goodnite, m'love,

Your loving wife,

Lottie (Chocolate)

P.S. I bought 25 pennies today, - I really got quite a bargain, - only paid a quarter for them. Nighty night. Mommie

February 28, 1945

Wednesday

From:	To:
Cpl. James G. Barr 11057933	Mrs. James G. Barr
4514th A.A.F. B.U., Tinker Field	65 Houghton St.
Oklahoma City, Oklahoma	Worcester 4, Mass.

My darling wife,

Your loving husband felt damn good this afternoon, when the man handed him his seventy bucks. He even felt better when he was able to send to his wife the forty that she received before this letter. Now you'll be able to pay back your mother all the money you owe, and I imagine that they'll be enough left for your account with the Book of the Month Club. And, maybe you need a Persian lamb coat!!!

If that stationery that you have is new stuff, you got cheated. When I received to-day's letter, the side had been opened. At first I thought someone had slit it with a knife, thinking that there was money in it, because of the way you seal the envelope with mending tape. On closer examination, I saw that it was the paper, it's all dried out and brittle, and the least amount of handling, tears it at the fold. It looks nice, but it won't stand up.

I'm glad that Barb isn't going overseas, it's no life for anyone. Does she have any future plans that you know of?

I got a big kick out of your hoping that I'll stay in Oklahoma. I hope that I do, too, but not because Oklahoma is supposed to have a nice landscape. If I had a car and plenty of time to drive around the state, then I imagine that we could appreciate it, but being in the army doesn't help. And as you said, damn the army!!

The main reason that I'd like to remain here is that it is near a large town and when you come out to me, it will be much easier for both of us, than if I were still in G.B. I don't want you to be disappointed, but I want you to know what the story is. When I first came down here, things looked good, as I wrote, but I don't know now, how good it will remain. This doesn't look like a permanent outfit.

I don't know why you showed Dave the cup, I wouldn't think he'd be interested. That bastard figures that if you get the raise, you won't leave later on, but that if you have a child, then you'd have to leave. It's not that he's mercenary, I just think he is no good!

We didn't do much of anything to-day but throw snowballs. The boys and I were having an uproarious time hitting one another. People have more fun than anyone I know. (O.K. so it's corny, come on out and wash my face in the snow!)

Maybe Alma Herck takes care of the kids, or she just didn't have anything else to do. Why else was she there?

I don't think I got all the money that was due me, so I may be able to send you a few bucks next month also. Good huh!

I'm going to be very glad when I can cross my wife off of my mailing list. Here's hoping that it will be soon.

Your husband, who loves you very much,
George

March 1, 1945
Thursday

From:	To:
Cpl. James G. Barr 11057933	Mrs. James G. Barr
4514th A.A.F. B.U., Tinker Field	65 Houghton St.
Oklahoma City, Oklahoma	Worcester 4, Mass.

Dearest Lottie,

When you come out where I am, I'll hold you tight, kiss you, and run my hands thru your beautiful hair. Not only because you want me to, but I'll thrill to every hug, kiss, and strand of your hair. Do I sound silly? Like hell I do!!! When we are to-gether again, we'll make up for all the time lost.

By this time, you should know whether Sam is in the army or not. I don't know why, but I didn't think Sam would be called in the army, and it's the same way I feel about Irving. Last Sunday certainly was a day for you. I feel so bad when I hear about those kind of days that you have, I want so much to be with you that I ache all over.

I'm glad that we married young, because we can have a long life of love to-gether.

I'm in town to-night. Norman and I are going to see the "Blythe Spirit", we hear it's very good, and if I remember correctly you've already seen it.

I got two letters from you again to-day, and these also were slit were the envelope cracked, so you'd better get new envelopes. You can send me my glasses, I don't think I'll get shipped out that soon, and even if I did, they would finally get to me, but as yet, we're staying and April might still find me at Tinker Field.

Darling, your husband (that's me) loves you more and more and more!

Your loving husband,
George

P.S. Almost sent this to my folks, even had it addressed to them, that would have been something. Papa

March 2, 1945
Friday

From:	To:
Mrs. J.G. Barr	Cpl. James G. Barr 11057933
65 Houghton St.	4514th A.A.F. B.U., Tinker Field
Worcester, Mass.	Oklahoma City, Oklahoma

My dearest George,

I certainly felt like a stinker this morning when I passed the mailbox and didn't have a letter to mail to you, but I was so darn tired last nite, all I could do was flop in bed. So please forgiveth me, eh wot?!!

Received your money order today and was very pleased, - to say the least. Your little note was cute, - so I can do what I want with the money, eh? Well, I could buy a very nice dress, - or have it towards a suit, - or.........I could put it in the bank, which is certainly what I'm going to do. But it was sweet of you to let me decide what to do with it, altho I have a faint idea you knew where the money was going.

Went over your house to-night for supper and had a very enjoyable evening. Your mother and dad fell asleep in the parlor while Narky, Charlotte, Toby, and I sat in the kitchen eating pistachio nuts, - I'm so full of nuts I even feel nuts! I had my dessert, then Narky and Charlotte drove me home and Narky kissed me goodnite. Hmmm, twas very good. But no matter how good it was, I knew it wasn't you, - and that spoiled it.

Last nite my mother and I had dinner down Water St. After we ate we saw Irving go into Ralph Garber's store so we went in after him. Irv introduced me to Ralph and when he heard I was married to you, - well, he couldn't stop raving about you. He thinks you are positively wonderful. While he was saying all these nice things about you, I couldn't help thinking that you said you disliked him!! You must remember from now on to like Ralph Garber!!

Things at the office are in a terrible state. Monday Charlotte is being transferred to a new department, which makes me the head of our department, - and I don't like it! I have a new girl whom I'm teaching the work, and altho she tries very hard, it's not easy to grasp all the work at once. If I had known Charlotte would be transferred, I never would have gone back to New England. But I'm still hoping that I won't be there too much longer, so I guess I can stick it out!

My mother is beginning to question why we haven't heard from my brother Sam. I don't know what to tell her, - I'm truly worried. Incidentally, I'm awfully glad you wrote letters to Sam & Irv.

I'm also anxiously waiting for the song that Norman wrote. Barb is going back to N.Y. Thursday, - I hope I get it before then.

Every day it gets warmer and warmer and I get happier and happier because the sooner it gets warm, the sooner I can be with you, - and oh how I'm looking forward to that. I keep pushing the hours, the days, and the weeks.

I love you very much dear.
Your loving wife,
Lottie B.

P.S. - No p.s. tonight!! Mommie

March 2, 1945
Friday

From:	To:
Cpl. James G. Barr 11057933	Mrs. James G. Barr
4514th A.A.F. B.U., Tinker Field	65 Houghton St.
Oklahoma City, Oklahoma	Worcester 4, Mass.

My darling wife,

They finally caught up with me! To-morrow morning I have K.P. This will make my day very morose and unhappy. I don't like K.P. for some reason or other, even tho I usually don't exert myself (After rereading that last sentence, I've decided to change it to "I don't usually" – me and my split infinitives!!!) When this war is over and all the boys are home again, a good idea would be for me to take eighth grade grammar over again.

When I left you last night we wandered over to the theater where the "Blithe Spirit" was playing. In doing so, I got my feet wet by stupidly placing my number $9 \frac{1}{2}$ D's in a puddle of water. I was glad that the place was warm so I could dry up.

The play was excellent and I liked it very much, even tho Gladys George didn't star because she was sick. Her stand in did a very good job and got quite an ovation.

I had gone with Norman, and when the first act started, he moved over to some empty seats that were close to the center. I didn't want to change our seats so soon and I told him so, but stubbornly he refused, so we moved. Of course, five minutes later we had to go back to our old seats because the owners came in late. We had fun anyway.

I really put out some work to-day and surprised the boss. When I told him that another fellow and I had finished our work on two ships, he could hardly believe it. It even surprised me. But what the hell, we've got to get this war over with!

No letter from you to-day, which only makes me feel that much lonelier. I try to think of some comparison of loneliness, but fail to, there just isn't any comparison. I love you and want you, and there is only one remedy, which I hope we'll both be able to have soon.

All my love, all my life.
Your husband, George

March 4, 1945
Sunday nite

From:	To:
Mrs. J.G. Barr	Cpl. James G. Barr 11057933
65 Houghton St.	4514th A.A.F. B.U., Tinker Field
Worcester, Mass.	Oklahoma City, Oklahoma

My dearest darling sweetheart husband,

It seems this evening for some odd reason I feel in quite a gala mood. If you were home tonight, I'd probably pester and kiss you to death. If you remember correctly, darling, I do have my moods! Today was really beautiful. Spring was in the air, fresh and clean, and I loved it. My mother and I certainly made the most of it. After breakfast, we cleaned the house from top to bottom, then I was so filthy, I climbed into a bubble bath, - only, sad to say, there were no bubbles. It was the first time I had used the stuff Sol bought for me. I was never so disillusioned, - I waited and waited and not one bubble!! While I was in the tub Fran called, and said she was coming over in a few minutes to take us to Milford. Well, without even having a chance to dry off, I put my clothes on and was ready when she got here. When we got to Milford we found that they were preparing a party for that nite for Leon, Fran's brother, who was just discharged from the army.

Fran's sister Milly was making cake frosting and having piles of trouble, as a matter of fact, she was ready to throw it out when Fran and I saved the day. I took over as if I had done it all my life, - and surprisingly enough, it came out very, very good. Goodness, was I proud of myself. Anywho, I frosted three cakes and helped set the table. We couldn't stay for the party because Fran had to come home to feed Rickey.

On the way home, Fran drove us down to my aunt Rose's where we had supper. After supper, Zelda's inlaws and Zelda plus my aunt & uncle sat down to play poker. I didn't have any money so I borrowed a dime from my uncle. Anywho, - I really cleaned up, I came home with 85¢ to the good. We didn't play very long because my mother wanted to go home, but I won nearly every game. It was the first time in my poker playing life that I ever won! So now Michael is 85¢ to the good.

By the by, the Dickman's gave us a $25.00 bond as a wedding gift. I thought it was very nice of them. Also, I think it would be a nice idea if you wrote them a short thank you letter, I'm sure they would appreciate it. The address is:

Mr. & Mrs. A. Dickman
Pleasant St. - Milford, Mass.

Yesterday, my mother and I stayed in the store till about 9 o'clock. I sold more shoes than anything, and my mother and I nearly died laughing at the astronomical prices I was asking and getting. On the whole, we didn't take in very much. It's hard and dirty work, but I kinda enjoyed it, - or at least I did when I could sell something.

In Saturday's letter, I finally received the song. I tried to play it on the piano, but I don't know what the minor and diminished cords are, so I could only play the melody, which didn't sound like much with me playing it. Tomorrow nite I think Barb is coming over so I'll really hear what it sounds like. As for the words, - I don't particularly care for them. They are nothing out of the ordinary, and sound amateurish. Of course, my opinion means very little. For a gal who goes for Cole Porter and George Gershwin, this song is quite a comedown, but I'll hold further remarks and see what Barb has to say. Of course, you needn't tell Norman what I think about it, he might get discouraged, and furthermore if I could write anything as good as that, I'd consider myself O.K. - but I don't think it has enough to it to warrant publication.

Also, what does this Norman look like, and what kind of a guy is he? He's so much of your steady companion that I'd like to know more about him.

Got quite a kick out of the WAC's - and they're shacking. That expression was a brand new one for me. Tell Norman to wait until I get there so we can double date!! I always did want to see how one of dem kind act – and get results!!!!!!

If you could see me darling, you'd never know I was an old married woman. My hair has grown very long of late, so tonight I decided to put it in pigtails. Everyone (my mother, Jeanne & Mrs. Ciborowski) think it looks velly cute. I really look horrible, - but they liked it – so anything to make them happy. Sitting here on my legs I look like a ten year old!! And smoking a cigarette too, oh my, for shame!!

Well, my dearest, darling, sweetheart, me little hand is worn out from writing so much. Tomorrow is another day of woik! I'm very tired, - you know the old saying, I'se so tired, I'se so weary - pick I up and kiss I dearie! Oh, - how I wish you could.

Always yours,
Lovingly, Lottie

P.S. Fran & Irv received your letter and were very pleased. Mommie.

P.S.S. – About that mommie business, - confidentially, I'm worried!!!
Signed
Poor me.

March 4, 1945
Sunday

From:	To:
Cpl. James G. Barr 11057933	Mrs. James G. Barr
4514th A.A.F. B.U., Tinker Field	65 Houghton St.
Oklahoma City, Oklahoma	Worcester 4, Mass.

Dearest Lottie,

I guess now I don't have to keep track of our engagement anniversary, I have a more important one to remember, which comes up in three more days. We'll be married two months by the time you get this letter, the best two months in my life. Many months and years are coming that we'll be able to enjoy just as well, maybe better. Lottie darling, I love you very much and miss you just as much. I'm just waiting until you are with me again.

After putting in a very grueling day of K.P., I wasn't in any mood to write any letters, I hope you'll understand. If you knew where this letter was being written from, maybe you wouldn't want it, but the latrine is the only place where we have lights now. We just came back from town.

This afternoon we bummed into town and went to see the symphony. They're not bad, but I didn't like their selections. The ballet is coming to town, so we're planning to see that also. It was a funny and nice thing that happened when we went to get our tickets. We were expecting to pay, but we, and the other music lovers were allowed in for free.

Then we went up to the shule where there was a dance and food. I watched all the kids dance, danced a few myself and had a nice little feed afterwards.

Norman and I walked two of the girls to a movie, but because there was a crowd, they were going to go home, but Norman asked them to have a beer, to which they readily said yes. I had already shown them our wedding pictures, so Norman talked with one of the girls and I answered questions about you ect. and ect. with the other one. They think you are very sweet and want to meet you when you come down, if I'm in Okie City.

Here's a piece of gum to tide you over for a length of time. If you just look at it every day, it will last a very long time!!!! Aren't I a (b.-) stinker!

Here's a cute article that I found in a little paper. Probably Evelyn can use it in her paper, if she still puts it out.

Goodnight my darling wife.
Your loving husband,
George

When A Sailor Marries

While a lawyer in Edinburgh, Scotland, was engaged in cleaning ~~up~~ out an old deed-box, he came across a quaint document, a chart for married life. The author had evidently been a sailor.

In nine clauses, there are set forth the duties of wife to husband, and those of husband to wife. The full text of the document is as follows:

"Having also read to my espoused the Articles of War, I explained to her the conditions under which we were to sail in company on lifes voyage, namely:

1. She to obey signals without questions when received.

2. She to steer by my reckoning.

3. She to stand by me as a true consort in foul weather, battle, or shipwreck.

4. She to run under my guns if assailed by picaroons, privateers, or garda costas.

5. Me to keep her in due repair, and see that she hath her allowance of coats of paint, streamers, and buntings, as befits a saucy pleasure boat.

6. Me to take no other craft in tow, and if any be now attached, to cut their hawseres.

7. Me to revictual her day by day.

8. Should she chance to be blown on her beam ends by wind of misfortune, me to stand by her and see her righted.

9. To lay our course for the Great Hourbor in the hope that moorings and ground to swing may be found for two British built craft when laid up for eternity."

When contemplatin matrimony, thake the advice of and old salt, and make certain that your course is set----for the Great WAXX Harbor.

March 5, 1945
Monday

From:	To:
Cpl. James G. Barr 11057933	Mrs. James G. Barr
4514th A.A.F. B.U., Tinker Field	65 Houghton St.
Oklahoma City, Oklahoma	Worcester 4, Mass.

My darling,

    Last night's letter was very poor, I know, but I was half asleep and the atmosphere wasn't at all conducive to letter writing! To-night I will try to put out something that looks and reads like a sensible letter.

Your two letters of to-day hit the right spot and I love you for it. I guess the airmail service isn't too hot here, because I got a letter from Toby and one from Narky dated the same day as one of yours, and I got all of them at the same time. How are my letters coming in comparison to my old way of sending them?

I'll have to write Edie a letter one of these days when I haven't any other people to answer. I hope that she gets well soon, and tell her I send my almost best.

I think you got stuck when you bought your stationery. The envelopes are almost falling apart when I receive them.

Michael's fund is starting to climb, I think the box I have the pennies in is almost half full. Norman is contributing very generously and I get a few of the other boys at times. Our kid is going to do all right! Why should you have to buy pennies when I can get them for free, and you being much prettier than me too!!!

You have a vague idea of what I'm doing and it will have to remain vague, for I don't know whether it is secret or not, but I hadn't heard about it until we came up here. My job tho is very simple and most of it is hooking up wires for different types of equipment. First, we're shown how to do it, then we go out to a B-29 in the hangar and start connecting. I just don't want to go up on any of those ships until after a few flights at least!

One good thing about working like we are and that is that our boss is a civilian. If we want to work we work, if not, we don't – how wonderful.

If people want to know what I'm doing, I'm in the electrical installation department. Now have you a broader view of my doings, if not, fire the questions at me and I'll try within my meager power to answer them.

How's the store and its merchandise getting along? With you in the store, I bet the men just come to look at you and when they buy, they probably pay the price that you ask for. Am I right? How could I be wrong!!

The man with the "tonette" is Norman Katz, a jew boy, who I've known before, but just recently started to pal around with. If things go bad, he can always play his tonette and liven up the place. He's a good kid and we get along famously. You remember the phone call I made to his mother, don't you? That was one of the few times I left you alone while we were on our honeymoon!

Darling, I'll have to ask you not to have Barb play that song in New York. He doesn't have it copyrighted and I don't want him to blame me if someone thinks it's good enough to steal. So, if you've given the song to Barbara already, write her to use discretion when she plays it. I know you'll understand. That Norman I cannot understand him, it cost one buck to copyright it and yet he doesn't do it. There must be something else behind it that he hasn't told me. Oh well, it's his song and I guess he thinks he knows what he's doing.

My stay in Oklahoma may not be for any length of time. What may happen, as soon as we get another outfit in with us and things get organized, is that all the men physically qualified will be shipped out to tactical outfits (by tactical, I mean that they are preparing for overseas shipment). A few men have already left and may be overseas in a few weeks from now. Even tho it doesn't look good, as you said, "I dunno."

If I'm still here in the spring and you can come out, of course, I'll want you here with me. And if I go to another base, why you come along too. Whatever happens, even if it is for a short period of time, it will be worth it. I know what I've just written sounds as if I'm ready to leave for P.O.E. in a few minutes, but that isn't at all so, I just want you to know what the possibilities are. Here's one thing I've found about the army – don't worry about going overseas until you are actually on the boat!!!

I don't know about that "Chocolate", it's almost like Candy. I've always liked chocolate, maybe that's why I love you, at least one of the reasons anyway.

What do you mean I knew what you were going to do with the check? Maybe you wanted a down payment on a Persian Lamb, or something. Heck, don't I have to take care of my wife?! Besides, I had to pay back what I took from the bank, didn't I?

That Garber makes me laugh. Hell, he doesn't even know me. I bet if I walked into his store he wouldn't even recognize me. That guy wouldn't know whether I was good or an old bastard. Maybe he expects you to buy a lot of sundaes and cigarettes off of him now. I still don't like him. Period.

So, Dave got the better of you, huh? I was wondering why he fell all over you when you came back. I bet he had planned to move Charlotte to another department anyway, and he wanted you back because you've had the necessary experience to run the show. I imagine you also got the raise coming with the responsibility too. Dave is no damn good, but I think he got the better of you this time. You'll be a good boss anyway.

Have I done alright – I could have written to many people in the time I took to write this "note" and you notice I have note quotation marked!!! Surprised myself in doing it too.

Good night my darling, and if you knew how much I loved you, you'd come flying to me right now. Darling I need you. You are my one and only morale builder, there is absolutely nothing that can or ever will take your place.

Your, George

March 6, 1945
Tuesday

From:	To:
Cpl. James G. Barr 11057933	Mrs. James G. Barr
4514th A.A.F. B.U., Tinker Field	65 Houghton St.
Oklahoma City, Oklahoma	Worcester 4, Mass.

My very dearest wife,

I hope that I'll be able to call you to-night, even tho I never wanted to ever have to make such a call.

Early this morning I was told to pack, for I was shipping. No one knew where I was supposed to go until three in the afternoon, and then I was told I was being transferred to a very hot outfit on the field ready to go to P.O.E.!

I reported over there and I guess we're leaving to-morrow, anyway, by this time we'll be on our way to P.O.E. After last night's letter to you, this sounds so damn unreal that I can't (one "n") believe it. I'm shipping overseas!!!

There are a few satisfying things about it tho. First, I'll be with an Air Depot, which is way behind the lines and action of any kind, except of course work, is practically out of the question; secondly, it may bring me back that much faster. Hold on darling, I know it's going to be tough, but try and keep going. I know you will!! I know what kind of stuff you're made of and you're solid thru and thru, and in every respect.

I know a few of the fellows in the outfit, and it won't be as hard to get acquainted as I thought. There are just two radio men that are corporals and I'm one of them, so there may be a good chance for a rating. More money to build our castles of the future, dream castles with solid rock foundations. Don't worry, everything is going to turn out O.K.

You may not receive as many letters from me as you hope or like, but you know the reason why.

I don't know if the mail of my outfit is censored or not, so I'll give you my present address & the mail will be forwarded & when I get my A.P.O., you'll hear from me.

> 94th Depot Repair Sqd.
> 23rd A.D.G.
> Tinker Field, Okla. City, Oklahoma

What I wouldn't give for a sight of you now. Where's that crack you were telling me about?

I'm having Norman send you some of my stuff & suit case, I don't have much, so you'll be able to put them someplace out of the way.

Good night my darling, and you know that I'll always love you. All my love, all my life!

Your loving husband,
George

P.S. Kiss me quick! Papa

P.P.S. Michael's fund – what there is of it will also come with my stuff. Papa

March 7, 1945
Wednesday
Our 2nd Anniversary

From:	To:
Cpl. James G. Barr 11057933	Mrs. James G. Barr
94th Dep. Rep. Sq., 23rd A.D.G.	65 Houghton St.
Tinker Field, Oklahoma	Worcester 4, Mass.

OKLAHOMA CITY AIR DEPOT
TINKER FIELD
OKLAHOMA CITY, OKLA.

March 7th
Our 2nd Anniversary

My darling wife,

I imagine that this will be my last for maybe five days or so. While on the train, if we write, we'll be unable to send any mail, as I understand it.

We're out of our barracks, most of our belongings have been put onboard the train & the only things that we will carry is our pack. So far I haven't been as rushed about as I thought I would be.

Many of the boy's wives are here with them on the field and to tell the truth, it makes my heart ache to see them. If you had been here with me, I hope I would have had the sense (which I doubt) to send you home a day earlier then when we actually left, because the men knew when they were leaving.

Talking with you last night was the best thing that I could have done to help out my morale, because it was pretty low. The connection was wonderful, and I could hear your wonderful and lovely voice as if I were next door to you. I'm just sorry that I didn't have enough change to take care of the remainder of the telephone bill.

You'll have to get some better stationery to stand up under the gaff of overseas mailing, I doubt if the stationery you now use would last long under a little abuse.

Here we've been married two months now, and we were able to spend 38 days to-gether, more time than a lot of G.I.'s have had in two years of married life! Even tho it is considered a long time by more unfortunate people, I still want more time! Darling, there won't be one minute when you'll be out of mind, whether awake or sleeping. When we are to-gether again, we're going to make up for every second lost!!!

I don't think you need worry about Mama, because you told me yourself that you get periods very irregular, but maybe Michael knows about his fund, and he wants to spend it!!

There was something else that I wanted to write you, but my mind is just full of thought about you and everything else is just one big muddle.

All my love,
Your, George

P.S. Got the two Gazettes you sent – they were swell. I'm glad that you're able to get a little money out of the store, by this time it should be empty with that ad in the paper. Papa.

March 9, 1945
Friday

From:	To:
Cpl. Norman Katz 32875776	Mrs. James G. Barr
4514th A.A.F. B.U., Tinker Field	65 Houghton St.
Oklahoma City, Oklahoma	Worcester 4, Mass.

OKLAHOMA CITY AIR DEPOT
TINKER FIELD
OKLAHOMA CITY, OKLA.

Dear Lottie,

I hope you don't mind the informal salutation, but Jim has always referred to you as Lottie.

I last saw Jim (I know you call him George) Wed. evening until he had to meet a formation at 8:15 P.M. He asked me to get his dry cleaning out for him and send it home to you together with his suitcase, which he left me. I sent same via Railway Express yesterday. Enclosed in this letter you'll find the keys to the suitcase.

Within the suitcase, you will find a tin-topped candy box, which contains approximately $2.50 worth of pennies and also a quarter, which I paid for misguessing the number of pennies therein. That quarter, plus a good number of pennies which I contributed to the collection, entitles me to be a "part godfather" to "junior" who although not yet on his way, I hope will be forthcoming (with) after Jimmy's speedy return home. Please pardon the poor choice of vocab.!

Jim & I took some pictures last Sunday, which have not yet been developed. My situation here is as uncertain as Jim's was & so I am reluctant to give the film away to be developed until I'm reasonably sure of being somewhere for a while. I shall send some copies to you at the very earliest opportunity.

I'd like to know if you've received the suitcase & keys in good shape, so I'd appreciate a note from you at your convenience.

Your husband's friend,
Norman Katz

March 10, 1945
Saturday
On route – still!

From:	To:
Cpl. James G. Barr 11057933	Mrs. James G. Barr
94th Dep. Rep. Sq., 23rd A.D.G.	65 Houghton St.
Tinker Field, Oklahoma	Worcester 4, Mass.

My darling wife,

Even tho this trip is a long one, time seems to have passed quite rapidly. Thinking of and about you has helped matters considerably. I know if you could be here with me, we could both enjoy the beauty of the Rockies. If we're able to after the war, just we two will travel around the U.S. and see its entirety if possible, because unless you've traveled a lot, being in the army has given me a good chance, you can't realize how large a place we live in. That you can travel for days, I should say hours, and not see any human being or buildings. I bet you could evenly distribute the entire population of this country and their closest neighbors would be miles away!

Every once in awhile we stop to get water, change trains, and so forth. During these stops we're able to get out and stretch. The last place we stopped at, the A.W.U.S., a women's organization, came out and fed us cokes, candy, doughnuts, and cigarettes. This was the first time during our trip that someone had something for us. It's not unusual, because we haven't hit any large places at all, maybe there just aren't any such places out here.

I was up pretty early this morning to pull my tour of guard, and will be up even earlier to-morrow morning. I have the 3-5 shift next. Guards stand at each end of the train and are supposed to allow no one by except officers and those men with passes. It's really a farce, except that it still reminds you of military discipline and I imagine that's the main reason.

We can have these letters mailed by giving them to sort of a mail clerk, who gathers them all. Whether they're censored or not, I don't know, or if they're holding them until we get to our destination, I don't know, but we have to leave them unsealed. If they are censored let me know.

I met a friend of Narky's on the train. He's a truck driver in this outfit and seems a likable fellow. So now there are about five or six men that I know.

What were my folk's reaction to my future status?

If I knew definitely how long we were going to stay at P.O.E. and if we could get passes, I'd ask you to come a-running! Darling, knowing that I won't be able to see you when my next furlough comes up makes it that much harder to take. What happy people there'll be when this damn war is over with and we're all home.

I hope that'll be able to take my camera with me. If I had been in the outfit earlier, I could have had it packed with the rest of the fellow's personal equipment, but because I was too late, I may have to ship it home.

When you get my suitcase, you'll find among the pennies for Michael, a quarter donated by Norman, because he lost a bet. Norman bet another fellow there were over 200 pennies & the loser was to put the quarter in the saving fund. We couldn't lose!!

We're now passing thru some of the most beautiful country I've ever seen. The train is cutting thru a valley, following the most unique river I've ever had the pleasure to see. The coloring of it is unique in that it reminds me of the turquoise stone, changing with the light, but always a gorgeous pale blue. I sure would have enjoyed my geography lessons enormously more if I had classes out where we were studying. You can't imagine the vastness of the Rockies until you are among them and can see cloud formations covering some of the higher mountain peaks. This is a must in our post-war travels!!

The food on the train has been pretty good, and the cooks have to be given credit. From the voices of some of the other boys who have eaten meals on troop trains before, something for which I'm glad I never had to go thru, say the food is beyond comparison.

I was sorry that my glasses hadn't reached me before I left Okie City, but I hope that they'll catch up with me at P.O.E.

My sweet, did you ever realize just how much your husband loved you? Well, he loves you very much and only wishes he could express it much better than he does. A wife like his deserves the best of everything.

Your loving husband,
George

P.S. Also passing some of the time at poker. I couldn't even win 85¢, but why should I go into the horrid details!!! Papa

March 11, 1945
Sunday

From:	To:
Cpl. James G. Barr 11057933	Mrs. James G. Barr
94th Depot Repair Sq.	65 Houghton St.
APO 18217 c/o Postmaster	Worcester 4, Mass.
San Francisco, Cal.	

My darling wife,

We arrived early this morning and were instantly doing the necessary things to prepare us to go overseas. This sort of stuff will last for a few more days. Then we have a certain amount of freedom, then we are alerted, then we go. There is no definite length of time for any of these times, so that I cannot plan on anything.

If we wish to make a phone call or send a telegram, we first have to have an application filled and then signed by an officer. It's too late for me to get such a form, so I'll have to wait until to-morrow. It won't be as easy getting a call thru as it was at any of the other camps that I've been at. I'm just twice as far away from home than when at my last station. This letter is censored so I don't know whether I can tell you what City I'm near or not, but I'll try. I'm near [censored].

The food here is good and plenty of it, even tho we have to march a little distance to get it.

The letters that I wrote on the train were probably mailed to you when we came in, because all they did was pick them up in the train and saved them until we got to our destination.

I was able to wash quite a bit of my dirty clothing to-day, but as yet, I can't get near a shower to wash up. I also got me a G.I. haircut – so now I have to go overseas, people would run me out of this country just as soon as they saw me.

After being stationed in level country during my entire army career, walking up and down the hills we have is tiring me out. I feel like a see-saw, up and down (up & down to Bernie's farm!)

Your loving husband,
George

March 14, 1945
Wednesday

From:	To:
Cpl. James G. Barr 11057933	Mrs. James G. Barr
94th Dep. Rep. Sq., A.P.O. 18217 c/o P.M.	65 Houghton St.
San Francisco, Calf.	Worcester 4, Mass.

March 14th
Wed.

A. P. O. 18217

Dearest Lottie,

Here's that man you love again. I just love talking to you and only hope it won't be long before I can talk to you again soon. It was funny, but when you asked me if I had to go, I said, no, not realizing at first what you meant! But if you know what I went thru before I got the call thru, well it wasn't funny! I didn't want to leave before I did get to hear your wonderful voice. My, but I love you very much.

Yesterday we had lectures on censorship and security measures. The officer in charge told us of the many ingenious methods of sending restricted information. Some of those guys, instead of being reprimanded or court martialed, they should have been transferred into intelligence – well, it's at least one man's opinion.

How's Edie, is she getting any better? Also, has my aunt Sarah been hearing from her sister? Ask my mother.

The weather here has been P.P. (pretty punk – I have to write abbreviations out or else they may censor it, they don't want any abbreviations, also may be code – I know, tough war!!) I like the camp here, there are a bunch of trees all over the place – like a C.C.C. camp. I'd like it even better if the camp were on the level, by level, I mean flat.

Last night I went to the show and saw "Unseen." I liked the first half, but the last half stunk. What the hell, there's nothing else to do.

They allow a certain percentage of men out each night, and I was due to go out, but things got screwed up and I hope to go to town to-night.

I'll be going with a fellow that I knew down at San Antonio. He has already told his girl that we met, and she left instructions for me to look after him, but who's to look after me?!

I'm contemplating wiring you for a little money, but I haven't decided yet whether I will or not, but you'll know before you receive this letter whether I want it anyway.

When I left Tinker, I gave Norman a half-taken roll of film. I'm in one of the pictures, so I asked Norman to send it to you. How did it come out?

I have to go get a few shots now, so until later.

All my love,
Your, George

March 15, 1945
Thursday

From:	To:
Cpl. James G. Barr 11057933	Mrs. James G. Barr
94th Dep. Rep. Sq., A.P.O. 18217 c/o P.M.	65 Houghton St.
San Francisco, Calf.	Worcester 4, Mass.

My darling wife,
I sent you a small package with your letters to you. In the package, there is a couple of pictures I had taken in a joint in town, a few things that our mine, and a form that mother has to fill out, which she then returns to me. In turn, I give it to my squadron C.O. Whether she'll get the allotment, no one here knows, it will have to go thru the channels.

Those pictures are really luloos! But I had to send you something showing my haircut. Ow! If you want, keep them both (I wouldn't know of any good reason), or you can give my mother one.

When we went to town, we went to a nice place for supper. The food was good, but the service was the worst I've ever had. Irving wanted to go dancing, so we went to the Triannon Ballroom. It's a Johnny Hines, G.I. style. While we were standing on the side lines, a girl came up to us who recognized Irv. She's from his home in Minneapolis, and is working here.

I had three dances last night, all with her. Does that meet with your approval? Besides, the other girls looked at my haircut and said no!!! See darling, I need you, no one else wants me.

Good for you and mother for getting rid of the stuff in the store. You'll be millionaires in no time.

You don't have to warn all your girl friends to read a book, I just think it may help those ignorant on sex. Hell, you got along alright didn't you!!! Or did you?

Darling, why the hell don't you quit your job? The hell with Dave and the New England, leave and find something you'll like. I want you to leave, or else your morale will go completely down soon. Go away for a vacation or something, but leave that place and find a place where it won't be so damn petty. You said they promised you a raise, as yet, you haven't told me whether you received it or not, probably like your last raise. You don't have any obligations there, not even Charlotte, so let's go and do something else, or somewhere else!

Thanks darling, for the money. I'm sorry that I had to send for it, but I guarantee I'll repay it, maybe not sooner, but later. I got it around eleven o'clock this morning, you are right on the bean, and don't think I don't love you for it, for I do, very much.

I was on detail to-day at the clothing salvage warehouse. There wasn't much work to do, because we were able to get off early. I'm on it again to-morrow, so I have another day of comparative ease, I hope!!

I hope Barb gets a good break, but I don't think I'll be seeing her in Oklahoma, not now anyhow. What got me to thinking tho, was that you had to have Barb play the song for you and here I've been deceived into thinking that you knew how – for shame!

Yesterday was the first time I got a letter from you and that helped out one hell of a lot. Hope I get some more to-night. You're my favorite reading, if you didn't know already.

Don't think about your job anymore, just give Dave your notice.

Your, George

March 17, 1945
Saturday

From:	To:
Cpl. James G. Barr 11057933	Mrs. James G. Barr
94th Dep. Rep. Sq., A.P.O. 18217 c/o P.M.	65 Houghton St.
San Francisco, Calf.	Worcester 4, Mass.

Dearest Lottie,

This has been a pretty rough day for me. What with chasing around doing one thing and another, and a batch of wash, I got pretty tired, but what really got me in the dumps is that I haven't received any mail in two days. I hope very much that I get some to-morrow, or I will be a case. After this war, when my clothes get dirty I'm just going to throw them away and just make phone calls, no more washing or letter writing, besides, my spelling is too bad to write, how would you like to be my secretary? Swell!

Last night I was scheduled to go to town, but things got a bit mixed up and my pass was not available, so I had to resort to other methods of getting in. Irv and I dropped into the U.S.O. were we were offered a chance to go to a sorority dance at a college here. Irv talked me into it, so we hopped a bus and rode and rode, got off and walked and walked. Finally, we got there and were outnumbered by the Navy (you could have had a time, couldn't you!!!) There were four G.I.'s to about twenty sailors. But; but, who made the party, of course, the good old U.S. Army. I never ran across a deader bunch of gobs in my life! It's no wonder that me with my haircut, was able to dance with a girl.

The house mother was a panic, every time I looked at her, I had to control myself from laughing out loud - what a prude she was!

After the food was served, we got the hell out - who has time for a college education anyway!!!

The fellows are cutting each other's hair because we have to get G.I. haircuts. Earlier this evening, three of us cut one man's hair, one on each side, and me in the back with a pair of clippers - what a mess!! The guy is a sorry sight. What the hell, we may not make a lot of money, but we have a hell of a time!

No mail from you, woe is me! Goodnight my dearest wife, all my love, all my life.

Your, George

March 22, 1945
Thursday
Board Ship

From:	To:
Cpl. James G. Barr 11057933	Mrs. James G. Barr
94th Dep. Rep. Sq., A.P.O. 18217 c/o P.M.	65 Houghton St.
San Francisco, Calf.	Worcester 4, Mass.

Dearest Lottie,

Darling, I love you very much, that's the foremost thought on my mind, nothing else really matters.

I don't feel like writing, in fact, I don't feel like doing anything whatsoever, but I think I'll feel much better after writing you. As yet, we haven't had a ride that could be considered half smooth. The only time that the ship wasn't tossing and turning was when we were in the harbor. As yet, I haven't gotten sea sick, but I've been groggy most of the time, by the time this trip is over, I'll be able to be a good sailor (I'm very glad I got into the Army instead of the Navy).

We're fed twice daily and that's about all we do is wait until chow, then we line up and wait until we get into the mess hall. If I didn't get fruit, apples, crackers, and candy from Irving, I think I'd be half starved. He works (no more tho) in Merchant marines mess, and is able to purloin a few odds and ends, upon which I thrive. Now that his job is done, I don't know how I'm going to make out!

I started the first page of this letter yesterday, but by the bottom of the page, I got too sick to finish, but since I can't mail it anyway, it doesn't make any difference.

When we left the U.S.A., I hadn't received any mail for four days, so that didn't do my morale any good. I just hope when we get settled, there'll be a pile of mail waiting for me. At least there should be, because you've been sending your letters air mail.

I met the Chief of Polices' nephew onboard the ship, he's a member of the crew. I don't know whether Foley is Chief still or not, but it felt good meeting a fellow from Worcester. I'm going to write Dad to call the Chief up and tell him I saw him.

To-day's pretty nice out, if it will only keep up this way. I spent a few hours on deck taking in the sun, but until the war is over, I only want one more boat ride, and that's the return trip!!

The best part of the trip so far was when I dreamt of you last night. How nice it would have been if I could go on dreaming that way.

I imagine this letter is very incoherent and lousy, but my darling, so am I for the present. I guarantee that when I'm back in solid terra firma again, I'll snap back to what may be considered normal again. If not, they'll be able to send me back home as a Section 8!!!! (Medical officer please note!)

I'm going to give this to the censor now in hopes he'll censor it and give it to the first sea gull going in the direction of home, but I haven't any idea when it will be mailed.

Remember darling, I'm always thinking of you and loving you.

Your, George

March 25, 1945
Sunday
Board Ship

From:	To:
Cpl. James G. Barr 11057933	Mrs. James G. Barr
94th Depot Repair Sq., A.P.O. 18217 c/o P.M.	65 Houghton St.
San Francisco, Calf.	Worcester 4, Mass.

My darling wife,

Why I'm in a better mood to-day than I was a day ago, I don't rightly know. Maybe it's the weather, maybe because I won about thirty cents in a new card game I learnt, or maybe yet, it was our last meal that did it (we had ice cream). But whatever it is, I'm that much better.

Here is what life aboard a troop ship is. First, of course, everyone gets sick, no one shaves, washes or moves a finger. Then when they become a bit more accustomed to the sea, they take out the cards and play, some continually, and others like myself, occasionally. The first few days no one writes, but as soon as a mail deposit was posted, the pens and pencils come out and everyone wrote to their loved ones. Writing conditions are not the best in the world, but somehow or other, you manage to scribble a note of two (like me).

I'm writing you standing up, leaning against some sort of boom, leaning to and fro, depending upon the movement of the ship. I'm in what I consider a small piece of Revere Beach where everyone is in everyone else's business and place of rest. People, I should say men, keep kicking and stepping on you, but you don't care, because there is no sand to get into your eyes, mouth, or nose. To-day was especially an example, because around noon time, the sun really came out and we started shedding. I was still too hot in my fatigues, so I went below and changed into a pair of suntan pants and "T" shirt.

On board ship, we have a public announcement system whereby all notices are announced. For a few hours a day, we have musical programs, some of the recordings that the ship has, others picked up by radio. We had an operetta by Schubert to-day, something about a "mouse".

We even get to hear "Frankie!!" I'd appreciate it much more if they'd play at longer intervals. Before a notice is broadcast, the fellow doing the talking will say, "Now hear this!" This term has taken the boys over and everything is started by "Now hear this!"

The sea is now a beautiful blue and pretty calm. During the day, it is so blue, I think if I dipped my pen into it I could write with the sea water (that's if I could reach down low enough!)

Some of our time is spent watching the sea gulls, or albatross, as some people know them. The way I distinguish them is, seagulls are white, whereas, albatrosses are dark in color. They're very graceful in flight and are interesting to watch. There are quite a few flying around the ship now.

I was on K.P. yesterday, but in comparison to K.P. on shore it was easy, maybe the two meals a day we feed have something to do with it.

Cookie, going further and further away from you really brings out the loneliness spells I have for you. I miss you terribly. It's hard to think that in a few more months, when I'd ordinarily be sweating out a furlough, that I can't come home to you for a little longer time. When we do get to-gether again, we're going on a second honeymoon and forget all that has passed and live in the present and future. Gee! But I miss you like everything!!!

> *All my love*
> *Your, George*

> March 29, 1945
> Thursday
> Board Ship

From:	To:
Cpl. James G. Barr 11057933	Mrs. James G. Barr
94th Dep. Rep. Sq., A.P.O. 18217 c/o P.M.	65 Houghton St.
San Francisco, Calf.	Worcester 4, Mass.

Dearest Lottie,

"If you think I know what I'm going to write, you're crazy!" That's what I just told one of my fellow G.I.'s in answer to what I'm going to write. It's a funny thing, whenever someone is about to write a letter, they put down the heading, then stop, look into thin air for a matter of moments, or minutes, then laboriously start to write. I haven't seen it fail yet. I guess a fellow has to get used to writing a censored letter. Some of the boys get careless and have their letters returned. I guess the censor could cut out the censored parts and then pass it thru, but it probably would look as if a five year old had been playing with a piece of paper and scissors. Then it would worry the person receiving it trying to figure out what had been censored, this way it saves everyone but the writer a headache. I'm glad that I haven't had any returned, as yet.

Last night, or was it the night before, anyway, it was the first night of Pesach, and we had services in the mess hall. We had quite a few boys, and under the conditions we had a pretty nice affair. There was a little wine, matzos, and gefilte fish in cans. It wasn't a long service, fortunately, because it was hot as hell in the mess hall. To-night there is going to be regular Friday night services, so I'll be going to them too.

The weather has been good and the sea calm, not like the earlier part of the trip. This makes it a lot easier to write or read, so I've written a few letters and read a bunch of mystery stories. In the first place, you can't get to feel like writing because you know the letters won't be mailed for some time, and then after the first letter or two, there is nothing else to write about. A boat trip is a very, very monotonous journey, just like in that old song "And All I See is the Sea!"

Always yours,
George

April 4, 1945
Wednesday
Board Ship

From:	To:
Cpl. James G. Barr 11057933	Mrs. James G. Barr
94th Dep. Rep. Sq., A.P.O. 18217 c/o P.M.	65 Houghton St.
San Francisco, Calf.	Worcester 4, Mass.

My wonderful Cookie,
I know it has been a few days since I last wrote, but you won't know about it, because you'll probably receive all my mail at the same time.

Nothing unusual has happened, and am very glad of it. Everything aboard ship is the same, in fact, everything is the same and I'm hating every minute of it. It seems as if we're going someplace, but no one knows the destination or the time of arrival, we're just sailing sort of indefinitely.

When I look over the sides and all there is, is sea on all sides, nothing in view, I feel so all alone, sort of makes me feel like dreaming. Time passes heavily and reading is becoming a labor and sitting an agony.

My only consolation is that I know this can't last forever, so I can take it in my stride. Although the stride I now use would be totally unsatisfactorily on land. When I finally do have a chance to walk on land, I'll probably lean over just enough to be able to pick myself up and start all over again. Maybe I should start like I did many long years ago. First crawl, then slowly try to walk on my feet, but don't worry, I'll make out, even if I have to tie balloons around my head to keep me upright.

Sleeping is a problem now too. It's hot and stuffy and when you wake you're all covered with perspiration and you feel as tho someone has been draining your blood during the night.

If I could only receive one little letter from you, I'd feel that much better, for there isn't any time during my waking hours that I'm not thinking of you. Darling, loving you is the only reason I have now for being in this damn war. It seems after you're in the army for a length of time your patriotism takes a different slant. I know mine has changed considerably since I first entered the service. Time certainly changes a person's view points, but what the hell! When I'm back again and things are normal, I'll be able to look back at my life in the army and laugh, hoping that I was able to put more debits than credits on my ledger.

It has been lovely for the last few days, and I've been able to get quite a nice sunburn. I haven't taken too much of it, so I haven't been bothered with going on sick call and having them put some sort of stuff on it so it'll be less painful. I'll have plenty of time to get my tan in small doses! So soon I'll be short, dark, and – well just and.

Oh yes, I forgot to mention that for some unknown reason I'm letting my beard grow to what I hope will become one. I'll let it grow and if it doesn't need any eye brow pencil to darken it, I'll get me a picture of me and send it home to you. Then you can burn the picture, because by that time, I'll have shaved it off!!

Thru our ship's paper, I've been able to keep up with the news of the world and I can say I'm quite pleased to see what's happening. The Germans can't last much longer under the blows the allies are dealing them. By summertime, the European war may be over with. Let's hope so anyway.

Altho I know you are writing me all that is new back home, I just can't help wondering about everyone, especially you. It seems such a long time since I've heard from home.

I'm going to run off for chow, at least that's what they still call it (for a better name).

"Kiss me quick!"
Your loving husband, George

April 7, 1945
Saturday
Board Ship

From:	To:
Cpl. James G. Barr 11057933	Mrs. James G. Barr
94th Dep. Rep. Sq., A.P.O. 18217 c/o P.M.	65 Houghton St.
San Francisco, Calf.	Worcester 4, Mass.

My darling wife,

Happy anniversary dear! Although in actual time it has been short, these last three months seem like ages. Every second away from you is painful and until we're together again, that pain will not leave me. Your love is the thing I'm fighting this war for, otherwise, being in the army would be a load that I would be unable to carry, loving you makes it that much lighter, but when I can be with you, it lifts as if a cool breeze had blown it off. Darling, I love you more and more.

Although I don't need any anniversary to bring back all the wonderful times we've had together, it accents them so that they are very vivid in my mind. At least our being parted cannot take them away! After this is done and gone, we'll make new times for our memories to look back together!!

When I come home again you're going to have quite a job fattening me up. I don't know actually that I've lost weight, but it seems to me that I could use a few more pounds. The dried eggs that they try to feed us in the mornings is no help either, because I haven't been able yet to pass more than one mouthful down. I think I'll have steak three times a day until I can't look another steak in the eye. Then we'll buy a cow for fresh milk. No, I guess we'll stick to bottled milk, I can't imagine you milking a cow!!!

I'd better quit before I really get silly – besides, I can't think of anything interesting to write.

All my love, all my life
Your loving husband,
George

April 12, 1945
Thursday
"Somewhere in the Pacific"

From:	To:
Cpl. James G. Barr 11057933	Mrs. James G. Barr
94th Dep. Rep. Sq., A.P.O. 18217 c/o P.M.	65 Houghton St.
San Francisco, Calf.	Worcester 4, Mass.

My darling wife,

This is it, darling, I arrived safe, sane, and of course, unhappy. I think a little later on I'll be able to give you a little more information on where I am. It's really not very important because most of these islands are pretty near the same I'm told.

The scenery is really very nice, and I guess under ordinary circumstances, it could be called beautiful. Of course, there are coconut palms and pretty flowers. This morning I tried to climb a tree to get a coconut. I didn't realize how high it was and when I got about two feet away from the fruit, I couldn't go any further. It was too bad, but I had to slide down. I can remember when I was a kid, there wasn't a tree I couldn't climb, and now when I want to get something, I couldn't make it. Must be getting old!!

I was very surprised to find living conditions much better than what I visualized. We have running water and showers, and not the kind that you have to fill up either. On the island, we have our own radio broadcasting station that gives out with plenty of good programs. No commercials, except a few that are strictly G.I. They're rebroadcast, and the few I've heard are good.

When I came in the area that we're now in, I found out that the outfit that was harboring us for awhile was the outfit that [censored] was in. You remember him, don't you? He remembers you, and after all, he did write you a few very nice letters. Then there were a lot of the other boys that were with me when I was down in New Orleans. It seems that all of us radio men are to-gether again, well at least some of us. [Censored] was very kind to me and let me borrow his flashlight so I could find my pup tent in the dark. He also was kind enough to rummage up an old battered can of beer. Even tho it was warm, it was very good.

This morning before dinner (three meals now) we went over to the P.X. and he bought me a "cold" can of orange juice.

Did I feel good this afternoon - mail, and plenty of it. I can't remember now of what I should answer in the letters you wrote me, but don't worry, they'll be read and reread, so I'll be able to get everything out of them.

"I Wanna Get Married" is tres' cute – too bad we couldn't see it on our honeymoon. There'll be more and better musicals to see later on and we'll see them.

If you want to number your letters go ahead, but I won't be able to number mine, when you're overseas that is also taboo. I don't see too much sense to it, because if I don't receive one of your letters, I just don't get it. If a letter is lost that has something important in it, you'd have to rewrite it anyway as soon as I didn't answer it. But go ahead if you want to.

The outfit that [censored] is in lives in large tents that have wooden floors, and they have bunks and mattresses to sleep in. Over their heads, they have electric lights, so you can see it isn't too bad here. Of course, we're still in pup tents, sleeping on the ground, but that shouldn't last too long.

We even have a table and chair to write on. These conveniences are in the day room. It's built like a pavilion, open sides, and on the floor, is a fine almost powder sand. It reminds me of buckwheat flour, it is so fine. Hanging up on the wall is a 'bra' and a pair of panties, where they came from I don't know – maybe the native women wear them! The natives here, the ones I saw as we drove by, wear dresses and I can't remember if they had shoes or not, but you can see this place was pretty civilized.

I was very glad for Zelda and Phil because he was home. Well, at least the Lex has our O.K. if they are going to stay there when they go to New York.

Received a letter from Norman, and he tells me you write a very nice letter, as if I didn't know. The pictures I took, that I wrote you about, didn't come out and I can't imagine why, but such is the way of life. Also, we can't take pictures here, why, I can't understand, and no one else can either, but such are the wishes of the high command and they will be obeyed, and besides, we haven't our cameras on us!!!

I was just listening to the news and it sounds quite good. Even heard a little on the Chaplin versus Barry case, so we're right up there with the news.

Claude Thornhill is here to-night, but I couldn't go because I just had to write to you. Darling, I love you too much to run off to see a band, no matter how good a band it is. If I had written to you it would be different, but when I can, you come first!!

Mail from you, the last of your letters came in a week, is pretty damn good. How it is from me to you I don't know, but I imagine it will take a little longer.

I don't have to tell you to take care of Mother's Day, but I want you to tell mother I love her and miss her also. Say hello to Mrs. "Ci" that day too, you can tell her the next time she comes down for coffee, but also Mother's Day, O.K.? O.K.

Good night my very sweet darling, I'll write again to-morrow.

Your loving husband,
George

P.S. What's this that Nooky wrote me, baby Barr is not Martin but Michael!! The dirty crooks, we'll get them for plagiarism yet!! What! No, Papa.

P.P.S. The reason this letter is cut a little and crossed out is that as first it was returned to me, so I tried to see why and crossed out stuff that I thought "may" be censored. Then I went & found out just what had to come out, so that when I rewrote it I wouldn't get it back. When I brought it up to our adjutant, he said I could just cut out a few names & send it thru again because it was alright. So, I'll try again. If it were shorter, I would have written it over. Stuff like that burns me up. Papa.

[Editor's note: For the reader's information, George was stationed in the U.S. Island territory of Guam. Less than 9 months earlier (July 21st – August 10th 1944), the U.S. had recaptured Guam from Japan.]

April 13, 1945
Friday
"Somewhere in the Pacific"

From:	To:
Cpl. James G. Barr 11057933	Mrs. James G. Barr
94th Dep. Rep. Sq., A.P.O. 18217 c/o P.M.	65 Houghton St.
San Francisco, Calf.	Worcester 4, Mass.

Dearest Lottie,

Here's your rover boy again! I went to services to-night and I thought they were pretty good. Because of President Roosevelt's death we had a special service. While at the services I met another fellow I knew from

New Orleans. After the services, we went back to his hut and smoked a few of his cigars. The only reason I smoked a cigar, was that yesterday he became a proud pappy of a baby girl. I told him about Michael, and he got quite a kick out of it. He also let me take a flashlight so that I could find myself in the darkness. He's a good fellow – how did I know, I showed him our wedding picture, and he remembered you as 'my girl back home'!

The only reason I'm using this stationery is that it would be a walk to get mine, and besides, I know you don't particularly care on what kind of paper you get it (of course, I know there are exceptions), but as long as you get it.

We're going to get ten dollars to-morrow so that we'll have enough money to last us until our regular pay day. We also got our beer rationing cards, which entitles us to six cans of beer a week. There goes at least sixty cents a week of my money!

As yet, I haven't reread your letters, so I can't answer any of your questions as yet, but I'll get around to it. A Barr's word is always good!! It better be, don't you think so?!!

Last night we had a little rain, altho I didn't get wet, Irving did. He was sleeping underneath my half of the tent, and that side leaked like a sieve. So, to-day I went and swapped it for another one. I hope this one works out that much better, because he's going to make me (and I can't blame him) sleep underneath my own half of the tent from now on. It really wasn't my fault, because at P.O.E. I wanted to turn it in, but they said it was serviceable enough, they didn't have to sleep underneath it, the dogs.

I subtracted a few letters from my list to-day and I feel better for it. It's quite a job answering a lot of letters, - isn't it!!

I forgot to tell you last night, but you better do the picture taking since your camera is able to be serviced. You're the one I love, so you'll have to send pictures to me, because, darling, that's the kind of stuff I love.

Your loving husband,
George

April 17, 1945
Tuesday
"Somewhere in the Pacific"

From:	To:
Cpl. James G. Barr 11057933	Mrs. James G. Barr
94th Dep. Rep. Sq., A.P.O. 18217 c/o P.M.	65 Houghton St.
San Francisco, Calf.	Worcester 4, Mass.

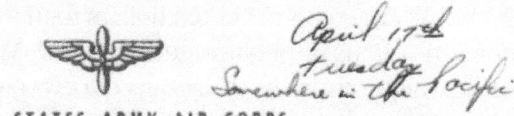

"For Christ also hath once suffered for sins, the just for the unjust, that He might bring us to God."
I Peter 3:18

UNITED STATES ARMY AIR CORPS

My darling wife,

Just this minute I came from seeing "A Song to Remember." Even tho the "seats" (a board held up by two empty gasoline cans) were hard, I didn't notice it until the picture ended, that's how much I liked it. Of course, the piano playing was excellent. If Jose' Iturbi ever comes out this way for a tour, I'll make it my business to hear him. I don't know if I'd be able to see him, you don't know the mess of G.I.'s that can congregate when there is something doing.

To-day I loafed just as hard as I worked yesterday. This afternoon I was even able to catch a nap, right beside the officer in charge too!! I pushed a couple of boards off a truck this morning, and when that was finished, so was I. I'm glad that nothing else showed up for us to do.

Got another one of those cute letters from my cousin in New York, one from Sid, and also one from Narky. I would have traded all those for one of your daily letters. Maybe I'll get two from you to-morrow. I really shouldn't kick, because, darling, your letters have been coming very good and the time that it takes is surprisingly fast. Whenever I receive one of your letters, my face lights up and a big smile comes across my homely face (you must have been crazy to have married me), I feel good all over, why? Because I got a letter from my sweetie!!! Darling, I miss you so very, very much. If they told me they'd let me go home if I'd swim, I think I'd even try that. I don't know how far I'd get, but it sure as hell would be worth a try. Every time I look at my band, I still thrill over our marriage, what a lucky guy I am to have married you!

Darling, on the end of each letter for a long time I'm going to add a P.S. for a package, so you'll have enough requests. O.K. If you ever need room in the package, add a package of soap suds. I'm going to write my folks the same.

Good night my life,
Your, George

P.S. Send Package.

April 25, 1945
Wednesday
"Somewhere in the Marianas"

From:	To:
Cpl. James G. Barr 11057933	Mrs. James G. Barr
94th Dep. Rep. Sq., 56th ADG	65 Houghton St.
A.P.O. 246 Unit #1 c/o P.M.	Worcester 4, Mass.
San Francisco, Calf.	

My darling wonderful wife,

You know that you are wonderful, don't you? You're the most wonderful thing that has ever happened to me. Darling, I love you with all my heart, and I miss you more than ever. Each day seems longer because we are so far apart. Time will stay still for me until I can once again hold you in my arms.

Darling, I think that someone is conspiring against me, because again to-night after I was ready to rinse the soap off of my body - no more water! Again, I had to run out naked and rinse off. Please, Lottie, come and take me from this awful place!

To-day they had me climbing around the high girders in one of the hangars. I'm now helping the electricians. Boy, will I be the handy man around our own home! What with the carpentry, wiring, painting, and general dirty work that I've done in the army, I should be (you notice, I said 'should') a 'jack of all trades' - by the way, do you know of any good contractors?!

I received a very cute letter from Toby to-day. She had written it during her spare time at school. She also told me that when I come back I'm going to have to get acquainted with quite a few of my new little cousins to be! By the way, how are you coming along in meeting, and remembering my relatives? (Also, yours now, you know)

There was a change made in our mode of living to-day. We now have tents that will accommodate three people, and sleeping in cots. Even tho I had done a little work in building a 'lean to' it didn't make me angry, for the tent will be many times nicer than anything I could have built, and so much quicker!

What do you know!! I didn't break or lose anything at all to-day. Isn't that wonderful! You bet your boots it is!

You should see the coconut palms from our tent. They are beautifully outlined against nice white fluffy clouds with the almost full moon shining down. This place can be really nice if it doesn't rain.

Of course, you know that I haven't received any mail from you in two days. And, of course, I can't blame you, because I know it isn't your fault, but I like to let you know, just in case some night you get weak, and want to put off what you can do to-day, to-morrow.

Did you happen to see Mackie Zitowitz while he was home? Toby wrote and said he stopped in the store.

Goodnight dear.
Always yours,
Your very loving husband,
George

P.S. Send Package.

April 26, 1945
Thursday
"Somewhere in the Marianas"

From:	To:
Cpl. James G. Barr 11057933	Mrs. James G. Barr
94th Dep. Rep. Sq., 56th ADG	65 Houghton St.
A.P.O. 246 Unit #1 c/o P.M.	Worcester 4, Mass.
San Francisco, Calf.	

My darling wife,

To-night my morale was boosted a thousand percent. Why you may ask, but you should know. I got two wonderful letters from you, one telling me that you received mail from me.

So, Mackie is finally scheduled to go overseas. He's missed going about three times now, and was pretty perturbed about missing the war. If he thinks that it is a picnic, he's crazy, even tho the air corps, especially the A.T.C., have it comparatively easy.

I can just taste that grilled American and coffee! I bet it was delicious. I can't see anything wrong in Mackie taking you out, because, wasn't I there also?! If I approved of anyone taking you out, it would be him. He's one fellow that I can trust. But can I trust you?!!

You don't know how Michael's fund came up, huh! I bet you practically put your beautiful hands in their pockets for their pennies!! I'd like to see anyone leave your presence without at least looking to see if they have any pennies. Besides, remember the night we all went to have "Pizza", and I collected about thirty cents. That night we made (I should say Michael made a clean up!).

Do you really think he's getting engaged? After all you did say her face was pretty good – and that's all you're supposed to see!!!!

Darling, what made me angry on the boat, should make any decent fellow start thinking, but I had already forgotten about it. That's the way I am, I'll bitch a hell of a lot, then I'll forget it, because I realize that it won't do me one bit of good to remain mad. If I remembered all the things that made me angry during this war, I'd be a mental wreck! As I said before, things aren't too bad on this island, and nothing here will change me. The length of time may make me a little sour at times, but it will be like a passing cloud.

If mother and you are going to wait on me hand and foot when I come home, I'll get real lazy and never want to go out and earn a living – you'll spoil me. About that cow, I wouldn't worry about it, for I really was kidding, you know!

I told you yesterday that we had gotten new tents, so that we could sleep on cots. Well, to-night after work, I came back to my area, and couldn't find the tent! They had moved it for a supposedly good reason (which I still can't see). It took me almost a half hour before I located it. In the first place, it wasn't up completely, which I didn't mind, but when I found all my stuff on the ground, that's when I cursed a rainbow, not a blue, but a rainbow streak!!!

Me and my tan are coming along pretty good. No more beard and have gained the poundage lost on the boat. All is well.

I got a chance to send you a cablegram, so I did, as you know. Pretty nice and for a grand total of sixty cents. If you wanted to send one, it would cost you seventy-five cents. I know, it's tough to be a civilian. Who am I kidding!

I was lucky and got half of a Pepsi-Cola. Emil Bazzy brought it over to me. There was a glee club meeting here at the Chapel and the members got colas. Emil is not a member, but he knows the Chaplin's assistant very well. It's good to have friends. And he is a good one. He may be able to do us both a wonderful favor soon. Time alone can tell. Just remember his name.

I'm sorry that I can't duplicate your nine-page letter, but after all, I haven't had a chance to go out with any women!!! I bet you'd be green with jealousy if I did take out another woman. - O.K. stop beating me, I'll leave them alone.

Goodnight, dearest.

Your, George

P.S. Send Package

April 28, 1945
Saturday
"Somewhere in the Marianas"

From:	To:
Cpl. James G. Barr 11057933	Mrs. James G. Barr
94th Dep. Rep. Sq., 56th ADG	65 Houghton St.
A.P.O. 246 Unit #1 c/o P.M.	Worcester 4, Mass.
San Francisco, Calf.	

My dearest wife,

I would have written you last night, but I honestly didn't have time. After putting in a dull day as an electrician's helper again, I ate supper. Right after supper, there was a meeting of all the men. All day long we tried to figure out what was up. There were all kind of ideas, but no one hit the correct answer. What it was, was a half hour of orientation. The only new thing we learned was that an army of occupation was in training. So, that lets out the chance of any of us, I hope, out of staying here after hostilities are over with.

My sweet, thank you very much for your birthday card. Don't be sorry that I got it too soon, because it wasn't your fault. I love you darling, for making sure that I would at least get it on time. I was going to wait until my birthday to tell you, but then, seeing how the mail has been coming thru, you'd worry thinking it had been lost. Speaking of birthdays, it seems to me that one of the people I love is also having one during the month of May. Try as I might, I can't seem to remember who the loved one could be! Ouch!!!

Right after the orientation, I went directly to services. Last night the colonel presented an Ark for the Torah to our Chapel. It was a very nice and impressive ceremony. There was quite a large crowd, even some officers came. I hadn't seen them there before, maybe the colonel being there had something to do with it - or, maybe they knew that a few nurses were going to be present! Anyway, they came.

It was nice to see a woman light the Friday night candles again. It's things like that, that bring back a little of home. I think that's the main reason I go, because I'm not that religious, or did you think I was getting to be real pious? Remember, I shaved the beard off!

After services, they had cake, chaley, gefilte fish, and salamis, also ice tea. Some of the bakers had baked a beautiful cake and had put the frosting in the form of the Ten Commandments. The whole affair was really very nice. Pictures were taken during the services and the cutting of the cake. I wish I could get a shot, but I doubt it very much.

Where did you get the very pretty daisies? A little sticker like that adds beauty to your letters, tho they don't need it.

Of course, you'll return all those muchly appreciated regards. How's Edie doing, gaining any weight? And Harriet, well you tell her she had her chance once, and opportunity has already knocked, and I feel sorry for her, because it has left, no longer to return. She may get another knock (at least I hope so), but it won't be from this direction, or maybe she's found out what it is like and wants variety!

Glad to hear that your dear old boss asked about me. It shows he has a heart someplace – tell him hello from the Marianas for me. I hope the hell that Paul does have more hair than me. I think I have too much, besides what a silly argument to get into to begin with. If he is short some, heck, I'll give him mine, all it is doing is keeping me from getting an even tan.

Dearest, if you're going to keep that stuff up, we're just going to have to sleep without pillows or sheets. If you think you're going to tear up our presents, you are mistaken! It's funny, you never did that while I was with you. Maybe it was that I held you so close that you were unable to roam around the bed tearing everything in sight.

To-day was another drippy day, and I think it all dripped on me. I got soaked to the skin, very easily too. I had no shirt on and was wearing a pair of shorts. Then it stopped raining and I dried up.

Sweetheart, I love you madly, and you are with me at all times. You are what I'm looking forward to after this is done and finished. My life is now on lease to the army, but my heart is with you. I hope soon I'll be able to give you the lease on my life.

Good night darling.

Your loving husband,
George

P.S. Kiss me quick.

P.P.S. Send Package.

Again P.S. The allotment for mother went thru. She should get two month's checks, for in my next month's pay, two payments are going to be taken out. J.G.B.

April 29, 1945
Sunday

From:	To:
Cpl. James G. Barr 11057933	Mrs. James G. Barr
94th Dep. Rep. Sq., 56th ADG	65 Houghton St.
A.P.O. 246 Unit #1 c/o P.M.	Worcester 4, Mass.
San Francisco, Calf.	

Dearest Lottie,

First of all, writing "Somewhere in the Marianas" is getting tiresome, so I'm going to discontinue writing it.

Guess who I met this afternoon? No, it wasn't the King of Siam – but it was "Uddy" Goff! Having this afternoon off, well, we were supposed to have from 12 noon to 12 midnight off, but just like last week, we didn't get our passes until late. I don't know what the hold up was, but it sure as hell is getting on the fellows' nerves. When we can have time off, they hold us up for two hours!

Irv and I bummed up to another field, just for the ride, and while driving by, I noticed the Bomb Squadron number that Uddy had in the states. He had told me when we were up at Salina that he expected to go over, so I had a pretty good idea he was here. After a little running around, at least three miles, I found him. He really found me – it was this way. I went from place to place until an officer directed us to the correct place. Just as I was about to get on a truck going in that direction, Uddy came out from somewhere and there we were! He even looks better now than when I saw him in the states. He even got a rating, he's now a tech sergeant. Also, he didn't have to endure the long ride on a boat, he flew here. I'm going up again next Sunday if I can.

On the way back, we were picked up by a couple of fellows who were going to our field, but first they were going to stop at the hospital to see a friend that was a medic, so we went along, not realizing how long we'd be there. When we finally located him, he was ready to go to chow, so he invited all of us along. After eating, he told his friend that a mutual friend was in the hospital, and that he was a casualty, so off we went to visit him.

It wasn't a very nice sight to see those boys all banged up, and some of them pretty badly. Irv and I had intended going to some boxing matches, but we were more than glad to miss them, because I know the fellows we talked to were thankful for our coming. They did most of the talking and didn't leave any of the facts out. It's surprising how their sense of humor holds out! I hope that I never have to experience any of the stuff they went thru. They were flown in from the fighting, and some are going back to the states.

One of the fellows who I talked to mostly was from New York and I told him that if he went back to the states he'd probably go to the General Hospital right near Mitchel Field, and his people would be able to see him. I think that was the best medicine he could have gotten to-day! Those boys went thru hell where they came from.

Darling, you didn't have to run around for a metal mirror. If I had brains, I would have just asked for a regular mirror, because I know you would have packed it so it wouldn't break. Now – why don't you tell me what kind of difficulties you had to go thru to get film! Hmm. I'm curious, who did you bribe, and how!

I'm sorry that, as yet, I haven't received any packages or your Easter egg. I'll get it tho, it may come a little late, but the U.S. Mail comes thru!

By the way, I think I know where the bra and panties came from. At the hospital to-day, I saw quite an assortment of the nurses unmentionables, could be a little 'midnight requisitioning on their part!

How come you ordered a Carstairs and coke, you know I'm a scotch and soda man. I'm glad tho that you got a couple of chances to get out. Mackie's a good fellow and I'm going to have to tell him so. Even tho his "idea" is quite farfetched!

I got my watch back with a crystal that one of the fellows made for me, and a damn good job too. The cost was a buck and a half, I at least, thought it would be three. Heck, it costs at least that back in the states!

The rumors flying around to-day, kept everyone here guessing. I certainly hope that the war with Germany is over with by the time you receive this letter.

After all my running about and having a terrible seat at the movie to-night, I'm tired and will proceed to hit the sack.

Your, George

P.S. Send Package.

P.P.S. I almost forgot. To-morrow I'm going to get a baldy. Remember you said I was losing my hair, well you'll be right. Besides I hear if you get one, you'll always have hair. – I hope. J.G.B.

April 30, 1945
Monday

From:	To:
Cpl. James G. Barr 11057933	Mrs. James G. Barr
94th Dep. Rep. Sq., 56th ADG	65 Houghton St.
A.P.O. 246 Unit #1 c/o P.M.	Worcester 4, Mass.
San Francisco, Calf.	

Dearest Lottie,

If you could see your old man to-night, you'd do one of two things, either split your sides or divorce me – maybe both! I look like a billiard ball that has the picture of a man painted on it. See what happens to me when I can't be with you, I get crazy ideas. Do you think you'll be able to tame me down when I come home? You'd better be able, or else you'll have a problem on your pretty hands.

A few packages came in the mail to-day, with many more promised to-morrow, so maybe I'll get that Easter egg yet! One of the men was playing "I'll be Loving You Always," on the chapel piano, and that's exactly what I'm going to do to you.

The only thing that I did to-day was to drill holes in wood. After a day's work of that sort, I felt like a Swiss cheese worker. I never know from day to day what I'm going to do next!

There is a U.S.O. show here to-night, but I had so much to do I couldn't get away to see it. I also wanted to go to the infirmary to see Emil Bazzy, he fell and hurt his knee, but no soap. My part of the tent was in such a mess that I couldn't find a thing and I just had to remedy it. Then when my house cleaning was finished, I put my clothes to soak. The army is making a good housewife out of me, as you can plainly see.

If you could read between the lines in my letter last night you could see I was dog tired, how I managed to write five pages, well I don't want to brag, but a good man can do those things!

The last few nights the sunsets have been gorgeous! The sky has the most beautiful colors that I've ever seen. To-night you could have swore that the horizon had burst into flames! It is a sight to travel many miles to see, but not this many! Maybe in twenty years or so, we'll get into our little plane and see the sight to-gether. Until to-morrow darling.

Your, George

P.S. Send Package.

May 1, 1945
Tuesday

From:	To:
Cpl. James G. Barr 11057933	Mrs. James G. Barr
94th Dep. Rep. Sq., 56th ADG	65 Houghton St.
A.P.O. 246 Unit #1 c/o P.M.	Worcester 4, Mass.
San Francisco, Calf.	

Dearest Lottie,

I just came from a show that some G.I.'s put on. They're a traveling unit, and are sort of a government U.S.O. group. The entire cast consisted of seven men, but they all did so much, it was like an entire cast with a band thrown in. I thought they did a mighty fine job.

Last night after finishing my letters, I played nine games of ping-pong!! I could hardly hold my ratchet the last game. The tough part was that I lost it!! Out of the nine, I won seven, pretty good, huh?!! Not really, the other guys were just a little out of practice. I wanted to play again to-night with someone who I know can beat me, but the table was being used by some of the fellows to write on. This fellow I wanted to play, showed me many things in the art of ping-pong playing and I'd like to pick up a few more pointers. How do I know he can beat me? When I was at San Antonio last year, he was in my outfit, and we used to play regularly. He used to spot me ten points and still beat me! He's good.

Darling, at the end of this month you may receive a phone call, I doubt if it will be a collect call, but if it is, accept it. I'm sorry it won't be from me, but it will be from someone who has seen me. Don't depend too much upon it, but I wanted you to know just in case it does happen.

I did a good day's work to-day by helping wire up one of the buildings here. I was helping the "boss" (what a character) so when I saw what he was doing, I did. When he saw that it was possible, he thought I was an old electrician and asked how long I had been one! I told him that I had never done it before, but that any fool could do the same thing, if he saw it done once. All you have to do; cut a piece of B.X. cable, put something on with a screw, place it in a metal box, screw a ring on, and then bang a few nails to hold the cable up. Simple isn't it!! No doubt the place will burn up when they put the power on – oh gee no!!! Then I'd have to do it over again!

I'm all written out now dear, after all, I haven't had any help from you in three days. Also, I didn't get the bundles I had hoped for, but as you say – for to-morrow is another day.

Goodnight darling.
Your loving husband, George

May 3, 1945
Thursday

From:	To:
Cpl. James G. Barr 11057933	Mrs. James G. Barr
94th Dep. Rep. Sq., 56th ADG	65 Houghton St.
APO 246 Unit #1 c/o P.M.	Worcester 4, Mass.
San Francisco, Calf.	

My darling wife,

I got your Easter egg yesterday, and when I opened it, I was very pleasantly surprised. Not only was the egg lovely, but it tasted excellent! The four weeks that it had been on its way here, didn't seem to affect the taste of it at all! If it had been anything else, but a fruit cake, I doubt if it would have stayed good. You packed it so well it didn't even get dented! You're marvelous! The boys think so too!

To-day I got my folks package and everything but the Nestles chocolate was in good condition. The chocolate, I think, would have run out if I had broken the paper. Now that I have both packages, I can say, "All comes to he who waits!"

I think the fellow who I work with is crazy. All day long he's been rushing the other two fellows and let me do almost nothing. He's been overseas for a very long time, and I think it has affected him a little. I shouldn't kick tho – he leaves me alone, so that is just some more time I can think about you.

This evening I puttered around my tent and made it a little more comfortable and I hope cooler. Then I went up and showered and to-night I was able to go thru the entire procedure without the water being turned off!! Surprised me also! Now I feel wonderful. Gee, it's easy to wash my head now!

My haircut darling, even tho you may not like it, is a great morale builder. People just have to laugh when they see it. I have a few varied answers to their questions – "How come?" "Lost my comb," "Had an automobile accident," and, "that's the way I woke up this morning!" We don't make much money, but we have a hell of a time!

Darling, your letter of to-day was beautiful. I liked the way you put our marriage as being made in heaven, very much, and of course, I agree with you. Because it was so, you don't ever have to think about 'what if our paths hadn't crossed, because my dearest, they would have eventually. There is nothing about you I don't love and cherish, this I'll do for the rest of my life.

I received a V-mail from Uncle Barney from Washington, and he sends his best to you. I was going to write to him to-night, but I don't think

I'll have time. There are a few before him that I have to answer. Also, Lenny DiPietro sends his love. Emil Bazzy, well, he's going to call you up and give it to you personally! He left for the states, and when he's home, he promised he'd call you. That's what I call luck!

Until to-morrow, good night,
Your, George

P.S. You can get some fruit juices from dad to put in a package – no tomato tho. J.G.B.

May 4, 1945
Friday

From:	To:
Cpl. James G. Barr 11057933	Mrs. James G. Barr
94th Dep. Rep. Sq., 56th ADG	65 Houghton St.
APO 246 Unit #1 c/o P.M.	Worcester 4, Mass.
San Francisco, Calf.	

Hello my darling,

Here's that man you love (I hope!) again. I'm dripping wet and somehow or other I don't care, maybe the rain cleaned my fatigues a bit and will save that much washing on my part.

I didn't feel like going to services to-night, but went to the movies instead. The picture was "Barbary Coast Gent," entertaining, but nothing to go out of your way for. That's the way I got wet, during the show the rain came down. For the last few times that I've gone, it hadn't rained, so this time I left my raincoat at home. Oh well, maybe the rain will help my crop grow faster! No comments please!!!

I just had the fellow playing the piano play "Take Me in Your Arms." Darling, whenever I hear that song, I really travel back to you. It's because you like it so much and because I love you so much. Anything that reminds me of you makes me like it.

I'm glad you didn't go out and buy me a birthday present because I don't think I need anything. You were wise in doing what you did. It's very seldom that a fellow gets a wife with brains and is beautiful to boot. But I was lucky and got both when I got you.

To-morrow we should get paid and I hope I can get enough time to run up to the post office and get a money order, so that our little nest egg can grow that much larger. Every little cent saved is a penny earned, so they say! What's come over me, since when do I save money! I guess that's another reason I married you, someone else would probably have spent it all by now. What a callous fellow I am! You're stuck with me, so what can you do about it!

I'll be on again to-morrow night, same guy, same place, same time.

All my love, all my life
George

P.S. Kiss me quick! J.G.B.

May 5, 1945
Saturday

From:	To:
Cpl. James G. Barr 11057933	Mrs. James G. Barr
94th Dep. Rep. Sq., 56th ADG	65 Houghton St.
APO 246 Unit #1 c/o P.M.	Worcester 4, Mass.
San Francisco, Calf.	

My darling Lottie,

See, I kept my promise to you. I got two wonderful letters from my darling today. Not only from you, but five others besides. One from Sol, with a picture of Fran and Martin (we'll call him Martin), one from Narky, one from the folks, my family really did alright by me to-day. I also got two V-mails, one from Sid and the other from Dave. The funny thing about their letters, were that they were both written on the same day and I got them both on the same day and from different parts of the world!

We got paid to-day after a few hours' delay. First, we had to go to work, but we managed to get off a bit early. Remember I wrote you I was going to get over a hundred dollars. Well I didn't, I got eighty-four. I thought it might have been a mistake in my figgering, but I went over it again and still think I'm right. I talked it over with our finance clerk and we're going to recheck it to-morrow when he has time. I hope I'm the one that's right!!!

A funny thing happened this morning while I was going to work. While passing a tent down from me, I noticed "The Telegram" lying on a bunk. The fellow who owned them comes from Worcy and used to work with Irving Kirch at Paul Hats. So now I have access to the paper. I like to read them occasionally, but they are usually so old, the papers don't have much value. It's good to see the old home town paper tho. Did you know that in comparison to other newspapers in the states, we have one of the best papers from a city of that size! It's nice to know about little things like that. Other papers that I've read aren't half as good, and the journalism was nothing compared to what we have. Worcester, Ra-Ra-Ra!!!

Hell, you tell Shirley that there are plenty of guys nicer than me to get hooked to. And I doubt very much if it is my eyelashes, probably my bald head now (altho, it is growing back fast.) All she has to do is wait until the boys come home, maybe you could fix her up with Jackie, he's a nice kid!

I kinda feel bad for Edie, but not too bad. If you remember, I had my troubles too. (O.K.! No more salt in the wounds.)

Did you get the promised ride to Natick? If so, how's our new cedar chest. Find any pennies in it, or did they grow into dollar bills.

I'm so glad you liked the cablegram. Hell, there is no need to expect the worst when you get news of that kind. Nothing is going to happen to me. How could it, haven't I you to look forward to? I'd never forgive myself if I let anything happen to me!!!

Darling, here is where I prove a little stubborn. Since I've been in the service I've written two letters to Irv and Fran and two to Sam and Jeanne. Jeanne has answered all but my last one, but Fran has yet to write. I like a little appreciation myself. When a letter is written to me, I answer it, it's not that they can't write!

I bought a pair of ear rings and a pin made out of shell for Toby to-day. The clasps are made out of plastic, so I doubt if they'll stand up long. I wouldn't have gotten them, only she wrote that she wanted something. If I can pick up something real nice I'll send it to you, but as yet, I haven't seen anything worth spending my money on. As yet, I haven't been able to get any wrapping paper to send you, that Hawaiian paper, but I'll keep looking.

I found out we can't send money orders except certain times during the month. Our outfit has to wait until my birthday, isn't that nice of them, and I wanted to send you some to-day.

Yes, darling, I do know you love me, and I'm that much happier knowing about it. It is a funny thing, I feel that way about you also!

Your loving husband,
George

May 6, 1945
Sunday

From:	To:
Cpl. James G. Barr 11057933	Mrs. James G. Barr
94th Dep. Rep. Sq., 56th ADG	65 Houghton St.
APO 246 Unit #1 c/o P.M.	Worcester 4, Mass.
San Francisco, Calf.	

Dearest Lottie,

Guess what? I just saved me about twenty-five dollars! I was watching a crap game and made mental bets, I didn't come out so good, but if I had put up money, it would have been much worse!

The boys over here really go all out for gambling. So far, I've seen two dice games. These aren't among the boys, but a few run house games and seem to be cleaning up. Money has no value here, why a bottle of whiskey will bring forty dollars and up!

I bet that the earrings I bought will be at least five dollars the next time the fellow makes a batch. He'll catch on mighty soon.

After traveling around all afternoon, Irving and I didn't accomplish a solitary thing! I went to Uddy's place of work, only to find he had moved, but no one knew exactly where. We searched for three hours, but no Uddy. It was hot as blazes and wandering around in the hot sun got me tired. We gave up the search, but I left him "Telegrams" on his bunk, so that he'll know I was there. I'm going to write him a letter and give him holy hell!

I straightened out my pay, finally, and of course, I did have to add where I was supposed to subtract. Are there any first grade teachers around! Anyhoo, I'll be sending home fifty bucks, better than nuthin' anyway. See what a stupid person you married! I bet everyone wonders how you could have married such a mental wizard!

To-night I saw superman, before 'Superman' became famous. The picture was "Tarzan Triumphs," tra-da-da!!! Hell, what do you want for nothing, and besides, it didn't rain, - well, not enough to count.

And that is how I spent a quiet uneventful day.

Good night, Cookie, - gee, I haven't called you Cookie for a long time. Good night Cookie.

Your, George

May 7, 1945
Monday
Our Anniversary

From:	To:
Cpl. James G. Barr 11057933	Mrs. James G. Barr
94th Dep. Rep. Sq., 56th ADG	65 Houghton St.
APO 246 Unit #1 c/o P.M.	Worcester 4, Mass.
San Francisco, Calf.	

My very dearest wife,

Our marriage grows older, but oh, how much sweeter! It seems ages ago since we were married and I long for you terribly. If I could only be with you, that's all I need to make me happy. Your love for me is what makes life a joy, instead of a drudge. Sweetheart, I love you very much. Happy anniversary, darling!

I have so many letters to answer that I'm not going to the movies, but will try to get most of them answered to-night. Two wonderful letters from you to-day, two from the folks, a birthday card from Narky, and a nice letter from Jeanne. I'm glad that the mail situation here is very good.

I thought it was very nice of Edie Richards to call you when she heard the news broadcast of the ending of the war in Germany. It would have been nice if it had ended, but it's almost over now, according to the news of last night.

You were very thoughtful in giving Sam Namath a Bar Mitzvah gift. If Becky hadn't got angry, she wouldn't have appreciated the gift as much as she did. If I never told you that you were wonderful, then I am now. But I'm sure that I mentioned it several times before.

I don't know if there is quite a difference between 'going for her', and 'going for it'. I think when used in that way, they are synonymous! But I won't argue with you. I could be wrong.

By this time, you'll have a million dollar smile. Now by this time you can look back and say, "Heck, it didn't hurt much at all." I'm talking about the pain, not the bill!

Bye for now, my darling,
Your ever loving husband,
George

May 8, 1945
Tuesday

From:	To:
Cpl. James G. Barr 11057933	Mrs. James G. Barr
94th Dep. Rep. Sq., 56th ADG	65 Houghton St.
APO 246 Unit #1 c/o P.M.	Worcester 4, Mass.
San Francisco, Calf.	

Dearest Lottie,

I received two very nice birthday cards to-day from Toby and the folks. The only trouble was, that was all I got, no letter from you. You must have missed the last plane out!

The name of our field was changed to-day, so there was some sort of dedication. I didn't go to it, but we got the morning off, after ten o'clock. That was the best part of it. I hope they change the name again, under the same conditions.

When I went back to my tent, I scanned a bunch of old Telegrams and kept up with "Terry and the Pirates." The last I read was that he was in a pretty tight fix. Now I am anxiously waiting for the next installment to see how he gets out of this fix!

By this time, you should be getting over the hangover that you got on V-E day! What you didn't get drunk, too bad. As yet, it isn't official here, but the President is going to speak at 2300 (11:00 P.M. civilian time) and I think he'll make the official announcement. Then with the rumors that Russia is going to fight Japan – heck I'll be home before long!

I saw "Tennessee Johnson" to-night, it was the first time that I ever heard the title. It was a pretty good historical picture on the life of President Johnson. One thing it brought out was that you can get pretty drunk on brandy on an empty stomach!

This is a terrible letter, but darling, I love you. And if you remember, you said that is enough.

Goodnight my love, I'll try harder to-morrow night.

Your, George

May 9, 1945
Wednesday

From:	To:
Cpl. James G. Barr 11057933	Mrs. James G. Barr
94th Dep. Rep. Sq., 56th ADG	65 Houghton St.
APO 246 Unit #1 c/o P.M.	Worcester 4, Mass.
San Francisco, Calf.	

My darling wife,

I just came back from seeing, "Can't Help Singing." The reason I enjoyed it so much, was that it brought back the endless pleasant memories of our wonderful honeymoon. Remember the two sailors who gave us the passes, only they were good for servicemen only. You not being a serviceman, I had to buy a ticket for you. Oh, happy memories!

We missed the first few minutes of the picture, but all it was, was that she met her supposed fiancée and her father had him sent away for business. I wish that you could have been with me to see the beginning, just as you were with me to see the rest of the picture. Darling, I love you very, very much.

Not very much mail came in to-day, but I was lucky enough to get three V-mails. Two from the Shapiro's (Harry & Rebecca), and one from Rose Lisabitsky. The oldest one was dated April 24th, so you can see V-mail isn't as fast as air mail. To-morrow tho, should bring at least two letters from you. That's what I look forward to each new day – a letter from my wife, whom I love dearly.

I finally managed to snag some wrapping paper, and just as soon as I can get it censored, I'll mail them out. You'll only get the newspaper and a little booklet on Hawaii, and Toby's earrings and pin. But don't worry, just as soon as I see something nice enough for you, I'll get it.

I had an easy job to do to-day. All I did was sit down and assemble lamps and shades. To-morrow we have to hang them. Then we'll get a new building to wire.

I wish I could get a picture of my head before all my hair grows back!! Why, I can almost feel it now!!

After supper Irv wanted a can of beer, and since he went for it last night, I had to go to-night. First I had to wait in line, then I had to pay for it and get my beer ration card punched. On the way back, I met a couple of the fellows who wanted a "taste." Taste, - hell, all they left me was one mouthful!! No more, next time I drink my beer alone!

Last night before I fell asleep I was reminiscing. It was wonderful to remember all the sweet and thoughtful things about you. I don't know why, but the one that stayed mostly in my mind, was the time I came home to become engaged to you. On the train, I was thinking, who am I to kiss first, you, or mother. Fortunately, you foresaw the situation and let mother come forward first. Little things like that are what made me love you. You say you're selfish with those you love, I can't seem to believe it.

All my love, all my life
George

P.S. Enclosed I'm sending a one dollar Hawaiian bill that I got onboard the ship. I had a few fellows sign their names, but it got wet & sort of washed off. J.G.B.

May 11, 1945
Friday

From:	To:
Cpl. James G. Barr 11057933	Mrs. James G. Barr
94th Dep. Rep. Sq., 56th ADG	65 Houghton St.
APO 246 Unit #1 c/o P.M.	Worcester 4, Mass.
San Francisco, Calf.	

My dearest Lottie,

I'm sorry about last night, I didn't write you. After showering and a general clean up, I laid down in my bunk for a cigarette. I smoked the cig, threw it away and laid back for a few minutes' rest. When I awoke, it was well into the night! I don't know what caused it, I know I didn't overwork myself, and I know I didn't eat too much, maybe it was the cig, or could have been the air. Anyway, I had twelve hours of sleep last night!!

It seems that everyone that owns a watch, has a metal watch band here on this island. The bug hit me, and I am now the owner of one stainless steel watch band. Guaranteed not to rust, shrink, or anyway detract from the looks of the watch! I would have made myself one, but my workmanship isn't worth a damn, so I bought one off of a fellow whose usual price is ten, cost me five because I know him pretty well. It's worth at least three, so he made himself a living for the day. He has a wife and four children to support!

Did you know darling, that if we had children, they'd be worth twelve points apiece for discharge! You only can count three of them tho, the other twenty-one wouldn't count. To get out now, you need eighty-five points. I don't have enough, so I'll stay in awhile.

Irv got a hold of a book, "Married Love", and read it, even after I had told him it was no good. I told him about "The Torch of Life," so he sent home for his girl to get it for him. The funny part was that the next day after she received his request, an advertisement came to her about the book. She's sent for it so Irv will be able to get an education, altho I gladly offered to teach him!

She also wanted to know how we both looked, and if you were better looking than her. Darling, she can't hold a candle to you!

Congrats to the Talbots, heck he must have known about his new point system before hand (the rain just chased me inside and I'm now writing standing up). Maybe Nate wasn't nervous, could be Irene was too lazy!!!!

No I don't know any Kulin girl, but I'm glad you went and even happier to know you enjoyed yourself.

I have a watch crystal as I wrote you, so there isn't any rush. If Kumin needs the watch and case number, I have it someplace around and could send him it (maybe I have it in my wallet – one sec.) (Nope). But I'm pretty sure I have it around, and if I remember correctly, I have it posted inside my wardrobe at my mother's.

It's funny you writing me about Uddy, because you know I've met him at least a week ago. Thanks for telling me anyway.

Is the cedar chest small, because you tried to put more stuff in it? Or is it small? If it is small enough to make a difference, how about changing it, or is it too much trouble?

In your letter of to-day, I got the air mail stickers, another thing I want to thank you for. Darling, you're so good to me, I'll be thanking you for the rest of my life. I love you very much.

I can't see what you see in my drippy boring letters, but if you like 'em, I'll write 'em.

I went to services to-night, and half way thru, the lights went out. We finished by candle light and I think it was more impressive that way. We even had G.I. Chaley after services ended.

I feel sorry for Evelyn, but if she had just a minute part of you, she'd be married a long time ago. Mothers also have a lot to do about it too!

Irv's birthday is to-day, so he bought the beers, because mine is to-morrow, I'll buy them. So, neither one of us is getting cheated.

Good night, darling.
Your loving husband,
George

May 12, 1945
Saturday

From:	To:
Cpl. James G. Barr 11057933	Mrs. James G. Barr
94th Dep. Rep. Sq., 56th ADG	65 Houghton St.
APO 246 Unit #1 c/o P.M.	Worcester 4, Mass.
San Francisco, Calf.	

Hello, my darling,

I know if you were with me, you'd wish me a happy birthday, so thank you very much.

For the last three years, I haven't been home on my birthday, so the chances are with me that on my next birthday, I'll be home with you for good. That will be one birthday that I'll really enjoy. It's funny tho, my age grows older, but I don't seem to feel it. I used to think of a person twenty-two as being well along the road to life, and I just started mine when I married you.

Darling, being able to love you has done wonderful things to me. I have an outlook in life that I never could have if I were single. I'm one damn lucky fellow to have you!

To-morrow we have the whole day off because of V-E day. Now I'll be able to sleep as late as I want. I hope it rains all morning so it will be nice and cool and nothing to do except remain in bed. It's been a long time since I've been able to sleep one morning late, and to-morrow, I hope to make the most of it. Ain't I the lazy one?!

Remember (how could you forget) how we stayed in bed for the entire morning days at a time? That's as close to heaven as I'll be able to get! Darling, every minute that we were to-gether is stored up in me and lasts me a day over here. When that supply runs out, where will I be? It just better not, that's all!!

My birthday only seems to remind me of your birthday; the time you had the measles, or the mumps (I can't remember). I had to throw your present to you. I get a big chuckle out of that one every time. I even think you would have kissed me, if you weren't sick!!!

Oh, for happier days of yore, but for better days to come!

We had a very easy day, except for a few pieces of metal I cut and a few screws I turned, I didn't do a thing. We had our officer inspect the work and he said it was pretty good. I could have told him that before, but he doesn't ask my advice. (I wonder why!)

Here at last is the money order I promised you. At mail call, it was the only thing I got. I would have much rather received a letter from you tho.

I was thinking to-night, that if I ever get back into radio again, I'm going to try a venture. Since everyone here is making one thing or another, I thought I might try building radios for the boys and importing the necessary parts from home. Until I have someplace where I can work at night, the idea will have to wait. It's a good idea anyway. I bet a good working set would bring in anywhere from thirty to fifty dollars, at a cost of maybe ten to fifteen to me, not counting my work!

I thought that to-morrow afternoon I'd be able to go shell hunting, but as yet, I haven't been able to get a piece of glass to fit my super deluxe shell finder. As yet, I haven't planned on what I'll do, maybe I'll end up remaining in bed!

And off to bed I go. Nighty night.
Your, George

P.S. Kiss me quick!!!

May 13, 1945
Sunday

From:	To:
Cpl. James G. Barr 11057933	Mrs. James G. Barr
94th Dep. Rep. Sq., 56th ADG	65 Houghton St.
APO 246 Unit #1 c/o P.M.	Worcester 4, Mass.
San Francisco, Calf.	

Dearest Lottie,

I just came back from "A Tree Grows in Brooklyn." I enjoyed it very much. Have you had a chance to see it as yet?

This afternoon our outfit got a truck to go sight seeing with. We left at one-thirty and didn't get back till five o'clock. It turned out to be quite a Cooke's Tour of the island. I was surprised a little to see what I saw and it is a happy surprise. The trip was a bit rough when we hit the dirt roads, but I guess I can't ask for the turnpike!

I didn't sleep as late as I wanted to, but I did manage to get breakfast in bed! Irv got up for breakfast and I asked him to bring me back a cup of coffee. He did, and also brought with him a piece of bread with plenty of jam on it.

I went back to sleep again for about an hour, couldn't go back, so I continued to read "Sons" by Pearl Buck, which I got out of our library last night. I don't like it as well as "The Good Earth," but it is still a good book.

Received five letters at mail call and after what I didn't get yesterday, it was wonderful - two from you!

Darling, I don't want you or anyone to send me any money unless I ask for it, because darling, what could I do with it, unless gamble it away, or buy a bunch of junk that the fellows make.

Sometimes I can say so much and no more. At the time I wrote you about Emil, I didn't know whether I could tell you about his going to the states or not. Remember darling, that I'm writing a censored letter.

I bet you looked real swell playing with the younger generation! How many home runs did you get? Don't you worry about our children 'taking' to you, as others are now, because darling, it is you liking children that does it and when we have our own, the love you'll have for them will bring them as close to you as you want. And, of course, they'll be beautiful. In fact, you are an example, a perfect example too, I may add!! Are you spoiled – no, and you are beautiful, so put that in your pipe and smoke it.

Again, I have to thank you for your thoughtfulness. Darling you are the best wife a man could love. Now you can be sure of receiving all your mail by air.

Tell Doc hello and to treat you mighty easy, or else; or else I won't give him my teeth to play around with anymore.

Michael is doing pretty good. That kid's going to be a millionaire, but I don't know about this mother, she gambles away his savings!! Shame on her!

Good night my darling.
All my love,
Your, George

P.S. What happened, you quit numbering your letters? J.G.B.

May 14, 1945
Monday

From:	To:
Cpl. James G. Barr 11057933	Mrs. James G. Barr
94th Dep. Rep. Sq., 56th ADG	65 Houghton St.
APO 246 Unit #1 c/o P.M.	Worcester 4, Mass.
San Francisco, Calf.	

My darling wife,

What a grand and wonderful surprise I got to-day. Three cablegrams!!! One from you, the folks, and Toby. I couldn't ask for a better family, darling, above all, you are the most wonderful, and I'm saying that without any prejudice. I bet every fellow at mail call was jealous of me, because who heard of a fellow getting three cablegrams at one time! Also, I received your daily letter, what a marvelous day it was for me!

I would have loved to have seen you when you got up after that dream with Danny Kaye. What has that guy got that I haven't – and where can I get it! I bet if I made faces like him, you'd throw me out. Heck, I bet he doesn't have a haircut like mine!

(I left you for awhile and saw "Xmas in Connecticut," which was very good. I enjoyed it so much that I sat thru it and got soaked! Boy, what I wouldn't give for a pair of eye glass wipes!!)

I don't think Sid Burach is such a terrible fellow, unless he's changed since I last talked to him. I'd never have wanted him for a close friend, but I thought he was a pretty good guy. As I remember him, he wasn't vulgar when he was around any women. Could be I didn't know him as well as I thought tho. I don't know why I wrote so much about him, it doesn't make any difference, but there isn't much else to write about.

I intended drawing a diagram for my intended radio to-night, but I have a few letters I must answer before I can do it. Got a letter from Norman and he sends his love, the stinker!

Lousy letter, lousy night, but to-morrow, you know, the sun will be shining, and so will I.

Your loving husband,
George

May 15, 1945
Tuesday

From:	To:
Cpl. James G. Barr 11057933	Mrs. James G. Barr
94th Dep. Rep. Sq., 56th ADG	65 Houghton St.
APO 246 Unit #1 c/o P.M.	Worcester 4, Mass.
San Francisco, Calf.	

My darling wonderful wife,

I just returned from seeing a command movie, "Two Down and One to Go." It told us how we are supposed to be discharged. It was what we already knew and I think a waste of time and money. The film would have had to been made some time ago, because our five star General Marshall, still had his four stars on. This, in my mind, was planned a long time ago, because it is not new stuff and the information had already come to our attention one way or another. I'm glad I'm not essential or I'd never be able to get out.

Darling, what did you mean that the glasses were too heavy to send by air, wouldn't the post office accept them? First class doesn't mean a damn thing after a package leaves the states. I doubt very much if it will come in the week you thought it would, that's why I told you to send it by air. Oh well, I'm getting along without them and I can wait, you know me, patient as they make them.

It was very nice of Doc Glixman to say I could send them back if they didn't please, and when you see him again, give him my regards also.

Sweetheart, with the prayers you make up, you could go into religion. Hell, my hair is growing back pretty fast, why in another month, I'll be able to run a comb across the ole' bean!!

My boss got kind of peeved at me to-day, because I must have made a million mistakes, I don't think I did anything right. Nope, I doubt if I'll be classified essential. He has more than the required amount of points to be discharged, and yet he can't see how he's going to get out for sometime, and yet, there are men in the states with less points than he and they are getting out. I think this essential stuff is a lot of baloney, for I have yet to see a man essential in the army. Heck, even if a man really is good, he doesn't get any credit for it. My boss, again for example, he's a corporal and yet he has men with higher ranks under him. Like Irv says, "See what I mean!" Good night darling.

Your, George

May 16, 1945
Wednesday

From:	To:
Cpl. James G. Barr 11057933	Mrs. James G. Barr
94th Dep. Rep. Sq., 56th ADG	65 Houghton St.
APO 246 Unit #1 c/o P.M.	Worcester 4, Mass.
San Francisco, Calf.	

My darling wife,

To-night we were presented with the play, "The Man Who Came to Dinner." Moss Hart, the author, played the lead, and other good actors played along with him. The show was worthy of a Worcester showing! That's how good it was!

By the time Irv and I came to the theater, every seat had been taken, so we had to go back for something to sit on, or stand like hundreds of others. I waited a good hour before the play started, so you can imagine how long the others had been there to fill every available seat.

It's a funny thing, but when we stopped over at Hawaii, we read in the newspaper that Moss Hart and his company was touring those islands and would travel on to the Pacific. I never imagined that I'd be seeing him, instead of reading about him. Now if Barb had gone across, I'd probably have seen her also. If I did, I bet the other fellows would have been mighty jealous!

Another peculiar thing happened to-day too. While showering, the water suddenly changed from cold to hot! We haven't any means of heating the water and I can't see how it got so hot. It felt damn good though. It's been almost three months since I've bathed in hot water. My, but it seems eons ago!

I received a letter from Jack W. to-day, I had thought he had forgotten about me. He didn't say anything about the enlargements of the picture of the wedding, so I don't know what he intends doing about them. I'll have to ask him again. Also, got a letter from our Uncle Barney in Washington, who sends his love.

My little head is weary and my, ahem, is very tired, so after I write a brief note (also) to the folks, I'll retire in my antique four poster!

Goodnight, Cookie, my darling,
Your, George

P.S. Kiss me quick! J.G.B.

May 17, 1945
Thursday

From:	To:
Cpl. James G. Barr 11057933	Mrs. James G. Barr
94th Dep. Rep. Sq., 56th ADG	65 Houghton St.
APO 246 Unit #1 c/o P.M.	Worcester 4, Mass.
San Francisco, Calf.	

My dearest wife,

This evening I saw quite an amusing picture called "Practically Yours." It was a war farce, but good. You know if I had come a few minutes later I would have missed "Popeye," then my evening surely would have been spoiled!

I may start to do a different type work to-morrow, I don't know. Some other shop wants some men and a few of us were on the list, the trouble is that the shop I'm working out of now, wants us to remain, but we want to go. Now we have to wait until we get replaced. I had a little talk with our shop sergeant and told him that I wanted to go, otherwise, it would have a definite effect on my work. He didn't like it one bit, but I'm tired of this job. Hell, I've worked at it a month and nothing new happens. And I'm afraid to learn one thing too well or I'll never get into radio again. We'll see what happens to-morrow.

If you have noticed the days and dates of my letters, you may see that I get them mixed up occasionally. Don't mind it, because the only day I keep in mind is Sunday, my day off. Otherwise, the days might not even have names.

You will not refer to me as "Cue ball," anymore. You may ask why, so I'll be kind enough to tell you. – I had a trim to-day!! Yes dear, there is now enough hair on my head so that there is a little excess around the edges that will need occasional trimming.

My, this is a dull life. It gets dark after work, so you can't do anything, unless you go to the show or the chapel. I'll be glad when we get set up in our new area so that I won't have to run all over before I can accomplish something. There's too much noise and goings on at the chapel to do much, and I don't want to make myself concentrate (which is bad, I know). I still haven't finished the drawing of my contemplated radio and I'm ashamed of myself. I wish you were here to give me hell, boy that I would certainly love.

What a bunch of dribble!!! Good night my darling.

All my love, all my life,
George

May 18, 1945
Friday

From:	To:
Cpl. James G. Barr 11057933	Mrs. James G. Barr
94th Dep. Rep. Sq., 56th ADG	65 Houghton St.
APO 246 Unit #1 c/o P.M.	Worcester 4, Mass.
San Francisco, Calf.	

My wonderful wife,

My, but I feel good to-night. First I received two letters from you to-day after a wait of two days, and I just came from services. I really shouldn't be so happy because I ran into a little trouble with my boss. I thought he'd blow his top! Of course, I goaded him along, I'll get out of that place yet!

I'm trying to make some sort of a washing machine, but I can't get enough material to build it quickly, so I take everything in sight that I can use. I took some connections that I shouldn't have and that's where my dear boss started seeing colors. When I apologized, he got madder, because he thought I'd try to get out of it someway, but you know me, another George Washington!! Yeah!!!

In the April 6th Civic Leader that I received to-day, on the servicemen's page, there's a little article on Passover services here. It was nice to read in a paper far away about something that happened here.

What you did for all our mothers was just like you. Darling, did you know that the wife Cpl. J.G. Barr is the most wonderful person in the world! Gee, but I love that gal!!!

Don't you worry about mother liking her new pocketbook. I know that anything you give her would be as much appreciated, as her gifts are appreciated by you.

Phil did get a very lucky break, tho I hope I don't have to spend two years out here to get one similar to his! I want home and you quick like. All I did noon hour was lie on my bunk and think of you. I love you very much my sweet.

I can't wait until I have the pictures you mentioned in my hands. Please hurry up with them Army mail service!

Mother should start putting up an entry fee. Look at all the money she could have collected so far. No wonder so many men want her, she's a wonderful woman. Give my love to mother will you, please. That's a good girl. Now, kiss me quick! Already, I'm a different man.

After writing a letter to the folks, I shall continue where I left off in my hair brain scheme of a radio.

Good night, Cookie.

Your ever loving husband,
George

May 20, 1945
Sunday

From:	To:
Cpl. James G. Barr 11057933	Mrs. James G. Barr
94th Dep. Rep. Sq., 56th ADG	65 Houghton St.
APO 246 Unit #1 c/o P.M.	Worcester 4, Mass.
San Francisco, Calf.	

Dearest Lottie,

After a brief interlude of a day, I'm back with you again. Last night, instead of writing to you, I played ping-pong! Can you ever forgive me? Well, you'd just better.

A friend of Irv's came to visit him. He's stationed in a different section of the island and because he had yesterday off, he came to visit Irv. We talked for quite some time, then went to the P.X. to get some beer, but because they didn't have any cold beer, we went without. The chapel was our next stop, where we played ping-pong for the rest of the night. I didn't get a work out like that for ages, and I really enjoyed it.

By this time it was late, so Art, Irv's friend, decided to sleep over. We managed to get him a cot, and while these two talked, I fell asleep.

This morning I didn't do a thing, but after dinner, I went back to the shop to work on the washing machine I started. Darling, I never realized that there was so much work in a hand-operated machine, such as I'm building. I worked for over five hours on it, and it is now completed, except for a paint job. I just hope it works out, it should, but the way I have it, the clothes may get tangled in it and rip. I had a lot of fun and experience building it, so there is nothing lost if it doesn't work, but if it does it should make washing pretty simple.

Irv got a record of his girl's voice and he invited me to go along and hear it with him. I think that he's going to get a pretty nice girl and she is going to get stuck, but so did you. Love certainly was blind when you chose me! I'll make it up to you tho, don't you think I won't.

I got one letter from you yesterday, but there is a few days interval between the last one I received from you and this one, so I should be getting the ones that were in the middle to-morrow.

The Sunday that our family went to Boston sounded swell, except for the news of the aunt in Chesea dying. I remember her very well, she was at our engagement and wedding. She was very nice.

You're a very good aunt, taking over the duties of your sister-in-law and changing the diapers on our little nephew. I hope you didn't stick him when you were putting those three cornered pants on him. I know – I ought to be ashamed of myself for saying a thing like that to my wife, – funny thing tho, I'm not ashamed. I'm glad, you'll need practice, after all you'll have to take care of twenty-four of them.

I'm still waiting to get out of the shop, but so far no luck. It looks as if I'm stuck. Essential – phooey!!

Goodnight, my love.

Your, George

Cpl. George Barr using his handmade washing machine in Guam.

~ 1945 ~

Cpl. George Barr with two buddies in Guam (notice George's handmade washing machine on the left)

May 21, 1945
Monday

From:	To:
Cpl. James G. Barr 11057933	Mrs. James G. Barr
94th Dep. Rep. Sq., 56th ADG	65 Houghton St.
APO 246 Unit #1 c/o P.M.	Worcester 4, Mass.
San Francisco, Calf.	

My darling wife,

I did get the letter I knew I should get. It must have gotten mixed up some way or another. This one was written on my birthday when you wished me a happy birthday. Thank you my sweet, I love you – oh, so much!

Your little feast with the "girls" sounded very nice. Just because you are a little younger, all right, a lot younger, doesn't mean a damn thing, except of course, that you can associate with people of all ages and have them like it. Even babies.

Our sister-in-law Charlotte is giving me a pain in the you know where. Charlotte is too damn selfish, and I wish I were able to do something about the situation. But as everything else, I can only wish. 'Nuff said on that subject.

It looks as if I'm going to remain just where I am. I cornered the man in charge and had a Tech. Sergeant to Cpl. talk. He can't let me go unless he gets authority from higher quarters and he said they won't give it to him. Maybe I should go around telling everyone that I just adore working for Shop Maintenance and I'm very happy there. Then maybe I'd get a transfer.

Put the final touches on my brain child and hope to test it out soon. Keep your fingers crossed. At least I got a few compliments on my work and they are all pulling for me. If they'd only come around and help me turn the crank when I wash, that would be much more appreciated!

I bet the rattles you got Martin were swell. Hell, what do we care for a little money, anyway. I hope you went out and got something for yourself with the check I sent (money order). If you haven't, you are hereby given a direct order by a non-commissioned officer, and it will be carried out. If you don't comply, I'll have to have you court martialed!! And besides, I want you to.

Thank the girls at the office for their singing of Happy Birthday. I bet it sounded good!

I bet your hair looks even more beautiful now that it has grown longer. Boy, wouldn't I love to run my fingers thru your lovely hair. It's so nice and soft and glossy. Darling, everything about you is beautiful and don't I know it, no wonder I love you.

With wonderful thoughts of you in my head, I bid you good night –
I want to dream of my Cookie.

Yours for ever and ever,
George

P.S. Kiss me quick!!!

May 22, 1945
Tuesday

From:	To:
Cpl. James G. Barr 11057933	Mrs. James G. Barr
94th Dep. Rep. Sq., 56th ADG	65 Houghton St.
APO 246 Unit #1 c/o P.M.	Worcester 4, Mass.
San Francisco, Calf.	

Dearest Lottie,

I finally mailed out Toby's earrings, I kept saying to-morrow, to-morrow, until I finally got around to it to-day. I didn't tell her she wasn't worth getting a souvenir, but that the souvenirs I saw weren't worth getting because of their price. The pin and earrings didn't cost much, that's why I got them. I doubt if they'll hold up if she tries to wear them often tho.

I finally got around to washing in my machine. Everything worked out swell, except it leaks like a sieve. I'll have to fix it before it will be real practical. For the first time, it worked out pretty good, I think!

I got a pleasant surprise to-day when I got the mail, besides a letter from you, I got a letter from dad. He doesn't usually write, Toby does the honors.

Darling, I'm sorry you asked me to write Fran and Irv, because even if they did treat us very nice at our wedding, I don't think that it should be bought kindness. That would be what is called a 'brown noser', or 'apple polisher' in the army and that would be very 'chicken' of me. I'm sorry, but I can't see it. If I did keep writing, I'd feel very cheap, and I know you wouldn't want me to feel that way. Darling, when you give someone a gift, I know you don't want any favors because of it. Shall we forget about it now?

I'm no longer an electrician's helper. I had it out with my boss and I'm now doing regular detail work, such as picking up lumber and paper and anything that requires moving. I got mad to-day, because I was sent to work on wires, right next to some other wire that had electrical current going thru them. That would have been all right if they were properly insulated, but they weren't. That was enough for me and I told them I wanted a change of jobs and I got it. To-morrow morning a few other radio men and myself are going to see our C.O. and see if he can get us into radio work, but I doubt it, because it seems as if the only jurisdiction the C.O.'s here have over their men is when they are in their immediate areas. All we can do is try.

What really got me mad tho, was that when I asked to be changed, my damn boss said, "Well, if you really don't want to work, we can't make you." And here I was the one that asked for a change, not the man right over me. When I asked him if anyone had ever complained that I hadn't done my work before, he said no. Then I said, "What the hell gave you the idea then, that I didn't want to work." He didn't answer that.

I felt better later tho, because everything annoyed him after that and he was boiling. I don't know how to handle men, but he knows less. He's a tech. sergeant, but I've worked under better privates! This is the army!!!

As you say, darling – to-morrow is another day. Goodnight, sweet.

Your, George

May 23, 1945
Wednesday

From:	To:
Cpl. James G. Barr 11057933	Mrs. James G. Barr
94th Dep. Rep. Sq., 56th ADG	65 Houghton St.
APO 246 Unit #1 c/o P.M.	Worcester 4, Mass.
San Francisco, Calf.	

My darling wife,
Our radio station is putting on its own "Pop's Concert" to-night, which only brings back the time we went to-gether. Darling, we can have the most wonderful times to-gether and I loved every minute of it and I cherish those moments in my heart. They are playing "Le Parisien" now, and tho that brings back memories, it wasn't with you that I saw the ballet of it! That was the time I asked you to come out to Boston with Charlotte, and Narky and I were going to take you both to see the "Ballet Russes." My dearest, we'll make up for that, now don't let me forget. (As if you would).

The only mail I got to-day was an announcement that the Glick's had a baby born to them, a boy. He was the cousin that took us to luncheon at the Waldorf. It is a very cute announcement, we should give him all our work. If my folks haven't shown it to you, ask them next time.

My little washing machine is getting a good work out, even tho it leaks, everyone wants to use it! I hope I don't have a tough time getting to use it myself! Heck, if the boys cooperated, a bunch of them could be built, and with good mechanics, they wouldn't leak. Maybe we could even get a few small motors to run them. If this had been in the old 4503rd, it would have been done a long time ago.

I had a very funny thing happen to me this afternoon. A couple of the boys and myself were dropped off at the edge of a salvage place and they forgot about us the entire afternoon. I fell asleep and had a dream. I dreamt that my mother had flown over here to visit me. I showed her around the island, which was very different in my dream, and before I had a chance to find her a place to sleep, someone woke me up to go back to the area! Now why couldn't you have come along with her!

Now I'm going to try and dream of you. Goodnight.

Your, George

May 24, 1945
Thursday

From: Cpl. James G. Barr 11057933 94th Dep. Rep. Sq., 56th ADG APO 246 Unit #1 c/o P.M. San Francisco, Calf.	To: Mrs. James G. Barr 65 Houghton St. Worcester 4, Mass.

My darling wife,

Here I am sucking on root beer drops in the chapel, writing you a letter. Now isn't that sweet of me? Also, very silly I think.

I can see that this is going to be a very P.P. letter, but darling, not much of anything has happened to me to-day, except I didn't receive anything in the mail.

To-night I banged away on a box I had, and put hinges and a back on it. Now I have a very nice foot locker to throw all my belongings in. To-morrow I'll try and make some sort of cabinet out of another box I have. When this is all completed and I have a place for everything and I know just where everything is – we'll move.

This evening I saw the movie "Pardon My Sarong." If they had girls on this island like the ones in the picture, – just wow! It gives fellows ideas!!! O.K. innocence!

I spent the day demolishing empty wooden crates that had airplane parts in them. I wish we could use dynamite, it would make a faster job out of it. It's a good job, there is no one there to bother us and when we get tired, which is often, we sit in the shade and take a break. Yes darling, it's a tough war!

The nights lately have been beautiful and I yearn for you in my arms so that we can see them to-gether. What good are romantic scenes if you can't be romantic? When I get home again, I'll pay off in dividends, how's that! I like it too!!!

I think this war has gone for enough and it's time it ended. I'm getting good and tired of the whole thing. I think I'll write a letter to the President or someone!

That's all – and it is.

Goodnight, Cookie, and how I love that woman!

Your, George

May 26, 1945
Saturday

From:	To:
Cpl. James G. Barr 11057933	Mrs. James G. Barr
94th Dep. Rep. Sq., 56th ADG	65 Houghton St.
APO 246 Unit #1 c/o P.M.	Worcester 4, Mass.
San Francisco, Calf.	

Dearest Cookie,

I didn't forget about you last night, I thought of you continuously. Last night there was a big shindig at the chapel and it ended late, too late to write a letter. After services, there was a program, then food and ice cream. A good time was had by all.

Yesterday I was commissioned to put latches on a new building. It would have been alright if we had the latches, but I also had to make them! I put them all up, but to-day I was told I had forgotten to put one on the colonel's private door! It was off to a side, and I don't look for work, so of course, I missed it. It's in now tho, I did it first thing this morning.

Darling, tho the pictures aren't the kind I take, I thought they were wonderful. I love you and whenever I have the good fortune of getting a picture of you, you can't imagine how thrilled I am. Your hair has grown long, and I'm waiting for the chance of running my hands thru it. If you can, keep the pictures coming, because darling I love them.

To-morrow afternoon I hope to go shell hunting. I haven't been down to the beach for a month now, and tho I can't go swimming there, I'm sure to enjoy it. Hope I can get a lot of pretty shells.

Mail, this week, has been coming in quite poorly, I hope this coming week it will perk up a bit. I had a letter returned that I sent to Bob (the baby cup) again, it seems that his old address couldn't locate him. I have his home address, so I'll send it to his parents to forward it.

This morning we had a shoe inspection and I flunked. It seems that the goo I was to put on wasn't put on correctly. This stuff is to make our shoes waterproof, and to-morrow morning I have to see our C.O. and he will check me again. Yes dear, it's a tough war. The more inspections of this sort will bring the war to an end sooner.

If you run into any more trouble with the stove, I'll send you my gas mask. I doubt if I'll ever have to use it. You have to be careful around the house, I don't want you to be hurt because of some little thing. I bet it scared mother half to death, to see you sleeping on the couch, with the smell of gas in the air.

Anne Joselowitz also wrote me a letter and she's hoping to leave around August, and she invites us down to Africa anytime we wish to come. I know how she feels, she's been away from home over twice as long as I have. She's been in the states now almost six years!

You know darling, that you still haven't gotten away for a few weeks as you promised me you would. Nothing would please me so much now, but to hear you went off to take it easy for awhile.

Good night, my darling.

Your, George

May 27, 1945
Sunday

From:	To:
Cpl. James G. Barr 11057933	Mrs. James G. Barr
94th Dep. Rep. Sq., 56th ADG	65 Houghton St.
APO 246 Unit #1 c/o P.M.	Worcester 4, Mass.
San Francisco, Calf.	

My darling wonderful wife,

I'm a very tired man to-night, and how did I become so fatigued? I went shell hunting this afternoon as planned, and after plodding around in the water bending down in search for those damn shells, who wouldn't get tired!!! Never again will I go shell hunting, unless it is to hunt up someone who wants to sell some. No kidding, I thought I had broken my back - Sunday afternoon, a day for relaxation - phooey. By the way, I did manage to find a shell!!!

The first ten minutes of my search it poured and the rain felt like someone was dripping ice water on my back as I had my feet in a pan of warm water. After my futile hunt, I got talking to a marine and when he heard I was giving up shell hunting, he wanted to buy my box (the box is used to see thru the water). I just wanted to give it to him outright, but he refused to take it unless he gave me a dollar. So, I took it and became a dollar richer.

The money you find here is Jap invasion money. No, I didn't kill any Japs for it, I just bought a few for souvenirs to send home. I could have gotten some before, but then the prices asked for them were too high, but they were quite reasonable. I hope you like them.

The three letters I received from you to-day was just what I needed. I had just finished a large washing and needed building up. And because you are such a wonderful wife, you came thru with flying colors. Darling, I love you very much and miss you just as much.

By this time the prophecy of Mrs. Silver should have come true, that is, the part were you get the phone call. Let's hope that the rest is going to be true also.

Let's see, - Irv is about 5' 11", has black wavy hair and is quite a good looking fellow. He's dark and has a sort of negroid look about him, lips that are a trifle wide and a wide nose. He's a conceited kid, but if handled right, you can get along with him. He definitely is not the understanding type, and a little selfish. That's not painting too good a picture of him, I know, but it's the truth. If we hadn't been to-gether before, I doubt very much if we'd pal around now.

Sylvia is an average looking girl and I think quite clever. They've been going steady ever since they were in high school, so now she won't even look at another fellow. Which isn't as clever as I said she was. They'll get along fine, because she thinks she's going to be boss, and when Irv puts his foot down he's going to be quite angry and peeved and won't listen to reason, and because Sylvia loves him, she'll give him his way, so he'll never have a chance to become unspoiled.

No darling, I have much better friends to spend occasions with, but because it is war, I can get along.

It's too bad that Bonnie contracted the measles, Charlotte must be going mad. Does the quarantine affect Toby or not?

Goodnight, my dearest.

All my love,
Your, George

P.S. Kiss me quick!!!

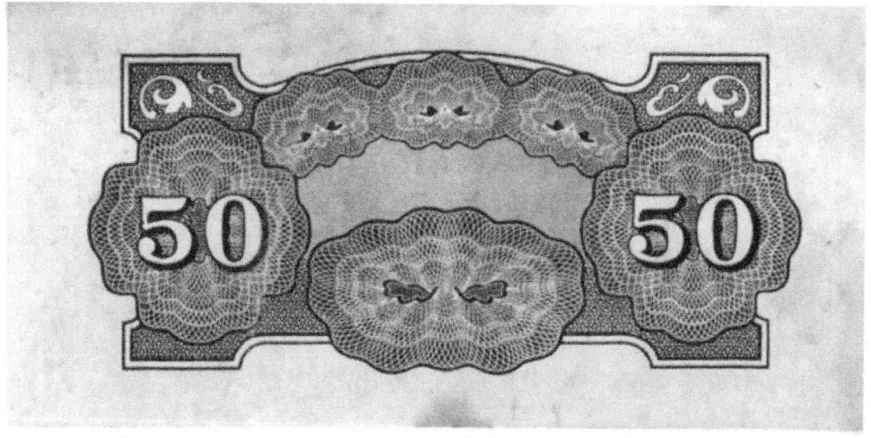

May 29, 1945
Tuesday

From:	To:
Cpl. James G. Barr 11057933 94th Dep. Rep. Sq., 56th ADG APO 246 Unit #1 c/o P.M. San Francisco, Calf.	Mrs. James G. Barr 65 Houghton St. Worcester 4, Mass.

Dearest Lottie,

To-day came and went and all I got was a Civic Leader, and that didn't have any engrossing news. Do you think I'm selfish when I want mail from my Cookie everyday? Of course, I'm not, but something always screws up and I have to wait a day or two before I get the mail I wait for. Am I complaining, of course I am, even if it's unjustly so. O.K, now I feel better and I'll start my letter to you.

This morning I had a wonderful time. I did an hour's work and then had to have the rest of the morning off. The crew I was working with had to go off of the field for something, but since a few of us didn't have our shirts on we couldn't leave. To get off the field, you have to wear a complete uniform. So, the crazy sergeant, instead of telling us to get our shirts, or driving us to our area, said we could have off. I didn't argue with him one bit and headed straight for my tent. When I got there, the cupboard was bare – wait a minute, how did that get in!!! Stupid of me wasn't it.

Anyhow, I wrote two letters and washed my dirty clothes. So all in all, my morning was well spent. I should have made the washing machine a long time ago, it works pretty damn good. (It doesn't leak as much as it did, - I put less water in it!!!).

Irv got a package from his Sylvia to-day, and besides all the goodies it had, there was a wallet for his birthday. The only trouble is that he doesn't want to use it because he's afraid he'll ruin it. It's a nice wallet too. I told him to use it, because when he needs another, Sylvia will get him one, at least I think she would. The moral to the story is when you get a present you should use it. What did Confucius have that I haven't? And I don't want any answers!!

It rained like hell after supper, so I lay on my comfortable bunk and smoked away. The only trouble with our tent tho is that when the water runs off the tent it drains onto the floor and makes it very muddy. I've been thinking of piling dirt around the tent to stop such things, but – I'm still thinking of it. Aren't I the lazy one tho!

Boy, wouldn't I love to be home now, storing up energy to give you your twenty-one whacks to-morrow. Guess I'll have to wait until next year.

Darling, you don't know how badly I need you. I love you so much that thoughts of anything else are pushed out of my mind because of you. My sweet, as long as I can love you, I'll never be completely unhappy, because without you, I know thru the years something would come up to knock me flat on my back. But with you it will only take me down on one knee. My darling, you are my strength!

All my love, all my life
Your, George

May 30, 1945
Wednesday
Your birthday

From:	To:
Cpl. James G. Barr 11057933	Mrs. James G. Barr
94th Dep. Rep. Sq., 56th ADG	65 Houghton St.
APO 246 Unit #1 c/o P.M.	Worcester 4, Mass.
San Francisco, Calf.	

Dearest Lottie,

Here it is your birthday again, and again I'm not with you. The next one dear, I just have to be with you, so we can celebrate to-gether. It's like my birthday, the odds are with us. My darling, a happy birthday! What I can't say, is in my heart and you should know what's in it, because my dear, it belongs to you.

If it wasn't your birthday, I wouldn't have written to you to-night. I feel dirty and grimy, no water to-night to wash with. I think a main broke or something. I have a few more letters that I should answer but I won't.

In the mail to-day, I received two more birthday cards, one from Sol and Fran, and the other from Martin. Fran also wrote me a letter telling me the life of our nephew.

I went to the movies to-night, but was quite disappointed in the picture. There were a few, too few, good parts, but on the whole I thought it stunk. The picture was "Stage Door Canteen."

I didn't have it so easy to-day as I did yesterday. I loaded and unloaded enough lumber to put Sawyers to shame! I don't mind too much tho, it keeps me out in the sun and fresh air.

Thank mother for bringing you the letter. Yes, darling, only a mother could be so sweet and considerate. Didn't I always say that mother was good, even tho at one time I thought she must dislike me. That's one of the nights I shall never forget.

Goodnight my beloved.

Your, George

May 31, 1945
Thursday

From:	To:
Cpl. James G. Barr 11057933	Mrs. James G. Barr
94th Dep. Rep. Sq., 56th ADG	65 Houghton St.
APO 246 Unit #1 c/o P.M.	Worcester 4, Mass.
San Francisco, Calf.	

My dearest Lottie,

Do you know what happened to-day? I asked and got the afternoon off!! I heard that Bob Orgain's outfit was here, so I wanted to see him. After going to a lot of bother to find the place, I was told that he had been shipped out before the outfit went across. The lucky dog. The afternoon wasn't wasted entirely, for I saw a different part of the island that I hadn't been to before. Another fellow and I went up there and he met a buddy of his, so at least some good was accomplished. I hadn't heard from Bob in a long time and I thought that I had found the reason why. But such is life, and we have to put up with all sorts of disillusionments.

To-day my dear, was pay day, and after donating a buck for the upkeep of the permanent K.P.'s, it left me with a grand sum total of twelve dollars and twenty cents. Don't worry now that I won't have enough money, because I spent a little over ten dollars last month on what I need to get along on. This month no more souvenirs!

For about a half hour before writing you, another radio man (and I say that seriously!) and I tried working out a formula, but we didn't get to first base, in fact, we struck out. I should worry, they're not using us as radio men, so what can you expect when a person is out of practice.

To-day was a terrible day, not only did it rain, but I didn't get a thing in the mail. Well to-morrow is another day. Wouldn't it be awful if I were a pessimist!

I mailed out the coconuts to-day and also enclosed your letters that I had saved up so you can get them from the folks.

Boy, I'm getting sick and tired of this place. It's getting more chicken by the day! To-morrow morning we are going to have roll call and march off to work. I admit a few have been reporting to work late, but why the hell should they punish everyone. This will almost be like basic training with roll calls and formations!

My right arm is sore and I don't know why, unless it's from thumbing, but how dumb of me, if it were, it would be my thumb that would be sore. I haven't written enough for that. I'll awake to-morrow bright and early, at least early, and it will be as good as new.

Now I'll leave you my darling, good night.

Your, George

June 1, 1945
Friday

From:	To:
Cpl. James G. Barr 11057933	Mrs. James G. Barr
94th Dep. Rep. Sq., 56th ADG	65 Houghton St.
APO 246 Unit #1 c/o P.M.	Worcester 4, Mass.
San Francisco, Calf.	

Hello Darling,

To-night my morale has moved down another notch. I haven't received any sort of mail in two entire days. I really shouldn't complain, because there must be a good reason for it, but still in all, I want my mail. Even better, I want you!

There is beauty in war, and when you see it, it is hard to realize that war is hell. A little while ago a plane of ours flew over and some of the searchlights put their lights on it. The plane seemed like a slow moving, silver insect, caught in webs of broad silver. It was a very nice picture and one I'd like, if I were able, to photograph.

Irv got a salami in a package and it came in real good condition, they waxed it completely, so we are over at the chapel to get some coffee and some bread so we can have a real feast. It will be like a picnic because we're on a nice green lawn sitting on beach chairs. Oh, the life of a soldier.

Tried to get out of my shop again, but still no luck. I hope something breaks soon, because the longer I'm in there, the less work they get out of me.

I didn't feel like going to services, so of course, I didn't. Instead, I went to see a movie named, "Jitterbugs," which reminded me of the "Latin Quarter" on our honeymoon. We had fun didn't we? You bet we did. I even remember when you turned down my bed!! Oh, you kid!!! But I love you darling, just the same and always will.

If I don't get a letter from you to-morrow my sweet, I'll, I'll – well, I'd better!

Good night, sweet dreams.

All my love,
Your, George

June 2, 1945
Saturday

From:	To:
Cpl. James G. Barr 11057933	Mrs. James G. Barr
94th Dep. Rep. Sq., 56th ADG	65 Houghton St.
APO 246 Unit #1 c/o P.M.	Worcester 4, Mass.
San Francisco, Calf.	

My darling wife,

I just came back from one of the screwiest pictures I've seen in a long time. It was called "Brewster's Millions." This Brewster fellow had to spend a million dollars within sixty days to get seven million permanently. It wasn't as easy as I thought, because he wasn't allowed to have any assets. The only way he was able to manage it was thru a lucky break. Just give me a million and I wouldn't want to throw it away.

I finally received a letter from you in which you received my birthday card. I just hope by now that you have received something else I planned.

I'm sorry to hear that you have a cold, but for not wanting to get near you, well darling, you're all wrong. I hope that you're over it by now.

Monday night we move into barracks, but tho barracks are better than tents, it's going to be very crowded. That's one advantage to a tent, and that was we had enough room. They're short of barracks and we have to get in them before the rain really comes down. It will be nice to be able to have lights tho, and I won't have to run miles or yards to write letters.

We'll also have our own mess hall and I hope that the mess lines I've stood in disappear.

I hate to tell you what I did to-day, but it was painting latrines! I hope that's not what the government spent all that money on me for!

It's raining now and it sounds real nice beating against the roof. Now if I only had you in my arms - that would be a piece of heaven. Darling, your husband, that's me, loves you dearly.

I was gigged again to-day at inspection, they claimed I didn't have my mess kit showing, so to eliminate any argument, I'll have to put it on my bunk to-morrow morning. First my shoes, then my mess kit. What will it be next week?

Did I tell you that I have sent the list of parts to the folks - yup! I remember I did - how foolish of me.

Bye for now.

Your ever loving husband,
George

P.S. Thanks for giving me hell for not completing the drawing of the radio. Only with your help will I ever amount to anything. J.G.B.

June 3, 1945
Sunday

From:	To:
Cpl. James G. Barr 11057933	Mrs. James G. Barr
94th Dep. Rep. Sq., 56th ADG	65 Houghton St.
APO 246 Unit #1 c/o P.M.	Worcester 4, Mass.
San Francisco, Calf.	

My dearest Lottie,

I'm glad that I received the letter yesterday that said you had a slight nose cold and to-day the one in which you are well again. You know yourself, darling, that I don't want you to be sick so from now on don't be, I hope.

Now that you told me you're not going to tell me about why you're not going to Washington, I'm even more curious to know what I might misinterpret. Of course, I think it's your job, and I know you know how I feel about it, so that's why you may not want to tell me. But there I go jumping to conclusions and that's bad. So, come across and don't try to compromise with that. Kiss me quick! Altho darling, I'd give anything if I could. You're the one I love and I love making love to you.

I don't know why you think I'm so clever, because my brain child was about the fourth to be made and the others are run by an engine. The Blondie cartoon was real cute and we all got a kick out of it.

This morning at work I made a pair of shower clogs out of wood. Everything came out fine, but I have two left feet!!! I still can't figger out how that ever happened. I'm a great guy, first I build a washing machine that leaks, then a pair of left foot shower shoes, I wonder what I'm going to do next.

We were allowed to get our cameras, so that we could clean them. I got mine, and cleaned it up real good. It felt good to hold it in my hands and monkey around with it.

For to-morrow morning, I managed to be able to get a small truck. If I hadn't, I don't know what I would do when the time came to move. I must have a million things to take along with me. Then when I get in the barracks, I don't know where I'll put it because there isn't too much room as it is.

This afternoon I washed and shaved real good, then put on clean sun tans. We then went to visit a friend of Irv's at a different part of the island.

Irv's friend wanted to know how come we were so spruced up, so we told him.

We played ping-pong there, he has a nice day room and it was nice to play there. At night, they're able to get ice cream sodas. Maybe we'll be able to get something like that for our day room when it's built up. I hope so anyway.

After eating supper there, and it was better than what we get here, we were driven back by Irv's chum. I'm glad that I don't drive with him everyday. What he needs is a month of good instruction, then maybe I'll consider it. We almost hit two natives on the road, and I still don't understand how we missed a sign in the road. We made it tho, and now I'm a tired boy.

Also in to-day's mail, Toby sent me a picture of herself. She sure is growing up. If she'd only have her hair taken off she'd look so much nicer. Maybe you could take her with you sometime that you have your hair set.

I hope you had a very nice time at your little gathering in honor of your birthday. How I was wishing, hoping, and miracle wishing that I could be with you.

By the way, I may have more business for Jackie if I can manage it. I'm going to try anyway.

Goodnight Cookie.

Your, George

June 4, 1945
Monday

From:	To:
Cpl. James G. Barr 11057933	Mrs. James G. Barr
94th Dep. Rep. Sq., 56th ADG	65 Houghton St.
APO 246 Unit #1 c/o P.M.	Worcester 4, Mass.
San Francisco, Calf.	

Hello Darling,

I'm almost all settled in my new abode. All we need now is running water and lights, which shouldn't take more than a week, then we'll be living quite comfortably, but a bit more crowded than we were.

I don't know what I would have done if I were unable to get some sort of transportation to take all my junk up to the new area. One box I had must have weighed close to a hundred pounds, and all it had in it was a few small articles. Irv is in another barracks, but he's trying to get into mine.

He's been writing to his Sylvia all about me and she wrote back that I must be a pretty good kid. Oh, that poor misinformed creature!

Dave wrote me a letter and he said that you were a bit worried because I'm overseas. Please darling, believe me when I say that this place is quite as safe as back in the states. Heck, I haven't even had a cold or anything that put me in bed for four days! So there!!!

I feel sorry for Dave, here he's been over there for over a year, and now he may have to come over here. At least he may get a chance to go home on furlough, at least I'm hoping he does.

I wonder how he and Rhoda are getting along? I wonder how cooled off Rhoda has gotten, or whether her love for Dave still burns. I hate to see him get hurt, he's had too much tough luck in his short life.

That's all, my darling sweetheart, good night.

Your, George

June 5, 1945
Tuesday

From:	To:
Cpl. James G. Barr 11057933	Mrs. James G. Barr
94th Dep. Rep. Sq., 56th ADG	65 Houghton St.
APO 246 Unit #1 c/o P.M.	Worcester 4, Mass.
San Francisco, Calf.	

Dearest Lottie,

Darling, you are the dearest person in the world to me, and I love you more than anything that a lowly soul, like me, could put into writing or words. Even tho the miles between us are many, my loving thoughts of you are that many times multiplied. If I could just hold you in my arms, I know I wouldn't have to say a thing, because you'd know. Darling, I miss you so.

Of course, I'm worried now that I haven't heard from you in two days. I'd blame it on the mail situation again, but your attack of grippe is playing upon my mind. You must know how much I want you to keep well and any little thing that bothers you makes me feel terrible. I hope it is the mail situation, very badly. Please try and not let me down.

This evening I saw "My Favorite Wife." It was very good, because it reminded me of my favorite wife - you! Cookie, your husband (that's me!), loves you madly.

We had a job to do to-day, but first we had to wait for a truck to pick us up. We waited and waited until someone called and said the truck broke down and couldn't make it. That, of course, made us very angry! I'm telling you darling, that if I keep working this way, I'll waste away to nothing!!!

Toby wrote me a letter where she is trying to get her driving license. It doesn't seem possible that she's old enough to drive. I'll have to get over the idea that she's not a child and think of her more grown up. Heck, when I was seventeen, I met the girl I was to marry! Gee, but you must have made an impression on me!!

I've been trying to get some radio stuff for our day room and some test equipment, so that we could fix any of the boy's sets when they go bad. So far, all I've run into is opposition, but there are a few more angles and people I have to see before I call it quits. I'd like very much to get hold of that stuff, because then I could be doing something instead of going to the movies every night. We'll see how things work out.

Goodnight my darling.

Your, George

June 6, 1945
Wednesday

From:	To:
Cpl. James G. Barr 11057933	Mrs. James G. Barr
94th Dep. Rep. Sq., 56th ADG	65 Houghton St.
APO 246 Unit #1 c/o P.M.	Worcester 4, Mass.
San Francisco, Calf.	

My dearest wife,

I was a happy man to-day, because my dearest, I received two wonderful sweet letters from you. The best one, of course, was the one that was written on your birthday. Darling, I'm so glad that you liked the flowers. You don't know what I was going thru until I heard you received them.

It wasn't an overnight plan and I had written to Fierer's a long time ago and enclosed the note with full instructions. The only trouble was that he didn't let me know that he got my letter (I can see now a little of it was my fault). I waited and waited to hear from him, but I didn't, so I worried and worried. I finally wrote to the folks to check up on it for me and when I got a letter from Toby telling me she had gone to see Fierer and that he had received my letter and would take care of everything. Then I had only to wait to hear from you. My sweet, it was worth every little worry I had about it. I'm so relieved and happy, that tho I'm far away, I could bring you a bright hour. Darling, my life is devoted to making you happy.

Your description of taking the roses one by one and kissing them and watering them with a tear, touched me, touched me, did I say. Darling, it took hold of me. There is none sweeter than my wonderful wife!

Your cocktail party sounded glorious. I'm glad it was a success. I bet the 'Three Feathers' and the rum hit the spot, or was it the head. I knew that my wife was an excellent hostess and entertainer, but now all those that were there know it too. So now they'll be saying – "that George Barr is a lucky guy to have such a wife." And of course, I'll agree with them.

Some people have difficulties when they throw a party, but not us, I can see that. The birthday cake that mother got you must have been super. I thank her from the bottom of my heart for looking after Mrs. J.G. Barr for me while I'm away. Also, tell Edith and Charlotte that the stationery is lovely and just fits you. It's flowery, delicate and above all nice. Tell them thanks, too, for helping mother look after you.

Sweetheart, love is such a wonderful thing and I'm glad it is you to whom I can give my love, altho it isn't worth much.

Goodnight darling.

Your very own,
George

June 8, 1945
Friday

From:	To:
Cpl. James G. Barr 11057933	Mrs. James G. Barr
94th Dep. Rep. Sq., 56th ADG	65 Houghton St.
APO 246 Unit #1 c/o P.M.	Worcester 4, Mass.
San Francisco, Calf.	

My dearest wife,

Well dear, this is the first night that I'm writing in my new barracks. Altho we had lights since yesterday, I didn't have a chance to write. Last night Irving was able to get a Jeep, so we went for a ride and then looked up Uddie Goff. We had a little difficulty finding him, but we did find him.

He was out on the line checking up on the ships that he takes care of. They had come back from a raid. It was quite interesting getting first hand information on a bombing raid. We talked and talked, then after promising to see each other again, we came back to our camp.

I just finished G.I.ing my part of the barracks and I can tell you it was a job. This place is the dustiest place I've ever been in.

Received a letter from you written on the night of your birthday, but it came a day after the one you wrote earlier, and yet it was postmarked the same time!

Had a little trouble with my boss again, he even tried to threaten me and two others with a court martial. That's when I got mad! He was told by our second in command that the three of us had 'goofed off', but when I told him the facts, he still didn't believe it. When we said we were going to see our C.O. and straighten things out, he quieted down and put us working with the C.B.'s. Now we work until four in the afternoon, and the C.B.'s are real nice men to work with.

The C.B.'s worked at their jobs in civilian life and know what to expect of their men and how to treat them. We get along fine with them and I think now, as long as we're with them, everything will go well.

A few of us radio men wanted to start building a little place where we could take care of the fellow's sets, but we won't be able to start building for sometime, because our area isn't ready. When it is, we'll be allowed to start on it. Now we're trying to get equipment, so that when we do have a place, we'll have something to work with. So far tho, we've only run into difficulties.

I'm sorry that it isn't warm in Worc., but maybe I can send you a little of our hot weather here to compensate it.

I'm awfully glad that the folks remembered you on your birthday. Heck, now you'll have enough money to pay for your poll taxes. You know now darling, that you can vote. Won't we have some lovely arguments on who we should, or should not put into office!

Don't you worry about me taking my time the next time I kiss you darling. I just hope I can control myself so I won't crush you!! Darling, I love you very much!

Goodnight dear.

Your, George

June 9, 1945
Saturday

From:	To:
Cpl. James G. Barr 11057933	Mrs. James G. Barr
94th Dep. Rep. Sq., 56th ADG	65 Houghton St.
APO 246 Unit #1 c/o P.M.	Worcester 4, Mass.
San Francisco, Calf.	

My very dearest Lottie,

Again, this evening I was fortunate in being able to get a little night ride. One of the boys got a Jeep, so off we went. We had a hell of a good time, just ribbing one another and commenting on how the driver drove. You never saw such a back-seat driver as I am, when I feel like it! We had fun, that was the main thing.

We came back early because there was a U.S.O. show here to-night and we planned on going. Out of the entire cast, just one could have been left out. The girl singer couldn't sing, but she had something else that the wolves liked, that's why she got so many encores, Awoooa! (I let that slip!)

You know I could have gone to sleep instead of writing you, but no! Here I am writing you, all because I love you and want to write, so you couldn't stop me even if you wanted!!!

The lights are out and everyone is either sleeping, or trying to sleep, but I'm not. That was easy to figger out, now wasn't it! If this letter is hard to read, blame it on the poor lighting I have – it's being done by flashlight. I'm writing with my right hand and my left is holding the light, paper and my writing folder (And here I am dying for a cigarette – oh well, we all have to make some sort of contribution to the war effort and I guess that this is it!)

I don't have the good deal that I had yesterday, because this morning I again was transferred to do something else. It seems that the colonel wants a lawn around his office and we had to get the loam for it. Dig, Dig, Dig!!! Well all right! Well anyhoo, that's what I have been doing. Oh yes, they say they are short of man power and yet they take me off of some sort of work to do this. I hope that in some way this will help win the war sooner. This "Chicken" stuff is going too damn far!

Listen baby, when you get that two piecer, I want a glamour shot. How would you look in a two-piece bathing suit – how would Venus De Milo look with arms!!!

Good night my darling.

Always your,
George

P.S. Don't forget that pin up picture! J.G.B.

P.P.S. I love you some more. Your husband.

June 10, 1945
Sunday

From:	To:
Cpl. James G. Barr 11057933	Mrs. James G. Barr
94th Dep. Rep. Sq., 56th ADG	65 Houghton St.
APO 246 Unit #1 c/o P.M.	Worcester 4, Mass.
San Francisco, Calf.	

My dearest Lottie,

I spent a very lazy day doing almost absolutely nothing. The almost was to wash a little clothes, the nothing was sleeping. I didn't feel like bumming around the island and nothing else drew my fancy, and besides, I was tired.

Yes, darling, I worked on the Colonel's lawn again to-day, but to-morrow I don't think I'll be on the illustrious crew, at least I hope not. Personally, I think the Colonel can do very well without the lawn, but I'm not one to say, now am I?

On the island here we have a newspaper, and one of the G.I.'s is a critic on all the movies that are shown, and he gives a write up of each one. I happened to read his opinion of "To-night and Everynight," which wasn't any too complimentary, but I still went to see it to-night. After seeing it, I thought it was pretty good, even weighing the bad parts against the good. Maybe he likes brunettes (I prefer them myself), because Rita Hayworth and Janet Blair were the leads. Enough of this pitter pat.

In the mail, I received no mail from you, but I did get one from Sam and also one from Mackie Z. When I write Sam, I'm going to write it to Wash., because you said he had been discharged. Mackie says he's due to go across soon and hopes to come here. He could be sent to worse places. At least whenever I felt blue, I could look him up and let him chase the blues from me. I hope he does come here if he does go P.O.E.

For the last few minutes I've been trying to think of something else to write about, but I'm sorry dear, that I'm unable to – soooo!

Good night sweetheart 'till we meet to-morrow – Good night.

Your, George

June 11, 1945
Monday

From:	To:
Cpl. James G. Barr 11057933	Mrs. James G. Barr
94th Dep. Rep. Sq., 56th ADG	65 Houghton St.
APO 246 Unit #1 c/o P.M.	Worcester 4, Mass.
San Francisco, Calf.	

Hello darling,

Do you know what I want in my arms more than anything right now? Yes, sweet you, no one else but you. The rest of the men can have their pinups, but you are for me! I love you, my darling!

This afternoon I went to the hospital. No, I wasn't sick, but I needed a little screw in my G.I. glasses. Instead of just being able to leave the glasses at our dispensary, they make you take them with you to the hospital. Not that I particularly cared, I was able to have the afternoon off, but it's the principal of the thing. Here they yell you have to work, and yet they'll have you take the afternoon off for something that could have been easily taken care of without you being there. If the army ever makes sense to me, it will be when they hand me that discharge paper!!

I wrote Sam and Narky letters, as I don't have to write to anyone else to-night except my beloved. Isn't that nice – well at least I think so!

Cookie, you wrote that Charlotte and you discussed what you'd do if I had walked into the Eden at that time. Well – don't keep me in suspense, would you have ordered a drink for me, or what!! Boy, how I wish I could have been there, I'd like to see you with a few drinks in you. I've seen you act silly, but with a few drinks and you in a good mood – anything could happen, couldn't it?

Anne must have told you all the details of her proposed trip home. I wonder if she's going to have as many evening gowns with her this time as she did when she came to America. If I remember rightly, she said twenty-nine!! A different one for every night on the boat. And did you know that she was just about your age when she started?!

About us taking the trip some day. I hope that we can, because I'd like to travel on my own when I can get the chance. I don't like G.I. travel!

You don't know how happy you made me when you said that you're going away for a few weeks. When I come back, we'll go back to the Lex, and go over our honeymoon step by step. Altho we'll have to ask Mackie to go back to where ever he was, so that I can call him!

I hope the pictures you and Charlotte took will be on the way soon, I'm waiting very patiently for them. Also, I'm waiting for that pin-up picture that you're going to take in your new bathing suit. Whistle, whistle, whistle!!!

So, little Frankie was having ideas! This modern generation, my, my! I can't blame him tho, you're too beautiful to pass up, but if I had been there, I would have knocked him flat. Besides, I'm jealous of him, you never even attempted to teach me how to dance, see what you missed? I'm only saying that, 'cause it's true!

I wonder what happened to me after everyone greeted me when I came home, in Charlotte's dream! When I go to sleep to-night, I'll try to find out.

Almost went for another ride to-night, but someone else got it before Irv did, so I had to content myself with a G.I. movie. It was an invasion film and quite exciting, but horribly true!!

I just finished up the last of my stationery, but I do have a few more of my own envelopes. When I bought it, the fellows ribbed me and said I'd never be able to finish it up and I'd probably would have to throw most of it away, because I'd be a civilian before it was gone. I fooled them tho, I'm not a civilian, and it's just a little over a year since I received it!

I'll have to write a hell of a lot more on this stationery than I did on the other, or else my letters won't look like anything but notes. Maybe I'll cut this stuff in half, huh?!! O.K., I was just kidding!

This evening I showed my picture album to a few of the fellows and they all think you're quite good looking, and asked how the hell did I manage to get you. I told them it was a trade secret and that a little money would loosen my tongue. Little do they know, that I don't know how I did get you. How about letting me know, will ya huh? Please.

My goodness did I write all this by myself? I have been a good boy, I wonder if I'll get the good conduct medal for it?

All my love, all my life
Your, George

June 12, 1945
Tuesday

From:	To:
Cpl. James G. Barr 11057933	Mrs. James G. Barr
94th Dep. Rep. Sq., 56th ADG	65 Houghton St.
APO 246 Unit #1 c/o P.M.	Worcester 4, Mass.
San Francisco, Calf.	

Dearest Lottie,

Here I am in my barracks writing to you. Tonight, I'm a little earlier than usual because I didn't go to the movies. I would have gone, but I had seen them all and none were worth seeing over. So, I'm taking it easy, ahem! for a change!

Of course, you know I didn't receive a letter from you to-day, which doesn't help me out in the least. I can't see how the postman can be so inconsiderate of me. Here I'm fighting desperately to sustain civilization, but does anyone besides my loving wife and family care? No!

I had very little to do to-day, so I can consider myself quite fortunate in not having to help shovel dirt for the Colonel's lawn. They got some other poor unfortunates to do the job to-day.

I have to-morrow off, but I don't know what to do with it. Another fellow and I were thinking of trying to get a flight to one of the other islands, but we have to go thru a little trouble, so we may abandon the idea. If it is real hot, we could go to the beach. I hear that they fixed it up nice since I was last down there. The beach has been cleaned of all sharp coral and a place has been dredged so that the water is over your head. I wonder if they will build a wharf so that we can dive. I'm not a diver, but I'd like to practice.

While unloading lumber from a truck this afternoon, the sergeant called me and another fellow off to go on another detail. We drove to another section of the field, but whatever we went for wasn't there, so we rode around some more until the sergeant gave up and we came back and went home. I still don't know what he was looking for, but it was nice to get off of unloading lumber.

Please forgive this dull, drab, and uninteresting missive, but such is the way of life when nothing of interest happens.

Good night, sweet dreams my love.

Your, George

June 13, 1945
Wednesday

From:	To:
Cpl. James G. Barr 11057933	Mrs. James G. Barr
94th Dep. Rep. Sq., 56th ADG	65 Houghton St.
APO 246 Unit #1 c/o P.M.	Worcester 4, Mass.
San Francisco, Calf.	

My very dearest wife,

I certainly hit the Jackpot!! I received three packages and three letters to-day!!! I had so much stuff I didn't know where to start to put things so I'd know where they were! Thanks darling, for all the things you got me. I never knew five pounds had so much stuff. I had a swell birthday just because my wife is such a wonderful and thoughtful wife, I love you darling, more than anything in life.

My folks sent me some hankies too, so now I doubt very much if I'll have to worry about my nose for a long time. You can't imagine how I felt when I received the stocking and handkerchiefs, it was the most important thing in anything I received. It meant to me that my darling wife was looking after me, and making sure that any little want would be satisfied. Dearest, that is an awfully comfortable feeling.

Emil is in Calif. now and I had been waiting and waiting to hear from you telling me that he had called. I hope that my faith in him isn't shattered, because I think I know Emil pretty good and if he can come thru, he will.

Another thing to make me happy, my darling is going to the beach to rest and have a good time. I wish I could have seen you and mother when Aunt Annie called and invited you. I hope she doesn't get you into one of those hot poker games!

This shirt business is only going one way, remember darling, how modest you are - or are you!! What would people say (besides whistling) if you were to go to work without a shirt? After all we have to look out for Michael, we have to give him parents that have a good reputation!

Listen darling, why should I be jealous of Irv just because he got a wallet? If I wanted one, I would have written to you. I don't want or even need a wallet, all I want or need is you, my sweet and adorable Cookie. And if you want to beat Syl, you did, because everyone admires my new flashlight and the way Irv is ribbing me about it, I know he'd like to own one. In fact, I don't think there is anything he doesn't want of mine, he's always borrowing one thing or another. When he saw that I had asked you for air mail stickers, he immediately wrote for some. Don't worry about a thing, you're tops!

Even if you had a coconut, what would you do with it? You know those shells are pretty hard to crack, altho you'd probably run down to the corner and have the trolley run over it!!

Now when I asked you about accentuating the positive, I just wanted to see if I was right. Now that I know I'm right, well a fellow can dream, can't he?

I thought I wrote you that I intend building a radio. What I want mostly is the practice and the experience. I don't know what I'll do with it when it's finished, but I know I can get at least twice what it cost to buy.

Now don't you worry your pretty little head about how much money I have. What kind of guy did you marry, if I can't take care of money, well you got stuck! You got stuck anyway, but that's beside the question. It isn't me darling, who I'm afraid of running short, look at all the things I get for free in the army, it is you who I want to have enough money for all the things you need. Hell, if seventeen dollars doesn't last me a month over here, I may as well give my money away! In fact, m'love, I hope to live on less!

I hope Morty does get a chance to get home, at least I'll have a little satisfaction in knowing that someone is being allowed to get home.

I guess you know that without the help of my very brand new flashlight, I'd have difficulty in writing you this letter. It is past ten o'clock and the lights went out a few minutes ago.

So soon we'll be in the upper brackets, that is nice to hear. I'll say it again, I have the most beautiful, the most clever, the sweetest, charming wife a guy could ever hope to have!

It is nice of Rita and Dot to confide in you, but they don't know how very lucky they are to have someone like you to confide in! They know when they have a good thing, that's why they always invite you to go with them. That's the same reason that Molly and Sam like you, 'cause you're so sweet and charming, "there I said it again!"

I'm even more jealous of Frankie now. It took me a long time to learn how to dance and he gets it in such a short length of time, but I didn't have such a talented teacher, now did I?

I guess now I can tell you what I did the entire day. First thing I did this morning was to get up. Wasn't that original? Then I had breakfast, came back and went to sleep. About an hour later, the carpenters came in and started to bang and saw, so I just lay in bed and read a little, then I said to myself that I should write a few letters to some people who may want to hear from me, so I wrote a letter to Aunt Dora in New York and one to Aunt Sarah in New York. I loafed until dinner, ate, came back and got all of my mail.

In the afternoon, I watched this other fellow wash his clothes in my machine and just took things easy. Even tho we planned on flying or going swimming, we weren't too enthused about either, and just took things easy.

After supper, we went to the movies, saw "Home in Indiana," which I had seen a long time ago in Kansas, and here I am!

Our area is really going to shape up nice. Shelves were put in to-day, and a wire to put on clothes hangers, and in front of the barracks it is being leveled off. I think they're going to make coral paths and just make it look neat and nice. In back they're building an orderly room, and as soon as that is done, they'll start on our own day room, then I can write letters after ten o'clock without having to use flashlights.

That was my day and now, my love, good night. I had a wonderful day. All my love, all my life.

Your, George

June 14, 1945
Thursday

From:	To:
Cpl. James G. Barr 11057933	Mrs. James G. Barr
94th Dep. Rep. Sq., 56th ADG	65 Houghton St.
APO 246 Unit #1 c/o P.M.	Worcester 4, Mass.
San Francisco, Calf.	

My dearest Lottie,

For what I didn't do yesterday, I did to-day! I must have shoveled ten million tons of dirt and I don't think I ever got so dirty in my life! No matter where I stood to throw the dirt on the truck, the wind would change its direction and blow the flying dust all over me. Soap and water got the dirt off, but a rest such as I had yesterday is what I need now to recuperate. What a way to win a war!!

This noon time at mail call they had just one letter and who do you think got it? I did! And was just as surprised as everyone else. Irv was jealous as hell and tried to belittle it because it wasn't from you. The poor fellow, he doesn't know that now I'll get two from you tomorrow.

To-night I saw "Leave It to Blondie." I thought it was going to be much better than it was. After awhile Dagwood's antics started to bore me. I think I was too tired to appreciate it, although I raised hell with the guys I went to the show with. There was a short that was a 'community sing' and we didn't try to harmonize, so you can just imagine how we sounded. I thought that someone was going to shoot us to keep us quiet!! And after, the boys called me "Frankie"!!!!!!!

Darling, it's rumored that we may take pictures soon, so if you get any extra film, you can send it. I do hope that they will allow us to take pictures.

Looking back at this afternoon, as I was walking to the showers, with just a towel around me, one of the boys called to me, only he had a question in his voice. I was so dirty, that he wasn't sure it was me, and at a distance he thought I had tanned awfully suddenly!! P.S. Everyone recognizes me now.

Goodnight darling, and may to-morrow bring you a longer letter from me.

Your, George

June 15, 1945
Friday

From:	To:
Cpl. James G. Barr 11057933	Mrs. James G. Barr
94th Dep. Rep. Sq., 56th ADG	65 Houghton St.
APO 246 Unit #1 c/o P.M.	Worcester 4, Mass.
San Francisco, Calf.	

My darling wife,

Again, I hit the jackpot! Two packages to-day!!! One from you and one from the folks. What swell people I have and I love them all, but most of my love is for my wonderful wife.

Darling, everything you sent was marvelous. Altho the picture album wasn't exactly what I asked for, it's better! I wish you hadn't spent so much money on it tho, it is beautiful, everyone is admiring it, but what really makes it is your picture on the first page. I had a few extra wash clothes, but I got rid of the ones I had to someone who needed them, and I'll now use the ones you sent me, they're much better than the ones I have. Olives, olives, olives! Thanks, my sweet ("Falling in Love with Love" is playing – Ah!). The atlas is just the thing, if you were able to send a better one, it would have been just too good, I didn't realize it before; but now I do.

There is one thing you needn't send me anymore tho, and that is sardines, or anything like that because I don't particularly care for them and getting bread is a bother, and greens to go with it, is almost out of the question. Juices I'd love. Don't want any cheese either. What a difficult person I am to please. I really don't need much of anything, so don't bother your pretty little head about what am I going to send George!

My folks sent me anchovies, soap powder, pineapple juice, and my tennis shorts. You should have heard the whistles when I put them on. What a crazy bunch of fellows I live with, but I guess I'm just as crazy!

I hardly did a thing at work to-day, but when I came back to the barracks, I did a good job of housekeeping. We're not going to have an official Saturday inspection, but what I think is that if this one is good they'll not give us one next Saturday, and if it is poor, we'll probably have on Sunday. No matter what happens, I'll be ready.

To-morrow night we are going to have a lottery for cigarette lighters and fountain pens. There is going to be about sixty items, so my luck will have to be good to get one of them.

When we were still on the boat, some one had "Forever Amber", and there was quite a lot of discussion on it, so Irv sent Sylvia a request and he got it to-day. After he finishes reading it, I'll delve into the dirt myself (Who the hell said I had a high moral standard?!!).

That's all the dirt for to-night, my sweet.

Your loving husband,
George

P.S. I'm going to like your stationery – it's small. Ain't I terrible. J.G.B.

June 16, 1945
Saturday
"Somewhere in Guam"
(As if you didn't know!)

From:	To:
Cpl. James G. Barr 11057933	Mrs. James G. Barr
94th Dep. Rep. Sq., 56th ADG	65 Houghton St.
APO 246 Unit #1 c/o P.M.	Worcester 4, Mass.
San Francisco, Calf.	

Dearest Lottie,

So now you know where I am! What a hell of a distance from home. There isn't anymore I can tell you about it, but there have been articles written about it that let out more military and other information than I'd be allowed to tell. So, if you want to know what kind of a place this is, you'll have to read it in the newspaper.

What do you know, I didn't even get close to winning a chance to buy anything. I'll have a better chance next time, because those that won this time will not be able to get in it until everyone has a chance to at least win one. That way I'm bound to win even if my name comes up last!

We managed to get a steam shovel to load trucks we've been using for our lawn project. After a comparatively easy day, we figgered that we did five days' work in one!! If we had dump trucks, we could have done the entire thing in three days, this way it will be about three weeks from start to finish! I still say it's a hell of a way to win a war!

To-morrow afternoon I'm going down to the beach, for it's a 'great day Mariana'. What is so exciting that I should go to the beach? To-morrow is Massachusetts Day at the beach! Who knows who I'll run across, maybe the governor, I doubt it tho, because he'd be silly as hell to be out here, when home is so much better.

No mail from you again, which makes two entire days that I've received naught from you. I did get the glasses tho, and the crystal. The glasses fit fine, but the crystal doesn't. I'll try to get rid of it here, but if I can't, I'll return it. Just for the fun of it, what did the glasses cost? Sixteen to eighteen dollars? How good am I?

I went to see a stinker picture to-night. "Circumstantial Evidence." If I weren't so comfortably seated, I would have walked away and not given it a second thought. Even if I had left, what would I have done? Gone to sleep early? Could be!

Have you made any further plans on your vacation?

Darling, I love you.
Your, George

P.S. Kiss me quick!

~1945~

Photo of "Steam Shovel" George mentions in his letter dated June 16, 1945.

June 17, 1945
Sunday
"Guam"

From:	To:
Cpl. James G. Barr 11057933	Mrs. James G. Barr
94th Dep. Rep. Sq., 56th ADG	65 Houghton St.
APO 246 Unit #1 c/o P.M.	Worcester 4, Mass.
San Francisco, Calf.	

My darling wife,
      When I arrived at the beach this afternoon, I thought I had come to Revere Beach! Massachusetts may be a little state, but it sure has a hell of a lot of people. The larger cities have designated areas so the fellows could congregate and find their own. Altho I spent a lot of time around the Worcester area, I didn't see one person who I knew or even remember seeing! Most of them were quite older than me and only gave me a glance, must have thought I was an intruder!

I did go swimming tho, the beach had been cleared and you could go into the water without your shoes on!! The water was deep enough to swim in too! I could swim about fifteen yards and then I had to stop and rest, I'll have to practice more often, because maybe I'll want to swim home one of these days!

Again, this morning I helped win this war. We had to move the Colonel from his hut to a new building. Our outfit can hardly get ice, but he has his own private refrigerator!! When we emptied it out, we found at least two dozen cans of juice in the bottom shelf. They had been in there so long, they had rusted to the enamel! I haven't felt like a dog as I did to-day when I saw the way guys like him live. A poor G.I. doesn't amount to a hill of beans, and yet they want compulsory military training for kids just out of high school. It would be good training for them, only if the army had a better system, something more like a glorified R.O.T.C., but not in the army! I don't want our children to take chicken like we have to! I'm not bitter now, I was, but I like to let you know things like that, I think you want to know what's happening. I just hope our children don't want to know "Daddy, what did you do in the big war?"

Another day has gone by and still no mail, the mail has been coming in quite slow, so just as soon as it speeds up, so will I.

Until to-morrow my sweet, good night.

Your, George

P.S. Darling, I almost forgot to tell you of my noon meal. Before I went to chow, I found that they had turkey, so I took out my can of cranberry sauce and the jar of olives you sent me, got two of my buddies and went to eat. Boy, with added trimmings like that, the meal took on flavor. We all had a wonderful Sunday afternoon dinner because of the thoughtfulness of my gorgeous, wonderful, and dear wife. Thanks again darling – I love you with all my heart. J.G.B.

June 18, 1945
Monday
"Guam"

From:	To:
Cpl. James G. Barr 11057933	Mrs. James G. Barr
94th Dep. Rep. Sq., 56th ADG	65 Houghton St.
APO 246 Unit #1 c/o P.M.	Worcester 4, Mass.
San Francisco, Calf.	

My dearest Lottie,

After what seemed like a three week wait, I got a letter from you, how happy that made me! I'd rather receive a letter from you than anything else, why you may wonder? It's because I love you so much, that's why! Darling, if this damn war doesn't hurry up and end, I'll go crazy, I want to be with you so much that I won't be me, until I am with you. I miss you terribly.

It was too bad that after rushing thru your work you didn't have much time to yourself. When I'm home again, you'll be able to have as much time as you want, that is, before we start getting our brood of twenty-four? Kind ain't I?

The last time I saw Uddy, he said something about Helene Rosoff coming overseas in a U.S.O. unit. If she does happen to play here, I'll make sure and look her up. Maybe she'll introduce me to one of those hot singers! Oh boy! Oh, what a lot of bull!

Is Barb still with a U.S.O. unit, or is she with a road band? I never did find out what happened after her troupe wasn't accepted for overseas.

We finally got a place to fix up a radio shop. This afternoon during our lunch hour we cleaned up the place and knocked off all the unnecessary boards. To-night we made a work bench and strung some wires, so that we'll be able to have lights. When we finish fixing it up, it should be a pretty nice place.

If we had a certain tube to-night, we could have had our first business, but the tube that the fellow wanted is an impossibility to get, even in the states. When we get some testing equipment and some more parts, we have a few, we may be able to improvise something.

Darling, I wish you were here when I banged my finger. I didn't have anyone to console me, or even bandage it up! All I could get out of my buddies was, "You stupid ass!" See what kind of guys I work with!! By the way, I think I'll live!

Before I sat down to write you, I got hungry, so I took a package of stuffed dates out that the folks had sent me. Before I had a chance to eat three myself, they were all gone! Of course, I got up and stopped at each bed and passed them out. They were really good too, aren't you jealous, I bet you don't have any stuffed dates at the house now!

With a wish that I could have a date with you now, goodnight my darling.

Your ever loving husband,
George

June 20, 1945
Wednesday

From:	To:
Cpl. James G. Barr 11057933	Mrs. James G. Barr
94th Dep. Rep. Sq., 56th ADG	65 Houghton St.
APO 246 Unit #1 c/o P.M.	Worcester 4, Mass.
San Francisco, Calf.	

My darling Cookie,

What a wonderful day I had, four letters and a card from you! Darling, that's what I live for out here, is mail from you. Now all the mail is caught up, but I'm so far behind in writing that I don't know when I'll find time to answer them. This week has kept me busy day and night. Our radio shop is shaping out, but it is taking a bit more work than we figgered on. Last night we worked until it was too late to write, but because I missed writing you last night, I wasn't going to repeat it. I took off a bit early, showered, and here I am, madly in love with you.

Since we started fixing up the little place we have, other men wanted to come in. Naturally we couldn't refuse, but it will make it more crowded than we had planned. There's going to be a watch repair man, a painter (paints coconuts for souvenirs), and a fellow who makes shell jewelry, and someone who I don't know what he does, probably a shoe shine boy or a fuller brush man.

Do you remember Lenny DiPietro, the little Italian fellow I used to pal around with in Philly & New Orleans? I just received an invitation to his graduation. He's to become a navigator and will be a flight officer, pretty good for an old radio man! Also, got a letter from Bob Orgain, who is in Kelly Field, Texas. He's also with a bunch of boys who were with us at New Orleans. The lucky stiff is going to school there.

I'm glad that you had a nice time at Barb's party. It really does me good to know that you go out and have a good time. Naturally, I'd love to be there to take you out, and will too soon, - soon's they let me out of this damn war!!

Too bad that it has to rain whenever you get a tennis permit, but at least you were in the house, dry as toast. Whereas this afternoon, while unloading a truck, we heard a roar in the jungle and that was our cue! Off the back of the truck and inside the cab, because that's how it rains here! I wasn't fast enough and had to sit on the outside, the cab being opened on the side, I got that side soaking wet. A few minutes later it stopped suddenly as it had come, the sky was blue again, and we continued to unload. All in a day's work.

Darling, I'm terribly sorry that I enclosed your letters in the box I sent to the folks, I should have thought, but like a dumbbell that I am, I figgered since I'm sending a package, why not enclose them and they could give them to you. I tell you what, I'll still save them, if you want, and next time I'll make sure that I mail them to you, but if not, I'll destroy them, howz at?

I'm glad that you cleaned our room so nice and neat. Now when I come home you'll be in such good practice that you'll be able to look after my clothes also. O.K. it was just a suggestion!!

After reading your letter of the Play, I closed my eyes and could just imagine us on the couch, listening to the radio, me running my fingers thru your beautiful hair, you with your arms around me, kissing me. Then darling, I just had to open my eyes again, because it made me fell very lonely and forlorn. My dearest, being away from you is the hardest thing I ever had to take and I hate every second we have to be apart.

Darling, your house coat that you made, I'm sorry, beach coat, sounds wonderful, and I bet looks gorgeous, just like my wife who made it. How's about a pretty picture of you in it? Huh, pretty please!

I was lifted up again when you told me definitely that you and mother are going to Washington. I'm so glad that you are taking some time off for yourself, whether you need it or not (I think you do) it will do you good. Give my love to Sam & Jeanne and the children and don't forget to call my Aunt and Uncle, their address is 816 Sheridan St. N.W. and their phone is GE orgia 5587. Uncle's name is Barney and Aunty is Jenny. When I write to Sam and Jeanne again I won't mention anything about the earlier difficulties.

Irv's girlfriend is from Minneapolis, Minn. so it would make an awful long telephone call. You have a good time in New York, and try to make as few calls as necessary. If Charlotte #1 comes down, you two can have a wonderful time shopping, at least you won't have to sit her on a chair and tell her to wait!

About Dave, there really isn't too much to tell, altho he was much worse off than you or I, that is in money relations. Then when he did go out and make a little money, it went to his doctor bills. You know how that puts a slice in the bank roll, then his family relations weren't like ours. A lot of things like that affect a person. If there is anything else that you'd like to know, I'll tell you, but I can't think of anything else right now.

What the hell were we dressed up like that for in your dream! I know for one thing, that if we were in bed, Jackie sure as hell wouldn't be there, the idea of him!!

The card you sent me surprised some of the fellows when I showed it to them. They thought for a minute that not only was I going to be a father, but also was going to get twelve more points toward discharge. I straightened them out tho. Maybe I shouldn't have and let them think that they were going to get cigars!!

Goodnight, dearest, I hope I'm lucky enough to dream of you.

All my love, all my life
George

P.S. Kiss me quick!

June 24, 1945
Sunday

From:	To:
Cpl. James G. Barr 11057933	Mrs. James G. Barr
94th Dep. Rep. Sq., 56th ADG	65 Houghton St.
APO 246 Unit #1 c/o P.M.	Worcester 4, Mass.
San Francisco, Calf.	

My darling Cookie,
This morning I felt pretty good, I was given some men and a job to do. The job that we had was carrying lumber and I was told it would take this morning and probably to-morrow morning. I had carried lumber myself and had a fair idea that it could all be done this morning, if we'd work a little harder, only of course, if we could get a little benefit from it. I asked the sergeant if I could tell the men that they could leave just as soon as the job was done, no matter what time it would be. He agreed whole heartedly, so I told them if they wanted to quit early this morning they could, if they worked, or else work their regular way and quit at the regular time. Usually when a thing like that is offered to a G.I., he thinks twice about it, because promises aren't worth a damn. After a minute of hesitation, they agreed with me and off we went. We finished the complete job in two and a half hours, which gave them an extra hour off this morning. Pretty good, huh? (Pardon

the black ink, that's all I could bum – I think I'll have to buy me a bottle, if I ever think about it!)

Because I had an extra hour off, I washed a bunch of clothes, and it was a good thing I did have a little extra time too, because just as I had the last of my clothes hung up, the line broke, and the clothes were once again dirty! I didn't like rewashing them, but I had to do it. Now at least I know that the clothes are clean.

The dinner we had at noon was pretty good. Listen and drool! Roast turkey, mashed potatoes, peas, apple pie, corn on the cob, and ice cream with cold chocolate to drink. Pretty snazzy. We're pretty damn lucky to have come over when we did, because earlier all they fed was "C" rations, and all that was, was canned food that was heated; sometimes. Now we get field rations or what is fed similarly back in the states. The food problem here is also the same as the states, not the food, but how it is cooked. Every once in awhile they get careless and we have a meal, such as the one we had to-day.

This afternoon I put to good use by writing letters. I wrote four letters, isn't that marvelous? I answered one from that girl that fed me when I was up in Salina, Kans. Remember. She and her husband are dying to meet you. I'm afraid she may have a chance sooner than she thinks, because she writes and says that he's in his overseas training. You two will have to meet when she does come home. I think you'll like Anne and Dante because they're real people. I don't think they have an act in them.

This afternoon I wrote in our radio shop mainly for two reasons. First, it was quiet, and secondly, it was the coolest place I could find. It's funny, but it hasn't rained to-day!!

I'm reading "Forever Amber" – it's a long book, I ran into two good descriptive chapters, one was on the plague that London went thru in the seventeenth century and the other was on the great London fire years later. The trouble with her writing is, I think, what is wrong with mine, when it is written it stays written.

Another thing we're planning on is saving a beer a week, then getting some ice and a truck and then going down to the beach and have a picnic. Sounds good doesn't it? The only trouble is that we plan on saving for a month and if I drink four beers, I may get drunk!

Good night, darling.

All my love,
George

June 28, 1945
Thursday

From:	To:
Cpl. James G. Barr 11057933	Mrs. James G. Barr
94th Dep. Rep. Sq., 56th ADG	65 Houghton St.
APO 246 Unit #1 c/o P.M.	Worcester 4, Mass.
San Francisco, Calf.	

My wonderful darling,

Did I get three swell letters from you to-day!! Darling, those wonderful marvelous letters put me in seventh heaven. I don't know why, but the last few days of waiting seemed longer than any other time that I had to wait for mail.

The gift we got for dad was very nice. I couldn't think of anything else we could have gotten him. I bet he knows what a wonderful daughter-in-law he has – I bet you!

The next time you see Edie L. tell her I hope this one's a boy (She did have a girl, didn't she?). Why don't you ask Edie if she has another hobby, she may have!

The belt that Charlotte is sending you sounds real western. I bet if I saw it, I'd like to own one so that I'll be able to look sharp the next time I'm astride a saddle. Then I'd have to get a cowboy outfit to match. At least the ten gallon hat would cover my head until I got all my hair back!

Your P.P. party (Pajama) sounded awful nice! Wish I could have sat in with you girls (If you think I'm a wolf, I'll show my colors). When are you going to take that picture that's going to knock my eyes out! But darling, I can't see the sense in such a party, unless of course, everyone was living at the house. By the way, how does one go to such a party? Do they dress in pajamas and go to the party, as is, or do you take your pajamas along and change? If you do the latter, then why bother to change, because then you'll have to change all over again when the party is over. Then again, I'll never be able to figger women out, and I hope I'll never be able to, because then life will become dull.

The only reason I asked what you'd do if I had come into the Eden, was that I wanted to hear you say it. I had a slight idea, of course, but I wanted to make sure. Aren't husbands terrible?! Even tho the girls that aren't married have to worry about getting one. See how lucky you are that you married me? You would have been an old maid like some of your friends.

Hell darling, if you want to take the trip with Anne, even if the boat is packed with G.I.'s, go right ahead. The only thing that I ask of you is be home when I get there, otherwise you'd make me very angry! Of course, I'm only saying that, because I know they wouldn't let you go with her, and besides, I don't think you'd like Africa without me, who'd protect you from the elephants and stuff?

Gee whiz, has Frankie been down again? What's the matter, aren't there any other women around in the neighborhood? I don't blame the guy for wanting to see you out of the rest of them, but "Gee Whiz."

So, that's how I got you, huh, I thought you were Lana Turner! Darling, I wouldn't trade you for all the other women in the world!! It is you I love, and it is you I'm going to love, whether the moon is full or if it's raining.

Don't dogs and cats have mouths? You said I'd have 27 mouths to feed, but you forgot to include our pets. What are they going to do, go out and work for themselves?

Now what did I do to-day to keep me busy? In the morning, we scraped a lot of mud away from the entrance to a hangar. We attached a large metal scoop behind a small truck and one of us held the scoop, while the other drove. I felt like a farmer behind a plow when I took my turn at it. I wouldn't have minded it, but I put on a clean pair of fatigues this morning, but by this afternoon, you'd think they'd never had been washed! Then in the afternoon, we swept the ramp in front of the hangars and where the planes are parked. The dust we threw up was terrific, so we had to quit. This made me feel like a strut cleaner. You know how those machines are back home! After that we moved a few extra large generators, not by hand, but with this tractor I told you about before. There are two of us who run it, but both of us never drove the things before a few days ago. Now we're called on to do experienced work!! How do you like dat! That was all for to-day, don't you think it was enough?

The radio we were working on last night needs a tube. How did we go about finding out? Well, last night I told you we thought a tube was bad, so to-night we borrowed a similar tube from one of the boys sets and exchanged it for the one that was thought bad. The set played like new. Now all we have to do is find a good tube and everything will be O.K!

Just because my stationery is larger means I'll have more to write about because unless something different happens, it doesn't.

Darling, I hate to mention this, but I have to. Another deal like Bazzy's may come up, but this time I think you'll be on your vacation. But if it does go thru, then we'll try and figger out some way of you receiving a call. I have Sam's phone number, just in case it has to be used.

Even with the big paper, I did purty good, didn't I - well, didn't I?

Bye for now.

Always yours,
George

July 7, 1945
Saturday

From:	To:
Cpl. James G. Barr 11057933	Mrs. James G. Barr
94th Dep. Rep. Sq., 56th ADG	65 Houghton St.
APO 246 Unit #1 c/o P.M.	Worcester 4, Mass.
San Francisco, Calf.	

My dearest Lottie,

I gave your address and telephone number to one of the boys who is lucky enough to go back to the states. I hope that he gets in touch with you. I was certain last time that you'd receive a call, but because of that – well, I'm just hoping.

I received a letter from Sol to-day, in which he wrote me that Fran will not talk or write to me until I refrain from calling the baby anything but Michael! Mrs. Anthony, what should I do?

I went to see Irv to-day, and he's quite O.K. now. His stitches (he had seven) were taken out to-day and he's now walking around. He'll be there for another week or so, and then he'll probably have a month or two of taking things easy until they consider him strong enough to go back to work.

Sid Plotkin wrote me a letter, which was very interesting. He has to make 40 flights, and then he'll be able to come home. Of his letter, he has had one of the necessary missions in. He said he was scared a bit, but it wasn't as bad as he had expected. Personally, he can have that life, I'll be satisfied to sweat the war out this way. I've seen planes after they've come back from missions, and after having an accident on the field, I don't want to take any chances, after all I have to come home and take care of my wife who I love very dearly.

All afternoon we drove up and down the apron in front of the hangars, picking up anything we saw, such as nails, bolts, wood, paper, and rags. After awhile I got tired of jumping off the truck, picking something up, then hopping back on. We took our time and came back just in time to quit.

I don't have any plan for to-morrow afternoon, but I would like to go for a cool swim. I don't know as yet, because the weather may be bad, or something will come up to change my mind, we'll see what we shall see.

I want a smoke, but I left my cigarettes back in the barracks and I'm too lazy to go out and get them. What a guy! Goodnight darling.

Your loving husband, George

July 9, 1945
Monday

From: Cpl. James G. Barr 11057933 94th Dep. Rep. Sq., 56th ADG APO 246 Unit #1 c/o P.M. San Francisco, Calf.	To: Mrs. James G. Barr 65 Houghton St. Worcester 4, Mass.

My darling wife,

How very stupid and inconsiderate of me, I forgot to wish you a happy anniversary. Here it was our six months of marriage, and I forgot. Please forgive me. I'll try and not let it happen again.

I just came back from not seeing Eddy Bracken and Peggy Ryan. The show was to start at seven thirty, but to make sure we'd get seats we were there at a quarter to six! Did we get seats tho, - like hell! Every seat was taken so we sat on some cans (the metal kind!) (and also - well you know). Five minutes later it poured so that I gave it up as a bad venture and came back. I would have remained, but last night I went to see "The Corn is Green," which was very good, only I got soaked seeing that, I didn't think getting wet two nights in a row was going to make me feel better, so here I am instead.

It was a long show and I was too wet to write last night, so I'll have to ask forgiveness again.

Here it is again! Three days have come and gone, but no mail from the one I love. I wish the mail was coming in the way it did when we first arrived, then every day I'd be receiving my sugar reports from you. Darling I love reading your letters.

The last few days I've been running a sweeper around the apron in front of the hangars. It's an awfully monotonous job for eight hours, so starting to-morrow night I'm going to work the night shift. The night shift is half as long as the day shift, so I'll be a little better off – I hope. Then when it rains, and it usually does now at night, I don't work!

Instead of going anywhere yesterday afternoon, I finished "The Razor's Edge." I didn't like it quite as well as I thought I would. Maybe it was that it was too hot to concentrate upon the philosophy that was being given out. At least I got some laughs out of the author's style of writing.

We have a few radios to repair, because our generator acted up one night and blew a few tubes in some of the sets. If we could get the right tubes we could repair them, but unfortunately, we don't have the facilities, as yet. There are some on the island someplace, so we may be able to get some yet.

Our day room for our squadron is getting along very nicely. Within a short length of time we'll be able to use it. The boys are doing a very nice job and they should be congratulated.

Within a few days, you'll be leaving on your vacation. Darling, I hope you have a good time. What else can I say, except that I want to be with you – I miss you very much.

Goodnight my sweet darling,
Always yours,
George

P.S. Kiss me quick! J.G.B.

August 11, 1945
Saturday

From:	To:
Cpl. James G. Barr 11057933	Mrs. James G. Barr
94th Dep. Rep. Sq., 56th ADG	65 Houghton St.
APO 246 Unit #1 c/o P.M.	Worcester 4, Mass.
San Francisco, Calf.	

My darling Lottie,

After last night, to-night I'm in a much better mood. We heard the news last night, and of course, we celebrated, even tho it was a bit premature.

It was about forty-five minutes after lights out, when there was a commotion outside. We didn't think anything of it until someone shouted, "the war is over." Rumor or not, I got out of bed to investigate.

There was our illustrious first sergeant running around naked yelling, "Get everyone up, the war is over!" Everyone got up, and danced around, yelling and singing, and just raising hell in general. Out came the beers and cokes and everyone drank up! A few of us went up to the radio shop and listened to the radio. Then we heard that the Japs offered to surrender. This didn't stop us tho, because we knew that the end was in sight. Back to the barracks we went and sang until one o'clock in the morning. I'm still hoarse and still tired from lack of sleep. We had a lot of fun and I think that by the time you read this, I personally think the peace will be signed.

I received a letter from Jack to-day, telling me that Sol Z. opened up his own radio shop on Lincoln Street and that he had been helping him fix his place up. He also said that he could get a little enlarging paper, so maybe at long last, we'll be able to get a few more of our wedding pictures.

To-morrow I know what I'm going to do before I attempt anything else, and that's wash some of my clothes. I certainly have accumulated a mess of dirty clothes.

I thought I'd be able to get a few extra letters written to-night, but a few of the boys came in and we talked about what our ideas were on the war. Time passed and it's getting late. I'll try to get at least a couple out, but I'm not making any promises.

Goodnight my one and only darling.

Your loving husband,
George

UNIT HISTORY

of

94TH DEPOT REPAIR SQUADRON
56th Air Depot Group
20th Air Force
Army Air Forces POA

For the month of

OCTOBER 1945

Losses in action	Negative
Awards and decorations	Negative
Organization (changes)	
strength of Personnel	1 October 1945: 2 Officers 337 Enlisted Men
	31 October 1945: 2 Officers 303 Enlisted Men
Strength of Airplanes	Negative
Losses of Airplanes	Negative

October didnot go by without leaving a few lasting impressions. One of the main morale boasters was when the entire squadron was out to say goodbye to all the twenty-two men with sixty points and over leaving for organizations due to move stateside. The more fortunate men with film and camera snapped pictures of the lucky returnees in all phases of leaving, from the packing of their duffle bags to their happy jump into the truck which would start them on their first leg of the journey stateside and most coveted discharge.

Instead of being sad, the men were quite happy to see these men leave. Not because we did not like them, but because it put us low pointers that much closer to home.

The most famed to leave was our First Sergeant. He who had led us across the smooth Pacific, had left us behind. We who wanted to go with him again, had to remain here, waiting for our trip back on the "Magic Carpet".

As of the fifteenth of the month, all Privates, Privates First Class and Corporals were put on a daily K. P. roster. Many of the men, after pulling a day's K. P. would have gladly increased the old K. P.'s donation to two dollars.

We lost one of our squadron barbers, so now the

one barber we have left will have a tough time keeping the men trimmed.

An interesting and intensified athletic program was put into effect this month. The highlight of the program was the squadron Ping Pong tournament. With prizes for the winners announced, competition doubled. The singles was taken, not easily by T/Sgt. Guptill from Cpl. Levine. After a very hard series, S/Sgt. Dodge and S/Sgt. Schwartz won the doubles from Cpl. Gallina and Cpl. Levine. Because the tournament proved a success, another one is scheduled for the near future.

Our basketball team is heading the Group League and is second in the Depot League.

This month, Wednesday and Saturday afternoons were given the men for off time. To ensure the men of something to do, two volly ball courts were erected. Facilities for the fisticuff fans were made available in the form of light and heavy punching bags. Another Ping Pong table was also added to our Day-room. More and More men can be found in the reading room lately as many new books have been added to our growing collection. On the musical side, new records are also being brought in; now "Caldonia" isn't being played as ofen as before; thank goodness!

Several men in the Squadron Orderly Room are on the next list to leave the organization. To avoid any

mix up in case they leave at a moments notice, men in the
low point bracket were brought in the orderly room to learn
the jobs of the clerks that may leave soon. Acting First
Sergeant Zeh has taken over the duties of the first soldier.
We think Zeh was a good selection.

The Saturdays inspection of the last of this month
was a well earned Superior.

With the close of the month the fifty pointers are
still sweating out their homebound transportation.

During the course of the month many men left the
Squadron for stateside, but the strength was quickly
built up by the arrival of several new men.

*Darling, this is some of
our squadron diary also written
by me. Not because I wanted to but the C.O.
because I was told. maybe now often the C.O.
has read it, he will no longer lock me
with it the next month. no, I didn't type it
us. your still tops in this family as the
literary genius of the family.*

All my love
George

THOMAS L. PARELLO
Capt, Air Corps
Commanding

Harmon Field, Guam
January 6 1946

Senators ,
David I. Walsh
Leverett Saltonstall

Dear Sir,

      Here, on Harmon Field, we soldiers, as well as many other, 'round the world which we have just made peaceful, want to know what is happening to our demobilization plan. Is it deteriorating, or has it deteriorated already? We want an answer. Just a few months ago General Marshall, then our Chief of Staff, promised us that all men with at least two years of service would be eligible for discharge on March 20, 1946. We were also told that points were frozen of September 2, 1945. Just a few days ago, on this very island, Secretary of War Robert P. Patterson in an interview with the press, was asked about these two dates, and he indicated complete surprise. If we cannot depend upon the chief of the department in charge of demobilization, who can we trust? Again, we want an answer. Also, when Secretary Patterson was asked when the next point drop would be, he said that he could not divulge this information because "I don't want to steal the show from the men in Washington." What kind of a show is this? We are not enjoying it, and neither are our parents, wives, and friends who are so dear to us. We want action, and we want to get home! We, who participated in the waragainst our enemies have fulfilled our mission; available troop ' space is not being utilized completely; we are now performing duties not related to the emergency; and the confusing and conflicting statements by high military authorities are seriously denting our morale. We, the overseas veterans cannot help but feel we are the victims of alibis, distortions and broken promises. Is this true? I suggest that a $a Congressional Committee be appointed to investigate this situation, and if necessary form a demobilization committee to draw and enforce a new discharge system.

      Was Mr. Patterson misunderstood on Guam? The enclosed clippings from the Navy News of today, supplies the answer.

Sincerely,

Cpl James G. Barr
11057933
94th Dep. Rep. Sq. 56th A.D.G.
APO 264 c/o San Francisco Calif.

January 8 1946
Harmon Field
APO 254, Guam

To the Editors of The Telegram &
Evening Gazette:

Dear Sirs,

Last night I attended a mass meeting of the men from
my field on Guam. There were at least 7,000 men there,
almost a 100% participation. What prompted such a meeting ?

We who have served our country during the war,
feel that we are not getting home "as soon as shipping space
is available". This statement was made just
after V-J Day. Now that shipping is available, we have to
wait for replacements that we don't need. Folks we are
getting the run around.

Secretary of War Patterson said he was unaware that
points were frozen as of V-J Day. He also said, when asked
about the next drop in points, "I don't want to steal the
show from the men in Washington". As Secreatary of War, I
think he's a big part of the Show! We do not want to wait
until "the men in Washinton" decide to put on the show!

Here is what we want. We want the War Department
to come out with a just and fair demobilization plan. One
which we can trust and know will be carried out. One that
will tell us when we are going home!

During the war, I for myself, when writing home
have told the folks that everything is O.K., I'm alright and
not to worry. During the war everything was not alright, but
yet because of the war we wanted to cause as little worry and
confusion as possible, Ask the boys who are now home if all
the hardships that they went thru were neccessary.
There is many a story that they will tell you.

Here is all I ask. Write to our Congressmen, and
have them get the War Department to come out with a definite
policy. If you want me home, If you want to see your
boy or girl home as soon as is justly possible, then you
will let our representatives know.

The faster the army is demobilized the faster they
will have a known number of men to work with. This will make
for a more efficient and more organized army to protect us,
if the nee ever arised.

Sincerely

Cpl James G. Barr
94th Dep. Rep. Sq.
56th Air Depot Group
Harmon Field, Guam

[Editor's note: Apparently, George had endured enough of being on the
island of Guam after the war had ended, that he wrote these letters to the
editors of the Telegram and Evening Gazette, and to the Senators of
Massachusetts. It is interesting to note that between the time George wrote
these letters and was on a ship back home, he was promoted to the rank of
Sergeant.]

February 6, 1946
Wednesday

From:	To:
Sgt. James G. Barr 11057933	Mrs. James G. Barr
94th Dep. Rep. Sq., 56th ADG	65 Houghton St.
APO 246 Unit #1 c/o P.M.	Worcester 4, Mass.
San Francisco, Calf.	

My very dearest darling wife,

Honey, if this is a little blurred or short, you will please not blame it upon me, but upon what I had to drink!!!

I'm not exactly drunk, but then again, I'm not what you might consider sober, but happy anyway! We had a little party to-night because we didn't want a party to-morrow night. The reason for to-night is simple – in case we feel rotten to-morrow morning, it will be O.K. because it isn't until the day after to-morrow we get on the boat.

Yes, my precious darling (I love you madly), our orders to ship have been out since this morning! We'll leave the morning of the 8th and no doubt, be on a boat headed for home two days afterward, from Saipan.

The pictures were just enlarged this afternoon, but since I'm leaving, Ed had to hurry up and make them, so that I could send them out to you. When I get home remind me I have to call his wife, will you please? I know you will, so here is a kiss for it, - Darling, I love kissing you – I can't explain it, but I do!! Kiss me again.

No kidding darling, I'm tired so I think I'll go hit the sack – Goodnight my little spare rib.

All my love, all my life
George

P.S. Kiss me quick!!!

February 11, 1946
Monday

From:	To:
Sgt. James G. Barr 11057933	Mrs. James G. Barr
94th Dep. Rep. Sq., 56th ADG	65 Houghton St.
APO 246 Unit #1 c/o P.M.	Worcester 4, Mass.
San Francisco, Calf.	

My darling wife,

We were told late last night we are leaving this morning. I just got up and there is still some work for me to do.

I just want to tell you we are on our way home! One more boat ride and that is all.

All my love, all my life
George

Kiss me quick!!! ---- Soon the real thing!

[Editor's note: The following pages are telegrams that George sent to Lottie as he was making his way back home.]

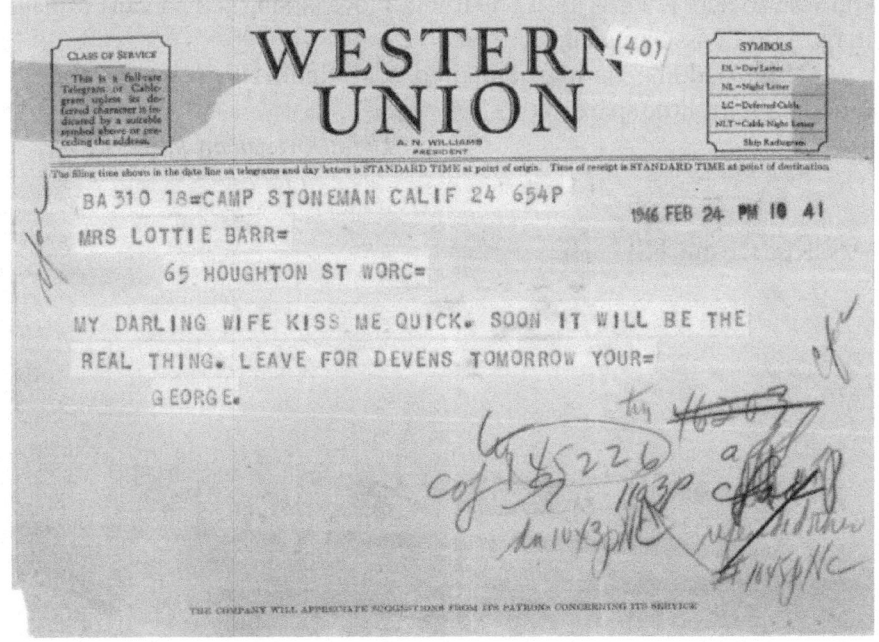

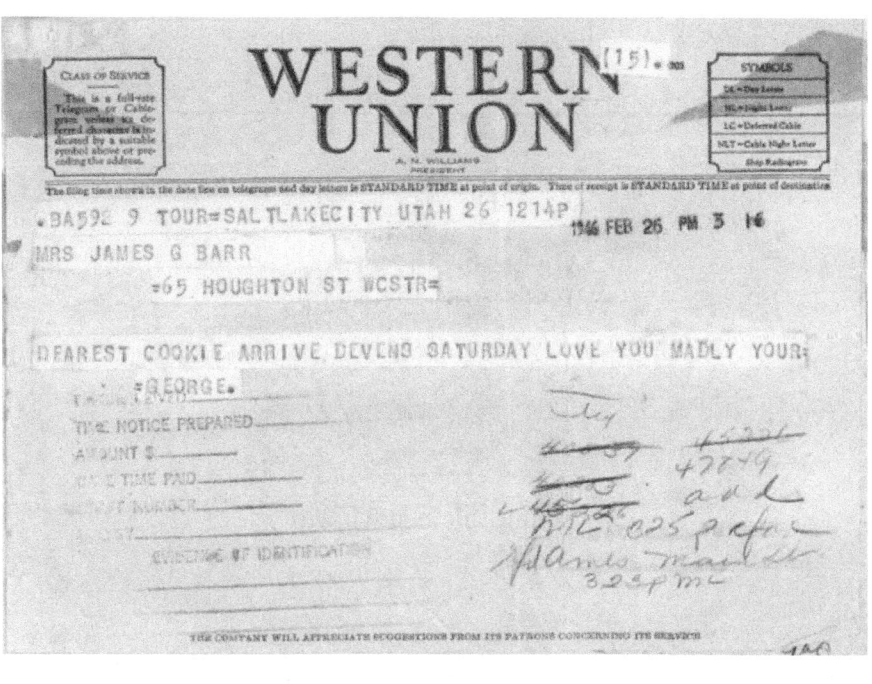

WESTERN UNION

BA59 9 TOUR=SALT LAKE CITY UTAH 26 1214P   1946 FEB 26 PM 3 16

MRS JAMES G BARR

=65 HOUGHTON ST WCSTR=

DEAREST COOKIE ARRIVE DEVENS SATURDAY LOVE YOU MADLY YOUR=

=GEORGE.

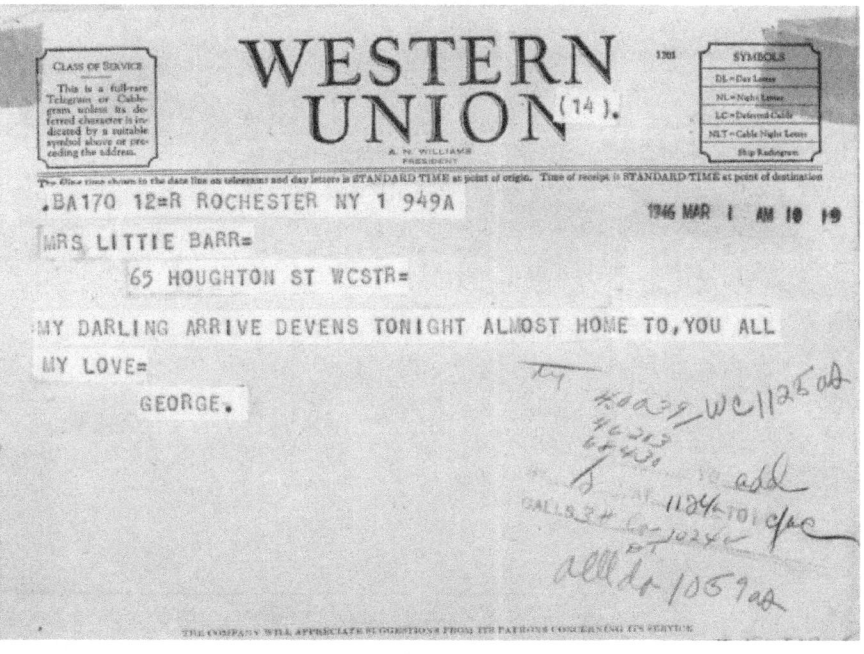

WESTERN UNION

BA170 12=R ROCHESTER NY 1 949A   1946 MAR 1 AM 10 19

MRS LITTIE BARR=

65 HOUGHTON ST WCSTR=

MY DARLING ARRIVE DEVENS TONIGHT ALMOST HOME TO, YOU ALL

MY LOVE=

GEORGE.

219-6695

Army of the United States

Honorable Discharge

This is to certify that

JAMES G BARR   11 057 933   SERGEANT

94TH DEPOT REPAIR SQUADRON 23RD AIR DEPOT GROUP

Army of the United States

is hereby Honorably Discharged from the military service of the United States of America.

This certificate is awarded as a testimonial of Honest and Faithful Service to this country.

Given at   SEPARATION CENTER
FORT DEVENS MASS

Date   4 MARCH 1946

E E MITCHELL
MAJOR   INF

ENLISTED RECORD AND REPORT OF SEPARATION
HONORABLE DISCHARGE

2745578

1. LAST NAME—FIRST NAME—MIDDLE INITIAL	2. ARMY SERIAL NO.	3. GRADE	4. ARM OR SERVICE	5. COMPONENT
BARR JAMES G	11 057 933	SGT	AC	ERC

6. ORGANIZATION	7. DATE OF SEPARATION	8. PLACE OF SEPARATION
94 DEPOT REPAIR SQD 23 AIR DEPOT GROUP	4 MAR 46	SEPARATION CENTER FORT DEVENS MASS

9. PERMANENT ADDRESS FOR MAILING PURPOSES	10. DATE OF BIRTH	11. PLACE OF BIRTH
65 HOUGHTON ST WORCESTER (WORCESTER) MASS	12 MAY 1923	WORCESTER MASS

12. ADDRESS FROM WHICH EMPLOYMENT WILL BE SOUGHT	13. COLOR EYES	14. COLOR HAIR	15. HEIGHT	16. WEIGHT	17. NO. DEPEND.
SEE 9	GRN	BLK	5'8½"	150 LBS.	2

18 RACE	19. MARITAL STATUS	20. U.S. CITIZEN	21. CIVILIAN OCCUPATION AND NO.
WHITE X	SINGLE X	YES X	SALES CLERK 1-70.10

MILITARY HISTORY

22. DATE OF INDUCTION	23. DATE OF ENLISTMENT	24. DATE OF ENTRY INTO ACTIVE SERVICE	25. PLACE OF ENTRY INTO SERVICE
	24 NOV 42	6 AUG 43	FORT DEVENS MASS

26. EFFECTIVE SERVICE DATA	27. REGISTERED YES / NO	28. LOCAL S.S. BOARD NO. COUNTY AND STATE	29. HOME ADDRESS AT TIME OF ENTRY INTO SERVICE
	X	WORCESTER MASS	7 HARTSHORN AVE WORCESTER MASS

30. MILITARY OCCUPATIONAL SPECIALTY AND NO.	31. MILITARY QUALIFICATION AND DATE
RADIO REPAIRMAN AIRCRAFT EQUIP 647	SS CARBINE

32. BATTLES AND CAMPAIGNS

NONE

33. DECORATIONS AND CITATIONS

VICTORY MEDAL ASIATIC PACIFIC THEATER CAMPAIGN RIBBON AMERICAN THEATER CAMPAIGN RIBBON

34. WOUNDS RECEIVED IN ACTION

NONE

35. LATEST IMMUNIZATION DATES				36. SERVICE OUTSIDE CONTINENTAL U.S. AND RETURN		
SMALLPOX	TYPHOID	TETANUS	OTHER (specify)	DATE OF DEPARTURE	DESTINATION	DATE OF ARRIVAL
4 OCT 45	4 OCT 45	7 SEP 44	TY 22 JUN 45	18 MAR 45	APT	11 APR 45
				11 FEB 46	USA	24 FEB 46

37. TOTAL LENGTH OF SERVICE					38. HIGHEST GRADE HELD
CONTINENTAL SERVICE			FOREIGN SERVICE		
YEARS	MONTHS	DAYS	YEARS	MONTHS	DAYS
1	7	22	0	11	7	SGT

39. PRIOR SERVICE

NONE

40. REASON AND AUTHORITY FOR SEPARATION

CONV OF THE GOVT AR 615-365 RR 1-1 DEMOBILIZATION

41. SERVICE SCHOOLS ATTENDED	42. EDUCATION (Years)		
NONE	Grammar 8	High School 4	College 0

PAY DATA

43. LONGEVITY FOR PAY PURPOSES			44. MUSTERING OUT PAY		45. SOLDIER DEPOSIT	46. TRAVEL PAY	47. TOTAL AMOUNT, NAME OF DISBURSING OFFICER
YEARS	MONTHS	DAYS	TOTAL	THIS PAYMENT			
3	3	11	$ 300	$ 100	none	15.30	YOU 357.95 4 MAR 46

F A NYQUIST MAJOR FD

INSURANCE NOTICE

IMPORTANT: If premium is not paid when due or within thirty-one days thereafter, insurance will lapse...

48. KIND OF INSURANCE	49. HOW PAID	50. Effective Date of Allotment Discontinuance	51. Date of Next Premium Due (One month after 50)	52. PREMIUM DUE EACH MONTH	53. INTENTION OF VETERAN TO
Nat. Serv. X	U.S. Govt.	Direct	Allotment X	28 FEB 46	31 MAR 46	$ 6.50	Continue X

54.	55. REMARKS (This space for completion of above items or entry of other items specified in W.D. Directives)
[fingerprint]	ISSUED LAPEL BUTTON ASR SCORE 2 SEP 45 ERC 24 NOV 42 TO 5 AUG 43

56. SIGNATURE OF PERSON BEING SEPARATED	57. PERSONNEL OFFICER (Type name, grade and organization—signature)
James G. Barr	M L CARLETON 1ST LT AC

WD AGO FORM 53-55
1 November 1944

This form supersedes all previous editions of WD AGO Forms 53 and 55 for enlisted persons entitled to an Honorable Discharge, which will not be used after receipt of this revision.

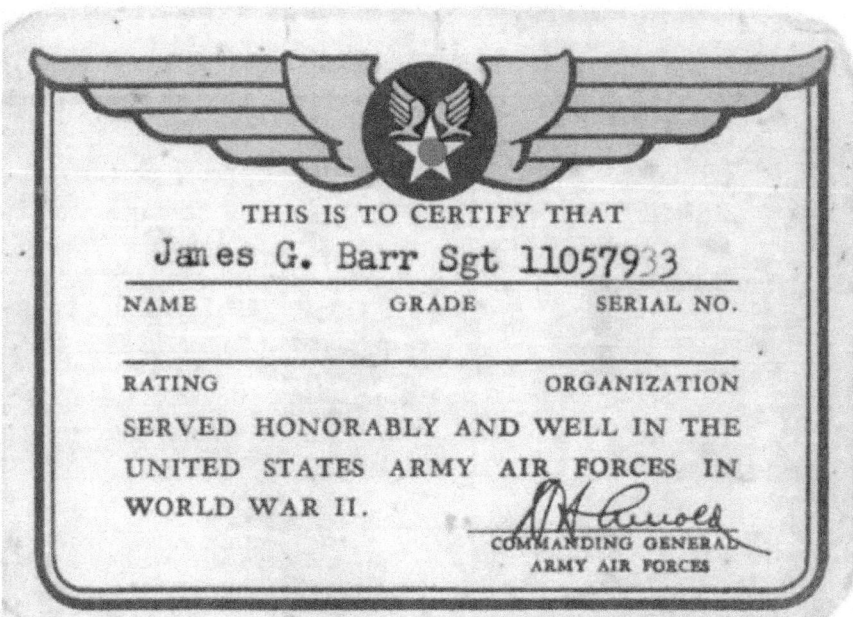

Lottie & George

(Circa 1940-1946)

George Barr H.S. Graduation Picture, 1941

Lottie Sniderman H.S. Graduation Picture, 1942

Sgt. James George Barr

George and Lottie Barr, Wedding Picture, January 7, 1945.

Lottie Barr, Wedding Picture, January 7, 1945.

Lottie & George, dated December 1943. Picture taken when George was on his first furlough after joining the Army.

Lottie Sniderman sitting in Jackie Waxler's car, dated May 1944

- GLAMOR -

Lottie Sniderman (Age 14 or 15) For those who knew her, this picture, above all others, really shows her humorous character. Dated: 1940

SEPT - 1946

Family

Referenced

In

Letters

(Circa 1940-1946)

Sara Sniderman (Lottie's Mother)

Max Sniderman (Lottie's Father)

Jacob & Rose Barr (George's Parents)

Jacob & Rose Barr (George's Parents)

Toby Barr (George's sister)

Nathan "Narky" Barr (George's brother)

Nathan "Narky" Barr (George's Brother), with wife, Charlotte, and daughter, Bonnie. Dated: 1944

Fran Barr and Solomon "Nooky" Barr (George's Brother) Date:
1/06/1942

Sol "Nooky" Barr (George's Brother), with wife, Fran Barr

Fran Barr (George's brother Sol's wife) with Michael (a.k.a. Martin to Lottie & George in their letters)

Sam Pemstein (Lottie's Half-Brother)

Erwin Pemstein (Lottie's nephew), Jeanne Pemstein (Lottie's sister-in-law), and Sandy Pemstein (Lottie's niece).

Sam Pemstein (Lottie's Half-Brother) in his Record Store in Washington D.C.

Irving "Jerry" Walker (Lottie's Half-Brother)

1945

Irving "Jerry" Walker (Lottie's Half-Brother), with wife Fran, children
(Barry 'Buzzy' and Ricky), and Lottie's mother, Sara Hoffman
Sniderman.

Dave Hoffman and wife Mary (Lottie's Aunt & Uncle), Lottie Sniderman Barr

Back row: Jennie Barr, Isaac "Izzy" Barr, Sarah Barr, Barney Barr (George's Aunts & Uncles). Knelling: Frumel & William "Willy" Barr (George's Cousins)

Left to Right: Rose Barr (George's mother), Aunt Jennie Barr, Aunt Sarah Barr, Aunt Dora Kaplan, Aunt Lena Barr, and Aunt Leah Barr

Left to Right: Uncle Abe Barr, Uncle Barney Barr, Jacob Barr (George's father), Aunt Dora Kaplan, Uncle Simon Barr, and Uncle Isaac Barr

Barr Creamery Store, with Jacob Barr (George's father) pictured.

Barr Creamery Store (Left to right: George Barr, Nathan "Narky" Barr, Toby Barr & Jacob Barr)

Barr Creamery, with Jacob Barr (George's father) serving a customer. Notice Sid Plotkin (George & Lottie's friend) was the photographer.

**Sol Barr, Edie Megans, and George Barr. Photo taken in Lottie's house at
Lottie & George's Wedding on January 7, 1945.**

Toby Barr (George's Sister)

ZELDA L. GREENGUS
"Zel"
Girls' Glee Club

Zelda Greengus Siegel (Lottie's Cousin and Bridesmaid) Dated: 1940
Worcester High School of Commerce

Friends

Referenced

In

Letters

(Circa 1941-1945)

EDITH M. MEGANS
"Edie"   "Migs"
United States History Club
Chemistry Club

BARBARA C. COPPERSMITH
"Bobbie"
Orchestra A

JACK B. WAXLER
"Jackie"
Camera Club—President
Chemistry Club
Principal's Cabinet

DAVID GROSSMAN
"Dave"

SYLVIA COBLENTZ
"Sylvy"
U. S. History Club   Britomart

MINNIE KAPLAN
"Min"

RITA J. SCHEYER
"Blondie"
Euphemia Debating Society
U. S. History Club

HARVEY G. COBLENTZ
"Harve"

BERNARD SHAPIRO
"Shap"
Band B   Orchestra B

CHARLES FREEDMAN
"Chas." "Shorty"

PEARL S. RITZ
"Fritzie"
Chemistry Club   Britomart

PHYLLIS JACOBSON
"Phil"
Girls' Glee Club   Mixed Chorus

CHARLOTTE M. PLOTKIN
Girls' Glee Club   Latin Club

SARAH SREIBERG
"Sorki"

GEORGE A. PILSON
"Pil"
Caduceus Editorial Board
Assistant Class Treasurer (4)
Mercury Staff—Assistant Editor
Class Day Committee
Class Day Sketch

George Pilson

IRENE J. GRACE
"Hockey"
United States History Club

BELLA SILVER
"Bait"
Mercury Staff

BELLA SANDMAN
"Sandy"
Britomart   U. S. History Club

SYDNEY R. STEIN
"Willie"
Assembly Debating Society
Table Tennis Club

JOSEPH COHEN
"Joe"

BEATRICE F. GOLDMAN
"Bea"   "Beadie"
Mercury Staff—Assistant Editor
Bumble Bees
Caduceus Editorial Board
Honor Pupil

EVELYN LEVINE
"Ev"

EVELYN AVERS
"Eve"
Bumble Bees

SYLVIA BERMAN
"Syl"
Bumble Bees

EVELYN COHEN
"Quinn"
Biology Club   U. S. History
Camera Club   Table Tennis Club
Euphemia Debating Society Tennis
Mercury Staff—Mailing Clerk
Honor Pupil

Edith "Edie" Megans

Beverly "Bev" Kaplan

Pauline "Polly" Cohan

Barbara "Barb" Carole Coppersmith. Stage name: Barbara Carroll

Freda Reck

Max "Maxie" Rothstein

Joseph "Joe" Cohen

Pictured from left to right: Ruth Miller, Dorothy "Dottie" Potash, Pearl Ritz Greengus, and Miriam "Mimmie" Sigel (dated: May 1944)

1944

Jack "Jackie" Waxler and his car, which Lottie references in her 9/8/43
letter to George.

Jack "Jackie" Waxler

Evelyn Isaacman & Jack Waxler

Lottie Sniderman, Sol Zitowitz, and Barbara Coppersmith, dated July 1941.

Edith "Edie" Megans & Lottie Sniderman Barr, dated Dec. 1945.

George Barr and His Army

Buddies

Referenced

In

Letters

(Circa 1943-1946)

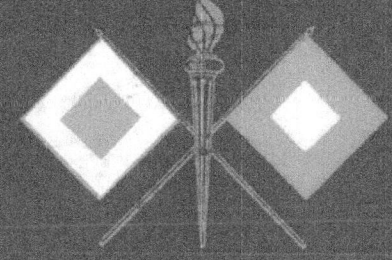

SIGNALS

1943

JAMES GEORGE BARR
"GEORGE"
20 years, unmarried

Lives at 57 Arlington Street, Worcester, Mass. Education, High School Graduate, Commerce High, Worcester, Mass. Hobbies, photography, member "Signal Corps Cavaliers".

EMIL BAZZY
"NO 'COUNT"
20 years, unmarried

Lives at 26 Walnut Avenue, Norwood, Mass. Education, High School, ½ year College, at Tufts. Experience: Airport Field Worker. Hobby, model airplane builder.

LEONARD DiPIETRO
"LENNY"
24 years, unmarried

Lives at 100 Brooks Street, East Boston, Mass. Education, Graduated from English High, 1936; Lowell Institute School (M.I.T.) 1939. Experience: Glenn L. Martin Co., Instrument Technician; General Electric Co., Engineering Draftsman. Hobbies, music and aviation.

Dave Grossman

George Barr & Sid Plotkin

Sid Plotkin

Sid Plotkin

Norman Katz

"19.45 ~

"UDDY"

"Uddy" Goff and George Barr in Guam, dated 1945

Left to Right: Lenny DiPietro and unknown soldier.

Bob Orgain

Bob Orgain

Irv & George Barr in Guam, 1945.

Unknown soldier (Irv's Friend), Irv & George Barr in Guam, Nov. 1945

George Barr (2ⁿᵈ from left) with some of his "Radiomen" in Guam, Sept. 1945.

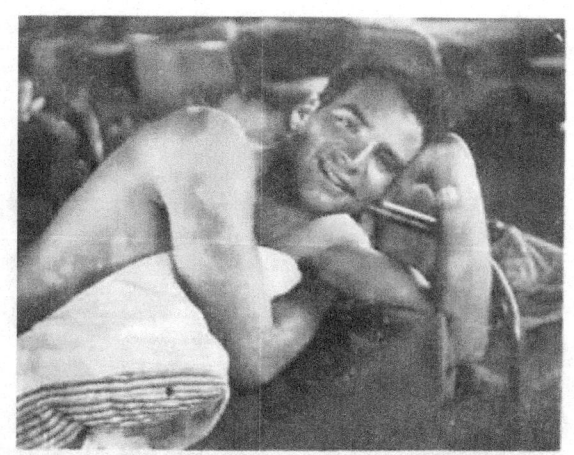

George Barr, Dated October 1943

George Barr with fellow Army mates in Guam, dated: 1945

AFTERWORD

George and Lottie (Sniderman) Barr would go on to have a wonderful and happy life together. True to all the love they proclaimed to each other throughout the three years of letter writing during the war, they were both still deeply in love when they celebrated their 59th wedding anniversary, a few months prior to Lottie's death in 2004.

George and Lottie went on to have four children (not the twenty-four they mention in their letters). Their firstborn, Michael, arrived in July of 1949. Two years after Michael was born, in August of 1951, Lottie and George had their second son, Jay, followed by Scott, in January of 1954. Last, but not least, in May of 1961, a daughter arrived, which they named Vickie.

In April of 1952, George took a job as a salesman for a packing and staples company (Alles Corp.). When the company decided to open a new South Florida office in 1955, George and Lottie left the cold winters of New England and moved the family to sunny North Miami, Florida. George would continue to work for this same company his entire working career, until finally retiring in 2006.

As promised in his letters, George did take Lottie to see many places throughout the United States and the world after the war, with vacation trips that included Canada, Australia, Israel, Italy, France, and Egypt, to name a few. Likewise, George's love of photography never waned, and he always had the latest camera or video recorder to capture the beauty of the world and his family, although Lottie never did get over her dislike of having her picture taken.

Upon moving to Florida, George took up another hobby, fishing. This would turn out to be a lifelong love, and George would often go fishing on a pier or commercial drift boat in his free time.

Lottie would spend most of her time looking after the children and filling the house with love. She always kept her sharp wit and sense of humor, many times laughing so hard she cried. Going shopping with her daughter, Vickie, was a favorite pastime, and like many women of her generation, Lottie had a standing appointment at the hair salon every Saturday.

Discovering such a detailed account of the daily lives of Lottie and George through letters and pictures between 1943 and 1946 was truly a unique and rare find, and one which I believe would not have occurred without the catalyst of a war, and dare I say it, without a "digital age", where communication was done with handwritten letters, rather than short text messages and tweets.

My hope for creating this book was to preserve these special memories which occurred in a unique time of our history, not only for the Barr/Sniderman family, but for others to see that our parents, grandparents, great-grandparents, and beyond, were once kids just like us, with the same dreams, desires, love, and sometimes even loneliness.

George and Lottie were both loving parents and grandparents, and if this book helps to keep their memory alive, then that is the best "love letter" I could hope to give to my wonderful mother and father-in-law.

Editor and son-in-law, Daniel R. Mazza.

Authors James George Barr and Charlotte Loretta (Sniderman) Barr
Photo dated: November 1997

Made in the USA
Las Vegas, NV
01 April 2024

88092353R00400